The Who's Who of
MIDDLESBROUGH

The Who's Who of MIDDLESBROUGH

Middlesbrough FC

First published in Great Britain in 2007 by
The Breedon Books Publishing Company Limited
Breedon House, 3 The Parker Centre,
Derby, DE21 4SZ.

This edition published in Great Britain in 2012 by The Derby Books Publishing Company Limited, 3 The Parker Centre, Derby, DE21 4SZ.

ISBN 978-1-78091-122-9

Printed and bound by Copytech (UK) Limited, Peterborough.

Contents

Written and compiled by

Dave Allan, Graham Bell, Gordon Cox, Claire Foy, Harry Glasper, Peter Harris, Dean Hayes, Mark Hooper, Nathan Judah, Mike McGeary and Dave Robson.

Foreword

From Sam Aitken to Bolo Zenden, they have won the Middlesbrough shirt with pride. From the rudimentary surroundings of the Linthorpe Road Ground to the state-of-the-art Riverside Stadium, the star players we will never forget – and others consigned to misty memories – come to life in the *Who's Who of Middlesbrough*.

This is not a conventional history book. The epic tale of Boro's birth as a Football League club, including its dramatic ups and downs, is recorded in detail elsewhere. This book is about the players – hundreds of them. Every player to have represented Middlesbrough FC, whether for five minutes or 500 games, is recorded here.

The *Who's Who of Middlesbrough* will entertain and rekindle memories. For many supporters, it will also throw new light on players from the past who have played influential, if largely forgotten, roles in the making of our modern football club.

Join as we flick back through more than 100 years of matches, from our first Football League game in October 1899 to the UEFA Cup Final and beyond, to review the men who have weaved dreams or had us throwing up our hands in exasperation! They're all here.

Players

AGNEW William Barbour

Full-back
Born: New Cumnock nr Kilmarnock, 16 December 1880.
Died: 20 August 1936.
Career: Kilmarnock 1900. Newcastle United 1902. MIDDLESBROUGH 1904. Kilmarnock 1906. Sunderland 1908. Falkirk 1910.

■ Blond-haired Scottish defender Agnew was the first man to pull on the three shirts of the North East's big clubs in League football. A full-back of the finest pedigree and comfortable on either side of defence, Agnew was a stocky man renowned for his bravery in combating opposing attacks.

Having performed well in Newcastle's side following a £200 move from Kilmarnock, Middlesbrough took two attempts to sign Agnew. The club had earlier offered the maximum wage allowed but Newcastle quickly signed him to a new contract and the player was happy to stay at St James' Park.

When he was finally recruited by manager John Robson, Agnew stepped in for a debut at left-back in the opening game of 1904–05 – a 3–1 home defeat to Sheffield Wednesday. After dropping out of the side for six games, Agnew was a regular for two seasons.

A return to his first club Kilmarnock came in the summer of 1906 and it was at Rugby Park that Agnew won international honours with matches against Ireland and Wales. Agnew returned to England for a spell with Sunderland before acting as trainer for Third Lanark and East Stirlingshire. He died in August 1936.

AITKEN Andrew

Half-back
Born: Ayr, 27 April 1877.
Died: 15 February 1955.
Career: Ayr Thistle. Ayr Parkhouse 1894. Newcastle United 1895. Kilmarnock (loan) 1898. MIDDLESBROUGH 1906. Leicester Fosse 1908. Dundee 1911. Kilmarnock 1912. Gateshead Town 1913.

■ Middlesbrough's first ever player-manager also held the distinction of being one of the rare men to hold that post and still be capped by their country. A versatile performer, Aitken was a fine tackler, strong in the air and adept at comfortably halting opposition attacks from his half-back position before getting the ball forward to attackers, rarely wasting possession.

One of the greats of Edwardian football, Aitken was a brilliant all-rounder who came to Middlesbrough having played in every position but goalkeeper at Newcastle and earning his place among St James' all-time greats.

The former grocer's delivery boy, known in the game as 'Daddler', earned his reputation with local clubs in Ayr, and Manchester United and Preston showed interest before he joined Newcastle who he helped to win the League and reach two Cup Finals.

The quality of Aitken's play did not suffer on Teesside despite also assuming the responsibilities of club secretary within a fortnight of his arrival. Under his stewardship on and off the pitch, the club lifted from a Christmas position at the bottom of Division One to a mid-table finish and then to sixth in the following season.

Aitken left the club on a point of principle following a disagreement and clash of personalities with chairman Thomas Gibson-Poole and he accepted the player-manager job at Leicester Fosse (now City), who were newly promoted to Division One. He enjoyed less success at Leicester and reverted to playing in Scotland after relegation in his first season, his playing career coming to an end following a groin injury. Aitken applied for the vacant Boro job when Andy Walker was suspended by the Football League along with chairman Gibson-Poole in 1911 but the position went instead to Darlington manager Tom McIntosh. He later scouted for Arsenal and became a publican on Tyneside. Aitken died in Ponteland in February 1955.

AITKEN George Bruce

Centre-half
Born: Dalkeith, 13 August 1928.
Career: Hibernian. Edinburgh Thistle. MIDDLESBROUGH 1946. Workington 1953.

■ Manager David Jack made commanding centre-half George Aitken wait five years to make his debut for Middlesbrough against Fulham in

September 1951. The Scot had been transfer-listed in January of that year along with Martin Reagan and Jimmy Hartnett and was immediately left out again following the 2–0 victory over the bottom of the table Londoners. A run of games did come later that season and his patience looked to be rewarded when he was recalled midway through the following campaign. But Aitken was dropped by Walter Rowley after a 3–1 FA Cup defeat at Aston Villa in January 1953 and never played for the club again. A regular place was won at Workington and he stayed on at the club as trainer, later spending three years as manager. Coaching stints came at Brighton and Grimsby, and Aitken worked as a scout for Graham Taylor at Watford and Aston Villa, linking up again subsequently as part of the England set-up.

AITKEN Samuel

Right-half/Centre-half
Born: 1879.
Career: Ayr. MIDDLESBROUGH 1903. Raith Rovers 1910. Ayr United 1911.

■ Wing-half Aitken served Middlesbrough for seven seasons, captaining the side for his final three years. A talented player with a good head for business, the Scot was chairman and captain at Ayr and was bought by Boro on the recommendation of Andy Davidson, who had played with him at Ayr.

He replaced David Smith in the half-back line midway through the club's first season at Ayresome Park, making his debut in a 2–1 North East derby defeat at Newcastle in November 1903. He became an immediate fixture in the defence alongside Davidson and Abe Jones as Boro established themselves in the First Division.

Aitken was made club captain in 1907 when Alf Common was stripped of the role and guided Boro to sixth in his first season. However, he was sold by his namesake, Andy Aitken, at the end of the 1909–10 campaign and returned to Scotland with Raith, later going back to Ayr.

ALLEN Michael

Defender
Born: South Shields, 30 March 1949.
Career: MIDDLESBROUGH 1966. Brentford 1971.

■ A regular first-team place eluded Allen at Middlesbrough but he showed his versatility by operating in a number of defensive and midfield positions in Stan Anderson's side. The teenager broke into the team late in 1967, making his debut in central defence in place of Frank Spraggon in a home game versus Bolton. His next chance came three months later in midfield as Anderson built for the following season but the first five months of 1968–69 were spent in the reserves before another short first-team run, even playing left back in place of Gordon Jones on one occasion. Allen's first good run came in October 1969 on the left side of midfield and in the 1970–71 season he played several games at right-back as a crop of youngsters were given a chance. A quiet man off the pitch, Allen was a good ball-winner and always gave 100 percent effort. Third Division Blackburn enquired about him, together with Eric McMordie and Alex Smith, in September 1971, only to be told by Anderson they were not available, yet a month later Allen joined Brentford where he secured a regular place. Allen later worked for ICI at Wilton, having returned to Teesside to live in Marton.

ALLPORT Henry George

Wing-half
Born: details unknown.
Career: Ironopolis 1893. MIDDLESBROUGH 1894.

■ Wing-half Harry Allport holds the distinction of being the only player to represent both of Middlesbrough's teams in the Football League. He joined Middlesbrough Ironopolis when they turned professional and joined the Football League in 1893. A year later, with Nops out of business, he made the short move to Northern League Middlesbrough and helped them win the FA Amateur Cup in 1895, playing in the Cup Final win over Old Carthusians as Boro came from behind to win. Three years later he was again in the side as the Amateur Cup was won for a second time, this time Uxbridge beaten in the Final at Crystal Palace. He was one of only three players to appear in both Finals. Allport was a club veteran by the time Middlesbrough joined the Second Division in 1899 and played in the club's first ever League game at Lincoln at right-half.

However, Allport was released at the end of that first League season.

ANDERSON John Robert

Goalkeeper
Born: Prestwick, 9 November 1924.
Died: November 1994.
Career: Blackhall Colliery. MIDDLESBROUGH 1945. Blackhall Colliery. Crystal Palace 1951. Bristol Rovers 1953. Bristol City 1954.

■ Goalkeeper Bob Anderson must have had nightmares about the one and only occasion he played for the Middlesbrough first team. As a young and inexperienced custodian, he was handed his debut away at Highbury on March 26, 1948. Anderson – in for regular 'keeper Derek Goodfellow – picked the ball out of his own net seven times on that ill-fated day and it was a performance littered with elementary handling errors. He was at fault for the majority of the goals, even conceding one when he hit a free-kick against the back of retreating Arsenal forward Ronnie Rooks. Until that disastrous debut for the first team, he had shown much early promise for the club's reserves but his confidence was so badly hit that he never recovered form. At the end of the season, Anderson returned to Blackhall but was given another chance at League football by Crystal Palace. He enjoyed happier times, later winning Division Three South honours with Bristol Rovers in 1953 before repeating the feat with Bristol City two seasons later. Anderson died in November 1994 just past his 70th birthday.

ANDERSON Stanley

Wing-half
Born: Horden, 27 February 1934.
Career: Sunderland 1951. Newcastle United 1963. MIDDLESBROUGH 1965.

■ Best remembered for his lengthy stint as Middlesbrough manager, Stan Anderson was also an excellent player who is the only man to have captained each of the North East's big three teams. A strong-tackling and consistent wing-half, he was also a constructive and dominant influence on the pitch with a fine footballing brain.

Anderson was signed by Middlesbrough towards the end of his career but could have started it on Teesside had manager David Jack not rejected him as a youth with an abundance of other wing-halves at the club. The former apprentice plasterer and plumber instead became a legend at Roker Park for over decade after making his debut as a teenager. Anderson won international recognition at Sunderland but his full England career was hampered by a sending off for the Under-23 team, though he earned caps against Austria and Scotland in 1962 and travelled with England's World Cup squad to Chile in the same year.

Raich Carter signed Anderson as player-coach after he had captained Newcastle to the Division Two Championship in 1965. He proved to be an astute signing for the relegation-threatened side, capable of spraying 40

and 50 yard passes at will, though it was a poor team and after Carter was sacked in February 1966, 32-year-old Anderson was appointed manager. Having found it hard to combine playing and coaching, Anderson hung up his boots following his appointment but couldn't prevent the inevitable relegation to Division Three.

Success came with instant promotion back to the Second Division and he signed a string of excellent players including Stuart Boam, Graeme Souness, Jim Platt and John Hickton but despite coming close several times, he couldn't get Middlesbrough into the top flight. Anderson resigned in January 1973 following an early FA Cup exit but left a good side that Jack Charlton took to promotion. After trying his hand in Greece, Anderson also managed Doncaster and Bolton.

ANDERSON Vivian Alexander

Right-back
Born: Nottingham, 29 July 1956.
Career: Nottingham Forest 1974. Arsenal 1984. Manchester United 1987. Sheffield Wednesday 1991. Barnsley 1993. MIDDLESBROUGH 1994.

■ The former England international right-back arrived at Middlesbrough as assistant to former Manchester United teammate Bryan Robson and in the process became Boro's oldest ever debutant when called up as an emergency centre-half. Well past his 38th birthday, Anderson gave impressive displays in two away games late in the successful 1994–95 promotion campaign, a 3–1 win at West Bromwich Albion and a hard-fought draw with his old club Barnsley, where he had spent a season as player-manager.

The vastly experienced defender had earlier become the first black England player and won two League Championships and two European Cups with Nottingham Forest, where he made his name as an attacking right-back. Known as 'Spider' due to his long legs, he scored two goals against Boro in the 1977–78 season that manager Brian Clough described as 'the two best goals I've ever seen by one player in a match'. He hung up his boots in the summer of 1995, continuing his role as Robson's

number two. When Robson left Boro in 2001 Anderson departed too and has not returned to football since. He received an MBE for services to football in the Millennium honours list.

ANGUS Michael Anthony

Midfield
Born: Middlesbrough, 28 October 1960.
Career: MIDDLESBROUGH 1978. Scunthorpe United (loan) 1982. Southend United 1983. Darlington 1984. Billingham Synthonia. South Bank.

■ Local boy Mike Angus played in central defence and midfield for his hometown club and was a whole-hearted performer in either role. Angus started an apprenticeship as a plumber and welder at a shipyard in Haverton Hill on leaving school and after five months joined Boro as a non-contract amateur player before signing as an apprentice in March 1978 and professional a few months later.

His debut came as replacement for Tony McAndrew at centre-back in a 3–1 defeat at Bristol City in April 1980 and he enjoyed regular opportunities in the following campaign as he tussled with Billy Ashcroft for the centre-back berth. Although not tall for the position, he was a hard tackler who gave everything and was occasionally used as a workhorse midfielder where he operated in the 1981–82 relegation season.

At the start of 1982–83, Angus joined Scunthorpe on loan and he left Middlesbrough the following summer. He later played Northern League football for Billingham Synthonia and South Bank and became a policeman after a knee injury ended his career.

APPLEBY Robert

Goalkeeper
Born: Warkworth, 15 January 1940.
Career: Amble Welfare. MIDDLESBROUGH 1957. Hereford United 1966.

■ Goalkeeper Bob Appleby came out of the shadows of Peter Taylor and Esmond Million to become Boro's first choice custodian for almost two seasons during the early 1960s. A talented shot-stopper, he was a centre-forward as a boy but had found his niche as a 'keeper by the time he was spotted playing for local League side Amble Welfare as a 17-year-old. He joined Boro's ground staff and progressed through the juniors and reserves before Bob Dennison gave him his debut in a 1–0 Second Division home win over Stoke City in April 1960. He displaced Taylor as the regular 'keeper but missed the second half of the 1960–61 season after injuring his back in an FA Cup tie at Manchester United. However, he was again the first choice throughout the 1961–62 campaign before being dropped for Arthur Lightening and Morris Emmerson. A good shot-stopper, Appleby sometimes struggled on crosses due to his lack of height. Always the dressing room joker, he was infamous among his teammates for spinning the ball when throwing it out, making it difficult for them to control. It is also said he would often make bird noises during the game.

The arrival of Eddie Connachan brought three years in the reserves and only occasional first-team opportunities

and he was placed on the transfer list in September 1965. One of his final games for the club was a disastrous 5–3 defeat at Cardiff that resulted in relegation to the Third Division in 1966. Appleby played his final games for Boro in Division Three before joining Southern League Hereford United, where his teammates included ex-Boro colleague Eddie Holliday. However, a niggling back injury that had dogged him since the Old Trafford Cup tie in 1961 forced his early retirement from the game. He later worked as a water bailif in Cumberland where his responsibilities included catching poachers. He now lives in retirement in the village of Reeth in the Yorkshire Dales.

ARCA Julio

Midfield
Born: Quilmes, Argentina, 31 January 1981.
Career: Argentinos Juniors 1999. Sunderland 2000. MIDDLESBROUGH 2006.

■ The talented Argentinean became Gareth Southgate's first signing as Middlesbrough manager after making the short trip from Sunderland in summer 2006. Boro paid £1.75 million for the adopted North-Eastener who became a folk hero in his six years with the Black Cats. Arca arrived at the Stadium of Light from Argentinos Juniors in 2000 and made 157 appearances for Sunderland, scoring 17 goals. Signed as a replacement for Franck Queudrue, he found his best form in midfield. Arca endured a nightmare start

to his Boro career when he broke his foot during the opening day defeat to newly-promoted Reading. During his lengthy rehabilitation, Andrew Taylor took over at left-back with considerable success and Arca eventually found himself redeployed in the unfamiliar role of central midfielder alongside George Boateng. As playmaker, he became one of Boro's most consistent performers and became a popular figure with the Riverside faithful. Nimble-footed and an accurate passer, he grew into the role and won several Man of the Match accolades. He scored his first Boro goal in the crucial 2–0 win over Charlton Athletic in December – a result that saw Addicks boss Les Reed sacked the following day – and ended his first season with three in all. Arca made Boro tick during their best spell in early 2007 and was instrumental in an exciting FA Cup run that ended in a quarter-final replay defeat to Manchester United. He picked up a groin injury shortly afterwards but regained his place towards the end of the season.

ARMES Samuel

Outside-right
Born: New Seaham, 30 March 1908.
Died: August 1958.
Career: Howden. Dawdon Colliery. Carlisle United 1930. Chester 1932. Blackpool 1933. Wigan Athletic 1934. Leeds United 1935. MIDDLESBROUGH 1938.

■ Pacy winger Armes lost the chance to make a success of his move to Middlesbrough when war broke out just months after joining the club. The outside-right had earlier played for a

variety of north-west clubs after turning professional at Carlisle and once scored nine goals in three games for Chester. He had drifted out of the Football League with Wigan before resurrecting his career at Leeds. Armes made his Middlesbrough debut when Bolton visited Ayresome Park and after just three League games played some wartime matches for the club in late 1939. He was placed on the transfer list in the summer of 1945 for £500 but no offers were forthcoming for the 38-year-old and he was freed in the summer of 1946 as the club prepared for the resumption of League football with Johnny Spuhler firmly entrenched in the right-wing berth. Armes died in Sunderland in August 1958.

ARMSTRONG Alun

Striker
Born: Gateshead, 22 February 1975.
Career: Newcastle United 1993. Stockport County 1994. MIDDLESBROUGH 1998. Huddersfield Town (loan) 2000. Ipswich Town 2000. Bradford City (loan) 2003. Darlington 2004. Rushden & Diamonds 2005. Doncaster Rovers 2006. Darlington 2006.

■ Injuries ruined what might have been a great Middlesbrough career for Geordie striker Alun Armstrong. The former Newcastle United front man burst onto the Riverside scene with a goal-a-start average but was struggling for a first-team place in the bottom divisions by the time he was 30. Armstrong celebrated his 23rd birthday by scoring on his Boro debut as substitute against local rivals Sunderland and then notched a brace against Oxford United in the final game of the 1997–98 season to secure promotion to the Premier League. But he had been struggling with a back injury in the lead up to the win-or-bust last match and following a summer operation suffered further woe when he ruptured his Achilles' tendon in pre-season training, missing most of the subsequent campaign. A clinical finisher with good composure in front of goal, Armstrong had been shown the door by Newcastle manager Kevin Keegan without making the first-team breakthrough and made his name in the lower Leagues with Stockport County after a £35,000 move. He played against Boro in the 1997 Coca-Cola Cup semi-final and obviously impressed Bryan Robson, who signed

him the following season for £1.6 million. The club announced his signing at half-time in a game at the Riverside as Robson strengthened his attack, purchasing Marco Branca and Hamilton Ricard within weeks of Armstrong. He had been set to join former Stockport boss Dave Jones at Southampton until hearing of interest from Boro and Nottingham Forest. His signing paid immediate dividends as he and Branca netted the goals that helped secure automatic promotion. After recovering from his Achilles injury, he found himself behind Ricard and Brian Deane in the pecking order of strikers and his days were numbered when Alen Boksic and Joseph-Desire Job also arrived at the Riverside. A £500,000 fee took him to Premier League newcomers Ipswich Town in December 2000 and he rewarded his new employers with two goals against Southampton on his home debut. Armstrong then enjoyed a perfect Riverside return by scoring both Ipswich goals in a 2–1 over Boro in April 2001, helping the Portman Road club qualify for the UEFA Cup. However, injuries again disrupted his career and he returned to the North East with Darlington, where he returned after unsuccessful stints with Rushden and Doncaster Rovers. He was released by Darlington at the end of the 2006–07 season, after scoring only twice in 29 League Two appearances.

ARMSTRONG David

Midfield
Born: Durham, 26 December 1954.
Career: MIDDLESBROUGH 1972. Southampton 1981. Bournemouth 1987.

■ Jack Charlton's 'little gem' was a familiar sight on the left side of Middlesbrough's midfield for a decade, setting an incredible club record when he played 305 consecutive League games from March 1973 to August 1980. Lying eighth in Boro's all-time appearance list, Armstrong is also the youngest player to have enjoyed a testimonial for the club – he was only 25 when the 1980 Boro team took on the 1973–74 Division Two Championship team he had starred in, to honour Armstrong's service.

Known to all as Spike, Armstrong had been at the club since the age of nine and made his debut at 17. Many believed he was older than he actually was as he was virtually bald from the age of 21. As a teenager, Armstrong was a vital part of Jack Charlton's promotion side, where he had a great understanding with Bobby Murdoch and Graeme Souness, and once the place in Division One was secured, he continued to impress. He had a roving role on the left side of midfield, covering every blade of grass, and, with a great left foot, showed good vision, enthusiasm, excellent long range passing and composure on the ball. He was also deceptively good in the air and had a useful habit of scoring goals, regularly taking penalties, as well as setting up countless strikes for others with his pinpoint crossing. The only criticism that could ever be levelled at him was that he was not the sort of player to get stuck in.

Always a favourite of the fans, who consistently campaigned for an England call up, Armstrong continued to improve throughout his Boro career and after winning the club's player of year award in 1979–80, when he was also top scorer, he finally made his full England debut against Australia in May 1980 after earlier winning caps at schools, Under-23 and B levels. In November 1980 newspaper stories linked Armstrong and teammate Craig Johnston with Leeds United but manager John Neal claimed that £1 million wouldn't buy either player. Nevertheless, he became Boro's record sale when he moved to Southampton, as Boro's midfield broke up with Proctor and Johnston also departing. At the Dell, he continued to star alongside Kevin Keegan and won further England caps.

Although he was keen to break into football management, Armstrong has held a number of other roles since retiring from the game. He was commercial manager of Waterlooville for some years, coached Andover Town, worked as sports liaison officer for Hampshire Schools and was a soft drinks salesman. He also occasionally works as a radio reporter, commentating on Southampton games.

ARNOLD Ian

Forward
Born: Durham, 4 July 1972.
Career: MIDDLESBROUGH 1990. Carlisle United 1992. Kettering Town. Stalybridge Celtic.

■ Teenage forward Ian Arnold was handed his first-team chance by Colin Todd after impressing in the Boro reserves and covering for injured John Hendrie. He made his entrance as a late substitute for John Wark in a 3–0 win over Newcastle at Ayresome Park. Another short appearance followed against Watford two weeks later. Once Lennie Lawrence had taken over as Boro boss only brief chances came again, one League opportunity against Wolves and another substitute appearance in the Zenith Data Systems Cup, but Arnold

never really impressed. Arnold, who had signed Schoolboy forms for Boro aged 14 and starred as Boro reached the FA Youth Cup Final, was released in the summer of 1992. He couldn't command a regular place at Carlisle and joined non-League Kettering Town for £10,000, later playing for Stalybridge Celtic where he won England semi-professional caps.

ASHCROFT William

Forward
Born: Liverpool, 1 October 1952.
Career: Wrexham 1970. MIDDLESBROUGH 1977. Twente Enschede (Holland) 1982. Tranmere Rovers 1985.

■ A big bear of a man, with his curly hair and beard, Billy Ashcroft was a distinctive figure on the football field. The lively Liverpudlian was a character off the pitch but all too often frustrated when playing, even though his effort could never be questioned and he was a threat in the air. Unselfish and hard working in his frontman role, Ashcroft was never a prolific goalscorer in his five-year spell at Ayresome Park.

He had been a big favourite at Wrexham, having asked for a trial after joining Blackpool on schoolboy forms. The highlight of his time in Wales came when he earned the nickname 'the Bear of Bruges' from Anderlecht fans following a European Cup quarter-final clash and the Belgian side tried unsuccessfully to sign him for £150,000.

He was signed at Middlesbrough by his former Wrexham boss John Neal for a club record fee of £135,000, becoming Boro's first six figure buy, and scored on his home debut against Birmingham, also making his mark early on by scoring two in a famous 4–2 First Division win at Newcastle. But Ashcroft never quite fulfilled the expectations of the club and fans, who often barracked him and were disappointed that Neal saw Ashcroft as the answer to the club's long-standing goalscoring problem. He never scored more than six in a season and, in truth, failed to bridge the gap to Division One football. He is also unfortunately remembered for a bad miss in an FA Cup quarter-final against Orient in March 1978, when six yards out and with an open goal at his mercy, denying Boro a place in the semis.

Ashcroft was tried at centre-half with some success when Stuart Boam joined Newcastle and won over the fans with his aerial power and strength. But he was back at centre-forward under Bobby Murdoch and was joint top scorer in 1981–82 with just five as Boro were relegated from the top flight, after which he was released. He moved to Holland when, on the recommendation of former Boro teammate Heine Otto, he won a contract with Twente Enschede. He was a cult hero in Holland where he toured the country judging talent contests and even recorded a song, and was widely known as 'the crazy Englishman'. He returned to England in 1985 to join Tranmere but was troubled by a back injury and became a publican in Merseyside.

ASHMAN Donald

Full-back/Half-back
Born: Staindrop, 9 October 1902.
Died: 1984.
Career: Cockfield Albion. MIDDLESBROUGH 1924. Queen's Park Rangers 1932. Darlington 1935.

■ Composed, unruffled half-back Don Ashman saw as much action in Boro's reserve team as he did in the Football League but was a vital squad member who could be relied upon to give full commitment to the cause with tenacious displays, full of energy and stamina. Initially a miner who played part-time football for Cockfield Albion, Ashman was brought to Ayresome Park by Herbert

Bamlett for a £10 fee and the guarantee of a friendly at Cockfield's ground. He was pushed into the North Eastern League reserve side and made his first-team debut six months later in a 1–0 home win against Stoke City. He was an established member of the side which romped to the Second Division championship in 1926–27. Limited opportunities came in Division One and even fewer in the 28–29 promotion campaign but he enjoyed an extended run at full-back in 1929–30. He moved on to Division Three South QPR but was back in the North East with Darlington shortly before the outbreak of World War Two.

ASKEW William

Midfield
Born: Great Lumley, 2 October 1959.
Career: MIDDLESBROUGH 1977. Gateshead. Hull City 1982. Newcastle United 1990. Shrewsbury Town (loan) 1991. Gateshead. Whitley Bay. Spennymoor United. Workington.

■ Being David Armstrong's reserve on the left-side of midfield was an unenviable task for Billy Askew, with Armstrong a permanent fixture in the side. Red-haired Askew had joined Boro from Lumley Juniors and was a small, tenacious midfielder with a good left foot and plenty of energy. A run of games came following Armstrong's departure in the summer of 1981 but Askew missed a penalty v Manchester United in a 2–0 defeat in September 1981 and was unable to make the number-11 shirt his own. He had a loan spell at Blackburn without making the first team and was released following relegation in 1982. Askew initially dropped out of the Football League and played some games for Gateshead before signing for Hull in October after a trial. He went on to make his name in the lower divisions with Hull where he was a firm favourite, winning promotion from Division Four in 1983 and Division Three in 1985. Newcastle paid £150,000 for him at the age of 30 to bolster their midfield but he suffered from injuries and was given few chances. Askew was loaned to Gateshead and Shrewsbury in 1991–92 before joining Gateshead on a free transfer in the summer of 1992. He later played for Whitley Bay, Spennymoor United and Workington, and was assistant coach at Darlington in 1996.

ASTLEY Henry

Forward
Born: Bolton, 1882.
Career: Bolton Wanderers 1900. Millwall Athletic 1902. MIDDLESBROUGH 1904. Crystal Palace 1905. Heywood United. Bury 1907. Heywood United.

■ Lancastrian Harry Astley was brought back into the Football League from Southern League Millwall but failed to provide the answers to Middlesbrough's goalscoring problems. After making his debut under John Robson in the half-back line in the opening day meeting with Sheffield Wednesday in 1904, Astley moved up to join the forwards for his other infrequent call-ups to the first team. He ended the campaign as top scorer with a measly five goals as Middlesbrough struggled to maintain their First Division status. At the end of the season, Astley followed manager Robson to newly formed Southern League side Crystal Palace, later returning to Lancashire with Bury.

ATHERTON Robert William

Inside-right
Born: Bethesda, 29 July 1876.
Died: 1917.
Career: Dalry Primrose. Heart of Midlothian. Hibernian. MIDDLESBROUGH 1903. Chelsea 1906.

■ Atherton became only the second player to win an international cap while with Middlesbrough when he represented Wales in a 2–2 draw with England in February 1904. His first cap came just two days after helping Boro to a crucial 1–0 First Division win over Notts County as the club struggled for survival. After joining the club from Scotland, Atherton made his home debut in the first ever League match at Ayresome Park, having played his first Middlesbrough game at Sheffield Wednesday a week earlier. Initially a wing-forward, he was switched to inside-forward after five games and scored his first goals in a 6–0 victory over Manchester City in October 1903. He missed only one League game in his first season with the club and that was the week after his international debut when he was again in action for Wales, this time becoming the first Boro player to score an international goal, in a 1–1 draw in Scotland. It was certainly a busy season for Atherton, as the following March he again represented his country in a 1–0 defeat against Ireland in Bangor just two days after scoring in his club's 2–1 First Division defeat at Aston Villa. Atherton was appointed club captain in his second season on Teesside before moving on to Chelsea.

AULD Walter Bottomley

Outside-left
Born: Bellshill, 9 July 1929.
Died: 1988.
Career: Bellshill Athletic. MIDDLESBROUGH 1950. Berwick Rangers.

■ After scoring on his debut, Wally Auld must have hoped he had earned a place in the Middlesbrough team but, despite being one of the select group to record a goal in their first appearance, the outside-left was given just two games. Having been brought to Ayresome by David Jack from Belshill Athletic, his memorable debut was a home meeting with Sheffield Wednesday in January 1951 when he struck the back of the net after 80 minutes to secure a 2–1 win but he was omitted from the next fixture and his only other chance was in a 1–1 home draw with Liverpool six weeks later. He returned to Scotland and died in 1988.

BAILEY Ian Craig

Left-back
Born: Middlesbrough, 20 October 1956.
Career: MIDDLESBROUGH 1974. Doncaster Rovers (loan) 1976. Carlisle United (loan) 1977. Minnesota Kicks (United States). Bolton Wanderers (loan) 1981. Sheffield Wednesday 1982. Blackpool (loan) 1984. Bolton Wanderers (loan) 1985.

■ With his overlapping runs to link up with the Boro attack, Bailey was the model of a modern-day wing-back. The local defender was good with the ball at his feet and quite skilful, though he had an annoying habit of taking his eye off the ball and allowing it to go out of play while looking up for a pass.

Having played his early football as centre-forward at Easterside Junior School, Bailey, who also attended Bertram Ramsey School, was converted to outside-left for Middlesbrough Boys before finding his natural position at left-back after being tried there by Boro trainer Harold Shepherdson in a practice game. His early progress was blocked by Terry Cooper and Frank Spraggon but Bailey made his debut in the Anglo-Scottish Cup before his League baptism against Tottenham in December 1975. Less than a month later he played in the first leg of the League Cup semi-final against Manchester City, still aged just 19. This was followed by loan spells at Stan Anderson's Doncaster and Carlisle as well as a stint in the US with Minnesota Kicks.

A regular place back at

Middlesbrough brought him one sub appearance for the England Under-21 side against Yugoslavia but he then missed five months with a knee cartilage injury in 1977–78. For much of his time, Bailey was not an automatic choice in the left-back berth, often contesting the place with Peter Johnson.

Another cartilage injury forced him out in 1978–79 and he was involved in a contractual dispute with the club in the summer of 1980 and placed on the transfer list. He still trained with the club and manager John Neal eventually persuaded Bailey to sign a one-year deal. He enjoyed his best campaign in 1980–81 but was out in the cold at the start of the following season following the arrival of Joe Bolton and was loaned to Bolton Wanderers. Though he won back his place, Jack Charlton returned to Boro to sign Bailey in August 1982 after Boro's relegation. Boro had put a one-year contract on the table but Charlton stepped in with a three-year offer. Boro valued him at £300,000 but Wednesday offered only £80,000. A tribunal was called but Charlton said he would pull out if the tribunal decided higher than his estimation and Boro accepted the original offer. His career was ended prematurely through a leg injury and he went on to become physiotherapist at Sheffield United.

BAIRD Ian James

Forward

Born: Rotherham, 1 April 1964.

Career: Southampton 1982. Cardiff City

(loan) 1983. Newcastle United (loan) 1984. Leeds United 1985. Portsmouth 1987. Leeds United 1988. MIDDLESBROUGH 1990. Heart of Midlothian 1991. Bristol City 1993. Plymouth Argyle 1995. Brighton & Hove Albion 1996.

■ The blood and thunder, robust style of striker Ian Baird made him a big favourite with the Ayresome faithful. A centre-forward with a big heart and battling instincts, Baird was strong and aggressive, good with his back to goal and a superb header of the ball. He enjoyed physical encounters and unsettling defenders but also had a deceptive element of skill to his game.

After winning England Schoolboy caps, and playing for Hampshire schoolboys alongside Paul Kerr, Baird started his career at Southampton and almost joined Boro when Willie Maddren agreed a £50,000 fee and talked to the player, but Baird was reluctant to join a team in danger of relegation to Division Three. He eventually came to Ayresome after mixed fortunes, having enjoyed success in two spells at Leeds including a Player of the Season award and a Division Two Championship medal, but asked to leave after the arrival of Lee Chapman.

Baird was Bruce Rioch's last signing at the club and was seen as the target man Boro had missed since the departure of Archie Stephens, but he had a disappointing first season. Boro were struggling for goals and he didn't provide the answer, waiting nine games for his first goal, though he did score twice in a 4–1 victory over Newcastle to keep Boro in Division Two.

However, more success came in 1990–91 under Colin Todd when he scored 10 in 18 early in the season and linked up well with Bernie Slaven as Boro challenged for promotion. But the goals dried up as Boro drifted out of the automatic promotion places and his last game was the Play-off defeat against Notts County. Baird walked away with the supporters' club Player of the Year award at the end of the campaign but was soon on his way to Scotland, deciding to leave after comments from Boro chairman Colin Henderson criticising players who did not choose to live in the Teesside area. He was a boo boy target at Hearts when the goals didn't come and joined Bristol City for £275,000. Baird retired in 1998 because of a knee injury and later played and coached in the Far East.

BAKER Steven Richard

Defender
Born: Pontefract, 8 September 1978.
Career: MIDDLESBROUGH 1997. Huddersfield Town (loan) 1999. Darlington (loan) 2000. Hartlepool United (loan) 2000. Scarborough 2001.

■ A versatile young defender, Steve Baker is perhaps best remembered for a fine man-marking job on Liverpool winger Steve McManaman in the semi-final of the 1998 Coca-Cola Cup. Sadly, he soon lost his way at the highest level and quickly dropped out of League football altogether. By the time of the memorable occasion at Anfield, Baker had already appeared several times in Boro's promotion-bound Division One side, following a debut in the earlier rounds of the Cup against Barnet. A hard-tackling defender, Baker had been in the same YTS intake as Andy Campbell and Anthony Ormerod but missed most of the 1996–97 season with a serious knee injury. He had, however, already appeared for the Republic of Ireland Under-21 side, qualifying through Irish parentage. When more injuries disrupted his season in 1998–99, he made his one and only Premier League start at right-back in a 2–1 win at

Coventry City in April 1999. He was loaned to Huddersfield, Darlington and Hartlepool over the next two years before joining non-League Scarborough on a free transfer in 2002. He was made captain of Gateshead when transferred there in 2006.

BARHAM Mark Francis

Right-winger
Born: Folkestone, 12 July 1962.
Career: Norwich City 1980. Huddersfield Town 1987. MIDDLESBROUGH 1988. West Bromwich Albion 1989. Brighton & Hove Albion 1989. Shrewsbury Town 1992. Sittingbourne.

■ Earlier in his career, Barham's performances on the right-wing had brought him England caps, but when he arrived at Middlesbrough on a short-term contract, he was a shadow of his former self. The ex-England Youth international had looked a tremendous prospect at Norwich and was only 20 when he earned two full caps on England's 1983 Australian tour. But a serious knee injury was sustained in 1984 which nearly ended his career and kept him out of action for 13 months. He failed to recapture his earlier form for the Canaries and was not a big success following his £100,000 transfer to Huddersfield. Bruce Rioch beat off competition from Crystal Palace to recruit Barham on a free transfer, hoping to restore him to former glories. Arriving at the same time as another ex-England man, Peter Davenport, Barham spent four months in the Boro reserves before his debut in a 1–1 Division One draw with Wimbledon at Plough Lane, then enjoying a fine home debut against Everton on Easter Monday. Yet, though he had a couple of good games, Barham was clearly incapable of playing at the top level and the club and player agreed by mutual consent to his departure in the summer, following relegation from the top flight. He returned to Norfolk before joining West Brom, initially on trial, and enjoying some success at Brighton.

BARKER Frederick Malcolm

Defender
Born: Middlesbrough.
Career: South Bank. MIDDLESBROUGH 1906.

■ Local defender Barker was recruited from South Bank into Middlesbrough's Division One team but made just one appearance in League football. Barker was one of five players to operate at right-back in the 1905–06 season, getting his chance in front of an Ayresome Park crowd estimated at 17,000 for the visit of Sheffield Wednesday on September 15, 1905. The visitors triumphed 3–1 and Barker was never seen again in a Middlesbrough shirt.

BARKER William Charles

Wing-half
Born: Linthorpe.
Died: May 1937.
Career: South Bank. MIDDLESBROUGH 1905.

■ Barker enjoyed just two seasons as a first-team regular in the Middlesbrough side but was a loyal club servant for well over a decade under four different managers. The local lad operated across the half-back line, making his debut in a 1–1 draw at Bury in February 1906. He was straight out of the side again but was recalled to play six of the last seven games of the season as Middlesbrough struggled badly and just avoided relegation.

Barker's only recorded goal was in the opening game of 1906–07 in a 2–2 home draw with Everton and he played in the club's opening games, though just one victory was secured in nine matches. Barker made way when player-manager Andy Aitken arrived at the club in November and over the following seasons, chances were rare with other new recruits, including Teddy Verrill and Bob Young, taking the full-back positions.

In fact it was five seasons before Barker won a more regular place, taking over from Sam Aitken and playing most games in two successive campaigns. He missed the start of the 1912–13 season after injuring his knee in a practice game and Barker's last game was against Manchester United in October 1912. He became assistant trainer after the Great War and one of his duties was to meet new players at the train station. He died in May 1937.

BARMBY Nicholas Jonathan

Midfield/Forward
Born: Hull, 11 February 1974.
Career: Tottenham Hotspur 1991. MIDDLESBROUGH 1995. Everton 1996. Liverpool 2000. Leeds United 2002. Nottingham Forest (loan) 2004. Hull City 2004.

■ When Nick Barmby was recruited by Bryan Robson in the summer of 1995 he was the first current England international to sign for Middlesbrough since Steve Bloomer 90 years earlier. The skilful young forward came with a reputation as one of the brightest talents in the game and made a brilliant impact on Teesside, netting on his debut at Highbury, and either scoring or making the final contribution to each of Boro's first 10 goals of the campaign.

The son of a former York player, Barmby was a graduate of the FA National School at Lilleshall and had trials at Manchester United, Liverpool and Arsenal before joining Tottenham. International recognition came early with caps at Schools and Youth level – appearing in the 1993 World Youth Cup with Jamie Pollock – and then chances at Under-21, B and ultimately full level, drawing comparison with Peter Beardsley thanks to his impish build, good passing ability, tricky skills and eye for goal.

Robson had tried to sign Barmby early in the 1994–95 season amid rumours that he was unsettled at Spurs but had to wait until the following summer to tie up a £5.25 million deal which smashed Boro's transfer record four times over. In his early days on Teesside, Barmby struck up a good relationship with Craig Hignett – they were dubbed the Midget Gems – and finished top scorer in his first season. Despite this success, the arrival of Juninho during the season had clearly affected him and Barmby had become far less effective. They were similar players who liked to attack from deep and play off forwards, and the balance of the team was not quite right, ultimately leading to Barmby's departure for a £5.75 million record fee to Everton. For some time before the sale, rumours had circulated that he would be moving on and that he had fallen out with Robson on a pre-season tour of Malaysia. Though this was denied by both parties, the rumours of his departure did become a reality after just 14 months on Teesside. After initial success at Goodison, Barmby suffered a loss of form and lost his England place, missing out on the 1998 World Cup. However, he returned to the national side and was a member of Sven-Göran Eriksson's England team that famously thrashed Germany 5–1 away. He made the rare move from Everton to Liverpool in 2000 before a less successful stint with Leeds, eventually returning home to Hull, helping them to promotion to the Championship.

BARNARD Raymond Scholey

Full-back
Born: Middlesbrough, 16 April 1933.
Career: MIDDLESBROUGH 1950. Lincoln City 1960. Grantham Town.

■ In 10 years at Ayresome Park, Ray Barnard was always contesting a place in the side with several rivals but was a reliable performer when required in the right full-back berth. A former England schoolboy international and apprentice motor mechanic, Barnard was given his Middlesbrough debut by David Jack aged 18 in the cauldron atmosphere of a

Division One Tees-Wear derby at Ayresome Park in December 1951 while still completing National Service, being stationed near York.

A steady no frills player, solid in the tackle, Barnard faced early competition from Dicky Robinson and also Ray Bilcliff – the man he would contest the shirt with for most of his time at Middlesbrough. Following Jack's resignations, he played only once in almost two years under Walter Rowley. However, for three seasons in the mid–1950s, following the appointment of Bob Dennison, Barnard was a regular sight in the red and white shirt. Bilcliff was still on the scene but Barnard played the majority of games, only missing out when suffering a broken leg against Bristol Rovers in 1955–56. Midway through the following campaign, Bilcliff was reinstated following a 1–0 home defeat against Rotherham and, with Derek Stonehouse also contesting the full-back places, Barnard spent two years on the sidelines before getting another chance. He went on to play for Lincoln and then non-League Grantham for four years, retiring after open heart surgery, and becoming a machine shop foreman and living near Lincoln.

BARNESS Anthony

Born: Lewisham, 25 March 1973.
Career: Charlton Athletic 1991. Chelsea 1993. MIDDLESBROUGH (loan) 1993. Southend United (loan) 1995. Charlton Athletic 1996. Bolton Wanderers 2000. Plymouth 2005. Grays Athletic 2007.

■ Lennie Lawrence knew all about Barness from his days as Charlton manager and recruited the young full-back – by then in the reserves at Chelsea – for the start of Boro's 1993–94 Division One campaign. Chelsea had paid £350,000 to sign Barness from Charlton as a teenager but he had failed to make the breakthrough at Stamford Bridge. Barness hoped for first-team football during his loan spell at Ayresome Park but instead it was another youngster, Richard Liburd, who made the left-back berth his own for the recently relegated side. Barness played just one game for Boro, in the Anglo-Italian Cup against Grimsby, in place of the rested Liburd, in a disappointing but ultimately meaningless 2–1 defeat. Comfortable on either flank, Barness was re-signed by Charlton for £165,000 in 1996 and enjoyed a lengthy spell with Bolton.

BARRON Michael James

Defender/Midfield
Born: Chester-le-Street, 22 December 1974.
Career: MIDDLESBROUGH 1993. Hartlepool United 1997.

■ Reserve team captain and a talented young defender, Barron was unfortunate not to make a real breakthrough at the club, though his lack of height probably cost him at the highest level. The determined centre-back was a calm and composed performer when given a first-team chance. Barron was given his debut as an 18-year-old, one of several youngsters blooded by Lennie Lawrence following a summer clearout and

subsequent injury crisis. He had been non-playing substitute on three occasions before his First Division debut against Portsmouth in November 1993, out of position at right-back alongside fellow debutant Ian Johnson.

Establishing himself as captain of the second string, Barron impressed when he made his first League start for two years when called upon to replace Steve Vickers against Everton in March 1996 – a 2–0 defeat which proved to be his only Premier League game. Barron initially joined Hartlepool on loan before securing a permanent deal, going on to win the supporters' club Player of the Year award at the Victoria Ground in 1997–98. He became club captain throughout their many highs and lows of the next decade and had made 325 League appearances for Hartlepool by the end of the 2006–07 season.

BATES Matthew David

Defender
Born: Stockton, 10 December 1986.
Career: MIDDLESBROUGH 2005. Darlington (loan) 2005. Ipswich (loan) 2006.

■ Another successful Academy product, Bates moved through the ranks and was given his full debut by Steve McClaren as an 18-year-old in the Premiership match at Tottenham in August 2005. A gifted centre-back, he was a regular England youth international highly regarded for his speed off the mark and timely interceptions. He was part of the Boro side that won the FA Youth Cup in 2004. Calm and strong on the ball, the youngster was admired by many other clubs before committing his long-term future to Boro. Bates produced a Man of the Match performance in the UEFA Cup semi-final first leg with Steaua Bucharest and made 12 League starts during the 2005–06 campaign. He also showed versatility by deputizing at right-back. The arrival of Jonathan Woodgate and Robert Huth in summer 2006 saw him drop down the pecking order and he was loaned to Ipswich where, in his second game, he ruptured cruciate and medial knee ligaments. Bates worked hard on his rehabilitation with a view to regaining full fitness for 2007–08.

BAXTER Michael John

Central defender
Born: Birmingham, 30 December 1956.
Died: 1989.
Career: Preston North End 1974. MIDDLESBROUGH 1981. Portsmouth 1984.

■ Gentle giant Mick Baxter was a tall, well-built centre-half but lacked the aggression to become a top defender. The son of former Villa and Wolves player Bill Baxter, the ex-Preston apprentice left Deepdale following relegation to Division Three and became Bobby Murdoch's first signing – though the Boro manager had just failed to sign St Johnstone's young striker Ally McCoist who had opted for Sunderland instead.

Baxter made his debut in the same game as Heine Otto, a home defeat against Tottenham, and suffered relegation from Division One in his first season. He was in a poor team but did struggle in the top flight. As Boro floundered in Division Two, Baxter had few highlights but chipped in with the odd goal including a blasted effort in the 100th Tees-Wear derby – a 2–0 win in April 1982 – and also scored the winner in a famous 3–2 FA Cup win over Arsenal in January 1984. In May of that year, he was released by Willie Maddren who needed to cut costs and Baxter was among the top wage earners. He joined Portsmouth but his contract was cancelled when he was diagnosed with Hodgkin's Disease. He returned to Preston to work in the Football in the Community programme but collapsed at Deepdale and died in 1989, aged just 32.

BAXTER Robert Denholm

Centre-half/Inside-left
Born: Gilmerton, 23 January 1911.
Died: April 1991.
Career: Musselburgh Bruntonians. MIDDLESBROUGH 1932. Heart of Midlothian 1945. Leith Athletic.

■ One of Middlesbrough's greatest centre-halves, Bob Baxter was an inspirational captain and defender in the club's excellent pre-war team.

Skilful, good in the air and a great tackler, Baxter was a leader, not just on the pitch but also in the dressing room, a hero on the terraces, and rated by many as the club's best ever captain.

Baxter was actually spotted by accident. Manager Peter McWilliam went on a scouting mission to Scotland, only watching Baxter play as the fixture he intended to see was postponed. He was impressed with the young miner in the Bruntonian Juniors team and persuaded him to give up his sideline running dance bands to come to Teesside. Baxter was signed as a forward and made his debut at inside-left at Birmingham in October 1932. He played in nine different outfield positions before finding his home at centre-half following the sale of Tom Griffiths in 1935.

With his square jaw and sunken eyes, together with black, centre-parted slicked-down hair, Baxter cut an imposing figure on the pitch. He also had a wicked sense of humour, shown most frequently when he displayed a tendency to try to dribble past forwards in his own box. Goalkeeper Dave Cumming would shout 'Baxter, Baxter, get rid of it!', but the centre-half would merely laugh at the panic he caused and rarely made errors.

But he accepted no insolence from those he oversaw. Like the other senior players, he was called 'Sir' by the younger players and a young Wilf Mannion once made the mistake of calling him by his first name, ending up in a cold bath fully clothed for his troubles.

Capped three times by Scotland, war brought a premature end to Baxter's Middlesbrough career and denied him a genuine title challenge. The Scot played in four wartime internationals and his last game for Middlesbrough was against Newcastle at Ayresome in 1940. He returned to Scotland to work as a miner, also running a newsagent and tobacconists shop as well as guesting for Hibernian and Hearts. He was transferred to Hearts after the war and later managed Leith Athletic and the Edinburgh Monarchs speedway team. He returned to Teesside in retirement and was an accomplished accordionist and low handicap golfer. His son, also called Bob, played for Darlington, Brighton and Torquay. Baxter senior died in Middleton St George in April 1991.

BEAGRIE Peter Sydney

Winger
Born: Middlesbrough, 28 November 1965.
Career: MIDDLESBROUGH 1983. Sheffield United 1986. Stoke City 1988. Everton 1989. Sunderland (loan) 1991. Manchester City 1994. Bradford City 1997. Everton (loan) 1998. Wigan Athletic 2001. Scunthorpe United 2001. Grimsby Town 2006.

■ Exciting winger Beagrie displayed massive potential when he broke into the Middlesbrough team as a fresh-faced youngster. A naturally confident player, Beagrie tormented defenders with his skills and array of tricks. But he blotted his copybook in the eyes of Boro fans by leaving the club in its darkest hour.

A member of the Middlesbrough Schoolboys team which won the English SFA Shield, Beagrie was on schoolboy forms at Hartlepool but joined Boro as an apprentice, featuring in the same junior team as Colin Cooper and Alan Kernaghan. He was given his Boro debut as a centre-forward against Birmingham by former Pools youth coach Willie Maddren in a relegation-threatened side. During his Boro career he was mostly used as an out and out winger and impressed the supporters with occasionally brilliant performances, though he was erratic.

After being sent off in the final game of 1984–85 against Shrewsbury, Beagrie was a regular sight in the following campaign as Boro were relegated to Division Three. With the club in liquidation, Beagrie opted for a cut-price move to Sheffield United. The decision meant that the local lad was heavily barracked whenever he returned to Middlesbrough as it was perceived that he had deserted the club in its hour of need.

At Stoke, Beagrie became an Under-21 international, later winning two B caps. He later made a million pound move from Everton to Manchester City in 1994, though he had something of a wild boy image off the field. Famed for his back flips after scoring goals, Beagrie built up a reputation as a talented, if inconsistent, traditional winger with the ability to win a game when on form. He returned to the Premier League in 1999 as part of the unfancied Bradford City team, playing against Boro before dropping into Division Two with Wigan. Months later he switched to Scunthorpe, managed by his former Boro teammate Brian Laws. A regular scorer despite entering the veteran stage, he helped them to promotion to League One in 2005. A year later he switched to Grimsby but injury forced him to hang up his boots a few months short of his 41st birthday, having made 653 League appearances for 10 clubs over 22 years.

BEATON Simon

Right-half
Born: Inverness 1888.
Career: Aston Villa 1907. Newcastle United 1908. MIDDLESBROUGH 1909. Huddersfield Town 1910.

■ Contemporary reports suggest that Middlesbrough were fined 10 guineas for playing half-back Beaton twice during the 1909–10 season. It seems the club landed themselves in hot water with the Football League as the player was still registered with Newcastle United. Beaton was on the books of both Aston Villa and Newcastle without playing a first-team game and was allowed to join Boro in February 1910, making his debut in a 2–1 defeat at Chelsea and retaining his place for the following match against Spurs. When Beaton returned to St James Park, he was told that he would not be retained and joined Huddersfield where he played over 100 games before retiring in 1914. He later came out of retirement to guest for Crystal Palace and Spurs during World War One.

BEATTIE Thomas Kevin

Central defender
Born: Carlisle, 18 December 1953.
Career: Ipswich Town 1971. Colchester United 1982. MIDDLESBROUGH 1982. Sandviking (Sweden). Kingsberg (Norway). Clacton.

■ Kevin Beattie was a fantastic centre-half in his prime, winning the PFA Young

Player of the Year Award and England caps in his time at Ipswich. He arrived at Ayresome Park having played a handful of games for Colchester in Division Four, two years after 'retiring' at Portman Road, and well past his best. Beattie had been given his chance at Bobby Robson's Ipswich when the future England boss had failed in a bid to sign Boro's Willie Maddren. He showed power, pace and command in the air as he rose to fame at Portman Road but had always been injury prone. A serious injury had prompted his decision to retire from Ipswich in 1980 and the Suffolk club were annoyed when he made his comeback at Colchester as they had paid up his contract and given him a testimonial. They demanded £100,000 but never got it. Malcolm Allison brought him to Teesside and raved about the former England international's performances when fitness allowed him to appear. Sadly he was unable to overcome the injury problems and recapture his earlier heights, while a refusal to move to Teesside cannot have helped him settle at Ayresome. Beattie left Boro after a contract dispute and hung up his boots once again.

BECK Mikkel Venge

Striker
Born: Aarhus, Denmark, 12 May 1973.
Career: B1909 (Denmark). Odense (Denmark) 1992. Fortuna Cologne (Germany) 1993. MIDDLESBROUGH 1996. Derby County 1999. Nottingham Forest (loan) 1999. Queen's Park Rangers (loan) 2000. Aalborg BK (Denmark) (loan) 2000. OSC Lille (France) 2000. Aalborg BK (Denmark) (loan) 2002.

■ Beck was the first player to sign for Middlesbrough under the transfer regulations initiated by the Bosman ruling. The Danish international was recruited shortly before appearing in the Euro 96 tournament in England. Yet Beck never fulfilled the high expectations of him and had a sometimes difficult relationship with the club's supporters. The son of an Aarhus player, Beck scored twice on his debut for Odense when he was 17 and broke into the Denmark squad after moving to Germany, scoring on his international debut versus Finland. He was recruited from German Second Division side Fortuna Cologne at the same time as Boro had tried to sign fellow Dane Michael Laudrup. Fortuna wanted £1 million for Beck and it took a long legal wrangle before the striker was able to make his Middlesbrough debut. That came in a Coca-Cola Cup tie at Hereford in which he scored.

In his first season, Beck struggled to adapt to the physical demands of the English game and was undermined by strike partner Fabrizio Ravanelli openly criticising him on the pitch. As the goals failed to flow in Boro's relegation, he also became unpopular with sections of the crowd. After scoring in the semi-finals of the 1997 FA and Coca-Cola Cups, Beck played in the Coca-Cola Cup Final draw with Leicester but was substitute in the replay and was also on the bench for the FA Cup Final.

Better fortunes came in 1997 alongside Paul Merson, shown by his award as Nationwide Player of the Month in November 1997, and he finished top League scorer as Boro won promotion. But, prone to frustrating fluctuations in form, Beck was still a boo boy target and it was no surprise when he lost his place late in the season following the arrival of Marco Branca, Alun Armstrong and Hamilton Ricard.

Out of favour at the start of the following campaign, injuries to Armstrong and Branca, coupled with the departure of Merson, handed Beck the chance to build a promising partnership with Ricard and earn a recall to the Danish national side. Yet once Brian Deane had been signed from Benfica, Beck was once again on the sidelines for club and country, eventually joining Derby on transfer deadline day for a £500,000 fee. He failed to sparkle at Derby but enjoyed success back in Denmark on loan to Aarlborg, returning to the Denmark side for Euro 2000. Another £500,000 fee took him to Lille but a series of injuries forced him into early retirement, despite an attempted comeback with Crystal Palace in 2004. He is now an agent.

BELL Henry Davey

Wing-half
Born: Sunderland, 14 October 1924.
Career: Hylton Colliery. Sunderland. MIDDLESBROUGH 1945. Darlington 1955.

■ Middlesbrough boss David Jack's sideline as manager of Sunderland Greyhound Stadium came in handy when he spotted a young footballer impressing in a wartime five-a-side competition at the venue. The tenacious youngster Harry Bell was serving in the RAF and on the books at Sunderland but, once League football resumed, he was plying his trade down the road at Ayresome Park.

Sunderland had spotted Bell playing for Hylton Colliery and he played some

wartime games at Roker Park before making his Middlesbrough debut as a guest in the wartime Football League North in November 1944, regularly travelling back to play for Boro with Cec McCormack and becoming a fixture in the side in 1945–46 after formally transferring to his new club. He went on to play more than 300 times for Boro's post-war side.

Bell had joined Boro as an inside-forward but was switched to right-half in an emergency and it became his regular position. Although never a flair player, he was a tenacious but fair tackler, only once being sent off in his career – in a derby clash with Sunderland in December 1951. Bell was noted for his hard work and bravery, displayed when he continued to play after breaking his nose in a game against Huddersfield in November 1948.

Alongside his football talents, Bell was a county standard cricketer. He played as a professional for Durham County and Middlesbrough in the North Yorkshire and South Durham Leagues. In January 1952, he announced that he would concentrate on football after rejecting a three-year contract to play for Somerset. After leaving Middlesbrough, Bell spent one full-time season at Darlington and another four on a part-time basis. After hanging up his boots, he scouted for Liverpool and became a top executive with Tetley breweries.

BELL Ian Charles

Midfield
Born: Middlesbrough, 14 November 1958.
Career: MIDDLESBROUGH 1976. Mansfield Town 1981.

■ A slightly-built midfielder or right-winger, Charlie Bell was a hard-working, tidy player. He made his first-team debut aged 19 in a goal-less draw at Wolves in April 1978, replacing fellow youngster Craig Johnston in John Neal's side. Just one chance came in 1978–79 as stand-in for John Mahoney and he enjoyed a brief spell in place of Mark Proctor in the following campaign. Bell's final games came in John Neal's last season in charge and he left soon after the appointment of Bobby Murdoch as manager. Bell served under former Boro colleague Stuart Boam at Mansfield where he played some games at right-back but mostly in midfield. After giving up the game, Bell became a policeman. He played cricket for Marske and later managed Marske United football team.

BELL James

Inside-right
Born: Eston.
Career: Bolton Wanderers 1902. Grangetown. MIDDLESBROUGH 1904. Eston United. Barrow. Exeter City. Portsmouth.

■ Known to all as Daisy, Bell enjoyed a fleeting spell in Middlesbrough's struggling First Division side. Operating at inside-right, the local lad stepped into the side for a trip to Notts County in October 1904. The club had not enjoyed the best start to the season and the poor form continued. Only one win was secured in Bell's eight games in the side, that coming when he scored both goals in a 2–1 win over Blackburn. Two weeks later, Bell played his last match for Middlesbrough. Following a 5–0 New Year's Eve defeat at Sheffield Wednesday, he was dropped for the visit of Sunderland to Ayresome Park and soon returned to local League football.

BELL Joseph Nicholson

Winger
Born: Pegswood, 30 August 1912.
Career: Barrow 1932. MIDDLESBROUGH 1934. West Ham United 1935. Walsall 1936.

■ Bell was given just two first-team games at Middlesbrough as stand-in for regular left-winger Fred Warren. He was handed the chance as new manager Wilf Gillow looked to build a team that could put years of First Division struggle behind them. The 1934–35 campaign was another difficult season as Middlesbrough once again flirted with relegation and it was a tough baptism for Bell, making his debut in a 3–1 defeat at Spurs and then playing in a 2–2 home draw with fellow strugglers Wolves. He moved on to West Ham at the end of the season after Warren had returned to the side.

BELL Stephen

Left-winger
Born: Middlesbrough, 13 March 1965.
Died: March 2001.
Career: MIDDLESBROUGH 1982. Portsmouth 1985. Whitby Town. Darlington 1987.

■ Of all the young players to emerge as a stunning talent and be tipped as an international star of the future, Bell is arguably the biggest disappointment in the club's history. After equalling the club

record as the youngest ever player and drawing comparison with the great Wilf Mannion by showing incredible skill and ball control, Bell wasted his talent and was on the soccer scrapheap in his early 20s.

The slightly-built youngster made his entrance into League football aged just 16 years and 323 days, equalling the previous record held by Sam Lawrie to the day. He had already played for England at schoolboy and youth level and starred as a member of the Middlesbrough Boys team which won the English Schools Championship in 1982. He had been wanted by 14 Division One clubs but chose his hometown team.

Bell's debut proved to be his only game in the top flight but he was immediately installed as a first-team regular in Division Two and was ever-present in the 1982–83 campaign, exciting everyone with his burgeoning talents, tormenting defenders with his pace and skill on the wing, and scoring his fair share of goals. Manager Malcolm Allison secured his signature on a lucrative four-year contract while still aged 17 and the football world was at his feet. But the signs of trouble were emerging. Bell was severely reprimanded after a 'joyriding' incident and there were other reports of off-the-pitch problems as Bell mixed with the wrong crowd.

Inevitably his performances suffered. After being such a shining light in Allison's team, he was a shadow of his former self by the time Willie Maddren took over in 1984. His fitness had deteriorated and with it his ability to beat defenders had diminished. He would instead wait to get hit by a defender to win a free kick. Maddren was forced to continue playing the wayward youngster because of his wafer-thin squad but his behaviour was increasingly causing problems within the club and, after being substituted in one game, a row broke out between Maddren and chairman Alf Duffield that almost led to the manager's resignation.

By 1985, Bell had stepped out of line once too often and his contract was cancelled. He had clearly been unable to handle the pressure his talent brought. Even then, he was given another chance by Alan Ball at Portsmouth but Bell soon walked out and returned to the North East without explanation. Former Ayresome Park colleague Paul Ward offered him a further opportunity at Darlington but yet again Bell failed to make the most of it, playing his last League game at the age of 22. In his mid–20s, rather than playing for his country as many had predicted, Bell was playing for Hemlington Social and North Ormesby Institute. He died in March 2001 aged just 36.

BELL William

Left-half
Born: Middlesbrough.
Career: MIDDLESBROUGH 1899.

■ Left-half was a problem position for Middlesbrough manager John Robson in the club's first Football League season. He used six different players in the first nine games of the season, 'Nobby' Bell being given the chance for a trip to play New Brighton Town in the fourth match of the campaign. Middlesbrough came away from the south coast with a 1–1 draw but Bell was replaced for the following game against Grimsby by James Stott, another of the club's one-game wonders.

BENNION Chris

Goalkeeper
Born: Edinburgh, 30 August 1980.
Career: Edinburgh Celtic. MIDDLESBROUGH 2000. Scunthorpe United (loan) 2001. Shelbourne 2002. Dundalk 2004.

■ A former Scotland schoolboy international goalkeeper who was spotted by Middlesbrough scouts playing for Edinburgh Celtic. Bennion was offered a professional contract but found opportunities limited behind Mark Schwarzer and first-team deputies such as Marlon Beresford and Mark Crossley. His sole appearance for the senior side came against Macclesfield Town in the Worthington Cup during September 2000 when bigger names were injured. The youngster was loaned to Scunthorpe before making a permanent move to Irish side Shelbourne in summer 2002. He later moved to Dundalk after turning down strong interest from fellow rivals Longford Town.

BERESFORD Marlon

Goalkeeper
Born: Lincoln, 2 September 1969.
Career: Sheffield Wednesday 1987. Bury (loan) 1989. Northampton Town (loan) 1989. Crewe Alexandra (loan) 1991. Northampton Town (loan) 1991. Burnley 1992. MIDDLESBROUGH 1998. Sheffield Wednesday (loan) 2000. Burnley 2002. York City 2002. Burnley 2002. Bradford City 2003. Luton Town 2003. Barnsley 2004. Luton Town 2004.

■ Bryan Robson swooped for Marlon Beresford when nine goals conceded in two disastrous defeats threatened to derail Middlesbrough's promotion bid in 1997–98. Luckless Andy Dibble had played in the two defeats as cover for injured Mark Schwarzer and Ben Roberts but Beresford – rated as one of the best goalkeepers in the lower divisions – took over to make his debut in a 6–0 rout of Swindon Town, keeping clean sheets in each of his three appearances that season. Beresford had started his career at Sheffield Wednesday after being spotted playing Sunday League football but was kept out of the first team initially by England 'keeper Chris Woods and then Kevin Pressman. After a series of loan spells, regular football came following a £95,000 move to Burnley, where he built a reputation as a fine shot-stopper, renowned for saving penalties. He was named Division Two goalkeeper of the year in 1993–94 and played against Boro in Bryan Robson's first game as manager. Burnley's asking price put off prospective buyers until Robson arranged a cut-price £400,000 fee in March 1998 in the knowledge that Beresford would have been out of contract and entitled to a free

transfer that summer. Mark Schwarzer's consistency meant Beresford rarely featured in the Boro first team over the next four years and he eventually joined York City on a free transfer. That was the start of a nomadic couple of years that also saw him return to Burnley before moves to Bradford City, Luton Town and Barnsley. He was still Luton's first choice 'keeper at the age of 37, having helped the Hatters win promotion to the Championship in his first season at Kenilworth Road, though relegation followed two years later.

BEST Charles

Inside-right/Outside-right
Born: Boosbeck, 1888.
Died: 1965.
Career: Eston United.
MIDDLESBROUGH 1910. Hull City 1911.

■ Forward Best was recruited from local football and got his chance to appear in Division One football in the 1910–11 campaign. He made his debut in a 2–1 home win against Bury in March 1911, stepping in for regular right-winger Robert Gibson and also stood in for inside-forward George Elliott on occasions. His only goal came in a 2–1 defeat at Sheffield United as Boro slumped from eighth position on the day of his debut to a 16th place season finish. Best moved on to Hull for two seasons before retiring through injury in the 1913 close season, aged only 25. He later became a miner in the area.

BILCLIFF Raymond

Full-back
Born: Blaydon, 24 May 1931.
Career: Spen Juniors.
MIDDLESBROUGH 1949. Hartlepool United 1961.

■ Right-back Bilcliff made more appearances without scoring a goal than any other outfield player in the club's history. Despite his lack of talent in front of goal, the Tynesider was a useful defender who battled for the number-two shirt for almost a decade.

He was spotted by the club while playing for High Spen Juniors in Blaydon when scouts from Boro and Portsmouth attended a game to watch the opposing outside-left. Bilcliff hardly gave the player a kick and instead it was he who was offered trials with the two professional clubs. He signed professional forms with Boro for £7 a week but had to wait three years for his first-team debut. Two of those years were spent on National Service with the RAF in Nottingham with Bilcliff returning home on odd weekends to turn out for the club's reserves. He was promoted to the first time for a 1–1 draw against Liverpool in March 1952, replacing Ray Barnard at right-back for the Anfield trip and the pair were to contest the place for many years to come. With a gangly, angular frame, Bilcliff lacked finesse but was a clean tackler who always gave 100 percent. With more experienced full-backs Dicky Robinson and Ronnie Dicks also in the squad, Bilcliff found chances few and far between initially, though he had a good run of games in Walter Rowley's 1952–53 team. He spent 18 months out of the game through a mystery knee injury and looked to have played his last game for the club when he was placed on the transfer list. However, without the club's permission, he secretly paid a visit to a physiotherapist – known at the time as 'quack doctors' – who realised Bilcliff had a misplaced cruciate ligament and manipulated the knee back in place. Though he never revealed the secret to his sudden recovery, he asked new manager Bob Dennison for a chance to prove himself and duly won back his first-team place from Barnard. Bilcliff was installed as first choice in 1957–58, and the pair continued their rivalry right up until Barnard's departure in 1960. Even then Bilcliff was struggling to hold down a place with Derek Stonehouse and emerging youngster Gordon Jones as rivals. Bilcliff's own departure came after he had made comments to the press regarding Brian Clough's controversial captaincy, after which he was confronted by club chairman Stanley Gibson. Although he insisted he had been misquoted, the comments were clearly a black mark against his name and he was slowly eased out of the first-team reckoning. He was sold to Hartlepool where he enjoyed three more seasons of League football before more controversery surrounded his retirement from the game. Bilcliff ran the Plough Inn at Hutton Henry and the King's Head in Ferryhill before moving to the Nottingham area where he worked as a labourer and bricklayer on building sites. He also coached Blidworth Miners Welfare in the late 1960s.

BIRBECK Joseph

Left-half
Born: Stanley, 15 April 1932.
Career: Evenwood Town.
MIDDLESBROUGH 1953. Grimsby Town 1959.

■ Left-half was a problem position for struggling Boro manager Walter Rowley and Joe Birbeck was the fourth player to occupy that position in 1953–54. The 21-year-old Tynesider was thrown into the cauldron of a relegation derby at Roker Park for his debut and came out unscathed as Middlesbrough won 2–0 in front of over 41,000 people. A run of games followed but a 3–0 home defeat against Huddersfield prompted another reshuffle. Subsequently, it was newcomer Bill Harris and versatile Ronnie Dicks who operated at left-half once Bob Dennison had taken over as manager following relegation to Division Two in the summer of 1954. Birbeck's unconventional style was sometimes described as 'all arms' and he suffered from poor distribution. However, he was a good ball winner, hard and brave. While serving in the RAF, Birbeck found it difficult to force his way into the first team and opportunities were always few and far between. A good run came in the second half of 1957–58 when Dicks was dropped but Birbeck was back out in the cold in the following season and opted to move on to Grimsby a year later.

BIRKETT Ralph James Evans

Outside-right
Born: Newton Abbot, 9 January 1913.
Died: 1989.
Career: Dartmouth United. Torquay United 1929. Arsenal 1933. MIDDLESBROUGH 1934. Newcastle United 1938.

■ Ayresome favourite Ralph Birkett was a fast and tricky player who was an important part of Boro's strong late 1930s team. Alongside the likes of Fenton, Mannion and Baxter, Birkett helped steer the club from Division One strugglers to genuine title contenders. The ever-cheerful player was pacy and direct on the flanks, and able to cut inside with a powerful shot.

Born the son of a former Middlesbrough postman in Kent, Birkett first worked as a clerk and played for his local side Dartford United. His professional career began at Torquay before he stepped up with a £2,000 move to Arsenal. He was signed at Highbury as replacement for the legendary Joe Hulme, whose boots proved hard to fill, though Birkett's undoubted ability saw him break into the first team and win a Championship medal in 1934.

Brought to Boro by Wilf Gillow, he was the club's record signing at £5,900 – a figure not beaten for 14 years – arriving as a potential forward partner for George Camsell or young Micky Fenton and he made his debut in a 2–0 defeat at Preston. Soon after, he made an ill-fated return to Highbury as his new club lost 8–0. But

Birkett was performing well and he earned his only England cap in a 3–1 victory over Ireland in October 1935. He was selected to play against Germany in December but a pulled leg muscle ruled him out and Birkett never played again as a young Stanley Matthews took his place.

His goals helped the club's fortunes turn around and he finished second only to Camsell in 1935–36, also figuring in two Football League representative games. Birkett had become popular at Ayresome and the fans were dismayed when their blond-haired favourite joined Second Division Newcastle. But, in reality, Birkett wasn't getting a regular place by 1937–38 with Jacky Milne's arrival from Arsenal midway through the season, and the chances of resurrecting his England career were limited. The player reluctantly agreed to go and Boro used the money to buy Duncan McKenzie from Brentford.

In World War Two, Birkett served as an Army PT instructor and guested for several clubs including Middlesbrough and Reading. He also played in one wartime international alongside Wilf Mannion against Scotland, scoring one goal in a 3–2 defeat. Birkett returned to Devon after retirement but was a guest at the last League game at Ayresome Park; the oldest of the former players there at 81. He was the oldest living former Boro player until his death in 2002 at the age of 89.

BIRRELL William

Inside-right/Outside-right
Born: Cellardyke, 13 March 1897.
Died: November 1968.
Career: Inverkeithing United. Raith Rovers. MIDDLESBROUGH 1921. Raith Rovers 1927.

■ Crafty schemer Billy Birrell was a shrewd club captain and intelligent inside-right with an eye for goal. As skipper he led the side to the record-breaking Division Two Championship success in 1926–27 and became a big favourite of the Ayresome Park crowd.

Birrell had suffered hardships in World War One while serving with the Black Watch. He received a foot injury soon after arriving in France and was later captured at Beugy in 1918 and interned as a POW at Stralkvowo in Russian Poland. After his release he

played football for Raith Rovers but decided that his future lay in the New World and made plans to emigrate to America. He had finalised the arrangements when Middlesbrough made a late bid to sign him and he changed his mind. Boro manager Jimmy Howie saw him as replacement for winger Jackie Mordue but instead Birrell became one of the club's most influential midfield generals.

Boro suffered relegation from Division One in 1923–24 and Birrell's play suffered for a spell when his old war wound returned but, after a period of rest, he returned to form in 1925–26 and played a major role as captain of the following season's promotion side. Birrell still had plenty to offer and it was with great reluctance that the Middlesbrough board allowed him to leave months into the next campaign. Birrell was keen to try his hand at management and become player-boss at Raith, full-back Syd Jarvis moving from Raith to Boro as part of the deal.

Birrell's management career was mostly a struggle for success. He was forced to seek re-election with Bournemouth and had to work hard to keep Chelsea in the First Division. While at Chelsea, where former Boro teammate Stewart Davidson was his assistant, Birrell led them to two wartime Cup Finals with Boro's George Hardwick in the team and two post-war Cup semi-finals. Well-respected in the game, Birrell became a clerk in Kenton after leaving football in 1952. He died in November 1968.

BISSETT James Thompson

Right-back
Born: Lochee, 19 June 1898.
Career: Dundee. Everton 1920. Ebbw Vale. Southend United 1922. Rochdale 1923. MIDDLESBROUGH 1924. Lincoln City 1926.

■ Right-back Bissett made his debut in Middlesbrough's first game outside the top flight for 22 years. Manager Herbert Bamlett brought in the Scots defender from Third Division Rochdale after seeing Boro slip out of Division One in 1923–24. Bissett had spent an early spell at Dundee before becoming a reserve at Everton. He played non-League football for Ebbw Vale, getting his chance in the Football League with Southend and then Rochdale. His Middlesbrough debut came in a 2–0 home win against Barnsley and Bissett played for the first half of the season before losing his place to Walter Holmes as Boro struggled to stay with the promotion pace. After playing against South Shields in January 1925, he didn't win a recall for over 13 months. Bissett played the final games of the 1925–26 season but was placed on the transfer list at £500 at the end of the campaign. After a spell with Lincoln, he returned to Dundee as manager. His side made little impact on the First Division but once reached the Scottish Cup quarter-finals. Bissett later had a disastrous short spell at Barrow.

BLACKBURN Colin

Winger
Born: Thirsk, 16 January 1961.
Career: MIDDLESBROUGH 1979.

■ The promising youngster had the misfortune to break his leg twice in his fledgling career and had just one chance at first-team football. Having first joined Boro as a schoolboy, Blackburn was offered an apprenticeship and signed professional in June 1979. His Football League chance came 15 months later when he stood in for Terry Cochrane on the right wing for a 1–0 defeat at Nottingham Forest in March 1981. After being released at the end of the season, Blackburn decided to go to university.

BLACKETT Joseph

Full-back/Inside-forward
Born: Newcastle 1875.
Career: Newcastle United 1894. Gateshead. Loughborough Town 1896. Wolverhampton Wanderers 1897. Derby County 1900. Sunderland 1900. MIDDLESBROUGH 1901. Luton Town. Leicester Fosse 1906. Rochdale. Barrow.

■ Well-travelled full-back Joe Blackett was an important member of Middlesbrough's first ever promotion-winning side. Arriving early in the campaign, he made his debut at right full-back in a 3–0 win over Woolwich Arsenal and missed just one game as Boro secured their place in the top flight. Blackett was in the line-up for the club's first ever Division One game but was dropped after a 3–2 defeat at Derby in October 1901. Newcomer John Hogg took over, Blackett not returning until the final home game of the season – the last ever played at the Linthorpe Road ground. He appeared at left full-back in that fixture and, though he missed the opening game at Ayresome Park in the following campaign, Blackett made that place his own in 1903–04, also scoring three times from the penalty spot. The arrival of Billy Agnew in the summer of 1904 made life harder for Blackett and he agreed to a move to Luton a year later. He ended his football career with a short spell as player-manager at Rochdale.

BLACKMORE Clayton Graham

Full-back/Midfield
Born: Neath, 23 September 1964.
Career: Manchester United 1982. MIDDLESBROUGH 1994. Bristol City (loan) 1996. Barnsley 1999. Notts County 1999. Leigh RMI. Bangor City. Porthmadog.

■ Bryan Robson made his former Old Trafford teammate Blackmore one of his first signings after taking over as Middlesbrough manager. A versatile midfielder or full-back with intelligent passing and useful shot, he arrived on a free transfer after a successful career with Manchester United. Nicknamed 'Sunbed' at Old Trafford, he won FA Cup, Cup-winners' Cup and Premier League title medals in more than a decade, though he was often seen as a squad player rather than an automatic selection. His Boro debut came alongside Robson in midfield against Burnley and Blackmore was an important part of the First Division promotion side. He also saw a crowd of 20,000 attend a testimonial game against Manchester United at Ayresome Park early in the 1994–95 season.

Once in the Premier League, Blackmore found opportunities few and far between and was loaned to Bristol City in November 1996 having spent seven months out of the side. It was expected that the deal would become a permanent transfer but Blackmore was surprisingly recalled from the loan spell amid an injury crisis and thrust straight into the first team, scoring with a long-range effort in a 4–2 victory over Everton. He was back in Robson's squad on a regular basis, winning a recall to the Wales team, and playing at full-back in the Coca-Cola Cup Final replay and FA Cup Final in 1997. Blackmore started the opening fixture of 1997–98 against Charlton but limped off with a leg injury. After making just one further start, in a Worthington Cup tie with Wycombe, he joined former Boro teammate John Hendrie who was player-manager at Barnsley. Blackmore was released again in the summer of 1999 after Hendrie had been sacked.

He later spent six years with Bangor City in the League of Wales, with ex-Boro player Peter Davenport as his boss. Blackmore succeeded Davenport as manager before a playing spell with another Welsh side, Porthmadog, saw him again try his hand at management from May 2007.

BLACKMORE Harold Alfred

Centre-forward/Inside-left
Born: Silverton, 13 May 1904.
Died: December 1989.
Career: Silverton. Exeter City 1924. Bolton Wanderers 1926. MIDDLESBROUGH 1932. Bradford Park Avenue 1933. Bury 1934. Exeter City 1935.

■ The balding centre-forward with the rocket left foot was brought to Middlesbrough to provide competition for veteran frontman George Camsell. He had starred at Bolton, helping to win the FA Cup in 1929, and was tipped to take over in the striking role. But the free-scoring Camsell proved he still had plenty to offer by yet again finishing the season as top scorer. Blackmore finished in second place but was on his way out of the club at the end of the campaign. The newcomer had started the season in the centre-forward role but was dropped after failing to score in his first three games. Another chance came in November as Boro flirted with relegation. Camsell was tried at inside-forward and out on the wing while Blackmore found his form with nine goals in 10 games, including a hat-trick against West Brom. But the goals dried up and he played his last game for the club in a 2–0 defeat at Sheffield United in March 1933. Blackmore later worked as a butcher in Exeter where his career had started. He died in the city in December 1989.

BLENKINSOP Thomas William

Defender
Born: Bishop Auckland, 13 May 1920.
Career: West Auckland. Grimsby Town 1939. MIDDLESBROUGH 1948. Barnsley 1952.

■ Powerful and aggressive in defence, Tom Blenkinsopp was a versatile performer in Boro's post-war side. Having played for West Auckland before the war, he joined Grimsby as his first professional club. He made his first appearance in a Middlesbrough shirt as a wartime guest, making his debut in a thrilling 7–4 defeat at Newcastle. Blenkinsopp's Football League debut for the club was on the opening day of the 1948–49 season against Chelsea. He operated in a number of positions including full-back and inside-forward, as well as centre and wing-half in his first season. His form soon warranted a call-up to play for the Football League against their Irish counterparts for a 5–1 victory in September 1948.

Blenkinsopp was an unconventional character and it was well known that he liked a drink or two before a game. He was often seen in the pubs of Middlesbrough before making his way to Ayresome Park. Indeed, one rumour had it that drinks would be secretly brought to him at half-time from the Shaw's Club at Ayresome Park. After winning a regular place in his first season, he found life tougher in subsequent campaigns and his behaviour also brought him into conflict with club officials. After being caught sneaking out of a hotel with Wilf Mannion on the night before a match, Blenkinsopp was placed on the transfer list. But the final straw came when he was suspended for two weeks for a second confrontation with the club following an undisclosed incident after an away game at Wolves. He was immediately transferred to Barnsley where he played a handful of games before returning to live in his native Whitton Park in County Durham.

BLOOMER Stephen

Inside-right
Born: Cradley Heath, 20 January 1874.
Died: 16 April 1938.
Career: Derby Swifts. Derby Midland. Derby County 1892. MIDDLESBROUGH 1906. Derby County 1910.

■ Just a year after stunning the football world by paying £1,000 for Alf Common, Middlesbrough pulled off another sensational coup by recruiting an established England international and the finest goalscorer of his generation in the shape of Derby's Steve Bloomer.

Bloomer endured a baptism of fire in a 6–1 hammering at Anfield but quickly found his feet. Though he was slight in build and had an unhealthy complexion that prompted the nickname 'Paleface', Bloomer shook off the uncompromising tactics of defenders to entrance opponents with his body swerve and dribbling ability. He had the touch and skills needed to play in his inside-forward role but his biggest asset was his goalscoring. His goals came from all angles – tap-ins to 25 yard rockets – and he went on to set a contemporary record of 380 first class goals. Many of his strikes came from vicious first-time shots. He rarely passed or stopped to control the ball and attributed his success to getting to the ball first.

His direct style did not endear him to all and his critics commented that he was too selfish. He believed it was not his job to defend and that he needed to conserve his energy for scoring goals. His Boro teammates dreaded a Bloomer stare when the ball was not put to his feet. Should an attack break down, he would stop in tracks, place hands on hips and give the culprit the infamous stare before looking to the heavens for divine assistance.

Back in his Derby days, Bloomer had made an immediate impact on the international stage, scoring twice on his England debut in a 9–0 win over Eire in 1895. He once scored five in a 9–1 victory over Wales and was England's leading scorer at the time, a record that stood for half a century. He was also Boro's top scorer in the 1906–07 and 1907–08 campaigns as the club put relegation battles behind them to cement their place in the First Division.

After four years in the North East, Bloomer happily accepted a return to Derby. He received a hero's welcome at Derby station and captained the Rams to promotion. In all, he was top scorer at Derby for 14 seasons and played on until the age of 40, becoming the first player to reach the landmark of 500 games. In 1914, with unfortunate timing, Bloomer took a coaching position in Germany and was subsequently interned as a POW. After the hostilities, he coached Derby reserves and also worked abroad in Germany, Holland, Canada and Spain. He was still working as Derby general assistant when, in failing health, he was sent on a cruise but he died three weeks after his return, in April 1938.

In a letter to a friend Bloomer once wrote: 'Where the vision came from I don't know but when I had the ball I always seemed to know just where the goal was. I had an instinct, perhaps, so that I did not need to look up when shooting or when steadying myself to take aim.'

BOAM Stuart William

Central defender
Born: Kirkby-in-Ashfield, 28 January 1948.
Career: Kirkby BC. Mansfield Town 1966. MIDDLESBROUGH 1971. Newcastle United 1979. Mansfield Town 1981. Hartlepool United 1983. Guisborough Town.

■ The familiar chant of 'Six foot two, eyes of blue, Stuey Boam's after you!'

reverberated around Ayresome Park throughout the 1970s as the uncompromising defender made life tough for opposing forwards. The rugged, hard-tackling centre-half was commanding in the air, had deceptive pace and was a brilliant one-on-one defender – the ball might go past him or the player but very rarely both! He was a contact player who liked to attack the ball and had an unconventional but effective style that led to many tipping him for England honours.

Turned down by Nottingham Forest as a teenager, Boam was converted from inside-forward to centre-half at Mansfield. He joined Boro for a substantial fee and immediately helped end the club's reputation for scoring a lot but conceding plenty, after making his debut in the same game as Nobby Stiles at Portsmouth in August 1971. He won the MFC Player of the Year in his first season, a feat he repeated in his last season. In between he played enough matches to place him 13th in the club's all-time appearance list.

Boam's early partner was Bill Gates but the pair were too similar and it was alongside Willie Maddren that the defensive foundation was formed to launch the club to the Second Division title. Their incredible understanding brought the nickname 'The Telepathic Twins'. Jack Charlton initially criticised Boam's playing style but the problems were ironed out and he succeeded Nobby Stiles as captain for the 1973–74 promotion success, a position he held until his departure.

He was an essential member of the Boro side that challenged for the First Division title in 1974–75 though a last minute mistake against Derby proved costly as Boro narrowly missed out on the Championship. Boam himself openly criticised Jack Charlton for not buying the goalscorer he believed was needed to push for major honours. Under John Neal, he signed a four-year contract in October 1978 and had a newsagent shop in St Barnabas Road close to Ayresome Park but he was sold less than a year later to Newcastle when Irving Nattrass moved in the opposite direction. Boam later managed struggling Fourth Division Mansfield Town for just a season and a half. After leaving football he worked as a manager for Kodak before running a newsagents.

BOARDMAN Harry

Right-back
Born: Grangetown, 1887.
Career: Grangetown. MIDDLESBROUGH 1909.

■ Boardman had enjoyed success at Grangetown, earning recognition as an England amateur international. He played games against Switzerland, France, Denmark and Ireland before getting the chance to appear in the Football League with Middlesbrough. He made his debut at right-back, replacing regular Don McLeod in defence, in a 4–3 win over Spurs. In his third game, Boardman switched to left-back in place of Jimmy Watson and kept his place for the subsequent fixture at Old Trafford. But a 4–1 defeat to Manchester United proved to be his last game for the club and he returned to local football.

BOATENG George

Midfield
Born: Nkawkaw, Ghana, 5 September 1975.
Career: Excelsior 1994. Feyenoord (Holland) 1995. Coventry City 1998. Aston Villa 1999. MIDDLESBROUGH 2002.

■ The experienced Dutch midfielder became one of the club's best signings of the modern era when he arrived from Aston Villa for £5 million in August 2002. He started his career with Excelsior before learning his trade with Dutch giants Feyenoord, where he enjoyed Champions League experience. His move to England came with Coventry City who paid £250,000 for his services in 1998. He was an immediate hit with the Sky Blues and quickly became a target for Midlands rivals Aston Villa, who bought him for £4.5 million at the end of that season.

After taking some time to adjust to Villa's style, he came into his own in a midfield holding role. He produced some outstanding displays in the second half of the 1999–2000 season as Villa reached the FA Cup Final – the last to be played at the old Wembley – where they lost to Chelsea. teammates included Ugo Ehiogu, Gareth Southgate, Benito Carbone and Alan Wright, all later to feature for Boro. McClaren saw Boateng as a replacement for the ageing Paul Ince and he immediately became a regular following his move to the Riverside. He finished the 2002–03 campaign without a goal to his name, however, prompting European scout Don Mackay to promise him 12 bottles of champagne if he could score three goals the following season. Boateng claimed the bubbly with strikes against Blackburn Rovers, Bolton Wanderers and the winner at the Riverside against Spurs. Boateng was also a key figure in the 2004 Carling Cup success and was named supporters' Player of the Year. Injury sidelined him for three months at the start of 2005, forcing him to miss crucial UEFA Cup ties against Grazer AK and Sporting Lisbon. But he came back to enjoy a blossoming partnership with fellow countryman Bolo Zenden. The following year he featured in unforgettable ties against Basel and Steaua Bucharest before appearing in the UEFA Cup Final against Sevilla. Boateng's hopes of winning a place in Holland's squad for the 2006 World Cup Finals were boosted when he was handed his fourth cap for a friendly with Italy, but he missed the final cut. Southgate's elevation from captain to manager in summer 2006 saw the midfielder take over the armband. As committed as ever, he insisted on playing on with a knee injury that affected his mobility and form. Towards the end of the season he was back to his best, however, prompting speculation of interest from Birmingham City.

BODDINGTON Harold

Outside-left
Born: Darlington.
Career: MIDDLESBROUGH 1904.

■ Manager John Robson was struggling to find a regular for the left-wing berth in 1903–04. Boddington was one of six players used on the flank that season. His chance came in a trip to Sheffield United but he failed to impress in a 3–0 defeat and Dicky Roberts was signed from Newcastle to fill the slot for the next game.

BOERSMA Philip

Midfield
Born: Liverpool, 24 September 1949.
Career: Liverpool 1968. Wrexham (loan) 1970. MIDDLESBROUGH 1975. Luton Town 1977. Swansea City 1978.

■ Jack Charlton had tried for two years to sign Phil Boersma – the man he saw as the answer to the club's goalscoring problems – but the fee was always the stumbling block. Eventually a compromise was reached and Kevin Keegan's deputy moved to Ayresome Park. At Anfield Boersma had a reasonable goalscoring record but had hit the headlines after walking out on the club during the 1974 Cup Final against Newcastle. But he settled his differences and remained on the fringes of Liverpool's awesome first team.

Unfortunately, despite exhilirating speed, Boersma was not a big success at Middlesbrough. He failed to score in his first 18 games and never produced the goods, either up front or in an attacking midfield role. He was often said to look outstanding in training but didn't perform on the big stage. Despite his high work rate, he failed to impress the Boro fans and moved on to Luton. He later became assistant manager to John Toshack at Swansea as the Welsh club went from Division Four to the top flight. It was at Liverpool, where he was physiotherapist, that he linked up with former Boro teammate Graeme Souness. He became the Scotsman's assistant and subsequently worked with him at Southampton and Benfica.

BOKSIC Alen

Striker
Born: Makarska, Yugoslavia, 31 January 1970.
Career: Hajduk Split (Yugoslavia) 1987. AS Cannes 1991. Olympique Marseille. (France) 1992. Lazio (Italy) 1993. Juventus (Italy) 1996. Lazio (Italy) 1997. MIDDLESBROUGH 2000.

■ Boksic had seen it all when he arrived at the Riverside in summer 2000. He had first-hand experience of winning top honours, having collected a European Cup medal with Marseilles and two Serie A titles and a World Club Championship winners' medal Juventus. The powerful Croatian striker had been a long-term target for Bryan Robson and he paid £2.5 million for the 30-year-old. Blessed with tremendous skills and strength, Boksic went on to score some sublime goals during his three-year stay, but the picture was mixed. He missed long periods with niggling injuries and questions were also asked about his commitment. Boksic started out in his home country with Hajduk Split where he spent four highly-successful seasons before moving to France with Cannes and then Marseille. He scored a terrific 23 goals in 37 games for the French side in 1992–93 to become the domestic League's top scorer. He moved to Italy the following season for a six-year stay at Lazio, interspersed by a short spell with Juventus. In his best season, 1997–98, he scored 10 in 26 games – highly respectable by Italian standards. Boksic relished the chance to escape the goldfish-bowl atmosphere of Italian football and won instant acceptance at the Riverside by scoring a double on his debut against Coventry. He was top scorer in his first season, his 12 League goals vital in a nervous battle against relegation. Two of the spectacular goals he scored – against Newcastle and Leicester – will live long in the memory but fans were frustrated too with his apparently indifferent attitude to the game. It took Terry Venables to get him on the pitch on a regular basis. Venables's departure and the appointment of Steve McClaren as manager saw Boksic return to his most frustrating self, too often unwilling to play if not 100 percent fit. Even so, he again top scored with eight goals including the winner against Manchester United at Old Trafford. After playing for Croatia in the 2002 World Cup, his appearances and goals became less frequent and he scored for the last time in a Middlesbrough shirt in a memorable 3–1 Boxing Day win over eventual champions Manchester United. He played his last game for the club in early January 2003 before surprisingly announcing his retirement from the game aged just 32. He is remembered by Boro fans as much for his poor attitude as his sublime skills.

BOLTON Joseph

Left-back
Born: Birtley, 2 February 1955.
Career: Sunderland 1972. MIDDLESBROUGH 1981. Sheffield United 1983.

■ After almost a decade at Roker Park, stalwart defender Bolton was brought into a struggling Boro team by Bobby Murdoch. The strong-tackling full-back had been sent off against Middlesbrough, just months before joining the club, for head-butting Terry Cochrane but he settled in beside his former victim at the start of the 1981–82 campaign. Bolton was in a poor side but failed to impress. He struggled to justify the substantial fee paid for his services and became a boo boy target, losing his place in mid-season. Ian Bailey was preferred at left-back though Bolton returned later in the season in midfield as Boro slumped to relegation.

He was back at full-back as Boro resumed football in Division Two. Again the club struggled for form and Bolton fell out of favour once more after Malcolm Allison took charge. The new manager accused the defender of having an attitude problem and handed his place to teenager Gary Hamilton. He moved on to find happier times at Sheffield United, winning promotion from the Third Division in 1984 before a knee injury ended his career.

BOTTRILL Walter Gibson

Forward
Born: Eston, 8 January 1903.
Died: 1975.
Career: South Bank. MIDDLESBROUGH 1922. Nelson 1924. Rotherham United 1928. York City 1929. Wolverhampton Wanderers 1930. Huddersfield Town 1933. Chesterfield 1934.

■ A product of South Bank amateur football, Bottrill played at outside-right for the Boro. He made his debut in a 1–1 home draw with Newcastle on Boxing Day 1922 following an injury to George Elliott. He was in and out of team in the following months, eventually losing his place to Tommy Urwin in January 1924 after a string of three consecutive 1–0 defeats. He moved on to Nelson, the fee being reduced from £500 to £250 by the League. Bottrill later became top scorer in York's first League season (1929–30) and also scored their first ever League hat-trick. Some sources suggest his Christian name was William and that he was known as Billy.

BRAITHWAITE Robert Munn

Winger
Born: Belfast, 24 February 1937.
Career: Linfield. MIDDLESBROUGH 1963. Durban City (South Africa).

■ Wing wizard Bobby Braithwaite was a classy ball-player who represented his country at all levels. He came to Middlesbrough having already been capped three times for Northern Ireland while with Linfield, making his debut in the same game as George Best and Pat Jennings. In his home country, he had played school football at left-half and junior football at inside-left. He worked as a shipwright and played part-time football for Linfield, winning the Irish championship and Cup in 1962, before moving for a record fee for an Irish player.

Naturally skilful, Braithwaite went straight into the side at outside left – which had long been a problem position for Boro – for the opening game of the 1963–64 season, playing his part in a 5–0

home win over Plymouth. He then scored two brilliant goals in his third match – a 4–2 win at Charlton – as Boro started the season well, only to break his leg in a challenge from Newcastle's Jim Iley in the following game. The injury was to rule him out for three months. For the following two seasons, however, Braithwaite battled for a place with Don Ratcliffe as the club increasingly struggled in the Second Division. Sadly, he was never the same player after the injury and clearly didn't enjoy the physical side of the game. By the time relegation came at the end of the 1965–66 campaign, Braithwaite was on the sidelines and he then made only a handful of appearances in Division Three as Derrick Downing secured the left-wing berth. Halfway through the campaign he decided to emigrate to South Africa and was released from his contract. In the following years, he regularly wrote to the club with updates of his progress in South Africa where he lived close to other ex-Boro stars Ian Davidson, Bryan Orritt and Eddie Connachan.

BRANCA Marco

Striker
Born: Grossetto, Italy, 6 January 1965.
Career: Grossetto 1981. Cagliari 1982. Udinese 1986. Sampdoria 1987. Udinese 1988. Sampdoria 1990. Fiorentina 1991. Udinese 1992. Parma 1994. Roma 1995. Inter Milan 1995. MIDDLESBROUGH 1998. FC Luzern (Switzerland) 2000. Monza (Italy) 2000.

■ The experienced Italian made a stunning entrance into English football, scoring just four minutes into his debut. That strike against Liverpool helped secure a place in the 1998 Coca-Cola Cup Final and Branca continued his electric form by notching two against Sunderland on his League debut. The striker's £1 million arrival from Inter Milan proved to be a perfect boost in Boro's promotion push. The nine goals he scored in the end-of-season run-in helped see off the challenge of Sunderland and Charlton to secure a place in the Premier League. He showed great opportunism in front of goal including a fine hat-trick against Bury and a stunning overhead strike versus Swindon.

Branca made his first debut for Serie B side Cagliari as a 19-year-old, when Gianluca Festa was a junior at the club, moving into the Serie A with Udinese. He spent a season on the sidelines at Sampdoria before returning to Udinese and helping them win promotion back to the Serie A. Another spell at Sampdoria followed before Branca moved to Fiorentina and then back for a third spell with Udinese. After scoring 14 goals in 29 games, he joined Parma for a season, followed by a shorter spell with Roma. At Inter, he scored 19 goals in his first season but his appearances were limited following the arrival of Brazilian legend Ronaldo. Marseille tried to buy Branca before signing Fabrizio Ravanelli from Boro and Branca instead moved to Teesside in the second half of the 1997–98 campaign.

A knee injury sustained against Manchester City, however, meant that Branca missed the end of the season but there were still high hopes that he would make an impact on the Premier League. Yet Branca made only one substitute appearance in the top flight as he struggled for fitness. After seeking the opinion of several specialists, who each stated that his knee could no longer stand up to the pressure of professional football, Boro reluctantly cancelled his contract. Branca, amid some acrimony, contested the decision. He believed he could play on and made a short-lived comeback with FC Luzern in Switzerland and Italian Serie B side Monza before eventually admitting defeat. Since 2003 he has been technical director with one of his former clubs Inter.

BRANCO Claudio Ibraim Vaz Leal

Left-back
Born: Bage, Brazil, 4 April 1964.
Career: Guarany Bage (Brazil) 1981. Fluminense (Brazil) 1982. Brescia (Italy) 1986. Porto (Portugal) 1988. Genoa (Italy) 1991. Gremio (Brazil) 1992. Corinthians (Brazil) 1994. Fluminense (Brazil) 1994. Flamengo (Brazil) 1995. Internacional (Brazil) 1995. MIDDLESBROUGH 1996. Mogi Mirim (Brazil) 1997. Fluminense (Brazil) 1998. New York/New Jersey MetroStars (US) 1998.

■ A vastly experienced Brazilian international with more than 80 caps and a 1994 World Cup-winners' medal to his name, Branco arrived in a blaze of publicity and attracted over 15,000 fans to his reserve team debut. The full-back was a free agent after leaving Brazilian club Internacional and turned down offers from clubs in Japan and the USA to sign an 18-month contract with Boro. On his debut as a substitute against Everton, Branco came close to scoring with a rocket-like shot. In his first start he played alongside Juninho and, in the following season, also Emerson as Boro created history by fielding three Brazilians.

In his heyday, Branco had been famed for his dangerous free kicks and had been a skilful and mobile left-back but he failed to reach those heights on Teesside. Branco showed flashes of his talent, particularly from set pieces, but was badly out of condition and was no longer good enough for the Premier League. He still had eight months left on his contract when he departed, Boro deciding to cut their losses on a player who had fallen well below the expected standards. He had failed to impress staff at the club with a questionable attitude and a poor attendance at training. He departed with a tabloid attack on assistant manager Viv Anderson and first-team coach John Pickering for 'their inability to handle big name players' to further sour his reputation on Teesside.

BRAWN William Frederick

Outside-right
Born: Wellingborough, 1 August 1878.
Died: August 1932.
Career: Wellingborough. Northampton Town 1898. Sheffield United 1899. Aston Villa 1901. MIDDLESBROUGH 1906. Chelsea 1907. Brentford.

■ Billy Brawn was a player who truly lived up to his name, standing over 6ft tall and weighing in at more than 13 stone. Brought in to fill the outside-right berth, Brawn was a former England international with a strong reputation. He arrived in the same month as Steve Bloomer as Boro spent big to preserve their First Division status. At the time rumours were rife that Middlesbrough were being assisted to buy players by other clubs who were keen to see Bury relegated. An FA investigation, however, failed to uncover any evidence to back up the claim.

Brawn had played outside the League with Wellingborough Town and Northampton Town before joining Sheffield United. It was at his next club, Aston Villa, that he played for England, against Wales and Ireland in 1904, and won an FA Cup medal. He made his Middlesbrough debut in a 1–0 defeat against his old club Sheffield United but his arrival helped to preserve top flight status.

Brawn's last League club was Brentford where he reportedly became the game's first ever player-director. He was also advisory manager at the club and ran the King's Arms in Brentford until his death in August 1932.

BREARLEY John

Inside-right
Born: West Derby, Liverpool, 1875.
Career: Kettering Town. Notts County 1897. Chatham 1898. Millwall Athletic 1899. Notts County 1900. MIDDLESBROUGH 1900. Everton 1902. Tottenham Hotspur 1903. Crystal Palace 1907. Millwall Athletic 1909.

■ Forward Jack Brearley was the man whose goals shot Middlesbrough to their first ever promotion. He was the club's top scorer in 1901–02 to win a place in the First Division. After making his debut in the last game of 1900–01, he set Division Two alight in the subsequent campaign. He notched 11 in the first 11 games and later scored four in a 7–2 trouncing of Barnsley. The versatile player operated at inside or centre-forward and even played on the left wing or half-back in 1901–02.

But Brearley departed before Middlesbrough made their First Division debut, returning to his home city to sign for Everton. His second game for his new club saw him lose 1–0 at the Linthorpe Road Ground but he gained revenge by scoring a hat-trick in the reverse fixture in January 1903. Brearley then followed Everton manager John Cameron to Southern League Spurs where he was converted to half-back. In 1907 he was recruited by his former Middlesbrough manager John Robson at Crystal Palace for their first season of League football. He became player-coach at Millwall after leaving Palace and then coached at Berlin Victoria in Germany. Unfortunately, he was in Germany when the Great War broke out and was interned at Ruhlenben Camp, along with his former manager Cameron.

BRENNAN Mark Robert

Midfield
Born: Rossendale, 4 October 1965.
Career: Ipswich Town 1983. MIDDLESBROUGH 1988. Manchester City 1990. Oldham Athletic 1992. Sydney Olympique (Australia). Dagenham & Redbridge.

■ Brennan was a player that Boro manager Bruce Rioch chased for some time but one who never realised the potential seen in him. Having turned

down Second Division Boro in March 1988, he accepted the move a few months later when top flight status was secured. Rioch saw off competition from Norwich, Southampton and Sheffield Wednesday to sign his top transfer target under freedom of contract.

The Lancashire-born midfielder had played for Blackburn Boys but joined Ipswich as an apprentice after being recommended by a friend of Paul Mariner. The former England youth player won six Under-21 caps at Portman Road but was banned by international manager Dave Sexton for drinking during a tournament in France.

Rioch saw him as a midfielder who would add skill and guile to his newly-promoted side. Brennan had two good feet and vision. He was an excellent passer of the ball over 30 or 40 yards. Unfortunately, his first season on Teesside was curtailed by a troublesome shoulder dislocation as Boro were relegated and he struggled for consistency. He lacked physical presence and was nicknamed 'Brenda' by the crueller fans. In the following season, he scored a superb free kick in the first leg of the ZDS Cup semi-final against Aston Villa but, after Boro just stayed in Division Two, he was sold to First Division Manchester City. An earlier offer had been rejected by Boro but City manager Howard Kendall, who had previously tried to sign him at Blackburn, finally got his man.

BRIGGS Walter

Goalkeeper
Born: Middlesbrough, 29 November 1922.
Died: 1990.
Career: Cochranes. MIDDLESBROUGH 1947. Southport 1948. Hartlepool United 1949.

■ Talented goalkeeper Briggs had a difficult League baptism, Boro losing 4–0 on a trip to Grimsby in May 1946. He was one of four 'keepers used by manager David Jack in the first post-war League campaign as he searched for a replacement for ageing Dave Cumming. Paddy Nash and Norman Malan were also handed chances but none made a big impression. Derwick Goodfellow was brought in during the close season and Briggs had just one more opportunity as stand-in for the regular number one in a 3–1 win against Bolton in September 1947. The Middlesbrough-born player later spent three seasons at Hartlepool after a year at Southport. Briggs, who lived in Bishopton Road in Grove Hill, died in 1990.

BRINE Peter Kenneth

Midfield
Born: Greenwich, 18 July 1953.
Career: MIDDLESBROUGH 1970. Minnesota Kicks (loan) 1975. Whitby Town.

■ Versatile Brine was a valued squad man who struggled to win a regular first-team place. He spent much of his time at the club occupying the bench but was a lively and enterprising player who could play on the wing, midfield or up front. Born in London, the son of a Boro exile, he signed for the club as a junior after playing for Winns Wanderers. After a brief substitute appearance under Stan Anderson, Brine was given his first start by caretaker manager Harold Shepherdson against Queen's Park Rangers in January 1973. He soon scored his first goal in a 2–0 victory over Cardiff.

When Jack Charlton took over in the summer of 1973, Brine was a frequent substitute but played only a peripheral role in Boro's promotion and then impressive first season in Division One, though he did score twice in the final game of the 1973–74 Second Division-

winning campaign. Chances became more common in 1975–76 and in the subsequent campaign – Charlton's last. Yet only once did Brine start more than five consecutive game in his eight years at the club and then it was only a run of nine matches that he saw. A steady player, who always gave 100 percent, Brine also played for Minnesota Kicks in the North American Soccer League in the summer of 1975.

Brine – nicknamed 'Salty' by his teammates – was becoming increasingly troubled by a persistent knee injury and, after playing just three times in John Neal's first season in charge, he was forced to retire from the professional game in his mid–20s. He later captained Whitby Town for a season while working as pipefitter's mate before taking up a coaching appointment with Hobart Juventus in Tasmania, guiding them to a state Championship. After officially emigrating down under, Brine moved to Townsville in North Queensland, where he lives to this day, working as a gaming machines manager for a major casino.

BROWN Alexander

Centre-forward
Born: Beith, 7 April 1879.
Career: Glenbuck. Kilsyth Wanderers. St Bernards. Preston North End 1896. Portsmouth. Tottenham Hotspur. Portsmouth. MIDDLESBROUGH 1903. Luton Town. Kettering Town.

■ Rated as one of the best headers of the ball ever seen in a Middlesbrough shirt, Sandy Brown was a Scottish international centre-forward who played in the club's first season at Ayresome

Park. He made his home debut in the opening match at the new stadium and scored the second goal in a 3–2 defeat. He went on to finish top scorer in the season and would have been ever-present but for missing the game at Bury on 8 April after receiving a telegram from the Scotland selection committee advising him to make his way to Scotland to play England. Scotland lost the game 1–0 and it proved to be Brown's only international chance. He had to fight hard for a place in the following season with Harry Astley and Tom Green and returned south to Luton in 1905. Before joining Middlesbrough, Brown had two spells at Portsmouth, sandwiching his time at Southern League Tottenham where he won the 1901 FA Cup, scoring in every round and setting a record which still stands today of 15 FA Cup goals in a season.

BROWN Arthur Samuel

Centre-forward/Inside-forward
Born: Gainsborough, 6 April 1885.
Died: 1944.
Career: Gainsborough Trinity 1901. Sheffield United 1902. Sunderland 1908. Fulham 1910. MIDDLESBROUGH 1912.

■ The crazy world of Arthur Brown saw him play international football as a teenager but fail to hold down a regular first-team place with Middlesbrough in his late 20s. The former England centre-forward enjoyed only a brief spell at Middlesbrough. Brown was capped by England while with Sheffield United. He made his debut, aged just 18, against Wales in 1904 and also played against Ireland in 1906, when he scored in a 5–0 win but was subsequently dropped. His form for United had prompted Sunderland to pay a substantial £1,600 for his services. Brown played the opening four games of the 1912–13 campaign at Middlesbrough alongside a young George Elliott. But Middlesbrough only scored one goal in those games and Brown failed to find the net. Sam Cail was recalled by manager Tom McIntosh and Brown, an accomplished sculptor, left the club.

BROWN David James

Goalkeeper
Born: Hartlepool, 28 January 1957.
Career: Horden Colliery. MIDDLESBROUGH 1977. Plymouth Argyle (loan) 1979. Oxford United 1979. Bury 1981. Preston North End 1986. Scunthorpe United (loan) 1989. Halifax Town 1989.

■ The son of a Manchester United and Hartlepool goalkeeper, Brown followed in his father's footsteps by taking up a career between the sticks. Having played for St Bede's School and Hartlepool Boys, he signed for Boro as an amateur and continued to learn his trade as a plumber. He had to wait a year for his first-team chance when he was called upon to replace Jim Platt for the final 10 games of 1977–78. It was John Neal's first term in charge of the club and Platt and Pat Cuff had already had chances that season though neither had shown consistent form. Just two wins were secured in Brown's run of games and, though only eight goals were conceded, he was discarded for the following campaign. Jim Stewart was brought in from Scotland and Brown found himself

third choice behind Platt and the newcomer. After struggling to even win a reserve team place, he was loaned to Plymouth in August 1979 and moved on to Oxford two months later. He enjoyed a lengthy career in the lower Leagues, finding his biggest success with Bury where he won promotion from Division Four in 1985. He repeated the feat two years later with Preston and in the same season returned to haunt Boro as part of the Preston team that won 1–0 at Ayresome Park in a third round FA Cup shock.

BROWN James

Left-half/Outside-left
Born: Luton 1880.
Career: Luton Town 1899. MIDDLESBROUGH 1900.

■ Outside-left Brown made his debut for Middlesbrough on the opening day of 1900–01 season alongside fellow debutants Wilkie and Robertson in a 2–0 win over Lincoln. Although left out for the following games, he returned as a stand-in for club captain Bill Higgins at centre-half for a 2–0 defeat at Burnley at the end of September. However, he spent the rest of his time with the club in the reserves and was released at the end of the season.

BROWN John 'Jock'

Centre-forward/Inside-right
Born: Motherwell, 1876.
Career: Dalziel Rovers. Sunderland 1897. Heart of Midlothian. Portsmouth. MIDDLESBROUGH 1900. Luton Town.

■ Outside-left Brown spent only a season with Middlesbrough as the club looked to establish itself in the Football League. After signing from Portsmouth, the Scot made his debut in the opening away match of the 1900–01 campaign as Boro lost 4–0 at Newton Heath. He netted twice – including a penalty – in his third game as a 3–2 win at Chesterfield was secured and was the club's top scorer by the end of October with four goals. However, he was used as a utility man as the season progressed, sometimes playing at centre-forward or centre-half, and eventually lost his place. After being released, he played for Luton.

BROWN John Robert

Right-back/Outside-right
Born: South Bank, 1885.
Career: South Bank. MIDDLESBROUGH 1906. Bristol City 1908. Warrenby Athletic.

■ An apprentice jockey at the age of 14, Brown opted instead for a football career. Brown, who lived in Lavender Road, first played for South Bank Board School and joined Boro as an amateur. His first-team debut came towards the end of the 1906–07 season when he replaced Jack Tyldesley at right-back for a 1–0 defeat at Bolton. Brown's biggest asset was his pace and he made the right-back berth his own for the first half of the 1907–08 season. However, he was dropped after a 6–0 hammering at Aston Villa in early December 1907 and played just four more times shortly after Christmas. He moved on to First Division rivals Bristol City but was injured early in his City career. He broke his kneecap in a practice match and his career was ended when pneumonia set in. Brown returned to Teesside to run the Navigation Inn in North Ormesby. He was reinstated as an amateur and played for Warrenby Athletic.

BROWN Joseph

Wing-half
Born: Cramlington, 26 April 1929.
Career: Seaton Delaval. MIDDLESBROUGH 1946. Burnley 1952. Bournemouth 1954. Aldershot 1960.

■ Brown, who hailed from Northumberland, joined Boro as a junior and played most of his games at wing-half. He got his first-team chance in place of Ronnie Dicks after three years at the club in a 2–1 home defeat to Fulham. After that solitary appearance it was another eight months before a second opportunity came his way. But after figuring in four games at the tail-end of the 1949–50 campaign, it was another year on the sidelines for Brown. His final opportunity came when he was called up in place of Jimmy Gordon for the final six games of the 1950–51 season. But Boro's title challenge faded as they failed to win any of the games. Although quick and a good footballer, Brown was very slight and was probably not aggressive enough to be a big success.

He missed the whole of the 1951–52 season with a slipped disc and was not on the retained list at the end of the campaign. He joined Burnley and made his debut against Middlesbrough, though his new side were beaten 1–0 at Turf Moor. He found opportunities scarce and moved to Third Division Bournemouth for regular football. After hanging up his boots, he returned to Burnley working behind the scenes for many years coaching and scouting before promotion to assistant manager and eventually becoming manager in 1976. But Brown couldn't prevent relegation to Division Two and left after failing to halt the slide in the following season.

BROWN Thomas

Outside-right
Born: Middlesbrough, July 1898.
Career: MIDDLESBROUGH 1920. Accrington Stanley 1923.

■ Local winger Tommy Brown first joined Boro as an amateur in March 1920 and played in the club's North Eastern League side. He turned professional a year later and was called up to make his first-team debut in place of Jacky Carr at Chelsea, playing the last four games of the 1920–21 season on the right flank. But Brown was out in the cold in the following campaign and his only other chance came as cover for Carr once again in October 1922 after 17 months out of the team. He joined Accrington Stanley after being released by Middlesbrough.

BROWN Thomas Emmerson

Full-back
Born: Throckley, 8 September 1935.
Career: MIDDLESBROUGH 1953. King's Lynn.

■ Brown was first thrust into the Middlesbrough side as a teenager and was a regular at left-back throughout the 1954–55 campaign. He was given his chance in place of Bobby Corbett for a trip to Hull in mid-September as manager Bob Dennison tried to end a run of eight games without a win following relegation from the First Division. He was a regular for the remainder of the campaign but failed to

impress in what was a poor Boro team. It was National Service that disrupted Brown's career in 1955 though he continued to play part-time for the club. He was out of the first team right up until January 1957 by which time Ray Bilcliff and Derek Stonehouse were the main contenders for the left-back slot. Brown joined King's Lynn after being released.

BROWN William Hutchinson

Right-half/Right-back
Born: Bedlington, 11 March 1909.
Died: 1996.
Career: West Stanley. MIDDLESBROUGH 1928. Hartlepool United 1946.

■ Billy Brown was a miner playing part-time for West Stanley when he was signed by Middlesbrough manager Peter McWilliam. He had to wait three years for his debut when he stepped in as replacement for regular right-half John MacFarlane against Leicester City in August 1931. He won a regular place in the following season and was a stalwart of the club's successful pre-war side. As part of an impressive half-back line with Bob Baxter and Billy Forrest, he helped the club to seventh, fifth and fourth places in the First Division in the three seasons before the outbreak of war. Brown, who also operated at right-back on several occasions, was 30 when war broke out and he guested for Watford as well as Middlesbrough during the hostilities. A well-liked character at the club, he played just one competitive post-war game. His swansong was a 7–2 FA Cup hammering of Leeds United in January 1946. He moved on to Division Three North Hartlepool and enjoyed two good seasons before retiring in 1948. He died in 1996.

BROWNLIE John Jack

Right-back
Born: Caldercruix, 11 March 1952.
Career: Hibernian 1969. Newcastle United 1978. MIDDLESBROUGH 1982. Hartlepool United 1984. Vasalunds (Sweden). Berwick Rangers. Blyth Spartans.

■ Right-back Brownlie was recruited by fellow Scot Bobby Murdoch at Middlesbrough. While with Hibernian, Brownlie had emerged as a bright talent, winning caps for his country while still a teenager. In the early 1970s he attracted interest from a variety of top English clubs but he broke a leg and was out for over a season. He never quite regained his best form though Newcastle brought him south of the border and he was popular with the St James Park crowd who liked his ability to get forward and support the attack. He left Newcastle following a dispute over terms and joined newly-relegated Middlesbrough. He was brought in to fill the right-back berth vacated by John Craggs' move in the opposite direction but proved to be an inadequate replacement and past his best. Nicknamed 'Snakehips' by his teammates, Brownlie made a disastrous debut in a 4–1 home defeat to Burnley and also lost 4–1 in his second home

game two weeks later against Fulham. And when Malcolm Allison took over as manager, he lost his place to Paul Ward. After a season at Hartlepool, he played for Swedish Second Division team Vasalunds in Stockholm on the recommendation of Stuart Baxter, brother of former Boro teammate Mick. He later managed Cowdenbeath but was surprisingly sacked in 1992 a month after winning promotion to Division One.

BRUCE Robert Frederick

Inside-forward
Born: Paisley, 29 January 1906.
Career: St Anthony's (Glasgow).

Aberdeen. MIDDLESBROUGH 1927. Sheffield Wednesday 1935. Ipswich Town. Mossley.

■ Tricky inside-forward Bobby Bruce had the almost impossible task of taking the place of Middlesbrough legend Jacky Carr. A skilful and elusive player, he struggled to win over Carr's many fans despite being a more than useful player in his own right. Bruce had built his reputation in Scotland with Aberdeen and was brought in for a record fee as a ready-made replacement for the veteran Carr. Just before joining Boro, he had become the first player to score a hat-trick in a Scottish Cup tie and still finish on the losing side.

He arrived following Middlesbrough's record-breaking 1927–28 promotion campaign, making his debut in a 5–2 First Division defeat at Bolton midway through the following season. Bruce failed to prevent immediate relegation back to Division Two but played a vital role in ensuring an instant return to the top flight once again. He was small at only 5ft 6in but was a box of tricks with accurate passing skills and an ability to lose defenders. However, Bruce struggled for form in the First Division and after a bad patch in April 1930 he was so upset at the crowd's barracking that he asked for a transfer. Many members of the crowd still drew unfavourable comparisons with Carr. His style of play was different and the supporters often complained about his tendency to shoot from long distance and inconsistent displays. But the Scotsman recovered his form and won over many of the fans as Boro consolidated their position in the First Division. He scored a hat-trick in an incredible 10–3 win over Sheffield United in November 1933 and his performances brought him a Scotland call-up in the same month. Approaching his 30th birthday, and having lost his regular place, Bruce joined Sheffield Wednesday for a season before dropping out of the League to join Ipswich.

BRYAN Peter Anthony

Full-back
Born: Birmingham, 22 June 1943.
Career: MIDDLESBROUGH 1961. Oldham Athletic 1965.

■ Eccentric Peter Bryan is believed to be the tallest player in the club's history at 6ft 5in. With huge feet and a gangling frame, he lacked finesse and probably the talent to make it in professional football. It was at full-back that he later settled, but Bryan made his Middlesbrough debut as a surprise call-up at centre forward. He was aged 19 when his chance came in a weakened team for a League Cup defeat at Hull in October 1962. He had to wait another 23 months for his League debut when he stepped in at right-back in place of Bill Gates for a 4–2 home defeat at the hands of Ipswich. Three more games followed but a 3 3 home draw with Bury proved to be his last appearance and Gates was recalled. After playing a handful of games for Oldham, he returned to live in Middlesbrough.

BRYAN Raymond

Outside-right
Born: Bishop Auckland, 26 July 1916.
Career: Bishop Auckland. MIDDLESBROUGH 1936.

■ While his namesake Peter Bryan is Boro's tallest recorded player, Ray Bryan was one of the smallest, a full foot smaller at just 5ft 4in. His first-team chances were limited and Bryan's only first class game came at outside-right in a goalless First Division draw at Birmingham in place of Cliff Chadwick.

BUCKLEY Michael John

Midfield
Born: Manchester, 4 November 1953.

Career: Everton 1971. Sunderland 1978. Hartlepool United 1983. Carlisle United 1983. MIDDLESBROUGH 1984.

■ Starved of transfer funds, Boro manager Willie Maddren brought in the experienced midfielder as one of his first signings to bolster the side. Mick Buckley had been a schoolboy star in Manchester and could have joined United or City but opted for Everton where he added Under-23 honours to his Youth caps. Sunderland had paid £90,000 to sign him though he was affected by injuries at Roker Park. A small but aggressive midfielder, he arrived on a free transfer and was immediately installed in the team. However, Buckley never lived up to expectations and Maddren was disappointed with his contribution and lack of loyalty to the manager himself. He was released at the end of his one-year contract.

BUCKLEY Seth

Centre-forward
Born: Middlesbrough.
Career: Haverton Hill. MIDDLESBROUGH 1899.

■ A local player who played in Middlesbrough's first Football League season. Buckley's only first-team game came at centre-forward in a 7–1 Division Two defeat at Chesterfield in January 1900 in place of regular forward George Reid. Released from Boro, he later worked in the salt mines at Port Clarence, where he also lived.

BURBECK Ronald Thomas

Winger
Born: Leicester, 27 February 1934.
Career: Leicester City 1952. MIDDLESBROUGH 1956. Darlington 1963.

■ A former England Youth international, Ron Burbeck joined Middlesbrough from his hometown club Leicester City. He was spotted by manager Bob Dennison on a scouting mission to find a new outside-left. He made his debut in the same game as goalkeeper Esmond Million, a 3–1 victory over Port Vale. Burbeck then scored in his second match for the club a week later. His last minute goal at Rotherham led to a 3–2 success.

Burbeck played his early games as an

outside-left providing a good supply for the prolific Brian Clough. A good crosser of the ball, it was his style to hug the touchline and was a little dynamo with the ball at his feet, though he did not enjoy the physical side of the game.

Burbeck was never an automatic choice and lost his left-wing berth following the arrival of Edwin Holliday. The newcomer and Billy Day were the preferred wing pair of manager Dennison and Burbeck had to show his versatility by filling in on either flank. Further competition came later from Arthur Kaye and Bobby Hume and when Raich Carter took over as manager midway through the 1962–63 season, Burbeck did not fit into his plans. He played just one more season of League football at Fourth Division Darlington.

BURKE Mark Stephen

Winger
Born: Solihull, 12 February 1969.
Career: Aston Villa 1987. MIDDLESBROUGH 1987. Darlington (loan) 1990. Wolverhampton Wanderers 1991. Luton Town (loan) 1994. Port Vale 1994. Fortuna Sittard (Holland) 1995. Omiga Ardija (Japan) 2000. Rapid Bucharest (Romania) 2000. TOP Oss (Holland) 2001.

■ Burke was a talented midfielder with plenty of skill and flair who became popular with the Boro fans. But he was a player who was often seen as a luxury by manager Bruce Rioch. Known to all as 'Sooty', Burke was good with the ball at his feet and could be brilliant on his day but he wasn't always given the chance to shine and could be frustratingly inconsistent. He never got the opportunity in his career to fulfil his massive potential.

Having played at Youth and Schools level for England while with Aston Villa, scoring a hat-trick in a Schoolboy international against Holland, Burke was one of several players recruited from Villa's reserves by Rioch. He arrived midway through Boro's Second Division promotion campaign and then enjoyed a relatively good season in the top flight. Unfortunately, he made a bad mistake which many believe cost the club relegation from the First Division in 1988–89. With a minute to go, and 1–0 up against Aston Villa, Burke attempted a 60 yard backpass to goalkeeper Kevin Poole. The ball was cut out and Villa equalised. Then, in the final game of the season, he missed a golden opportunity to score against Sheffield Wednesday. Boro lost 1–0 and went into the drop zone for the first time all season.

Despite the errors, Burke had played well and he was expected to be a regular back in the Second Division but Rioch seemed to lose faith in him and he suffered from injuries. Rioch accepted a third request for a move in October 1989 and, when Colin Todd replaced Rioch in March 1990, he arranged a loan deal with Darlington. But Burke became the forgotten man of Ayresome Park, much to the frustration of his many admirers in the stands. He spent 14 months in the reserves before a cut-price move to Wolves. He showed flashes of brilliance and was linked with several Premiership

clubs including Liverpool, having a short trial at Tottenham. But first-team football eluded him again and he joined Port Vale where his 15 substitute appearances in the 1994–95 campaign broke a club record. He was released on a free transfer and moved to Holland where he enjoyed some success and regular football.

BURLURAUX Donald

Winger
Born: Skelton, 8 June 1951.
Career: MIDDLESBROUGH 1968. York City (loan) 1971. Darlington 1972.

■ Speedy winger Don Burluraux came through the junior ranks at the same time as Willie Maddren and David Mills but failed to make the impact on the first team as his contemporaries. An out and out winger, he was a talented player with a good left foot but never made a concerted breakthrough. Burluraux was a non-playing substitute at Leicester in September 1970 but had to wait another six months for his debut in wide midfield against Luton in March 1971 and played two more games in the end of season run-in. But he failed to progress in the following season, playing half an hour as substitute against Fulham before his final game in place of Derrick Downing at Blackpool. He was loaned to York before being released with a young David Armstrong breaking into the team ahead of him. At Darlington, his teammates included Billy Horner and his former Boro skipper Gordon Jones though the trio were unable to stop the club finishing bottom of the League in the 1972–73 season. He later worked at ICI Wilton as a process worker and in a shoebox factory at Skelton.

BURNS Michael Edward

Forward
Born: Preston, 21 December 1946.
Career: Skelmersdale United. Blackpool 1969. Newcastle United 1974. Cardiff City 1978. MIDDLESBROUGH 1978.

■ Micky Burns was not the tallest striker at 5ft 7in but he was full of tricks and a natural goalscorer. He came to Middlesbrough late in his career but still made an impact and is best remembered

for scoring four in a sensational 7–2 victory over Chelsea in December 1978, a season in which he finished top scorer.

The striker came into the game late, turning professional at the age of 23 after studying for a degree in economics at Manchester University and taking up a teaching career. He joined Blackpool after playing non-League with Chorley and Skelmersdale United where he was an Amateur Cup winner alongside Steve Heighway and England Amateur international. He scored on his Blackpool debut and helped the club into the First Division in 1969–70. A fee of £166,000 took him to Newcastle where he collected a Texaco Cup-winners' medal in his first season, scoring a spectacular goal against Boro on the way, but was on the losing side in the 1976 League Cup Final. Indeed, he developed a reputation for always seeming to score against Boro. He spent just two months at Cardiff. He was player-coach and in control of all team affairs but didn't settle in Wales and left after a conflict of opinion with senior officials.

Burns made an immediate hit at Boro, scoring on his debut at Old Trafford and enjoyed a good first season, only interrupted by a back injury. The goals were continuing to come in the following years but appearances became more infrequent for the veteran striker as youngsters like David Shearer and David Hodgson emerged. He joined the club staff as youth team coach in 1981 but there was still talk of him making a comeback in the 1981–82 relegation season amid a goal drought. But following the relegation, Burns, who had been working without contract, lost his job amid financial cutbacks. He took up a job with the PFA, co-ordinating the football in community scheme and the PFA's training and education programme. He left the post in 2003.

BURTON George

Centre-forward
Born: Middlesbrough.
Career: Grangetown.
MIDDLESBROUGH 1909. Cardiff City 1910.

■ A local centre-forward who deputised for regular frontman Sam Cail in the 1909–10 season. Burton's debut came in a goalless draw at Liverpool in December 1909 partnering England international Steve Bloomer. But Fred Pentland was preferred for the next game and Burton had to wait two months for another chance. He was recalled for a 2–1 defeat at Chelsea as Boro tried to end a disastrous run of just one win in 11 games but made little impact and moved

on at the end of the season. His brother also played League football for Cardiff.

BUTLER Geoffrey

Full-back
Born: Middlesbrough, 26 September 1946.
Career: MIDDLESBROUGH 1964. Chelsea 1967. Sunderland 1968. Norwich City 1968. Bournemouth 1976. Peterborough United 1981.

■ An early version of today's wing-back, Geoff Butler broke into the Middlesbrough first team as a teenager and earned a big money move to Chelsea but never made the grade at the top level. Having progressed through the junior ranks, Butler turned professional under Raich Carter and made his debut at right-back in a 6–0 defeat at Bolton. He played six games at the tail-end of the 1965–66 season but missed the final day defeat at Cardiff that consigned the club to Third Division football for the first time.

A good ball player, Butler was a regular in the subsequent promotion season, operating on either flank but usually at left-back. Boro started the 1967–68 season poorly but a shock League Cup victory over Chelsea proved to be a watershed for Butler. Chelsea boss Tommy Docherty raved about young Butler's performance after the game and soon forked out a club record fee to take him to Stamford Bridge. Despite the outlay, however, Butler got few chances, playing only eight games in four months. He struggled to settle in London and joined Sunderland for £65,000. It was another short spell before moving on to Norwich, where he played in the First Division, and then Bournemouth. He progressed to coach the reserves at his last club and then assisted former Norwich teammate Peter Morris at Peterborough as player-coach. Butler took over as player-manager of Salisbury in early 1983.

BUTLER Reuben

Centre-forward/Inside-right
Born: Stillington, 10 October 1890.
Died: 1958.
Career: Spennymoor Athletic. MIDDLESBROUGH 1912. Hartlepool United. MIDDLESBROUGH 1919. Oldham Athletic 1920. Bury 1923. Bradford City 1924. Crewe Alexandra 1925. Rochdale 1926. Accrington Stanley 1927. Great Harwood.

■ Forward Butler scored in the first three games he played for Middlesbrough's first team. Partnering George Elliott in attack, he played at centre-forward on his debut at home to Blackburn in the first season of League football after the Great War. He found the net in a 2–2 draw and was again on target in a 3–0 success over Sheffield Wednesday three days later. The goals continued to flow as Butler hit the only goal of the game against Sheffield United at Ayresome Park. By the end of October, he was out-scoring Elliott but the goals began to dry up as the season went on. He moved on to Oldham at the end of the season.

BUTLER Thomas

Outside-right/Inside-forward
Born: Atherton, 28 April 1918.
Career: Astley & Tyldesley Collieries. Bolton Wanderers 1936. Macclesfield. Oldham Athletic 1937. MIDDLESBROUGH 1938. Oldham Athletic 1946. Accrington Stanley 1947. Wigan Athletic.

■ The outbreak of World War Two prematurely ended Tom Butler's Middlesbrough career. He played just two League games for the club before the hostilities intervened. Butler had played his early football with Astley before joining Bolton, dropping into non-League football with Macclesfield after failing to break through at Burnden Park. Oldham revived his career but he was soon signed by Wilf Gillow at Middlesbrough. He played two of the last three games of the 1938–39 season but war was declared three games into the aborted 1939–40 campaign. Butler came through the conflict unscathed and made some wartime appearances for the club. However, on the resumption of League football, he was deemed surplus to requirements and returned to Oldham in time for the 1946–47 season kick-off. He soon went on to Accrington Stanley where he enjoyed his most productive years.

BUTLER William

Outside-right
Born: Stockton, 12 January 1901.
Career: Darlington 1922. MIDDLESBROUGH 1922.

■ Butler played in the final two games of the 1922–23 First Division campaign. He deputised at outside-right for Bottrill and was given the task of supplying chances for the strikeforce of George Elliott and Andy Wilson. However, both games, home and away against West Brom, ended in 1–0 defeats and Middlesbrough narrowly avoided relegation.

BYRNE Wesley John

Left-back
Born: Dublin, 9 February 1977.
Career: MIDDLESBROUGH 1994. Stoke City 1996. Darlington 1996.

■ A left-back tipped for a bright future, Irishman Byrne didn't make the progress expected of him. He played for Eire at Schools and Youth level and was named in Eire Under-21 squads alongside Boro teammates Alan Moore, Graham Kavanagh and Keith O'Halloran but never played at that level. A defender with pace and strong tackling, Byrne's only first-team action came in a 3–1 Anglo-Italian Cup defeat in Ancona when Curtis Fleming and Derek Whyte were the main contenders for the first-team left-back slot. Bryan Robson fielded a team of youngsters in the controversial competition and a crowd of just 1,500 saw Byrne play. He moved on to Stoke and Darlington without success.

CADE Jamie

Striker/Midfield
Born: Durham, 15 January 1984.
Career: MIDDLESBROUGH 2002. Chesterfield (loan) 2003. Colchester 2003. Crawley 2005. Lewes 2006.

■ The lively forward graduated from the Academy and represented England at all levels from Under-15 to Under-18. He began his career as a defender, playing at left-back for the reserves as well as in his normal position up front. Quick and enthusiastic, Cade made his first-team debut as a substitute in the 3–1 Worthington Cup defeat at Ipswich on 6 November 2002, turning in an energetic and eye-catching performance. However he failed to win a new contract and moved to Colchester in 2004 and is currently playing for Lewes in Blue Square South.

CAIG Hugh

Inside-right
Born: Dalry, 1894.
Career: Kilwinning. MIDDLESBROUGH 1914.

■ This Scottish inside-right played in Middlesbrough's last game before the Great War brought League football to an end. He played in the forward line alongside George Elliott, Andy Wilson and 26-goal top scorer Walter Tinsley in a 4–0 defeat at Blackburn.

CAIL Samuel George

Centre-forward/Inside-left
Born: Middlesbrough, 1888.
Died: 1950.
Career: Army. MIDDLESBROUGH 1906. Aberdeen. Stalybridge Celtic.

■ Middlesbrough paid for teenager Sam Cail to come out of the Army and he provided six years' good service to the club. An inside or centre-forward, he joined Boro after a year's suspension over an earlier transfer triviality and left the Army in India. He made his debut in March 1907 in a 1–0 First Division victory over Aston Villa. Cail had to wait until January of the following year for another chance but scored in a 1–1 home draw with Nottingham Forest. He set off on a goalscoring spree – finding the net in his next six games and finishing with 12 in 13 games as Middlesbrough finished sixth. He formed a good partnership with Steve Bloomer and Alf Common and, ending the season as joint top scorer, he stood out as a great talent for the future.

The signing of Jack Hall meant that Cail was out of the side for the first two games of 1908–09. He was soon back in the team but the goals never flowed in the same way again. Cail was frequently dropped as others were tried in the forward positions with little success and Cail was inevitably brought back into the side. However, he lost his regular place in the 1912–13 campaign as young Jacky Carr emerged. Cail had a benefit against Derby in 1913 before leaving to join Aberdeen and later Stalybridge Celtic. Cail played for Scotswood in the Northern Victory League after the war. He died in 1950.

CALLAGHAN James

Inside-right
Born: South Bank.
Career: South Bank. MIDDLESBROUGH 1899.

■ Callaghan played for South Bank in the 1898–99 season and signed to play for Middlesbrough's A team. He got just two chances in the Second Division team. Callaghan missed out on the club's first ever Football League game but his debut came at inside-right in the first home League game at Linthorpe Road. It was an unhappy start with a 3–1 defeat to Small Heath, though he helped Middlesbrough secure their first point in a 1–1 draw at New Brighton a week later. But Callaghan was axed for the following game in favour of Thomas Lamb. His contract was cancelled by the club directors as he was unable to train on a regular basis.

CAMERON Kenneth

Inside-forward/Outside-left
Born: Hamilton, 1905.
Career: Parkhead. Preston North End 1926. MIDDLESBROUGH 1929. Bolton Wanderers 1933. Hull City 1935. Queen's Park Rangers 1936. Rotherham United 1937.

■ The much-travelled forward made a sensational start at Middlesbrough. Cameron scored twice from the left-wing on his debut in a 5–3 defeat at West Ham in September 1929 and found the net again two days later in a 3–1 win at Sheffield United. The Scotsman was unable to sustain his goalscoring form and was axed midway through the season with tough competition arriving in the shape of wingers Ernie Muttitt and Fred Warren, who were signed as the 1929–30 season went on.

Cameron returned to the First Division side in the 1930–31 campaign, winning a regular place at inside-left with Warren firmly ensconced in the wing role. The goals did not flow but he provided able support to the prolific George Camsell. He reverted to the wing in 1931–32 and played some games at inside-right. The arrival of Bob Baxter in 1932, however, curtailed Cameron's opportunities. He found himself increasingly out in the cold and moved on to Bolton early in the 1933–34 season. He enjoyed a nomadic career after leaving Ayresome Park.

CAMPBELL Alexander

Full-back
Born: Inverness 1885.
Career: Inverness Clachnacuddin. MIDDLESBROUGH 1906. Leeds City 1911.

■ Scottish full-back Campbell was recruited from his hometown club Inverness Clachnacuddin in time for the

start of the 1906–07 season. Brought in as a replacement for Kilmarnock-bound Billy Agnew, he made his debut in the opening day clash with Everton. Playing at left full-back, he saw his new side draw 2–2. Campbell was in and out of the side as new player-manager Andy Aitken tried to put together a winning team. And when Aitken brought in left-back Jimmy Watson from Sunderland in April 1907, Campbell was dropped. He did play the occasional game at right-back in the following season but a regular return to first-team action eluded him and Campbell moved on. Unfortunately, he played just one game for Leeds City in which he broke his leg, ending his professional career.

CAMPBELL Andrew Paul

Striker
Born: Stockton, 18 April 1979.
Career: MIDDLESBROUGH 1996. Sheffield United (loan) 1998. Sheffield United (loan) 1999. Bolton Wanderers (loan) 2001. Cardiff City 2002. Doncaster Rovers (loan) 2005. Oxford United (loan) 2005. Dunfermline Athletic 2006. Halifax Town 2006.

■ Andy Campbell's Boro career was very much a case of what might have been. The lightning fast striker made history when he became the first 16-year-old to appear in the Premier League, but he was playing for Halifax Town in the Conference 10 years later when he might have expected to have been one of the game's top stars. Campbell was an unknown prospect when he was brought on as substitute against Sheffield Wednesday in April 1996. It was an even bigger shock when he was named in the starting line-up for Boro's trip to Anfield three weeks later as a lone striker. Unfortunately, a shirt with his name and number had not been packed and physiotherapist Bob Ward was dispatched to find a supporter wearing a Boro away shirt for Campbell to wear. After his early baptism, the local lad – formerly of Nunthorpe School – found progress hard to make. Although extremely fast, he was slight of frame and lacked confidence in front of goal. He scored against Boro's deadly rivals Sunderland in a Coca-Cola Cup win in October 1997 but, having been linked with Sheffield United and Huddersfield, enjoyed his best first-team run in 1999–2000 when he scored four times in 25 League games. He again fell out of favour under Terry Venables and then Steve McClaren, though he scored one of the goals in a memorable FA Cup win over Manchester United in January 2002. Having scored seven goals in eight games on loan to Second Division Cardiff – including a hat-trick in a 7–1 win at Oldham – former Boro manager Lennie Lawrence took him to the Bluebirds on a permanent basis for a £950,000 fee. Despite struggling for a regular starting place at Ninian Park, he scored the Play-off winner against Queen's Park Rangers that won promotion to Division One. Having lost his first-team place, one of three loan spells saw him join Scottish Premier League side Dunfermline and he played in their 3–0 defeat to Celtic in the Scottish League Cup Final in March 2006. He suffered more injury problems during his first season with Halifax Town.

CAMSELL George Henry

Centre-forward
Born: Framwellgate Moor, 27 November 1902.
Died: 1966.
Career: Esh Winning. Tow Law Town. Durham City 1924. MIDDLESBROUGH 1925.

■ Middlesbrough's all-time top scorer, Camsell's astonishing record in front of goal stands as testimony to his supreme talent as a centre-forward. Recording almost a goal a game in his 14 seasons in a Middlesbrough shirt, Camsell tormented defences as an intimidating leader of the line who matched his physical presence with brilliant opportunism and quick acceleration, scoring goals with both feet and from all angles and distances. His 59 goals in the 1926–27 season shattered all records, only to be narrowly eclipsed by Everton's Dixie Dean a year later.

Born in a coalmining village, Camsell went down the mines at the age of 13 and only took up football when he was spotted taking part in a pit-top kickabout to pass the time during a strike. He joined Tow Law before turning professional with Third Division Durham City. Camsell came to Boro in payment of a £500 debt owed by Durham, Middlesbrough also writing a £100 cheque to the cash-strapped club. Camsell was reluctant to make the move because of the form of regular centre-forward Jimmy McClelland and it took persistence and the offer of a £10 signing on fee for manager Herbert Bamlett to tie up the deal.

Camsell's hesitance looked well-founded when he was restricted to just four games in the 1925–26 season. He had scored 36 goals in the reserves, including nine in one game against Bedlington, but failed to dislodge McClelland and Camsell came within a whisker of leaving the club. He was

placed on the transfer list in the summer of 1926 for just £300. Only Barnsley showed interest, they persuaded Boro to knock £100 off the price and a deal was struck. Fortunately for Middlesbrough, Barnsley then found difficulty raising the cash and Camsell stayed at Ayresome Park.

When the 1926–27 season started there was little suggestion of what was to come. It was only after a disastrous start that Camsell was given his chance in the fifth fixture. He scored twice to seal the club's first win and started his incredible run of goals, showing clinical finishing, including nine hat-tricks, taking full advantage of the change to the offside law that had been introduced in 1925. Boro romped to promotion.

A year later Dixie Dean pipped Camsell to the all-time goalscoring record by notching 60 League goals. The Everton forward sent a commiserating telegram mentioning that he had received a watch in recognition of his feat and asking what Camsell had received. The modest Middlesbrough man, who shied away from the hero worship he received, replied: 'Nothing, and rightly so.' But it could so easily have been Camsell who held the record. As well as missing the opening games of the season, he also missed a penalty against Millwall and was so upset at the ribbing he received from his teammates that he refused to take any more. Four other penalties were scored that season.

Camsell continued his brilliant form for years to come. His finishing ability was unrivalled and teammate Jacky Carr was so confident that Camsell would score that he would often squat down and watch after playing the ball through to his striker. With most goalkeepers staying on their line, many of his goals were scored from close in – called babyliners at the time – and his great skill was being in the right place.

Camsell scored 24 hat-tricks for Middlesbrough – a club record – and was top scorer for 10 consecutive seasons from 1926 to 1936. He also won nine caps for England, scoring in every game and amazingly totalling 18. He was unlucky to be in the shadow of Dixie Dean and several other contenders for the centre-forward slot. Camsell was 37 when war broke out. He was still at the club after the hostilities ended working on the coaching staff. He looked after the Colts, then scouted for the club and finally worked as assistant secretary before retiring in 1963. He lived just five minutes from the ground in Devonshire Road. Camsell died in March 1966 shortly before the club he had served so well were relegated to the Third Division for the first time.

CARBONE Benito

Midfield
Born: Italy, 14 August 1971.
Career: Torino 1988. Reggina 1990. Casertana 1991. Ascoli 1992. Torino 1993. Napoli 1994. Inter Milan (Italy) 1995. Sheffield Wednesday 1996. Aston Villa 1999. Bradford City 2000. Derby County (loan) 2001. MIDDLESBROUGH (loan) 2002. Como (Italy) 2002. Parma 2003. Cantanzaro 2004. Vicenza 2005. Sydney 2006.

■ The term 'much-travelled striker' could have been invented for Benito Carbone, who briefly starred for Boro on loan from Bradford in Steve McClaren's first season. Carbone has represented no less than 16 clubs, starting his career in his native Italy with Torino before graduating to giants Inter Milan. Sheffield Wednesday signed him for £3 million in 1996 and he quickly became a crowd favourite at Hillsborough. Able to play as a striker, linkman or wide on the right, Carbone did his best to impress the new Owls boss Ron Atkinson, but with Booth and Di Canio forming a good strike partnership he wasn't always guaranteed a starting place. However, he was outstanding in 1998–99 and, as well as chipping in with his usual supply of goals, he created many more for his teammates and deservedly won the supporters' Player of the Year competition. Early the following season he went into dispute with the Owls and was allowed to move to Aston Villa for a nominal fee. His goals provided a significant contribution to an FA Cup campaign that ended in defeat to Chelsea at Wembley. He then joined Bradford City and was ever-present until being dropped by boss Jim Jeffries in mid-January and placed on the transfer list. He eventually returned for the Bantams side and, although he was unable to prevent them slipping out of the Premiership, he won another Player of the Year award. His wages proved too expensive for the relegated club and he went on loan to Derby, where he linked up with Fabrizio Ravanelli, before another loan move to Boro until the end of the 2001–02 season. The diminutive striker scored his only goal for the club in the 13 appearances he made at the Riverside in a 2–1 win over one of his former clubs, Aston Villa. Carbone then rejoined Derby before returning to Italy in the close season to play for Como. After spells with other Italian lower League clubs, he played a handful of games for Sydney in 2006–07 as a replacement for Sunderland-bound Dwight Yorke.

CARR Andrew

Centre-half/Left-back
Born: Burradon, 1909
Died: 20 December 1983.
Career: Percy Main. MIDDLESBROUGH 1930. Mansfield Town 1934. Crewe Alexandra 1935. Rochdale 1936.

■ Reserve centre-half Carr was given just a handful of chances on the first-team stage. He made his debut as stand-in for Billy Forrest in November 1930 in a 4–2 defeat against Manchester City as fellow debutant Johnny Holliday scored twice. Carr had to wait 15 months for another opportunity when he replaced Jack Elkes in April 1932 once Boro were safe from the threat of relegation. Eight months later he played two games midway through the 1932–33 season when the club was embroiled in a relegation battle. A year later he moved on to Mansfield. He died on December 20th, 1983.

CARR George

Centre-half/Inside-forward
Born: South Bank, 19 January 1899.
Career: Bradford Park Avenue. MIDDLESBROUGH 1919. Leicester City 1923. Stockport County 1932. Nuneaton Boro.

■ George was the youngest of four Carr brothers to play for Middlesbrough. He was the only one of the quartet not to start with South Bank. Signed as a youngster from Bradford Park Avenue, he played alongside his brothers Jacky and Willie 26 times – the only time three brothers have appeared in the same League team – the first occasion being a 4–0 victory over Burnley on New Year's Day 1920. When Boro went in to sign young Carr, it was rumoured that he would not discuss the move until the club promised his brothers benefit games. Only the League could sanction benefits but, sure enough, a game came less than three years after the signing.

Unlike his brothers, George was not a big crowd favourite. He was second top scorer in his best season, 1921–22, but failed to win a regular place at inside-forward. The crowd's barracking contributed to his decision to leave and Boro accepted an offer from Leicester. He spent 11 years at Leicester where the Foxes won the Second Division championship in his first season, beating Boro 5–1 at Ayresome Park on the way. He played against his brother Jacky on several occasions.

George ended his League career at Stockport before playing non-League football for Nuneaton Boro. He subsequently managed Cheltenham

Town in the Southern League for seven years, then returning to Teesside to scout for Leicester in the region. Billy Pease, a friend and playing colleague of George's brother Jacky, persuaded George to try his hand at running a pub and he was landlord at the Black Swan in North Ormesby for a spell, also coaching South Bank into the late 1940s.

CARR John (Jacky)

Inside-forward/Outside-right
Born: South Bank, 26 November 1891.
Died: 10 May 1942.
Career: South Bank East End. South Bank. Sunderland 1909. MIDDLESBROUGH 1910. Blackpool 1930. Hartlepool United 1931.

■ Jacky Carr was the most successful of the four brothers to play for the club and one of the finest players in Middlesbrough's history. A speedy and intelligent player, Carr was a master at providing the killer through ball for centre-forwards. His Middlesbrough career spanned three decades in which he established himself as a huge crowd favourite.

Rejected as too small by Sunderland, Jacky started his career as a right-winger with South Bank and collected an FA Amateur Cup runners'-up medal in 1910.

When he was called up to make his Middlesbrough debut, legend has it that the slight youngster had to have his kit taken in with safety pins. The frail, nine stone youngster scored twice on that debut on Boxing Day 1910. Despite this, it was more than a year before another chance came and it wasn't until October 1912 that he established himself as a regular when manager Tom McIntosh made wholesale changes after a 4–0 defeat at Sunderland.

Usually playing at inside-right, Carr was not a prolific goalscorer but was a consistent provider of chances. His tactic was to stay behind the forward line and release his teammates with balls through the middle. A teetotaller and non-smoker, he was a very skilful player who could evade challenges and was well known for goading opponents into fouling him, especially in the penalty box. His contribution was well recognised by the Ayresome regulars and it is folklore that after scoring two early goals in a game against Barnsley, the cheering disturbed the horses at Stockton Races so much that a race was held up for eight minutes! He also won Boro many penalties by verbally goading opposing defenders into committing fouls. Infamously, this was the case against Oldham in April 1915 when Latics defender Bill Cook upended Carr and was ordered off. Feeling badly done by, Cook refused to leave the pitch with the result that the game was abandoned and Boro given both points.

Carr served with the Royal Engineers and guested for Fulham and Bradford in the Great War but asked for a transfer after the hostilities following a row over a

£3 12s rail pass. Before the war, the club had paid his fare to and from his Redcar home, named 'Ayresome House'. But when the club stopped paying the fare, Jacky asked for a move until the club backed down.

Jacky's England debut came in the first post-war full international in 1919 against Ireland and he toured Belgium with the team only to end up running the line rather than playing. A second cap came against Wales in March 1923 but he was forced off the field with a pulled muscle after 80 minutes. Pneumonia set in during the summer and he was hospitalised for nearly two months. The England call never came again though he played three times for the Football League side.

Despite approaching the age of 35, Carr was still going strong in Boro's phenomenal 1926–27 promotion-winning season. It was his 16th year at the club but it was a regular sight to see him beating players and laying the ball into the path of George Camsell to smash into the net. He was even put on standby for England and played in a trial game at Middlesbrough in 1928.

Carr's Boro career finally came to an end when he was not re-signed for the 1930–31 season at the age of 39. He played on for a season at Blackpool, helping to win promotion to Division One, and was then player-coach at Hartlepool in July 1931. Jacky went on to manage Pools but lost his job as part of a cost-cutting exercise, only to be selected from 60 candidates to manage Tranmere. He was a popular manager who was highly regarded for his understanding of players and sense of humour. In his Boro days, he had been a well-known practical joker. On one occasion, after scoring a penalty, he rushed up to the goalkeeper he had just beaten and shook his hand. Carr later managed Darlington and undertook work at Head Wrightson's in Thornaby during World War Two until his sudden death, at Ayresome House, on 10 May 1942.

CARR Henry (Harry)

Centre-forward
Born: South Bank.
Career: South Bank. Sunderland 1910. MIDDLESBROUGH 1910.

■ The eldest of the four Carr brothers, Henry only played a handful of games for the club. The quartet's father George was a riverside foreman who never kicked a ball in anger in his life yet had four sons who all played for Middlesbrough. Known as Pep or Harry, Carr was an FA Amateur Cup runner-up with South Bank alongside brothers Jacky and Willie. They all played in a 2–1 defeat against Royal Marine Light Infantry in 1910. Henry made his debut in the same season as his brothers. A centre-forward, Carr scored on his debut, against Oldham in February 1911. He also scored two in the following game – a 6–2 defeat at Spurs. He had proved to be a capable stand-in for regular frontman Fred Pentland and was offered professional terms but turned them down, opting to stay amateur. Carr played some games for Sunderland as well as South Bank where he won England Amateur international honours.

CARR William

Centre-half
Born: South Bank.
Died: March 1943.
Career: South Bank. MIDDLESBROUGH 1910.

■ Centre-half Willie Carr was yet another of the famous South Bank Carr brothers. Willie, the second eldest, played alongside his brothers Jackie and George as the club made history by becoming the first, and only, club to play three brothers in the same League team.

Known as Puddin', Willie wore leg irons as a boy and his brothers often joked that he walked like a crab. He was rarely a regular choice for the Boro team. He made his debut in an away defeat at Bradford at the tail-end of the 1910–11 campaign and he was deputy to regular centre-half Andy Jackson in the years before the Great War. After Jackson's premature death in the hostilities, Boro signed William Ellerington as a replacement. Carr continued to deputise but finally won a regular place midway through the 1919–20 season and Ellerington was switched to wing-half. But it proved to be a short-term move and Carr was forced to contest the place once again with his rival. The signing of Maurice Webster pushed Carr even further down the pecking order in subsequent years and he left the club in 1925 after playing just a handful of games in the previous three years. Carr, who had been paid two benefits while at the club, in 1919 and 1922, died just 10 months after his brother Jacky in March 1943.

CARRICK Christopher

Outside-left
Born: Stockton, 8 October 1882.
Died: 1927.
Career: MIDDLESBROUGH 1900. West Ham United 1904. Tottenham Hotspur 1905. Reading 1906. Bradford Park Avenue 1907. Glentoran (Ireland).

■ Outside-left Carrick made an early impression at Middlesbrough as the club negotiated the treacherous route through the qualifying rounds of the FA Cup. Forced to play three ties before reaching the first round proper, it took three attempts to see off the opening opponents Willington Athletic. After a disappointing 3–3 home draw, Carrick made his debut in a goalless away game before scoring twice in an unlikely 8–0 victory in the second replay.

In between the ties, the local lad had made his League debut in a 1–0 defeat at Woolwich Arsenal. Carrick continued his good Cup form by notching two more goals in a 3–0 victory over Jarrow but played just one more game in the 1900–01 campaign. After 18 months out of the side, he returned for a run in the team during the 1902–03 campaign. However, he struggled to hold on to the shirt and was one of seven players tried on the left wing in the 1902–03 and 1903–04 seasons.

A keen billiards player away from football, Carrick moved on to West Ham. He was later signed by Spurs as replacement for John Kirwan but was involved in a misdemeanour and suspended for a breach of the club's training rules.

CARTWRIGHT Herbert Philip

Outside-right
Born: Scarborough, 8 February 1908.
Died: 1974.
Career: Scarborough. MIDDLESBROUGH 1925. Bradford Park Avenue 1927. Hull City 1929. Lincoln City 1930. Bournemouth 1933. Scarborough 1933. Carlisle United 1934. Rotherham United 1935.

■ Reserve outside-right Phil Cartwright was a highly-rated youngster but failed to make a real breakthrough into the first team. The teenager was given a chance at the end of the 1925–26 campaign but the signing of Billy Pease in the summer of 1926 effectively ended his opportunities. In Boro's record-breaking 1926–27 promotion season, Cartwright was stuck in the reserves. He scored more than 20 goals from the wing including four against West Stanley which was described in a contemporary report as an 'outstanding performance in a career bright with promise'. However, the brilliant form of Pease meant Cartwright had to move on for first-team football.

CASSIDY Joseph

Centre-forward/Inside-left
Born: Dalziel, 30 July 1872.
Career: Motherwell Athletic. Blyth. Glasgow Celtic. Newton Heath 1894. Manchester City 1899. MIDDLESBROUGH 1901. Workington 1906.

■ Scotsman Cassidy was captain of the first Middlesbrough team to run out at Ayresome Park for a Football League tie in September 1903. The inside-forward won the toss on that momentous day and decided to defend the new Linthorpe Road End. Cassidy's role did not end at that as he also had the honour of scoring the first competitive goal at the new ground, knocking the ball home in a goalmouth scramble – or 'scrimmage' as it was called at the time. Unfortunately, it was not a winning start as Sunderland spoilt the party by winning 3–2.

Cassidy had been an important part of the side for the previous two seasons. He had joined the club after helping Manchester City to promotion into the First Division and repeated the feat in his first season at Middlesbrough, subsequently appearing in the club's first ever First Division game. He had also scored on his Boro debut and on his first home appearance. Cassidy was tried in the half-back line for the 1904–05 season but lost his place in the following campaign.

CATTERMOLE Lee Barry

Midfield
Born: Stockton, 21 March 1988.
Career: MIDDLESBROUGH 2005.

■ Tough as teak and betraying no sign of nerves, Cattermole looked instantly at home in the Premiership and became one of the club's best young products for several seasons. The tenacious midfielder made a spectacular full debut as a 17-year-old on New Year's Day 2006, producing a Man of the Match display

during Boro's 2–2 draw with Newcastle at St James' Park and quickly becoming a fans' favourite. Cattermole had already sampled first-team football when he came off the bench to replace the injured Jimmy Floyd Hasselbaink in a UEFA Cup tie against Litex Lovech at the Riverside some two weeks earlier. Admired for his tough-tackling approach, he went on to make 24 League and Cup appearances in the same season despite not having played a game until after Christmas. The Stockton teenager, whose father Barry played for Boro's reserves in the 1970s, became the club's youngest-ever Premiership goalscorer when he netted the winner in a 1–0 win over Manchester City at Eastlands in April and helped Boro reach the FA Cup semi-final in the same year. He also became the club's youngest-ever captain when, at 18 years and 47 days old, he took over the armband from Colin Cooper – the previous record-holder – against Fulham at Craven Cottage on the final day of the season. Cattermole also starred in Europe, producing an inspirational display at the Stadio Olympico as Boro defeated Roma 3–2 on aggregate on the way to the UEFA Cup Final. He was a substitute in the defeat to Sevilla in Eindhoven. Next season he continued his progression under Gareth Southgate, signing a long-term contract and showing his versatility when playing right wing when required.

CHADWICK Clifton

Winger
Born: Bolton, 26 January 1914.
Career: Fleetwood. Oldham Athletic 1933. MIDDLESBROUGH 1933. Hull City 1946. Darlington 1947. Stockton.

■ Winger Cliff Chadwick was known as 'the poacher' by his teammates – he was always alert for half-chances or situations arising from opponents' mistakes. He was a member of Boro's successful pre-war side, though he had to fight hard for a first-team place. He helped the club to fourth place in the top flight in 1938–39 and many tipped Middlesbrough for the title but his last game for the club was against Stoke in September 1939, the final League fixture before war intervened.

Brought in at the age of 20 from Oldham, Chadwick was in the side at the start of the 1934–35 season at outside-right after a handful of appearances in the preceding campaign. However, he lost his place to Ernie Coleman. Ralph Birkett was signed to fill the right wing position and Chadwick was on the left flank when he returned in 1935–36. The subsequent signings of Arthur Cunliffe and Tom Cochrane made it tough for the Lancashire lad.

Chadwick switched between the two flanks but struggled to maintain his place. After infrequent games in 1937–38 he was not called up until December of the following season. It was then that he showed his best form. He scored two and helped Mannion get four in a 9–2 win at Blackpool on his recall. It was the start of an excellent run and Chadwick played his full part in a 4–1 win at top of the table Derby and in an 8–2 victory over Portsmouth, showing good goalscoring form. Some wartime appearances came but when League football resumed in 1946 Chadwick moved on to Hull. He later emigrated to Australia in 1989 at the age of 75.

CHADWICK David Edwin

Winger
Born: India, 19 August 1943.
Career: Southampton 1960. MIDDLESBROUGH 1966. Halifax Town 1970. Bournemouth 1972. Torquay United (loan) 1972. Gillingham 1974. Dallas Tornadoes (United States).

■ Southampton reserve winger Chadwick was one of Stan Anderson's first signings as Middlesbrough manager. Anderson had initially been offered Chadwick in part-exchange for star midfielder Ian Gibson but the deal broke down. However, once Gibson had signed for Coventry, Anderson used some of the money to go back in for Chadwick.

The diminutive winger signed for the club in time to make his debut in Boro's first ever game in Division Three. He was a regular in the side that immediately bounced back providing excellent service for the frontmen and using his fine dribbling skills. Full of tricks, he laid on many goals for John O'Rourke though he lacked physical strength. Once in the Second Division, he spent several months on the injury list and found chances were more limited on his return to fitness. He was used on the left wing as well as his more familiar right flank berth with competition coming from the likes of Mike Kear and Ray Lugg. After opportunities dwindled further, he moved on to Halifax and later played in the USA for Dallas Tornadoes. After emigrating to the States, he was coach at Fort Lauderdale when he signed Boro's John Hickton in 1978 and also later coached Atlanta.

CHAPMAN Neville

Right-back
Born: Cockfield, 15 September 1941.
Died: 1993.
Career: MIDDLESBROUGH 1958. Darlington 1967.

■ Fringe full-back Nev Chapman has the dubious honour of being the first Middlesbrough player ever to be substituted. He was replaced by Bryan Orritt against Preston in September 1965. A tidy player who perhaps lacked the necessary aggression, Chapman had always found opportunities scarce after initially waiting more than three years for his debut. His first chance came as a replacement for Derek Stonehouse who was out with a wrenched back.

Chapman enjoyed spells as first choice right-back in 1961–62 and 1962–63 but lost his place to Mick McNeil and then Cyril Knowles kept him out. By 1964–65 the struggling side preferred versatile Bill Gates and Ernie Ratcliffe; the emergence of Geoff Butler subsequently keeping him in the reserves. Chapman, who lived in Acklam, later scouted for the club on occasions but was working as a tanker driver when he was killed in a freak road accident in 1993.

CHARLTON Harold

Midfield
Born: Newcastle, 22 June 1951.
Career: MIDDLESBROUGH 1968. Hartlepool United 1976. Chesterfield 1976. Buxton. Darlington 1979.

■ A busy midfielder, Harry Charlton was rated by Boro's assistant manager Harold Shepherdson as one of the most promising youngsters in British football when he first broke into the first team. Further, manager Jack Charlton – no relation – said he had the best technique of all the club's players. Although he struggled to live up to such billing, he was a ball player who made up for his lack of strength and stature with much skill. However, he suffered heavily from injuries and underwent a cartilage operation and struggled to win promotion from Boro's reserves.

Having joined Boro from Redheugh Boys Club, Charlton's debut came against Watford in October 1970 and he retained his place for four games. It was 20 months before his next game at the start of 1972–73 when Charlton, who could also play up front, had the unenviable job of deputising for John Hickton. Yet he was soon back in the second string. Jack Charlton gave him only scarce opportunities in the 1973–74 promotion season, though he played the final half hour of an 8–0 thrashing of Sheffield Wednesday.

His only ever game in the top flight followed a number of outstanding performances for the reserves. He was called up in place of the injured Bobby Murdoch in November 1974 but Peter Brine was preferred for the following game and Charlton's only remaining matches came as stand-in for Murdoch in Cup competitions.

CHIPPERFIELD Francis

Left-half/Left-back
Born: Shiremoor, 2 December 1895.
Died: 1979.
Career: Leeds City 1914. Lincoln City 1919. MIDDLESBROUGH 1920. Blyth Spartans (loan) 1921. Carlisle United (loan) 1922. Ashington 1923. Frickley Colliery.

■ When Frank Chipperfield played for Lincoln in an FA Cup tie against Middlesbrough in 1920, the club's directors were so impressed that they agreed to sign him immediately after the game. However, his only ever appearance for the first team came at centre-half as stand-in for Willie Carr in a 6–2 First Division defeat at Wolves in October 1920. He was loaned to Blyth Spartans for the 1921–22 season on the understanding that he would be returned if required and Chipperfield went to Carlisle under the same conditions for the 1922–23 campaign. A transfer fee of £400 was set by Boro but Chipperfield applied to the Football League in February 1923 for the fee to be reduced. The League rejected his appeal but Boro gave him a free transfer at the end of the season and he joined non-League Ashington.

CHRISTIE Malcolm Neil

Striker
Born: Stamford, 11 April 1979.
Career: Nuneaton Boro. Derby County 1998. MIDDLESBROUGH 2003.

■ Steve McClaren went back to his old club, Derby County, in January 2003 to sign striker Christie and defender Chris Riggott in a combined £3 million deal. Christie came up the hard way through non-League football with Nuneaton Boro, where he was spotted by Derby coach Steve Round, who was later to join the backroom staff at Middlesbrough. Hungry to succeed as a professional, he scored his first two goals for the Rams in a 4–1 win over Boro at the Riverside on January 15 2000. Christie's form saw him win selection for the England Under-21 side and he scored the goal against Manchester United at Old Trafford that secured County's Premiership status for 2001–02. He was the club's joint top scorer with nine Premiership goals and had scored 35 goals in 129 games when he signed for Boro. Christie quickly slotted into the Riverside forward line and scored two goals on his full debut in a 3–1 win over Sunderland at the Stadium of Light. But injuries blighted his career on Teesside. He suffered double leg and foot fractures that involved lengthy recoveries. One of several comebacks came against Boro's first UEFA Cup opponents, Banik Ostrava, in September 2004, but he lasted just eight minutes before another five months on the sidelines. His next game came at Portsmouth in April 2006, where he scored in a 2–1 defeat, before playing 45 minutes in the home win over West Ham, his first appearance at the Riverside for 14 months. He picked up a stress fracture of his foot in his next game against Blackburn and was ruled out for the rest of the season. Christie scored his first goal in 21 months when he made a surprise start for Gareth Southgate at Aston Villa in November 2006, but although he remained fit he was unable to command a regular place in competition with Mark Viduka and Yakubu. He was released in summer 2007.

CLARK Ernest

Right-back
Born: Middlesbrough.
Career: MIDDLESBROUGH 1899.

■ One of many one-game wonders in the club's history, Clark played at right full-back in place of Bill Shaw for the home game against Burton Swifts in November 1899. A local player, Clark was given his chance as the club's directors struggled to find players of the necessary calibre after Middlesbrough's late election to the League at the end of the previous season. A resounding 8–1 win was secured in a game that also saw two other debutants in George Reid and Joe Murphy as changes were made following a run of only two wins in Middlesbrough's first 10 games as a Football League club. Despite the victory, James Cowan then stepped in to the right-back berth and Clark was released.

CLARK Joseph

Inside-right
Born: Dundee, 1879.
Career: MIDDLESBROUGH 1899.

■ A trialist from the town of Dundee, inside-right Clark was injured in his only game for Middlesbrough – a 3–0 home defeat to Bolton in April 1900. He had been given his chance as Boro, newly elected to the Second Division, struggled to find good quality players following their late elevation to the Football

League. Clark subsequently returned to Scotland.

CLARK Wallace

Outside-left
Born: Jarrow, 14 July 1896.
Died: 20 November 1975.
Career: Durham City. MIDDLESBROUGH 1919. Leeds United 1921. Birmingham 1922. Coventry City 1924. Boston Town 1925. Barrow 1926. Torquay United 1927. Connah's Quay.

■ A Geordie winger who could play on either flank, Clarke was a reserve player who only once played two consecutive games for Middlesbrough. His debut came as stand-in for Tommy Urwin on the left wing in a 3–1 defeat at Preston in January 1920. Infrequent chances followed and only one win was secured in his eight first-team appearances. He died in Jarrow in November 1975.

CLOSE Brian

Midfield
Born: Belfast, 27 January 1982
Career: MIDDLESBROUGH 2001. Chesterfield (loan) 2003. Darlington 2004.

■ Close represented Northern Ireland at Schoolboy, Youth and Under-21 level. Strong and combative, he proved his worth in other positions, notably at right-back, although he was also used on the left side of midfield. Close progressed through the junior ranks to play for the reserves during 2001–02. He made his League debut on loan to Chesterfield in 2002–03 before returning to the Riverside. His sole senior appearance came as a substitute in the 3–1 Worthington Cup defeat at Ipswich on 6 November 2002. He moved to Darlington on a free transfer in 2004 and became a regular in David Hodgson's League Two side. However, he was released by new boss Dave Penney in the summer of 2007.

CLOUGH Brian Howard

Centre-forward
Born: Middlesbrough, 21 March 1935.
Died: 20 September 2004.
Career: Great Broughton Juniors. MIDDLESBROUGH 1953. Sunderland 1961.

■ A goalscoring phenomenon, Brian Clough lays claim to being one of Middlesbrough's greatest centre-forwards. Better known in the wider football world for his managerial exploits, Clough was a Teesside legend for his undisputed ability to score hatfuls of goals from all distances. A supreme goalpoacher, he had quick reactions and unrivalled determination coupled with strength, pace and skill. His record of almost a goal a game puts him head and shoulders above any other post-war frontman and places him on a par with any of his predecessors in the number-nine shirt.

The sixth of nine children, Clough grew up in Grove Hill and watched Boro legends Hardwick and Mannion from the terraces. He played for Great Broughton as a boy and worked as a clerk at ICI. He was recommended to Boro by local headteacher Ray Grant and George Camsell went to watch him but was unimpressed. Grant eventually persuaded the club to play him in a trial game and Clough was subsequently signed as a junior. Two years' National Service interrupted his development but Clough was re-signed as a professional in the summer of 1955 on £7 10 shillings a week. Initially serving as deputy to Charlie Wayman and behind Doug Cooper in the pecking order, he had a steady first season but made his first of many transfer requests after just nine first-team games. Even in his early days, Clough was regarded as arrogant and cocky by his teammates.

It was in the 1956–57 season that Clough began to justify his self-confidence. The goals started to flow with regularity and he was the Second Division's leading scorer for three seasons, becoming the Football League's top marksman in 1958–59 and topping 40 goals every season from 1956 to 1960. He even scored five goals in one game against Brighton.

Despite Clough's goals, Middlesbrough couldn't get promotion and he publicly accused his teammates of betting against their own team and deliberately conceding goals. Sadly, there appeared to be some truth behind the accusations and on more than one occasion he exchanged blows with the colleagues he accused. Clough was often a controversial figure. He was a selfish goalscorer who was even known to barge his teammates off the ball to score. Transfer requests came with every season's close – Everton and Birmingham both made enquiries in 1958 – and he made several more in November 1959 following an infamous 'round-robin' when nine members of the first-team squad petitioned to have him removed as captain, quoting his 'harsh words on the pitch' and a tendency to sulk after defeats. He was barracked by the crowd in the next game against Bristol Rovers but showed his strength of character by scoring a hat-trick, all from more than 25 yards.

There were frequent calls for England recognition for Clough but he never made a significant international breakthrough. He travelled with England on an Iron Curtain tour without playing and was then left out of the 1958 World Cup squad. He eventually got his first cap in October 1959 against Wales. In the excitement, Clough forgot his boots and Boro manager Bob Dennison's wife had to take them to Cardiff. Unfortunately, Clough didn't impress in that or the following game against Sweden, despite having Boro teammate Eddie Holliday alongside him for both games.

In the summer of 1961, Middlesbrough finally conceded that Clough could leave. It took a club record fee to prise him away but there was dismay among supporters that Sunderland were his new employers. The goals continued until his career was cut short by a devastating knee injury at the age of 27. It was on Boxing Day 1962 that he was involved in an accidental collision with Bury goalkeeper Chris Harker. After several aborted comebacks, he retired in November 1964.

Clough's first chance in management was provided by former Boro favourite George Hardwick who made him youth coach at Sunderland. He subsequently went on to become one of the all-time managerial greats working alongside his former Middlesbrough teammate Peter Taylor. Clough won the League title with Derby and again with Nottingham Forest where he also won the European Cup twice in 16 years at the City Ground. A statue in his honour was unveiled in Albert Park, Middlesbrough, in the summer of 2007.

CLOUGH John (Jack)

Goalkeeper
Born: Murton, 13 May 1902.
Career: Fatfield Albion. MIDDLESBROUGH 1922. Bradford Park Avenue 1926. Mansfield Town 1932. Brentford 1933. Rotherham United 1934.

■ Clough was the goalkeeper who finally

brought the Tim Williamson era to an end. Williamson had been first choice in the Boro goal for the best part of 20 years but had conceded nine goals in his previous two League games and Boro had lost six successive matches. The time had come for change and manager Jimmy Howie handed Clough his chance. Clough kept a clean sheet in a 2–0 win against Arsenal and Williamson played just one more game.

Clough had mixed fortunes as regular number one, seeing relegation to the Second Division in his first full season. He enjoyed two seasons as a regular outside the top flight but moved on after manager Herbert Bamlett signed Jim Mathieson in June 1926. Clough, who had won a Military Medal and Bar as a stretcher bearer in World War One, was transfer listed at £1,000 but the fee was reduced to £500 by the League.

COCHRANE Alexander Fraser (Sandy)

Inside-forward/Outside-right
Born: Glasgow, 8 August 1903.
Career: Alloa Athletic. MIDDLESBROUGH 1922. Darlington 1926. Bradford City 1928. Chesterfield 1931. Llanelli 1932. Northampton Town 1933. Swindon Town 1935. East Stirling 1936.

■ Boro manager Jimmy Howie turned to Scottish inside-forward Cochrane as he tried to end a disastrous six game losing streak in early 1923. The Glaswegian was one of three debutants for the visit of Arsenal and the tide was turned with a 2–0 victory, Cochrane capping his debut by scoring the opening goal.

A diminutive figure at only 5ft 5in, Cochrane was in and out of the team as Boro were relegated in 1923–24. The arrival of Russell Wainscoat provided stiff competition for the number-10 shirt and Cochrane was moved to the wing on occasions. He eventually lost his place as the 1925–26 campaign went on when poor results scuppered Boro's promotion campaign with top place in November becoming ninth by the end of the season. Cochrane left before the club embarked on their record-breaking 1926–27 campaign.

COCHRANE George Terence

Winger
Born: Killyleagh, 23 January 1953.
Career: Derry City. Linfield. Coleraine. Burnley 1976. MIDDLESBROUGH 1978. Gillingham 1983. Dallas Tornadoes (United States). Millwall 1986. Hartlepool United 1987. Billingham Synthonia. ICI Wilton.

■ Terry Cochrane was an old-fashioned winger who liked nothing better than taking on full-backs. The Northern Ireland international teased and tormented opponents with skilful runs and a deceptive body swerve coupled with speed and guile. More of a goalmaker than taker, he could also score spectacular goals.

He was a latecomer to the professional game, playing part-time football for Derry City, Linfield and Coleraine while working as a labourer in a tannery and laying electrical cables. Cochrane had unsuccessful trials at Nottingham Forest and Everton as a teenager before eventually joining Burnley at the age of 23. He was a club record signing when he made the switch to Middlesbrough.

He was an instant hit with the Boro supporters and received a standing ovation after playing a part in both goals in a 2–0 victory over Norwich. His first goal came in his third appearance but his strikes were few and far between. A spectacular scissor kick against Swansea in 1980 lived long in the memory and his goal at Wembley for Northern Ireland in a 1–1 draw with England created plenty of headlines.

Cochrane occasionally came into conflict with his managers, especially when he felt he was being made a scapegoat for poor team performances, and was dropped by Bobby Murdoch for a trip to Nottingham Forest after refusing to be substitute. He subsequently handed in a written transfer request, stating that he never wanted to kick another ball for the club. He later submitted another written transfer request after being dropped for an away game at Newcastle in September 1982. His days were numbered when Malcolm Allison took over as manager and, together with Jim Platt, he was forced to train with the juniors. After being loaned to Hong Kong side Eastern, coached by Bobby Moore, he moved to Gillingham, where he was a big crowd favourite. Cochrane was coaching the Saudi Arabian Air Defence Team when the Gulf War broke out and also later played for several local sides including Billingham Synthonia and ICI Wilton. He was also player-coach of South Bank and Ferryhill in the Northern League. He took up a coaching position at Sedgefield Boro Council in the mid–1990s after also undertaking coaching with Boro's centre of excellence. In 1999, at the age of 46, he was still turning out regularly for the Navigation team in a Redcar Sunday League. More recently he has coached at Boro's Community Centre.

COCHRANE James Kyle

Left-back
Born: Glasgow, 14 January 1954.
Career: Drumchapel Amateurs. MIDDLESBROUGH 1971. Darlington 1975. Torquay United 1980.

■ A workman-like left-back or winger, Jimmy Cochrane was a reserve player who combined hard tackling with an excellent left foot and good crossing. His debut came at full-back as cover for Frank Spraggon in December 1973 at Sheffield Wednesday. His second game was at Luton at the end of March 1974 as a David Mills goal secured promotion to the top flight with six games still to play. He went on to make his home debut against Bolton a couple of weeks later but was never given a chance in the First Division, his final appearance coming in a 4–0 Texaco Cup defeat at Newcastle in August 1974. After finishing his playing career with Torquay, Cochrane switched his attention to law and took up a job as solicitor at a Darlington-based firm in 1995.

COCHRANE Michael

Right-back
Born: Belfast.
Career: Milltown. Distillery. Leicester Fosse 1900. MIDDLESBROUGH 1901. Distillery 1901.

■ Irish international full-back Cochrane spent just a few months in Middlesbrough after signing from

Leicester Fosse for a club-record £100 fee. His debut came at right-back in place of regular John Dow against Woolwich Arsenal in March 1901. He was switched between the flanks in the remaining games of the season as Boro finished sixth in the Second Division. He was given a free transfer at the start of the following season.

COCHRANE Thomas

Outside-left
Born: Newcastle, 7 October 1908.
Died: 1976.
Career: St Peter's Albion. Leeds United 1928. MIDDLESBROUGH 1936. Bradford Park Avenue 1939.

■ Forceful outside-left Tom Cochrane was an important part of Boro's exciting pre-war team. Contesting the place with talented rival Cliff Chadwick, Cochrane provided quality service for the frontmen as the club challenged in the upper reaches of the First Division. Cochrane was enticed to the club after a successful spell with Leeds. Having started his career with St Peter's Albion in the Tyneside League and having trials with Hull and Sheffield Wednesday, he was persuaded to join Leeds in 1928. He suffered from inconsistent early form and was barracked by some fans but won them over, going on to play almost 250 League games. He was a popular winger at Boro and many thought the excellent side he was part of could win the League in 1939–40. Once war broke out,

Cochrane played only a few wartime games for Bradford before retiring. He died in Cleveland in 1976.

COLEMAN Edward

Centre-forward
Born: Middlesbrough, 23 September 1957.
Career: MIDDLESBROUGH 1975. Workington (loan) 1977. Guisborough Town.

■ Local centre-forward Coleman was a prolific goalscorer for Boro's junior team but never made the grade. After banging in the goals as a youngster he also impressed in the reserves. Yet his lack of stature probably cost him and his solitary first-team appearance came in the last game of the 1975–76 season. He had a loan spell with Workington in the following season and had trials at Nottingham Forest and Halifax without success. The highlight of his career was an appearance in an FA Vase Final at Wembley for Guisborough Town.

COLEMAN Ernest (Tim)

Centre-forward/Inside-forward
Born: Blidworth, 4 January 1908.
Died: 1984.
Career: Hucknall Colliery. Nottingham Forest 1925. Halifax Town 1926. Grimsby Town 1928. Arsenal 1931. MIDDLESBROUGH 1934. Norwich City 1936. Linby Colliery.

■ An incisive goalscorer whether playing at centre-forward or inside-left, Coleman joined Boro after winning a League Championship medal with

Arsenal. He made his name as a prolific goalscorer at Grimsby – his record of 35 in 38 games in the First Division bringing him to the attention of the big clubs. Despite regularly finding the net at Arsenal, he wasn't an automatic first choice and they accepted Boro's approach. At Ayresome Park he helped turn a struggling side into title outsiders. Coleman was second top scorer in his first campaign behind the veteran George Camsell. Boro came close to relegation in that season and Coleman found greater success in 1935–36 in a role as goalmaker playing at inside-forward. He was a hard but fair player, his biggest regret being a red card against his former club Grimsby in a 1936 FA Cup sixth round tie after fighting with Harry Betmead. Coleman eventually lost his place to Norman Higham and was sold to Norwich. He later spent 10 years in various capacities at Notts County including two spells as manager. Coleman died in Nottingham in January 1984.

COLEMAN Simon

Central defender
Born: Worksop, 13 March 1968.
Career: Mansfield Town 1985. MIDDLESBROUGH 1989. Derby County 1991. Sheffield Wednesday 1994. Bolton Wanderers 1994. Wolverhampton Wanderers (loan) 1997. Southend United 1998. Rochdale 2000. Ilkeston Town.

■ When Bruce Rioch searched for a replacement for Gary Pallister in September 1989, he decided to move for Mansfield's regular left-sided central defender Simon Coleman. The youngster looked similar in build and style to Pallister and was also adept at bringing the ball out of defence. Unfortunately the comparisons with his predecessor did Coleman no favours and he ultimately moved on after suffering from inconsistent form.

Coleman made his Boro debut at left-back as a substitute against Watford in a 1–0 reverse before his full debut at right-back against Plymouth. He became a virtual automatic choice in his first season, partnering Tony Mowbray and then Alan Kernaghan in the centre of defence, capping the campaign by appearing in the ZDS Cup Final at Wembley.

Following Mowbray's recovery from injury in the summer of 1990, Coleman found himself out of the team and soon requested a transfer. He had a trial at Manchester City in October before a brief return to the Boro team as cover for the injured Kernaghan. When Lennie Lawrence took over as manager in the summer of 1991 he sanctioned Coleman's sale to Derby where he was signed as a replacement for England's Mark Wright who had joined Liverpool. He subsequently moved on to Sheffield Wednesday for £350,000, where he was mainly played at full-back, and then re-signed by Bruce Rioch at Bolton. Coleman scored in a 4–1 win at the Riverside during his time at Bolton but broke his leg in a challenge with Marco Gabbiadini in March 1995 and struggled to recover his form, dropping down the divisions to join Southend for first-team football.

COLLETT Andrew Alfred

Goalkeeper
Born: Stockton, 28 October 1973.
Career: MIDDLESBROUGH 1992. Bristol Rovers (loan) 1994. Bristol Rovers 1995. Rushden & Diamonds (loan) 1998. Darlington 1999.

■ A graduate of the club's youth system, Andy Collett spent a lot of time sitting on Boro's bench before later finding success in the lower Leagues. He first came to the club after being offered a trial by a Boro scout – despite conceding 11 goals for his Under-12 team. The youngster came into the first-team frame in the 1992–93 Premier League season and was named as substitute eight times before his debut. It was an impressive first start when the 19-year-old was called upon to replace the injured Steve Pears for the vital game against Sheffield Wednesday. He was one of the star performers as Boro won the game but it was to be a sad day for Collett as results elsewhere saw the club relegated. A home debut in a 3–3 final day draw with Norwich followed and he was hailed as a potential star of the future. Yet, despite a handful of games in minor Cup competitions, Collett never got another chance. He was named reserve 'keeper on 38 occasions before slipping below Ben Roberts in the pecking order. Collett was loaned to Bristol Rovers in October 1994 before signing permanently on transfer deadline day. A confident and competent goalkeeper, he was regular number one for three years with the Pirates before falling out with manager Ian Holloway when he refused to join Norwich on loan. He returned to the North East to join Darlington in the summer of 1999.

COMFORT Alan

Outside-left
Born: Aldershot, 8 December 1964.
Career: Queen's Park Rangers 1982. Cambridge United 1984. Leyton Orient 1986. MIDDLESBROUGH 1989.

■ Traditional winger Comfort looked to be an excellent signing for Middlesbrough in the early games of the 1989–90 season, only to see his career brought to a shuddering halt by a serious knee injury. Comfort was a wide man with plenty of skill and accurate crossing. His displays made a big impression with the club's supporters before he was forced to give up the game at the age of 25.

A former England Youth international, Comfort had established his reputation with Leyton Orient, finishing top scorer as the O's won promotion to the Third Division via the Play-offs in 1989. He was on the verge of

joining Bournemouth when Orient manager Frank Clark persuaded him that Boro was a better career move.

Comfort was ever-present at the start of the season but the turning point came in a game against Newcastle in November 1989. Trying to retrieve the ball out on the wing, Comfort twisted and went down. He was carried from the field with a serious ligament injury. His leg was put in plaster but despite three operations, disease had set in behind the kneecap and his career was over. Comfort received a £55,000 pay-off instead of the testimonial he requested and was aggrieved when the club made public the details of the financial arrangement.

The mild-mannered Comfort made several attempted comebacks outside the League without success and decided to take up a career in the clergy. He studied theology in Durham and then went to Cambridge on a training course, becoming a Church of England vicar in County Durham and then East London where he was also appointed club chaplain at Leyton Orient.

COMMON Alfred

Forward
Born: Millfield, County Durham, 25 May 1880.
Died: April 1946.
Career: South Hylton. Jarrow. Sunderland 1900. Sheffield United 1901. Sunderland 1904. MIDDLESBROUGH 1904. Woolwich Arsenal 1910. Preston North End 1912.

■ The football world was in uproar when Middlesbrough shattered the transfer record by paying £1,000 for Alf Common. The first four-figure fee was widely condemned as almost immoral and the matter was even raised in Parliament. The *Athletic News* wrote: 'As a matter of commerce, 10 young recruits at £100 apiece might have paid better, and as a matter of sport, the Second Division would be more honourable than retention of place by purchase.'

Despite the criticism, Middlesbrough believed Common was a vital investment to avoid the potential financial ruin that could follow relegation. They anticipated that the experienced, bustling frontman could ensure survival and it proved to be

money well spent. Common was not the best player of his time and had only played twice for England but he was a strong, aggressive centre-forward with deceptive pace and an eye for goal. His transfer brought instant dividends when he helped end the club's dismal record of not winning away from home going back two years – and staved off relegation.

Boro appointed Common as club captain on his arrival and he finished top scorer in his first full season, linking up well with another high profile signing, Steve Bloomer. His form prompted an England recall against Wales in March 1906 and he was also the first Middlesbrough player to represent the Football League.

Common did cause more controversy when he was stripped of the captaincy by the club's directors in 1907 for reported drunkenness and violence. He continued in the team but eventually lost his place to the emerging George Elliott. Common played some games at centre-half before being transferred to Arsenal after cash-strapped Middlesbrough had failed to provide a £250 benefit he was due. Common later retired to Darlington and became a publican in the town. He died in April 1946.

CONNACHAN Edward Devlin

Goalkeeper
Born: Prestonpans, 27 August 1935.
Career. Dalkeith Thistle. Dunfermline Athletic. MIDDLESBROUGH 1963. Falkirk.

■ Manager Bob Dennison made Scottish

international Eddie Connachan one of his first signings at Middlesbrough. The goalkeeper had risen to fame at Dunfermline where he helped win the Scottish Cup, earning rave reviews along the way and was selected for Scotland and the Scottish League. However, he had lost his place for club and country when Dennison swooped to sign the part-time player who also worked as a miner.

Connachan had played right-back for an Edinburgh Juvenile side but found his niche between the sticks when the goalkeeper was injured and he managed to save two penalties in the game. Middlesbrough had struggled to find a consistent goalkeeper and had used three players in the 1962–63 campaign. Famed for his long goal-kicks, the Scot immediately established himself as a regular and was selected as the club's Player of the Year for the 1964–65 season. However, he looked slightly overweight and wasn't always commanding on crosses.

The 1965–66 season was to be one of disappointment, however. Connachan sustained a broken arm in a game against Coventry but there had already been calls for him to be axed after conceding nine goals in the previous two games. That was his last game for the club. Young Des McPartland took over in goal as the club slumped to relegation into the Third Division for the first time. Connachan returned to Scotland but later emigrated to South Africa – along with former Boro players Bryan Orritt, Bobby Braithwaite and Ian Davidson – and worked for the country's biggest plumbing firm.

COOK Henry (Harry)

Wing-half
Born: Middlesbrough.
Died: January 1917.
Career: MIDDLESBROUGH 1912.

■ Cook was one of several Middlesbrough players who lost their lives in World War One. The local half-back had been a reserve player in the years before the war getting his biggest chance in the first team as stand-in for Andy Jackson in the 1913–14 campaign as Boro achieved the best ever position of third in the First Division. He had made his debut in the previous season and enjoyed more games in 1914–15, appearing in the club's last pre-war fixture, a 4–0 defeat at Blackburn. Cook was killed in January 1917.

COOK John (Jack)

Inside-right/Outside-left
Born: Sunderland, 27 July 1891.
Career: MIDDLESBROUGH 1911. Notts County 1919. Northampton Town 1924.

■ Young forward Cook was establishing himself as a Boro regular when World War One intervened. He made his debut in February 1912 in a 2–0 home defeat to Arsenal on a day that manager Tom McIntosh fielded three debutants. Cook had to wait a year for another chance when he scored in a 3–2 First Division win at Manchester United while standing in for Jimmy Windridge. Having played all his early games at inside-forward, Cook was moved to outside-left midway through the 1913–14 campaign with some success. He replaced James Nichol as the regular left winger as Boro finished third in the top flight – a record that still stands. After the war, Cook started the club's first four fixtures in the friendly Northern Victory League (1918–19) but when League football resumed it was Tommy Urwin who won the number-11 shirt and Cook had moved on to Notts County.

COOK Mitchell Christopher

Midfield/Left-back
Born: Scarborough, 15 October 1961.
Career: Scarborough. Darlington 1984. MIDDLESBROUGH 1985. Scarborough 1986. Halifax Town 1989. Scarborough (loan) 1990. Darlington 1991. Blackpool 1992. Hartlepool United 1994. Guiseley Town. Scarborough 1996.

■ Cash-strapped Boro manager Willie Maddren recruited Mitch Cook as a player of potential. He joined the club as part of a deal that saw Alan Roberts and Paul Ward move to Darlington with Cook and £5,000 coming to Ayresome Park. He was an orthodox left-footed midfielder who failed to fulfil the potential seen in him. After a handful of games, his contract was cancelled by mutual consent and he dropped out of the League to join Conference side Scarborough. He helped his new side into the League in 1987 and spent the rest of his career travelling around the lower Leagues.

COOPER Colin Terence

Defender
Born: Sedgefield, 28 February 1967.
Career: MIDDLESBROUGH 1984. Millwall 1991. Nottingham Forest 1993. MIDDLESBROUGH 1998. Sunderland (loan) 2004.

■ Defender Colin Cooper distinguished himself as a Middlesbrough player during two very distinct periods of the club's history, with his first and final appearances for the club separated by nearly 21 years. By the time he hung up his boots to join the club's coaching staff, he had forged a place in the hearts of Boro fans as one of the most popular players of the modern era. Early in his career Cooper was a mainstay of the Boro side that rose from the depths of near extinction in the mid–1980s before returning to play his part in the Riverside revolution. At an early age, Cooper was small but big-hearted and manager Willie Maddren saw him as an ideal sweeper, though he was only made a regular through necessity by Maddren's successor, Bruce Rioch. It was Rioch that moved Cooper to left-back, despite the player being right-footed, and he proved himself as a strong tackler who liked to get forward. His form was excellent as Boro rose through the divisions and he was rewarded with eight England Under-21 caps alongside teammate Stuart Ripley. Cooper's form began to suffer after he sustained a foot injury in the 1988–89 top-flight struggle when he carried on playing when rest was needed. Switched to right-back following relegation and the signing of Jimmy Phillips, he no longer looked the same player and made a £300,000 switch to Millwall to join up again with Bruce Rioch shortly after Lennie Lawrence replaced Colin Todd as Boro manager in the summer of 1991. Cooper's first game for Millwall was against Boro at Ayresome Park and he was barracked by the crowd as the home side won 1–0. It was Rioch's successor Mick McCarthy who converted Cooper to central defence and his value rocketed with several top clubs being linked before he made a £1.7 million move to Nottingham Forest. At the City Ground, he won two full

England caps and played against Brazil on the day Juninho mesmerized the national side and made himself Bryan Robson's number one target. Having succeeded Stuart Pearce as Forest captain, he helped his side pip Boro to the First Division title in 1998 before a £2.5 million fee saw him reunited on Teesside with Gary Pallister in the heart of Bryan Robson's new-look Boro defence. Cooper remained a regular member of the squad under Terry Venables and Steve McClaren beyond his 38th birthday, showing admirable courage and dignity following the tragic death of his young son Finlay. He made his final appearance in a Boro shirt as a late substitute against Fulham on the last day of the 2005–06 season. Receiving the armband from the club's youngest ever captain, 18-year-old Lee Cattermole, Cooper in turn became the oldest player to captain Boro, aged 39. He coached under Steve McClaren, regularly appearing for the reserves the following season, before being appointed reserve team coach under Gareth Southgate and then promoted to first-team duties when Steve Round moved on in December 2006.

COOPER Douglas

Forward
Born: Eston, 18 October 1936.
Died: 1998.
Career: MIDDLESBROUGH 1953. Rotherham United 1959. Hartlepool United 1960.

■ At the start of the 1956–57 season it was Cooper who was preferred to his young rival Brian Clough for the number-nine shirt. Many expected greater things of 19-year-old Cooper than of Clough as the club searched for a replacement for veteran Charlie Wayman.

A big, bustling centre-forward and a prolific scorer for the club's juniors, Cooper had made his debut on the final day of 1954–55 at Bristol Rovers, aged 18. He waited 10 months for a second chance in March 1956 but was then named in the line-up for the opening day fixture with Stoke in August of that year. Unfortunately for Cooper, strained ankle ligaments kept him out of the following game and Clough never looked back, scoring 38 times in 41 games that season. Cooper had just two more chances, when he failed to score, spending a lot of time in the club's reserves before dropping into the lower divisions. Again, success eluded him and he left the professional game before his 25th birthday. Cooper died in 1998.

COOPER Terence

Left-back
Born: Castleford, 12 July 1944.
Career: Leeds United 1962. MIDDLESBROUGH 1975. Bristol City 1978. Bristol Rovers 1979. Doncaster Rovers 1981. Bristol City 1982.

■ Terry Cooper had been one of England's finest post-war defenders in a great Leeds side. When Jack Charlton brought his former teammate to Ayresome Park, there were doubts as he had missed almost two full seasons after breaking his leg. But, though he had lost some of his pace, he was still an excellent attacking left-back with dribbling skills and brilliant delivery on his left foot.

Wearing his distinctive white boots, Cooper had starred in Don Revie's Leeds side, winning two League titles and the European Cup. He also became an England regular and appeared in the 1970 World Cup. He joined the Middlesbrough team that was among the contenders to take the First Division title in 1974–75, replacing Frank Spraggon

from the team that had been promoted a season earlier. He showed great attacking flair and provided another option as Boro came forward.

Cooper enjoyed two full seasons as a regular and many believed he should have won further England caps before an injury handed the chance to young Ian Bailey. In the summer of 1978 he was suspended by the club for refusing to go on a pre-season tour of Norway. With a year of his contract remaining, he asked for a transfer and was soon on his way to Bristol City where he linked up with another former Leeds man Norman Hunter.

Cooper went into coaching and management with mixed fortunes. He suffered relegation in his first season at Bristol Rovers and was sacked but later won promotion from the Fourth Division with Bristol City and Exeter. He was linked with the Boro job in 1991 and coached at Southampton before taking up a European scouting role for the Saints.

CORBETT Robert

Full-back
Born: Throckley, 16 March 1922.
Died: October 1988.
Career: Throckley Welfare. Newcastle United 1943. MIDDLESBROUGH 1951. Northampton Town 1957.

■ Corbett was a converted winger who used his attacking ability to good effect from the full-back position. He was a cheerful, happy character who always played with a smile. Indeed, he was also something of an eccentric. A pigeon fancier, he would often take a basket full of homing pigeons with him on the train to Boro's away games, releasing them on arrival at the ground they were visiting. Corbett lost his early years to the war and played some wartime matches for Newcastle before making his League debut at St James' Park. He enjoyed several good years at Newcastle including the FA Cup winning run in 1951.

He was approaching 30 when he came to Middlesbrough but still had pace and was an accurate crosser from the left flank. Corbett, with his unconventional playing style, had plenty of rivals for the number-three shirt including the likes of Derek Stonehouse, Ray Bilcliff and Tommy Brown. His appearances dwindled as he approached his mid–30s and he moved on for a season at Northampton. Corbett later managed Brierly Hill. He died in Newcastle in 1988.

CORDEN Stephen

Defender/Midfield
Born: Eston, 9 January 1967.
Career: MIDDLESBROUGH 1984. Guisborough Town.

■ Two young home-grown defenders lined up for their Boro debuts in the first game of the 1985–86 season. One was Gary Pallister and the other was Steve Corden. However, while Pallister went on to play for England, it was to be Corden's solitary appearance in the professional game. The son of former Boro director Richard Corden, who was also later chairman at Darlington, Corden was a workman-like defender or midfielder with plenty of aggression. He joined the club as a youth trainee and his chores included cleaning the boots of then manager Malcolm Allison. Not a bad job as Big Mal rarely got his boots dirty! His only appearance came at left-back when he was 18 in a game against Wimbledon. The luckless youngster broke his leg 10 minutes into the second half. He eventually battled back to fitness, only to break his leg a second time, this time in a training accident. He was released at the end of the season and, after unsuccessful trials with Chesterfield and Northampton, was restricted to non-League football with Guisborough. He also ran his own Yarm-based structural engineering firm after gaining a university degree.

COWAN James

Right-back.
Career: MIDDLESBROUGH 1899.

■ Defender Cowan appeared in half of Middlesbrough's games during the club's first League campaign. His debut came at right full-back in November 1899 in a goalless against Gainsborough Trinity. A right-back, Cowan also served as a policeman.

COX Neil James

Defender
Born: Scunthorpe, 8 October 1971.
Career: Scunthorpe United 1990. Aston Villa 1991. MIDDLESBROUGH 1994. Bolton Wanderers 1997. Watford 1999. Cardiff City 2005. Crewe Alexandra 2006.

■ Boro's first million pound buy was part of the rollercoaster ride of Bryan Robson's first few years as manager. A key role in the promotion side in his first season, Cox was tipped for England honours by Robson but later fell out of favour and never fully won over the club's supporters.

The strong-tackling Cox had been seen as a utility player at Villa, who had paid Scunthorpe a record fee for a lower division player of £400,000. He subsequently won six Under-21 caps. Robson earmarked him for the right-back position and he was subsequently named in the 1994–95 First Division team of the season. The only blackspots in the season were a broken collarbone and a penalty miss in the final League game at Ayresome Park against Luton.

Cox was a regular as Boro consolidated in the Premier League in 1995–96, missing only three League games. His committed displays and regular wing forays made him an automatic choice. It was towards the end of the following season as Boro slumped to relegation that he lost his place. Curtis Fleming and Clayton Blackmore took over at right-back. Cox also missed the FA Cup Final after allegedly fighting with Fabrizio Ravanelli on the morning of the game when the Italian took exception to comments made by the defender in the press. He was soon on his way to join

former Boro manager Colin Todd at Premier League newcomers Bolton but suffered immediate relegation once again. Cox then missed out on an immediate return when he was on the losing side in the 1999 Play-off Final.

COXON Thomas

Outside-left
Born: Hanley, 10 June 1883.
Died: 30 January 1942.
Career: Burslem Port Vale 1902. Stoke 1903. MIDDLESBROUGH 1905. Burslem Port Vale 1906. Stoke 1907. Grimsby Town 1908. Leyton. Grimsby Rovers.

■ Coxon left his home in the Potteries to come to Teesside for a season. The 22-year-old left-winger was handed his

debut in the fifth game of the 1905–06 campaign but was a part of a 4–0 reverse at Manchester City. Five matches later another chance came and he enjoyed a run of 10 successive games. However, Boro were struggling badly and enjoyed just one win in his appearances. He was dropped after a 7–0 hammering at Birmingham and replaced by James Thackeray.

COYLE Ronald Paul

Defender/Midfield
Born: Glasgow, 19 August 1961.
Career: Glasgow Celtic 1979. MIDDLESBROUGH 1986. Rochdale 1987. Raith Rovers 1988. Ayr United 1996. Albion Rovers 1997. East Fife 1998. Queen's Park 1999.

■ Midfielder Ronnie Coyle initially joined Boro on a month's loan in December 1986. He made just one substitute appearance in the spell before returning to Parkhead. A few month's later Bruce Rioch decided to recruit the Scot on a free transfer as Boro pushed for promotion from the Third Division. He was immediately handed his full debut against Bristol City but failed to impress. He sat on the bench on several occasions but was unable to win a place, with the likes of Gary Hamilton, Gary Gill and Paul Kerr ahead of him. He left following Boro's promotion.

CRADDOCK Thomas

Forward
Born: Darlington, 14 October 1986.
Career: MIDDLESBROUGH 2005. Wrexham (loan) 2006.

■ A prolific scorer for Middlesbrough at both junior and reserve-team levels, Tom Craddock was given his chance at senior level in the last game of the 2005–06 season against Fulham at Craven Cottage. Although he appeared for only the last nine minutes, he was part of both club and Premiership history as one of 16 Englishmen fielded by Boro that afternoon. With an average age of only 20, it was also the youngest-ever team to play in the Premiership. Craddock was the eighth member of Boro's 2004 FA Youth Cup-winning side to progress to the first team following James Morrison, Tony McMahon, Andrew Taylor, David Wheater, Matthew Bates, Adam Johnson and Jason Kennedy. He went on loan to Wrexham in October 2006 after hitting form for the reserves and opened his scoring account with a late goal in a 2–0 win over Bristol Rovers. However, he picked up a serious knee injury during the same game and spent the rest of the season undergoing rehabilitation with a view to being fit for pre-season training in summer 2007.

CRAGGS John Edward

Right-back
Born: Flint Hill, 31 October 1948.
Career: Newcastle United 1965. MIDDLESBROUGH 1971. Newcastle United 1982. Darlington 1983.

■ Craggs was a fine attacking right-back for over a decade at Middlesbrough. Unlucky never to be capped by England, he was a mainstay of the side throughout the 1970s and fully justified the record fee paid for his services. Known as Craggsy and also nicknamed Ted by his teammates who were amused to see a letter with his full name arrive at the club, he is fourth in the club's all-time appearance list.

At Newcastle, Craggs had played in the 1969 Fairs Cup semi-final and was on their bench for the final success. The former England youth international left St James' Park for first-team football after struggling to dislodge David Craig. Boro paid a sizeable fee for a reserve player and had to sell Hugh McIlmoyle to finance the deal but manager Stan Anderson was confident that it would be money well spent.

Strong and determined in defence, Craggs was comfortable on the ball and loved to make overlapping runs. He was a firm tackler who also scored some spectacular goals and was renowned for his long throws and excellent crosses. When Jack Charlton took over as manager and won promotion to the top flight he rated Craggs as the best attacking right-back in the game and he performed well in the top flight.

Craggs was a consistent performer throughout his time at Ayresome Park. He was suspended for seven days by Charlton in April 1976 for a double V-sign to a section of the crowd that had been barracking him but was mostly a

well-appreciated figure. He was appointed club captain for the start of the 1981–82 but his form dipped and Tony McAndrew, who had been unsettled, was reinstated. He was awarded a testimonial against Newcastle in 1982 but, with Boro recently relegated, his efforts were poorly recognised when just 3,572 attended and Craggs left following relegation to the Second Division. After returning to Newcastle for a spell, he spent two seasons with Darlington. Craggs later joined Bobby Moncur as youth coach at Hartlepool before taking up work in a Teesside sports store, initially working for ex-Boro teammate Willie Maddren.

CRAIG Thomas

Right-back
Born: Glasgow.
Career: MIDDLESBROUGH 1904. Falkirk 1905. Sunderland 1906.

■ Craig was brought in from Scotland two months into the 1904–05 season. He operated at left and right full-back in games against Preston and Stoke as stand-in for Joe Blackett. When Donald McCallum was signed in December, the new man formed a regular full-back partnership with Billy Agnew and Craig soon returned to Scotland.

CRAWFORD Andrew

Forward
Born: Filey, 30 January 1959.
Career: Filey Town. Derby County 1977. Blackburn Rovers 1979. Bournemouth 1981. Cardiff City 1983. MIDDLESBROUGH 1983. Filey Town. Stockport County 1984. Torquay United 1985.

■ Andy Crawford was a much-travelled striker who failed to fulfil his early promise, dropping out of the League at the relatively early age of 26. He was signed by Boro manager Malcolm Allison after calling in at Ayresome Park to train and then scoring twice in a reserve game. Crawford had left his most recent club Cardiff and was playing for non-League Filey Town when he dropped in at Ayresome. He enjoyed a brief run in the side but his only goal came against his former club Cardiff.

Crawford had earlier been an apprentice at Derby and had scored on his debut against Liverpool. He was subsequently leading scorer when Blackburn won promotion from the Third Division in 1979–80 and also won promotion from Division Four with Bournemouth in 1981–82. Crawford returned to Filey Town on a non-contract basis after being released by Boro, returning to the League for brief spells with Stockport and Torquay.

CRAWFORD James

Outside-right
Born: Leith 1877.
Career: Abercorn. Reading 1897. Sunderland 1898. Derby County 1900. MIDDLESBROUGH 1901.

■ Scottish outside-right Crawford played his part in Middlesbrough's first promotion success and then appeared in the club's top flight debut. Arriving midway through the season from Derby, the former Sunderland player was a regular on the right-wing as Boro finished second in Division Two. He was in the starting line-up for the opening game in the First Division, a 1–0 victory over Blackburn, but then lost his place to James Robertson. Crawford's daughter Eleanor later married Middlesbrough star Andy Wilson.

CREAMER Peter Anthony

Defender
Born: Hartlepool, 20 September 1953.
Career: MIDDLESBROUGH 1970. York City (loan) 1975. Doncaster Rovers 1975. Hartlepool United 1976. Gateshead 1978. Rochdale 1978.

■ Versatile reserve Creamer was an England Schoolboy international at football and cricket but found it hard to break into the Middlesbrough first team. Seen mostly as a right-back he found his path blocked by John Craggs. A reliable, steady player, Creamer's debut came at left-back in place of Frank Spraggon following a 4–0 defeat at Oxford. A strong, mobile defender, he retained his place for three games and later in the season also played in midfield and at right-back. It was almost a year since his last game when Jack Charlton played him at right-back against Bristol City and Sunderland over Christmas 1973 but with Craggs in top form there was only one more game, at Bolton in April 1974, once promotion had been secured. His final appearance came in front of 36,000 people at Ayresome Park in a goalless League Cup draw with Manchester City in December 1974. He was loaned to York before joining Doncaster where he was signed by ex-Boro manager Stan Anderson. Creamer later managed Whitby Town and Evenwood Town and ran a pub in Bishop Auckland. His son Chris joined Boro as a YTS trainee but didn't make the grade.

CROSIER Joseph

Wing-half
Born: Middlesbrough, 4 December 1889.
Died: 1960.
Career: MIDDLESBROUGH 1910. Bradford Park Avenue 1914. Grimsby Town 1922.

■ Local right-half Crosier enjoyed just one season in which he was consistently in the first-team frame. Having made his debut against Manchester United in March 1911 as stand-in for Billy Barker, he made sporadic appearances before getting his big chance in place of Eddie Verrill in December 1912. A run of games followed as Boro struggled in the bottom half of the First Division. However, when Stewart Davidson was signed in the summer of 1913, Crosier was back in the reserves and moved on to Bradford a year later.

CROSSAN John Andrew

Inside-forward
Born: Derry, 29 November 1938.
Career: Coleraine. Sparta Rotterdam (Holland). Standard Liege (Belgium). Sunderland 1962. Manchester City 1966. MIDDLESBROUGH 1967. Tongren (Belgium).

■ A skilful and creative inside-forward with an eye for goal, Johnny Crossan failed to recreate the form at Middlesbrough that had made him a big favourite at Manchester City and Sunderland. A club record signing, he suffered from injuries and failed to provide the expected spark to assist the club's ambition of returning to the top flight.

Crossan played Irish League football for Derry City and Coleraine but problems over a proposed move to Bristol City resulted in a 'life' suspension by the FA. He was banned for receiving an illegal payment as an amateur with Coleraine and the League refused to register him. He joined Sparta Rotterdam instead where he won his first Northern Ireland cap in 1959. After moving to Standard Liege, where he played in the European Cup, he joined Sunderland when his ban was lifted. He twice won promotion to the First Division with the Rokerites and then Manchester City and joined Boro after the club had won promotion from the Third Division.

Crossan had impressed when playing against Middlesbrough but was something of a disappointment as Boro consistently failed to win promotion from the Second Division. He played just once more for Northern Ireland when he was captain but missed a penalty and was then dropped for the next game. He was injury prone and needed medical treatment after suffering a severe bout of insomnia. He returned to playing in 1969–70 after abdominal surgery but was released at the end of the season and went on to play for Tongren in Belgium.

CROSSLEY Mark Geoffrey

Goalkeeper
Born: Barnsley, 16 June 1969.
Career: Nottingham Forest 1987. Millwall (loan) 1998. MIDDLESBROUGH 2000. Stoke City (loan) 2002. Fulham 2003. Sheffield Wednesday (loan) 2006. Oldham Athletic 2007.

■ The experienced Yorkshireman became the latest in a long line of deputies to Mark Schwarzer when he signed from Nottingham Forest in 2000 – and he was more talented than most. The Midlands club released him to reduce their wage bill after he had appeared in 395 matches for them over 13 years, largely as first-choice keeper. He and another ex-Forest keeper, Dave Beasant, remain the only goalkeepers to have saved a penalty in an FA Cup Final. Crossley's big moment came when he denied Gary Lineker in Forest's 1991 final defeat to Spurs and he is also the only keeper ever to have denied Matt Le Tissier from the penalty spot. Inevitably he found his chances limited at the Riverside, such was Schwarzer's consistency, but always impressed when called into the fray. His best run of games came in 2001–02 when injuries to Schwarzer gave him the chance to start 17 League games. He also earned a recall to the Welsh national side. His form was so good that Steve McClaren was faced with a difficult selection when Schwarzer returned to fitness, the manager recalling his first-choice keeper. Crossley was bought by Fulham in 2003 for £500,000 as cover for Edwin van der Sar. He again had to settle for reserve team football, although he gave Tony Warner a run for his money in 2005–06 when he started 13 League games. Midway through the 2006–07 campaign he had a successful loan spell at Sheffield Wednesday, where he scored the first League goal of his career, before joining Oldham.

CUFF Patrick Joseph

Goalkeeper
Born: Middlesbrough, 19 March 1952.
Career: MIDDLESBROUGH 1969. Grimsby Town (loan) 1971. Millwall 1978. Darlington 1980.

■ An England schoolboy international, goalkeeper Cuff waited patiently for his first-team chances in nearly a decade at the club but found it hard to dislodge the consistent Jim Platt. Having initially been deputy to Willie Whigham, he was then cover for Platt and it was in a loan spell at Grimsby that his first taste of League football came in 1971. Back at Middlesbrough, it wasn't until the end of the 1973–74 promotion campaign that he was given a chance when Platt was rested once Boro's place in the top flight was secured. Cuff was brave and a good shot-stopper though inconsistent.

It was almost two years before another game came in an Anglo-Scottish Cup tie at Newcastle before Cuff made his First Division debut in April 1976 in a 2–0 home win over Ipswich. After waiting so patiently in the reserves, his big chance came in late December 1976 when Platt was dropped by manager Jack Charlton following a tactical disagreement over his positioning on corners. Cuff played 23 consecutive League and Cup games but John Neal then reinstated Platt when he took over in the summer of 1977. Although an enthusiastic, hard working player, he possibly lacked the physique to establish himself as a top rate goalkeeper. Another run of games came midway through the 1977–78 season but Cuff left when he found himself third choice behind Platt and the emerging David Brown, and Jim Stewart was then signed. He retired early with a back injury and joined his brother in setting up a partnership of bookmakers. He later coached at Boro's centre of excellence.

CUMMING David Scott

Goalkeeper
Born: Aberdeen, 6 May 1910.
Died: 1993.
Career: Aberdeen 1930. Arbroath 1933. MIDDLESBROUGH 1936.

■ Cumming was a fine goalkeeper with quick reflexes and excellent handling, and a great reader of play. The Scot was denied the chance to fully establish himself as one of the club's greats by the outbreak of World War Two. He had been a highly-rated 'keeper in Scotland and established his reputation in England with some brilliant displays as Middlesbrough challenged at the top of the First Division.

He was signed by manager Peter McWilliam as a replacement for Fred Gibson. Cumming stepped straight into the side for a 3–3 draw with Liverpool at Ayresome Park and was initially bewildered by the pace of the English game. It was a tough baptism as he conceded 10 goals in his first three games, but he adapted quickly and established himself firmly as first choice.

Cumming made his Scottish international debut in the same game as Boro teammate Jacky Milne, against England at Wembley in April 1938, as the Scots recorded a famous 1–0 victory. As Boro gradually improved in the late 1930s he was part of a formidable side that was tipped by many to win the League in 1939–40. Instead, though, war ended the club's hopes. Cumming played more than 100 wartime games for Boro and also won one wartime cap, a 6–2 defeat to England. During the war he drove a bus from Middlesbrough to Newcastle and this possibly explains how he came to be the only Middlesbrough player who guested for the Geordies. He quickly became a crowd favourite at Newcastle despite his Middlesbrough allegiances.

He was back in the Middlesbrough goal after the war and in the first League season he was involved in an infamous incident at Ayresome Park. Cumming generally wore a wide grin on the pitch but he also had a temper. During a match against Arsenal in December 1946, opponent Les Compton kicked him in a penalty area melee following a corner. Cumming walked up to the 6ft 4in centre-half and struck him with right-hook. He then took off his jersey and handed it to Johnny Spuhler as he walked off the pitch before the referee could give him his marching orders. He continued for most of the season before suffering a dislocated kneecap against Blackpool in April 1947 after falling awkwardly when going to punch the ball. An operation and lengthy stay in hospital followed and he was forced to retire. Cumming died in 1993.

CUMMINS Michael Thomas

Midfield
Born: Dublin, 1 June 1978.
Career: MIDDLESBROUGH 1995. Port Vale 2000. Darlington 2006.

■ An Irish Under-21 international who made his debut in the final game of Boro's 100th Football League season. The versatile defender or midfielder got his chance at right wing-back in a 4–0 defeat at West Ham. After playing his junior football in Dublin, he turned down Chelsea and Blackburn and signed

schoolboy forms for Boro at 15. Cummins had been a regular in the reserves for several seasons and starred in the 1997 World Youth Cup in Malaysia when Eire reached the semi-finals. He later moved to Port Vale and Darlington.

CUMMINS Stanley

Midfield
Born: Ferryhill, 6 December 1958.
Career: MIDDLESBROUGH 1976. Sunderland 1979. Crystal Palace 1983. Sunderland 1984. Minnesota Kicks (United States).

■ Diminutive frontman Stan Cummins was billed as Boro's first million pound player when the transfer record was half that figure. But Jack Charlton's comments probably placed an unfair burden on the young striker and he failed to fulfil his early potential. Despite his obvious talent, he struggled for consistency and was in and out of the side under Charlton and his successor John Neal before moving on to Sunderland.

Cummins, like Brian Clough, was unearthed by Ray Grant, a retired headmaster and honorary scout of the club. As a boy he had trials with Chelsea, Manchester United, Aston Villa and Arsenal but was persuaded to sign for Boro. He emerged as a genuine discovery in 1977–78 when he starred alongside David Mills and Billy Ashcroft and he is remembered for his brace in a 4–2 win over Newcastle in January 78.

The teenager with the dangerous left foot was becoming a first-team regular only to suffer a knee injury in a pre-

season friendly in the summer of 1978. Opportunities were scarcer following the signings of Micky Burns and Bosco Jankovic. Cummins scored on his Sunderland debut and helped the club to promotion into the First Division. Cummins, who also played for the Seattle Sounders and Minnesota Kicks in the US, joined Crystal Palace on a free transfer in 1983 but couldn't settle and returned to Roker Park. He later emigrated to the US, where he was a football coach, before returning to live in the North East.

CUNLIFFE Arthur

Outside-left
Born: Blackrod, Bolton, 5 February 1909.
Died: August 1986.
Career: Adlington. Chorley. Blackburn Rovers 1929. Aston Villa 1932. MIDDLESBROUGH 1935. Burnley 1937. Hull City 1938. Rochdale 1945.

■ Boro manager Wilf Gillow travelled to Birmingham to sign former England international Cunliffe and found him at 11.20pm taking part in a whist drive! The winger signed on the dotted line before midnight and joined his new teammates at Portsmouth to make his debut. Despite the fairly sizeable fee, he was far from a regular at Ayresome.

Cunliffe had made his name at Blackburn where he was a speedy winger with a lethal turn of pace and excellent ball control. From the left wing he would also cut inside and score plenty of goals. His only England caps came in 1933. Villa had paid £8,000 for his services.

Cunliffe was a Boro regular in the second half of 1935–36 and, most notably, scored the opener in an incredible 6–0 win over Sunderland in March 1936, just months before Sunderland were crowned champions. He also played well enough to gain selection as an England trialist that same month. After playing for Burnley and Hull, Cunliffe joined Rochdale after the war and became trainer at Spotland and then at Bournemouth. He was also physio at the club and stayed into the mid–1970s. Cunliffe died in Bournemouth in August 1986.

CURRIE David Norman

Forward
Born: Stockton, 27 November 1962.
Career: MIDDLESBROUGH 1982. Darlington 1986. Barnsley 1988. Nottingham Forest 1990. Oldham Athletic 1990. Barnsley 1991. Rotherham United (loan) 1992. Huddersfield Town (loan) 1994. Carlisle United 1994. Scarborough 1997.

■ Strong-running forward 'Kid' Currie was a good dribbler with an excellent left foot. He was a composed finisher but was let down by a handful of bad misses that knocked his confidence. After an impressive start, he was released but went on to find success, particularly in the lower Leagues.

A Stockton schoolboy, Currie made his Boro debut as a substitute in the last game of the 1981–82 relegation season. In his early days Currie had been the victim of Mickey-taking from some senior players and thought about leaving the club or even quitting football before making his first-team breakthrough. He got his chance in 1983–84 when he finished top scorer, creating chances for others as well as scoring his share of goals in a poor Boro side. However, mixed fortunes followed and he is unfortunately remembered for one of the worst misses in the club's history. In a crunch relegation match against Carlisle in April 1985, he rounded the 'keeper only to place the ball wide of an open goal from no more than six yards. Boro stayed up despite the 2–1 defeat but Currie's confidence took a knock. He was exceptional on his day but that didn't come often enough at Boro. He was deemed surplus to requirements by Bruce Rioch and released during the liquidation crisis.

In his first season with Darlington Currie was sent off for retaliation on his return to Ayresome. He recovered his form and became Barnsley's record signing at £150,000 in February 1988. He was a big star at Oakwell and won a £750,000 move to Brian Clough's First Division Nottingham Forest. But it was a frustrating time at the City Ground and he became Oldham's record signing before returning to Barnsley.

CURRIE Robert

Centre-forward
Born: Glasgow.
Career: Arthurlie. MIDDLESBROUGH 1902. Bury. Arsenal.

■ Centre-forward Currie spent just a few months at Middlesbrough and made only a handful of appearances. A £60 signing from Scottish side Arthurlie, he made his debut in a 1–0 victory over Newcastle in February 1902. His only goal came in a 1–1 draw with Stoke in the last ever game at the Linthorpe Road ground. He was demoted to the A team as the club tried unsuccessfully to sign Alf Common from Sheffield United in the search for a regular goalscorer.

CURTIS John Joseph

Outside-right
Born: South Bank, 13 December 1888.
Died: 1955.
Career: South Bank St Peter's. South Bank. Sunderland 1906. Shildon Athletic. Gainsborough Trinity 1908. Tottenham Hotspur 1909. Fulham 1913. Brentford 1914. Stockport County 1914. MIDDLESBROUGH 1919. Shildon Athletic.

■ Local lad Curtis returned to Teesside after more than a decade with

Tottenham. He spent a season at Ayresome Park but played just a handful of games in the first League campaign after the war. He started the first game of the season at outside-right but had to wait until November for another chance when he played four consecutive games.

DAVENPORT Peter

Forward
Born: Birkenhead, 24 March 1961.
Career: Cammell Laird. Nottingham Forest 1982. Manchester United 1986. MIDDLESBROUGH 1988. Sunderland 1990. Airdrie 1993. St Johnstone 1994. Stockport County 1995. Southport 1996. Macclesfield 1997.

■ Striker Davenport had an unsuccessful time at Boro, mainly thanks to stormy relationships with managers Bruce Rioch and Colin Todd. Having lost his place at Manchester United to Mark Hughes and Brian McClair, Davenport arrived at Ayresome Park in 1988 for a record fee of £700,000, breaking a record that had been held by Irving Nattrass for nine years. Bruce Rioch said Davenport would play down the middle, rather than wide on the left where he was at Old Trafford, and he was expected to be final piece in the jigsaw, but Boro's first ever half-million pound buy didn't quite pay off.

The goals never came for Davenport and it was thought that his big wages upset the dressing room stability that had been built since liquidation. To make matters worse, Davenport didn't link up well with popular frontman Bernie Slaven. Davenport was denied a stunning debut goal by Liverpool 'keeper Mike Hooper and it took him two months to score his first goal. Ironically it came against his old club, Manchester United, in January 1989. He became many people's scapegoat after relegation in 1988–89 and was dropped for a match against Watford in October 1989, but dismissed speculation he was about to leave the club. Davenport had a stormy relationship with Rioch and in March 1990 he was banned for two weeks and transfer-listed. In the meantime Sheffield Wednesday enquired about him but the offer didn't meet club requirements.

When Colin Todd took over in March 1990, Davenport was restored to the team, playing on the left wing and performing well in the ZDS Cup Final. He was then suspended and picked up an ankle injury but things were to get even worse when he was involved in a heated dressing room argument with Todd.

Davenport joined Sunderland in the summer of 1990, becoming one of the few post-war players to go from Teesside to Wearside in the process. He later scored a stunning goal against Boro in 1991–92 to jeopardise promotion hopes. Davenport's career started when he signed for Everton as an amateur but he failed to make the grade and played non-League for Cammell Laird, alongside his job as a civil servant. He was spotted by Nottingham Forest and joined them at the age of 20. Davenport came to fame at the City Ground and won an England cap against Eire in 1985, as well as playing in the controversial UEFA Cup semi-final v Anderlecht. In 1995 he became player-coach at Macclesfield, where he made occasional appearances, and managed to score his 100th League goal in the final game of the 1997–98 campaign. He eventually succeeded Sammy McIlroy as Macclesfield manager but was sacked. He returned to management with Welsh Premiership side Bangor City, where another former Boro player Clayton Blackmore was a member of the squad. After four years at Bangor he resigned and spent six months in charge at Colwyn Bay, before returning as manager of Southport in January 2007.

DAVIDSON Andrew C.

Left-half/Centre-half
Born: Ayr 1878.
Career: Ayr United. MIDDLESBROUGH 1900. Bury 1906. Grimsby Town 1908. Southampton. Grimsby Town 1909. Grimsby Rovers.

■ Scottish half-back Andy Davidson could not only boast of playing the last ever game at the Linthorpe Road ground, but also Boro's first ever Division One match in 1902 and the first game at Ayresome Park in 1903. Davidson was delighted to join Boro on a professional contract from then non-League Scottish side Ayr United, as he had previously earned a living as a miner. Once described as a little slow but consistently reliable, he was part of the promotion-winning half-back line in 1901–02 alongside Dave Smith and Abe Jones. After six good seasons at the club Davidson had a benefit game against Woolwich Arsenal on 21 April 1906 before moving on to Bury.

DAVIDSON Ian

Wing-half
Born: East Lothian, 8 September 1937.
Career: Kilmarnock. Preston North End 1962. MIDDLESBROUGH 1965. Darlington 1967.

■ Despite being rated by many as a talented wing-half, Davidson, who once famously missed an FA Cup Final for Preston due to suspension and was replaced by a young Howard Kendall, ended up being placed on the transfer list with Frank Spraggon, Nev Chapman and Alex Smith in May 1967. Davidson had struggled to make a first-team spot his own and tussled with the likes of Don Masson and Billy Horner for a place in the Boro side. Luton enquired about his services and Boro were also considering an offer from Durban United in South Africa when Darlington came in for him. He was club captain at Feethams for a spell and then made the move to South Africa where he worked as a salesman for Coca-Cola.

DAVIDSON Stewart

Right-half
Born: Aberdeen, 1 June 1889.
Died: 26 December 1960.
Career: Aberdeen Shamrock. Aberdeen. MIDDLESBROUGH 1913. Aberdeen. Forres Mechanics.

■ A player who played the majority of his games at right-half after making his debut against Manchester City on 6 September 1913, Davidson was actually a legal clerk by profession. He guested for Chelsea in World War One but was wounded on active service. However, he was able to resume his career at the end of the war and went on to play over 200 games for Boro. Davidson's proudest moments came when he took over as club captain from George Elliott in 1920 and when he won his only Scotland cap in a game against England in 1921.

During his Boro career Davidson lined up alongside the likes of George Elliott, Jock Marshall and Walter Tinsley and was rewarded for his services with a benefit game against Derby on 20 November 1920. He was placed on the transfer list in May 1923 at a price of £500 but Davidson appealed against the size of the fee and the League Management Committee reduced it to £250 to the pleasure of his former club Aberdeen who snapped him up. He later became player-manager at Forres Mechanics then coached for the Kent County FA and in the summer of 1939 joined former Boro teammate Billy Birrell who was boss at Chelsea, as his assistant manager. Davidson stayed at

Stamford Bridge for 18 years until his retirement in July 1957 and passed away on Boxing Day 1960.

DAVIDSON William

Outside-left
Born: Glasgow.
Career: MIDDLESBROUGH 1910. Queen's Park Rangers 1911. Everton 1911. St Mirren 1913.

■ Outside left Davidson made his handful of appearances during the 1910–11 season in a side that included Boro record appearance maker Tim Williamson and England international George Elliott. He failed to score any goals and struggled to pin down a first-team place and made the move to Queen's Park Rangers at the end of an unimpressive campaign that saw Boro finish 16th in the top flight.

DAVIES Albert Stanley

Outside-left
Born: Swindon, 1 March 1894.
Died: 1976.
Career: West End Juniors. Swindon Town. MIDDLESBROUGH 1914. Swindon Town 1920. Luton Town 1927. Garrards Athletic.

■ Ouside-left Albert Davies made just one League appearance in a brief spell at Boro and ironically it was at The Hawthorns, against his old club West Brom, during the 1914–15 season. The only other game in which he featured was a 9–3 FA Cup thrashing of Goole Town during the same campaign.

DAVIES Andrew John

Central defender
Born: Stockton, 17 December 1984.
Career: MIDDLESBROUGH 2002. Queen's Park Rangers (loan) 2005. Derby County (loan) 2005.

■ Davies was just 18 when he made his Premiership debut for flu victim Gareth Southgate against Aston Villa in January 2003. He had captained the club's youth team through to just their second-ever FA Youth Cup Final and, in the summer of 2002, was called up into the England Under-19 UEFA Championship squad. The following season he had acted as understudy to the likes of Gareth Southgate, Ugo Ehiogu and Chris Riggott, and had worked his way into David Platt's England Under-21 side when he fractured his tibia and fibula in a reserve game at Blackburn. On Davies's return to full fitness, he was loaned out to Queen's Park Rangers, where his form prompted manager Ian Holloway to ask

about a permanent transfer. In 2005–06 he was loaned to Derby County but, following an injury crisis at the Riverside, he returned to Boro, where he was thrust straight into the injury-ravaged side. He then enjoyed regular first-team football both in the Premiership and the UEFA Cup during the closing stages of the campaign. Although he had risen through the ranks as a centre-back, most of his games at senior level have been at right-back. Davies enjoyed a productive season in 2006–07, starting 21 matches in the problem number-two position in competition with Abel Xavier and Stuart Parnaby.

DAVIES Benjamin E.

Goalkeeper
Born: Middlesbrough.
Died: 1970.
Career: Shildon Athletic. MIDDLESBROUGH 1910. Cardiff City 1920. Leicester City 1923. Bradford Park Avenue 1924.

■ The highly-rated 'keeper arrived at Ayresome Park from County Durham side Shildon with high hopes of a successful career. However, he was to struggle to get into the side, mainly thanks to the consistency of record appearance maker Tim Williamson, and in his eight years at the club managed to play just 31 games. Following the Great War, Davies also played for Hartlepool in the Northern Victory League before returning to the Boro reserves.

DAVIES William Arthur

Outside-right
Born: Bod Howell 1886.
Died: November 1949.
Career: Wrexham St Giles. Wrexham. Druids. West Bromwich Albion 1904. MIDDLESBROUGH 1904. Wrexham Nomads.

■ Having impressed with his local side Wrexham, outside-right Arthur Davies was given his chance at League level with West Bromwich Albion. After appearing in 12 games for the Throstles, he joined Middlesbrough in December 1904 and made his debut in a 1–1 draw against Nottingham Forest. He also appeared in 12 League and Cup games for Boro but failed to find the net, having scored once while with Albion. He later returned to his native North Wales to end his career with Wrexham Nomads.

DAVISON Joseph W.

Full-back
Born: Byers Green, 6 July 1897.
Career: Blyth Spartans. MIDDLESBROUGH 1919. Portsmouth 1923. Watford 1927.

■ Half-back Davison was part of the side that lost 3–1 at Chelsea in the 1919–20 season – but he never played for Boro again. He was placed on the transfer list at the end of 1922–23 for £350, a fee that was reduced to £200 by the Football League.

DAY William

Outside-right
Born: Middlesbrough, 27 December 1936.
Career: Sheffield Wednesday. South Bank. MIDDLESBROUGH 1955. Newcastle United 1962. Peterborough United 1963. Cambridge United 1964.

■ Exciting outside-right Billy Day played as part of the late 1950s explosive forward line that included Brian Clough, Alan Peacock and Eddie Holliday on the other wing. Day, who started off as an amateur at Sheffield Wednesday and then played for South Bank Juniors, gave up his job as an apprentice fitter to sign professional forms with Boro. He made his debut against Leicester in October 1955, and became very popular at Ayresome Park for being an excellent touchline player who loved to attack defenders. Day's main qualities were that

he displayed a lack of nerves and possessed control, speed and accuracy.

Day served his National Service in Germany with the 7th Royal Tank Regiment, and was Army sprint champion, but he was so vital to the Boro side that the club paid for the expensive flights from his Army camp for weekly games and flew him back afterwards. This happened more than 20 times, and he would have to leave the barracks at mid-day on Friday, arriving in Middlesbrough in the early hours of Saturday before playing and flying back that evening, all for £1 a week retainer and £5 per match.

Day later lost his place because of a broken leg picked up in a practice match at the Hutton Road training ground but made a quick return to the Boro side. However, he had been impatient and hadn't allowed his leg to heal properly, and manager Bob Dennison agreed to a transfer request. He joined north-east rivals Newcastle and scored on his debut but the leg trouble returned and Day was soon on his way again to League newcomers Peterborough. Sadly, his career was to end early, at the age of just 29, during a spell at non-League Cambridge United due to a bad attack of pneumonia. He later returned to Teesside and became a racecourse bookmaker.

DEANE Brian Christopher

Forward
Born: Leeds, 7 February 1968.
Career: Doncaster Rovers 1985. Sheffield United 1988. Leeds United 1993. Sheffield United 1997. Benfica (Portugal) 1998. MIDDLESBROUGH 1998. Leicester City 2001. West Ham United 2003. Leeds United 2004. Sunderland 2005. Perth Glory (Australia). Sheffield United 2006.

■ Until joining Middlesbrough from Benfica for £3 million in October 1998, Deane was best known to Boro fans for his goal as a Leeds player in the last match of the 1996–97 season – a header that condemned Bryan Robson's side to relegation. That was forgotten when the much-travelled front man arrived at the Riverside and formed a partnership with Hamilton Ricard over a two-year period that saw the Colombian score the bulk of the goals with target man Deane often the provider. Having struggled for goals during the first half of the 2000–01 campaign, Deane never started a League game once Terry Venables arrived at the club to save Boro from what had appeared inevitable relegation. Although he scored the opening goal in Steve McClaren's first win as Boro manager, he fell out of favour and was allowed to move on to Leicester for £250,000. Not the most aesthetically pleasing of players and never a crowd favourite at the Riverside, Deane was certainly a 100 percent man. He had played for Leeds City Boys and Yorkshire Amateurs, recovering from a broken leg to join Doncaster as a 17-year-old. He progressed up the divisions with two prolific spells at Sheffield United, with four years at Leeds United sandwiched in between. He then spent a year in Portugal with Benfica under the management of former Boro hero Graeme Souness. After leaving Boro, Deane's goals could not retain Leicester City's Premier League status but his 13 goals in 2002–03 helped them bounce back at the first time of asking before he moved on to West Ham and then returned to Leeds. His nomadic career continued with a brief spell at the Stadium of Light as Sunderland clinched promotion to the Premier League in 2005. A year later, after playing for Perth Glory in the Australian A-League, he returned for a third spell with Sheffield United, making two substitute appearances as they clinched promotion to the top flight. Deane hung up his boots that summer, aged 38.

DEBÈVE Mickaël

Midfield
Born: Abbeville, France, 1 December 1970.
Career: Toulouse 1986. Lens (France) 1994. Le Havre (France) (loan) 1999. MIDDLESBROUGH 2002. Amiens (France) 2002. Abbeville (France) 2004.

■ The vastly-experienced French midfielder signed on a short term contract from Lens midway through the 2001–02 season and made his debut from the bench in a 3–0 FA Cup quarter-final victory over Everton. With skipper Paul Ince suspended and Jonathan Greening injured for the semi-final, he started against Arsenal at Old Trafford and had a fine game in the unlucky 1–0 defeat. All of his four appearances for the first team – three of which were from the bench – ended in defeat and in the close season he returned to France to continue his career with Amiens. In 2004 he became player-trainer of French lower league side Abbeville, his home-town club. Earlier on in his career he won the 1998 French League title with Lens.

DELAPENHA Lloyd Lindberg (Lindy)

Forward
Born: Jamaica, 20 May 1927.
Career: Arsenal. Portsmouth 1948. MIDDLESBROUGH 1950. Mansfield Town 1958. Burton Albion. Heanor Town.

■ Famed for his rocket-like shot, Delapenha was the first black player to represent Middlesbrough. The Jamaican forward was a loyal club servant for almost a decade, during which time he earned a place in the hearts of all Boro fans who saw him play. With his fierce shot, said to be one of the most powerful in the game, speed and bite, he was a key player in an era which spanned three managers, David Jack, Walter Rowley and Bob Dennison.

Delapenha was born on the same day Charles Lindberg successfully flew solo across the Atlantic, hence his rather strange middle name. His first break in the game came when he approached Arsenal manager Tom Whittaker with a letter of introduction and duly signed amateur forms at Highbury. However, first-team opportunities did not come his way and, following National Service with the RAF, he had trial offers from Chelsea, Plymouth and Portsmouth, choosing the latter on the recommendation of an Army friend. Pompey boss Bob Jackson was so impressed by the 21-year-old that he didn't bother to wait for the end of the game to sign him and Delapenha made history when he became the first black player from overseas to play League football.

Although small, he was a sturdy, powerful and speedy forward. Indeed, it was even suggested that he should run for Great Britain in the 1948 Olympics in London but Delapenha preferred to stick with the beautiful game. At the time Portsmouth were at their all-time peak and won the League title in both of Delapenha's seasons at Fratton Park, meaning first-team chances were few and far between. David Jack persuaded him to make the move north to Boro and he made his debut on the final day of the 1949–50 season at Fulham. He was the club's regular outside-right throughout the following season as Boro finished sixth and scored his first goal against Arsenal, the club who had rejected him as a teenager. Equally at home on the wing or at inside-forward, he was entrusted with penalty kicks and rarely missed, though on one occasion against Sunderland, he was adjudged to have missed when the ball had in fact gone through a hole in the back of the net. In truth, there was a fault with the net but rumours quickly spread that the power of his penalty had actually broken the net! Delapenha was three times Boro's top scorer, including the 1953–54 relegation season, by which time he had turned down a £12,000 transfer to Manchester City, insisting there was little point in moving when he was already on the maximum wage allowed by the Football League.

He was no longer guaranteed a first-team place by the time he left for Mansfield in 1958 but was a regular for three seasons at Field Mill before playing

non-League football for Burton Albion and Heanor Town. He eventually retired from the game due to damage caused by an untreated groin injury and went on to hold a senior job with the Jamaican Broadcasting Corporation.

DESMOND Peter

Inside-forward
Born: Cork, 26 October 1926.
Died: 16 September 1990.
Career: Waterford. Shelbourne. MIDDLESBROUGH 1949. Southport 1950. York City 1951. Fleetwood. Hartlepool United 1953.

■ During his year with Middlesbrough, Irish forward Desmond actually played more times for his country than he did for his club. A skilful inside-forward who relied on a sharp burst of speed rather than fancy footwork, he made his name with Shelbourne where he and Arthur Fitzsimons represented the League of Ireland. Both were signed for a combined £18,000 fee in May 1949 but neither player had made their first-team debut for the club when they helped Eire to a shock 2–0 win over England in September of the same year. Desmond played his part by winning the penalty for Eire's first goal. Three days later, he and

Bill Linacre made their Boro debuts in a 3–0 win over Charlton. Desmond retained his place for the following week's home draw with Manchester City but spent the rest of the season in the reserves and was never called into the first team again, despite continuing to be selected by his national side. He made only limited appearances in the lower Leagues with Southport, York and Hartlepool before retiring on Teesside. He died in Stainton on 16 September 1990.

DEWS George

Inside-forward
Born: Ossett, 5 June 1921.
Career: MIDDLESBROUGH 1946. Plymouth Argyle 1947. Walsall 1955.

■ Inside-left Dews was one of the lesser-known players of Boro's talented team immediately after World War Two. While teammates such as Mannion, Hardwick and Fenton earned the plaudits, Dews was a hard-working member of the Boro forward line which challenged for the title for much of 1946–47 only to fade in the final months of the season.

An Army corporal, he was stationed at Whitby when he signed as an amateur for the club, after scoring two goals in an Ayresome Park trial game in 1945. He received orders to return to London but instead signed professional, signing on in the pavilion at Egbaston cricket ground where he batted at number three as Worcestershire's captain. After playing games in the League North and FA Cup, he was joined by five others –

including Dicky Robinson and Jimmy Gordon – in making his First Division debut for the club on the opening day of 1946–47 against Aston Villa. He was a regular throughout the first half of the campaign, of which the highlight was a two-goal performance in a 4–2 success at Wolves, watched by a crowd of over 45,000. He lost his place to Cec McCormack early in 1947–48 and agreed to join Second Division Plymouth in an £11,000 deal which also saw Bobby Stuart make the move to Home Park. In a successful career with Plymouth, Dews was relegated but later won a Division Three South championship medal.

DIBBLE Andrew Gerald

Goalkeeper
Born: Cwmbran, 8 May 1965.
Career: Cardiff City 1982. Luton Town 1984. Sunderland (loan) 1986. Huddersfield Town (loan) 1987. Manchester City 1988. Aberdeen (loan) 1990. MIDDLESBROUGH (loan) 1991. Bolton Wanderers (loan) 1991. West Bromwich Albion (loan) 1992. Glasgow Rangers 1997. Luton Town 1997. MIDDLESBROUGH 1998. Altrincham 1998. Carmarthen Town 1998. Hartlepool United 1999. Carlisle United (loan) 1999. Stockport County 2000. Wrexham 2002. Accrington Stanley 2005.

■ Goalkeeper Andy Dibble had the misfortune to concede nine goals in two disastrous games as Boro's promotion challenge almost went off the tracks in

1998. But he should also be remembered for a much more successful loan spell on Teesside under Colin Todd's management in the early 1990s.

Dibble made his League debut for Cardiff on his 17th birthday before making his name with Luton Town, where he picked up a Littlewoods Cup-winners' medal in 1988, saving a penalty in an exciting 3–2 victory over Arsenal in the Final. A £250,000 fee took him to Manchester City and he helped them to promotion in 1990, only to lose his place to Tony Coton in the top flight.

His first spell with Boro came on loan midway through the 1990–91 season when Stephen Pears broke two fingers in a training accident. Despite Boro's inconsistencies, he did well and displayed safe handling as a place in the promotion Play-offs was secured. He needed special persmission from the Football League to take part in the Play-offs but was unable to help the club avoid a 2–1 aggregate defeat to Notts County. He returned to Maine Road as he knew Pears would be first choice again once he was fit. Dibble made a surprise return to Boro in 1998 after being on a month-by-month contract with Luton. He initially came as cover for Mark Schwarzer and Ben Roberts but when both 'keepers were injured, he was given his chance against Nottingham Forest, only to concede four goals as Boro were humbled in a top-of-the-table clash. Schwarzer had conceded only four in the previous seven games. Things went from bad to worse when Queen's Park Rangers romped to a 5–0 win three days later and it was clear that Dibble's confidence was shattered. Bryan Robson immediately signed Marlon Beresford and Dibble never played for the club again. After 23 years as a player, taking in 16 clubs, he retired aged 40 and had spells as goalkeeper coach at Accrington, Coventry and Peterborough.

DICKINSON Percival E. (Peter)

Outside-right
Born: Langley Moor, 19 January 1902.
Died: 1985.
Career: Willington Athletic. MIDDLESBROUGH 1924. Annfield Plain.

■ Outside-right Dickinson stepped up from non-League football to make his Second Division debut as Middlesbrough lost 1–0 at home to Hull in October 1924. His only goal came in a 2–2 draw at Coventry the following month but he lost his place to Billy Birrell and spent the remainder of the season in the cold. The club placed Dickinson on the transfer list for £250 at the end of the season but the Football League intervened and insisted that he be given a free transfer. After leaving Boro, he played for Annfield Plain.

DICKS Ronald William

Wing-half
Born: Kennington, 13 April 1924.
Died: 2005.
Career: Dulwich Hamlet. MIDDLESBROUGH 1943.

■ Such was the versatility of Ronnie Dicks that Boro manager David Jack nicknamed him 'The Handyman of Ayresome Park'. Dicks played in every position for the club, including goalkeeper, even keeping a clean sheet as replacement for the injured Rolando Ugolini against Leicester in 1954.

And yet, given the choice, Dicks would never have played a League game for Middlesbrough. He played wartime football for the club while stationed in the forces at an artillery training camp in Marske and signed professional terms before seeing active service in Burma. However, the Londoner wanted to return home to the capital when peace returned. The situation needed the firm

intervention of David Jack who told Dicks that he would not play football for any other club as Middlesbrough held his resignation. With little choice but to return to the North East, he made his First Division debut on the same day as Bill Whittaker and Derwick Goodfellow on the opening day of the 1947–48 season as Manchester United were held to a 2–2 draw at Ayresome Park.

Dicks' early games came at outside-left or outside-right but the form of Geoff Walker and Johnny Spuhler saw him switched to inside forward. He continued as a forward until an injury to wing-half Jimmy Gordon in August 1949, after which he mainly played in defence. Equally at home in either full-back berth or at half-back, he personally preferred the latter position and it was from there that he captained the club for two seasons 1956–58. A long throw specialist, Dicks possessed speed, deceptive body swerve and the ability to kick with either foot. He preferred not to chase the ball but would loiter until the ball came to him.

His excellent form and attitude in all positions brought him to national attention and he was asked to represent the Football League in February 1950, only to be denied by an Achilles injury. Another injury then cost him his place in the England B team for a game against Holland and his high hopes of joining Wilf Mannion in the England squad for the 1950 World Cup Finals came to nothing. Dicks retired from the game in 1958, aged 34, and stayed on Teesside, working for many years at Jack Hatfield's sports shop on Boro Road. Ronnie's younger brother, Alan, played for Chelsea, Southend and Brighton before managing Bristol City.

DICKSON Ian William

Centre-forward/Inside-right
Born: Maxwelltown, September 1902.
Career: Queen of the South. Aston Villa 1920. MIDDLESBROUGH 1923. Wesbrough.

■ Record signing Dickson failed to reproduce the form at Middlesbrough that had persuaded the club's directors to spend £3,000 to bring him to Ayresome Park. After making his name at Aston Villa, the centre-forward was signed midway through the 1923–24 season as replacement for the great Andy Wilson who had recently joined Chelsea. The transfer fee smashed the club's record set by Love Jones 15 years earlier but the directors were growing increasingly concerned about relegation from the First Division. After making his debut alongside William Wainscoat in a 2–1 defeat to Preston, he scored a hat-trick in his second home game as Burnley were beaten 3–0. It was Boro's first win in seven games. However, the anticipated goal rush never came and relegation followed at the end of the season. He was initially left out of the side in the Second Division as George Elliott was given his chance but won a recall for the second half of the season and ended the campaign as seven-goal joint top scorer with Owen Williams. He was given a free transfer in May 1926 after spending an entire season in the reserves.

DIXON Charles

Full-back
Born: Sacriston, 22 July 1891.
Career: Darlington. MIDDLESBROUGH 1919. Hartlepool United 1922.

■ Local lad Dixon played his first games for the club during Middlesbrough's championship success in the Northern Victory League of 1919. A right full-back, he made his First Division debut in the opening game of the 1919–20 season as League football resumed following the hostilities. However, he lost his place following a 4–1 home defeat to Aston Villa and spent the rest of the season in the reserves as Jock Marshall established himself as first choice right-back. Dixon played his final game for the club as Marshall's stand-in as a 40,000 crowd saw Boro lose 2–0 at St James' Park in February 1921.

DIXON Thomas

Outside-right/Inside-forward
Born: Cramlington.
Died: 1941.
Career: Bedlington United. MIDDLESBROUGH 1907. Watford 1911. Bristol Rovers 1913. Blyth Spartans.

■ Versatile forward Dixon played in every attacking position for Boro but was never able to make the leap from the reserves to first-team football on a regular basis. Playing at inside-forward, he made the perfect start to his career with the club, scoring as he and Eddie Verrill made their Middlesbrough debuts in a 2–0 win over Manchester City at Ayresome Park in November 1907. Dixon again rose to the challenge of standing in for England international Steve Bloomer the following week before being switched to centre-forward in the absence of another England star, Alf Common. He played further games as a winger, scoring twice from outside-right in a 3–1 home win over Chelsea on New Year's Day 1908. The majority of the following season was spent in the

reserves before responding to a call-up for the opening away game of the 1909–10 season, scoring the opening goal in a 5–1 win at Sheffield Wednesday and another two in the following week's 5–2 home victory over Woolwich Arsenal. But a return to the reserves followed soon afterwards and he played his final game for the club at Bradford City in April 1911.

DOBBIE Harold

Inside-forward
Born: Bishop Auckland, 20 February 1923.
Died: 1988.
Career: South Bank. MIDDLESBROUGH 1946. Plymouth Argyle 1950. Torquay United 1953.

■ Dobbie was Boro's reserve centre-forward in the era immediately after World War Two, during which he had seen active service with the Gordon Highlanders. Signed from South Bank St Peter's, he hit the headlines by scoring on his First Division debut as stand-in for the great Micky Fenton in February 1947. Although Boro lost the match 4–2 to Sheffield United, he was given another chance, at inside-forward, against Wolves five weeks later and again delighted the Ayresome Park crowd by finding the net, this time in a 1–1 draw. Fenton's form meant first-team chances remained few and far between, though he was given a run in the side in place of inside-forward Cec McCormack early in 1948–49 and scored two late goals in a 4–1 win over Burnley. However, the signing of Andy Donaldson was the directors' way of saying they did not see Dobbie as

Fenton's long-term replacement and the player moved on to Plymouth in March 1950, later enjoying his greatest success with Torquay in the Third Division South. He later returned to live on Teesside and died in 1988.

DOIG Thomas

Right-half
Born: Dundee, 1873.
Career: MIDDLESBROUGH 1900.

■ Scot Tom Doig's Middlesbrough career lasted just three weeks as the people of Teesside prepared to celebrate the first 20th-century Christmas. Although very little is known of the player, we do know that he made his Second Division debut at right-half in a 3–1 win over Blackpool at the Linthorpe Road ground on 1 December 1900. He retained his place for the next three games, one of them an FA Cup victory over Bishop Auckland, before new signing David Smith took his place. Doig was never called upon again and was released at the end of the season.

DONAGHY Peter

Centre-forward/Left-half
Born: Grangetown, 13 January 1898.
Career: Grangetown St Mary's. MIDDLESBROUGH 1919. Bradford City 1923. Carlisle United.

■ Left-half Donaghy's brother, Ted, was also on Middlesbrough's books and, like Peter, later played for Bradford before moving on to Derby. While Peter was the only one of the siblings to play first-team football for the club, he was never more than a squad player in four seasons as a professional at Ayresome Park. After playing his first games for the club in the Northern Victory League immediately after the Great War, local lad Donaghy left St Mary's to sign professional terms with Middlesbrough. He made his First Division debut in a 1–0 win at Bradford City in the penultimate game of 1919–20 and retained his place for the final match at Bolton. He was also in the side for the first two games of the following season, playing once at outside-left, before making way. His first run in the team came at the end of that season, replacing Bill Ellerington in the half-back line. As Boro again finished in the top half of Division One in 1921–22, he was unable to retain his regular place in competition with Bob Pender. He made a surprise first-team return against Sunderland in February 1923 as a stand-in for centre-forward Andy Wilson and duly scored his first goal for the club. Another strike followed against Everton a week later and he was given further opportunities at outside-left as relegation was narrowly avoided. However, he moved on to Bradford at the season's end after rejecting terms offered by the club of £5 in the summer, £6 in the season and £8 when playing.

DONALDSON Andrew

Centre-forward
Born: Newcastle-upon-Tyne, 22 March 1925.
Died: Peterborough, 20 June 1987.
Career: Vickers Armstrong. Newcastle United 1943. MIDDLESBROUGH 1949. Peterborough United 1951. Exeter City 1953. Peterborough United 1955.

■ It is not recorded whether Donaldson ever ran over a black cat but it is fair to say that he did not enjoy the best of luck in his football career. Not only did he have the misfortune to be a centre-forward at Newcastle at the same time as the legendary Jackie Milburn but, just when he was looking set to become a Boro star, he had his ankle broken – by one of his own players!

A tall, leggy forward, Donaldson was built like a greyhound and was a strong header of the ball. The Tynesider played his early football for South Benwell Boys and Vickers Armstrong before joining hometown club Newcastle during World War Two. He was highly rated at St James' Park but was a direct rival to Milburn, meaning chances were few and far between. By early 1949 he had already turned down moves to Manchester City, Spurs and Huddersfield but Boro were desperate to find a replacement for the ageing Micky Fenton. With that in mind, manager David Jack was sent to St James' with the order from the club's directors to sign the player 'irrespective of the fee'. Donaldson duly became Boro's first five-figure buy, his £17,000 fee almost trebling the club's previous transfer record for Ralph Birkett.

After an inauspicious debut in a 2–0 defeat at Charlton, the goals began to come and he netted several vital strikes as Boro avoided relegation by a single point. Crucial winners were scored against Huddersfield and Derby, while a sixth goal in 14 games snatched a point at Aston Villa on the final day of the season. Donaldson would have retained his place at centre-forward the following season but had the misfortune to break his ankle in a clash with Boro 'keeper Rolando Ugolini in a pre-season practice match and duly spent the entire season on the sidelines. It was November 1950 before he played again and his old sharpness had deserted him, Johnny Spuhler proving to be immovable as the new first choice centre-forward.

After leaving Boro, he enjoyed two spells with non-League Peterborough, becoming a huge crowd favourite and establishing himself as an all-time Posh great. Donaldson lived in Peterborough until he died in June 1987.

DORIVA Dorival Ghidoni

Midfield
Born: Landeara, Brazil, 28 May 1972.
Career: Sao Paulo 1993. Piracicaba 1995. Atletico Mineiro (Brazil) 1995. Porto (Portugal) 1997. Sampdoria (Italy) 1999. Celta Vigo (Spain) 2000. MIDDLESBROUGH 2003.

■ The Brazilian international was so successful as a cover player that his short-term contracts kept being renewed on an

annual basis so that he spent three-and-a-half useful seasons at the Riverside. Doriva's arrival from Celta Vigo in January 2003 did not make headlines, coming at the same time as Michael Ricketts, Chris Riggott and Malcolm Christie all joined, but he quickly proved his worth. The tough-tackling midfielder had played for some of the continent's biggest clubs – including Oporto and Sampdoria – enjoying European competition along the way while he had also been a member of Brazil's 1988 World Cup Squad. Doriva made 20 Premiership appearances in his first full season, won a Carling Cup-winners' medal and he was voted the club's Player of the Year by his teammates. The following year he was an integral part of Boro's first UEFA Cup campaign and made another 26 appearances. In his final 2005–06 season, he helped the club to the UEFA Cup Final but did not appear in the Eindhoven meeting with Sevilla. After being released he returned to Brazil but was surprisingly unable to find a club despite training with Serie A side America.

DOUGLAS Harry

Outside-right
Born: Hartlepool.
Career: South Bank. MIDDLESBROUGH 1902.

■ Outside-right Douglas was brought in from South Bank halfway through the 1902–03 season as Middlesbrough's directors desperately tried to end a poor run which threatened to bring relegation in the club's first top flight season. After making his debut in a defeat at WBA in January 1903, he made his home debut as Notts County were beaten 2–1 at Linthorpe Road the following Saturday. The club's biggest crowd of the season – 20,000 – saw his following match as Newcastle were beaten but Douglas played his final match for Boro at Liverpool two weeks later.

DOUGLAS John Stuart

Wing-half
Born: Hartlepool, 1 December 1917.
Career: Trimdon Grange. Hartlepool United 1938. MIDDLESBROUGH 1945. Hartlepool United 1948. Halifax Town 1950.

■ The Middlesbrough career of tireless left-half Douglas was sandwiched in between two spells with Hartlepool United. Douglas played his first League football for hometown club Hartlepool before World War Two and continued to play as an amateur throughout the hostilities, when he served with the RAF. He played his first games for Boro in the League North in 1945–46 in a half-back line which also included Jimmy Gordon and Harry Bell, making his official competitive debut for the club in a 4–4 FA Cup draw with Leeds United in January 1946. He netted his only goal for the club in the Ayresome Park replay, a 7–2 win. However, his chances were restricted following the arrival of Jimmy McCabe and Douglas played only twice in Division One alongside the likes of Mannion and Hardwick. He spent two years in the reserves before returning to Hartlepool in the Third Division North, later joining Halifax but failing to make any first-team appearances.

DOVE Craig

Forward
Born: Hartlepool, 16 August 1983.
Career: MIDDLESBROUGH 2000. York City (loan) 2003. Rushden & Diamonds 2004. Chester City 2005. Forest Green (loan) 2006.

■ A fast, quick and agile forward, Dove was highly rated as a schoolboy but struggled to make an impact at first-team level. The Hartlepool-born player was a member of the Boro side that reached the semi-finals of the FA Youth Cup in 1999–2000 season. Capped at Schoolboy and Youth levels for England, Dove featured regularly for the reserves and made his first-team debut as a late substitute in the 4–1 Worthington Cup second round win at Brentford in October 2002. He later had a brief run-out against Ipswich in the same competition. Dove failed to make a League breakthrough, however, and after a brief spell with York City he moved to Rushden and Diamonds in 2004, scoring six goals in 31 matches. He later moved to Chester City and had a loan spell with Conference side Forest Green.

DOW John M.

Right-back/Centre-forward
Born: Dundee 1873.
Career: Newton Heath 1893. Glossop North End. Luton Town 1898. MIDDLESBROUGH 1900. West Ham United. Luton Town 1905.

■ Dow was Middlesbrough's regular right full-back during their second season in the Football League in 1900–01. Signed from Luton Town, he made his debut along with eight others in a 2–0 home win over Lincoln City on the opening day of the season. He remained part of John Robson's side until early the following season but lost his place on the arrival of Joe Blackett. After spending the majority of the campaign in the reserves, it was no surprise when he was released in the summer of 1902.

DOWNING Derrick Graham

Winger
Born: Doncaster, 3 November 1945.
Career: Frickley Colliery. MIDDLESBROUGH 1965. Leyton Orient 1972. York City 1975. Hartlepool United 1977. Scarborough. Mexborough. Hatfield Main.

■ Flying winger Downing was a fixture in the Boro side for seven seasons and is

best remembered by those who saw him for the many goals he scored with brave diving headers. Downing was a clerk on leaving school and played for Doncaster at Youth and reserve team level before signing for Cheshire League side Frickley Colliery. His form brought him to the attention of Raich Carter who brought him to Boro midway through the 1964–65 season, though the player initially believed he was set to join Burnley. After several months in the reserves, he and Stan Marshall were given their debuts at home to Norwich in October 1965, Downing replacing Don Ratcliffe in the starting line-up.

He was given his first run in the side in place of Eddie Holliday in late January as relegation began to loom large and netted his first goal in only his third game for the club in Carter's final game in charge, a 3–1 home defeat to Huddersfield Town. The season ended in the disaster of relegation to the Third Division for the first time in the club's history but Downing was one of the stars of Stan Anderson's side as promotion was secured at the first time of asking. Sporting long sideburns and receding hair, Downing provided strong and speedy wing play, was a non-stop runner and boasted an excellent shot. He was also a hard, crisp tackler when the need arose, an attribute which further endeared him to the club's loyal supporters, the Ayresome Angels. He missed much of Boro's return to the Second Division through injury but he ended the 1968–69 season as the club's top scorer after John Hickton. A long throw specialist, he could reach the far post from throw-ins near the corner flag but he was particularly noted for his diving headers, a prime example of which came in a famous FA Cup victory over an all-star West Ham side in 1970.

The goals and crosses continued to flow but Boro constantly fell short of promotion to deny Downing his dream of top flight football. Boro blocked a move from Crystal Palace manager George Petchey but Downing was released at the end of 1971–72 following a knee injury and Petchey, by then at Orient, finally got his man. At Brisbane Road, Downing was converted to left-back and, despite a reoccurence of the knee injury, enjoyed several good seasons before becoming unsettled and joining York. Further moves came to Billy Horner's Hartlepool and non-League Scarborough and Mexborough before a spell at Hatfield Main as player-manager. After retiring from the game, Downing, a keen angler and tropical fish enthusiast, tried his hand at the nightclub business before working in a garage. He now lives in retirement in Doncaster.

DOWNING Stewart

Midfield

Born: Middlesbrough, 22 July 1984.

Career: MIDDLESBROUGH 2001. Sunderland (loan) 2003.

■ The Middlesbrough-born winger is one of the Academy's finest products and is firmly established for his club and England. Downing's pinpoint deliveries from the left wing have become a vital weapon in Boro's armoury and he has also weighed in with vital goals. He stepped up to the professional ranks in September 2001, making his debut aged 17 at Ipswich Town towards the end of the 2001–02 season. The youngster had to be patient for his chance the following year, with Bolo Zenden and Jonathan Greening also competing for places on the flanks. He did, however, score his first goal in a 4–1 Worthington Cup win over Brentford. It was not until the 2003–04 campaign that he really began to flower – initially on loan at Sunderland. Downing scored three goals in seven appearances for the Black Cats, who were keen to make the deal permanent while Wigan were also interested. But his form did not go unnoticed by Steve McClaren, who gave him another chance towards the end of the season. Downing never looked

back. Although he did not make the Carling Cup Final team, he soon won England Under-21 recognition. A long-term contract followed and he established himself as a first choice in the 2004–05 season when Zenden moved inside to central midfield. He missed just three of the club's 51 games and won his first full England cap against Holland at Villa Park in February 2005. He enjoyed another England call-up for the end-of-season tour in America, but had to fly home for knee surgery. Ongoing problems caused him to miss most of the first half of the busy 2005–06 season, but he returned to play a key part in the historic UEFA Cup victories over Roma, Basel and Steaua Bucharest that culminated in defeat to Sevilla in the Final. Downing was selected for Sven Goran Eriksson's 2006 World Cup squad in Germany where he made three appearances from the bench. New Boro manager Gareth Southgate made Downing a central part of his plans and rebuffed interest from Spurs and Everton. He was also in demand at international level, where his former boss, Steve McClaren, picked him in place of the injured Joe Cole in a stuttering start to the Euro 2008 qualifying campaign. At the end of another fine season at club level he had collected 14 England caps, more than any player but Wilf Mannion in Boro's history. He also scored his first two goals for England B in a friendly with Albania.

DOWSON Francis

Left-half/Inside-left
Born: North Ormesby 1897.
Career: MIDDLESBROUGH 1920. Hartlepool United 1922. Spennymoor United.

■ Few players can boast a two-goal display against Manchester United but that is exactly what inside-left Dowson achieved in one of only seven appearances for Middlesbrough. Originally joining the club as an amateur during the 1919–20 season, he signed professional forms and made his debut in a 1–1 draw at Sheffield United in January 1921, playing in a Boro side that included greats like Jacky Carr, George Elliott and Tim Williamson. Nicknamed 'Sankey', he was given only occasional chances by the club's directors but his moment of glory came with a two-goal display as Boro beat Manchester United 3–1 at Ayresome Park in a First Division match in late March. Instead of being the lift off to a great career, he played only three more times for the club and spent the entire 1921–22 campaign on the sidelines.

DUFFY Christopher Francis

Outside-left
Born: Jarrow 1885.
Career: Brentford 1905. MIDDLESBROUGH 1905. Newcastle United 1906. Bury 1908. North Shields Athletic. Bury 1914. Bradford City. Leicester City 1919. Chester-le-Street 1920.

■ Speedy Tynesider Duffy was brought to Middlesbrough in an attempt to solve the team's problem position of outside-left. The club's directors had chopped and changed the number-11 position throughout the 1904–05 season and Duffy became the third player to be given a chance to fill the gap in 1905–06, even though the season was little more than a month old. He made his debut as an amateur in an emphatic 5–1 victory over Bury at Ayresome Park as George Reid netted a hat-trick and retained his place for the next three games. However, Tom Coxon was recalled following a 4–1 defeat at Newcastle and Duffy spent the remainder of the season in the reserves.

He returned 'home' to Newcastle in the summer of 1906 as wing cover and played seven times during United's championship success of 1906–07. Although born in Jarrow, he attended school in Hammersmith and turned to football after winning several prizes as a sprinter and qualifying as a teacher. He played as an amateur for hometown club Jarrow before joining Brentford while completing his further education in Hammersmith. Regular football finally came his way at Bury, who were then in Division One, before returning to the North East with non-League North Shields Athletic. After World War One, he joined Leicester and then Chester-le-Street before becoming a teacher on Tyneside on his retirement from the game.

DUGUID William

Wing-half/Centre-half
Born: Wishaw.
Career: Albion Rovers. MIDDLESBROUGH 1910.

■ Versatile Duguid spent three seasons as a Middlesbrough reserve, making occasional first-team appearances to cover for the club's regular defenders. The Scot made his debut in Boro's half-back line in a 2–0 First Divison home win over Tottenham in October 1910, standing in for the injured Billy Barker. Two weeks later, Duguid was selected again, this time at inside-left alongside a young George Elliott. Later in the same season he again stood in for first choice defenders and even played at left full-back on one occasion. He was given a short run in the side in place of Andy Jackson early the following season but again played most of his football for the club's second string, before further showing his ability as a utility player when he was selected at right full-back several times during the 1912–13 campaign. Nothing is known of his career after leaving Ayresome Park in 1913.

ECKFORD John

Outside-left
Born: Buckhaven, 13 February 1878.
Career: Raith Rovers. Luton Town 1899. MIDDLESBROUGH 1900. Raith Rovers 1900.

■ Left-sided forward Eckford was handed his Football League chance in November 1900 after impressing in FA Cup victories over non-League sides Willington Athletic and Jarrow. He was picked at outside-left for a trip to Woolwich Arsenal which Boro lost 1–0. He played the following two games at inside-left but was dropped after a 1–0 home defeat to Small Heath and returned to his native Scotland.

EDWARDS William Inman

Centre-forward
Born: Bowburn, 10 December 1933.
Career: Bowburn. MIDDLESBROUGH 1952.

■ Bill Edwards made an impressive debut at centre-forward seven months

after his arrival. He scored the first goal after 11 minutes with an excellent header in a 3–3 draw at Molineux in October 1952. Boro had struggled for a consistent frontman since the retirement of Micky Fenton a few years before but Edwards was not the answer. He vied with Ken McPherson throughout the 1953–54 season but went part-time in 1954–55. The arrival of Charlie Wayman ended his first-team hopes and he was released at the end of the campaign.

EGLINGTON Robert

Inside-left
Born: Thornaby.
Career: Thornaby. MIDDLESBROUGH 1899.

■ Inside-left Eglington scored on his Middlesbrough debut and helped secure the club's first point in the Football League. After three defeats, he scored his goal in a 1–1 draw with New Brighton. In the following game, Eglington's strike against Grimsby Town at the old Linthorpe Road ground gave Boro their first ever Football League victory at the fifth time of asking. However, he played his final game for the club just six weeks later and was released at the end of the season.

EHIOGU Ugochuku (Ugo)

Defender
Born: Hackney, 3 November 1972.
Career: West Bromwich Albion 1989. Aston Villa 1991. MIDDLESBROUGH 2000. Leeds United (loan) 2006. Rangers 2007.

■ Ehiogu became Bryan Robson's last major signing when he joined from Aston Villa for a record £8 million in November 2000. The commanding centre-back spent the next seven years at the Riverside and saw a club fighting for survival transformed into an established Premiership force. He re-established the partnership he had formed with Gareth Southgate at Villa Park and the high point of his Boro career came when he helped the club to Carling Cup success in 2004. Ehiogu started his career at West Bromwich Albion where he made only a handful of appearances before being snapped up by Villa in 1991. He won his first League Cup-winners' medal with the Midlands club and had an outstanding game in their losing 2000 FA Cup Final against Chelsea. After 303 appearances for Villa, he was thrust into a relegation battle with Boro. He endured a nightmare debut at Charlton where he was forced to leave the pitch with a calf injury after only five minutes. On his return two months later he was sent off against West Ham at Upton Park. He really proved his worth over the next

two seasons in helping Boro to preserve their top-flight status. His excellent form in the early Steve McClaren era won him a recall for England, scoring in a 3–0 victory over Spain. He went on to win his third and fourth caps against Holland and Italy in 2001–02. The following season, despite suffering broken ribs and a punctured lung in an aerial challenge with Blackburn's Brad Friedel, he continued to succeed alongside Southgate. He then missed the first half of the 2003–04 season with a torn posterior cruciate ligament, but on his return he continued to produce outstanding displays, not least in the famous Cardiff victory over Bolton. Further injuries blighted his 2004–05 campaign, although he managed to end the season on a high note by featuring in the closing games as Boro clinched a second season in Europe. Ehiogu was sent off in the opening game of the 2005–06 campaign against Liverpool, and despite more injuries managed 16 League appearances and was an unused substitute in the UEFA Cup Final. New manager Southgate allowed him to join Leeds on loan in 2006 and he later joined Rangers on a free transfer during the January transfer window. He totalled 150 games in a Boro shirt. Ehiogu became an instant cult icon at Ibrox when he scored a spectacular overhead winner in an Old Firm derby with Celtic.

ELKES Albert John

Inside-left/Centre-half
Born: Snedshill, 31 December 1894.
Died: Rayleigh, 22 January 1972.
Career: Wellington St George's. Stalybridge Celtic. Shifnal Town. Birmingham 1919. Southampton 1921. Tottenham Hotspur 1923. MIDDLESBROUGH 1929. Watford 1933. Stafford Rangers. Oakengates Town.

■ Jack Elkes was 33 when he came to Middlesbrough at the end of a successful career, particularly with Spurs. He played most of his games at half-back but could also operate at inside-forward where he had played at the start of his career. Elkes had come close to England caps at White Hart Lane. He was named as reserve and toured Australia with an FA party in 1925. A tall, intelligent footballer, Elkes was brought to Ayresome by former Spurs manager Peter McWilliam. Although primarily a defender, he scored twice in a 5–2 defeat at Liverpool while standing in for George Camsell at centre-forward in December 1929. He contested a place in the defence with Maurice Webster for several seasons but lost out when Tom Griffiths arrived. Elkes died in January 1972 in Rayleigh, Essex.

ELLERINGTON William

Centre-half/Left-half
Born: Sunderland.
Career: Darlington. MIDDLESBROUGH 1919. Nelson 1924.

■ Bill Ellerington was a bargain purchase from amateur Darlington and proved to be an astute buy. He was a regular for several seasons in the years after World War One alternating between the centre and left-half positions. He made his debut in the club's first post-war fixture – a 1–0 victory at Sheffield Wednesday. After three and a half seasons as a first-team player, he lost his place to Maurice Webster following a 3–0 defeat at Burnley. After a handful of games in the next year, he moved on Nelson. His son, also Bill, was an England international in 1949 with Southampton.

ELLIOTT George Washington

Centre-forward/Inside-forward
Born: Sunderland, 7 January 1889.
Died: November 1948.
Career: Redcar Crusaders. South Bank. MIDDLESBROUGH 1909.

■ Elliott went against the wishes of his family to pursue a football career and Middlesbrough reaped the rewards with more than 15 years great service and a glut of goals. He was a phenomenal centre-forward with a great strike rate. Elliott was the first of several homegrown frontmen who starred for their club and won England recognition.

The son of a sea-faring captain also named George, he had moved with his family to the town as a boy and excelled at Middlesbrough High School. He was expected to go to Cambridge University but resisted, preferring to play football and winning the Northern League with South Bank before signing for Middlesbrough. Elliott was tucked up in bed at 10pm on 23 May 1909 when a Boro director called at his Southfield Road home. He was taken together with his father to a nearby hotel where he signed on the dotted line.

After playing his early games at inside-right, he was moved into the centre-forward berth with great success. He was the club's leading scorer for seven out of nine seasons from 1910 to 23 and is second in Boro's all-time scorers list. Elliott holds the record for the most goals scored in a competitive Boro game, scoring 11 in a 14–1 reserve victory over Houghton Rovers. Captain from 1913 to 1921, he was also the Football League's top scorer in 1913–14 – the first Boro player to achieve that feat – in a season where the club finished in its highest ever position of third in the old First Division. In that season he had a great partnership with inside forward Walter Tinsley, shown clearly when they combined for Elliott to notch a hat-trick in a 3–0 win over the eventual champions Blackburn.

After winning his first international cap against Ireland in 1913, Elliott played against the same opponents in only the second international to be played at Ayresome Park. War intervened and Elliott's final international was against Wales in the first home official post-war international.

As he got into his 30s Elliott slowed down and was unable to avoid the crunching tackles as he had before. After several injuries, he played his last game against Southampton in April 1925 and, despite attractive offers from Sunderland and Newcastle, he decided to retire in that summer. Elliott's father had always insisted that he had a job to fall back on and throughout his playing career he was a cargo superintendent at Middlesbrough Docks. He continued his trade but soon hit the headlines when he was involved in a reported drink-driving incident that resulted in the death of a young boy. Elliott died in Middlesbrough General Hospital in November 1948 and was interned in Acklam Cemetery.

EMERSON, see MOISES COSTA Emerson

EMMERSON George Arthur Heads

Outside-right
Born: Bishop Auckland, 15 May 1906.
Died: 1966.
Career: Jarrow. MIDDLESBROUGH 1928. Cardiff City 1930. Queen's Park Rangers 1933. Rochdale 1935. Tunbridge Wells Rangers. Gillingham 1937.

■ Outside-right Emmerson made an impressive impact on the Middlesbrough first team when he scored a hat-trick in his second game for the club. Emmerson

had impressed in the reserves after signing from Jarrow but had found his progress blocked by the excellent Billy Pease. His chance came in mid-season in 1928–29 when he played against Oldham, Millwall and Swansea, scoring all three in the 3–0 win over the Lions, before Pease returned. His only other appearance that season was in the final game of the campaign when a 3–0 win over Grimsby secured the Second Division title and Emmerson set up one of the goals for Camsell. Pease continued to shine for several seasons and Emmerson moved on in search of regular football.

EMMERSON Morris

Goalkeeper
Born: Sunniside, 23 October 1942.
Career: MIDDLESBROUGH 1959. Peterborough United 1963.

■ England Schoolboy international goalkeeper Morris Emmerson made his big first-team breakthrough shortly after his 20th birthday. His debut came against Bury in mid-November 1962 following injuries to Arthur Lightening and Bob Appleby. Although small for a 'keeper, it was a commendable performance from the youngster but he made only 13 first-team appearances before Lightening and then Appleby returned to the team. After a short spell at Peterborough he worked in computing at ICI for many years.

EUELL Jason

Midfield/striker
Born: Lambeth, 6 February 1977.
Career: Wimbledon 1995. Charlton Athletic 2001. MIDDLESBROUGH 2006.

■ The Londoner was one of Gareth Southgate's first signings and his ability to play as striker or advanced midfielder made him a useful squad member. Euell started his career at Wimbledon where he suffered relegation from the Premiership. Charlton signed him for £4.75 million in 2001 and he enjoyed five eventful seasons at The Valley where he helped them to bounce back to the top flight in 2004 after relegation the previous year. He scored 34 goals in 134 games for the Addicks. Euell settled into his new surroundings on Teesside and made an impressive debut at the Emirates Stadium, where he laid on a skilful pass for James Morrison's opener in a 1–1 draw. The consistency of Mark Viduka and Yakubu meant he enjoyed few chances in the forward line and had to be content with long periods on the bench. Jamaican international Euell, who made nine League starts in his first season on Teesside, also picked up a knee injury in the second half of the campaign.

EUSTACE John

Midfield
Born: Solihull, 3 November 1979.
Career: Coventry City 1996. Dundee United (loan) 1999. MIDDLESBROUGH 2003. Stoke City 2003.

■ Steve McClaren signed the midfielder on loan in 2003 from Coventry City with a view to a permanent transfer, but Boro never took up the option. Eustace made only one substitute appearance when he replaced Malcolm Christie in the 87th minute during a 1–1 draw with Liverpool at Anfield. The former Highfield Road favourite moved to Stoke City at the end of the season and was loaned out to Hereford United in 2006–07.

EVANS R. William

Inside-left
Born: Thornaby, 1875.
Career: Whitby Town. Bury 1898. Gainsborough Trinity 1898. MIDDLESBROUGH 1899.

■ Just two first appearances came the way of inside-left Evans. Arriving from Bury, he played in a 1–0 victory over Woolwich Arsenal before a 5–2 defeat at Barnsley ended his brief Middlesbrough career. The Boro directors were looking for the right calibre of player following the club's elevation to the Football League and obviously didn't feel Evans fitted the bill.

EYRE Edmund

Outside-left
Born: Worksop, December 1884.
Died: 1943.
Career: Worksop West End. Worksop. Rotherham Town. Birmingham 1906. Aston Villa 1908. MIDDLESBROUGH 1911. Birmingham 1913.

■ Known to all as 'Ninty', Eyre operated at outside-right in the seasons immediately before World War One. He was thrown straight into the starting line-up for the opening game of the 1911–12 campaign and held his place for the majority of the season. James Nicholl was Eyre's main rival for the left wing berth and he gradually fell out of favour as Nichol and then converted inside-forward John Cook took his place.

FABIO, see MOREIRA DA SILVA Fabio

FALCONER William Henry

Left-back/Midfield
Born: Aberdeen, 5 April 1966.
Career: Lewis United. Aberdeen 1982. Watford 1988. MIDDLESBROUGH 1991. Sheffield United 1993. Glasgow

Celtic 1994. Motherwell 1996. Dundee 1998. St Johnstone 2001. Grimsby Town (loan) 2002. Clyde 2002.

■ Many Boro fans will remember Willie Falconer with mixed feelings. For the first few weeks after his arrival on Teesside, he looked capable of establishing himself as one of the greats of the club's recent history but injury and loss of form meant he never fulfilled that early promise.

A Scotland Schoolboy and Youth international, Falconer joined Aberdeen from Lewis United and made his first-team debut in the semi-final of the 1983 European Cup-winners' Cup. Although he did not appear in the final victory over Real Madrid, he was a fringe member of Alex Ferguson's squad as they won two League titles, plus Scottish Cup, League Cup and European Super Cup honours. His ability as a goalscoring midfielder brought him to Watford's attention and he joined them in the First Division in 1988 for £300,000. After three seasons, during which Watford were relegated, he was ready to move on and spoke to two other clubs before joining Boro in a deal which also saw Paul Wilkinson make the switch to Ayresome Park and Trevor Putney move in the opposite direction.

A left-sided midfielder, Falconer made an immediate impact with a string of outstanding early season performances. An excellent passer of the ball, his willingness to get stuck in made him a hit with the fans but his true value was as a playmaker who revelled in racing into the box to join the attack. He scored four goals in six games during August and September, including a sensational strike on his return to Vicarage Road to play Watford. However, a bad knee injury sidelined him for six months and he was not the same player on his return to the side in March. He did, however, come desperately close to claiming a place in the club's hall of fame on his return to first-team action in the second leg of the Rumbelows Cup semi-final against Manchester United at Old Trafford. His header looked goal-bound all the way but a wonder save from Peter Schmeichel kept United in it and their star-studded team went on to clinch an extra-time victory. Falconer was a regular as promotion was secured to the inaugural Premier League, playing several games at left-back in place of the injured Jimmy Phillips, but he no longer had the influence of his earlier appearances.

He was, however, watched by Scotland boss Andy Roxburgh late in the season but turned down the chance to join the 1992 European Championships squad as his wife was due to have a baby. He was never called up again. Injury and loss of form meant he was in and out of the side as Premier League status was lost after only one season and he moved on to Sheffield United the following summer as he was keen to continue in the top flight. Lennie Lawrence wanted £600,000 for Falconer but the Blades offered only half that amount. A tribunal finally set the fee at £450,000. However, he returned to Scotland with Celtic a year later, where he was frequently used out of position in attack, before moving on to Motherwell.

FEATHERSTONE Thomas Frederick

Outside-right/Centre-forward
Born: Darlington.
Career: MIDDLESBROUGH 1993. Bolton Wanderers 1994. Leyton.

■ Centre-forward Featherstone played just one match in a Middlesbrough shirt before moving on to Bolton. The Darlington-born player was snapped up from local football to stand in for regular centre-forward Sandy Brown when Boro's top scorer missed his only game of the season in April 1904. The First Division game at Bury ended in a 1–1 draw and Brown returned for the following match.

FENTON Michael

Centre-forward
Born: Stockton on Tees, 30 October 1913.
Died: Stockton on Tees, 5 February 2003.
Career: South Bank East End. MIDDLESBROUGH 1933.

■ One of Middlesbrough's greatest ever servants, Micky Fenton was a prolific goalscorer over a 15-year career that would have produced even more had it not been interrupted by World War Two. Blessed with pace and a blistering shot with either foot, he stands fifth in the list of the club's all-time top scorers with 147 League goals. We will never know how many more Fenton might have scored had the war not denied him seven seasons of football when he would have been at the peak of his game.

On leaving school, Fenton worked in a butcher's while playing for Princess Street juniors and then South Bank East End. As a teenager, he accepted a month's trial with Wolves, but returned after one day and signed professional for Middlesbrough, aged 19. He was given his First Division debut at inside-forward in place of Bob Baxter on the final day of the 1932–33 campaign and scored in a 4–0 win over Blackburn. More games followed at inside-forward and even as an outside-right over the next three seasons but he did not win a regular starting slot until 1936–37 when, for the first time, he was given the chance to show he could succeed the legendary but ageing George Camsell at centre-forward. Never the biggest of players, he weighed only 9st 12lb when he signed for the club and put on only a further 6lbs over the next five years. Indeed, the club's directors were so concerned at his slim physique that they considered sending him to a health farm to beef him up. Initially, Fenton frequently partnered Camsell in attack but the directors began to realise that he was fulfilling his early promise and blossoming into the complete centre-forward. That season he ended Camsell's run of 10 consecutive seasons as the club's top scorer.

With a blistering turn of pace, good control and a terrific shot, Fenton was the perfect leader of the line. Goals came quick and fast, including two against champions elect Arsenal in March 1938 in front of then record Ayresome Park crowd of almost 47,000. He fully deserved his call-up to the England team against Scotland in April 1938 and celebrated with a four-goal performance for Boro against WBA on the final day of the League season. Sadly, it was to be his only England cap though he toured South Africa with the FA team the following year. Fenton's shooting ability continued to terrify opposing goalkeepers as Boro challenged for the title in 1938–39, while he also proved to be lethal from free kicks and was an excellent header of the ball. The only criticism that could be made of him was that he had a tendency to fiddle about with the ball in the penalty area and would always shoot rather than pass. But perhaps that was the hallmark of a great goalscorer.

With Fenton, a young Wilf Mannion and experienced stars like Bob Baxter and Duncan McKenzie in the side, Boro looked certain to challenge for the League title in 1939–40 but war denied them that chance. Fenton joined the RAF and saw service in North Africa and Egypt, while winning one wartime cap and guesting for Blackpool. Indeed, the Seasiders were keen to buy him when peace returned and Everton tried to sign him as a replacement for England legend Tommy Lawton in 1946. By then, Fenton was approaching his 33rd birthday but was still a lethal marksman, having scored four goals against Stoke the previous month. With much conjecture about his future, Fenton was dropped for a trip to Derby but club chairman Bill Kelly insisted that the player himself should decide whether to stay or go. Fenton opted to remain at Ayresome Park, though it was said he might have joined the Goodison club if they had offered him a business opportunity once his playing days were over. He went on to top Boro's scorers for the first three seasons after the war, playing his final game in an emergency in January 1950 as a replacement for Peter McKennan. Fenton had travelled to Villa Park as coach but was drafted in when Jimmy Gordon failed to make the team. He remained a member of the club's coaching staff and trainer to the reserves until 1965, also running a newsagents. He was still a regular visitor to Middlesbrough's home games in his late 80s.

FERGUSON Charles

Outside-right/Inside-left
Born: Dunfermline, 22 November 1910.
Died: 1995.
Career: Yoker Athletic. Glasgow Benburb. MIDDLESBROUGH 1933. Notts County 1936. Luton Town 1937. Aberdeen.

■ Forward Charlie Ferguson won more acclaim as a scout for Sunderland than he ever did as a player with Middlesbrough, Notts County or Luton. The Scot was responsible for taking nine of Sunderland's 1973 FA Cup winning team to Roker Park.

Ferguson was an apprentice plater in Glasgow shipyards while playing part-time football before turning professional with Boro. He picked the wrong match in which to make his First Division debut as his side lost 3–0 at home to Birmingham that day in September 1933. However, he retained his place at outside-right and gave George Camsell a regular supply of chances while netting five times himself in a run of just four games. Even so, his goal and excellent overall performance in a memorable 10–3 win over hapless Sheffield United in November 1933 was reported to have justified the directors' persistence in playing him when he was out of form.

A shin injury caused Ferguson to sit out the entire 1934–35 season and he was given only more first-team chance, standing in for Ralph Birkett in a 2–0 home defeat to Birmingham in December 1935. The following summer he moved on to Notts County. After the war, he scouted for Sheffield United and Burnley and was manager-coach of Newcastle United's youth team, the Corinthians. He also had the dubious distinction of being Gateshead's last League manager, having been appointed shortly before the club was voted out of the Football League in 1960.

FERGUSON Robert

Goalkeeper
Born: Grangetown, 27 July 1917.
Career: Hurworth Juniors. Sunderland 1933. MIDDLESBROUGH 1936. York City 1939. Peterborough United. Goole Town.

■ Goalkeeper Bob Ferguson played the majority of his games for Middlesbrough while still a teenager. After playing his early football with Hurworth Juniors, he was on Sunderland's books without making the first team. His big break came when Wilf Gillow snapped him up for a £2,000 fee and made him Boro's first choice 'keeper in preference to the ageing Fred Gibson at the start of 1936–37. He played just eight First Division games before being dropped and replaced by new signing Dave Cumming when he conceded 11 goals

in away games against Stoke and Grimsby. Although he didn't play again that season, he was recalled briefly early the next season but then found himself behind both Cumming and Paddy Nash in the pecking order. He was out in the cold for almost two full seasons before accepting a move to York City shortly before the outbreak of World War Two.

Ferguson played a few post-war games for York before turning his attentions to his other sporting talent, cricket. An excellent wicketkeeper and batsman, he was a prolific run scorer in the Bradford League and played the game until his late 40s when he took up bowls with considerable success.

FERGUSON Robert Gibson

Centre-half/Right-back
Born: Glasgow.
Career: Battlefield. Queen's Park Rangers. Sunderland 1921. MIDDLESBROUGH 1924. Crystal Palace 1931.

■ Although not always popular with the fans, Bob Ferguson was a reliable defender for eight seasons at Ayresome Park, during which he played his part in two Second Division championship successes.

Having joined Sunderland from Battlefield Juniors, he became a Middlesbrough player midway through the 1924–25 season. Although signed as a centre-half, he was rarely given the opportunity to play in that role in his first year at the club after making his debut in place of Maurice Webster in a 3–1 Second Division defeat at Derby in February 1925. Quiet and uncomplaining, he struggled to win over the Boro fans, who were especially critical of his recall at centre-half in October 1926 when Webster was ruled out through injury. However, he went on to play a key role in that season's record-breaking promotion and remained a regular first teamer for the next three seasons as First Division status was lost and then regained at the first attempt.

Ferguson's gait gave the appearance of slowness but he actually had deceptive speed. He was also versatile enough to be converted to right full-back early in the 1929–30 season until the signing of Jack Jennings. His final first-team appearances came at left full-back but the arrival of Tom Freeman saw him relegated to the reserves. Transfer listed at the end of the 1931–32 season after a year in the second team, he joined Crystal Palace early the next season and took charge of Northwich Victoria in 1933. Ferguson was also a talented cricketer and was wicketkeeper for Darlington RA.

FERNIE William

Inside-forward
Born: Kinglassie, 22 November 1928.
Career: Leslie Hearts. Kinglassie Colliery. Glasgow Celtic 1948. MIDDLESBROUGH 1958. Glasgow Celtic 1960. St Mirren 1961. Alloa Athletic 1963. Fraserburgh 1963. Coleraine 1964. Bangor 1964.

■ In his day, Scotland international Willie Fernie was a mesmeric and masterly dribbler, capable of turning a game with one piece of skill. Unfortunately, his best days were behind him when he joined Boro and he stayed only two years on Teesside before returning to Glasgow Celtic, the scene of his greatest glories.

Fernie had played for Leslie Hearts in a Scottish juvenile Cup Final before joining Celtic at the relatively late age of 21. A ball playing inside-forward, he boasted a beautiful silky touch, though he often took his skill to extremes and his goal return was disappointing for a player of his talents. In nine years at Celtic, he won Scottish League and Cup medals, together with two League Cup honours, while representing Scotland at B and full level, including appearances in the 1954 and 1958 World Cup Finals.

Boro were a mediocre Second Division side when manager Bob Dennison and director George Winney drove to Glasgow to sign him midway through the 1958–59 campaign for a fee which matched the club's previous record, paid out for Bill Harris four years earlier. However, he didn't get on with Brian Clough at Ayresome Park and the pair disagreed over principles and style. Fernie had been told by Dan Murphy, the scout who took him to Celtic, never to pass the ball unless it was to his team's advantage. That became his football philosophy though it didn't always

endear him to supporters or teammates, least of all Clough. Fernie's renowned independent streak resulted in frequent angry exchanges with Clough, who disproved of his tendency to beat another defender rather than pass. Clough would often turn away in disgust and with his nickname for him of 'My Ball Fernie' helped turn Boro's supporters against him.

Fernie left Boro to return to Parkhead for a season before a £4,000 move to St Mirren. He later left Scotland for a spell with Bangor in Ireland and turned down the chance to be Drogheda's player-manager to take up a role as Celtic's youth coach in 1967. He managed Kilmarnock during the mid–1970s before running a Glasgow taxi firm.

FESTA Gianluca

Central defender
Born: Cagliari, Sardinia, 15 March 1969.
Career: Cagliari 1987. Fersulcis (loan) 1987. Inter Milan 1993. AS Roma (loan) (Italy) 1993. MIDDLESBROUGH 1997. Portsmouth 2002. Cagliari 2003. Nuorese (Italy) 2004.

■ Defensive performances and an off-the-pitch character full of passion made Gianluca Festa one of the most popular overseas players to have appeared for Boro. Among Boro's myriad of controversial foreign signings, Festa stood out both on and off the pitch as a perfect ambassador for overseas players. Signed by Bryan Robson from Italian giants Inter Milan in a bid to stave off

relegation during the 1996–97 season, many believed Festa would follow the example of Boro's other Italian import, Fabrizio Ravanelli, and leave the club when Premier League status was lost. Instead, the defender stayed loyal to his new employers and over the following years earned a reputation as a talented and physical centre-back who always played with his heart on his sleeve. A Sardinian, rather than an Italian, Festa played for his hometown club Cagliari for seven years, having made the first team as a 17-year-old. After helping them into Serie A and the UEFA Cup, he earned a move to star-studded Inter Milan. With first-team football not always easy to come by at the San Siro, he spent a season on loan with Roma before establishing himself with Inter where his teammates included Paul Ince and Christian Ziege. He played against Boro in Willie Maddren's benefit match in 1996. After losing his place and falling out with officials at Inter, he joined Boro midway through the 1996–97 campaign, signing in the same week as Vladimir Kinder. Replacing Derek Whyte in central defence, Festa scored on his Boro debut in a crucial 4–2 home win over Sheffield Wednesday but was unable to help the club avoid relegation. He did, however, appear in both the 1997 Coca-Cola and FA Cup Finals, having a headed goal ruled out for offside in the latter.

His passionate displays, with trademark hard tackling and commanding headers, made him a big crowd favourite, a popularity which resulted in his selection as the supporters' club Player of the Year for 1998, a season in which he helped clinch promotion and played in his third Wembley Cup Final in just 12 months. Although naturally at home in the centre of defence, he showed his versatility by covering at right-back and in midfield when the need arose. Despite strong competition from the likes of Ugo Ehiogu, Gary Pallister, Steve Vickers and Colin Cooper, he remained a regular choice under Bryan Robson and Terry Venables. Injury meant he missed much of Steve McClaren's first season in charge but he returned to the side, only to suffer the misfortune of scoring an own goal that proved crucial in Boro's FA Cup semi-final with Arsenal in April 2002.

That summer he left Boro on a free transfer, joining Portsmouth, helping them to win promotion to the Premiership before returning to Italy with his first club Cagliari. He then continued in the Italian lower Leagues, helping Nuorese gain back-to-back promotions.

FITZSIMONS Arthur Gerard

Inside-forward
Born: Dublin, 16 December 1929.
Career: Shelbourne 1946. MIDDLESBROUGH 1949. Lincoln City

1959. Mansfield Town 1959. Wisbech Town.

■ Only two players, Mark Schwarzer and Wilf Mannion, won more international caps as Middlesbrough players than Fitzsimons. A scheming inside-forward, he was a skilful player who spent a decade with Boro after initially struggling to win a first-team place.

Fitzsimons arrived on Teesside from Irish side Shelbourne along with Peter Desmond during the 1949 close season, having foresaken his apprenticeship as a motor mechanic to turn professional. Both players were still waiting for their first-team debuts when they won their first caps for the Republic of Ireland. Indeed, Fitzsimons was not called up by Boro manager David Jack until April Fool's Day when he covered for the injured Peter McKennan, with Alec McCrae switching to centre-forward. He spent most of the following season in the reserves before injury to Mannion gave him another chance as Boro's once promising Championship challenge stumbled towards a disappointing conclusion. A regular place came in 1952–53, when he was occasionally used on the wing, though he was dropped midway through the following year's relegation campaign. Fitzsimons came into his own in the Second Division, though he had an unfortunate tendency to dribble around two or three defenders and blast the ball over the bar. When Brian Clough arrived on the first-team scene, the goalscoring sensation would regularly take the ball off his more experienced teammate's toe to score and, on one occasion, actually barged him off the ball. Clough was reported to have shouted at Fitzsimons: 'You make the bloody goals and I'll score them.'

A genial man, the Irish star lost his place to Alan Peacock and turned down a move to Scunthorpe in March 1959 before joining Second Division Lincoln. Seven games later he joined former Boro teammate Lindy Delapenha at Mansfield for a club record fee, though they were relegated to Division Four at the end of his first season there. After retiring, he coached Drogheda and Shelbourne in the League of Ireland and was in charge of an Irish League select beaten 7–2 by their Football League counterparts. He later played for Wisbech Town in the Southern League but asked to be released to take up a coaching contract in Libya, where he remained until the Arab-Israeli war broke out in 1967. Fitzsimons retired back home to Ireland.

FJORTOFT Jan-Åge

Forward
Born: Aalesund, Norway, 10 January 1967.
Career: Hamkameralene (Norway) 1987. Lillestrom (Norway) 1988. Rapid Vienna (Austria) 1989. Swindon Town 1993. MIDDLESBROUGH 1995. Sheffield United 1997. Barnsley 1998. Eintracht Frankfurt (Germany) 1998. Stabaek (Norway) 2001. Lillestrom (Norway) 2002.

■ Spectacular goals followed by aeroplane-style celebrations were the forte of Norway legend Fjortoft during his two-year stay on Teeside. And yet it was his disappointing scoring record in the Premier League that ultimately cost him his place in the Middlesbrough first team.

Fjortoft's excellent strike rate in Norwegian football brought him to the attention of crack Austrian side Rapid Vienna in 1989 and he was a prolific goalscorer for four years there, during which he was three times a losing Cup finalist. After playing for Norway in the 1994 World Cup Finals, a £500,000 transfer took him to Swindon Town for their first year in the top flight. A complete goal drought in the Premier League almost resulted in his return to Lillestrom on loan but he hit form late in the season, though it was too late to save Swindon from the drop. He was a regular goalscorer in the First Division and scored in both League games against Boro before Bryan Robson made him a club record signing on transfer deadline day 1995. In fact, at £1.3 million, it was widely believed that Boro had got a bargain as many had rated Fjortoft in the £3 million bracket.

Capable of amazing skills and clumsy errors in equal measure, he initially struggled to find his top form and failed to hit it off with Uwe Fuchs in the Boro front line, though he did score a tremendous goal at Barnsley to cement his record as the division's top scorer. Playing as a lone striker in the Premier League, he scored the second goal against Chelsea in the first ever game at the Cellnet Riverside Stadium and another astonishing solo effort in an otherwise forgettable Coca-Cola Cup win over Crystal Palace. He initially linked up well with Nick Barmby and Craig Hignett and his goal against Leeds United in November 1995, running on to debut boy Juninho's through-ball, was voted the club's goal of the season. Alas, the goals dried up and he was relegated to the subs' bench by the end of the season.

Never a typical footballer, off the pitch he was an opera-loving teetotaller who campaigned against drug and alcohol abuse while always insisting that journalists coming from Norway to interview him should bring with them some brown goat's cheese. Intelligent and intellectual, he impressed all who met him with his excellent grasp of the English language. Sadly, he found Bryan Robson harder to please and was out in the cold following the arrival of Fabrizio Ravanelli in 1996. He did, however, score in his final appearance for the club, in a memorable 3–2 FA Cup win over non-League Hednesford.

After leaving Sheffield United, he was later signed for Barnsley by his former Boro teammate John Hendrie but moved

to the German Bundesliga where his final day goal saved Eintracht Frankfurt from relegation in 1999. After retiring, having scored 20 goals in 71 games for Norway, he became sporting director with former club Lillestrom.

FLEMING Curtis

Defender
Born: Manchester, 8 October 1968.
Career: St Patrick's Athletic (Ireland) 1987. MIDDLESBROUGH 1991. Birmingham City (loan) 2001. Crystal Palace 2001. Darlington 2004. Shelbourne 2005. Billingham Synthonia 2006.

■ But for two quirks of the game Oldham Athletic or Swindon Town might easily have benefited from the loyal service of Curtis Fleming. But their loss proved to be Middlesbrough's gain with Fleming spending 10 years with the club following his bargain £50,000 signing during the summer of 1991. Born in Manchester, Fleming's mother – an Irish actress – moved back to Ireland when he was still a baby and, after playing for Belvedere Boys Club, he joined top Irish side St Patrick's in the Inchicore district of Dublin. He made his St Patrick's debut in September 1987, aged 18, and became a popular figure at the club, earning the nickname The Black Pearl of Inchicore Mark II – Mark I being another ex St Pat's star Paul McGrath, of Manchester United fame. Fleming's outstanding performances not only won him Irish Under-21 and B honours but brought him to the attention of several top clubs, including Aberdeen and Manchester City. Swindon

were set to sign him during the summer of 1989 after a loan spell but the deal fell through when manager Lou Macari was sacked following an infamous scandal. A year later and by now the Irish Under-21 Player of the Year, he impressed while on trial with Oldham but turned down an offer he described as derisory, instead returning to Dublin to continue his job in a clothes shop. It was Colin Todd who made the decision to sign Fleming for Boro and the deal might have fallen through when the manager left the club. Fortunately, his successor, Lennie Lawrence, stood by the deal and Fleming moved to Teesside. Having played in the European and UEFA Cups for St Patrick's, the full-back took time to win a regular place in the Boro first team but was a member of the side which clinched success to the inaugural Premier League with victory at Wolves in May 1992. His hard-tackling, 100 percent style won him many admirers at Ayresome Park and he was the first choice right-back for three years until the arrival of Neil Cox in 1994, winning the supporters' club Player of the Year award for 1993–94. However, he showed his versatility by switching to left-back, only for injury to rule him out of the second half of the promotion season under Bryan Robson. He spent almost a year on the sidelines but returned to win back the regular left-back spot and appeared in both the 1997 Coca-Cola and FA Cup Finals, while finally winning full Irish caps. He was again used at right-back as he helped Boro to a third promotion in 1998 – though injury ruled him out of the Coca-Cola Cup Final – and was occasionally used as cover in central defence, though a knee injury forced him to miss much of the 1998–99 campaign and the early stages of 1999–2000. Hugely popular with the Boro fans, Fleming's role in the side changed many times in his 10 years and 317 appearances with the club. He remained first choice right-back under Terry Venables, but lost out to Robbie Stockdale early in Steve McClaren's managerial reign. Following a loan spell with Birmingham City, he parted company with the Riverside club and signed for Crystal Palace for £100,000. He was made Palace captain, but knee problems meant that he spent much of his time at Selhurst Park on the treatment table. Following his release by Palace, Fleming returned to the North East to play for Darlington, where he was a steadying influence at the heart of the Quakers defence before returning to Ireland to play for Shelbourne. In 2007, while working as a coach for Boro's Academy, he played his part in helping Billingham Synthonia reach the semi-final of the FA Vase. During the summer of 2007, he accepted a role as assistant manager to his former Boro teammate Mark Proctor at Scottish Division One side Livingston.

FLINT William

Outside-right
Born: Eastwood, 21 March 1890.
Career: Hebburn Argyle. MIDDLESBROUGH 1909. Watford 1910. Gateshead 1911. Ashington 1912.

■ Bill Flint replaced Fred Pentland at outside-right for his only first-team game in a Middlesbrough shirt in a 2–1 defeat at Chelsea in February 1910. Picked up from non-League Hebburn Argyle two years earlier, Flint was only 19 and still an amateur at the time of his debut. He moved on to Notts County where he faced Middlesbrough in First Division games.

FOGGON Alan

Winger
Born: Chester-le-Street, 23 February 1950.
Career: Newcastle United 1967. Cardiff City 1971. MIDDLESBROUGH 1972. Manchester United 1976. Sunderland 1976. Southend United 1977. Hartlepool United 1977. Consett.

■ For a player who was immediately recognisable by his rotund physique, it is astonishing to think that Alan Foggon owed much of his success as a Middlesbrough player to his deceptive pace. It was that ironic combination that earned Foggon the nickname of The Flying Pig among supporters who both adored and mocked him in equal measures during a colourful four-year stay on Teesside.

An England Youth international, the lad from a Durham pit village broke into

the Newcastle United first team as a teenager and scored a brilliant goal in the 1969 Fairs Cup Final. Despite much early promise, he was never a regular at St James' Park and, by his own admission, went off the rails and was eventually transferred to Second Division Cardiff City. With his career seemingly in freefall, he was rescued by Boro manager Stan Anderson in 1972 after much wrangling between the two clubs. However, in his first training session with Boro, his new teammates were shocked to find he looked at least a stone-and-a-half overweight and seemed totally inept in front of goal. But Foggon quickly proved to everyone that looks could be deceiving and became a regular in the side under caretaker manager Harold Shepherdson. Like Anderson before him, new boss Jack Charlton ordered Foggon to lose weight and put him on a food allowance at a local butchers in an attempt to improve his diet. But Foggon was living proof that beer and professional football could mix and often enjoyed an unconventional match preparation of a gin and tonic together with a few cigars with his friend and equally rotund roommate Bobby Murdoch.

Despite his unhealthy habits, Foggon was perhaps the key player in Boro's record-breaking run to the Second Division championship in 1973–74, scoring 19 League goals to end John Hickton's six-season run as the club's top scorer. Charlton utilised Foggon's speed to great effect, playing him behind the front two and asking him to make deep runs into the channels as the defence tried to play offside. With Souness, Murdoch and Armstrong making inch perfect passes over the top, Foggon's turn of pace enabled him to burst through defences and score many crucial goals. But his game was not only about speed, as he was an excellent finisher, always keeping a cool head in one on-one situations with opposition goalkeepers. With long flowing hair, socks rolled down and shirt outside his shorts, Foggon was a sight to behold in full flight while also proving very difficult to knock off the ball. He was again top scorer as Boro challenged for the First Division title in 1974–75 but his effect was diminished as opposing teams began to suss Boro's unique style and he eventually lost his place.

He made a surprise transfer request to chairman Charles Amer on a club tour of New Zealand in 1975 and the board agreed to grant the request. Manchester United manager Tommy Docherty flew to Montreal to see Foggon play for Hartford Centennials in the North American Soccer League during the summer of 1976 and duly signed him as cover for United's UEFA Cup run. Sunderland had also expressed an interest in signing him but Charlton had refused to sell him to Boro's north-east rivals. However, four months after moving to Old Trafford, he made the switch to Roker Park to join a select band of players who have appeared for all three of the north-east's big clubs. After ending his playing days, Foggon, who also played for Rotchester in the NASL, ran a pub and has more recently worked for a Tyneside security firm.

FORREST William

Left-half
Born: Tranent, 28 February 1908.
Died: February 1965.
Career: Haddington. Musselburgh Juniors, St Bernard's, MIDDLESBROUGH 1929.

■ A copper by trade, Billy Forrest had made his mind up to become a Policeman until the intervention of Middlesbrough manager Peter McWilliam. After meeting with club officials at the North British Hotel in Edinburgh, Forrest decided to join the Boro beat and so began an outstanding career for one of the club's greatest servants.

The eldest of 10 children, he played his early football in Scotland for Haddington and Musselburgh Juniors before joining Edinburgh St. Barnard's where he attracted the attention of several professional clubs. He became close friends with Middlesbrough teammate Bob Baxter after recommending his fellow Scot to McWilliam when he scored five goals in a junior game. Indeed, the pair later married sisters, with Forrest eloping to Gretna Green to tie the knot. Along with John Martin, the duo formed a great half-back line for several years in the mid–1930s. A stylish, uncompromising left-half, Forrest was one of the stars of the side that looked destined to win the League, only to be thwarted by the outbreak of war in 1939. He played more than 100 war-time games for Boro and even scored a hat-trick against York while playing at centre-forward but, at the age of 37, decided to retire from the game when peace returned in 1945.

He coached the club's juniors for a short time before taking over as Darlington boss, where he attracted record crowds as the Quakers briefly challenged at the top of the Third Division North. Forrest later ran the Station Hotel in Billingham but in 1956 was partially paralysed in an accident which eventually led to his death in Middlesbrough in February 1965.

FORRESTER Paul

Forward
Born: Edinburgh, 3 November 1972.
Career: Heart of Midlothian 1989. Musselburgh Windsor 1991. MIDDLESBROUGH 1993. Berwick Rangers 1994. Stenhousemuir 2000.

■ The Middlesbrough career of Paul Forrester lasted just 25 minutes. A promising wide midfielder, he spent two years with Hearts but appeared to have missed the boat and was playing for Musselburgh until offered a trial by Boro in December 1992. He later returned for a second trial and was awarded a short-term contract. His only taste of first-team action came under Lennie Lawrence when he replaced Phil Stamp during the second half of a 1–0 First Division home defeat to Bolton in November 1993 in front of a sparse Ayresome crowd of less than 7,000. After being given a free by Boro, Forrester became a regular with Berwick Rangers in the lower divisions of Scottish football and was a regular goalscorer for his new club.

FOWLER Henry Norman

Full-back
Born: Stockton-on-Tees, 3 September 1919.
Died: 1990.
Career: South Bank. MIDDLESBROUGH 1937. Hull City 1946. Gateshead 1949. Scarborough.

■ Norman Fowler had the misfortune to develop as a promising left full-back at the same time as George Hardwick. Indeed, after winning England Schoolboy caps, he joined Middlesbrough from South Bank and actually made his first-team debut just

five months after Hardwick. Fowler stood in for Bobby Stuart in a 1–0 win at Leicester in April 1938 and was preferred to Hardwick on several occasions as Stuart's stand-in the following season. The outbreak of war sadly brought his career to a grinding halt before it had really got going and he joined the RAF in 1940, though he did make a number of war-time appearances for both Boro and Leeds. Unable to win a first-team place on his return from the services, he was placed on the transfer list at £500 at the end of the 1945–46 season and subsequently joined Hull in the Third Division North for a knock-down £425. He was later in the Gateshead team that narrowly missed out on promotion to the Second Division in 1950. After his playing days were over, Fowler trained Stockton when another ex-Boro player, Bill Harris, was in charge in the mid-1960s. He died in 1990.

FOX William Victor

Full-back/Left-half
Born: Middlesbrough, 8 January 1898.
Died: Manchester, 17 February 1949.
Career: South Bank Juniors. MIDDLESBROUGH 1919. Wolverhampton Wanderers 1924. Newport County 1930. Exeter City 1931. Manchester Central. Nantwich.

■ Victor Fox is one of only two players throughout Middlesbrough's history whose father also played for the club's first team. The defender's father, Billy Fox, was a star of Middlesbrough's pre-League team in the 1880s. Indeed, Fox Snr, the owner of a sports shop in the

town, was coaching the club's juniors while his son was in the team. Although World War One delayed the onset of Fox's career, he made up for lost time by helping Boro to the Northern Victory League Championship in 1918–19 before making his League debut at Sheffield Wednesday when First Division football resumed in August 1919. Initially a left-half, he was converted to left full-back with great effect and was the club's regular in that position for two seasons before losing his place to Alf Maitland. A sturdy tackler, Fox was a vigorous but occasionally erratic kicker. He was placed on the transfer list during the close season of 1924 and, when his transfer fee was halved to £250 by a Football League Management Committee tribunal, he was snapped up by Wolves. Although he was never a regular at Molineux, like his father, he enjoyed much success playing county cricket for Worcestershire between 1923 and 1932, three times scoring more than 1,000 runs in a season. Fox died in Manchester on 17 February 1947.

FRAIL Joseph Martin

Goalkeeper
Born: Burslem, 1869.
Died: Hanley, 4 September 1939.
Career: Burslem Port Vale 1892. Gorton Villa. Glossop North End. Derby County 1897. Chatham. MIDDLESBROUGH 1900. Luton Town 1902. Brentford 1903. Stalybridge Rovers. MIDDLESBROUGH 1903. Stockport County 1905. Glossop 1905.

■ There is no doubt that goalkeeper Joe

Frail was one of the more colourful characters in Middlesbrough's long history. A traditional gypsy, Frail lived in a caravan during his playing days and was renowned for always wearing a knotted handkerchief around his neck while keeping guard between the sticks. For many years, he ran a Middlesbrough town centre market stall where punters paid to take penalty shots against him. Indeed, he was such a good penalty stopper that he once saved three spot-kicks in the same game while playing for Brentford. Born in the Potteries, he appeared in Burslem Port Vale's first ever Football League game in 1892. He began the first of two spells with Middlesbrough when leaving non-League Chatham in time for the club's second season in the Football League in 1900 – though it was his former Football League club Derby that recived a £25 fee – and made his debut in a 2–0 win over Lincoln at the Linthorpe Road ground. Indeed, all but two of the Middlesbrough team were making their debuts for the club that day. An imposing shot stopper, he established a still unrivalled record of conceding an average of less than a goal a game throughout his time with Boro and was first-choice 'keeper as promotion to the First Division was secured in 1902. However, he was dropped for the final games of the season after failing to advise the club that he was appearing in the police courts for a misdemeanour. With Tim Williamson showing the form that would eventually win him England caps, Frail was allowed to join non-League Luton that summer. However, in 1903 he returned for a brief spell as cover for Williamson and played one final game for the club, in a 1–0 First Division win at Sheffield United in February 1905. The style of his second exit had echoes of his previous departure as Frail was handed his papers after another police conviction.

FRASER Alexander

Inside-left/Centre-half
Born: Inverness, 1883.
Career: Inverness Thistle. Newcastle United 1903. Fulham 1907. Bradford Park Avenue 1908. Darlington. MIDDLESBROUGH 1911. Darlington.

■ Replacing the great George Elliott was the onerous task given to inside-forward Alec Fraser on his Middlesbrough debut against WBA at Ayresome Park in April 1912. However, although Elliott returned for the following match, Fraser retained his place in the Boro forward line for the next two games before switching to half-back for a trip to Bradford City. Fraser, whose shoot-on-sight playing style with Darlington had brought him to the attention of Middlesbrough, played his fifth and final game for the club in the opening day defeat at WBA in September 1912 before returning to Feethams.

FREEMAN Reginald Vincent

Full-back
Born: Birkenhead, 20 December 1897.
Died: Rotherham, 4 August 1955.
Career: Wallasey Rovers. Harrowby. Northern Nomads. Oldham Athletic 1920. MIDDLESBROUGH 1923. Rotherham United 1930.

■ A stylish and graceful full-back, Reg Freeman was a star of leading amateur club, Northern Nomads, immediately after the Great War before joining the professional game with Oldham at the relatively late age of 23. His sterling displays in the First Division soon earned him the club captaincy and trials for the full England squad before Boro paid the considerable fee of £3,600 for his services. Known not only as a skilful footballer but as a gentleman, Freeman proved to be an excellent purchase despite suffering the pain of relegation in his first season with the club. He was made club captain in 1924 and quickly became a key figure in defence. He turned in one of his most outstanding performances in a 5–1 FA Cup victory over Leeds in January 1926, although he was criticised for poor form late in that same campaign and lost his captaincy to Billy Birrell as promotion to the First Division was achieved in record-breaking style in 1926–27. Equally at home on either side of the defence, Freeman was rated one of the best full-backs in the country throughout his time at Ayresome Park but eventually lost his first-team place. After leaving Middlesbrough, he gave Rotherham 22 years' service as player and then manager. After steering the penniless club away from re-election troubles, he developed a knack of moulding untried youngsters into skilled professionals and, after several close calls, led his club to the Third Division North Championship and promotion in 1951. He won the Second Division Championship in his first season in charge of Sheffield United and was still manager at Bramall Lane when he died after a long illness in Wickersley, near Rotherham, on 4 August 1955.

FREEMAN Thomas

Left-back
Born: Brandon, 26 January 1907.
Career: Durham City. MIDDLESBROUGH 1930. Chester 1933. Blyth Spartans.

■ A bricklayer by trade, Tom Freeman was brought to Middlesbrough by Peter McWilliam after making his name as an outside-left for Durham. At Ayresome Park, he was switched to left full-back though he was forced to wait almost a year for his first-team debut. With regular left-back Don Ashman injured, Bob Ferguson had filled the vacant position for the opening three First Division games of the 1930–31 season but Freeman – known as 'Duck' to his teammates – stepped in for a 3–0 win at West Ham and remained the first choice until an 8–1 mauling at Aston Villa at the end of January. He regained his place from Syd Jarvis and was Boro's regular left-back as relegation was successfully avoided the following season, only to again find himself in the second team midway through the 1932–33 campaign. He left Boro six months later.

FREESTONE Christopher Mark

Forward
Born: Nottingham, 4 September 1971.
Career: Eastwood Town. Arnold Town. MIDDLESBROUGH 1994. Carlisle United (loan) 1997. Northampton Town 1997. Hartlepool United 1999. Cheltenham Town (loan) 2000. Shrewsbury Town 2000. Rugby United. Forest Green Rovers.

■ Expectancy among the fans probably ran too high from the day Chris Freestone scored on his full Boro debut. The goal, together with an outstanding scoring record for the club's reserves, brought a pressure that the striker was never able to live up to and it was no surprise when he eventually moved on to Northampton Town.

As a youngster, Freestone had trials with several League clubs, including Nottingham Forest, Notts County and Carlisle, but played local League football while serving as a swimming pool lifeguard in his spare time. After a spell with Eastwood Town, his prolific goalscoring record for Arnold Town in the Northern Counties (East) League brought the striker to Boro's attention and, at the age of 23, he signed professional forms midway through the 1994–95 season after impressing for the reserves during a short trial spell. He was a regular scorer for the reserves before making his first-team debut as substitute along with Craig Liddle at Tranmere on the final day of the promotion campaign. A goal-a-game average for the reserves brought him his first start at home to Sheffield Wednesday in the Premier League in place of the injured Nick Barmby the following April and he scored Boro's third goal in a 3–1 win. Freestone utilised his main strength of breathtaking speed to good effect but lacked the physical stature and ball skills to unlock top class defences.

He was largely overlooked by Bryan Robson over the next two years and joined Second Division Northampton Town for a fee of £75,000 after impressing during a loan spell. His goals helped take his new club to the promotion Play-offs in 1998 but he lost form the following season and returned to the North East with Third Division Hartlepool for just £50,000.

FRENCH John Proctor

Right-back
Born: Stockton-on-Tees.
Died: Southend 1954.

■ Although he made just one appearance in a Middlesbrough shirt, Jack French went on to carve out a reasonable career in the game. The only first-team game he played for Boro ended in a humbling 5–1 home defeat to Leicester City on 3 January 1925. Having stood in for regular left full-back Reg Freeman, he was never called upon again and left for Southend at the end of the following season. Known as 'Carnera French' after the famous boxing champion, he was something of a gentle giant during his playing days. He later opened a stall selling jellied eels in a Southend amusement arcade while he is also said to have helped introduce bingo to these shores. He died in Southend in the early 1950s. His nephews, John and Jim French, were both on Boro's books during World War Two and John went on to play for Nottingham Forest and Southend.

FUCHS Uwe

Forward
Born: Kaiserslautern, Germany, 23 July 1966.
Career: Hamburg SV 1984. Stuttgart Kickers 1986. Fortuna Cologne 1987. Fortuna Dusseldorf 1989. Cologne 1990. Kaiserslautern 1993. MIDDLESBROUGH (loan) 1995. Millwall 1995. Armenia Bielefeld (Germany) 1996.

■ The term 'cult hero' could have been invented for Uwe Fuchs. A strong running striker with an unorthodox style, the German was a goalscoring sensation during a four-month loan spell with Boro during Bryan Robson's first season as manager. It would not be an exaggeration to say that his goals were almost solely responsible for kick-starting Boro's promotion bid that was to eventually lead them back into the promised land of the Premier League. Until the arrival of the 6ft forward, a promotion which had once looked a formality was slipping out of the club's grasp and the nervous fans welcomed

Fuchs with open arms, despite the fact that he was unknown outside his own country.

He began his career at Hamburg but it was only on the intervention of his father, Fritz, Hamburg's coach and himself once a professional footballer, that he was switched to an attacking role. He became something of a football journeyman in Germany while a serious injury caused him to miss almost two years before helping Kaiserslautern finish second in the Bundesliga in 1994. Tony Woodcock, a former Nottingham Forest teammate of Boro'a assistant manager Viv Anderson, recommended Fuchs to Boro as 'an English style centre-forward' when Swindon refused to sell Jan Fjortoft and he duly signed on loan from Kaiserslautern until the end of the season with a view to making a permanent £500,000 move if he impressed. Certainly, he could not have done more in place of the out-of-sorts Paul Wilkinson. A clever goal just 15 minutes into his full debut against Charlton was followed by an impressive hat-trick against Bristol City as he netted seven times in his first five starts. However, although a natural goalscorer, Fuchs was not a team player and often looked clumsy on the ball. The record signing of Jan Fjortoft saw the pair briefly partnered in attack but Fuchs was sent off for retaliation in a bruising encounter with Sheffield United in what turned out to be his last competitive game for the club. Two days after the season had ended with the First Division title, he was informed that his move would not be made permanent – Robson insisting that he was not good enough for the Premier League. The fans who had hero-worshiped Fuchs were initially dismayed at the decision but Robson was proved right when the striker failed dismally with Millwall the following season as they fell to relegation to Division Two. However, Fuchs' tearful farewell in Stephen Pears' testimonial match in the last ever game at Ayresome Park was a fitting way to end his short love affair with the people of Teesside. After finishing his playing career back in Germany, he enjoyed coaching roles with Fortuna Dusseldorf, Fortuna Cologne and the Wuppertaler Sports Association.

GALLACHER Connor

Inside-forward
Born: Derry, 24 April 1922.
Career: Lochee Harp. MIDDLESBROUGH 1947. Hull City 1947. Rochdale 1948.

■ Irishman Gallacher enjoyed only a brief spell in English football, finding little fortune at three League clubs. An inside-forward, he joined Boro from Irish League side Lochee Harps but made just one first appearance on a trip to Fratton Park in March 1947. Boro lost 3–1 and Gallacher was not on the retained list at the end of the season.

GALLAGHER James

Left-back/Centre-forward
Born: Dipton, 17 February 1897.
Died: 1972.
Career: Liverpool. Northern Nomads. Oldham Athletic 1919. MIDDLESBROUGH 1920. Millwall Athletic 1921. Durham City 1923.

■ George Elliott's brother-in-law did not enjoy the success of his far more famous relation. Left-back Gallagher played a couple of Central League games for Liverpool and then played for Northern Nomads before joining Oldham. His only game for Boro came against Manchester United in April 21 – a 4–2 defeat. Gallagher's son Donald played for Boro during the war and also played for Middlesbrough Cricket Club.

GANNON John Spencer

Midfield
Born: Wimbledon, 18 December 1966.
Career: Wimbledon 1984. Crewe Alexandra (loan) 1986. Sheffield United 1989. MIDDLESBROUGH (loan) 1993. Oldham Athletic 1996.

■ Boro manager Lennie Lawrence had his First Division squad stretched to the limit by injuries when he recruited midfielder Gannon on loan from Premier League Sheffield United. A former Wimbledon apprentice, Gannon had followed Dave Bassett to Bramall Lane and established himself as creative and gritty left-sided midfielder who was also a dead ball specialist. Having scored on his debuts for the Dons and Blades, he failed to repeat the feat at Ayresome Park. In truth, he didn't stand out in a poor Boro team and soon returned to Sheffield.

GARBETT Terence Graham

Midfield
Born: Lanchester, 9 September 1945.
Career: Stockton. MIDDLESBROUGH 1963. Watford 1966. Blackburn Rovers 1971. Sheffield United 1974. New York Cosmos (United States) 1976.

■ Diminutive forward Garbett scored on his first-team debut in a friendly against Sunderland but struggled to make a breakthrough. His only appearance came in a relegation season but he found better fortune away from Teesside. Having played his junior football for Pelton Fell and also for a Chester-le-Street boys' team captained by Howard Kendall, he joined Stockton before signing for Boro as an amateur. He had to wait until the early part of the 1965–66 season when he replaced Bryan Orritt in a struggling side. His only goal came in a 3–2 victory over Ipswich and he made only fleeting appearances as Boro dropped into the Third Division for the first time. Following relegation, Boro rejected an initial offer from Watford but accepted an increased £8,000 fee. He became a big favourite and leading goalscorer at Watford, scoring on his debut and later netting the headed goal that beat Middlesbrough at Vicarage Road in October 1966. After helping the Hornets to win Division Three in 1969, Garbett followed manager Ken Furphy to Blackburn and then Sheffield United. He also played for New York Generals in the USA, linking up with Furphy for a fourth time.

GARDNER John Robert

Centre-half
Born: Hartlepool, 1905
Career: Hartlepool United, June 1927, Aldershot, May 1929, £300.

■ Centre-half Gardner was a solid reserve player but failed to feature in the Football League side. His only first-team chance came as stand-in for Maurice Webster in an FA Cup fourth round meeting with First Division West Bromwich Albion. He was allowed to leave at the end of the season on the condition that Aldershot would give Middlesbrough 50 percent of any subsequent fee received.

GASCOIGNE Paul John

Midfield
Born: Gateshead, 27 May 1967.
Career: Newcastle United 1985. Tottenham Hotspur 1988. Lazio (Italy) 1992. Glasgow Rangers 1995. MIDDLESBROUGH 1998. Everton 2000. Burnley 2002. Gansu Tianma (China) 2003. Boston United 2004. Algarve United (Portugal) 2005.

■ One of the most famous and often controversial players of his generation, Gascoigne spent his whole career in the media spotlight. During his time with Boro the midfielder made his debut in a Cup Final and helped the club to promotion. But 'Gazza' also spent time in a private hospital amid a variety of personal problems and was dropped by England on the eve of the 1998 World Cup, eventually leaving the club on a free transfer a little over two years after his £3.45 million signing. Gascoigne had trials with Boro as a schoolboy but accidentally stood on a piece of glass and cut his foot so was unable to complete the trial. He instead made his name with Newcastle before starring in the national side's march to the 1990 World Cup semi-final while on Tottenham's books, having joined Terry Venables' side for a British record £2 million fee. Having agreed an £8.5 million move to Italian side Lazio, his own rash challenge on Nottingham Forest's Gary Charles 15 minutes into the 1991 FA Cup Final saw him sidelined for 12 months. He eventually moved for £5 million but suffered more injury problems before returning to the UK with

Glasgow Rangers in a £4.3 million deal, helping the Ibrox club to two Premier League titles and success in both Cup competitions before joining Middlesbrough. He had been linked with Boro as far back as 1994 when he saw the club take on Watford but it was March 1998 before he linked up with his former England teammate Bryan Robson just days before the Coca-Cola Cup Final. Having made his debut as substitute at Wembley, he helped Boro to win promotion from the First Division and played in warm-up games leading up to the World Cup in France. He was, however, controversially omitted from the final squad following an infamous tale of a late-night kebab and drinking session with showbiz pals Danny Baker and Chris Evans. His response to the axe was a furious row with national boss Glenn Hoddle. Gascoigne then made his return to top flight football in England after a long absence, scoring spectacular trademark goals against Leicester and Southampton. However, he missed part of the season after going into a rehabilitation clinic as he tried to deal with alcohol and psychological problems. He returned to the side to a hero's welcome, helping the club to a respectable ninth place in the Premier League. Although lacking the pace that made him a world star, his skill and inventiveness were still major parts of his game and he remained a crowd favourite and entertainer. It became the subject of national debate whether he should be recalled to the England team to solve the national side's creative problems but new boss Kevin Keegan overlooked the charismatic midfielder. Injuries again kicked in and Gascoigne started only seven games in 1999–2000, his final season on Teesside. His final game, in a dismal 4–0 home defeat to Aston Villa, was best remembered for a painful challenge on George Boateng that left Gazza with a broken elbow and a red card. He moved on to Everton in the summer of 2000 after just 41 league appearances for Boro, initially making a big impact at Goodison before fading. A downwards spiral began with a short spell with Burnley followed by an unsuccessful trial in the US with DC United and an unlikely and short-lived move to China with Giansu Tianmu. Then came a short stay with Boston United as player and coach and two months in Portugal in a similar role with newly-formed Algarve United. A 39-day spell as manager of Kettering Town resulted in the sack. Early in 2007, he announced plans to star in a sci-fi film called *Final Run*.

GATES William Lazenby

Centre-half
Born: Ferryhill, 8 May 1944.
Career: MIDDLESBROUGH 1961.

■ Bill Gates was a great all-rounder who was used in a variety of positions in his long Middlesbrough career. A former England youth captain, Gates was a strong tackler and hard worker who was also a good talker on the pitch. Known as a football hard man, he saw Boro relegated to the Third Division for the first time but hung up his boots after top flight status had been attained.

The brother of England star Eric Gates, the youngster was initially torn between football and accountancy as a career but football won and he was allowed to continue his business studies. He made his first-team debut as a teenage amateur, aged 16, while still at Spennymoor Grammar School. Despite this early promise, however, Gates had fluctuating fortunes at Middlesbrough. He often only won a first-team place because of injuries to other players and was regarded as a utility player. Gates was

used in eight positions, from defence to centre-forward, though he was perhaps most comfortable at centre-half.

Unable to win a regular place in the side in 1963–64 he asked for a transfer but the board turned down his request. Gates was subsequently given more chances but missed the end of the 1965–66 relegation season after chipping a bone in his ankle. After years of narrowly missing promotion under Stan Anderson, Gates played only twice in the 1973–74 promotion season but enjoyed a well-attended testimonial against First Division champions Leeds United in 1974, following Boro's Division Two success. Gates invested the income in a sports shop business and the venture's success enabled him to later retire to the Caribbean.

GAVIN Jason Joseph

Defender
Born: Dublin, 14 March 1980.
Career: MIDDLESBROUGH 1997. Grimsby Town (loan) 2002. Huddersfield Town (loan) 2003. Bradford City 2003. Shamrock Rovers (Ireland) 2005. Drogheda United (Ireland) 2006.

■ A product of the Boro youth system who joined the club straight from school, Jason Gavin developed into a tough and uncompromising defender and his early displays for the club led to him winning Under–21 honours for the Republic of Ireland. The central defender had a tough baptism to Premiership football, getting the call to replace Colin Cooper in an away game at Newcastle before making his home debut against Manchester United at the end of the 1998–99 season. Gavin represented his

country at Schoolboy and Youth levels and also appeared in Eire's European Under-20 championship-winning side in 1998 and the 1999 World Youth Cup in Nigeria but struggled to progress at club level. With the experienced Cooper, Gianluca Festa, Steve Vickers and Gary Pallister all ahead of him in the defensive pecking order, first-team chances were few and far between over the next two years and it was at right-back that he was eventually given an extended run under Terry Venables towards the end of the 2000–01 campaign. With Curtis Fleming injured, Gavin played the final eight League games, playing his part in crucial three-goal wins at Arsenal and Leicester City. His 40th and final Boro appearance came the following season but he was clearly not fancied by new boss Steve McClaren, who allowed him to spend loan spells with Grimsby and Huddersfield. Released by Boro, Gavin linked up again with Bryan Robson at Bradford City, but the player lost his place following injury and the sacking of his former Riverside boss and he eventually returned to Ireland with first Shamrock Rovers and then Drogheda United.

GEREMI Njitap Fotso Geremi Sorele

Midfield
Born: Cameroon, 20 December 1978.
Career: Racing Baffousam (Cameroon) 1995. Cerro Porteno (Paraguay) 1997. Genclerbirligi (Turkey) 1997. Real Madrid (Spain) 1999. MIDDLESBROUGH (loan) 2002. Chelsea 2003. Newcastle United 2007.

■ The talented African midfielder spent a memorable year on loan to Boro from Real Madrid in 2002–03. An Olympic gold medallist with Cameroon in 2000, Geremi had played in Paraguay and Turkey before signing at the Bernabeau in July 1999. He did well in Spain but enjoyed one of his busiest and most productive seasons at the Riverside. Geremi could also play right wing-back and was lethal from set-pieces. He made 33 starts and scored seven goals, including a memorable free-kick strike against Liverpool at Anfield. Steve McClaren was unwilling to meet Madrid's £7 million asking price for a permanent deal, but his Chelsea counterpart Claudio Ranieri had no such qualms. Geremi was on his way to Stamford Bridge where he was used all across in midfield in his first season. Under new manager Jose Mourinho, he was confined to appearances from the bench but an injury crisis in the dying embers of the season allowed him to claim a Premiership-winners' medal in 2004–05. Geremi played a more prominent role in the club's second Premiership success and continued to feature regularly at international level, collecting his 85th cap for Cameroon. After making just 48 League starts in four years at Stamford Bridge, he joined Newcastle United in the summer of 2007 after Boro had denied suggestions that they might re-sign a player linked regularly with a Riverside return.

GETTINS Edward

Inside-forward
Born: Date unknown.
Career: Gainsborough Trinity 1898. MIDDLESBROUGH 1903. Reading 1905.

■ Right-winger Gettins signed in time to appear in the first ever League fixture at Ayresome Park. The former Gainsborough man was a regular in the 1903–04 season under manager John Robson as Middlesbrough finished 10th in the First Division. Gettins, however, lost his place in the following campaign with competition from the likes of Bill Davies and Charlie Hewitt. He signed for Reading after being released.

GETTINS Joseph Holmes

Centre-forward
Born: Middlesbrough, 19 November 1874.
Died: Molesley, August 1954.
Career: Millwall Athletic. MIDDLESBROUGH 1891, 1893, 1894, 1895, 1896, 1898, 1899, 1900. Also Millwall Athletic. Corinthians.

■ Pacy and tricky forward Joe Gettins left the town of Middlesbrough in 1893 to go to teacher training college in London. But he still regularly turned out for the town's team when he returned to the North East during the school holidays over the next decade, often playing for the first team over the Christmas and New Year period. He won the FA Amateur Cup with Boro in 1895 and the Northern League in 1894 and 1895. He was also able to appear in Middlesbrough's first ever Football League fixture against Lincoln City in 1899.

Gettins, who played first class cricket for Middlesex, was an amateur throughout his playing career and played for Millwall Athletic and the great amateur side Corinthians throughout the 1890s, together with his occasional games for Middlesbrough. He appeared in the FA Cup semi-finals of 1900 and 1903 for Southern League Millwall.

GIBSON Frederick William

Goalkeeper
Born: Somercotes, 18 June 1907.
Career: Laughton Common. Frickley Colliery. Denaby United. Dinnington Colliery. Hull City 1927. MIDDLESBROUGH 1932. Bradford City 1937. Boston United.

■ Fred Gibson was a technically competent goalkeeper who was brave and agile. Standing at 6ft 2in, he was an imposing figure in the Boro goal in the mid–1930s after replacing long-serving Jimmy Mathieson. The former miner was mostly a regular until the arrival of Dave Cumming in 1936.

Gibson had reached an FA Cup semi-final with Hull in 1930. His performance in the quarter-final victory over Newcastle prompted opposition forward Hughie Gallacher to describe him as 'a superman'. At Middlesbrough he missed most of the 1934–35 season when his place went to Joe Hillier but returned as a regular in the following campaign. After leaving to join Bradford, Gibson also played for Midland League Boston United before the war.

GIBSON Ian Stewart

Midfield
Born: Newton Stewart, 30 March 1943.
Career: Accrington Stanley 1958. Bradford Park Avenue 1960. MIDDLESBROUGH 1962. Coventry City 1966. Cardiff City 1970. Bournemouth 1972. Whitby Town. Gateshead. Guisborough.

■ Gibson was one of several young players tagged 'the new Wilf Mannion' in the years after the Golden Boy's retirement. It was a tough act for the Scot to live up to and he never truly realised his vast potential. He was a star in a struggling Boro team but he failed to hit the heights expected of him.

Having played four times for Scotland Schoolboys, Gibson had the chance to join Rangers but his father advised him against the move and he joined Fourth Division Accrington Stanley where he became the club's youngest player at 15 years and 358 days. He was soon on his way to Bradford Park Avenue – the Football League allowing the move after protests from Accrington – and he was only 18 when Boro swooped with a club record bid.

Manager Bob Dennison aimed to carefully nurture the young midfield playmaker but injuries forced his hand and he quickly established himself as a regular. He emerged as an exciting talent whose vision and passing seemed to be above that of his teammates and he was a pleasure to watch when on form. After finishing top scorer in 1963–64, he was appointed club captain in succession to Mel Nurse in 1965–66, aged just 22, but it was inevitable that the only real star of the side would leave when Boro were relegated to the Third Division. However, he performed particularly poorly in the final day 5–3 defeat to Cardiff which condemned Boro to the drop.

Jimmy Hill took him to Coventry for a club record fee as Boro sought to raise cash for a promotion bid. He soon had a dispute with Hill over his role in the team and demanded a transfer but returned to the side in a role that gave him more freedom. Gibson was a big favourite at Coventry despite his appearances being restricted by knee injuries and helped to win the Second Division title in 1966–67. Injury problems and off-field controversies blighted him and he moved on to Cardiff where he was again a record signing. It was at Bournemouth that his career was ended by an Achilles injury.

Gibson spent some time in South Africa before returning to play for Whitby, Gateshead and Guisborough. In 1983 he was reported to be working on Port Stanley airport in the Falklands and he also worked on North Sea oil rigs and as a scaffolder in Holland. Since hanging up his boots, Gibson has also scouted for Coventry in the North East and ran a hairdressing salon in Redcar.

GIBSON Robert James

Outside-right
Born: Scotswood, Newcastle-upon-Tyne, 1887.
Career: Scotswood. Bury 1908. Crystal Palace. MIDDLESBROUGH 1910. Newcastle United 1911. Lincoln City 1912. Third Lanark. Newcastle United 1919.

■ Geordie outside-right Gibson spent a season on Teesside before going to his native Tyneside. He appeared in most of Boro's First Division fixtures in 1910–11 but the signing of Jock Stirling in the summer of 1911 provided a new man for the right flank and Gibson moved to St

James' Park where he struggled to win a place. After a spell in Scotland with Third Lanark, Gibson returned to Newcastle after the war.

GILL Gary

Midfield
Born: Middlesbrough, 28 November 1964.
Career: MIDDLESBROUGH 1982. Hull City (loan) 1983. Darlington 1989. Cardiff City 1992.

■ Hard-working midfielder Gill was one of several young players thrown in at the deep end following liquidation in 1986. The local lad was a regular in a defensive midfield role as promotion was secured from the Third Division. First-team football was hard to come by in subsequent years and after a spell in the reserves his resurgence in 1989 was cut short by a broken leg. Known to all as Gilly, his main strengths were his fitness and ball-winning ability. Unselfish and a good marker in defensive positions, he was not an obvious crowd pleaser and was, on occasions, a boo boy target.

Gill joined the club as an apprentice after leaving Stainsby School and was a member of the Boro Boys' team that won the FA Youth Cup in 1982. He made his League debut in a loan spell at Hull before being handed his chance while Jack Charlton was in temporary command. Gill was out of the first-team frame in 1987–88 following the signing of Dean Glover and captained the reserves until getting another chance in the second half of the 1988–89 campaign. He was playing some of his best football and enjoyed what was regarded as his best ever game, eclipsing Everton's England internationals on Easter Monday 1989, only to break his leg at Ayresome Park in a game against Southampton in April 1989. He was famously told to run off the injury by the club's physio, who hadn't realised the leg was broken.

Gill made a full recovery but was not on the best terms with manager Bruce Rioch until he was surprisingly recalled and made team captain as stand-in for Tony Mowbray for a Cup tie against Halifax. The following League game was postponed and Gill never played for the club again. Told he could leave, he rejected a £100,000 move to Scunthorpe, before signing for former Boro youth team boss Brian Little at non-League Darlington. Having missed promotion from the Conference with injury, he was a key player in the club's successive promotion to the Second Division and Lennie Lawrence at one time tried to bring him back to Middlesbrough. After retiring through injury, Gill was appointed as Boro's Football in the Community Officer in January 1992 and later became a reporter on Boro's games for BBC Radio Cleveland. He also worked as a buyer for a men's leisurewear store in the town. After a spell off air, he returned to commentary duties as Paul Kerr's successor alongside Paul Adison.

GITTENS Jonathan Antoni

Central defender
Born: Birmingham, 22 January 1964.
Career: Paget Rangers. Southampton 1985. Swindon Town 1987. Southampton 1991. MIDDLESBROUGH (loan) 1992. MIDDLESBROUGH 1992. Portsmouth 1993. Torquay United 1996. Exeter City 1998. Nuneaton Boro.

■ Gittens scored one of the most important goals in the club's history to help take Boro into the inaugural Premier League. It was the highlight of a mixed spell on Teesside after initially joining the club on loan. Manager Lennie Lawrence made the deal permanent but Gittens was left out when the boss lost faith in him and he was released a year later.

Gittens was brought to Teesside from Southampton where he was in his second spell after playing for Swindon.

He was playing for Paget Rangers at 22 when spotted by the Saints, who sold him to Swindon for £40,000. Southampton signed him back for £600,000 after Gittens had been part of the Swindon side promoted and then 'relegated' after the infamous wages scandal. He turned down moves to Wimbledon and Newcastle to join Boro and arrived as cover for the central defenders Alan Kernaghan and Nicky Mohan. Gittens was not the most gifted on the ball but had pace and was a strong defender. He made occasional appearances before replacing injured Kernaghan for the final run-in. His moment of fame came when he scored a vital scrambled equaliser for 10-man Boro at Wolves in the game that won promotion.

Gittens was signed permanently on a one-year contract but a week later defenders Chris Morris and Derek Whyte were signed from Celtic after disastrous pre-season results. Lawrence later said that he had signed Gittens out of sympathy, having done so well the season before. But the manager didn't think he was good enough for the top flight. Gittens was only recalled when Kernaghan was injured and his relationship with Lawrence deteriorated. He subsequently joined Portsmouth on a free transfer and was a good performer for several clubs in the lower Leagues.

GLOVER Dean Victor

Central-defender
Born: West Bromwich, 29 December 1963.
Career: Aston Villa 1981. Sheffield United

(loan) 1986. MIDDLESBROUGH 1987. Port Vale 1989.

■ No-nonsense Glover was one of several players recruited from Aston Villa in Bruce Rioch's early years as Boro manager. A central defender at Villa Park, Glover was used as a midfield player by Rioch. Along with Gary Hamilton, he provided the engine room for Boro's successful Division One promotion campaign with Pallister and Mowbray settled at the back.

Known as Spamhead by his fellow players and Deano to the fans, Glover was a popular, tough-tackling player who was adept at breaking up opposition attacks, legally or otherwise! Once top flight status had been attained, first-team chances were more limited and, after failing to impress, Glover made a hasty departure early in 1989. There were rumours in the town that he had fallen out with the club management which the player denied. Glover insisted that he wanted to revert to central defence and also sought first-team football. He became Port Vale's record signing at £200,000, winning promotion to the Second Division through the Play-offs in his first season and played with former Boro teammates Bernie Slaven and Paul Kerr in the 1994 Autoglass Trophy Final. After a decade at Vale Park, much of it as captain, he enjoyed a testimonial in 1998 and later joined the Port Vale coaching staff.

GODLEY William

Forward
Born: Durham 1879.
Career: MIDDLESBROUGH 1902. Stoke 1904. Plymouth Argyle. Reading. New Brompton.

■ Godley, who went by the nickname 'Snip', was a centre-forward who appeared just twice in the Middlesbrough first team. His first appearance was at centre-forward in a 2–0 defeat at Wolverhampton Wanderers in December 1902. It was another 14 months before Godley was recalled, this time on the left wing, for a 1–0 victory over Notts County at Ayresome Park.

GOOD Hugh Jardine

Centre-half/Right-half
Born: Motherwell, 2 July 1901.
Career: Kilmarnock. Wishaw YMCA. MIDDLESBROUGH 1924. Exeter City 1926. Bristol City 1927. Torquay United 1927. Raith Rovers. Bo'ness. Glentoran. Montrose.

■ Scottish half-back Good was given his chance in the Middlesbrough side early in the 1924–25 campaign. Playing at centre-half, he enjoyed a short run of games as Boro hovered around the middle of the Second Division table. After sporadic chances later in the season, Good's final games came in February 1926 and he joined Third Division Exeter at the end of the season.

GOODFELLOW Derwick Ormond

Goalkeeper
Born: Shilbottle, 26 June 1914.
Career: Gateshead 1935. Sheffield Wednesday 1936. MIDDLESBROUGH 1947. Exeter City 1948.

■ A native of Northumberland, former marine commando Goodfellow was a tough customer. In one game for Middlesbrough he was regularly impeded by Manchester City centre-forward Eddie McMorran. After one foul, though, the 6ft 1in goalkeeper jumped to his feet and with one hand screwed the front of McMorran's jersey tightly under his chin, lifting him into the air and carrying him slowly to the penalty-spot advising not to come closer to the goal than that.

Goodfellow had played for Sheffield Wednesday before the war but made only seven post-war appearances at Hillsborough before moving to Ayresome Park. He made his Middlesbrough debut in a 2–2 draw with Manchester United and was a regular in his only season at the club. He left when Rolando Ugolini was brought in but didn't make a first-team appearance at Exeter.

GOODSON Leonard

Inside-left/Outside-left
Born: Details unknown.
Died: Doncaster, 1922.
Career: Doncaster Rovers 1901. MIDDLESBROUGH 1902.

■ Left-sided forward Goodson – comfortable on the wing or at inside-forward – arrived midway through the 1902–03 season. It was a difficult start as the team drifted out of the top half of the First Division table, ending in 13th place. The final game of the season – in which Goodson played – proved to be the last game at the Linthorpe Road ground but the former Doncaster man was missing from the side at the start of 1903–04 and didn't feature in the first game at Ayresome Park. Goodson was in and out of the side in that campaign and his final game came in a 1–0 victory over Everton early in the 1904–05 season. Goodson, who had three spells at Doncaster in his career, died in the Yorkshire town in 1922.

GORDON Daniel

Right-back
Born: West Calder, 1883.
Career: Everton 1903. Southampton. St Mirren. MIDDLESBROUGH 1908. Bradford Park Avenue 1908. Hull City 1909. Southampton.

■ Gordon's only Middlesbrough appearance came at right full-back in a nine-goal thriller at Old Trafford. Replacing regular full-back Jimmy Watson, Gordon saw Boro concede six goals to Manchester United with only three in return. The Scotsman made way for Campbell a week later and soon left the club.

GORDON Dean Dwight

Full-back
Born: Croydon, 10 February 1973.
Career: Crystal Palace 1991. MIDDLESBROUGH 1998. Cardiff City (loan) 2001. Coventry City 2002. Reading (loan) 2004. Grimsby Town 2004. Macclesfield 2005. Apoel Nicosia (Cyprus). Blackpool 2006. Albany United (Australia) 2006. Auckland City (Australia) 2006. New Zealand Knights 2006. Torquay United 2007.

■ Dean Gordon's Boro career was very much a case of what might have been. An outstanding and ever-present first season in the left wing-back role made him a big crowd favourite, but he never reached the same heights after suffering a cruciate ligament injury early in the 1999–2000 campaign. A £900,000 signing from Crystal Palace at the same time as Gary Pallister returned to the club, Gordon was adept at getting forward well to provide telling crosses and the occasional spectacular goal. His strike against Manchester United in the famous 3–2 win at Old Trafford was voted as the club's goal of the season in 1998–99. Following the arrival of Christian Ziege, Gordon started the 1999–2000 season in central defence, covering for the injured Pallister, but suffered the cruciate ligament damage in the third League match, a 3–1 win at Derby. His one further appearance that season came as a substitute the following March. The 2000–01 season saw Gordon again blighted by injuries though he did score the winner against Chelsea in Terry Venables' first game in charge. In November 2001 he joined Cardiff City on loan and then returned to the Riverside to make his one appearance under Steve McClaren as a substitute in an important 1–0 win at Sunderland. His free transfer move to Coventry began a nomadic end to his career as he appeared for 10 clubs in seven divisions over the next five years, taking in spells in both Cyprus and Australia. He also played briefly for Crook Town in the Northern League while opening a sports shoe business in Darlington. He spent the second half of the 2006–07 season with Torquay United as they finished bottom of the Football League. Before joining Boro, Gordon won 10 caps at England Under-21 level after coming through the Crystal Palace youth ranks. He played alongside Gareth Southgate at Palace before being snapped up by Bryan Robson following his club's 1998 relegation from the Premier League. He had played 241 games for Palace and made a further 71 for Boro.

GORDON James

Wing-half
Born: Fauldhouse, 23 October 1915.
Died: Derby, 29 August 1996.
Career: Wishaw Juniors. Newcastle United 1935. MIDDLESBROUGH 1945.

■ When World War Two came to an end, Newcastle United believed the career of their 30-year-old wing-half Jimmy Gordon was all but over. One director described him as a '20 minute footballer' and he had lost his place to a stream of promising youngsters. The Magpies were happy to offload Gordon to Middlesbrough but the tenacious Scot proved his critics wrong by enjoying many good years on Teesside.

Gordon was in fact one of the mainstays of Boro's post-war side. He was among the fittest players at the club despite his age and was a regular into his late 30s. Gordon was a polished wing-half, a firm but fair tackler and also a talented ball-player who commanded the midfield. He was a specialist at the long throw, rarely flustered and made the most of his new lease of life on Teesside as part of a fine half-back line with Harry Bell and Bill Whitaker. Boro struggled in the seasons after the war but the trio helped lift the club to a ninth place finish in 1949–50. He was appointed club captain for 1951–52 but the arrival of Eddie Russell late in the season limited his appearances. He was still an important squad man though and played his last game in February 1954, past his 38th birthday.

Gordon was placed in charge of Boro's juniors in 1955 before joining the coaching staff at Blackburn. Gordon had come into contact with Brian Clough at Middlesbrough and he subsequently became the third member of the celebrated Clough Taylor management team at Derby, Leeds and Nottingham Forest, once leading Forest out in a League Cup Final at Wembley. Gordon died in Derby in August 1996.

GOWLAND Norman

Goalkeeper
Born: Butterknowle, 1902.
Career: Chilton Colliery Welfare. MIDDLESBROUGH 1925. Stockport County 1930. Rotherham United 1931.

■ Goalkeeper Gowland found life tough as deputy to the consistent Jimmy Mathieson. He came into the first-team frame as cover for Jack Clough in the 1925–26 campaign, making his debut in a 2–1 win over Oldham in October 1925 before getting another chance in the final two games of the season. Mathieson was signed in the summer of 1926 and it was October 1928 before Gowland was given another opportunity. A defeat at Clapton Orient and home draw with West Brom proved to be his last games. Gowland fell below Joe Hillier in the pecking order in 1929–30 and was released at the end of the season, later playing some games for Stockport County.

GRAHAM Daniel Anthony William

Forward
Born: Gateshead, 12 August 1985.
Career: Chester-le-Street Town. MIDDLESBROUGH 2004. Darlington (loan) 2004. Derby County (loan) 2005. Leeds United (loan) 2006. Blackpool (loan) 2006. Carlisle United (loan) 2007. Carlisle United 2007.

■ Having first made his name with

Northern League outfit Chester-le-Street Town, the former window fitter, who was a prolific scorer with Middlesbrough's Under-19 team, went on loan to Darlington in 2003–04 to gain some valuable experience of senior football. After finding the net a couple of times in his stay with the Quakers, he returned to the Riverside and made his debut off the bench in a 1–1 draw with Manchester United in October 2004. He scored his first goal a few weeks later in a 3–0 Carling Cup victory over Coventry and scored his one and only Premier League goal in a 2–2 draw at home to Charlton in February 2005 – although he knew little of it after suffering a broken nose while netting the ball. In 2005–06, Graham had loan spells with both Derby County and Leeds United but failed to find the net. A further loan to Blackpool early in 2006–07 was followed by 11 minutes as a Boro substitute at Watford. It was to be his only action under new boss Gareth Southgate as a successful loan to Carlisle United resulted in a free transfer to the League One side in the summer of 2007.

GRAY Robert S.M.

Outside-left
Born: Stirling, 27 February 1872.
Died: November 1926.
Career: King's Park. Aston Villa 1894. Grimsby Town 1895. Bedminster. MIDDLESBROUGH 1899. Luton Town 1900.

■ One of a huge number of players tried in Middlesbrough's first Football League campaign, Scottish inside-forward Gray had plenty of League experience. His League debut came in a 4–1 defeat and he was left out following a goal-less home draw with Luton. Gray was recalled for the reverse fixture at Luton in February 1900 and it was the Hatters that subsequently signed him.

GREEN Thomas

Outside-right/Centre-forward
Born: Rock Ferry, 25 November 1883.
Career: Liverpool 1901. Swindon Town. Stockport County. MIDDLESBROUGH 1904. Queen's Park Rangers. Stockport County 1907. Exeter City. Preston North End 1910.

■ Middlesbrough manager John Robson swooped to sign centre-forward Tom Green as the club desperately tried to avoid relegation. The signing was, however, soon eclipsed by the sensational £1,000 purchase of Alf Common. Green did help retain First Division status but was moved on to the right-wing in 1905–06 with Common preferred in the central role. The well-travelled frontman had been a regular at all his clubs after leaving his first – Liverpool – and moved on in the summer of 1906 following the signings of Steve Bloomer and Billy Brawn. Green was later a wireless operator at Cable & Wireless and lived in Aldershot.

GREENING Jonathan

Midfield
Born: Scarborough, 2 January 1979.
Career: York City 1996. Manchester United 1998. MIDDLESBROUGH 2001. West Bromwich Albion 2004.

■ Boro boss Steve McClaren went back to his old club Manchester United to make Greening one of his first signings in August 2001. Greening had been a fringe player at Old Trafford and was valued at £2 million when he arrived with fellow midfielder Mark Wilson in a combined £3.5 million deal. Born in Scarborough, Greening joined York City in 1996, making his professional debut in March 1997. He stayed for two years at Bootham Crescent before

moving to Old Trafford for £1 million in March 1998 as the second signing of Sir Alex Ferguson. Competition was tough against the likes of Ryan Giggs, Paul Scholes, Jordi Cruyff, Nicky Butt and Roy Keane, and he managed 27 appearances in three-and-a-half years. He made his Boro debut in McClaren's first game, a 4–0 home defeat against Arsenal and became a fixture in the side over the next two seasons. One of the fittest players on the staff, he covered a huge amount of ground from left midfield. Greening was unlucky to miss out on the 2001 semi-final with a rare injury. His second season was his most successful and he was named supporters' club Player of the Year. He was also called up to an England training camp, having been a regular at Under-21 level. Greening was a League ever-present in 2002–03 but, by his own admission, should have scored more goals – he managed only four League strikes in three seasons, in which he made 109 appearances. The arrival of Bolo Zenden and the graduation of Stewart Downing meant that

Greening's chances became more limited in 2003–04 and he missed out on the Carling Cup victory over Bolton. West Bromwich Albion and former Boro manager Bryan Robson snapped him up for £1 million in summer 2004 and he quickly became a fixture in the Baggies' promotion and relegation campaigns.

GRIFFITHS Thomas Percival

Centre-half/Right-back
Born: Moss, 21 February 1906.
Died: Wrexham, 25 December 1981.
Career: Ffrith Valley. Wrexham Boys Club. Wrexham 1922. Everton 1926. Bolton Wanderers 1931. MIDDLESBROUGH 1932. Aston Villa 1935. Wrexham 1938.

■ Griffiths was rated by many as Middlesbrough's greatest ever centre-half. He seemed to have an uncanny ability to hang in the air longer than his opponent and was a brilliant defensive header of the ball, excellent at judging crosses and high balls. He rarely missed a tackle and his only arguable weakness was his poor distribution – Griffiths was of the opinion that defenders should relieve themselves of the ball as quickly as possible.

Griffiths had been a contemporary of Dixie Dean at Everton but was part of the first ever Toffees side to be relegated – a fate he also suffered later in his career with Aston Villa. He came to Ayresome Park via a short spell at Bolton. He had

excelled when playing against Boro and prompted Peter McWilliam to splash out a Boro record fee for his services. He arrived with a big reputation, was immediately installed as captain and soon made a good impression on the club's supporters with a string of superb displays.

In 1934–35, inside-forward Bob Baxter was tried in more defensive positions with great success and by the start of the following season, Griffiths had to content himself with a few games at right-back as Baxter settled in at centre-half. Struggling Aston Villa saw the Boro skipper as the man to steer them away from relegation danger and the club's vice-chairman Norman Fell came to Teesside in Nov 1935 with full authority to buy him whatever the price. In the later years of his career, the Welsh international returned to his first club to become player-coach at Wrexham. An accomplished celloist, he was also a publican in the town and was a director of the club. Griffiths died in Wrexham on Christmas Day 1981.

GROVES James Albert

Full-back
Born: South Bank, July 1883.
Career: South Bank. Lincoln City 1903. Sheffield United 1903. MIDDLESBROUGH 1907. Wingate Albion.

■ Full-back Groves returned to his roots to spend five years at Ayresome Park but made only 27 first-team appearances. Groves had played early football for Grangetown before moving to London to join Arsenal. He had spells at Lincoln and Sheffield United – where he played in a North v South England trial game – before joining Boro. His debut came in the opening game of the 1907–08 season but it was February before another chance came. He was used sporadically in the following season and scored two goals from the right-wing when given a rare chance on a visit to White Hart Lane in October 1909.

HALL Berthold Alan Couldwell

Centre-forward
Born: Deepcar, 29 March 1908.
Died: Saxilby, 9 February 1983.
Career: Sheffield Park Labour Club. Doncaster Rovers 1926. MIDDLESBROUGH 1928. Bradford City 1930. Lincoln City 1931. Tottenham Hotspur 1933. Blackpool 1933. Gainsborough Trinity 1935.

■ Teenager Allan Hall was cast in the unenviable role of understudy to the prolific George Camsell when he joined Boro late in the 1927–28 season. The centre-forward was only 19 when Middlesbrough paid Third Division North side Doncaster a very significant fee of £3,500 but Hall was unable to live up to his transfer value in the few first-team opportunities he was afforded. He did, however, make a promising start by scoring on his debut in an impressive 4–2 away at then mighty Huddersfield Town. But Boro slipped to relegation a month later and Camsell's goalscoring feats ensured further appearances were strictly limited over the following two years. Hall eventually moved to Second Division Bradford City for a much reduced fee. A prolific goalscorer for Tottenham's reserves, he again found first-team opportunities rare and was playing for Blackpool at the outbreak of World War Two, during which he guested for Manchester City. Hall died in Lincolnshire in February 1983.

HALL John Henry

Centre-forward
Born: Hucknall, 3 July 1883.
Died: Nottingham, 1947.
Career: Newstead Byron. Newark. Nottingham Forest 1902. Mansfield Town. Stoke 1904. Brighton & Hove Albion. MIDDLESBROUGH 1908. Leicester Fosse 1910. Birmingham 1910. Hucknall Town.

■ Forward Jack Hall was a big hit during a two-year stay at Ayresome Park, finishing as the club's top scorer in both seasons. Brought to Boro by Andy Aitken from Southern League Brighton during the summer of 1908, he stepped straight into a forward line which also included ex-England stars Steve Bloomer and Alf Common. After a slow start, scoring only once in his first seven games, he found the net more regularly than both of his more illustrious teammates. His hat-trick

in a 6–2 win over Leicester Fosse in January 1909 was part of a run of eight goals in six games. He was less prolific in a struggling Middlesbrough team the following season but it was still something of a surprise when he left for Second Division Birmingham in the close season of 1910.

HAMILTON Gary James

Midfield
Born: Glasgow, 27 December 1965.
Career: MIDDLESBROUGH 1983. Darlington (loan) 1991. Billingham Town.

■ It is testimony to the consistency and quality of Gary Hamilton that he played over 250 games for Middlesbrough, despite the fact that he made his last appearance for the club aged only 23. The battling Scot may well have gone on to play twice as many games for the club had injury not cruelly cut short his career.

Spotted by Boro while playing for Eastercraigs youth side in Glasgow, he made the move south and was handed his first-team chance by Malcolm Allison at the tender age of 17. Indeed, only four younger players have appeared in a first-team game for the club. Allison frequently played the teenager at left-back but it was in a central midfield role that he was to establish himself as a first-team regular. A naturally physical player but also a good footballer, Hamilton's obvious will to win made him a firm favourite with the fans, though his whole-hearted displays were not enough to stop Boro suffering relegation to the Third Division in 1986. However,

despite having been on the transfer list, he displayed great loyalty to the club when declining a two-year contract with Charlton Athletic when Boro went into liquidation during the summer of 1986. Charlton's loss was Boro's gain as Hamilton played a pivotal role in the club's successive promotion successes under Bruce Rioch. Always keen to drive forward, he scored with a typically fierce finish to see off Bradford City in the 1988 Play-offs as Boro returned to the top flight. Despite carrying an ever-worsening injury to his right knee throughout the 1988–89 campaign, he refused to undergo treatment and missed only two games. Sadly, his bravery was all in vain as a final day defeat at Sheffield Wednesday confirmed Boro's relegation. The match proved to be his final appearance for Boro's first team as his knee proved beyond repair, despite three operations and several attempted comebacks. In 1991, he had a short loan spell with Darlington and seemed destinated to return to the Boro first team two-and-a-half years after his last appearance. Manager Lennie Lawrence named him as substitute for a League game, only for the problem knee to give way again during a reserve team match.

As always wearing his heart on his sleeve, Hamilton announced his retirement from the game at half-time during a game against Manchester United later that season. He was given a well-deserved testimonial match against Sunderland during the 1993–94 season and later played local League football for Billingham Town. He emigrated to the United States in the mid–1990s and still lives there to this day, having achieved much success coaching youngsters. He is still a regular visitor to the Riverside whenever he returns home to Teesside.

HAMILTON William Murdoch

Inside-forward
Born: Airdrie, 16 February 1938.
Died: Calgary, Canada, 22 October 1976.
Career: Drumpelier. Sheffield United 1956. MIDDLESBROUGH 1961. Heart of Midlothian. Hibernian. Aston Villa 1965. Ross County.

■ Willie Hamilton was a mercurial talent who never fulfilled his huge potential, always capable of delighting and disappointing in equal measures. Fans who saw him in action for Boro will no doubt look back on his all too short stay with the club and wonder what might have been. For the inside forward was described by some who saw him play at his best as 'a wayward genius'. Certainly it is no criticism of Bob Dennison to say he failed to get the best out of this likeable rogue, as none of his managers – who included Joe Mercer and Jock Stein – could claim to have done so. Hamilton made just 12 appearances in 14 months on Teesside at a time when Boro were struggling to win promotion to the First Division.

One of those rare talents, a player with the ability to win a game on his own, Hamilton had brilliant ball skills and was particularly difficult to dislodge from the ball. Alas, he also had a self-destructive side that made him his own worst enemy. He was given his break in professional football by the legendary Joe Mercer at Sheffield United when still only 17. After moving to Boro, he scored against Plymouth just 13 minutes into his debut and played the next seven games before losing his place. However, teammates recall how, in training, Hamilton could hit the crossbar with a shot nine times out of 10, such was his accuracy. They also remember how more than once he slept the night in his car outside Ayresome Park ready for training the next day.

He was made available for transfer after a long spell in the Ayresome Park reserves, where he was watched by representatives from Hearts. He eventually joined the Edinburgh club and revitalised his career, helping them to a Scottish League Cup triumph in 1963. He remained in Edinburgh with a move to Hibernian where he played under Jock Stein and was capped by his country while also representing the Scottish League. He later made his English First Division bow during a two-year spell with Aston Villa but off-the-field problems were never far away. It seemed that Hamilton simply lacked the temperament to become a top player and he ended his playing days in South Africa. His death was reported in Canada in early November 1976 at the age of just 38.

HANKIN Raymond

Forward
Born: Wallsend, 21 February 1956.
Career: Burnley 1973. Leeds United 1976. Vancouver Whitecaps (Canada) 1980. Arsenal 1981. Vancouver Whitecaps 1981. MIDDLESBROUGH 1982. Peterborough United 1983. Wolverhampton Wanderers 1984. Whitby Town. Blue Star FC. Guisborough Town. Hamrun Spartans (Malta).

■ Although he was just 26 at the time, Hankin was past his best when he joined Boro early in the 1982–83 season. Bobby Murdoch's last signing as Middlesbrough manager, he was sent off against Grimsby on his debut for the club as Second Division Boro crashed to a 4–1 defeat for the third successive home game. It would perhaps be unfair to say it was all downhill from there but a return of just one goal in 21 League games was a huge disappointment for the fans who remembered Hankin as a bustling centre-forward of the highest order from his days with Burnley and Leeds.

He had won England Youth and Under-23 honours with Burnley when his form attracted the attention of several top clubs. A well-built target man, he almost joined West Ham but told Hammers boss Ron Greenwood that he preferred to stay in the north and, instead, moved to Leeds United for £172,000. He was United's 20-goal top scorer in 1977–78 but knee problems dogged his progress and he decided to try his luck in the North American Soccer League with Vancouver Whitecaps, where he won a North-West Division medal. In November 1981 it was reported that Arsenal were willing to pay £400,000 to bring Hankin back to England but the Gunners released him after a short trial. He returned to Vancouver via a brief spell in Ireland with Shamrock Rovers before Boro signed him in a bid to solve a disastrous start to the season. Sadly, Hankin was no longer the free-scoring striker of old, though he remained a regular under Malcolm Allison and occasionally captained the side.

After leaving the professional game, Hankin returned to the North East and worked in a mental hospital while playing for Guisborough Town in the Northern League. He actually returned to Ayresome Park with Guisborough for an FA Cup tie with Bury in 1987 but suffered an unwanted case of déjà vu when he was shown the red card for refusing to wear the captain's armband. He later managed Darlington, Northallerton Town and worked as Newcastle United's Football in the Community Officer.

HANLON Edward

Centre-half
Born: Darlington.
Died: 1925.
Career: Darlington. MIDDLESBROUGH 1908. Darlington. Barnsley 1911. Darlington.

■ Centre-half Eddie Hanlon added his name to Middlesbrough's list of one-game wonders when he made what proved to be his only appearance for the club in the opening away game of the 1906–07 season. Signed from Darlington, he was handed his First Division debut at Woolwich Arsenal alongside fellow rookies, Hickling and Priest. All three were dropped by manager Alex Mackie after Boro's 2–0 defeat and neither Hanlon nor Priest were given another first-team chance. Mackie's successor, Andy Aitken, allowed Hanlon to join Barnsley in 1907. After finishing his playing days, Hanlon had a spell as Darlington's trainer.

HARDWICK George Francis Moutry

Full-back
Born: Saltburn, 2 February 1920.
Died: Stokesley, 19 April 2004.
Career: South Bank. MIDDLESBROUGH 1937. Oldham Athletic 1950.

■ Glance through any books of football's all-time legends and you will almost certainly discover the name of George Hardwick. Captain of club, country and, on one unique occasion, Great Britain, 'Gentleman George' was a stylish, composed left full-back and an inspirational skipper.

The grandson of a former Middlesbrough Ironopolis player, Frank Hardwick, he was born in Saltburn though he lived his early life in Lingdale. He played his first football for South Bank East End's junior side, displaying his enthusiasm and fitness by frequently cycling from Lingdale for games. Arsenal and Glasgow Rangers were among a whole host of clubs who showed an interest in the talented youngster but Hardwick signed amateur forms with Middlesbrough after leaving school at 15. He worked as a costing clerk at Dorman Long during his early days at Ayresome Park, where his chores included cleaning the boots of his Boro hero Bob Baxter. Hardwick made a disastrous start to his first-team debut against Bolton, scoring a first minute own goal after receiving an early touch from Billy Forrest. Without looking, the 17-year-old passed the ball back to Dave Cumming, not realising the

Boro goalkeeper had come off his line to receive the ball. Despite the gaffe, Hardwick was given a run in the side as Bobby Stuart's deputy but was not called upon again the following season, the last before the outbreak of war. An RAF sergeant during the hostilities, he made his name while guesting for Chelsea (managed by former Boro star Billy Birrell) and played in two War Cup Finals while playing in 17 war-time England internationals. His blossoming career was threatened when he was wounded in both legs during an air raid attack on an RAF base on the Isle of Sheppey but he made a full recovery to fulfill all of his early promise.

A classy, cultured defender, he was England's automatic choice at left full-back when peace returned and captained the side in all 13 of his post-war international appearances. Perhaps the pinnacle of his career was the day he skippered Great Britain against a select side representing the Rest of Europe in 1947, a game in which Boro teammate Wilf Mannion also played a starring role. He would almost certainly have won many more caps but lost his place through injury and, with Billy Wright installed as captain, he was not allowed to return. Hardwick and Mannion were the undoubted stars of a First Division Middlesbrough team that rarely threatened to win honours. A great reader of the game, Hardwick was a hard and accurate tackler who rarely wasted a pass. He was also charming and debonair and it was no surprise when he revealed his ambition to move into management.

In November 1950, Boro reluctantly agreed to the 30-year-old's transfer request, though they demanded £15,000, a hefty fee that represented a club record sale and the largest ever fee paid for a full-back. Hardwick turned down the offer of a player-coach's role at Everton to take up an appointment as player-manager of Third Division North side Oldham Athletic and led the Latics to promotion. He combined the two roles with great success and actually went on to play more times for Oldham than he had for Middlesbrough. However, relegation followed and he left the club on a point of principle when the Oldham board refused to sanction his signing of George Eastham. Hardwick spent eight years abroad, initially coaching the US Army in Germany before accepting exciting roles as coach of PSV Eindhoven and director of coaching for the Dutch FA, during which he introduced the original version of total football. He returned to Boro during the early 1960s to coach the club's youth team before becoming manager of Sunderland. He took the Roker club to their highest post-war position but was controversially sacked after just 169 days in the job. He later managed non-League Gateshead and was a columnist in the *Evening Gazette* before moving into quality assurance. Hardwick and Mannion were belatedly granted a benefit game by the Middlesbrough directors in May 1983. Hardwick rarely missed a Boro game in his latter years when he was honoured with the unveiling of a statue outside the Riverside Stadium.

HARKINS John

Wing-half
Born: Musselburgh.
Died: 1915.
Career: Black Watch Regiment. MIDDLESBROUGH 1906. Broxburn Athletic. Bathgate. Leeds City 1910. Darlington. Coventry City.

■ Defender Jack Harkins was one of no fewer than 15 players given their Middlesbrough debuts during a chaotic two-month spell early in the 1906–07 season. Having guided the club to First Division safety the previous year, Alex Mackie and his directors reverted to what appeared to be desperate measures in a bid to avoid another relegation battle. Boro had taken just two points from their opening seven games when Harkins was given his chance in the heat of a north-east derby clash against Newcastle United in October 1906. Despite a 3–0 home defeat, he retained his place as Boro won their first match at the ninth time of asking at Aston Villa a week later and he missed only one game throughout the remainder of the campaign. Scotsman Harkins, who was equally at home as centre or right-half, partnered player-manager Andy Aitken at the heart of the defence as a respectable mid-table finish was achieved. However, he struggled to hold his form the following season and found himself relegated to the reserves following the arrival of Eddie Verrill and moved to Bathgate in 1907. He later returned to League football with Leeds City and Darlington before serving the famous Black Watch during World War One.

HARRIS Joseph

Wing-half
Born: Glasgow, 19 March 1896.
Died: Glasgow, 29 October 1933.
Career: Strathclyde Juniors. Partick Thistle 1913. MIDDLESBROUGH 1923. Newcastle United 1925. York City 1931.

■ Tenacious right-half Harris was a far bigger success at Newcastle United than he was with Middlesbrough. Manager Jimmy Howie signed the Scotland international from Partick Thistle late in the 1922–23 season. Harris, who could be both commanding and dainty footed, was an automatic choice under new boss Herbert Bamlett for much of the 1923–24 campaign but Boro finished rock bottom and were relegated to Division Two. As Boro struggled to bounce back, Harris lost his first-team place and was placed on the transfer list for £1,000 in May 1925, joining Newcastle for a knock-down £750 four months later. He was a popular player at St James' Park and helped them win the First Division Championship in 1926–

27. He was still on the books of York City when he died, aged 37, in Glasgow Infirmary after a short illness in 1933.

HARRIS William Charles

Inside-forward/Wing-half
Born: Swansea, 31 October 1928.
Died: Acklam, December 1989.
Career: Swansea Town. Llanelli. Hull City 1950. MIDDLESBROUGH 1954. Bradford City 1965.

■ Middlesbrough supporters took Welshman Bill Harris to their hearts during his 11-year stay on Teesside despite the fact that he was unable to lead them back to the promised land of Division One. Dubbled 'the Red Dragon', he combined a winger's pace and trickery with a half-back's ability to spot the vulnerable point in the opposition's defence and regularly exploited those weaknesses with his forward runs or defence-splitting passes. He was also famed for his thunderbolt shot. However, he lacked ball-winning ability and it was no surprise when he was moved up to inside-forward as his Boro career progressed. His ability to create and control a game meant he was directly responsible for making many of the prolific Brian Clough's goals though it is believed that Harris instigated an infamous petition demanding that Clough be relieved of the club captaincy.

Harris himself captained the side soon after joining Boro from Hull City for a club record £18,000 fee. He had been on the books of Swansea Town immediately after the war but he was released by his hometown club on completion of his National Service and dropped into non-League with Llanelli. His obvious talent brought him to Hull's attention and he moved to Boothferry Park for a £2,000 fee, quite a sum for a non-League player. His arrival at Boro four years later was not enough to prevent relegation to the Second Division and, after just nine games, Harris' top flight career was over. Noted for his consistency, he rarely missed a game and played in 127 consecutive League games between September 1954 and September 1957. While his main role was as Boro's creative influence, Harris boasted a fine scoring record and in January 1962 he scored the fastest recorded goal in Boro's history after just 11 seconds into an FA Cup tie with Shrewsbury. Given his undoubted ability, it is only a wonder that Harris did not win far more than just six caps for his country. However, aged 34, he was on the verge of quitting Boro in 1963 and even contemplated retirement to run a hotel, only to be given a second wind with the appointment of Raich Carter as Boro's manager. Carter, who had earlier signed him for Hull, convinced Harris he still had a big part to play in the side and the player responded in style. Although he no longer boasted the speed and stamina that had once been the hallmark of his game, his excellent positional sense and precision passing meant he was still running games after his 36th birthday.

He eventually left Boro to take up a position as Bradford City's player-manager but failed to find success and returned to the North East and had a spell as coach of local side, Stockton. Harris died in Acklam in December 1989.

HARRISON Craig

Defender
Born: Gateshead, 10 November 1977.
Career: MIDDLESBROUGH 1996. Preston North End (loan) 1999. Crystal Palace 2000.

■ Craig Harrison experienced the contrasting highs and lows of the game in his all-too-brief playing career. The left-back made an immediate impact

when given his chance by Bryan Robson in the 1997–98 promotion season and, having signed a new four-and-a-half year contract, received the club's Young Player of the Year award. However, injury and the arrival of Dean Gordon curtailed his progress in the Premier League the following season. He suffered a further setback during the summer of 1999 when a burst appendix ruled him out of the game for at least six months. It was later revealed that Harrison had had a lucky escape as he might have died had surgeons not operated quickly. Although he grew up as a Newcastle fan and played for Tyneside's Redheugh Boys Club, Harrison was spotted by Boro scout Peter Kirtley and attended the club's Centre of Excellence. He was given a two-year professional contract in March 1996 after impressing as a trainee. Along with Steve Baker, he made his first-team debut in a Coca-Cola Cup tie at Barnet in October 1997 after impressing for the reserves and went on to play more than 20 times that season. Indeed, he could consider himself very unfortunate not to have played at Wembley in his first season, as he played in the six games either side of Boro's 1998 Coca-Cola Cup Final defeat but was left out for the big match. Competitive and gutsy, Harrison displayed good composure and an ability to get forward down the left flank. Harrison joined Crystal Palace for a fee of £200,000. His performances improved game by game for the Eagles until he suffered a double fracture of the leg in a match against Reading in January 2002, an injury that forced his premature retirement from the game. He returned to the North East to open a pet training centre.

HARRISON Henry (Harry)

Goalkeeper
Born: Redcar, 21 November 1893.
Career: Grangetown. MIDDLESBROUGH 1919. Darlington 1924. Durham City 1925. Hartlepool United 1926. Darlington 1928.

■ The eldest of three goalkeeping brothers, Harrison was forced to wait six years for his first-team debut for Middlesbrough. Tom McIntosh signed Harrison after spotting him in a game between Redcar West End and Lackenby in 1913 but the form of the legendary Tim Williamson and the outbreak of war meant it was October 1919 before he was given his First Division chance in a 1–1 draw at Manchester United. Williamson returned after a few games and it was another 15 months before Harrison was called upon again. This time he was given a long run in the side but he was relegated to third choice behind Williamson and Jack Clough in 1922–23. He played his final Boro games in the relegation season of 1923–24 before joining Darlington. Throughout his playing days, Harrison continued to ply his other trade as a fishmonger on Redcar's Coatham Road.

HARTNETT James Benedict

Outside-left
Born: Dublin, 21 March 1927.
Died: June 1988.
Career: Dundalk. MIDDLESBROUGH 1948. King's Lynn. Barry Town. Hartlepool United 1957. York City 1958.

■ Irish outside-left Jimmy Hartnett is best remembered by older Boro fans for the hat-trick he scored against Sheffield United at Ayresome Park in April 1949, less than two months after his first-team debut. That day's 3–1 win over the relegation-bound Blades saved Middlesbrough from a similar fate, David Jack's side avoiding the drop by a single point.

Signed the previous summer from Dundalk, where he had won Irish League representative honours, Hartnett scored on his Boro debut in a 4–4 home draw with Wolves. After struggling to build on his fine start he returned home to Ireland in the summer of 1950 but was

persuaded to return in a telephone call from the Boro manager. Despite scoring against the 1950–51 champions Spurs, first-team opportunities were few and far between and he was transfer listed twice, in January 1951 and again in the summer of 1953 after playing non-League football for a year with King's Lynn. Boro had continued to hold Hartnett's registration and he made a surprise return in place of Geoff Walker in October 1953 almost two years after his previous first-team game.

Boro were relegated to the Second Division at the end of that season and he was released to join non-League Barry Town in 1955, though he did briefly return to League football with Hartlepool and York. Hartnett died in 1988 when complications set in after being admitted to hospital for an exploratory operation.

HASSELL Albert Arthur

Goalkeeper
Born: Bristol.
Career: Bolton Wanderers 1906. MIDDLESBROUGH 1907. Nottingham Forest 1909. Swindon Town.

■ Like eight other goalkeepers over a 20-year period, Hasell discovered that being understudy to Tim Williamson was a thankless task. He had his one and only first-team appearance shortly after joining the club from Bolton, Boro losing 2–0 to Everton at Ayresome Park. Hasell moved on to non-League Swindon shortly afterwards.

HASSELBAINK Jerrel (Jimmy Floyd)

Forward
Born: Paramaribo, Surinam, 27 March 1972.
Career: Telstar (Holland) 1990. AZ Alkmaar (Holland) 1991. Campomaiorense (Portugal) 1993. Boavista (Portugal) 1996. Leeds United 1997. Atletico Madrid (Spain) 1999. Chelsea 2000. MIDDLESBROUGH 2004. Charlton Athletic 2006.

■ By the time Jimmy Floyd Hasselbaink joined Boro on a free transfer, £29 million had been spent on transforming the one-time Dutch non-League player into one of Europe's finest strikers. Born in Surinam, the career of Jimmy, real name Jerrel, took him to the Netherlands and Portugal, where he helped Boavista win the domestic Cup, before he signed for Leeds United in 1997. He scored 44 goals in his first two seasons for the Yorkshire side, helping them to fourth place in the Premiership. His 18 League goals in his second season made him joint Premiership top scorer alongside Michael Owen and Andy Cole. He signed for Atletico Madrid in summer 1999 and had one season in the Spanish League. Scoring 24 goals in 34 appearances. He came back to England the following year when Chelsea paid a record £15 million for him. He became outright Premiership top scorer in his first season with the Blues, scoring 23 goals in 35 appearances. He spent four seasons at Stamford Bridge, finishing top scorer in three of them and ending with 87 goals in 177 games. Steve McClaren signed him on a free transfer in summer 2004 to add experience for the club's first season in Europe. Hasselbaink scored 16 goals in 45 appearances in his first season as McClaren rotated his front line to accommodate Mark Viduka and Yakubu. He was the first Boro player to score in the UEFA Cup when he hit the opener in a 3–0 win over Banik Ostrava. He also scored in both legs against Grazer AK and his final goal of the domestic campaign in a 1–1 draw at Manchester City guaranteed European football for a second year. He was second top-scorer to Yakubu in 2005–06, netting 18 goals. Vital strikes included the winners against Grasshoppers and AS Roma and one of the two that helped Boro win in Stuttgart. He also scored in the incredible UEFA Cup quarter-final against Basel when Boro came back from three goals down to win 4–3. Hasselbaink's last appearance came in the final against Sevilla and he ended his stay on Teesside with 34 goals from 89 appearances. He moved to Charlton on a free transfer but lasted just one season at The Valley, scoring just four goals in their relegation season.

HASTIE John

Outside-right
Born: Details unknown.
Career: Plymouth Argyle. MIDDLESBROUGH 1920. Dundee.

■ Signed from Third Division Plymouth Argyle, John Hastie played his only game for Middlesbrough on the opening day of the 1920–21 season. Playing at outside-right, he was the novice in a quality forward line which also included George Elliott, Jacky Carr, Walter Tinsley and Tommy Urwin. The First Division match ended in a disappointing 2–1 home defeat to Oldham and the club's directors never called upon his services again. He left for Dundee soon afterwards.

HAWKINS George Henry (Harry)

Inside-forward/Centre-forward
Born: Middlesbrough, 24 November 1915.

Died: Middlesbrough, 11 March 1992.
Career: South Bank Princess Street, South Bank East End. MIDDLESBROUGH 1935. Watford 1937. Southport 1938. Gateshead 1945. Hartlepool United 1947. Blyth Spartans. Murton Colliery.

■ Another member of the one-match wonders club, Harry Hawkins appeared at inside-right alongside England stars George Camsell and Ralph Birkett in a 4–1 First Division defeat at Huddersfield in February 1936. Signed from the famous production line of Middlesbrough players at South Bank East End, he had a long spell in the Ayresome reserves before joining Watford in the Third Division South. He did, however, return to Ayresome Park as a Southport player in 1945 to receive specialist treatment for an injury from Middlesbrough trainer Charlie Cole. Hawkins died in 1992.

HAWORTH John Houghton

Right-back/Left-half
Born: Bolton, 1887.
Career: Turton. Brighton & Hove Albion. MIDDLESBROUGH 1911.

■ A £600 signing from Brighton midway through the 1911–12 season, Haworth made his Middlesbrough debut at left-half in a 2–0 home defeat to Arsenal in February 1912. John Cook and Joe Hisbent were also awarded their first-team debuts that same day. Haworth partnered Willie Carr and Eddie Verrill in the Boro backline for the remainder of the season but lost his place the following season. He was more successful when switched to right full-back and was the club's regular in that position when Boro achieved their highest ever top flight

finish of third in 1913–14. He continued as a regular in 1914–15 but the Great War brought an end to his playing days.

HEALEY Richard

Inside-right/Centre-forward
Born: Darlington, 20 September 1890.
Career: Bishop Auckland. Sunderland 1909. Bishop Auckland. Sunderland 1911. Bishop Auckland. MIDDLESBROUGH 1913. Darlington 1921.

■ A member of the exclusive club who can claim to have scored on their Middlesbrough debut, Richard Healey made the step up from Bishop Auckland to the First Division in April 1914. He was on target in a 4–1 home win over Preston North End but found the form of Boro's quality forwards severely limited his chances. Healey was behind the likes of Walter Tinsley, George Elliott, Andy Wilson and Jacky Carr in the pecking order, though he did score again when standing in for top scorer Tinsley in a 3–1 home defeat to Bradford Park Avenue in November 1914. After the Great War, the former Darlington Grammar School boy appeared for Sunderland and his hometown club, Darlington.

HEARD Timothy Patrick

Midfield
Born: Hull, 17 March 1960.
Career: Everton 1978. Aston Villa 1979. Sheffield Wednesday 1983. Newcastle United 1984. MIDDLESBROUGH 1985.

Hull City 1986. Rotherham United 1988. Cardiff City 1990. Hull City 1992.

■ Willie Maddren once described Pat Heard as his most disappointing signing. Recommended to Maddren by former Boro manager Jack Charlton, Heard was watched playing for Newcastle reserves and duly arrived at Ayresome Park on loan. He was highly impressive during the loan, starring and setting up the vital winner over Sheffield United with an excellent left wing run. That convinced Maddren to make the deal permanent and Heard signed on the dotted line soon afterwards. Sadly, that proved to be a turning point as the player's form immediately dropped off and Maddren questioned his attitude and commitment, only persevering with him due to the lack of options. With Boro in deep relegation trouble, Maddren's successor Bruce Rioch dropped the ineffective Heard and he moved on to Hull the following summer. A left-sided defender or midfielder, Heard had enjoyed a bright career as a teenager but was unable to claim a regular place at any of his high profile clubs. Signed by Aston Villa for £100,000, he was among their substitutes for their 1981 European Cup Final success over Bayern Munich.

HEDLEY George Thomas

Right-back
Born: County Durham, 1882.
Died: 1937.
Career: West Stanley.

MIDDLESBROUGH 1905. Chester. Heart of Midlothian. Hull City 1905. Leicester Fosse 1907. Luton Town. Brandesburton.

■ It is perhaps no surprise that right full-back Hedley played just three games in a Middlesbrough shirt when it is considered that Boro conceded 13 goals in his three first-team appearances. He and George Henderson made their debuts for the club in a 4–1 hammering at Aston Villa in November 1905 and Hedley retained his place a week later for a 5–1 home defeat to Liverpool. A month later he was again called upon for a 4–4 Ayresome Park draw with Bolton. Hedley moved on to Hearts at the end of the season and later played League football for Leicester Fosse.

HEDLEY Graeme

Midfield
Born: Easington, 1 March 1957.
Career: MIDDLESBROUGH 1975. Sheffield Wednesday (loan) 1978. Darlington (loan) 1979. York City (loan) 1981. Horden Colliery. Hartlepool United 1984.

■ Hedley can perhaps count himself unlucky to have been at Middlesbrough at a time when a number of talented young players were also emerging. Although never a first-team regular during six seasons with the club, he was noted for his fine passing ability and will long be remembered for a fabulous goal against Sunderland at Ayresome Park in

1981. Standing in for the injured Craig Johnston, Hedley curled a superb free-kick over the Roker defence into the top corner for what proved to be the only goal of the match. It was typical of his luck that Johnston was fit to return for the following match and Hedley found himself back on the sidelines.

He might easily have made his name in another sport as he once opened the batting for an England schoolboys cricket team which also included David Gower and Mike Gatting. He was later offered terms by Northants but turned them down to join Boro. His initial first-team opportunities came in an attacking role as Jack Charlton looked to find a replacement for the ageing John Hickton. However, his skills were more suited to a midfield role and it was in that position that he was called upon infrequently by John Neal. Slight, small and particularly recognisable for his mass of blond hair, Hedley had two loan spells with Jack Charlton's Sheffield Wednesday but suffered the ill fortune to break his ankle just when the move looked set to be made permanent. Released by Boro following relegation to the Second Division, he later played in the Fourth Division for Hartlepool United.

HENDERSON George Hunter

Right-half
Born: Ladhope Selkirk, 2 May 1880.
Died: Scotland 1957.

Career: Queen's Park Rangers 1900. Dundee 1902. Glasgow Rangers 1902. MIDDLESBROUGH 1905. Chelsea 1905. Glossop 1909.

■ Right-half Henderson was a disappointment during his short stay on Teesside, having joined Middlesbrough as a player of much promise. As a Glasgow Rangers star, he had played in a 1–1 draw for Scotland against Ireland in 1904 and joined Boro for £130 the following year. A 4–1 defeat at Aston Villa was not the best game in which to make his debut and he was given only one short run of seven games in the first team, one of which was a 7–0 defeat at Birmingham. Although Middlesbrough narrowly avoided relegation, Henderson was allowed to move on to Chelsea after less than a year with the club.

HENDERSON Raymond

Outside-right
Born: Wallsend, 31 March 1937.
Career: Ashington. MIDDLESBROUGH 1957. Hull City 1961. Reading 1968.

■ Tynesider Henderson played for a number of local outfits before joining Boro from North Eastern League side Ashington during the summer of 1957. An inside-forward, he was handed his Second Division debut in place of the injured Arthur Fitzsimons at Blackburn in November of that year and scored 10 minutes into his home debut against Sheffield United a week later. However, the emergence of Alan Peacock meant it was almost three years before Henderson won another first-team chance – and he again responded with goals. Partnering Clough and Peacock, he scored four times in five games. Though he was soon back in the Ayresome Park reserves, his performances were enough to persuade Hull City to snap him up and he became a firm favourite at Boothferry Park, mainly playing as a right-winger and helping Hull to the Third Division Championship in 1966. After a short spell as Hull's assistant coach, he became player-coach at Reading before taking up his first managerial position at Halifax. Disillusioned with management, he moved to Everton as reserve team coach before having another unsuccessful crack at management, this time with Southport in their penultimate season as a Football League club.

HENDRIE John Grattan

Winger/Forward
Born: Lennoxtown, 24 October 1963.
Career: Coventry City 1981. Hereford United (loan) 1984. Bradford City 1984. Newcastle United 1988. Leeds United 1989. MIDDLESBROUGH 1990. Barnsley 1996.

■ Barrel-chested John Hendrie is remembered by Middlesbrough fans as a player who wore his heart on his sleeve, an all-action committed forward whose direct attacking style was always exciting to watch. It was astonishing that he was never capped by Scotland as for several seasons players of lesser ability seemed to be given the nod ahead of him.

The Scot turned down Celtic to join Coventry as a 16-year-old after impressing for Glasgow's Lennoxtown Boys Club and Possil YM. However, he made only limited first-team appearances at Highfield Road before being released and joined Third Division Bradford City, where he became an immediate hit. Switched from the flanks to a central striking role, he played a pivotal role in Bradford's promotion to the Second Division and very nearly helped them into the top flight, City losing to Boro in the 1988 promotion Play-offs. His tricky skills and turn of speed had impressed Bruce Rioch and the Boro manager tried to sign Hendrie for the club's return to the First Division. To Rioch's frustration, Hendrie had already agreed to join Newcastle United in a £500,000 deal, though the move did not come off and United were relegated in his one season at St James' Park.

After a short spell at Leeds, picking up a Second Division championship medal, he finally joined Boro when Colin Todd agreed a £500,000 transfer during the summer of 1990. Soon afterwards, Hendrie gave notice of his enormous talent by scoring a goal that would be talked about by those who saw it for many years to follow. Picking up the ball outside his own box, he ran half the length of the pitch before shooting into Millwall's goal. Despite that strike, Hendrie sometimes flattered to deceive in that first season on Teesside, too often flitting in and out of games from his position wide on the right wing. His rise to cult status on Teesside only really began when Todd's successor, Lennie Lawrence, reverted Hendrie to a central striking role and the goals began to flow. Sadly, the switch came too late to save Boro from relegation from the Premier League in 1992 but he was the supporters' club Player of the Year for 1992–93, while also being the run-away choice for readers of the fanzine, *Fly Me to the Moon*, who had voted him their most disappointing player two years earlier. Hendrie enjoyed a lethal strike partnership with Paul Wilkinson, his speed and tricky skills being the perfect foil for Wilkinson's aerial ability. Made club captain during the 1993–94 season, Hendrie was among the nation's top scorers in the early part of the season, netting 15 times by the end of October, only for injury to rule him out for four months. However, he was still named in the PFA First Division team of the season and continued his form into Bryan Robson's first season in charge. Indeed, it was Hendrie who scored both goals in a 2–1 win over Luton that all but ensured promotion and the First Division Championship in the last ever competitive match at Ayresome Park. That was to prove the pinnacle of his Boro career as injury dogged him throughout the following season and he was pushed down the pecking order with the big money signings of Nick Barmby, Juninho and Fabrizio Ravanelli.

He renewed his partnership with Wilkinson at Barnsley and helped the Tykes to promotion to the top flight for the first time in their history, winning the club's Player of the Year award into the bargain. However, he enjoyed less success as the club's player-manager, despite signing former Boro favourite Craig Hignett, and was sacked after less than a season in the role. Hendrie's older brother, Paul, played League football for Birmingham while Paul's son is Lee Hendrie of Aston Villa fame. Noted as something of a dressing room prankster, Hendrie's autobiography, *Don't Call Me Happy*, was popular among fans of all of his former clubs.

HEPPLE Gordon

Full-back
Born: Sunderland, 16 September 1925.
Died: 1980.
Career: North Sands.
MIDDLESBROUGH 1945. Norwich City 1954.

■ Although never a regular, left-footed Hepple was a member of Middlesbrough's first-team squad for eight First Division seasons. The Wearsider made his Boro debut at left-half at Huddersfield on the last day of the 1946–47 season and was given a run in the side the following year when Jimmy Gordon was injured. However, he usually played at left full-back when called upon, either as cover for George Hardwick or Ronnie Dicks. He was enjoying a short run in the side in March 1951 when he broke his leg against Stoke City. Although he made a full recovery from the injury, he did not play again for almost three years. Hepple was sold to Norwich City following Boro's relegation to the Second Division in 1954.

HEWITT Charles William

Inside-forward
Born: Greatham, nr Hartlepool, 1882.
Died: Darlington, 31 December 1966.
Career: West Hartlepool.
MIDDLESBROUGH 1905. Tottenham Hotspur 1906. Liverpool 1907. West Bromwich Albion 1908. Spennymoor United 1910. Crystal Palace 1910. Hartlepool United 1921.

■ Though he played for several top clubs as a quality forward, it was in management that Charlie Hewitt found his true niche. His stay with Middlesbrough lasted little more than a season, though the goals he scored in a 2–0 win at Blackburn in April 1905 did much to stave off the threat of relegation. He was a regular in the forward line for much of the 1905–06 season but lost his place when manager Alex Mackie signed England legend Steve Bloomer.

He moved on to Spurs but within weeks announced he wanted to leave after hearing that Liverpool were ready to offer £400 for him. However, the Football League ruled that Hewitt should honour his one-year contract at White Hart Lane and he joined Liverpool 12 months later. He was in his late 30s when he played for Hartlepool in their first ever Football League season.

He took up his first managerial role with Wrexham and enjoyed immediate success, winning the Welsh Cup and steering Chester into the Football League. In 1936, he accepted a lucrative offer to manage Millwall where he reversed their fortunes, taking them to the Division Three South championship and the FA Cup semi-final. However, he left the club in disgrace when sacked for making illegal payments to players. After serving as a Naval skipper during the war, he returned to Millwall via a spell at Leyton Orient. Although nicknamed 'Mr Millwall' for his loyalty to the club, Hewitt was unpopular with many of his players due to his abrasive manner. Consequently, it was reported that the players were so relieved when he was eventually sacked that they enjoyed a celebratory drink! Hewitt died in Darlington in December 1966.

HEWITT John

Midfield
Born: Aberdeen, 9 February 1963.
Career: Middlefield Wasps. Aberdeen 1979. Glasgow Celtic 1990.
MIDDLESBROUGH (loan) 1991.
Deveronvale. St Mirren 1991.

■ The undoubted highlight of John Hewitt's career came when he was just 20 years old. Hewitt scored the winner for Alex Ferguson's Aberdeen against Real Madrid in the 1983 European Cup-winners' Cup Final in Gothenburg. As a teenager, the attacking midfielder turned down Boro to join Aberdeen from Middlefield Wasps. He picked up his first Premier Division Championship medal while still just 17 and, as a forward, he was a regular player and goalscorer in Alex Ferguson's outstanding side which

won two further Championships, four Scottish Cups and a Scottish League Cup. One of his Aberdeen teammates was Willie Falconer. He moved to Parkhead but was a utility player with Celtic when he finally came to Boro on loan in October 1991. Hewitt and fellow Scot Rab Shannon were brought in by Lennie Lawrence with a view to making the moves permanent if they impressed at Ayresome Park. However, neither player shone and Hewitt made only two short substitute appearances, the first lasting just four minutes in a 2–1 Second Division defeat at Bristol Rovers. He returned to Celtic, moving on to St Mirren later that season.

HICK William Morris

Centre-forward
Born: Beamish, 13 February 1903.
Died: 1972.
Career: Consett Celtic. Hartlepool United 1921. South Shields 1922. MIDDLESBROUGH 1923. Southend United 1924. Bristol City 1928. Exeter City 1928. Grays Athletic. Scunthorpe & Lindsey United. Notts County 1929. Rotherham United 1930.

■ Centre-forward Hick was a makeweight in a deal which saw Jimmy McClelland move from Southend United to Middlesbrough in March 1925. For Hick, it was a disappointing end to what had looked certain to be an exciting career at Ayresome Park. Snapped up from Second Division South Shields, he burst on to the first-team scene with a debut goal in a 2–0 home win over Blackburn Rovers. But it was a case of too little too late for Herbert Bamlett's side who had failed to win any of their previous nine League games – and didn't manage a single victory in their final nine fixtures after the Rovers success either. Hick did, however, cover himself in more personal glory with both his side's goals in a 3–2 defeat to Sunderland at Roker Park. Sadly, his form deserted him in the Second Division and he was no more than a fringe player until his move to Roots Hall.

HICKLING William

Left-back
Born: Details unknown.

Career: Somercotes United. Derby County 1903. Tottenham Hotspur 1905. MIDDLESBROUGH 1906.

■ Left full-back Hickling was a reserve defender at each of his three major clubs. Snapped up by Derby from Somercotes United, a Derbyshire mining district club, he played just nine times before moving on to Tottenham Hotspur. He made only one Western League appearance for Spurs against West Ham before joining Middlesbrough. His debut came in the opening away match of the 1906–07 season at Woolwich Arsenal along with Hanlon and Priest. He was released a year later after making only a handful of appearances.

HICKTON John

Forward
Born: Chesterfield, 24 September 1944.
Career: Sheffield Wednesday 1962. MIDDLESBROUGH 1966. Hull City (loan) 1977. Fort Lauderdale Strikers (United States) 1978. Hartlepool United. Whitby Town.

■ John Hickton was one of Middlesbrough's most popular players ever. The archetypal centre-forward, he was a goalscoring machine who converted into a battering ram for the good of the team. Whatever his role, he enjoyed an excellent relationship with even the most critical of supporters and fully deserves his place in the club's hall of fame.

Hickton joined his first club, Sheffield Wednesday, as a full-back though he was also tried at centre-half and centre-forward and once scored eight times in an FA Youth Cup match. Having made his first-team debut at left-back, his versatility ensured he was used in a variety of positions, though he was unfortunate to miss out on a Wembley appearance when he was left out of the team for the 1966 FA Cup Final.

Hickton was a bargain £20,000 signing by Stan Anderson soon after Boro's relegation to the Third Division for the first time. He made his debut at centre-back and scored the first of many penalties for the club in a 3–2 win over Workington Town. Over the course of a memorable season, Hickton also played at right-back and up front, grabbing 15 League goals as promotion was secured at the first time of asking. There was no

doubting what Hickton's best position was as he finished each of the next six seasons as the club's top scorer, heading the Second Division scoring list no fewer than three times. Famed for his 20-yard run-ups before blasting his penalty kicks, Hickton had a powerful shot, was excellent in the air and was a brave, whole-hearted player. Despite his goals, Boro narrowly missed out on promotion several times and the striker became impatient to taste top flight football. He made several transfer requests and it was no surprise that several clubs were interested in signing the prolific goalscorer. Indeed, Hickton almost moved on in 1972. Huddersfield offered cash plus striker Frank Worthington while Queen's Park Rangers were prepared to meet Boro's £100,000 asking price. Thankfully, the Boro board got cold feet and pulled out of the deal at the last minute.

It took the arrival of Jack Charlton to turn Boro's potential into results and much of that success was down to Hickton's new role as a target man and battering ram, releasing others to score rather than trying to claim all the glory himself. He made his long awaited First Division debut, aged 29, at Birmingham City in August 1974 and celebrated by scoring the opening goal in a 3–0 win. In his latter years with the club, Hickton converted once again to utility player, though Boro were never able to find his replacement in attack. He enjoyed a testimonial match against Sunderland in 1977, scoring a hat-trick in a 6–1 win, before trying his luck in the North American Soccer League with Fort Lauderdale Strikers, coached by former Boro star Dave Chadwick. Sadly, he broke his leg in his first week in the States to effectively end his professional playing career. He did play two reserve games for Hartlepool but declined an offer to return to League football and later turned out for Whitby Town for a brief spell. Only two players made more appearances for Boro than Hickton while he is fourth in the club's all-time list of goalscorers. He now lives in Chesterfield where he worked in the insurance business.

HIGGINS William (Sandy)

Centre-half
Born: Smethwick, 1870.
Career: Woodfield. Albion Swifts. Birmingham St George. Grimsby Town 1892. Bristol City 1897. Newcastle United 1898. MIDDLESBROUGH 1900. Newton Heath 1901. Grimsby Town 1902.

■ Centre-half Higgins was a fearless player and a fine passer during his short spell with Middlesbrough. Nicknamed 'Sandy', he succeeded John McCracken as club captain in Boro's second season of League football and made his debut along with no fewer than eight fellow debutants on the opening day of the 1900–01 season against Lincoln City at the old Linthorpe Road ground. Noted for his sweeping passes out to the wings, Higgins also boasted a stinging shot. However, he achieved an unwanted 'first' against Small Heath in December 1900 when he became the first Middlesbrough player to be sent off in a Football League game. His punishment for retaliating against Bob McRoberts was a month's suspension. He left for Newton Heath after just one season on Teesside. Higgins initially made his name at Grimsby and joined Boro from Newcastle, where he had shown his versatility by playing in midfield, full-back and at centre-forward.

HIGHAM Norman

Inside-forward
Born: Chorley, 14 February 1912.
Career: Chorley. Everton 1933. MIDDLESBROUGH 1935. Southampton 1939.

■ The night before making his Middlesbrough home debut in the heat of a Tees-Wear derby, Norman Higham would no doubt have hoped for a positive outcome. His dreams, however, could not possibly have matched reality. Sunderland were top of the League at the time and on their way to claiming the First Division championship, while Boro were a mediocre mid-table side. But Wilf Gillow's team turned the form book upside down and humbled their illustrious neighbours to the tune of an incredible 6–0, with Higham playing a starring role and netting the fifth goal into the bargain.

That was March 1936 and the inside-forward had waited almost two years before making his Boro debut after being snapped up from Everton. Although he had been unable to claim a regular first-team place at Goodison, he had displayed an eye for goal that convinced Gillow that he was a player for the future. The following season, Higham was a regular alongside such luminaries as Camsell and Fenton as Boro briefly challenged for the title only to fade at the crucial time. However, his inconsistency cost him his place midway through the 1937–38 campaign. Despite scoring in the first minute against Leeds at Elland Road, Higham was made the scapegoat for a 5–3 Christmas Day defeat. For the return match two days later, the club's directors gave his place to a teenage protégé who had impressed for the club's second string. Enter Wilf Mannion.

Higham rarely played again for Boro and it was no surprise when the club sanctioned his move to Second Division Southampton in May 1939. He never even had the chance to prove his former employers wrong, the war effectively ending his playing days three games into the 1939–40 campaign.

HIGNETT Craig John

Winger
Born: Prescot, 12 January 1970.
Career: Liverpool. Crewe Alexandra 1988. Stafford Rangers (loan). MIDDLESBROUGH 1992. Aberdeen 1998. Barnsley 1998. Blackburn Rovers 2000. Coventry City (loan) 2002. Leicester City 2003. Crewe Alexandra (loan) 2004. Leeds United 2004. Darlington 2004. Apollon (Cyprus) 2005. Bishop Auckland 2006. Hartlepool 2007.

■ It is often claimed that some players are never given a fair crack of the whip by their managers. In the case of Craig Hignett, the argument does carry much strength. Neither Lennie Lawrence nor Bryan Robson ever displayed absolute faith in the midfielder's ability and when the 11 players did not perform on a Saturday afternoon it was often Hignett's name that would be missing from the team-sheet for the following game. It is to the bubbly Scouser's eternal credit, therefore, that he is still revered on Teesside as one of the most popular

players of recent times. Certainly, if he had been able to please his managers as much as he had delighted the supporters then Hignett would surely have claimed legendary status at Middlesbrough. Instead, cult status is probably a more apt description of his position in the club's history.

A probing, attacking midfield player, he was a fine passer of the ball, equally at home hitting long-range passes to his forwards or running on to balls to score himself. He arrived on Teesside from Crewe Alexandra after attracting the attention of Lennie Lawrence as a prolific goalscorer from midfield in the lower divisions. Like David Platt before him, Hignett's career had been saved by Crewe boss Dario Gradi who turned his potential into reality after the player had failed to make the grade with Liverpool as a teenager. Boro were deep in relegation trouble at the time Hignett was signed and as a last throw of the dice he was probably the wrong choice to ensure Premier League status was retained. The leap from the Third Division was a big one and, though he adapted well to the elevation, Hignett did not have the know-how at that level to halt Boro's alarming freefall. Despite two goals at Everton on his first return to Merseyside, he was frequently dropped throughout his first season and he later criticised Lawrence for sapping his confidence. Following Boro's demotion to the First Division, there were rumours that he would be sold but he stayed on and enjoyed excellent early season form, scoring four goals in a Coca-Cola Cup tie with Brighton – the first Middlesbrough player to achieve such a feat for 15 years. However, he again ended the season out of the side and Bradford City expressed a strong interest in taking him to Valley Parade.

Instead, he stayed on and was a fringe member of the squad which lifted the First Division Championship in Bryan Robson's first season in charge before being told he could leave if any club was willing to pay a £500,000 asking price. Determined to prove he was up to the challenge of Premier League football, Hignett declined the offer and actually took a pay cut to stay on at the club. Robson was rewarded with a series of excellent displays and he formed an instant partnership with record signing Nick Barmby as Boro settled comfortably into the top flight. Hignett's name will be forever listed in the record books as the scorer of the first goal at the Riverside Stadium, Barmby setting up a fine strike against Chelsea. A deadball specialist and accurate finisher, such was Hignett's form that it was different to tell which of the look-alike 'Midget Gems' was the England star. Sadly, it did not last and the arrival of Juninho brought demotion back to the reserves, though he did make appearances in both the Coca-Cola and FA Cup Finals the following season. Perhaps the cruellest blow, however, came when he was not even included among the substitutes for the 1998 Coca-Cola Cup Final against Chelsea, having scored several crucial goals in the earlier rounds. The newly-signed Paul Gascoigne, who probably took Hignett's place on the bench, recognised the injustice and made the noble gesture of donating his losers' medal to the unfortunate star. Unable to agree terms with the club, Hignett made the decision to leave Boro on a Bosman-style free transfer but signed off in story book fashion with two goals against Oxford United as Boro clinched promotion back to the Premier League on the final day of the 1997–98 season.

He moved on to Aberdeen but stayed only briefly before rejoining his former Boro teammate John Hendrie at Barnsley to be nearer to his estranged children. He immediately became a popular figure at Oakwell, scoring twice and missing a penalty on his debut as Huddersfield were humbled 7–1. The final years of his playing career were spent with several different clubs, including a Football League comeback with Hartlepool in 2007 after a spell in Cyprus and a flirtation as a football agent. In the summer of 2007 he replaced Livingston-bound Curtis Fleming as a coach at Boro's Academy.

HILLIER Ernest John Guy (Joe)

Goalkeeper

Born: Bridgend, 10 April 1907.

Career: Bridgend Town. Swansea Town 1926. Cardiff City 1927. MIDDLESBROUGH 1929. Newport County 1936.

■ A makeweight in a three-way deal which also saw Jack Jennings and Fred Warren leave Cardiff City for Middlesbrough, Hillier spent the majority of his six-year stay in the North East as the club's reserve team goalkeeper. Club officials had gone to Ninian Park to

sign only Jennings but decided to take all three players for a combined £8,500 fee when they discovered the others were available. Hillier, who worked in a butcher's shop before turning professional with Cardiff, made his Boro debut alongside his two fellow newcomers in a disappointing 4–1 First Division defeat at Leicester on April Fool's Day 1930 and saw no further first-team action until the following November. The consistent form of first choice custodian Jim Mathieson meant opportunities remained few and far between and it seemed his hopes of regular first-team football were doomed when manager Peter McWilliam sold Mathieson only to hand his place to new signing Fred Gibson. Hillier finally got his chance in the 1934–35 season when he missed only a handful of games before again losing out to Gibson. Keen to find regular first-team football, he moved to Newport County in the Third Division South in 1936 for a £275 fee paid in three installments.

HINES, Sebastian

Defender
Born: Wetherby, 29 May 1988.
Career: MIDDLESBROUGH 2006.

■ A big future is predicted for this talented young defender from Wetherby who is another product of Boro's Academy who was a boyhood schoolmate of Manchester City and England defender Micah Richards. Hines worked his way up through the junior ranks for both club and country, representing England at Under-16, Under-17 and Under-19 level. He can play anywhere along the back line and has also played in midfield at junior level. He captained England Under-16 in the Nordic Tournament in Finland in May 2003 and also scored and skippered the side in a 3–1 win over France in the Pepsi Tournament in England. In 2003–04, he was awarded a scholarship with Boro, helped the club win the prestigious Nike Cup Youth tournament in Oregon and travelled to his father's native America for trials with San Diego. Hines also played in the quarter and semi-finals of Boro's winning FA Youth Cup campaign. He suffered a serious knee injury in October 2005 that kept him out for much of the season and also broke his arm during a 5–0 win for England Under-17s in Slovenia. Hines holds two passports and could still elect to play for the US. Playing at left-back, his first-team debut was marked in style as he scored the opening goal in a thrilling FA Cup third round replay win over Hull City at the Riverside. His second Boro appearance came in an FA Cup fourth-round replay with Bristol City, this time at right-back. In July 2007 he signed a two-year professional contract with Boro. Whether he will progress as a full-back or in his favoured central-defensive role remains to be seen.

HISBENT Joseph S.

Right-back
Born: Plymouth, May 1882.
Died: November 1949.
Career: Green Waves. Aston Villa 1905. Portsmouth. Brentford. MIDDLESBROUGH 1911.

■ A member of the squad that achieved Middlesbrough's highest ever position in the Football League – third in 1913–14 – Hisbent was a right full-back versatile enough to switch to the left when the need arose. He made his debut against Arsenal at Ayresome Park on the same day as John Haworth and Jim Nichol, replacing regular right-back Don McLeod in the defence. Known as 'Gentleman Joe', he was never able to win an automatic place in the starting line-up and played his last game during the final season before the outbreak of World War Two.

HODGSON David James

Forward
Born: Gateshead, 6 August 1960.
Career: MIDDLESBROUGH 1978. Liverpool 1982. Sunderland 1984. Norwich City 1986. MIDDLESBROUGH (loan) 1987. Jerez (Spain) 1987. Sheffield Wednesday 1988. Mazda (Japan) 1989. Metz (France) 1990. Swansea City 1992.

■ The name of David Hodgson went down in the club's folklore the day he joined Boro supporters on the terraces of Ayresome Park's Holgate End to watch a game he was forced to miss through injury.

An adopted Teessider, 'Hodgy' was actually born on Tyneside, the son of a former Northern League player. At school, he fancied himself as a goalkeeper but found his niche as a speedy attacker with Redheugh Boys Club, while showing his all-round sporting talent by representing Gateshead and District Boys at cross country running and swimming. He had trials with Ipswich and Sheffield Wednesday while Bolton offered him a two-year apprenticeship and a guarantee of a further two years as a professional. Hodgson turned them all down to join Boro and made his first-team debut as substitute in a 2–2 draw at champions Nottingham Forest in 1978 shortly after turning 18. After a season on the first-team fringe, John Neal made him a regular in the attack and Hodgson never looked back, installing himself as a firm favourite with the traditionally critical

Ayresome fans. With Craig Johnston and Mark Proctor, he was one of three England Under-21 players in a team boasting an exciting blend of talented youngsters and experienced stalwarts. A determined and tireless worker, Hodgson's biggest asset was his speed which he frequently used to tear past defenders before hooking in accurate crosses from the byline. His crossing ability meant he was occasionally used on the wing but he was at his most effective when playing through the middle, where his extreme pace and unselfish play was a godsend for the likes of Micky Burns and Billy Ashcroft. The only real criticism that could be made of Hodgson was that he should have scored far more goals than he did for he was not a clinical finisher. On one memorable occasion in 1980, however, he answered his critics in style scoring a marvellous hat-trick against Tottenham to end a barren run of just one goal in his previous 22 outings. He was also a key instigator of a famous 5–0 FA Cup victory at Swansea a couple of weeks later, scoring twice and crossing for Terry Cochrane's superb scissor kick.

Boro's relegation to Division Two brought Hodgson's inevitable departure and he followed in the footsteps of Graeme Souness and Craig Johnston by joining the mighty Liverpool for £450,000. He made an impressive start at Anfield but, faced with formidable opposition from the likes of Kenny Dalglish and a young Ian Rush, he struggled to hold on to a regular first-team place and returned to the North East with Sunderland. He had become something of a journeyman footballer by the time Bruce Rioch brought him back to Teesside for a loan spell in 1987 and the deal was cut short in controversial fashion. Although still only 26, his former zest and sparkle had deserted him and he was sent back to Norwich after being sent off in his second game for a bad foul on Bristol City's Joe Jordan. He later had a short spell in the Spanish Second Division with Jerez where he again made the newspaper headlines for all the wrong reasons, being photographed behind bars following a contractual dispute with his club. After hanging up his boots, he worked as a football agent before joining forces with former Boro goalkeeper Jim Platt as joint manager of Darlington. The two fell out and Hodgson resigned, only to be reinstated in sole charge following Platt's dismissal. He lost the job again in 2000 but returned for a third spell in charge in 2003, only to leave in controversial circumstances in September 2006.

HODGSON George

Goalkeeper
Born: Details unknown.
Career: South Bank. MIDDLESBROUGH 1900.

■ Goalkeeper George Hodgson was understudy to regular number one Joe Frail in Middlesbrough's second season in the Football League. He played just four Second Division games, making his debut in a 2–0 defeat at Grimsby in December 1900 and playing his last match for the club on New Year's Day 1901.

HODGSON John Percival

Goalkeeper
Born: Seaham, 10 May 1922.
Career: Murton Colliery. Leeds United 1943. MIDDLESBROUGH 1948.

■ It was two impressive performances against Boro that won goalkeeper Jack Hodgson a transfer to Ayresome Park. Hodgson was Leeds United's custodian when he performed a brilliant, single-handed defence against a rampant Boro attack in a League North match on Boxing Day 1945. Middlesbrough won the match 4–1 but the result would have been far more convincing but for a string of outstanding saves from Hodgson. He again shone when making his competitive debut for Leeds against Boro in a 4–4 FA Cup draw a couple of weeks later and manager David Jack made a mental note of his ability between the sticks. When Jack needed cover for Derwick Goodfellow in 1948, he remembered those scintillating performances of two years earlier and brought him to Teesside in exchange for centre-half Jimmy McCabe. Hodgson, Stan Rickaby and Martin Reagan all made their Boro debuts against Derby at Ayresome Park in March 1948. Though Goodfellow moved on, Rolando Ugolini became the new first choice 'keeper and Hodgson remained his deputy for seven years. He had originally joined Leeds as an amateur from Seaham Colliery, conceding eight goals against York on his wartime debut for United.

HOGG John

Right-back
Born: West Calder, 1881.
Career: West Calder Swifts. Heart of Midlothian. MIDDLESBROUGH 1902. Luton Town 1906.

■ Right full-back Hogg joined Middlesbrough at a momentous time in the club's early history. Signed from Hearts for a £200 club record fee to strengthen a squad newly promoted to Division One for the first time, Hogg got his opportunity in the team when regular full-back Joe Blackett was injured in a match at Derby. He was to make the position his own for two full seasons, during which he appeared in the last ever match at the Linthorpe Road ground and the first competitive game at Boro's new home, Ayresome Park. Injury caused him to miss much of the 1904–05 season and he moved on to Luton during the close season of 1906.

HOLLIDAY Edwin

Outside-left
Born: Leeds, 7 June 1939.
Career: MIDDLESBROUGH 1956. Sheffield Wednesday 1962. MIDDLESBROUGH 1965. Hereford United. Workington 1968. Peterborough United 1969.

■ Middlesbrough have Eddie Holliday's mother to thank for the fact that the speedy winger made his name at

Ayresome Park rather than Oakwell. Holliday began his career with Barnsley boys, his hometown club, but his mother, who had once lived in Brotton, wrote to Bob Dennison asking him to give her 17-year-old son a trial. He came to Boro with his father and elder brother, both miners, and duly signed on the dotted line after impressing in two trial games.

The nephew of Sheffield United and England star Colin Grainger, he made his League debut at West Ham in December 1957 and played so well that Ronnie Burbeck, the club's regular number 11, rarely got a look-in again that season. A fast, skilful winger, Holliday's hard and accurate crossing was a key part of Boro's attack and main supply line for the goals of Brian Clough and Alan Peacock as promotion was chased unsuccessfully. Despite playing with an unglamorous Second Division club, Holliday's dazzling wing play caught the eye of the England selectors and he won three full caps in 1959, two of them alongside Clough.

But the sparkle didn't last and by March of 1962 he was in the reserves and available for transfer when he was watched by Sheffield Wednesday manager Vic Buckingham and Sunderland scout Charlie Ferguson. He signed for the Owls but was unable to recapture his form of old and returned to Boro during the 1965 close season. Raich Carter hoped that Holliday, still only 26, would rekindle his former glories but the gamble did not pay off and Boro were relegated to the Third Division for the first time. Sold to Southern League Hereford United, he later returned to the Football League for brief stays with Workington and Peterborough but a broken leg forced him into early retirement from the game.

HOLLIDAY John William

Centre-forward/Inside-left
Born: Cockfield, 19 December 1908.
Died: 1987.
Career: Cockfield Albion.
MIDDLESBROUGH 1930. Brentford 1932.

■ The unenviable task of deputising for the great George Camsell was a burden centre-forward Johnny Holliday carried admirably well in the limited opportunities he was afforded. Snapped up from non-League Cockfield, he was an amateur when he scored twice on his first-team debut as Camsell's stand-in at Manchester City in November 1930. Alas, Boro lost 4–2, though the rookie had done enough to retain his place for the following match against Birmingham. He also found the net in his only other appearance that season in a 5–1 First Division home win over Blackpool and hit the winner against the Seasiders the following October. Holliday was one of several Boro players who joined Brentford in 1932 and helped them to the Division Three South championship a year later. The Bees later took the Second Division title to win promotion to the top flight and there was a hostile atmosphere when a Brentford team including five former Boro players were beaten 3–0 at Ayresome Park in November 1936.

HOLMES Walter

Full-back
Born: Willington, 9 May 1892.
Died: July 1978.
Career: Willington Athletic.
MIDDLESBROUGH 1914. Darlington 1928.

■ Football was considered as no more than 'an interesting sideline' by the man they nicknamed 'Squire'. Certainly, Walter Holmes answered to an authority far greater than the Middlesbrough manager. For Holmes was a deeply religious man and a Methodist lay preacher who would regularly take 'Sportsmen's Services' at local chapels where he would take another Boro player along with him to read the scriptures. But he was also a talented footballer and a loyal club servant for 14 years.

Teetotaller Holmes played his early football at outside-right for Bede College, where he was training to be a teacher, and took up his first teaching post in 1912, signing amateur forms with Boro the same year. He turned professional in 1914 after helping hometown club Willington Athletic to the Northern League title and was granted special permission by the club to continue as a schoolmaster.

A full-back equally at home on the left or right, his early progress was interrupted by the war and he saw active service in France as an officer in the RAMC. He developed bronchial pneumonia but made a total recovery to become a regular member of the first-team squad after the war and was awarded a benefit by the club in 1921. His appearances became less frequent in his final season but he played his part in a record-breaking promotion success when he was called upon as an emergency centre-half when Maurice Webster was injured early in the season. He was reported to have played extremely well in the role, looking cool on the ball and displaying excellent positional play. Having moved on to Darlington in 1928, there was concern over the birth of his son so, when a telegram arrived at the ground just before half-time of a match he was playing in, officials decided not to give it to him in case it was bad news. However, it turned out that the message brought the good news that all was well. Accompanied by his old teammate Maurice Webster, headmaster Holmes was a regular spectator at Boro games until his death in the summer of 1978 and the club sent a red and white ball-shaped wreath for his grave.

HONEYMAN John William

Outside-right
Born: Middlesbrough, 29 December 1893.
Died: 1972.
Career: Cargo Fleet Works.
MIDDLESBROUGH 1919. Dundee.
Maidstone United. Grimsby Town 1923.
Maidstone United. J & P Coats (Rhode Island).

■ Middlesbrough-born Honeyman let nobody down on the day he made his one and only appearance for his hometown club. Standing in for Bill Fox, he was asked to make the leap from his usual Saturday game with the Cargo Fleet Works team to a clash at Manchester United in October 1919. The game finished 1–1 but Honeyman was never called upon again and he left for Dundee a year later.

HORNE Brian Simon

Goalkeeper
Born: Billericay, 5 October 1967.
Career: Millwall 1985. MIDDLESBROUGH (loan) 1992. Stoke City (loan) 1992. Portsmouth 1992. Hartlepool United 1994.

■ Middlesbrough were having a goalkeeping injury crisis during Horne's loan spell with the club early in the 1992–93 season. Brought in to cover an injury to Stephen Pears, he became the first substitute goalkeeper to play for Boro when Ian Ironside picked up a hip injury during the second half of a 2–2 Premier League draw with Ipswich. A former England Under-21 'keeper, he hadn't played for 18 months when Lennie Lawrence brought him from Millwall but he kept clean sheets in his next two games before conceding three at Queen's Park Rangers. He returned to Millwall when they refused to allow him to become Cup-tied by playing in a League Cup match against Newcastle. Horne had been made available for £50,000 but was carrying a few extra pounds at the time after suffering a number of injury problems. He eventually joined Portsmouth on a free transfer shortly after his brief stay on Teesside.

HORNER William

Defender
Born: Cassop, 7 September 1942.
Career: MIDDLESBROUGH 1959. Darlington 1969.

■ One of Boro's finest stalwarts through the roller-coaster ride that was the 1960s was Billy Horner, who was revered for his ball-winning but stylish displays at wing-half.

Having won representative honours for Durham County as a youngster, Horner was an inside-forward until Jimmy Gordon moved him back to his natural position and his obvious talent blossomed in the Boro first team. Given his debut in a Second Division match at Leyton Orient in March 1961, he was a strong tackler and hard battler with strength and a fierce long-range shot. A loyal club servant for a decade, his Boro career could have been much shorter had his transfer request not been turned down by the directors when he failed to see eye to eye with manager Raich Carter in the early 1960s. Although unable to help the club avoid relegation to Division Three, he was a key figure in the promotion success under Stan Anderson but lost his place the following season after suffering a knee ligament injury. He took on coaching the club's reserves while turning out for the second string but many fans were shocked when Anderson allowed him to join Darlington, aged only 26, as it was felt he was a valuable squad member.

He played six full seasons at Feethams, where his teammates included former Boro players Gordon Jones and Don Burluraux, though the trio were unable to stop the club from finishing bottom of the entire League in 1973. After hanging up his boots, he managed Darlington, had two spells in charge of Hartlepool and coached at York City.

HORSFIELD Arthur

Forward
Born: Newcastle, 5 July 1946.
Career: MIDDLESBROUGH 1963. Newcastle United 1969. Swindon Town 1969. Charlton Athletic 1972. Watford 1975. Dartford.

■ When Horsfield scored on his Boro debut in September 1963 he set a club record that remains to this day. Standing in for the injured Alan Peacock, the rookie centre-forward netted his team's final goal in a 6–0 rout of hapless Grimsby just two months after his 17th birthday to become Boro's youngest ever goalscorer.

England youth international Horsfield created goalscoring records in junior football and Boro beat a crop of clubs – including Newcastle, Sunderland and Preston – to his signature. Having grown up a goal-kick away from St James' Park, it was a tough decision for the teenager to make to turn down his boyhood heroes, though he was to play

for them some years later. A good team player, Horsfield was neither fast nor flamboyant but he was a good striker of the ball and his goal ratio was always impressive. He did well whenever called upon by Raich Carter but made only fleeting appearances as Boro were relegated to the Third Division. However, the appointment of Stan Anderson gave him his big chance and he took it with both feet as he formed an excellent partnership with John O'Rourke and Boro stormed to promotion at the first attempt. By the time he struck a devastating hat-trick at Doncaster at the end of March, he had scored no fewer than 22 League goals in just 27 games. Sadly, his form began to suffer and he was dropped after a six-game barren run and was pipped as the club's top scorer by O'Rourke. He spent the first half of the following season back in the reserves but was recalled when O'Rourke left for Ipswich.

He was John Hickton's regular strike partner until, still aged just 22 but keen to sample First Division football, he moved to hometown club Newcastle as a stop-gap striker midway through the 1968–69 campaign. He moved on to Swindon, where he twice won the Anglo-Italian Cup, scoring a hat-trick in the 1969 Final. The goals continued to flow at Charlton Athletic, where he also set a club record of 156 consecutive League and Cup appearances. After retiring from the game, Horsfield lived in Gravesend, working as a postman and later managing a social club.

HOWLING Edward

Goalkeeper
Born: Stockton 1885.
Died: 1955.
Career: South Bank. MIDDLESBROUGH 1910. Bristol City 1913. Bradford Park Avenue 1919.

■ Teddy Howling was the only amateur to play in goal for Middlesbrough in the First Division. An England amateur international, who won caps against Switzerland during the 1909–10 season and against Belgium in 1912–13, he also won the Amateur Cup while with South Bank. It was unfortunate for Howling that England star Tim Williamson was the club's custodian at the time, otherwise he would surely have been a regular. Instead, he played for the Boro first team only once, in a 1–0 home defeat to Aston Villa in April 1911. He moved on to Bristol City and Bradford Park Avenue, turning fully professional shortly before World War One. When an ankle injury ended his career at Pontypridd, he returned to live in South Bank where he worked as a commission agent's clerk. He died in 1955.

HUDSON Mark

Midfield
Born: Bishop Auckland, 24 October 1980.
Career: MIDDLESBROUGH 1999. Chesterfield (loan) 2002. Carlisle United (loan) 2002. Chesterfield 2003. Huddersfield Town 2005. Rotherham United 2007.

■ Hudson made his Middlesbrough debut when replacing Christian Karembeu 20 minutes from time in a 1–0 win over Liverpool at the Riverside on Boxing Day 2000. But chances were limited for the midfielder with the likes of Paul Ince, Robbie Mustoe, Paul Okon and Karembeu in the squad. He made four appearances that season, all from the bench. A loan spell with Chesterfield the following season brought 19 appearances and much acclaim. But back with Boro he managed just two more games, both against Ipswich Town, each time coming off the bench to replace Carlos Marinelli and Robbie Stockdale. In between, he again went on loan, this time to Carlisle United where he made 15 appearances. He made a permanent move to Chesterfield in March 2003 and went on to become captain. After making 82 appearances for Chesterfield, he was transferred to Huddersfield Town in June 2005 and was released in summer 2007 after 69 games.

HUGHES Martin

Goalkeeper
Born: Fauldhouse.
Career: MIDDLESBROUGH 1899.

■ Scot Hughes was goalkeeper for Middlesbrough's first ever Football League home game. He was called up for the 3–1 defeat to Small Heath after missing the club's first two games as a professional club. Three teammates – Redfearn, Callaghan and Murphy – all made their debuts that same day. He was the club's regular 'keeper throughout that momentous season but was released to make way for Joe Frail in 1900.

HUME Robert

Outside-left
Born: Kirkintilloch, 18 March 1941.
Died: Johannesburg, South Africa, 1997.
Career: Glasgow Rangers 1959. MIDDLESBROUGH 1962. Aberdeen 1963. Highlands Park (South Africa).

■ Ex-paratrooper Hume suffered poor vision and was one of the first footballers to wear contact lenses. Although small and lightweight, he was a talented footballer and made his name at Glasgow Rangers, playing in the home leg of their 1961 European Cup-winners' Cup defeat against Fiorentina in front of a crowd of 80,000. An outside-left, he was seen as the ideal replacement for Eddie Holliday when he moved to Ayresome Park early in the 1962–63 season. However, he fell out of favour shortly before Bob Dennison's dismissal and was recalled for only four games under new manager Raich Carter. He returned to Scotland that summer with Aberdeen and later emigrated to South Africa where he played alongside his brother, Ronnie, for Highlands Park, helping them win the national Championship in 1966. Hume was murdered in 1997, the victim of a carjacking as he drove to his Johannesburg home.

HUNTER Herbert

Goalkeeper
Born: Details unknown.
Career: MIDDLESBROUGH 1905. Crystal Palace.

■ Goalkeeper Hunter's Boro career was yet another victim of the brilliance of Tim Williamson. He made his debut in a 1–0 First Division home win over north-east rivals Newcastle in March 1906 but played only twice more for the club before joining former Middlesbrough manager John Robson at Crystal Palace.

HUTH Robert

Central-defender
Born: Berlin, 18 August 1984.
Career: Chelsea 2001. MIDDLESBROUGH 2006.

■ The highly-rated centre-back finally joined Boro for £6 million on the last day of the summer 2006 transfer deadline, ending a three-month chase by new Riverside manager Gareth Southgate. Huth joined Chelsea from German side Union Berlin as a scholar and came up through the ranks with the London club. His appearances were restricted by the vast resources at Chelsea's disposal but he quickly made his mark at international level and was a member of Germany's 2006 World Cup squad, where an ankle injury restricted his availability. Huth was used sparingly by Chelsea, serving as an understudy to John Terry, William Gallas and Marcel Desailly. With the arrivals of Ricardo Carvalho and Paulo Ferreira, he became increasingly frustrated at a lack of first-team opportunities. Jose Mourinho rejected a bid from Bayern Munich in summer 2005 but agreed to sell him to Boro the following year. Huth managed just 14 games with Middlesbrough in his first season, his debut coming in a Carling Cup defeat against Notts County at the Riverside. He suffered a stress fracture of his foot and then incurred an ankle injury that restricted his availability. A summer ankle operation meant the start of his second season on Teesside was also delayed.

ILLMAN Neil David

Forward
Born: Doncaster, 29 April 1975.
Career: MIDDLESBROUGH 1993. Eastwood Town 1994. Plymouth Argyle 1996. Cambridge United (loan) 1996. Exeter City 1997. Northwich Victoria.

■ Unpredicatable left-winger turned centre-forward, Illman played just 17 minutes of League football for Middlesbrough, when Lennie Lawrence brought him on as a substitute against Bristol City in 1993–94 amid an early season injury crisis. This was after he had made his debut in a 3–1 away defeat in Pisa in the Anglo-Italian Cup. Illman was a quick and lively forward who never fulfilled his potential at Boro, and after a couple more Anglo-Italian Cup games and an eight minute League Cup substitute appearance against Sheffield Wednesday he moved on to Plymouth, where he spent two seasons. Illman later joined Exeter on a non-contract basis before moving to non-League Northwich Victoria.

INCE Paul Emerson Carlyle

Midfield
Born: Ilford, 21 October 1967.
Career: West Ham United 1985. Manchester United 1989. Inter Milan (Italy) 1995. Liverpool 1997. MIDDLESBROUGH 1999. Wolverhampton Wanderers 2002. Swindon Town 2006. Macclesfield 2006.

■ England international Paul Ince was an aggressive and stylish presence in the centre of the Boro midfield for three Premier League seasons, captaining the side under Bryan Robson, Terry Venables and Steve McClaren. At just £1 million, Ince was undoubtedly one of Robson's most astute signings, while the ball-winner's decision to leave Liverpool for Boro was vindicated when he was recalled to the England team just two months after arriving at the Riverside. Ince, who won 53 international caps, started out with West Ham United on a YTS scheme in the summer of 1984 before signing professional forms the following year. However, he left his adoring Hammers fans with a sour taste when he posed in a Manchester United shirt while still registered with their club. Although considered by some as hot-headed, he quickly established himself at Old Trafford following his £1 million move in 1989 and was a midfield regular alongside Bryan Robson as Alex Ferguson's side gradually established themselves as the nation's top side.

Ince went on to win two League Championships, two FA Cup-winners' medals, a League Cup and a European Cup-winners' Cup medal, as well as being voted Footballer of the Year in 1993. Two years later, after appearing in 273 games for the Reds, the self-styled 'Guvnor' was forced out of Old Trafford and moved to Inter Milan for £8 million. Shortly afterwards, he threatened to quit Italian football after Cremonese supporters hurled racist abuse at him.

After two years in Italy, he returned to the UK to play for Liverpool in a £2 million deal, though he struggled to inspire the Anfield club to their former glories and lost both his England captaincy and place after being sent off in a crucial World Cup qualifier against Sweden. Despite the setbacks, Ince was still rated one of the country's finest midfielders, so there were raised eyebrows when news leaked out of Anfield during the summer of 1999 that Liverpool would be prepared to let him go for as little as £1 million. Boro manager Bryan Robson wasted no time in beating several other Premier League and European clubs to his signature. In truth, Boro fans craving a return to exciting football were not initially hugely impressed by the signing of Ince but they were quickly won over as he stamped his authority on every game, including an early 1–0 win over his former employers from Merseyside. His recall to the England set-up by Kevin Keegan was fully justified and he went on to win eight caps over the next year, appearing in the European Championship Finals over the summer of 2000. Having succeeded the departed Andy Townsend as club captain, Ince led the team by example. Although his ability and commitment remained unquestioned, he clearly found it more difficult to get up and down the pitch in his third season on Teesside and it was no surprise when Steve McClaren allowed him to leave on a free transfer during the close season of 2002. After 106 games for Boro, he joined Wolves on a free transfer. Determined to show that he still had a lot to offer, he helped the Molineux club win promotion to the Premiership. When he later missed out on succeeding Glenn Hoddle as Wolves manager, he moved to Swindon Town before taking up his first management role with Macclesfield, who he guided to safety from seemingly inevitable relegation from the Football League. Eager for a further challenge, he then took up a job in charge of MK Dons in the summer of 2007.

IRONSIDE Ian

Goalkeeper
Born: Sheffield, 8 March 1964.
Career: Barnsley 1982. Matlock Town. North Ferriby United. Scarborough 1988. MIDDLESBROUGH 1991. Scarborough (loan) 1992. Stockport County 1993. Scarborough 1995. Oldham Athletic 1997.

■ Ironside kept it in the family by becoming a professional goalkeeper, as his father Roy had previously been between the sticks at Rotherham and Barnsley. Ironside Junior's road to Middlesbrough wasn't an easy one as he drifted into non-League football after failing to follow in his father's footsteps as a youth player at Oakwell. He then went to college to study for a City and Guilds Diploma before becoming a joiner, a job he supplemented with spells playing for Matlock Town and North Ferriby Town. Ironside was plucked from non-League football by Scarborough during their first season in the Football League, and he made his debut at the age of 24 alongside a certain Martin Russell. In the summer of 1991 he was invited to Ayresome Park for a trial and after a successful two week period was signed for £40,000 as cover for Stephen Pears. However, Pears' consistency made life difficult for Ironside to hold down a first-team spot. Following an excellent debut in the last game of the 1991–92 season, when Boro won 2–1 at Wolves to win promotion, he went on to be Boro's first ever nominated goalkeeper substitute and played in goal for the first ever Premier League match at Ayresome Park v Man City. Tall and athletic and solid rather than inspirational, he proved

himself a capable deputy for Pears but he was released following the emergence of Andy Collett and joined Stockport. He later went to Oldham but retired after suffering a series of injuries.

IRVINE James

Centre-forward
Born: Whitburn, 17 August 1940.
Career: Dundee United. MIDDLESBROUGH 1964. Heart of Midlothian. Barrow 1970.

■ A Scotland Schoolboy international, Jim Irvine had trials with Manchester United and Notts County but preferred to remain in his native Scotland and signed for Dundee United. His prolific scoring feats from his position at inside-left alerted the clubs south of the border and in May 1964, Boro boss Raich Carter paid £25,000 for his signature. After a few games he was switched to centre-forward and ended his first season on Teesside as the club's top scorer, with 23 goals including an FA Cup hat-trick against Oldham Athletic. Irvine missed the first three games of the ill-fated 1965–66 season while serving a two-week suspension, but once restored in

the team he proved he could still find the net in a struggling side. He missed a couple of months in mid-season after undergoing an emergency operation for appendicitis but then returned to top the scoring charts for a second successive season. The goals dried up the following season and with O'Rourke and Hickton the club's new strike force, Irvine lost out. In the summer of 1967 he was suspended by Stan Anderson for an undisclosed breach of club discipline and he left the club two days after promotion had been won. He returned to Scotland with Hearts but after helping them reach the Scottish Cup Final, he missed out on the game after colliding with a teammate in training. Irvine later returned to the Football League with Barrow but couldn't prevent them from finishing bottom of the Fourth Division.

JACKSON Andrew

Centre-half
Born: Cambrose Mount.
Died: 1918.
Career: MIDDLESBROUGH 1910.

■ When Jackson lost his life in battle during World War One Middlesbrough and Scotland lost a player who many believed would go on to establish himself as one of the greats of the game. Jackson was born into a footballing family as his father, Alex, was a Scotland international while his uncle, Jim, played for Glasgow Rangers, Newcastle, West Ham and Arsenal. The family were also related to former Liverpool captain James 'Parson' Jackson. Andy was brought to Middlesbrough by manager Andy Walker as replacement for centre-half Bob Young who had moved to Everton. Although only 5ft 8in, he was a commanding central defender with firm resolve, his grit and determination making him a terrace hero at Ayresome Park. He was the dominant centre-half the team had lacked since the departure of Andy Aitken in 1908.

Jackson was not the only player to make his debut against Everton on the opening day of 1910–11. Weir, Gibson, McClure and Nichol were also new faces in Walker's Boro side. Jackson was a kingpin in the side that achieved the club's highest ever League placing of third in Division One in 1913–14 and he earned the captaincy on merit, succeeding Tim Williamson for the final season before World War One. Always well groomed and smartly dressed, Jackson, who loved playing golf, was a close friend of centre-forward George Elliott and the pair were similar in looks and appearance. When war broke out in 1915, Jackson initially guested for Chelsea before enlisting with the Army and rising to the rank of sergeant. He was tragically killed shortly after arriving at the front line in France in 1918 and football fans were left to ponder what might have been.

JAMES William E.

Outside-left/Centre-forward
Born: Stockton, 1882.
Died: Portsmouth, 10 December 1960.
Career: MIDDLESBROUGH 1910. Portsmouth 1920. West Ham United 1920.

■ Centre-forward James was strike partner to the great George Elliott in one of Middlesbrough's most successful pre-war seasons. He made his debut at outside-left on the same day that Teddy Howling and Henry Leonard began their Boro careers. He was out of Tom McIntosh's first games in charge at the start of the 1911–12 season but was called up in place of the out-of-sorts Leonard at centre-forward against Spurs in October, scored a 15th minute opener and won a regular place in the side. James scored twice, one a penalty, as Manchester City were beaten 3–1 two days before Christmas to take Boro into second spot and fans began to dream of a first title success. It didn't last, of course. James' goals dried up, the Championship challenge faded and the forward was eventually dropped. Thankfully, McIntosh steadied the ship and a creditable seventh spot was achieved. James spent a season in the reserves before agreeing to join Portsmouth, where he spent seven seasons. His death was reported in Portsmouth on 10 December 1960.

JANKOVIC Bosco

Forward
Born: Sarajevo, 22 May 1951.
Died: Kotor, November 1993.
Career: Zeljeznicar (Yugoslavia) 1967. MIDDLESBROUGH 1979. Metz (France) 1981.

■ There can have been few less likely looking Boro heroes than Jankovic. Balding and overweight, he looked at least 15 years older than he really was but proved that looks could be deceiving. Skilful and full of invention, he was also an excellent finisher and had become a firm crowd favourite by the time he left the club in 1981.

Spotted by Zeljeznicar as a 13-year-old, he helped them win the Yugoslavian Championship in 1972 and played against Derby County in Europe. He came to Boro's notice after winning several caps for his country and John Neal sent Harold Shepherdson and Jimmy Greenhalgh to Yugoslavia to watch the striker in action. He impressed during a two-week trial back on Teesside and was signed late in the 1978–79 campaign. Although not a big name outside his own country, Boro fans were keen to see Jankovic in action as the club had never previously moved into the foreign transfer market despite attempts to bring Argentinian Rene Houseman and Dutchman Arie Haan to Teesside. He was initially blooded in the club's reserves to help build up fitness as it had been the mid-season break in Yugoslavia. He scored his first goal for the club in a

3–0 Division One win at Derby in the penultimate game of the season. With Billy Ashcroft switched to the centre of defence, Jankovic partnered Micky Burns for the start of his first full season and scored in a memorable opening day win at Spurs. The goals did not flow, however, and Jankovic struggled to adapt to the fast and physical English game. He also had the annoying habit of straying offside, much to the consternation of hecklers in Ayresome Park's infamous 'Chicken Run'.

He began the 1980–81 campaign as second choice to David Shearer but a last minute equaliser as sub against Manchester City was a turning point that transformed his fortunes. Within a fortnight, he was the toast of Teesside after scoring the only goal of the game against Sunderland at Roker Park, a high point which was followed by two terrific strikes in a 6–1 destruction of Norwich City. Jankovic finally began to get to grip with First Division defences and his strong running and tricky ball skills were a delight to watch in an attack-minded Boro side that included the likes of Craig Johnston, David Hodgson and David Armstrong. He had netted eight times by early November but missed two months through injury and was again in competition with Shearer on his return. But Jankovic was saving his best till last. He scored twice against Ipswich in the penultimate game of the season to deny Bobby Robson's side the Championship and head Boro's scorers.

It came as a surprise to everyone when he announced his intention to return home to work as a civil lawyer, a career he had trained for throughout his playing days. He declined the offer of a new contract but, instead of returning to Yugoslavia, played in France with Metz. However, Middlesbrough retained his registration and, when Neal tried to sign for his new club Chelsea, Boro's directors blocked the deal. Both clubs were called to a tribunal and a panel ruled that Chelsea would have to pay Boro £60,000 if they wanted to sign the player. It was a fee the Blues were unwilling to pay and Jankovic returned to Yugoslavia. He was later forced to abandon his law practice and his property in the war torn Bosnian capital, Sarajevo, and his death was reported in November 1993, aged just 42.

JARVIS Sydney

Full-back
Born: Sheffield, 1905.
Died: Perth, Australia, June 1994.
Career: Hull City 1924. Kettering Town. Raith Rovers. MIDDLESBROUGH 1927. Darlington 1936.

■ For a player who spent the best part of a decade with the club, Jarvis was something of a peripheral figure at Middlesbrough. The full-back arrived at Boro in November 1927 as part of a deal that took Billy Birrell to Raith as player-manager. The form of Frank Twine meant it was April before he made his first-team debut for the club, playing at right full-back in an impressive 4–2 win at Huddersfield. Sadly, with Jarvis in the side, Boro were unable to win any of their final five games and were relegated from the top flight. He was the club's regular right-back during the first half of the promotion season that followed but lost his place to Reg Freeman long before the title was clinched with a final day win over fellow challengers Grimsby. He was more of a reserve team player in the years that followed, making only occasional appearances in either full-back berth as Boro struggled to retain their top flight status. Placed on the transfer list at the end of the 1934–35 season, the club's directors demanded £1,000 but the fee was later cut to £500 by the League. With Boro retaining his registration, Jarvis sampled continental football in France before joining Darlington during the summer of 1936. He initially lived in retirement in Saltburn but later emigrated to Australia and died in Perth in June 1994, aged 89.

JENNINGS John (Jack)

Full-back/Right-half
Born: Platt Bridge, 27 August 1902.
Died: Northampton, April 1997.
Career: Wigan Boro 1923. Cardiff City 1925. MIDDLESBROUGH 1929. Preston North End 1936. Bradford City 1937.

■ Right full-back Jennings served Boro with distinction as a fine captain and a stylish defender. He also distinguished himself on several different fronts after his playing days were over. He was working as a railway fireman while playing non-League football for Wigan Boro when Cardiff snapped him up as a youngster. His fine performances soon caught the eye and he toured Canada with the FA in 1926.

He moved to Boro a year after Cardiff had suffered relegation to Divison Two. Boro chairman Phil Bach and manager Peter McWilliam travelled to Wales to see Jennings in action. After expressing their interest in the defender, they were told that goalkeeper Joe Hillier and reserve winger Freddy Warren were also available. All three were snapped up for a combined fee of £8,500. The trio made their Boro debuts on the same day

– Jennings replacing Bob Ferguson in the line-up – though the game was lost 4–1 at Leicester. He was made club captain for the start of his first full season with the club, a position which he retained until the arrival of Tom Griffiths three years later. He missed several games in 1931–32 after undergoing a cartilage operation but was back to steer Boro clear of relegation. In 1934, he was 12th man for the Football League when they took on their Scottish counterparts.

After losing his first-team place to Bill Brown, Jennings moved on to Preston in his mid–30s and was trainer at Deepdale until the outbreak of the war. He served in the Army and guested for Northampton while posted at Bedford during the hostilities. When peace returned, he began a 25-year spell as the Cobblers' trainer coach and physio and was the club's caretaker manager for their first three games in Division Two in 1964. While with Northampton, Jennings was appointed trainer of England Amateurs in 1949, while he was also travelling physio for Northants cricket team, coach of the Oxford University side and two local schools. He also coached the Great Britain Olympic team in three Olympics. With such a record, it was no wonder that a legend such as Stanley Matthews should turn out for his benefit game. Jennings died in Northampton in April 1997 at the ripe old age of 94.

JENNINGS Samuel

Forward
Born: Cinderhill, 18 December 1898.
Died: Battle, August 1944.
Career: Coldstream Guards. Basford United. Norwich City. MIDDLESBROUGH 1919. Reading 1921. West Ham United 1924. Brighton & Hove Albion 1924. Nottingham Forest 1928. Port Vale 1929. Stockport County 1931. Burnley 1931.

■ Sam Jennings's time with Middlesbrough was one of the less interesting spells of a colourful life. A member of the Coldstream Guards during World War One, he guested for Tottenham and Notts County. When peace returned, he joined Norwich from Basford United. An inside-forward, he scored regularly for all of his clubs except Boro, where he found his hefty pricetag a weight around his shoulders. And yet it all started so well. He found the net just 15 minutes into his debut at Everton. Sadly, it was all downhill from there. Boro lost the match 5–2 and, though he scored the winner at Bradford two weeks later, the form of Jacky Carr greatly restricted his first-team opportunities throughout the 1920–21 campaign. He found greater success after moving on and was Nottingham Forest's top scorer in 1928–29. He later moved to the continent and coached Olympique Marseille long before Mr Ravanelli arrived on the scene. He had further spells coaching in Ireland with Glentoran and then in Switzerland. A short spell as manager of Rochdale was ended by ill health and Jennings died in Battle, Sussex, in August 1944. His brother, William, played for Northampton and Luton.

JOB Joseph-Désiré

Forward
Born: Vanissieux, France, 1 December 1977.
Career: Lyon 1997. Lens (France) 1999. MIDDLESBROUGH 2000. Metz (loan) 2002. Al Ittihad (Saudi Arabia) 2005. Sedan (France) 2006.

■ The Cameroon international will forever be remembered for his role in helping Boro win their first-ever major trophy. He scored the first and won the penalty that led to the second as Boro beat Bolton Wanderers 2–1 in the Carling Cup Final of 2004. Job was signed by Bryan Robson from French side Lens in the summer of 2000 as Boro fought off attention from Udinese for his signature. His debut was a goalscoring one in Boro 3–1 win at Coventry's Highfield Road, but he scored only three goals in 15 appearances in that first season. Job was blessed with pace and impressive ball skills, but he often found the physical side of the English game a challenge. He struggled for consistency under Steve McClaren and went on a half-season loan to Metz in January 2002. The following year he was in and out of the team, scoring five goals in 29 matches. He scored eight goals in 2003–04, and seven the year after. His spectacular overhead strike against Sporting Lisbon in a UEFA Cup tie on 10 March 2005 was voted by fans as the best ever goal at the Riverside. Job was on his way to Saudi Arabia next season to take up a contract with Al Ittihad, a sports club based in the Red Sea port of Jeddah. After just one season he moved back to France to play for Sedan, where he was part of the side that was relegated to the second division in 2006–07.

He had trained with Watford before the start of the 2006–07 season but was not offered a contract. Job, who has won nearly 50 caps with Cameroon and played in two World Cups, made 112 appearances for Boro, scoring 22 goals.

JOHNSON Adam

Midfield
Born: Sunderland, 14 July 1987.
Career: MIDDLESBROUGH 2005. Leeds United (loan) 2006.

■ The Wearsider is one of the most talented players to graduate from Boro's Academy. Blessed with eye-catching dribbling skills, he has had to be patient for his chance behind another gifted left-winger, Stewart Downing. He made his debut as a 17-year-old in the away leg of a UEFA Cup defeat to Sporting Lisbon in March 2005. Far from being overawed by the occasion, the youngster set about showing off his impressive ball skills in front of a national TV audience. He followed that up with an energetic full

Premiership debut in the 2–1 win over Arsenal at the Riverside in September 2005, with Downing missing through injury. Johnson was a fringe player in the 2004 FA Youth Cup-winning squad but progressed to the team the following year, scoring a wonder goal in a 3–0 win over his hometown club, Sunderland, at the Riverside. He has progressed to play for his country at Under-19 level and is held in high regard by national coaches. His progress was rewarded with an improved four-year contract in the summer of 2006. Johnson spent a month on loan at Leeds in autumn 2006. He returned to play reserve football with Middlesbrough but he also made a dozen first-team appearances for Boro before the end of the season, keeping his nerve to score the winning penalty in a dramatic FA Cup replay shoot-out over Bristol City.

JOHNSON Ian

Winger
Born: Sunderland, 1 September 1975.
Career: MIDDLESBROUGH 1994. Bradford City 1995. Blyth Spartans. Chester-le-Street. South Shields. Durham City.

■ Johnson must wonder what might have been when he looks back on his debut. The winger hit the post against Portsmouth just four minutes into his one and only League start for Boro. Whether things might have worked out differently had the shot gone in instead of rebounding back into play, we will never know. Having represented Sunderland and County Durham Boys, Johnson was spotted by Boro's youth development officer Ron Bone while playing as striker for Sunday League side Dunlop. Fast and direct, he was transformed into a flying winger as a Boro trainee before being handed his first-team debut at 18 along with several other youngsters amid an early season injury crisis under Lennie Lawrence. Both Johnson and fellow teenager Michael Barron made their first starts in a 2–0 First Division defeat at Portsmouth in November 1993. The England youth trialist played further games in the Anglo-Italian Cup in the weeks that followed but was given only 14 more minutes of League football as a sub in a 3–0 home win over Notts County a week before Christmas. That same season he helped the club's youth team clinch the Northern Intermediate League title, scoring 20 goals in 35 games along the way. However, Bryan Robson's arrival at the club saw Johnson's fortunes take a marked downturn and he was soon struggling for a place even in the reserves. The nearest he came to the first team was as a non-playing sub against Cesena in the Anglo-Italian Cup. His contract was cancelled to allow him to rejoin Lawrence at Bradford along with another of Boro's young professionals, David McKinlay. However, he had an unhappy spell with Bradford and stayed only five months before giving up the professional game and returning home to Sunderland. He spent six months without a job before a spell selling insurance. He later worked for Sunderland Council's housing department and played right wing for Durham City, having also appeared for Blyth Spartans, Chester-le-Street and South Shields.

JOHNSON Peter Edward

Left-back
Born: Harrogate, 5 October 1958.
Career: MIDDLESBROUGH 1976. Newcastle United 1980. Bristol City (loan) 1982. Doncaster Rovers 1983. Darlington 1983. Whitby Town. Crewe Alexandra 1985. Whitby Town. Exeter City 1986. Southend United 1986. Gillingham 1989. Peterborough United 1991.

■ Johnson found tough competition for the left-back post at Middlesbrough and never truly established himself at the club. Having attended school in Harrogate, he had trials with York before joining Boro and progressed through the ranks to make his debut late in the 1977–78 season against Chelsea. Most Boro fans, however, will remember the match for the other player making his debut, as David Shearer scored both goals in a 2–0 win. Johnson played two further games in central defence as cover for Alan Ramage but it was in his favoured left-back slot that John Neal handed him his first run in the side in place of Ian Bailey. A steady, reliable defender who liked to join in attacks, he only lost his place through injury but took almost seven months to win it back as Bailey and then Jeff Peters were preferred during the first half of the 1979–80 campaign. But with Bailey again given the nod, he became Arthur Cox's first signing for Newcastle after turning down a move to Carlisle. No more than a fringe player at St James's, he later became one of football's journeymen in the lower divisions.

JOHNSTON Allan

Winger
Born: Glasgow, 14 December 1973.
Career: Tynecastle Boys Club. Heart of Midlothian 1990. Rennes (France) 1996. Sunderland 1997. Birmingham City (loan) 1999. Bolton Wanderers 2000. Glasgow Rangers 2000. MIDDLESBROUGH 2001. Sheffield Wednesday (loan) 2002. Kilmarnock 2004.

■ Johnston began his career with Heart of Midlothian, winning three Under-21 caps. He moved from Tynecastle to join French side Rennes and then transferred to Sunderland in spring 1997. He became a huge favourite on Wearside where he formed an excellent partnership with Michael Gray on the left. He scored 11 goals in his first season and seven the next as the Black Cats won promotion to the Premiership. But he fell out with manager Peter Reid when he refused to sign a contract extension and spent a long time languishing in the reserves. After spells on loan at Birmingham City and Bolton, Johnston returned to Scotland in summer 2000, joining Rangers on freedom of contract. He made just 14 appearances for his boyhood heroes before joining Boro for £600,000 in the 2001–02 season. Johnston struggled to reproduce the form that had made him such a hero elsewhere in the North East but enjoyed one of his best games in a losing FA Cup semi-final with Arsenal. He scored one goal in 23 appearances and went on loan to Sheffield Wednesday before another return north of the border with Kilmarnock in August 2004. Johnston won 18 Scotland caps.

JOHNSON Christopher Patrick (Paddy)

Wing-half
Born: Dublin, 16 July 1924.
Died: 1971.
Career: Shelbourne. MIDDLESBROUGH 1947. Grimsby Town 1949.

■ For a player who Boro sold to Grimsby as an apology for an earlier misdemeanour, Johnston made a huge success of his career at Blundell Park. He had twice represented the League of Ireland before leaving Shelbourne for Ayresome Park in 1947 but the wing-half found First Division life very difficult. With survival assured, he was handed his first-team debut in place of Harry Bell for the penultimate game of 1947–48 season as David Jack's side were beaten 3–0 at Sunderland. He was again on the losing side a week later on his home debut against Aston Villa. He retained his place for the opening fixure of the following season at Chelsea, but was this time handed the number eight jersey. It was to be his final game for the club. Johnston moved to Grimsby in mid-season as the replacement for Norman Robinson. Six months earlier, Boro sold sold Robinson to the Second Division club but the player was found to have an injury that ended his career. When Grimsby approached Boro for compensation, Ayresome Park officials instead sold them Johnston for a cut-price fee and he became a big favourite at Blundell Park. Cool under pressure and a close marker, he was a stalwart of over 250 games, though Grimsby were in Division Three North by the end of his playing days. Having married Brenda Fisher, a famous Channel swimmer, Johnston later worked for the Ross Group. He died suddenly in 1971, aged only 47.

JOHNSTON Craig Peter

Forward/Winger
Born: Johannesburg, 25 June 1960.
Career: MIDDLESBROUGH 1978. Liverpool 1981.

■ Long before the likes of Harry Kewell, Craig Johnston became the first Australian to make it big in English football. Needless to say, his name is hugely famous Down Under, not only for his playing achievements but for his work in developing the renowned Predator football boot.

The son of a former part-time player Dundee, Johnston was born in South Africa but his family moved to Australia when he was very young. He was a member of the Australian youth squad when he saw Boro playing friendlies in his homeland while on tour with his school. He subsequently wrote to a number of English First Division clubs asking for a trial but Boro trainer Harold Shepherdson was the only one who bothered to reply. 'Shep' invited him over for a trial as long as he paid his own air fare and the enthusiastic youngster duly came to Teesside, only to be sent packing after a short stay. Undeterred, Johnston returned for a second trial a year later and eventually impressed enough to earn a contract.

By his own admission, Johnston had much to learn in his early days but was a truly dedicated young professional and would frequently stay back for extra training to practise his skills, often kicking the ball against Ayresome Park's car park wall time and time again. Indeed, so over eager was he to reach top condition, he suffered an injured pelvis that sidelined him for eight months. He

was less than two months past his 17th birthday and still a junior when picked to make his debut in an FA Cup tie against Everton in January 1978 but almost lost his life before the big day arrived. Johnston came close to drowning in a sea drama when he was stranded by the tide in Jersey but thankfully his swimming prowess came to his rescue. He remains the youngest player to appear for Boro in an FA Cup tie. Although he made occasional appearances over the next two seasons, John Neal only handed him a regular first-team place following the departure of John Mahoney in 1979 and Johnston immediately began to stamp his authority and enthusiasm on the game.

A fantastic athlete with natural fitness, pace and the ability to unleash a hard shot, he quickly won over the Ayresome Park fans with his hard-working displays and appeared regularly alongside fellow teenagers Mark Proctor and David Hodgson. All three progressed to England Under-21 honours, though in Johnston's case, a battle had to be won over fellow claimants, Scotland, Australia and South Africa. Nicknamed 'Roo' or 'Skippy', he was establishing his name as an attacking central midfielder of some note when he scored both goals in a 2–0 win at Everton, still aged just 19. His season was blighted by a mid-season injury but he bounced back to start a 5–0 rout of European Cup-winners' Cup finalists Arsenal on the final day. Despite his long, dark locks, he was also a fine header of the ball, as he displayed in rising for one of Boro's six goals against

Norwich in 1980. By Christmas of 1980–81, he led the club's scorers with an impressive tally of 10 goals in 22 games but had become frustrated with the club's lack of ambition. A public statement that he wanted to leave the club did not go down well with the supporters and his car was vandalised. The incident only hardened his resolve and he became briefly Boro's record sale when he left for Liverpool shortly after an infamous FA Cup quarter-final defeat to Wolves.

That game proved to be the start of a very slipperly slope that would eventually lead the club into liquidation. For Johnston, however, it was the start of an exciting new episode. Having turned down Brian Clough and Nottingham Forest to move to Anfield, he had to wait a year for his full debut but then established himself among Liverpool's all-star cast, winning European Cup, League championship and FA Cup-winners' medals in a glorious career. However, he shocked the football world when he walked out on his contract and, at 27, gave up the professional game in 1988 to return to Australia to take care of his sister who had been seriously injured in a freak accident. Liverpool retained his contract for several years afterwards but Johnston did not come back, except to comfort families after the Hillsborough Disaster. Back Down Under, he worked as a sports journalist before earning a fortune by developing the Adidas Predator boot. He later developed another boot design, The Pig, before being declared bankrupt. He lives in Florida, US. At Anfield, he is still remembered for another rather offbeat achievement, as the writer of their top five hit song, *The Anfield Rap*.

JONES Abraham

Centre-half
Born: Tipton, 1875.
Died: 1942.
Career: Cameron Highlanders. West Bromwich Albion 1897. MIDDLESBROUGH 1901. Luton Town.

■ It is not recorded why Abe Jones's nickname was 'Bullet'. It could have been reference to great pace or perhaps it was a description of the half-back's headers. Or maybe the cowboy reference was a pun

on the name of Jones and his defensive partner, Dave Smith. Whatever, Smith and Jones – not to mention their fellow half-back Andy Davidson – shot down many a strikeforce in their years together at Middlesbrough. Signed from WBA as a centre-half replacement for club captain Bill Higgins, Jones settled immediately into the Boro defence and the talented half-back line was the rock on which John Robson built promotion to the First Division. Ironically, Boro finished second behind Jones' former club. A great stopper, he could also take goals himself and found the net in impressive thrashings of Doncaster (6–0), Burton (5–1), Stockport (6–0) and Glossop (5–0) at the Linthorpe Road ground in a memorable first season. His forays forward were curtailed in the top flight and his only goals came from the penalty spot, though he did have the honour of playing in Boro's first ever game in Division One. A year later, he was again in the line-up as another piece of history was made as Ayresome Park hosted its first competitive match, against Sunderland. Despite his popularity, he was once criticized by a Gazette writer for doing 'so much unnecessary headwork'. Jones fell out of favour with new manager Andy Aitken and joined Luton at the end of the 1905–06 season.

JONES Bradley

Goalkeeper
Born: Armadale, Australia, 19 March 1982.
Career: MIDDLESBROUGH 1999.

Shelbourne (Ireland) (loan) 2002. Stockport County (loan) 2002. Rotherham (loan) 2003. Blackpool (loan) 2003. Blackpool (loan) 2004. Sheffield Wednesday (loan) 2006.

■ Jones is a tall angular goalkeeper who has been understudy to fellow Australian Mark Schwarzer for club and country. The form of Australia's number one has been such that first-team opportunities have been limited for the 6ft 3in custodian who was born in Armadale, Western Australia. Signed from Bayswater SC, Jones progressed through Boro's Academy system and had to wait four years before making his debut. That came in a 2–0 FA Cup third-round win over Notts County at the Riverside. By then Jones had been on loan with Shelbourne, Rotherham, Stockport County and Blackpool in the third tier of the English game, recording the impressive feat of five clean sheets in seven games and just one in each of the other games with the Tangerines. He returned for a further dozen games with the Bloomfield Road outfit in the 2004–05 season ending that season with five games for Boro. In 2005–06 he played in four of Boro's ties on the way to the UEFA Cup Final, including the never-to-be-forgotten second leg of the semi-final when Boro came from behind to defeat Steaua Bucharest. Season 2006–07 was an eventful one for Jones. He started by going on loan with Sheffield Wednesday for three months, returning to play in two FA Cup ties with Boro, the second a penalty shoot-out win at West Brom. Having previously been in the Australia squad for the Olympic Games in Greece and winning Under-23 honours, Jones won his first senior call-up in January 2007 for a game against Denmark at Loftus Road, winning his first cap in June 2007, a 2–1 defeat against Uruguay.

Highly rated by Boro's goalkeeping coach Paul Barron, Jones was keen to step up the fight for first-team duties with Schwarzer and fellow 'keeper Ross Turnbull.

JONES George Wilfred

Outside-right
Born: Crook, 28 June 1895.
Died: 1970.
Career: Crook Town. Gwersylit. Everton 1919. Wigan Boro 1922. MIDDLESBROUGH 1925. Southport 1926. Yeovil & Petters United. Great Harwood.

■ Outside-right George Jones spent only one season with Middlesbrough before dropping into Division Three South with Southend. It was Herbert Bamlett who brought Jones to the North East and he won his first chance in place of Jacky Carr for a 3–0 home success over Sheffield Wednesday in September 1925. He struck his only goal for the club two weeks later, his late strike clinching both Second Division points against Oldham as Boro challenged the early pace-setters. Sadly, the season deteriorated into mid-table mediocrity and Jones was allowed to leave.

JONES Gordon Edward

Full-back
Born: Sedgefield, 6 March 1943.
Career: MIDDLESBROUGH 1960. Darlington 1973. Crook Town.

■ The man who played more post-war games for Boro than any other player, Jones was a polished left-back who could consider himself unlucky not to have won full England caps. Although he did play his country's Under-23 side, it was probably only his lack of pace that denied him full international honours as there is little doubt that his overall game made him a match for most opponents.

It was Jones' own initiative that brought him to Boro when he put pen to paper and wrote to Ayresome Park asking for a trial. He was signed as an amateur after the club's officials had seen him in action for just 10 minutes of a trial game and the England youth star duly became a professional two years later. After making his first-team debut in a 4–3 League Cup defeat to Cardiff in October 1960, he was handed his League debut by Bob

Dennison in January 1961 when the 17-year-old, having travelled as 12th man, was drafted in after Derek Stonehouse was taken ill overnight. He was given just 20 minutes' warning of his shock call-up at right-back but performed well enough in a 3–2 defeat to Southampton to earn a long run in the side, though he was switched to his favoured left-back slot late in the season. He was never out of the first-team reckoning again in a Boro career which spanned 13 years.

Although a strong tackler, Jones was known for his unscrupulous fairness and was never sent off and booked only twice in well over 500 appearances for the club. He was also a model of consistency and quickly established himself in the side in 1961–62 when, after starting the season at right-back, he even displaced Boro's England star Mick McNeil on the left-hand side of the club's defence. He won the first of nine England Under-23 caps in November 1961, aged only 18, and was a mainstay in the team under both Dennison and his successor Raich Carter. However, after being dropped by Carter in January 1964 following a poor run of results, he demanded a transfer and was on the list until being reinstated. Despite Boro's ever-worsening plight in the lower reaches of the Second Division, he was strongly tipped for full England honours in the months before the 1966 World Cup Finals but was overlooked for Ray Wilson.

Boro's embarrassing relegation to Division Three that year only served to strengthen Jones' resolve and he led Stan Anderson's team to promotion at the first attempt as club captain, a position which he retained for six seasons. An astute skipper, he had a great left foot and was an excellent crosser of the ball – a skill he displayed to great effect as a main supply for the aerial dominance of Hughie McIlmoyle. He enjoyed a much-deserved testimonial in 1969, though appalling weather conditions spoilt his big night. However, he proved he had lost none of his old class and won the club's Player of the Year award for a second time in 1971, having previously received the accolade in the relegation season five years earlier. After losing his left-back slot to Frank Spraggon early in the 1972–73 campaign, he played some games in left midfield. Jones joined Darlington on a free transfer in January 1973, although caretaker boss Harold Shepherdson had initially blocked the move. At Feethams, he played alongside several former Boro teammates, including Billy Horner, but was unable to help them avoid finishing bottom of the entire League in 1973. After hanging up his boots, Jones went into business on Teesside and still lives in the area. Only Tim Williamson played more games for Middlesbrough than Jones.

JONES James

Full-back
Born: Details unknown.
Career: MIDDLESBROUGH 1899.

■ Full-back Jones enjoyed the majority of his success while Middlesbrough were still a Northern League side. He was a prominent player in the two seasons immediately before the decision to join the Football League in 1899. Indeed, Boro won the Amateur Cup in his first season on the club's books though he did not figure in the final win over Uxbridge. He made his Football League debut at left full-back in a home clash with Lincoln at the end of December 1899 when Andy Ramsay was injured but played only once more in that groundbreaking campaign, as Woolwich Arsenal were beaten at Linthorpe Road. He again played as Ramsay's stand-in the following season and played his final games at right full-back early in the 1901–02 promotion campaign. He remained on the club's books for several more seasons before being released.

JONES John Love

Outside-left/Centre-forward
Born: Rhyl, 1885.
Died: 1913.
Career: Rhyl. Stoke 1905. Crewe Alexandra. MIDDLESBROUGH 1908. Portsmouth.

■ For a player who smashed the club's transfer record and held it for the next 15 years, Jones was something of a disappointment at Ayresome Park. The outside-left made his name with Stoke City and was capped by Wales before his big money move to Andy Aitken's Boro. Whatever Aitken saw in his new signing is not recorded but, despite the fee, he chose to leave him on the sidelines for most of his two-year stay with the club. He made his debut in place of Jimmy Thackeray in a thrilling 3–0 First Division home win over Manchester City as England internationals Bloomer and Common got the goals. However, Thackeray returned after a run of just three games and was also preferred for the opening fixture of the 1909–10 campaign. Jones was then given a four-match run in the side, only to find himself back in the reserves for the next five months. He was recalled in favour of Thackeray once again when a bad run of form brought the threat of relegation and helped produce three wins from five games. He won a second Welsh cap as Ireland were beaten 4–1 at Wrexham in April 1910 but his final appearance for the club came as Boro were beaten 4–1 at Manchester United on the final day of the season. He spent the entirity of the following season in the reserves and joined Portsmouth as the Southern League side began their swift rise to fame.

JORDAN Brian Athol

Centre-half
Born: Doncaster, 31 January 1932.
Career: Derby County 1951. Denaby United. Rotherham United 1953. MIDDLESBROUGH 1958. York City 1960.

■ Left-half Jordan hardly had time to draw breath after signing for Boro before he was making his debut for the club as Scunthorpe United were drubbed 6–1, with a hat-trick apiece from Brian Clough and Alan Peacock. Rejected by Derby, he had joined Denaby United but quickly came to the attention of Rotherham. Bob Dennison signed him to fill a problem position as Boro had leaked eight goals in their two previous games. Jordan made his memorable debut the day after signing but, despite his promising start, it was clear things were no better a week later when Boro fell to another embarrassing defeat, this time 5–2 at Leyton Orient. A 5–0 mauling of Derby was followed by three successive defeats and Jordan played his last game for the club in the second of them, a 3–2 loss at home to Ipswich. Ray Yeoman made his debut alongside the recalled Ronnie Dicks the following week and Jordan was left to play reserve team football for 18 months until a cut-price move to York.

JUNINHO Oswaldo Giroldo

Midfield
Born: Sao Paulo, Brazil, 22 February 1973.
Career: Corinthians 1990. Ituano 1991. Sao Paulo 1993. MIDDLESBROUGH 1995. Atletico Madrid (Spain) 1997. MIDDLESBROUGH (loan) 1999. Vasco da Gama (loan) 2000. Flamengo (loan) 2002. MIDDLESBROUGH 2002. Glasgow Celtic 2004. Palmeiras 2005. Flamengo 2007.

■ Juninho is by far and away the most popular Boro player of modern times and many would argue that he is the best player ever to pull on the red and white shirt. Boasting astonishing skills, a heart as big as a lion and, at his peak, phenomenol acceleration, he was hero-worshipped on Teesside during his first spell, lauded on his year-long return and played a huge part in bringing the club its first-ever major silverware when he incredibly returned for a second time. For many Boro fans, Juninho was, and is, a god – or at least the nearest you can get to him in a pair of football boots!

And yet his career might never have even happened had his first club had their way. Brazilian side Juventus rejected a teenage Juninho as too small and he was forced to play as an amateur with Corinthians before joining Ituano, where his performances caught the eye of top Brazilian side, Sao Paulo, who paid a £350,000 fee for him. He helped them win the Super Copa in 1993 and the Recopa in both 1993 and 1994 before the big one, the World Club Championship, in 1994. A call-up to the Brazil squad soon followed and when Juninho was made Brazilian Footballer of the Year in 1995 it seemed he had the world at his feet. 'The Little Fella' caught the attention of Bryan Robson – who was assisting Terry Venables with the national squad at the time – when scoring a sensational free-kick in a 3–1 Wembley win over England during the 1995 Umbro Cup and the Boro boss set his heart on bringing him to Teesside. Robson and chief executive Keith Lamb flew out to Brazil and arrived at Sao Paulo unannounced in late June. An initial £3 million offer was turned down and the pair returned home empty-handed. But by October news reached them that Sao Paulo might now be prepared to sell and they returned to South America for five days of negotiations. The audacious signing, which took persistence and patience, was tied up despite an 11th hour attempt by

Arsenal to hijack the deal and snatch Juninho from Boro's grasp. Top European clubs were also interested but the player was tempted by the challenge of helping Boro win their first major trophy. Juninho's arrival on Teesside could not have been more high profile. Some 5,000 fans and a samba band were there to greet him at the Riverside Stadium, while over 200 members of the media were there for the press conference to announce his signing. Quite simply, Middlesbrough went samba-mad. Season tickets were sold out within days of his arrival and Juninho did not disappoint, setting up Jan Fjortoft's goal on his debut against Leeds with a pinpoint pass after a trademark driving run. The Brazilian's skill was there for all to see and he had the natural ability to bewilder opponents with tricks, dummies and exhilarating pace. That first season was not all a bed of roses, however. He took time to adjust to a new way of life, a new culture and the fast, physical nature of the English game. Some argued that his teammates were not on the same wavelength as Juninho but there was no denying that he was largely anonymous in some games, especially away from home as Boro slumped to a long run of defeats. His season was further disrupted by a return to South America to help his country qualify for the Olympics and he eventually won a bronze medal at Atlanta 96.

Juninho's second season in English football was everything the first was not. Now he began to get to grips with the pace of the game and the old inconsistencies vanished. The dream weaver's astonishing dribbling ability was a joy to watch and his appearance added thousands to the attendance wherever he played. Breathtaking skill and perfect control meant he frequently embarrassed opposing defenders while his killer passes were a godsend for a striker like Fabrizio Ravanelli. With his compatriot Emerson alongside him, Juninho turned in a series of awesome performances as Boro launched a bid for Cup success on two fronts. Though Boro's League form was poor, he was now a regular goalscorer, grabbing memorable goals against Everton and Derby. His best, however, was saved for Chelsea as Juninho started a move which culminated in his own diving header to meet Mikkel Beck's cross. It was rightly voted the club's goal of the season but the awards didn't end there. He was the club's and the supporters' Player of the Year, the Premier League Player of the Year and the runner-up to Gianfranco Zola in the Football Writers' award.

Sadly, it all ended in tears. The Coca-Cola Cup was snatched from Boro's grasp by Leicester with only seconds remaining and Juninho was marked out of the final and the replay by Pontus Kaamark. Relegation came on the final day of the season at Leeds, Brian Deane's headed goal leaving a weeping Juninho crestfallen on the Elland Road turf. Finally, there was defeat in the FA Cup Final and the fans' hero announced that he must leave to realise his ambitions of playing for Brazil in the 1998 World Cup Finals. Despite interest from Manchester United and Tottenham, Atletico Madrid won the race for his signature and a £12 million fee took him to Spain. It seemed the samba beat had sounded its last on Teesside. But Boro always said that they held first refusal on his signature if ever Atletico decided to sell and when a broken leg denied him a World Cup place and disappointing form followed, Boro looked to bring him back. He looked all set to sign for £10 million in January 1999, only for Atletico to have a change of heart. But Juninho was finally back at his adopted home in September when Boro beat off competition from Aston Villa to agree a short-term deal with the option to buy him outright at the end of the season. A 25,000 crowd for his debut in an otherwise low profile Worthington

Cup clash with Chesterfield was testament to the mark he had left on the town during his first stay on Teesside. This time, however, things did not run so smoothly, with Bryan Robson's surprising decision not to play him 'in the hole' behind the main strikers nullifying his ability to damage the tightest of Premier League defences. Even so, a midfield of Juninho, Paul Ince and occasionally Christian Ziege should have been a huge success, but the Brazilian often flattered to deceive, much of the lightning pace seemingly having vanished with the leg break. Juninho struggled to hold down a starting place during the closing months of a disappointing season for the club, though he rolled back the years with a stupendous individual goal in a final day win at Everton to sign off in style. Robson's decision not to turn his loan into a permanent deal shocked many fans and the following season's battle against relegation suggested that the boss got it wrong. It seemed certain that the Boro's Juninho love-in was over and the player enjoyed extended loan spells back in Brazil with Vasco da Gama, where he won the Serie A title, and Flamengo. Then, on the day England met Brazil in the quarter-finals of the 2002 World Cup, new Boro boss Steve McClaren asked Juninho if he would be interested in a third Riverside spell. Juninho's answer was an emphatic 'yes' and, as a consequence, Boro agreed a £3.8 million fee to buy him back from Atletico Madrid five years after selling him to the Spanish club. He completed the move back to Boro soon after helping a Brazil team that also included the likes of Ronaldinho, Rivaldo and Ronaldo win the 2002 World Cup. His second return sent a buzz around Teesside but it would be March 2003 before Boro fans would see their adopted hero on his second return. Juninho suffered an horrendous cruciate ligament injury on a pre-season tour of Holland. But he was back with a bang when scoring an equaliser against Everton when introduced as a half-time substitute, following it with a stunning strike against Leeds at Elland Road two weeks later. The following season he hit up a fine partnership with Gaizka Mendieta and finished as the club's joint-top scorer with nine goals, including two headers in a memorable 3–2 win at Old Trafford and the winner at Highbury in the first leg of the Carling Cup semi-final. His aim had always been to help Boro win a first major Cup and he fulfilled that ambition when playing a starring role in victory over Bolton in the final. Riverside regulars loved Juninho as much as ever – but McClaren had other ideas, believing him to have lost 'half a yard' of acceleration and told the fans ' idol that he would not be guaranteed a place in the side in 2004–05. As a consequence, just as Boro were embarking on their first European adventure, Juninho made a free transfer switch to Celtic, having scored 34 goals in 155 appearances for Boro. The move to Scotland was not a success and he switched back to Brazil with Palmeiras before the season was out, enjoying a fine spell there before a disastrous return to Flamengo. There, without playing a League game, Juninho was sacked after refusing to be substituted at half-time of a Copa Libertadores defeat to Uruguayan side Defensor in May 2007. He spent two months without a club before news broke that he was in shock talks over a proposed return to English football with Hull City.

KAMARA Christopher

Midfield

Born: Middlesbrough, 25 December 1957.

Career: Portsmouth 1975. Swindon Town 1977. Portsmouth 1981. Brentford 1981. Swindon Town 1985. Stoke City 1988. Leeds United 1990. Luton Town 1991. Sheffield United (loan) 1992. MIDDLESBROUGH (loan) 1993. Sheffield United 1993. Bradford City 1994.

■ Two talented young footballers, Chris and Steve, grew up together on the back streets of Middlesbrough's Park End estate and dreamt of one day playing for the Boro. One of them, Chris Kamara, fulfilled his dream, albeit late in a respectable career. The other, Steve Gibson, had to make do with becoming the club's chairman. Kamara's boyhood friendship with Gibson remains to this day and Gibson was a club director when his old mate joined Boro on loan midway through the 1992–93 season. A Boro fanatic as a teenager – and a member of the famous Holgate supporters, the Ayresome Angels – Kamara attended St Thomas' School in the town and almost signed for the club on three occasions. Indeed, along with another later famous friend, cricketer Bill Athey, he very nearly joined Boro as an apprentice but, on being rejected, he joined the Navy and was very nearly lost to football. Thankfully, eagle-eyed Portsmouth scouts spotted his talents and Kamara bought himself out of the forces within weeks of joining and signed professional forms for Pompey. A hard tackling, honest midfielder, he became something of a football journeyman and was sent off at Ayresome Park during a spell with Stoke City. After winning Stoke's Player of the Year award, he was all set to join Bruce Rioch's Boro but agreed to 'drop in' at Elland Road on the way and instead made a £150,000 switch to Leeds United. Belatedly, aged 35, he did play for his hometown club when Lennie Lawrence brought him in on loan from Luton and Kamara added steel to the midfield in a brief stay in the inaugural Premier League. Lawrence wanted to make the move permanent but the clubs couldn't agree the fee and the player returned to Kenilworth Road. Kamara later played for Lawrence again at Bradford and, after a spell as his assistant, succeeded him as City's manager. Surprisingly sacked, he later enjoyed a brief and unhappy spell in charge of Stoke. Kamara then became a regular football pundit on Sky Sports.

KAREMBEU Christian Lali

Midfield
Born: Lifou, New Caledonia, 3 December 1970.
Career: Nantes (France) 1990. Sampdoria (Italy) 1995. Real Madrid (Spain) 1997. MIDDLESBROUGH 2000. Olympiakos (Greece) 2001. Servette (Switzerland) 2004. Bastia (France) 2005.

■ The dreadlocked midfielder was one of the most decorated players to represent Boro when he arrived from Real Madrid for £2.1 million during summer 2000. Karembeu was born on the remote island of New Caledonia, a French Colony in Melanesia in the South Pacific. He started his career with Nantes before travelling to Sampdoria and Madrid, despite the Italian club president's attempts to move him to Barcelona. Along the way he collected a World Cup, European Championship and two European Cup-winners' medals. Accompanying him to Teesside was his wife, Slovakian model Adriana Sklenaříková, the Wonderbra model. The Oceania Player of the Year in 1995 and 1998, Karembeu refused to sing the French national anthem, La Marseillaise, before games as two of his uncles have been exhibited in a human zoo during the Paris Colonial Exposition of 1931. Karembeu made his Boro debut in a 3–1 away win at Coventry's Highfield Road in August 2000, and first goal came 10 games later against Manchester United at Old Trafford. His form was patchy in his one season on Teesside and the following season he left for Olympiakos after scoring four goals in 36 appearances. He played 68 times for the Greek side before moving to Swiss club Servette, for whom he made a dozen appearances. He was then signed on loan by French club Bastia, his last match action before he retired from the game in October 2005.

KAVANAGH Graham Anthony

Midfield
Born: Dublin, 2 December 1973.
Career: Home Farm. MIDDLESBROUGH 1991. Darlington (loan) 1994. Stoke City 1996. Cardiff City 2001. Wigan Athletic 2005. Sunderland 2006.

■ Boro beat a host of clubs to the signature of talented midfielder Kavanagh. The Irish lad was spotted by Boro's youth development officer Ron Bone playing for Home Farm in the annual Milk Cup tournament in Ireland and was persuaded to sign a two-year professional contract at Ayresome Park, despite interest from Liverpool, Leeds, Manchester City and Chelsea. 'Kav' progressed through the ranks alongside Jamie Pollock and was a non-playing sub for the Boro first team at Watford in September 1991. However, he had to wait until October of the following year for his full debut when he replaced Robbie Mustoe in the starting line-up for a disappointing 1–0 Premier League defeat to Nottingham Forest. He hit the post on his home debut against Sheffield Wednesday in the following game but was only used sparingly as Boro were relegated. Lennie Lawrence used him as a stop-gap striker the following season and the teenager responded with two goals in a 3–0 triumph over Notts County. Though the player himself preferred a midfield role, he was again pushed up front for much of Bryan Robson's first season at the club and finished as the reserve team's top scorer. However, it was as a creative midfielder that Kavanagh shone, his excellent control, passing and strong shooting frequently catching the eye. He played for Eire's Under-21 side alongside Alan Moore on several occasions but spent much of the 1995–96 Premier League campaign on the sidelines due to a broken big toe and torn ligaments. He hit the headlines for all the wrong reasons when he was arrested by police for an alleged assault but returned to the side and scored a vital penalty winner at Leeds that eased growing relegation fears. After beginning the following season back in the second team, he was loaned to Stoke before making the move permanent. Kavanagh was a key figure in the Wigan side that stormed through the divisions to the Premiership. He went on to win full international caps and later helped Sunderland to promotion in 2007.

KAY John

Right-back
Born: Great Lumley, 29 January 1964.
Career: Arsenal 1981. Wimbledon 1984. MIDDLESBROUGH (loan) 1985. Sunderland 1987. Shrewsbury Town (loan) 1996. Preston North End 1996. Scarborough 1996. Workington.

■ Committed right-back Kay is well remembered in the North East. It was not, however, on Teesside that he became a popular figure but on Wearside, where he played over 200 games for

Sunderland. After failing to make the grade with Arsenal, he came to Boro on loan from Wimbledon midway through the 1984–85 season as Willie Maddren desperately fought to find a formula to drag the club from the jaws of relegation. Darren Wood, Gary Gill, Gary Hamilton and Irving Nattrass had all been tried in the problem right-back position and Kay didn't last long either. He made his debut in a goalless draw at Wolves and Boro failed to win any of the eight games in which he appeared. He returned to London after two months and Maddren swooped for Brian Laws soon after. Kay was a consistent performer at Roker Park, winning a Division Three Championship medal in 1988 before dropping into the lower divisions.

KAYE Arthur

Outside-right
Born: Darton, 9 May 1933.
Career: Barnsley 1950. Blackpool 1959. MIDDLESBROUGH 1960. Colchester United 1965.

■ The rather unimaginative dressing room wits at Ayresome Park nicknamed Kaye 'Danny'. But playing against the outside-right was never a laughing matter. A fast-raiding winger with silky skills, his party trick was to push the ball past the opposing full-back in the opening minutes of a game and run full speed into him, willingly conceding a free-kick. It was Kaye's way of getting his retaliation in first and letting his opponent know that he would not be jostled out of the game.

One of the smallest players in Boro's history, the England Schoolboy international joined home-town club Barnsley straight from school and quickly developed an excellent reputation for his skill, tearaway style and creative ability. Unlike many wingers, he was also aggressive and abrasive. He represented the Football League, won Under-23 caps and was included in full England squads ahead of the 1958 World Cup Finals. Blackpool signed him as the intended replacement for Stanley Matthews but Kaye was unable to shift the legend from the Seasiders' wing and made do with roles at inside-forward before dropping into the reserves.

Moving to Middlesbrough rejuvenated his career and he was a regular maker and taker of goals for the side under Bob Dennison and his successor Raich Carter. However, he was unlucky to be at the club when talent was lacking and he played all his games in the Second Division. Kaye joined Fourth Division Colchester at the age of 32 and later played for them in their first ever visit to Ayresome Park during the 1966–67 season. He became a joiner back in Barnsley after finishing his playing days.

KEAR Michael Philip

Outside-right
Born: Coleford, 27 May 1943.
Career: Cinderford Town. Newport County 1963. Nottingham Forest 1963. MIDDLESBROUGH 1967. Berkon (Belgium). Barnsley (loan) 1970.

■ Mike Kear and Peter Worthington made their Boro debuts on the same day in September 1967 at Birmingham and neither will want to be reminded of the scoreline. Stan Anderson's side lost 6–1. For Worthington it meant a return to the reserves but Kear missed only two games throughout the remainder of the season and played his part in helping the club re-establish itself back in the Second Division. A right winger, he had been signed by Newport from non-League Cinderford Town but joined Nottingham Forest just four months later, where he was understudy to their talented wingers as a First Division runners-up spot was achieved. Craving regular first-team football, he moved to Ayresome Park but was in and out of the side in his second season, when he was

competing for a wide berth with Ray Lugg and Dave Chadwick. He was tried at inside-forward early in the 1969–70 campaign but was dropped after a 4–0 defeat at Blackburn and never played again. His contract was cancelled by the club in April 1970 and though Kear appealed the Football League tribunal found Boro not guilty of any misdemeanour. He later played in the Belgian First Division for Berkon, where a broken leg kept him out for 10 months before a brief return to England with Barnsley.

KELLY B.

Right-back
Born: Details unknown.
Career: Ashfield. MIDDLESBROUGH 1910.

■ Defender Kelly split his four appearances for the club between the right and left full-back berths. After signing from Ashfield, he was handed a debut in place of Boro's international right-back Don McLeod in a 3–1 home win over Sheffield United in November 1910. However, he spent five months out in the cold after a 5–0 mauling at Aston Villa. He returned briefly at left-back in place of James Weir late in the First Division season and again played against Villa before a final game – a Wear-Tees derby defeat at Sunderland.

KENNEDY Frederick

Inside-forward
Born: Radcliffe, April 1902.
Died: 1963.
Career: Rossendale United. Manchester United 1923. Everton 1924. MIDDLESBROUGH 1927. Reading 1929. Oldham Athletic 1930. Rossendale United. Northwich Victoria. Racing Club de Paris. Blackburn Rovers 1933. Racing Club de Paris. Stockport County 1937.

■ Although forward Kennedy enjoyed a reasonable football career, he should perhaps be best remembered for the occasion when he saved the life of a drowning woman. For his act of heroism, he was awarded a certificate by the Royal Humane Society. On the pitch, Kennedy's career began in the back waters of Rossendale United before moving on to Manchester United,

Everton and then Boro. His debut came in a First Division win over Blackburn in place of regular outside-left Owen Williams and he later stood in for Jacky Carr at inside-forward. The highlight of his short stay on Teesside came with a two-goal performance in a 5–3 home win over Bradford following relegation, while he was also a regular penalty taker. Kennedy later had a spell in France with Racing Club de Paris and ran a tobacconist's in Manchester once his playing days were over.

KENNEDY Jason Brian

Midfield
Born: Stockton-on-Tees, 11 September 1986.
Career: MIDDLESBROUGH 2005. Boston United (loan) 2006. Bury (loan) 2007. Livingston (loan) 2007.

■ A hard-working midfielder who started life as a striker, once scoring from the halfway line for Boro's Under-17 side. Kennedy was Boro's joint top scorer in their victorious FA Youth Cup campaign in 2004, scoring four goals in the eight games including the all-important winning goal in the 1–0 home leg victory over Aston Villa in the final. Born in Roseworth, Stockton, he has been with the club since he was 12 and was handed a two-year professional contract in 2005. His Premiership debut came against Fulham at the Riverside in April 2005 when he replaced Colin Cooper. The experienced defender repaid the compliment when he made his last Premiership appearance in May 2006, replacing Kennedy in the 85th-minute of a 1–0 defeat to the same side at Craven Cottage on a day when 15 of the 16-man squad were born within a 25-mile radius of the Riverside. He finished the campaign on seven appearances for

Boro, including the full 90 minutes of the 2–0 UEFA Cup win over Litex Lovech at the Riverside in December 2005. Kennedy impressed on a loan spell with League Two side Boston United in the 2006–07 season and finished the season at Bury.

KENNEDY Michael Francis Martin

Midfield
Born: Salford, 9 April 1961.
Career: Halifax Town 1979. Huddersfield Town 1980. MIDDLESBROUGH 1982. Portsmouth 1984. Bradford City 1988. Leicester City 1989. Luton Town 1989. Stoke City 1990. Chesterfield 1992. Wigan Athletic 1993.

■ Boro fans have always loved their midfield hard men so Mick Kennedy was a Holgate hero during his two-year stay at Ayresome Park. Aggressive and uncompromising, Kennedy would often crudely put his foot in to intimidate opponents but there was little doubt that he was a winner and the sort of player you would rather have playing for you than against you. An apprentice with Halifax, he made his name with Huddersfield and agreed a £100,000 move to Boro after meeting with manager Bobby Murdoch at Wetherby. Although a talented player, he was unfortunate to join Boro at a time of crisis and endured three 4–1 home defeats in his first month at the club, receiving his marching orders along with Ray Hankin in the last of the three against Grimsby. He showed his versatility by filling in at several positions under Malcolm Allison but spent a month on the sidelines early in the

1983–84 campaign after breaking his arm in a clash at Chelsea. He was sent off for a second time for elbowing an opponent in an off-the-ball incident at Brighton late in the season. When Kennedy was chased by Sheffield Wednesday and Portsmouth during the summer of 1984, Maddren dismissed an initial bid from Pompey of £80,000 but, with Boro desperate for cash, accepted an improved bid of £100,000. He later made his Portsmouth debut in a 1–1 draw against Boro before becoming one of the game's journeymen.

KENT Henry (Harry)

Centre-half
Born: Foleshill, 22 October 1879.
Died: 1948.
Career: Heanor Town. Ilkeston Town. Newark. Brighton & Hove Albion. MIDDLESBROUGH 1908. Watford.

■ Half-back Harry Kent's biggest achievement at Ayresome Park was not as a Middlesbrough player but as manager of Watford. Kent was in charge of the Third Division South club when they humbled top flight Boro by a 1–0 scoreline in an embarrassing FA Cup exit at Ayresome Park in January 1924. He had earlier played only a handful of games for Boro during the 1908–09 campaign as a respectable mid-table finish was achieved in Division One. He had, however, played more than 100 games for Brighton and enjoyed another successful time after leaving Ayresome for Watford. After initially being appointed player-manager, he was forced to sell to survive but took them to the Southern League Championship in 1915 and into the Football League in 1920.

KERNAGHAN Alan Nigel

Central defender
Born: Otley, 25 April 1967.
Career: MIDDLESBROUGH 1985. Charlton Athletic (loan) 1991. Manchester City 1993. Bolton Wanderers (loan) 1994. Bradford City (loan) 1995. St Johnstone 1998. Brechin City 2001. Clyde 2001. Livingston 2004. Falkirk 2005.

■ The watershed in Kernaghan's career with Boro was undoubtedly the appointment of Lennie Lawrence as the

club's manager in the summer of 1991. Until then, the versatile player had become a boo-boy target and looked destined to leave the club, ironically to join Lawrence at Charlton. Kernaghan had impressed while on loan the previous season and was keen to make the move a permanent arrangement. Instead, he was invited on to the pitch to meet Boro's new manager and was shocked to come face to face with Lawrence, who persuaded him to stay on Teesside. Such was the manager's faith in Kernaghan that he made him club captain on Tony Mowbray's departure soon after and the player responded with a string of fine performances at the heart of the Boro defence.

Although born in Otley, Kernaghan was brought up Northern Ireland and lived in Bangor for 14 years. After returning to England, he signed for Boro and progressed through the youth ranks alongside Colin Cooper and Peter Beagrie. Initially, he was seen as a striker and it was there that Willie Maddren handed him his first-team debut in a home defeat to Notts County in February 1985. He netted his first goal five weeks later to clinch three vital points against Sheffield United but was a peripheral figure for two years, making appearances up front, in midfield and in defence. He was regularly switched between centre-forward and central defender under Bruce Rioch, though he was also a regular substitute. Indeed, he holds the club's all-time record for sub appearances. A stunning hat-trick as a striker in a 4–2 win at Blackburn in November 1989 proved to be something of a false dawn as he could not find consistent form and became Tony Mowbray's defensive partner under Colin Todd. While dominant in the air, Kernaghan lacked pace and was prone to errors. Although regularly barracked by the fans, many believed he should have been named Man of the Match for a fine defensive display in the 1990 Zenith Data Systems Cup Final against Chelsea.

After being dropped by Todd, he twice came close to joining Charlton, with Lawrence offering Colin Walsh plus cash on the first occasion before Boro accepted a £300,000 bid. Then came Lawrence's surprise. A diabetic who regularly had to inject himself with insulin, Kernaghan missed the run-in to the successful promotion challenge of 1992 due to a knee ligament injury and spent nervous moments wandering around a local supermarket as promotion was clinched on the final day at Wolves. After captaining Boro in the Premier League, he won his first international caps. Despite playing six times for Northern Ireland Schoolboys as a youngster, he switched allegiances to Jack Charlton's Eire, having qualified through his grandparents. With the 1994 World Cup Finals on the horizon, Kernaghan was keen to remain in the top flight after Boro relegation and eventually moved to Manchester City when Brian Horton agreed to meet Lawrence's inflated request for £1.6 million. Kernaghan eventually lost form at Maine Road and played under Colin Todd at Bolton before a surprise move to Scotland with St Johnstone. He later took up a coaching career north of the border and briefly managed Dundee. Kernaghan is now a youth coach at Rangers.

KERR Paul Andrew

Midfield
Born: Portsmouth, 9 June 1964.
Career: Aston Villa 1982. MIDDLESBROUGH 1987. Millwall 1991. Port Vale 1992. Leicester City (loan) 1994. Wycombe Wanderers 1994. Waterlooville.

■ In his own words, Kerr was predictable in his own unpredictability during his four years as a Boro player. He was part of the Rioch revolution that clinched successive promotions, only to slump back at the first opportunity. The son of a Royal Navy man, Kerr was about to join Southampton as a youngster when Aston Villa moved in. As a striker, he was a prolific goalscorer for Villa's reserves but received only infrequent opportunities for their first team before becoming Boro's first cash signing since liquidation midway through the Third Division promotion season of 1986–87. The form of Bernie Slaven and Archie Stephens meant chances in the forward line were few and far between so, after making his debut on the left wing in a shock FA Cup defeat to Preston, he was mainly played in midfield, filling a gap left by the injured Brian Laws. As he would throughout the majority of his Boro career, Kerr struggled for consistency in his early months with the club and failed to find the target in any of his first 31 games for the club. However, the goal drought ended with a sweet moment when he scored the only goal of the match to clinch three important League points in a Second Division match against his old club, Villa, in September 1987.

A skilful, nippy attacking player with a good shot, Kerr had an unfortunate tendency to go missing in games. Nicknamed 'Nookie', he played his part in helping the club win promotion to the top flight via the Play-offs but missed a number of games in Division One through injury and loss of form. After giving up alcohol and working hard on his fitness during the 1988 close season, he was unfortunate to suffer a stress fracture to his ankle in the opening day win of the following campaign against Wolves. It was Christmas before he returned to the side, by which time Boro were in dire danger of a second consecutive relegation. The drop was narrowly averted though Kerr suffered Wembley heartbreak when left on the subs' bench in the Final of the ZDS Cup against Chelsea. The rejection was all the more gauling as he had scored one of the goals against Villa in the northern area final that had clinched the club's first ever Wembley appearance.

He was placed on the transfer list at his own request soon after but stayed on to enjoy his best ever form in the first half of the 1990–91 season as Colin Todd

chased promotion. After missing the first six games, he scored twice on his return as Leicester were humbled 6–0 and enjoyed a fine run in an attack-minded team. It didn't last, however, and he spent several months out in the cold before Bruce Rioch enquired about him for Millwall. Boro initially asked for £175,000 but a cut-price £100,000 fee was eventually agreed and Kerr moved on. Despite a fine scoring form, he never truly settled in London and joined former Villa and Boro teammate Dean Glover at Port Vale, joining Bernie Slaven on the scoresheet as his new club won the Autoglass Trophy Final at Wembley. He played his final football under Martin O'Neill as a non-contract player with Wycombe and scored in his only League game before retiring through injury, aged only 30. He later returned to live on Teesside, working as a financial advisor. He also spent several years as a co-commentator on Boro games for BBC Radio Cleveland.

KILGANNON Sean

Midfield
Born: Stirling, 8 March 1981.
Career: MIDDLESBROUGH 1999. Dunfermline Athletic 2002. Ross County 2004.

■ The Stirling-born midfielder made just one appearance for Boro after coming through the junior ranks. That came in a 2–2 draw with Newcastle United at the Riverside in May 2000. He was released in March 2002 and joined Dunfermline. He stayed at East End Park for two years before moving to Ross County. From there he moved to Partick Thistle, then closer to home in 2006 when joining Raith Rovers for whom he played 17 games in the 2006–07 season.

KINDER Vladimir

Full-back
Born: Bratislava, 9 March 1969.
Career: Slovan Bratislava (Czechoslovakia) 1990. MIDDLESBROUGH 1997. Petra Drnovice (Czech Republic) 2000. Artmedia Petrzalka (Slovakia) 2000. Interwetten (Austria) 2003.

■ Slovakian full-back Kinder was a popular player during his time on Teesside, though he always looked more comfortable with the ball at his feet than defending against a tricky winger. He gained a wealth of European experience with Slovan Bratislava, where he was voted the nation's Player of the Year on three occasions. He won his first international cap for the former Czech Republic before becoming a mainstay of Slovakia's side and came to Bryan Robson's notice. He impressed during a brief trial with the club and joined Boro in the same week as Gianluca Festa as reinforcements were brought for the looming relegation battle and Cup sagas. Kinder made his Boro debut in a memorable 3–2 FA Cup victory over Hednesford but found it hard to displace Curtis Fleming from the left-back slot, receiving most of his chances when Fleming was switched to the right in place of Neil Cox. He scored an excellent long distance strike on his Premier League home debut to set Boro on the way to a 6–1 rout of Derby but did not help Boro's cause when he was sent off for a foul on Kevin Davies during the first half of the FA Cup semi-final against Chesterfield. He did, however, play the full match of the Coca-Cola Cup Final replay and was a late sub in the FA Cup Final.

A pacy full-back who could cross the ball with accuracy, Kinder was a regular during the 1997–98 promotion success and appeared in the Coca-Cola Cup Final against Chelsea. Good with both feet, he was occasionally utilised at right-back under competition from Fleming and young Craig Harrison late in the promotion year and was completely in the cold following the arrival of Dean

Gordon. He did not start a game back in the Premier League, though he scored a spectacular effort at Coventry as a midfield substitute in his penultimate game for Boro. Told he could leave the club, he had trials in France and Spain but eventually joined Drnovice in the Czech Republic.

KINNELL George

Centre-half
Born: Dunfermline, 22 December 1937.
Career: Aberdeen. Stoke City 1963. Oldham Athletic 1966. Sunderland 1966. MIDDLESBROUGH 1968. Juventus (Australia).

■ Was it something he said? It's a strange quirk of Stan Anderson's management days that a peculiarly high number of

players moved abroad after he had rejected them. While the likes of Eddie Connachan, Bryan Orritt and Ian Davidson emigrated to South Africa, George Kinnell went Down Under to Australia. The cousin of Scottish legend Jim Baxter, the Scot was brought to England by Stoke and moved to the North East via Oldham, enjoying two seasons of top flight football with Sunderland. A left-half, he was not what could be described as a big success at Ayresome Park and his jittery defensive displays made him a boo-boy target. Cruelly, the fans would even sing: 'We paid £40,000 for Kinnell' (repeat it a few times and you'll get the joke). It was that song that gave him the unfortunate nickname of 'Foo'. Kinnell actually scored against Millwall in his last start for the club, just three months after joining Boro. He signed off late in the season with a sub appearance in a 3–0 defeat at Carlisle and was placed on the transfer list soon after. He later joined Juventus, though, sadly for Kinnell, this was not the Italian version but one based in Australia.

KIRBY Frederick

Centre-forward
Born: County Durham.
Career: Bishop Auckland. Durham City. MIDDLESBROUGH 1913. Halifax Town. Bradford Park Avenue 1914.

■ Centre-forward Kirby played all his games for the club in Boro's most successful League season, when Tom McIntosh's team finished third in Division One. Sadly, Kirby can take little credit for the success as he played only twice throughout the campaign and failed to find the net on either occasion. The holder of an FA Amateur Cup-winners' medal, he had played for Bishop Auckland before joining Durham City and then Middlesbrough. On his First Division debut, he stood in for George Elliott in a 2–0 defeat at Everton and was not given another chance for more than six months. He again stood in for Elliott for his home debut in April 1914 as Boro ran out 4–0 winners over Liverpool. Elliott returned for the final game of the season and Kirby never played for the club again. He moved to Bradford Park Avenue, newly promoted to the First Division, but war broke out a year later, during which he served in the RAMC and helped out at both Halifax and Bradford. After the war, Kirby worked as a surveyor for Morpeth Rural District Council.

KIRK Henry Joseph (Harry)

Winger
Born: Saltcoats, 25 August 1944.
Career: Ardeer Athletic. MIDDLESBROUGH 1963. Third Lanark. Dumbarton. Darlington 1967. Hartlepool United 1969. Scunthorpe United 1970. Stockport County 1973.

■ Kirk's star trek alongside the likes of Cyril Knowles and Bill Harris lasted just two games. The 18-year-old must have wondered what planet he was on when he ran out to the roar of a 30,000 Ayresome Park crowd within months of joining Boro from Ardeer Athletic, an ICI works team in Scotland. Raich Carter handed him his debut in September 1963 following an horrific injury to new signing Bobby Braithwaite and Kirk played at outside-left in a 2–2 Second Division draw with Rotherham United. That, sadly, was just about that. Left-back Gordon Jones was switched to the wing role for the next match at Preston and Kirk's only other first-team action came in a shock League Cup exit at the hands of Fourth Division Bradford in early October. Released at the end of the season, he returned to Scotland with Third Lanark. He later returned to the North East for spells with Darlington and Hartlepool before ending his playing days with Stockport.

KITE Philip David

Goalkeeper
Born: Bristol, 26 October 1962.
Career: Bristol Rovers 1980. Southampton 1984. MIDDLESBROUGH (loan) 1986. Gillingham 1987. Bournemouth 1989. Sheffield United 1990. Mansfield Town (loan) 1991. Plymouth Argyle (loan) 1992. Rotherham United (loan) 1992. Crewe Alexandra (loan) 1992. Stockport County (loan) 1993. Cardiff City 1993. Bristol City 1994. Bristol Rovers 1996.

■ Kite's career never took off on Teesside. The big goalkeeper was a stop gap loan signing by Bruce Rioch as cover for Stephen Pears late in the relegation season of 1985–86. Apart from Pears, there were no other 'keepers with first-team experience on Boro's books so Rioch brought in Kite from Southampton, where he was reserve to England's Peter Shilton. Kite played in Second Division games at Oldham and Bradford in April 1986, both of which Boro lost and the former England youth star returned to The Dell soon after while Rioch's boys were relegated. After leaving the Saints, Kite's career took in several lower division clubs.

KNOWLES Cyril Barry

Full-back
Born: Fitzwilliam, 13 July 1944.
Died: Middlesbrough, 31 August 1991.
Career: Monkton Colliery. MIDDLESBROUGH 1962. Tottenham Hotspur 1964.

■ Nice one, Cyril! Actually, the Boro directors are more likely to have smiled 'Nice one, Raich' the day Raich Carter sold the inexperienced Knowles to Spurs for a massive £42,500 fee. An attacking full-back, he was almost unheard of away from Teesside when he left Ayresome for White Hart Lane during the summer of 1964 but Knowles was to go on and become a Spurs legend.

Born in the mining village of Fitzwilliam, the son of a former professional rugby player with Wakefield Trinity, the young Cyril followed in his father's footsteps by playing as an amateur with Featherstone Rovers. However, while his nextdoor neighbour, Geoff Boycott, made his name in cricket, Knowles moved into football. However, this was no story of overnight success. He drove a pit pony in the mines at Fitzwilliam Colliery while turning out for Monkton Colliery Welfare and was rejected at 15 after a year with Manchester United for being too small. After a short spell as a junior with Wolves alongside his brother, Peter, he gave up football to become a Jehovah's Witness. He later had second thoughts and wrote to Boro trainer Harold Shepherdson asking for a trial and was offered an apprenticeship after impressing as an outside-left during a trial. He developed into a strapping six-footer and was no

shrinking violet even as a teenager, often drawing complaints from the club's senior pros for kicking lumps out of them in practice games.

Nevertheless, Knowles was about the leave the club when he was offered professional terms by Bob Dennison in October 1962 and duly made his debut at Derby the following April when regular right-back Mick McNeil was injured. He established himself as the regular right-back the following season, though he actually much preferred to play on the left-hand side of the field as he had a great left foot. Though Boro struggled to make any impact, teenager Knowles caught the eye as an attacking and stylish full-back who was an excellent crosser of the ball.

Signed by Spurs as a right-back, he initially struggled and only hit form when he was switched to left-back. The club's coaching staff smoothed out his rough edges and he began a sparkling career which saw Spurs win the FA Cup in 1968, the League Cup in 71 and 73, and the UEFA Cup in 72. England caps followed and Knowles was the inspiration behind the popular song 'Nice One, Cyril'.

After his playing days were over, he became Billy Bremner's assistant at Doncaster before accepting a job as Boro's reserve team coach from Bobby Murdoch, whom he had met on a coaching course at Lilleshall. He took up his first managerial post with Darlington and steered them to promotion and the Sherpa Van Trophy Final. While at Feethams, he also took a young Gary Pallister on loan and made a cheeky £5,000 bid for the future England defender. After a spell with Torquay, he again displayed his managerial talents by guiding Hartlepool to safety when they were in danger of losing their League status. However, tragedy was never far away. After losing his young son in a freak motorway accident, he himself became ill with a brain tumour in March 1991 and stepped down with Hartlepool on the brink of promotion. Sadly, he died on 31 August, aged just 46.

LAIDLAW Joseph Daniel

Midfield/Forward
Born: Whickham, 12 July 1950.
Career: MIDDLESBROUGH 1967. Carlisle United 1972. Doncaster Rovers 1976. Portsmouth 1979. Hereford United 1980. Mansfield Town 1982.

■ Geordie Joe Laidlaw progressed through Boro's junior ranks alongside Willie Maddren and David Mills in the late 1960s. It was a measure of Laidlaw's potential that it was the young forward, rather than Maddren or Mills, who many saw as the brightest prospect around the club. Like any youngster he had to wait patiently for his chance and there was a gap of more than a year between his first and second starts for the senior side,

having made his debut as a 17-year-old centre-forward in March 1968. His big breakthrough came when he replaced stalwart Derrick Downing for a home game against Norwich in April, 1969 and he was a regular for the next two seasons. The stockily built striker formed a fine partnership with John Hickton before moving on to the wing and eventually losing his regular place in the side in 1971–72. At Carlisle, he enjoyed arguably his best form, finishing as top scorer with 15 goals in 1972–73 and then spearheading the Brunton Park club's charge to the top flight – alongside Boro – in 1974. The First Division dream did not last for Carlisle though and Laidlaw was on the move again by 1976. He later switched to midfield to lengthen his career and played many more games for Doncaster, Portsmouth – who he skippered in a Cup tie against Boro – Hereford and finally Mansfield.

LAKING George Edward

Full-back
Born: Harthill, 17 March 1913.
Died: September 1997.
Career: Dinnington. Wolverhampton Wanderers. MIDDLESBROUGH 1936.

■ If you're younger than 70, you've probably never heard of George Laking but, if it wasn't for Mr Hitler, he might have become a Teesside legend. Boro were building a fine side capable of challenging for honours when war broke out in 1939. Hefty right full-back Laking signed from Wolves and made his debut in an amazing 5–5 draw with Sunderland at Ayresome in 1936. He was an ever present in the team which finished fifth in Division One – the highest in 25 years – in 1938. He lost his right-sided place at the start of the 1938–39 season to Billy Brown after an injury but soon re-established himself at left full back as Boro went one better and notched up fourth place. Laking was returned to right full-back at the start of that fateful 1939–40 campaign but the season was cancelled after only three games as Hitler invaded Poland. Like many of his generation he could claim the war robbed him of his best years as by the time hostilities ceased Laking was 32. During the war he played occasional games for Middlesbrough and guested for Doncaster but played just once more when the League restarted and retired in 1947. A talented cricketer, he represented Shropshire in the summer game. George Laking died in September, 1997.

LAMB Thomas John

Inside-right
Born: Details unknown.
Career: Newcastle United 1898. MIDDLESBROUGH 1899. Willington Athletic.

■ Inside-right Thomas Lamb was there when it all began, well, almost. He was snapped up from Newcastle in 1899 – where he had failed to play a game – as Boro began their journey in League football. Lamb made his debut at home to Grimsby on 23 September before 4,000 fans at Linthorpe Road and scored the first of his six goals with a brace against Barnsley a fortnight later. His stay by the Tees was short-lived as he moved on to Willington shortly after the turn of the century.

LAWRIE Samuel

Outside-right
Born: Glasgow, 15 December 1934.
Died: Bradford, 1979.
Career: Middlesbrough 1952. Charlton Athletic 1956. Bradford Park Avenue 1962.

■ If you are reading this book from cover to cover you are about to have a strange sense of déjà vu. Back in the B-section you will have come across a teenage sensation called Stephen Bell who burst on to the scene at 16 only for his Boro career to go off the rails and fizzle out.

A diminutive winger (it's uncanny, isn't it?), the Glaswegian had the chance to join either Rangers or Celtic as a 15-year-old. Boro boss David Jack thought he had pulled a masterstroke by bringing him to Ayresome instead, initially as a member of the groundstaff. A couple of years cleaning boots tempted him to stay on at Boro when he turned professional at 17. After banging in four for the reserves against Ashington he was handed a first-team debut as the youngest ever to pull on the red shirt against Arsenal in November 1951 alongside the likes of Mannion and Delapenha. Bell later equalled the record by making his debut at the same age to the day in 1982. Although possessing a burst of pace, Lawrie failed to find the required consistency in the opportunities he was afforded and was never more than a fringe first-team player. He also fell foul of the law. In 1956 he was fined £35 for taking a car without the owner's consent and driving without a licence or insurance, for which he was banned for a year. He left Boro that same year and had a brief spell in, of all things, dairy farming before being tempted back by Charlton Athletic and did enjoy six good years at the Valley. Clearly, fate dealt a bad hand to Lawrie when it came to Boro as he suffered a serious knee injury playing against them for Charlton. He fell out with Charlton over an unsanctioned trip to Canada to play for Montreal Concordia but it was the club, not Lawrie, who backed down to end the impasse. He later played for Bradford Park Avenue. Tragically, Lawrie died aged just 44 in Bradford in 1979.

LAWS Brian

Right-back
Born: Wallsend, 14 October 1961.
Career: Burnley 1979. Huddersfield Town 1983. MIDDLESBROUGH 1985. Nottingham Forest 1988. Grimsby Town 1994. Darlington 1996. Scunthorpe United 1997.

■ Geordie full-back Brian Laws is one of the many gems brought to Boro by Willie Maddren. After learning his trade at Burnley, where he won a Division Three

title in 1982, he had a spell at Huddersfield before becoming Maddren's first cash signing in 1985.

Laws was ahead of his time as an attacking full-back and helped secure Boro's place in the Second Division with a thunderous drive in a crucial last day game at Shrewsbury. He briefly became skipper in the heartbreaking season of 1985–86 as Boro finally went down and then went bust. But he was one of the stalwarts who gained strength in adversity and was part of the golden years of 1986–88 as Bruce Rioch's team stormed into the top flight with successive promotions. It was tinged with sadness for Laws, however. He suffered a cruciate knee ligament injury while taking a penalty – which he missed – against Bristol Rovers in 1987 as Boro fought for promotion to Division Two. Laws had been successfully converted to midfield and hit eight goals in 10 games as Boro got off to a dream start in Division Three. He regained his place the next year by scoring on his return in a 4–1 win at Huddersfield and played a significant role in the next promotion success only to miss out on the big day at Chelsea, when the return to the First Division was clinched.

Laws' Boro days ended that summer, however, after a contract wrangle with Rioch who, he claimed, had offered him only one year after initially agreeing to two years. It was the start of better things for Laws, though, as he was signed up by Brian Clough and won two League Cup medals as well as a Simod trophy win at Forest after a £120,000 move. He moved into management at Grimsby and guided Scunthorpe to promotion from Division Three in 1999. After a long spell at Scunthorpe he took charge at Sheffield Wednesday in 2006–07.

LAWSON James Joseph

Winger
Born: Middlesbrough, 11 December 1947.
Career: MIDDLESBROUGH 1964. Huddersfield Town 1968. Halifax Town 1976.

■ Winger Lawson could hardly have had a better tutor in his younger days. For the Middlesbrough lad asked the legendary Wilf Mannion for guidance when Wilf was a neighbour of his.

He achieved his dream of representing his home town club when signed from South Bank St Peter's by Raich Carter. The young Lawson's debut season in the first team was far from glamorous, however, as Boro slipped into the Third Division for the first time. Lawson had played only five games when Boro went to Cardiff for their last match needing a result to stay up, but new boss Stan Anderson spared him that ordeal as his number-11 shirt was passed to stalwart Gordon Jones. Boro lost 5–3 but relegation gave Lawson a chance to find his feet at a lower level. He played 17 games as Boro won promotion the following year, scoring twice, but missed out on the run-in as big John Hickton was converted from full-back to his more familiar centre-forward role.

He found first-team chances hard to come by and moved on to Huddersfield in 1968 where he enjoyed mixed fortunes. He played in a game at Ayresome in which his new club secured promotion back to the top flight, but was also part of a side that slid all the way back to the Fourth Division. He later helped Halifax avert re-election in a brief spell as player-manager.

LAYTON Arthur Edmund

Full-back
Born: Gornal, 14 February 1885.
Died: 1959.
Career: Royston United. Sheffield United 1905. South Kirby. Rotherham Town. Aston Villa 1908. MIDDLESBROUGH 1911. Whitby Town (loan). Cardiff City 1914. Stockport County 1920.

■ Full-back Layton was signed by Boro just in time to make his debut against his old club Aston Villa. But whatever inside knowledge the new man had didn't work as Boro lost at Villa 2–1. He played only six more games, at either left or right full-back, though the last could have been worse – it was a 3–0 thumping of Manchester United.

LEE Dong Gook

Forward
Born: Pohang, South Korea, 29 April 1979.
Career: Pohang Steelers (South Korea) 1998. Werder Bremen (Germany) (loan) 2001. Gwangju Sangmu (South Korea) 2003. Pohang Steelers 2005. MIDDLESBROUGH 2007.

■ The striker became the first South Korean to play for Boro when joining from Pohang Steelers on an 18-month contract in January 2007. It was the second time the player known as the Lion King by his fans had tried to make it in Europe, a previous spell with Werder Bremen in the German Bundesliga lasting just seven games. He made 11 appearances in his first half season at the Riverside and was still waiting for his first goal. Dong Gook was a member of the South Korea team in the World Cup Finals in France 1998 when just 19 and was top scorer with six goals in the Asia Cup two years later. However, he was controversially omitted from the 2002 World Cup squad by Guus Hiddink. National Service in 2002 took him to

military team Gwangju Samgmu, where he stayed for two years. He returned to Pohang in 2004 and was Korea's leading scorer in 2005 and 2006. A return to the national team was on the cards for the 2006 World Cup in Germany until he suffered a serious knee injury that needed surgery to repair cruciate ligament damage followed by a six-month recuperation period. He returned to the South Korea squad for the Asia Cup in the summer of 2007.

LE FLEM Richard Peter

Outside-left
Born: Bradford-on-Avon, 12 July 1942.
Career: Arsenal. Guernsey. Nottingham Forest 1960. Wolverhampton Wanderers 1964. MIDDLESBROUGH 1965. Leyton Orient 1966.

■ Dick Le Flem probably doesn't have the fondest memories of his time by the Tees. He was signed from Wolves by Raich Carter but lasted barely a year, playing only nine games. Nicknamed 'Flip', he played for Arsenal as a youngster but was freed by the Gunners. After a spell back at home in Guernsey he was picked up by Nottingham Forest where he established himself. His brief spell at Boro followed an even briefer spell at Wolves and sadly his career came to an end due to injury while at Orient, aged just 24.

LEONARD Henry Droxford (Harry)

Centre-forward
Born: Sunderland, 1886.
Died: 3 November, 1951.
Career: Sunderland West End. Southwick. Newcastle United 1907. Grimsby Town 1908. MIDDLESBROUGH 1910. Derby County 1911. Manchester United 1920. Heanor Town.

■ Centre-forward Leonard's goal return at Boro wasn't spectacular as he struck three times in 13 games in under a year with the club. Signed from Grimsby, he made his debut against Aston Villa on April Fool's Day 1911, as Teddy Towling and Billy James also started their Middlesbrough careers. He played alongside the legendary George Elliott but lost his place early in his second season to James. He was sold to Derby by new boss Tom McIntosh where he joined up with Steve Bloomer, scoring 17 goals as Derby won the Second Division title in 1914–15. He also had a spell at Manchester United. After World War One he did what so many old professionals do – he opened a pub. Leonard died on 3 November 1951.

LESLIE James

Inside-right
Born: Details unknown.
Career: Bolton Wanderers 1896. Sunderland 1897. MIDDLESBROUGH 1901. Clyde.

■ Had you landed on the planet around 22 February 1902, you would soon be under the impression that James Leslie was about to become a Boro great. The inside-right's second game for the club was a 7–2 thrashing of Barnsley in which he scored. He followed that with two more goals in the following games, 5–0 wins against Leicester and a 3–0 victory over Preston. Bizarrely, he played only three more games in which Boro remained unbeaten before disappearing. He was last heard of playing for Clyde.

LIBURD Richard John

Full-back
Born: Nottingham, 26 September 1973.
Career: Eastwood Town. MIDDLESBROUGH 1993. Bradford City 1994. Carlisle United 1998. Notts County 1998. Lincoln City 2003. Eastwood Town 2004. Boots 2005. Basford United.

■ Marauding left-back Liburd always seemed to play off the cuff. The young Liburd burst into Lennie Lawrence's Boro side after a post relegation clear-out. Regular full-back Jimmy Phillips moved on to Bolton and Liburd was asked to take on the job. He impressed most with his strong tackling and surging runs forward.

The Midlander had joined his local club Nottingham Forest as a junior but drifted into non-League football with Eastwood Town where boss Brian Chambers recommended him to Boro scout Peter Kirtley. He impressed in a trial with the youth and reserve teams and signed a two-year deal. Eastwood didn't do badly out of it either, picking

up a fee rising to £20,000 for a player they'd only had for four months. All looked good as he became a regular for Boro in the First Division season of 1993–94, as other youngsters like Jamie Pollock and Alan Moore also earned their chance, but his fortunes changed with the appointment of Bryan Robson.

The new boss saw him as a good athlete but with much to learn and he was allowed to move on to Bradford, where Lawrence was now boss. His career stuttered after that and almost ended completely after he was convicted of a nightclub assault and fired by the Bantams.

LIDDLE Craig George

Midfield
Born: Chester-le-Street, 21 October 1971.
Career: Aston Villa 1990. Blyth Spartans 1991. MIDDLESBROUGH 1994. Darlington (loan) 1998. Darlington 1998. Durham City.

■ 4 November 1995 was an historic day for Middlesbrough Football Club as a certain Brazilian made his Premiership bow. But Juninho wasn't the only one celebrating that day with Craig Liddle making his own Premiership debut. To say Juninho's presence took the spotlight away from Liddle would doubtless be the understatement of the decade but at least it allowed him to prosper unnoticed as he took on the task of marking Brian Deane.

Liddle had arrived at Boro from Blyth Spartans, having served his time with

Villa before being released. He was actually rejected by Boro after a trial in 1990 and was rescued from the dole queue when a second chance came around in 1994. He impressed in the reserves and made his debut in midfield against Tranmere as Boro celebrated promotion to the Premiership in the last game of 1994–95. That first year in the big League gave Liddle a chance to prove his versatility as he turned out in both defence and midfield. Although not a flashy player, Liddle was hard working and rarely let anyone down. Robson rewarded him with a new contract after a dozen Premiership games but his chances were limited as Boro went for star quality. He gave up reserve team football to move on to Darlington in the summer of 1998, where he quickly became a crowd favourite. He went on to play more than 300 games for the club until injury forced him to retire in 2005. He returned to Boro as a coach at the club's Academy.

LIGHTENING Arthur Douglas

Goalkeeper
Born: Durban, South Africa, 1 August 1936.
Career: Queen's Park (South Africa). Nottingham Forest 1956. Coventry City 1958. MIDDLESBROUGH 1962. Durban City (South Africa).

■ There were certainly a few storms in the life of keeper Arthur Lightening. The South African was brought to England by Nottingham Forest but was soon on the move to Coventry. When Sky Blues boss Jimmy Hill decided to sell him after 150 games for the club, Boro manager Bob Dennison stepped in. No sooner had he arrived, however, and he was facing court proceedings in Coventry. Lightening was fined for receiving stolen property and had been accused of breaking into two social clubs in the city and harbouring stolen cigarettes, spirits and wine. It was no better on the pitch as he let in six on his debut as Boro lost 6–1 to, of all sides, Newcastle. Dennison quickly recalled old professional Bob Appleby, though Lightening did win a recall a few weeks later – and kept a clean sheet against Preston. Vying with both Appleby and Morris Emerson, he managed only 15 games in that 1962–63 season and let in four in his final game, a 4–1 hammering at Rotherham. After another spell back in the reserves, Boro allowed him home after that to attend his brother's funeral in Durban. But Lightening never came back and it fell to Appleby to take over between the posts for the rest of the season. He was last heard of playing in his native country for Durban City.

LINACRE William

Forward
Born: Chesterfield, 10 August 1924.
Career: Chesterfield 1944. Manchester City 1947. MIDDLESBROUGH 1949. Goole Town 1952. Hartlepool United 1953. Mansfield Town 1955.

■ The story of Bill Linacre is not for the faint-hearted. When Linacre broke his leg playing for Boro against his old club Manchester City in 1950 there was none of the medical care of the modern game. When the leg was snapped the players had to look around for someone to help their stricken mate. In the end a City player had to hold down Linacre's leg before it was strapped while a loudspeaker announcement was made requesting a doctor to attend on the pitch! The talented Linacre was jinxed by injury and had broken a leg twice in the same season with Chesterfield and then again while playing for City. Linacre arrived at Boro in a deal which could have taken Wilf Mannion to Maine Road. City offered cash plus Linacre for Mannion but Boro refused. Speedy and noted for his body swerve, the outside-right also occasionally displayed a temper and was sent off in a Manchester derby in 1949. Boro were a fine side when he joined and good judges felt he could have made a big impression were it not for the injury. He did have time to become firm friends with Boro's Bill Whittaker and was later his best man. His career ended in the lower divisions.

LINTON Thomas

Centre-forward
Born: Details unknown.
Career: Stockton Vulcan. MIDDLESBROUGH 1899.

■ A member of Boro's fledgling League side in 1899–1900, Linton had few chances to impress after signing from the scarily-named Stockton Vulcan. As the club's directors searched for players of the right calibre, the centre-forward played only four games and failed to score. Not too surprising that he was freed, then.

LINWOOD Alexander Bryce

Inside-forward
Born: Drumsmudden, 13 March 1920.
Died: 26 October 2003.
Career: Mulkirk Athletic. St Mirren. MIDDLESBROUGH 1946. Hibernian 1947. Clyde 1948. Morton 1951.

■ Scot Linwood was brought in by boss David Jack because Everton were pursuing Boro's Micky Fenton. The move didn't materialise and Linwood found his chances limited. He mainly played as an inside-left but did cover for Fenton at centre-forward in his third game for the club when Fenton was left out. He will remember a home game with Portsmouth in which Mannion bagged a 28-minute hat-trick for the wrong reasons. He was left out for the next four months and suffered a bad knee injury in a reserve game against South Shields. Linwood moved back to Scotland after only a year.

LIVINGSTONE Joseph

Centre-forward
Born: Middlesbrough, 18 June 1942.
Career: MIDDLESBROUGH 1960. Carlisle United 1962. Hartlepool United 1966.

■ 'Just stick it in the onion bag, young man' was probably the kind of advice Brian Clough gave to his young understudy Joe Livingstone when he replaced the injured Clough at the start of the 1960–61 season. Boro won the game at Bristol Rovers and local lad Livingstone held his place against Derby a few days later. Sadly, that was the end of Livingstone's season as Clough came back and he failed to appear for the first team again that year. It was déjà vu as he started the following season at centre-forward, but this time Clough was permanently out of the way having moved to Sunderland. He did score in the opening match, a 4–3 home defeat to Derby, but got only one more game before Alan Peacock took his shirt. Livingstone played occasionally through that season – bagging a brace against Swansea in one game – but never really established himself despite a healthy goals return of six in 14 games. He was allowed to move to Carlisle where he established himself as a goalscorer. The Livingstone family continued to make their mark on the game as Joe's son, Steve, played for Coventry, Blackburn, Chelsea and Grimsby.

LLOYD Evan

Centre-forward/Inside-left
Born: Middlesbrough.
Career: Grangetown. MIDDLESBROUGH 1919. Bradford Park Avenue 1920. Tranmere Rovers 1921.

■ Lloyd's brief Boro career came as the game started up again following World War One alongside players like Jacky Carr and George Elliott. He had a memorable debut in the number-10 shirt against Liverpool as Boro ran out 3–2 winners with all the goals coming in the first half. Obviously Lloyd was completely exhausted by that as he played only once more, against Bradford Park Avenue. He soon joined the Bradford club and is thought to have had a spell with Tranmere.

LONGSTAFFE Geoffrey

Outside-right
Born: Details unknown.
Career: MIDDLESBROUGH 1894. Stockport County 1902. Burton United 1902.

■ Manager-secretary John Robson and the club's directors dabbled with no fewer than 39 players in Boro's first season of League football in 1899, many of whom didn't last too long at League level. Into this category fits Geoff Longstaffe, a regular in the amateur days and a member of the Amateur Cup-winning team of 1898 when Uxbridge were beaten in the Final. The outside-right also won a Northern League title the previous season. Longstaffe has the distinction of appearing in Boro's first ever Football League game against Lincoln as an inside-right. The last of his appearances came in a home defeat against Leicester.

LUGG Raymond

Midfield
Born: Jarrow, 18 July 1948.
Career: MIDDLESBROUGH 1965. Watford 1969. Plymouth Argyle 1972. Crewe Alexandra 1973. Fort Lauderdale Strikers (loan) 1977. Bury 1978. Chorley.

■ Ray Lugg hardly ever played for Boro but the fans gave him the ultimate accolade by thinking up his own song. The Holgate would sing 'All you need is Lugg' when the outside-left appeared in a variation on a Beatles song. Geordie-born Lugg joined Boro from Primrose FC as a 16-year-old but found his chances limited. He made his debut as a sub for Jim Lawson as Boro crashed 5–1 at Gillingham and, as stand-in for Derrick Downing, played a bit part as Boro recovered to win promotion from the Third Division. He had his best run in the 1968–69 season, as a winger or inside-forward, but lost his place to John Hickton, no less, and played his last game at Oxford the following year. Lugg later moved on to Watford and had his best spell at Crewe.

LYNCH Patrick

Forward
Born: Belfast, 22 January 1950.
Career: Cliftonville. MIDDLESBROUGH 1970. Kidderminster Harriers. Stourbridge.

■ Irishman Lynch followed Jim Platt to England and for a time Boro had high hopes for the hard-working front runner. He had an excellent goals record at Cliftonville but never established himself in Boro's first team. He was a non-playing sub during a mini injury crisis in January, 1972 against Cardiff and Bristol City and played only 30 minutes in the first team as a sub for David Mills in a 1–0 defeat at Queen's Park Rangers the same year. Stan Anderson released him that summer and he later had spells at non-League Kidderminster Harriers and Stourbridge.

MacAULAY William

Inside-right
Born: Glasgow, 1 November 1879.
Career: Cambuslang Hibernian. Glasgow Celtic 1898. Walsall 1899. Sheffield Wednesday 1899. Glasgow Celtic 1899. Aston Villa 1900. Portsmouth 1901. MIDDLESBROUGH 1902. Portsmouth 1903. Aberdeen 1903. Falkirk 1906. Hibernian 1907. Alloa 1909.

■ Inside-right MacAulay witnessed the end of an era with Boro – and starred as the club appeared in the top flight for the first time. He made his debut in Boro's first ever Division One game at Blackburn on 1 September 1902, as the side ran out 1–0 winners. A week later he played in their first home game in the top division, when Everton were beaten by a single goal. MacAulay flitted in and out of the side as Boro finished that season in a creditable 13th place. He netted twice – both from the penalty spot. The season was to be Boro's last at the old Linthorpe Road ground and MacAulay played in the last League fixture there against Stoke on 25 April 1903. However, he wasn't around to see the opening of the new Ayresome Park ground the following season as he moved on to Portsmouth in the summer.

MacDONALD Garry

Forward
Born: Middlesbrough, 26 March 1962.

Career: MIDDLESBROUGH 1980. Carlisle United 1984. Darlington 1984. Stockport County 1989. Hartlepool United 1989.

■ Big Garry MacDonald was thrust into first-team action as part of John Neal's team of young stars in the early–1980s. A Middlesbrough lad and former pupil of Stainsby School in Acklam, he represented the town and county schools teams. A tall and well-built striker, he quickly made an impression as a youngster, scoring regularly for the youth and reserve sides and learning his trade under Bobby Murdoch, then the youth coach.

MacDonald blasted a hat-trick on his reserve debut and proudly wore first-team colours in a top flight game at Brighton in November 1980, which Boro won 1–0. However, he made only occasional first-team appearances in the following seasons under John Neal, Murdoch, Malcolm Allison and Jack Charlton. He seemed to be making a breakthrough in the 1983–84 season when he became a regular name on the teamsheet, but his goals return wasn't enough. That season brought a highlight for MacDonald and the club as he scored the opening goal in an 3–2 FA Cup victory over Arsenal.

Although he held the ball well, it was felt by some that MacDonald lacked the dynamism or goalscoring prowess to make it at the highest level and he was released by Willie Maddren in 1984. He went on to enjoy success with Darlington's promotion winners of 1985 and finished his professional days at Hartlepool. He was also a feature in the Northern League with South Bank.

MacFARLANE John

Wing-half/Inside-forward
Born: Bathgate, 21 November 1899.
Died: 25 February 1956.
Career: Denbeath Star. Wellesley Juniors. Cowdenbeath 1919. Raith Rovers. Glasgow Celtic 1919. MIDDLESBROUGH 1929. Dunfermline Athletic 1934.

■ It took a clear-out at Celtic's Parkhead to bring polished left-half MacFarlane to Ayresome in 1929 and he went on to be a regular in a fine Boro side which finished seventh in the First Division. He joined Celtic from Fife junior side Wellesley and had a glittering career north of the border, winning two Championships and three Scottish Cups. A highly-regarded player, he was converted to right-half by Peter McWilliam to replace Joe Miller. He was blessed with a good positional sense, an excellent first touch and the ability to use a ball well. His skills were recognised when he was picked for the Scottish League side four times. His best year came in 1930–31, when he played in all but one game as Boro finished seventh with a side graced by the likes of George Camsell and Billy Pease. MacFarlane had some weaknesses, however, and was criticised for his occasional apathy. In all his time at Ayresome, he never once hit the net. He acquired the unfortunate nickname 'Jean' while at Celtic as Jean MacFarlane was a female character in a popular newspaper serial of the time. MacFarlane, whose brother Hugh starred for Hibernian, died in 1956.

MacFARLANE Robert

Goalkeeper
Born: Greenock, 1875.
Career: Greenock Rosebery. Greenock Morton 1894. Third Lanark 1896. Everton 1897. East Stirlingshire 1898. Bristol St George 1899. New Brompton 1900. Grimsby Town 1900. Glasgow Celtic 1901. MIDDLESBROUGH 1902. Aberdeen 1904. Motherwell 1909.

■ Poor Rab MacFarlane was a man in the wrong place at the wrong time. All was going well for the much-travelled Scottish international goalkeeper as he kept a clean sheet on his debut in 1902 in Boro's first ever top flight game at Blackburn. He then played every game up to a 2–0 Christmas win over Stoke – and was never seen in first-team action again. MacFarlane's time coincided with the emergence of the legendary 'Tiny' Tim Williamson. Once Tiny Tim had the goalkeeper's jersey he was never going to let it go and Rab became a reserve. MacFarlane had been capped while with Morton in 1896 as the Scots beat Wales 4–0.

MacFARLANE Thomas

Left-back
Born: Details unknown.
Career: Burslem Port Vale 1898. MIDDLESBROUGH 1900.

■ What can you say about full-back MacFarlane? Very little, actually. He vanished almost as quickly as he appeared and played only three games, all away from home at former club Burslem Port Vale, Barnsley and a Cup tie at Willington. He made his debut in the Cup tie as stand-in for left full-back Andy Ramsay in November 1900. His Second Division debut came four months later in a 2–0 win at Burslem and he was switched to the right to cover for John Dow at Barnsley three days later. MacFarlane, who had cost a £50 fee, was released in the summer of 1901.

MACCARONE Massimo

Forward
Born: Galliate, Italy, 6 September 1979.
Career: AC Milan 1997. Modena (loan) 1998. Prato 1999. Varese (loan) 1999. Empoli (Italy) 2000. MIDDLESBROUGH 2002. Parma (Italy) (loan) 2004. Siena (loan) (Italy) 2005. Siena 2007.

■ The Italian international became Boro's record signing when he joined from Empoli in 2002 for £8.15 million. He had impressed for Italy Under-21 against England and also appeared in the senior international team's follow-up game against Sven Goran Eriksson's side

at Elland Road. He thus became the first Serie B player for over 20 years to play for the national side. All his experience had been in the lower Italian Leagues following an early start in AC Milan's youth set-up. He made an immediate impact at the Riverside, scoring two goals in his second game, a 2–2 home with Fulham. Nine goals came from 34 appearances in his first year in England, plus another appearance for the full Italy team in a 2–1 European Championship qualifying defeat against Wales. But he failed to build on that promise, scoring just seven goals in 30 appearances in 2003–04 when he was left out of the victorious Carling Cup Final line-up. The following season he was loaned out to Parma and Siena. He failed to score in seven appearances for Parma, but seven goals came in 18 appearances with Siena. He returned to Boro for 2005–06, when he scored seven goals in 30 games. Maccarone achieved cult status thanks to two exquisite UEFA Cup goals. He put Boro through to the semi-finals with a last-gasp winner against Basel after his side had been three goals down. Then just three weeks later lightning struck twice. Boro were again three goals down on aggregate, this time to semi-final opponents Steaua Bucharest. Maccarone scored the opener in the second leg at the Riverside, then with less than a minute of normal time remaining he flung himself at a Stewart Downing cross to send Boro into the Final with a 4–2 win. He was a half-time replacement for James Morrison against Sevilla in the Feyenoord Final but couldn't weave his magic for a third time. He made just eight appearances for Boro in his final season before being freed to join Siena in January 2007. A player who had failed to live up to his status as a record signing departed amid controversy with a stinging verbal attack on the club, its staff and particularly former manager Steve McClaren. Maccarone made 102 appearances for Boro, scoring 24 goals.

MADDEN George

Inside-left
Born: Loftus.
Career: Haverton Hill.
MIDDLESBROUGH 1899. Stockport County 1901.

■ Loftus lad Madden joined Boro as a crop of local players were given their chance in the club's first season in the Football League. After signing from local League side Haverton Hill, his debut was watched by a crowd of 5,000 at Woolwich. Arsenal were beaten 1–0 at Linthorpe Road in February 1900. Switched from inside-forward to the wing, he also played the following game at Barnsley. However, he failed to make it with Boro and was on his way to Stockport later that year.

MADDISON James

Outside-left
Born: South Shields, 9 November 1924.
Died: 1992.
Career: South Shields.
MIDDLESBROUGH 1945. Darlington 1949. Grimsby Town 1950. Chesterfield 1959. Cambridge City.

■ Slightly-built wide man Maddison enjoyed a long career in the game but managed only one top flight appearance for Boro. He came to attention playing junior football with South Shields and played some wartime football for Middlesbrough alongside Micky Fenton and Johnny Spuhler. His one League game for the club came against Wolves in March, 1947, in a 1–1 draw when he played outside-left. He had a spell back at South Shields before a season at Darlington, a long spell at Grimsby and then ending his full-time career at Chesterfield. His last club was non-League Cambridge City. In later life he lived in Cleethorpes and the North East. Jimmy Maddison died in 1992.

MADDISON Neil Stanley

Midfield
Born: Darlington, 2 October 1969.
Career: Southampton 1988.
MIDDLESBROUGH 1997. Barnsley (loan) 2000. Bristol City (loan) 2001. Darlington 2001.

■ Like his close friend Alan Shearer, Neil Maddison started out at Southampton but ended up back in the North East. Darlington-born Maddison had trials with Boro as a 13-year-old but was rejected and joined the Saints, where he remained until 1997. A versatile and enthusiastic player, Maddison played 169 games on the south coast in every

position except goalkeeper. Bryan Robson drafted him into the Riverside squad to boost the club's promotion chances for a £250,000 fee and his versatility was quickly called upon as he played in midfield, at full-back and in central defence. He also weighed in with some important goals for the club, none better a stunning half-volley as Swindon were crushed 6–0 in March 1998. Maddison was in Boro's Coca-Cola Cup Final side which lost 2–0 to Chelsea, playing in midfield after some fine performances. He found his chances at the club restricted, however, with the likes of Paul Ince and Paul Gascoigne in Boro's midfield and was often used as a utility player in the Premier League. Unable to secure a regular place in the Boro side, Maddison had loan spells with Barnsley and Bristol City before signing for Darlington at the end of his Riverside contract. His early days there were hampered by injuries but when he did appear in the first team, Maddison showed his class with quality control and accurate passing from midfield. Although topping 100 appearances for Darlington, he began to move into coaching by studying for a UEFA 'B' qualification and briefly shared caretaker-manager responsibilities along with Martin Gray following David Hodgson's departure. Maddison hung up his boots in January 2007 to concentrate on his role as the club's youth team coach.

MADDREN William Dixon

Central defender
Born: Billingham, 11 January 1951.
Died: Stockton, 29 August 2000.
Career: MIDDLESBROUGH 1968.

■ One of the greatest players ever to pull on the red shirt, Willie Maddren would surely have achieved even more in the game were it not for a cruel knee injury which meant he played his last game at just 26. Not only was Maddren a great player, rated by many the best uncapped defender of his time, he has also been a great servant to Middlesbrough.

Maddren played for his local side, Port Clarence juniors, as a youngster and came to the attention of Leeds. He may have gone to Elland Road but broke his ankle just before a trial. As it was, he came to Boro but played initially as a centre-forward and made his debut for Stan Anderson's team against Bury in the final home game of the 1968–69 season as a replacement for Big John Hickton. It couldn't have started better as Maddren scored a first half opener for Boro, though the game ended in a 3–2 defeat and he suffered a broken nose. It was still unclear whether Maddren was going to spend his time up front or at the back as his next game, midway through the following season saw him replace centre-back Bill Gates (the victim of a broken jaw) for a run of 10 games. It was in 1970–71 that Maddren really established himself, starting out up front before switching to the defensive berth that from then on would become his own. Initially, he partnered Gates but the signing of Stuart Boam in 1971 saw the start of a partnership that would be forever famous on Teesside. By 1972–73, Stan Anderson's last in charge, Maddren had been named Boro's Player of the Year in a good side that consistently fell just short of promotion.

The following season, of course, was the year everything fell into place at Ayresome Park. New boss Jack Charlton's side won the Championship by a country mile and Maddren, Boam and co conceded only 30 goals. It was now time for the stylish Maddren, a tremendous reader of the game, to step on to the higher stage and Boro quickly made their mark on the top flight. Such were their defensive capabilities they became known as 'boring Boro' and perhaps, with a top class striker in the ranks, they could have achieved far more. Boro finished seventh in that first top flight season, though they had challenged for the Championship, before settling into mid-table positions in the following seasons. In this time Maddren should surely have won an England cap. He was called into a training squad by Don Revie but never made it into the side, kept out by the likes of Phil Thompson and Kevin Beattie. His troublesome knee, which had been a problem for many years, was gradually worsening and in the later stages of his playing career he couldn't train at all, but it is to his credit that his match performances remained of such a high standard. By the 1977–78 season, however, the pain was becoming too much. In his last game at West Brom, three matches into that season, he knew he was struggling and the operations and recuperation that followed were to no avail. Though his playing days came to such a premature end, he is still 19th on Boro's all-time appearance list, with well over 300 games to his name, and a run of 125 consecutive performances from April, 1973 to March, 1976. He was awarded a testimonial against Scotland's World Cup squad in 1978 before bowing out of the club.

After his playing days, he opened a

successful sports shop business in Stockton and kept an involvement with the game by coaching at Whitby and then Hartlepool. By 1983, he was back at his beloved Boro, initially working as a physiotherapist under Malcolm Allison. When Big Mal was sacked, the club asked Charlton to act as caretaker boss until the end of the season. Charlton then recommended his trusty old defender for the poisoned chalice of trying to halt Boro's desperate slide. Few would have wanted the job with the club having no money and seemingly doomed to a continued struggle for survival in the Second Division. He accepted low wages to take on the task – probably the lowest in the Football League – and threw himself into rescuing Boro for 18 long months. In 1984–85, relegation was avoided with a glorious final day win at Shrewsbury when Maddren was carried around the pitch by his jubilant players. It was only postponing the inevitable, however, and the drop finally came in 1986, by which time Maddren had departed. His final game was a miserable 3–1 home defeat against Charlton Athletic in February and his recently-appointed coach Bruce Rioch took over. Maddren's legacy, however, was to provide Boro with a platform for considerable success in the coming seasons. The little money he had was wisely spent on players like Stephen Pears, Bernie Slaven, Brian Laws, Archie Stephens and, of course, he was the man who saw talent in a young Gary Pallister and signed him on. They formed the nucleus of a side which ended up back in the top flight, along with youngsters like Ripley and Cooper who learned their trade under Maddren. The man himself stayed away from football and continued with his business interests.

In 1995, Willie Maddren was handed the greatest challenge of his life when he was diagnosed with the fatal muscle wasting condition Motor Neurone Disease. As with every other challenge in his life, Maddren came out fighting and used the illness to raise funds and awareness of the disease. Boro chairman Steve Gibson ensured a club that had profited so greatly from Maddren as a player and manager recognised his enormous contribution by organising a testimonial against Inter Milan before 20,000 Riverside fans in 1996. It was Teesside's tribute to a great man and a great player. He died in August 2000 but his name lives on in a pioneering education centre at the Riverside Stadium.

MAHONEY John Francis

Midfield
Born: Cardiff, 20 September 1946.
Career: Ashton United. Crewe Alexandra 1966. Stoke City 1967. MIDDLESBROUGH 1977. Swansea City 1979.

■ Welsh international John Mahoney was among John Neal's first recruits after his appointment to the Boro manager's job in 1977. The former Crewe midfielder had made his name at Stoke City and played as a substitute in their League Cup-winning side of 1972. A neat passing and competitive player, he decided to quit Stoke after they refused him a testimonial and heard from Wrexham boss Arfon Griffiths that Neal was looking for players at Boro.

As a man who was to end with more than 50 Welsh caps, he slotted into Boro's midfield alongside Graeme Souness and was briefly a club record signing until the arrival of Billy Ashcroft a few weeks later. His first game was on the day Kenny Dalglish made his Liverpool debut, in a 1–1 Ayresome draw. When Souness departed to Liverpool in 1978, Mahoney took his role on and hardly missed a game in two First Division seasons with the club.

In 1979 he joined his cousin John Toshack at Swansea and helped their climb to the First Division. He actually played against Boro in an FA Cup tie in 1981, which Boro won 5–0. Mahoney's career was ended by a triple stress fracture of his ankle and he retired to Colwyn Bay.

MAITLAND Alfred Edward

Full-back
Born: Leith, 8 October 1896.
Died: Leicester, 1982.
Career: Leith. Benwell Adelaide. South Shields 1919. MIDDLESBROUGH 1923. Newcastle United 1924. Jarrow. Northfleet. Salisbury City.

■ Colourful Alf Maitland was as erratic on the field as he was off it. A dashing and fearless full-back, he had only one season at Boro, 1923–24, which ended in turmoil. The club went down to the Second Division and Maitland, who had been in and out of the side since Christmas, had a bust-up with the management and was not resigned for the following campaign. He had never really settled and moved to Newcastle where he won a title in 1927. Despite being a mainstay of the United defence, he ran into more problems and was accused of being drunk on the pitch on a

tour of Hungary along with Hughie Gallacher. Newcastle put him on the transfer list in 1930 but, to Maitland's fury, they asked such a high fee that nobody would have him. He drifted into the non-League game with Jarrow, Northfleet and as a player-manager at Salisbury City. He later became a publican in North Shields before moving to Leicester. It was in Leicester that Alf Maitland died in 1982.

MALAN Norman Frederick

Goalkeeper
Born: South Africa, 23 November 1923.
Career: Defos (South Africa). MIDDLESBROUGH 1945. Darlington 1948. Scunthorpe United 1950. Bradford Park Avenue 1956.

■ South African goalkeeper Malan was spotted playing for Eastern Transvaal and South African League winners FC Delfos. At home he had worked as a turner and machinist but former Boro player Bob Ferguson recommended him to the club straight after the war and boss David Jack had the relevant forms sent out to him by air mail. He played only two games, the last two of the 1946–47 season, as Boro looked for a replacement for the veteran Dave Cumming. Both of the games Boro lost, 2–0 at Chelsea and 3–1 at Huddersfield. Following the signing of Derwick Goodfellow, he was allowed to join Darlington in 1948 but never played. He moved on to Scunthorpe where he became a regular.

MALCOLM George

Left-half
Born: Thornaby, 20 June 1889.
Career: Thornaby St Marks. Thornaby St Patricks. Darlington St Augustine's. Woolwich Arsenal 1909. Fulham 1909. Plymouth Argyle. MIDDLESBROUGH 1912. Darlington 1921. Durham City 1926.

■ Left-half George Malcolm was part of one of Boro's best sides. In 1914, a team containing Williamson, Carr and Elliott finished third in Division One and Malcolm missed only three games. His Boro career was sadly interrupted by the outbreak of World War One and Malcolm was robbed of some of his best years. The player also had a spell at Fulham but was playing for Darlington by 1920 and skippered the Quakers in 1921–22. He finished up in the local Leagues with Durham and was still playing in 1927.

MANNION Wilfred

Inside-forward
Born: South Bank, 16 May 1918.
Died: 14 April 2000.
Career: South Bank St Peters. MIDDLESBROUGH 1936. Hull City 1954. Poole Town. Cambridge United. King's Lynn. Haverhill Rovers. Earlestown.

■ The memories may fade, but half a century after he graced the Ayresome turf, Wilf Mannion remains arguably the greatest player ever to represent the Boro. Mercurial, breathtaking, inspirational, controversial, Mannion was in every sense the golden boy of Middlesbrough. A great runner over five yards or 50, he possessed a lethal shot from inside or outside the box. Mannion, the masterful dribbler and all-round entertainer, went on to become Boro's most capped player, appearing for England 26 times. Like so many of his era, he grew up in the community that would come to idolise him, to the extent that when he got married Boro fans had a whip round to buy him a present. It needs to be said that

had it not been for the draconian rules that chained players down in the 1940s, he would probably have moved on to a club that could win him some medals. As it was, all his best years were at Ayresome Park, and six more were taken from him by World War Two.

He started out at South Bank St Peter's, the club nearest to where he grew up. Even at a young age, Mannion didn't commit himself easily, in fact it took Boro director Bob Rand four visits to his home to get him to sign. It was midway through his first season at Ayresome that the public got their first glimpse of the golden boy, in a 2–2 draw against Portsmouth in January, 1937, when he was still only 18. Within a year, Mannion had become a fixture in the Boro side and the club's fortunes were transformed. When Mannion won a recall against Leeds at Christmas 1937, they were 15th in the First Division. They won that game 2–0, with Mannion among the scorers, and went on a run that would see them finish fifth. Mannion wasn't a regular scorer that season, but provided the ammunition for Micky Fenton. In the following season, Boro were again up with the best in the land, finishing fourth and Wilf played in all but four games. Now approaching his 21st birthday, he was coming into his own and was turning on the style with regularity. In one astonishing game that season, in a match against Blackpool, Wilf hit four as Boro won 9–2 at Ayresome. Later that year he hit another hat-trick as Portsmouth got off relatively lightly, beaten 8–2. In all, 93 goals were scored that season and notable results included a 2–1 win at Arsenal, Mannion scoring, and a double over Sunderland. Then came the war and Boro's dream of finally winning honours was brought to a shuddering halt. Mannion was conscripted in January 1940 and at one time was rumoured to be missing in action. Fortunately, he had only been forced into retreat as part of the 7th battalion The Green Howards and was in the 1940 Dunkirk evacuation. He played war games for Boro, Bournemouth and Tottenham and gained his first international recognition in those years.

When the League kicked off again in 1946, Mannion was 28 but he was soon making up for lost time. That famous run, with arms outstretched and palms facing downwards for balance was back with a vengeance. He scored Boro's first goal of the post-war era, with a last-minute winner at Aston Villa, in a season which saw Boro settle in mid-table with Mannion joint top scorer on 18 with Fenton. He was called up by England for the first post-war international and destroyed Eire with a brilliant hat-trick. Then a period of turmoil entered Mannion's relationship with the club. His form dipped and there were rumours of dressing room jealousy after the club gave a house to the star player. He turned in some brilliant individual displays nonetheless, notably in the game dubbed the Mannion Match against Blackpool in 1947 when Boro won 4–0 and Mannion turned on perhaps the best performance ever seen at Ayresome. Mannion was at the centre of everything that day and such was his confidence he is reputed to have juggled the ball on his head during the game. But, in some ways, he created a rod for his own back as some questioned why he couldn't play so well every week. At the end of the 1947–48 season, Mannion demanded a move and, unlike a similar dispute a year previously, this time he refused to back down and a stand-off ensued. He ended up taking a job selling chicken coops in Oldham while Boro steadfastly refused to accept offers from other clubs. Oldham were desperate to sign him and Aston Villa were willing to pay £25,000, offering Mannion underhand payments to get him to sign but pressures away from football were forcing Mannion's hand. His wife was expecting their first child and, needing to support his family, the Golden Boy was forced to resign for Boro. He returned to find a club in turmoil and Boro finished 19th in 1949. But with Mannion back in full swing, David Jack's team saw a marked upturn, finishing ninth and sixth in the next two seasons with Wilf teaming up with Johnny Spuhler. In 1950, he scored a remarkable goal against Chelsea in a match which saw Boro reduced to nine men and in the same year represented England at the 1950 World Cup. He continued to shine but Boro were on the slide after 1951 and were eventually relegated three years later. Now 36, Mannion decided to call it a day.

The most famous player in the history of Middlesbrough Football Club played his last game at Arsenal on April 24, 1954, as Boro lost 3–1 and were relegated. Hull did manage to talk him out of retirement and he agreed to play for them, doubling the Boothferry Park crowd on his debut. But while out of the game he had made comments that upset the Football League bigwigs and was ordered to appear before the management committee. Wilf refused and they suspended him from football in April, 1955. Mannion was then left to play on at non-League level, for Poole Town, King's Lynn, Havershill Rovers and Earlstown before finally hanging up his boots in 1962, aged 44.

MARCROFT Edward Hallows

Winger
Born: Rochdale, 13 April 1910.
Career: Bacup Boro. Great Harwood. MIDDLESBROUGH 1931. Queen's Park Rangers 1932. Cardiff City 1933. Accrington Stanley 1934. Rochdale 1936. Macclesfield.

■ Young outside-right Marcroft is another of those players who burst on to the scene and then vanished. He scored on his debut at Sheffield Wednesday in a First Division match in 1932 when he replaced the great Billy Pease. Within a few months, however, he was sold on to Queen's Park Rangers, having instantly lost his place to Pease. He then toured the lower Leagues, no doubt avidly following his hobbies, which included the piano, swimming and tennis.

MARINELLI Carlos Arturo

Midfield
Born: Buenos Aires, Argentina, 14 March 1982.
Career: Boca Juniors (Argentina) 1998. MIDDLESBROUGH 1999. Torino (loan) (Italy) 2003. Boca Juniors 2004. Racing Club (Argentina) 2004. Torino (Italy) 2005. Sporting Braga (Portugal) 2006. Kansas City Wizards (US) 2007.

■ So talented was the young Argentinean that he was dubbed the

new Maradona'. Skilful as he was, it was an impossible tag to live up to. Marinelli was arguably the most naturally-talented player to appear for the club in modern times, but he found it hard to transfer that ability to matchplay and basic team discipline. Marinelli was spotted by Middlesbrough manager Bryan Robson playing for Boca Juniors' youth side in the annual Irish Milk Cup tournament, though an initial request to bring him on trial was turned down by his club. Bryan Robson and Keith Lamb flew out to Argentina to seal a £1.5 million deal in October 1999 just days after arranging Juninho's Teesside return. After a frustrating delay due to a tax wrangle with the Argentinean FA, Marinelli made his debut for the club in a reserve game against Barnsley, boosting the Riverside attendance to almost 7,000. With bags of trickery and skill that astonished even Paul Gascoigne, Boro fans expected the teenager to make a huge impact, though he made only a couple of appearances off the bench in his first season with the club. Not surprisingly, it took time for him to adjust to life in a new country with its unfamiliar culture, but he was given occasional chances from the bench in the 2000–01 season. Steve McClaren arrived that summer and was fascinated to see what he could do. The attacking midfielder was given a run of games towards the start of the season and scored a memorable double in a 5–1 home victory over Derby County. But the magic didn't last. Marinelli faced criticism over his workrate – or lack of it – and in January 2003 he was given the chance to revive his career on loan to Italian Serie A side Torino. The Italians were keen to negotiate a deal but Middlesbrough were not prepared to accept anything less than the required £3 million. On his return to the Riverside, Marinelli scored Boro's first goal of the 2003–04 season against Fulham but McClaren was unimpressed with his overall display and he would never play for the club again. In November, his contract was terminated by mutual consent. To complete his fall from grace, Marinelli began a nomadic period that took him from one club to another across the world, each with little or no success. In February 2004 he rejoined Boca Juniors before briefly returning to Europe to play for Portuguese side Sporting Braga. Released after only a handful of appearances, he spent a year out of the game before trying his luck with American Major League Soccer side KC Wizards in 2007.

MARSHALL Dwight Wayne

Forward
Born: Jamaica, 3 October 1965.
Career: Grays Athletic. Plymouth Argyle 1991. MIDDLESBROUGH (loan) 1993. Luton Town 1994. Plymouth Argyle 1998. Kingstonian.

■ Speedy striker Marshall came into the game late, at 26, when Plymouth signed

him from Diadora League side Gray's Athletic. Having played for London sides Hampton Town, Leyton Wingate and Kingsbury Town, he became an instant hit at Argyle, scoring on his debut and was the club's Player of the Year in 1992. He scored a fine goal against Boro during their 1991–92 promotion campaign. But after a fall out with manager Peter Shilton, Lennie Lawrence brought him to Boro on loan to boost the Premier League survival chances. On his reserve team debut he scored a spectacular over head kick but his first League game was a disastrous 4–0 defeat at Chelsea. He came on as a sub in the last two games as Boro went down and never started a match. He later joined Luton and came back to haunt Boro by scoring twice as the Hatters beat Bryan Robson's side 5–1 in 1994. He missed out on a place in Jamaica's 1998 World Cup squad through injury.

MARSHALL John (Jock)

Right-back
Born: Saltcoats.
Career: Shettleston. St Mirren. MIDDLESBROUGH 1919. Llanelly. Belmont (New York). Brooklyn Wanderers. Newark Steelers. Brooklyn Wanderers. Bethlehem Steel.

■ Once a player's name was on a contract in the 1920s he could consider himself something of a prisoner for the duration. One such player was Jock

Marshall, who signed for Tom McIntosh in 1919 from St Mirren. A hardman defender, he become a mainstay of a First Division Boro side for four seasons before getting embroiled in an extraordinary dispute with the club. A right full-back who possessed enormous strength, he could apparently kick the old leather ball from one end of the pitch to the other without a run-up, a feat all the more remarkable for the fact the ball would swell with water as the game went on. So well-timed were his tackles, opposing strikers were said to carry on running after he had gracefully dispossessed them, blissfully unaware the ball had left them. By 1922, he was an established Scottish international, but that summer he told the club he wanted to return north of the border. Boro refused to release him from his contract and, incredibly, the Football League agreed to suspend him after he turned out for a five-a-side game in Scotland. He came back but again went walkabout the following season and was suspended by the club. Eventually his suspension was lifted but the rift could not be healed and Marshall showed that if he was going down, he was taking Boro with him. He told the League that Boro had made false promises about a benefit match and had given him a contract that was longer than allowed in the rules. Boro themselves were fined £100 and the League decided he could leave Boro for a fee of £2,000, only for Marshall to scrap his plans to go to Scotland and sign for Welsh side Llanelli instead. Later he moved to America to pursue business interests and played for Belmont FC in the USA.

MARSHALL Stanley Kenneth

Inside-forward
Born: Goole, 20 April 1946.
Career: Goole Town. MIDDLESBROUGH 1963. Notts County 1966.

■ Marshall was signed from Goole as a goalscoring youngster and looked set to break through to the first team after scoring 57 times for Boro's Northern Intermediate League side in 1964. He finally appeared at inside-left in the final days of Raich Carter's reign against Norwich at home in October 1965 but Boro lost 1–0. He played only once more, in a 3–1 reverse at Manchester City, three months later. Boro went down that season and new boss Stan Anderson had not been impressed. Marshall accepted his first-team chances were slim and agreed to a move to Notts County that summer.

MARTIN George Scott

Inside-forward/Outside-right
Born: Bothwell, 14 July 1899.
Died: Luton, 1972.
Career: Cadzow St Anne's. Hamilton Academical. Bathgate (loan). Bo'ness. Hull City 1922. Everton 1927. MIDDLESBROUGH 1932. Luton Town 1933.

■ Stylish inside-forward Martin didn't spend long at Boro but at least he could provide the entertainment at players' parties. After his career he became something of a pop star, releasing several records in the 1940s, though sadly he is not the same George Martin who worked with The Beatles. Martin will have remembered his time elsewhere rather more sharply than his brief stint at Boro. At Everton, he won promotion and played alongside Dixie Dean in his record breaking 60-goal season. After his playing days he managed Newcastle and took them to promotion and then fourth in the First Division. His move to Ayresome in 1932 had been part of a deal that also brought Arthur Rigby to the club but he played only six times, starting with a defeat at Villa and ending on December 17 with defeat at home to Leeds. He moved on that summer to Luton for a lengthy spell before managing Villa and Newcastle. All round clever clogs Martin was also an accomplished sculptor, golfer and tennis player. He died in Luton in 1972.

MARTIN John

Wing-half
Born: Sunderland, 6 October 1912.
Career: Horden Colliery Welfare. Portsmouth 1931. MIDDLESBROUGH 1932

■ A career severely curtailed by the war still reaped more than 100 Boro games

for flame haired wing-half Martin. He was spotted by boss Peter McWilliam playing for Horden CW and signed in exchange for a £10 donation from Boro He was handed a memorable debut in place of Billy Forrest on the same day Micky Fenton made his bow, in a 4–0 home win over Blackburn. He established himself the following season and flitted in and out up to the outbreak of war as Boro crafted a fine side that challenged at the top end of the First Division. He continued to play for Boro in wartime games and was taken on with a fresh contract when the war ended, despite having suffered a serious leg injury in a game in 1944. He did not appear as the Football League resumed though and was released. He was later a trainer at Huddersfield and Doncaster.

MARWOOD Brian

Winger
Born: Seaham, 5 February 1960.
Career: Hull City 1978. Sheffield

Wednesday 1984. Arsenal 1988. Sheffield United 1990. MIDDLESBROUGH (loan) 1991. Swindon Town 1993. Barnet 1993.

■ Skilful winger Brian Marwood came to prominence in a Hull City side that won promotion from the Fourth Division in 1983. He moved up the ladder with Sheffield Wednesday and won a Championship medal while with Arsenal in 1989. It was during his time with the Gunners that he earned an England cap against Saudi Arabia, a game in which Gary Pallister also played. He was with Sheffield United when Lennie Lawrence took him on loan to ease an injury crisis. His contribution to the promotion push was minimal, however, as he himself suffered from injuries in his first month on loan and his spell was extended for a further four weeks. He made only two starts, a defeat at Grimsby and a win at home against Port Vale. He later became chairman of the Professional Footballers Association and is now a broadcaster.

MASSON Donald Sanderson

Midfield
Born: Banchory, 26 August 1946.
Career: MIDDLESBROUGH 1963. Notts County 1968. Queen's Park Rangers 1974. Derby County 1977. Notts County 1978. Minnesota Kicks (United States). Bulova (Hong Kong). Kettering Town.

■ Don Masson's story is very much a case of one that got away. A Scot by birth, Masson was brought up in Middlesbrough, attended Marton Road School and played outside-left for the Middlesbrough Boys team. He initially broke into the Boro first team in 1964, replacing Taffy Orritt for a 2–0 home win over Norwich. That prompted a five-match unbeaten run with Masson getting off to a great start by scoring three times in that spell, including twice in a 4–1 win at Swindon. In all he played 14 games that season, chipping in with four goals. The following season Boro went down and it was a frustrating time for Masson as a broken ankle restricted him to just one start. He did establish himself in the second half of the promotion charge from Division Three in 1967 but struggled to hold a place on the return to Division Two. A fine passer of the ball, he was fighting for a berth in midfield with Crossan and McMordie and his cause wasn't helped by a fall-out with manager Stan Anderson.

In 1968, he was transferred to Notts County, along with Bob Worthington and that is very much where his story begins. In an illustrious career he won two promotions with County, was a First Division runner-up with Queen's Park Rangers and went back to County to help them into the top flight. In between this he became Derby's record signing when they paid £180,000 to Queen's Park Rangers. He was selected for Scotland's 1978 World Cup squad but missed a penalty in the notorious 3–1 defeat against Peru. He also had spells as captain of his national side. Masson finished playing in America for Minnesota Kicks and had a time with Hong Kong club Bulova. He moved into management with Kettering and Los Angeles Kickers. He went on to run a hotel in the Nottingham area.

MATHIESON James Adamson

Goalkeeper
Born: Methil, 10 May 1898.
Career: Dubbleside Hearts. Colinsburgh United. Partick Thistle. Raith Rovers. MIDDLESBROUGH 1926. Brentford 1934. Queen of the South.

■ Boro's board signed goalkeeper

Mathieson from Raith without even seeing him play. He came on the recommendation of Peter McWilliam, one day to become the club's boss, and made his debut at Chelsea in August, 1926. The directors may have had second thoughts after that first outing, a 3–0 defeat, but the new boy went on to give sterling service to Boro. Indeed, over the next five years he missed just seven games. He was an ever present in that first year as Boro ended up Second Division champions and, though they went straight back down, he was again between the posts as the championship took Boro back up in 1929. His performances were regularly described as brilliant in this time. It must have been hard work guarding Boro's net in those days, because even when doing well the goals were flying in. In 1931, for instance, Mathieson missed only four games but the side still conceded 90 – and they managed to finish seventh in the First Division after smashing in 98 at the other end! It was not unusual for them to get hammered out of sight, losing 7–0 at Leeds and 8–1 at Villa. Mathieson was clearly highly regarded, so the mind boggles at what would have happened if he hadn't played. Mathieson's last Boro game came in a 3–0 defeat at Derby in 1932 and his place was taken by Fred Gibson the following week. Along with several Boro teammates, he moved on to Brentford and helped them to two promotions. His days finished back in Scotland with Queen of the South.

MATTINSON Harry

Centre-half
Born: Wigton, 20 July 1925.
Died: 8 June 2001.
Career: MIDDLESBROUGH 1945. Preston North End 1949. Queen of the South.

■ Mattinson joined the Boro ranks at the end of World War Two and stayed for four years, though the greater part of his career was spent with Preston. The centre-half broke into the side in 1947, taking the number-five shirt from George Hardwick, who switched to a full-back place, for a game at Preston on 29 January, which Boro won 1–0. He held his place for a 4–2 home defeat against Sheffield United a few days later but

played only once more, for a defeat against Blackburn. He lived in Norton after his football days and his death was reported in 1997.

McALLISTER William

Wing-half/Inside-right
Born: Glasgow.
Career: Renton. St Mirren. Johnstone (loan). Ebbw Vale. Brighton & Hove Albion 1921. MIDDLESBROUGH 1924. Queen's Park Rangers 1926. Raith Rovers. Heart of Midlothian.

■ The Glaswegian right-half made his debut in place of Joe Harris at Derby in a 3–1 Second Division defeat in February, 1925 and held his place for the rest of that Second Division season. His appearances were spasmodic the following year and he played for the last time in a 3–3 draw at home to Hull. He was put on the transfer list at the end of the season at a price of £500 but moved on to Queen's Park Rangers after the League agreed that the fee should be halved to £250.

McANDREW Anthony

Central defender
Born: Glasgow, 11 April 1956.
Career: MIDDLESBROUGH 1973. Vancouver Whitecaps. Chelsea 1982. MIDDLESBROUGH 1984. Willington 1987. Darlington 1988. Hartlepool United 1988. Billingham Synthonia.

■ Aggressive Scot Tony McAndrew was at both ends of the Boro roller coaster, making his bow in the glorious promotion-winning season under Jack Charlton, through the promising days of John Neal's young side and he was still there to see relegation to Division Three and liquidation in 1986. He gave service to four managers over 11 years. The former Scotland youth player made his debut as a replacement for Graeme Souness in the midfield ball-winning role for a 2–1 win over Luton in 1973–74 but played only one more game for the next 18 months. Once established, however, he became a fixture in the side. At the end of the 1975–76 season, he became the youngest Boro player ever to score a hat-trick after playing in an emergency striker's role. He had just turned 20 when he put three past Sheffield United in a 3–0 win at Ayresome. That summer he went to America and played for Vancouver Whitecaps in the NASL. The following year he replaced Bobby Murdoch in midfield though he was a much more defensively minded player than his fellow Scot.

By 1978, John Neal had switched him to centre-half alongside Stuart Boam and McAndrew seemed most at home there. An uncompromising tackler and good in the air, he would always make his presence felt on the opposition. Boam's departure to Newcastle at the end of that season saw McAndrew awarded the Boro captaincy and he became a rock on which young talent like Johnston, Proctor and Hodgson could flourish. With luck he could have found himself leading Boro out at Wembley in 1981 but for that infamous quarter-final replay defeat at Wolves. As that team was broken up, McAndrew himself was in dispute with the club over the departure of John Neal and was stripped of the captaincy. He eventually made peace with the club, playing in all but three games and finishing as joint top scorer – with four – as Bobby Murdoch's team went down in 1982.

That summer Neal, now at Chelsea, returned to Ayresome to sign his former skipper for a fee of £92,500, set by a tribunal. He helped Chelsea win promotion to the First Division and actually scored in a game against Boro before suffering from injuries. Willie Maddren turned to him to add some steel to his struggling side. Young defender Darren Wood went the other way with Boro receiving £40,000. By now he was not the same player, however, and was released as Boro went down and into liquidation. He coached the juniors for a while before moving on to brief spells as a player with Darlington and Hartlepool. He later became assistant to Brian Little at Darlington and followed Little for coaching jobs at Leicester, Villa and Stoke. He is now a youth coach at Villa.

McCABE James Joseph

Wing-half
Born: Derry, 17 September 1918.
Died: 1989.
Career: South Bank. MIDDLESBROUGH 1937. Leeds United 1948. Peterborough United 1954.

■ McCabe's long spell at Ayresome was sadly punctuated by the war so he turned out in only 34 games in a nine-year association. Brought up in Billingham, he played for South Bank East End as a youngster before joining Boro in 1937. During the war he served in The Green Howards, alongside Wilf Mannion, and after the war played with the Golden Boy for Boro. The no-nonsense wing-half made his debut in a 2–2 home draw against Liverpool early in the first post-war League season and became a regular for the rest of that campaign. He was surprisingly sold to Leeds the following season for a fee of £10,000, plus keeper John Hodgson coming to Ayresome. At that time it was a record sale for Boro. He was converted to centre-half at Elland Road. He later played in the Midlands League for Peterborough and, after football, returned to Teesside and worked at ICI Wilton. Jimmy McCabe died in 1989.

McCALLUM Donald

Right-back
Born: Details unknown.
Career: Queen's Park Rangers. Liverpool 1902. Greenock Morton. Sunderland 1904. MIDDLESBROUGH 1904. Port Glasgow Athletic. Kilmarnock. Renton. Lochgelly United. East Fife. Mid-Rhondda. East Fife.

■ Right full-back McCallum established himself midway through the First Division season of 1904–05 as replacement for John Hogg. He held the berth for the rest of the season but Hogg won his place back in a struggling Boro side the following year and McCallum was released.

McCLELLAND James

Inside-forward/Centre-forward
Born: Dysart, 11 May 1902.
Career: Rosslyn. Raith Rovers. Southend United 1923. MIDDLESBROUGH 1924. Bolton Wanderers 1927. Preston North End 1929. Blackpool 1930. Bradford Park Avenue 1933. Manchester United 1936.

■ Poor Jimmy McClelland. A fine goalscorer in his own right, barrel-chested McClelland was unfortunate enough to be on the scene at the same time as the phenomenon that was George Camsell. He scored on his home debut against Sheffield Wednesday in March, 1925, after joining from Southend in a deal that saw Morris Hick go the other way, and was a consistent scorer from then on, hitting 32 in 1925–26. That included all five in a 5–1 FA Cup win over Leeds before 29,000 at Ayresome, at the end of which he was carried off by his ecstatic teammates. It was quite a day for McClelland as his son, Charles, later to play for Blackburn, was born the same day. A tally of 32 was then a club record, beating George Elliott's total by one, but the end was already in sight for Jimmy. The young Camsell made his debut the same season and the following year he could not be held back. McClelland was injured early on and lost his place to Camsell, who didn't need a second invitation. Camsell led Boro to the Second Division Championship with an extraordinary 59 goals in 37 games.

McClelland was frozen out for half the games, but did finish the season in tandem with Camsell and finished as top scorer for the reserves. He tried playing at inside-right or left and out on the wing to get a place in the side and even played a game at centre-half. He again played second fiddle in the top flight and moved on to Bolton before the season was out. His story had a happy ending as he won the FA Cup at Wanderers in 1929.

McCLURE Samuel

Inside-left
Born: Middlesbrough.
Career: Grangetown. MIDDLESBROUGH 1910. Aston Villa 1911. Watford.

■ Grangetown lad McClure made quite a start to his First Division career at Boro. Making his debut against Everton on the opening day of the season as an inside-left alongside George Elliott, he hit a late winner in a 1–0 win. A week later he scored again, this time in a 1–1 draw at Sheffield Wednesday. From then on he found it hard to hold down a place and was largely overshadowed by Sam Cail. He moved on to Watford the following summer.

McCORMACK John Cecil

Centre-forward
Born: Chester-le-Street, 15 February 1922.
Died: Canada, 1995.
Career: Gateshead 1941. MIDDLESBROUGH 1947. Chelmsford City 1949. Barnsley 1950. Notts County 1951.

■ Boro had long coveted the talents of Cec McCormack before they finally got their man in 1947. A slight and speedy outside-right, he had made a guest appearance for Boro during the war and boss David Jack watched him while he was playing for Gateshead. He replaced Mannion for a 4–0 defeat at Grimsby at the end of the 1946–47 season and established himself the following year, teaming up with Fenton and Mannion. He finished as second top scorer with 15, behind only Fenton, but missed the last few games. From then on his first-team appearances were limited and he moved on to Chelmsford City. Boro had

retained his registration and Barnsley paid £6,500 to take him to Oakwell. He became something of a legend in South Yorkshire by scoring 34 goals in a season for them, a club record for the Tykes. That tally included five in a 6–1 mauling of Luton. After a spell with Notts County, for the princely fee of £20,000, he emigrated to Canada and worked as a fitter in Toronto. He also played for the Canadian Select XI. Cec McCormack died in Canada in 1995.

McCORQUODALE Douglas

Outside-right
Born: Glasgow.
Career: MIDDLESBROUGH 1899.

■ Scottish outside-right McCorquodale was the original Emerson. He was brought in to boost Boro's squad for the first season but boss John Robson saw the new man play just twice, against Newton Heath and Sheffield Wednesday, both defeats, in December 1899. He returned home for Christmas after getting injured and never came back.

McCOWIE Andrew

Inside-forward/Outside-right
Born: Scotland, 1876.
Career: Liverpool 1896. Woolwich Arsenal 1899. MIDDLESBROUGH 1900. Chesterfield 1901.

■ Former Arsenal player McCowie took the number-10 shirt for his debut against Burton in 1900. The club record £75 signing flitted in and out before holding down a place for the last nine games. He did have some memorable moments despite such a brief stay with Middlesbrough, scoring two in a 9–2 hammering of Gainsborough Trinity in March 1901 at Linthorpe Road. He took no further part in the club's fortunes and moved on that summer, joining Chesterfield for a £50 fee.

McCRACKEN Peter J.

Left-half/Left-back
Born: Glasgow, 1867.
Career: Third Lanark. Sunderland Albion. Nottingham Forest 1892. MIDDLESBROUGH 1899. Chesterfield 1900.

■ McCracken was the first of a long line of people able to say they skippered the Boro in the Football League. McCracken led his charges into the first ever League season in 1899 and missed only one game. Given the vast number of players employed that year it must have been hard for him to get to know all his teammates. The centre-half, signed from Forest, was keen to return to the Midlands, however, and stayed for just the one season. He moved on to Leicester Fosse and William Higgins took his role as captain the following season.

McCRAE Alexander

Inside-forward
Born: Whitburn, 2 January 1920.

Career: Heart of Midlothian. Charlton Athletic 1947. MIDDLESBROUGH 1948. Falkirk. Ballymena United.

■ With Wilf Mannion away during his long contract dispute with Boro, the club snapped up versatile front man Alex McCrae from Charlton. The former Hearts player hadn't settled in London and rejected Sheffield United to sign on at Ayresome. McCrae could play in any forward line position but preferred inside-left. He started out in Mannion's absence early in the 1948–49 season with Boro struggling but his form dipped and he was dropped. He was soon recalled, this time alongside the prodigal son Mannion. An under-rated player who inevitably lived in Mannion's shadow, he nonetheless made a major contribution to Boro and was a star in his own right. Possessing pace and an inch-perfect pass, he had a fine shot and consummate ball skills. He was second top scorer in 1950 and topped the scoring charts in 1951 with 21 after switching to centre-forward following a freak injury to Andy Donaldson as Boro finished sixth in the First Division. In some games he could be breathtaking and had scored three hat-tricks before Christmas that season, against Everton, Huddersfield, and Blackpool. He would have achieved even more that season but was injured and it may be that losing McCrae robbed Boro of a Championship challenge. He had fewer games as Boro waned after 1951 and quit the club for Falkirk in 1953. After a spell managing Stirling Albion he returned to Falkirk and renewed his links with Boro by scouting for the club in Scotland from November, 1966. All at Ayresome should remain eternally grateful to McCrae for the tip off that recommended Jim Platt to Stan Anderson, while McCrae was managing the young 'keeper at Ballymena United. He stayed in touch with the club and was at the launch of the Boro's Best book, in which he naturally featured.

McCREESH Andrew

Full-back
Born: Billingham, 8 September 1962.
Career: MIDDLESBROUGH 1980.

■ Local lad McCreesh worked his way through the junior team coached by [illegible]

Murdoch, alongside players like Darren Wood and Kelham O'Hanlon. He made his League bow when Murdoch stepped up to manage the first team and started the second game of the 1981–82 season, replacing injured skipper John Craggs at European champions Liverpool. The young right-back gave away a hotly disputed penalty for a foul on Kenny Dalglish after Boro had led 1–0. Phil Neal scored the spot kick and McCreesh played only once more, in the following 2–0 defeat at Brighton. He could not dislodge Craggs and was freed that summer as Boro went down.

McCULLOCH Alexander

Inside-forward/Centre-forward
Born: Edinburgh, 1886.
Career: Bonnyrigg Rose Athletic. Leith Athletic. MIDDLESBROUGH 1907. Newcastle United 1907. Bradford Park Avenue 1908. Brentford 1909. Swindon Town 1909. Reading 1910. Swindon Town 1911. Coventry City 1912. Raith Rovers 1913. Edinburgh St Bernards 1915. Alloa Athletic 1915. Broxburn United 1916. Dunfermline Athletic 1917. Heart of Midlothian 1918. Lincoln City 1919. Merthyr Tydfil 1920. Llanelly 1921.

■ With more clubs than the most experienced of golfers, journeyman centre-forward McCulloch dropped in on Boro for a year from February 1907. As with most other clubs he played for, he didn't last long at Ayresome Park. He had to wait until the following season for a debut, in a 1–0 home defeat against Bolton in the First Division, as a deputy for Alf Common. Common's presence ensured he turned out just twice more, scoring once in a 1–1 draw at Preston. Boro boss Andy Aitken sold him to Newcastle in February 1908. He later played at inside-right for Hearts as they lost the 1919 Scottish Victory Cup Final 3–0 to St Mirren.

McGEE Owen Edward

Full-back
Born: Middlesbrough, 29 April 1970.
Career: MIDDLESBROUGH 1988. Leicester City 1992. Scarborough 1992. Guisborough Town.

■ Pocket battleship McGee made a brief but significant appearance on the Boro stage in the early 1990s. After being named as a sub on the day Boro went

down from the First Division at Sheffield Wednesday in May, 1989, he had to wait until January the following year to get on, as a sub in a 1–0 defeat at Sheffield United. A few days later he went on as sub as Boro won through to the semi-finals of the ZDS Cup with a last minute win over Newcastle at Ayresome. He was then pitched into the first leg of the semi-final at Aston Villa in place of Peter Davenport as Boro pulled off a shock 2–1 win in torrential rain. He was a substitute for the second leg at Ayresome but was quickly called into action as midfielder Trevor Putney suffered a broken leg in a tackle with Villa's Gordon Cowans. Boro went on to win the second leg, again 2–1, and McGee became part of the first Boro side ever to win through to Wembley. He held a regular place, at full-back or in midfield, in the run up to Wembley and the proud Teessider duly took his place in the Final against Chelsea on 25 March as Boro went down 1–0. McGee flitted in and out of the side as Boro desperately battled to avoid a second successive relegation.

When the last game arrived boss Colin Todd knew he needed a player with McGee's terrier-like presence in midfield and handed him the number-six shirt in preference to Stuart Ripley. That crunch Ayresome clash with Newcastle saw both sides needing a win, Boro to stay up and the Geordies to have any chance of automatic promotion. McGee endured the heartache of putting through his own net but all was well in the end as Boro won 4–1 and secured their Second Division place. After such a hectic start, the following season was an anti-climax for McGee as he started only six games. He did score his only Boro goal at this time, against Leicester in a 4–3 defeat, but was criticised by Todd for naïve defending. He moved on to Leicester on a non-contract basis followed by a stint at Scarborough. He quit the Seasiders after being asked to take a pay cut. He had been forced out of the side after being injured in a car crash and dropped out of the professional game. McGee went into full-time education and gained a maths degree at the University of Teesside. He also played for Guisborough Town in the Northern League.

McGUIGAN Andrew

Inside-left
Born: Newton Stewart, 24 February 1878.
Career: Newton Stewart. Hibernian. Liverpool 1900. MIDDLESBROUGH 1902. Southport Central. Accrington Stanley. Burslem Port Vale 1906. Bristol City 1907. Barrow. Exeter City.

■ Despite being a club record £300 signing from Liverpool, inside-right McGuigan played only one Boro game after signing from Liverpool. That came on the final day of the 1903–04 season, when he replaced Ted Gettins for a 1–1 draw at Nottingham Forest. He had been a Middlesbrough player since December 1902 but had arrived with a torn knee cartilage that left him incapable of playing. He was on the books for another year but did not appear in the first team again. McGuigan moved on to Southport Central in 1905.

McILMOYLE Hugh

Centre-forward
Born: Port Glasgow, 29 January 1940.
Career: Port Glasgow. Leicester City 1959. Rotherham United 1962. Carlisle United 1963. Wolverhampton Wanderers 1964. Bristol City 1967. Carlisle United 1967. MIDDLESBROUGH 1969. Preston North End 1971. Morton. Carlisle United 1974.

■ Despite being under 6ft tall, McIlmoyle is rated the best header of a ball ever to play for Boro. McIlmoyle will always be remembered on Teesside for a game against Queen's Park Rangers in 1970 that was to become known as the McIlmoyle Match. Boro were struggling at the wrong end of the Second Division

and were staring down the barrel at another defeat as they trailed Rangers 2–0. But the game turned spectacularly on McIlmoyle's head as he scored twice and set up a hat-trick for John Hickton as Boro ran out 6–2 winners McIlmoyle won everything in the air, to the annoyance of one Queen's Park Rangers player who punched him in the face for his trouble.

Boss Stan Anderson had hoped McIlmoyle's arrival from Carlisle in 1969 would be the final piece in the promotion jigsaw, but it didn't turn out that way. In his first season Boro gradually gathered pace after his arrival – though his debut against Blackpool saw him being taken off with a broken nose – and finished just short of a promotion place in third spot. In 1970–71 he and Hickton bagged 38 goals between them and formed an impressive partnership with Hickton feeding off McIlmoyle's knockdowns. Still, Anderson felt he never got the best out of the amiable Scot and he flattered to deceive. He was in dispute with the club by the end of the 1971 season and moved on to Preston. The most significant spells of his career were with Carlisle, who he joined several times, and he was in their side that played in the top flight in 1974–75 alongside Joe Laidlaw.

McKAY John Reid

Inside-forward
Born: Glasgow, 1 November 1898.
Died: 6 February 1970.
Career: Townhead Benburb. St Anthony's. Glasgow Celtic 1919. Blackburn Rovers 1921. MIDDLESBROUGH 1927. Bolton Wanderers 1935. Hibernian 1936.

■ Being brought in to replace Jacky Carr put considerable pressure on Johnny McKay when he signed for Boro in 1927 and it is fair to say he was never in Carr's class. A nippy and clever inside-forward, he broke into the side in place of Carr at the end of the 1926–27 Second Division Championship winning season. Carr kept him out for most of the next two seasons and it wasn't until the 1929–30 campaign that the new boy started to get the upper hand over Carr. The following season he was an integral part of a Boro side that scored goals for fun and finished seventh in the top division. That season included one of his sweetest moments in a red shirt when he was among the scorers as Boro beat Newcastle 5–0 on 14 February, a game that was to become known as the St Valentine's Day massacre. That was very much his Boro peak. McKay – known as Jock to teammates – was always a great provider of chances, a ball artist who skills delighted but inconsistencies exasperated. Opportunities became fewer the following season as Bill Scott took his shirt. He managed only occasional games until his departure to Bolton. During his pre-Boro days, he had played for Celtic before joining Blackburn, where he had earned a solitary Scotland cap, against Wales in 1924. He was Rovers' top scorer in 1922–23 and 1924–25 and was on target in an FA Cup semi-final defeat to Cardiff. However, his tendency for showmanship probably cost him further caps.

McKENNAN Peter Stewart

Inside-forward
Born: Airdrie, 16 July 1918.
Died: Troon, 1991.
Career: Whitburn Juniors. Partick Thistle 1935. West Bromwich Albion 1947. Leicester City 1948. Brentford 1948. MIDDLESBROUGH 1949. Oldham Athletic 1951. Coleraine.

■ Hefty centre-forward McKennan was not a man to be messed with – and he needed to be tough in the rough and tumble game of the 1940s. The big Scot had brought himself to Boro boss David Jack's attention in the most painful possible way, by smashing a hat-trick past Boro for Brentford to knock the club out of the 1949 FA Cup. By the end of that season he was at Ayresome Park and made his debut in a 1–0 defeat at Everton. He ended that season as top scorer, however, and had the honour of scoring the only goal as Boro beat Newcastle on the day Ayresome Park hosted its biggest ever crowd. A total of 53,802 fans packed in on December 27, 1949 to see Boro beat United for the

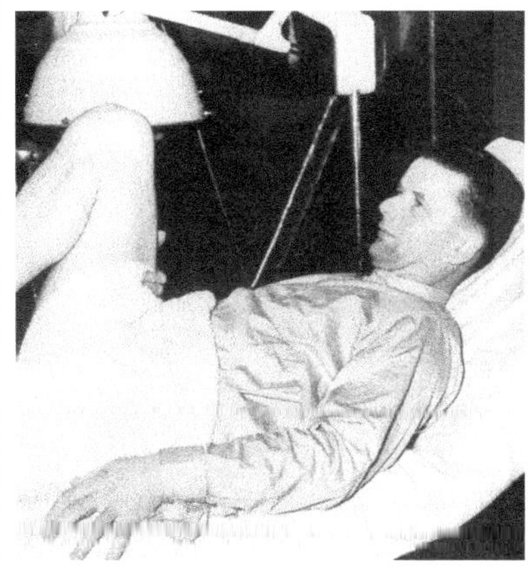

second time in 24 hours. McKennan missed out on the run-in after an horrific injury in a bruising clash at Chelsea on 29 March. His knee cap was shattered but the stricken forward had to lay on the pitch in agony for 10 minutes until a stretcher arrived and carried him to hospital. George Hardwick also had to be carried off and two other Boro players picked up knocks as Boro lost 2–1 with only nine men. McKennan fell out of favour the following season as Johnny Spuhler took his place and at the end of that season he was signed by old Boro captain George Hardwick for Oldham. McKennan later went to Coleraine as player-coach. He died in Scotland in 1991.

McKENZIE Duncan

Right-half
Born: Glasgow, 10 August 1912.
Died: 1987.
Career: Milton Parish Church. Albion Rovers. Brentford 1932. MIDDLESBROUGH 1938.

■ Unflappable right-half McKenzie was seen as the last piece in the jigsaw that could see Boro mount a serious Championship challenge when he joined in 1938. The club had finished fifth in 1937–38 but it was felt they needed some stability in the midfield positions to complement their effective attack and defence. He settled into the anchorman role and brought an unhurried calm to Boro's play. He had tough boots to fill having replaced Newcastle-bound England player Ralph Birkett but he did the job well and in 1939 Wilf Gillow's team finished fourth. He played in all three games of the 1939–40 season but it was all academic, of course, as war intervened and all Boro's ambitions were left in tatters. He played in the first North East regional game at York after the war began but that was to be his last for the club. McKenzie earned a Scotland cap in his Brentford days, against Ireland in November, 1937.

McLEAN John Derek

Inside-forward
Born: Brotton, 21 December 1932.
Career: MIDDLESBROUGH 1952. Hartlepool United 1961.

■ The young Derek McLean was in the best company as he worked his way through the Boro ranks. The Brotton lad broke through at a similar time as Brian Clough and Alan Peacock, though being in such illustrious company would inevitably limit his opportunities. He broke through at the end of the 1955–56 season, the same year both Clough and Peacock made their debuts. Although that first game ended in defeat at home to Bristol Rovers, he found his way on to the scoresheet twice before the season was out, in a 4–2 win over Lincoln and a 3–2 defeat at Port Vale. A hard working, 90-minutes footballer, he became a regular the following year and scored 10 goals alongside the young Clough, who was off the mark with 38 from just 41 games. McLean, Clough and Peacock were together in the starting line up in the next campaign as Boro moved up to finish seventh, but after that McLean found games much harder to come by. He continued to give good service when called upon. After his Boro days he had three seasons at Hartlepool and retired from the game to become a bricklayer in his native Brotton.

McLEOD Donald

Right-back
Born: Laurieston, 28 May 1882.
Died: Belgium, 6 October 1917.
Career: Stenhouse Thistle. Stenhousemuir 1901. Glasgow Celtic 1902. MIDDLESBROUGH 1908. Inverness Caledonian (loan) 1913.

■ One of the finest Scottish defenders of his generation, McLeod was drafted into the army at the end of his Boro career at the outbreak of World War One and was killed while serving as a gunner in the Royal Field Artillery at Dozinghem in Begium on 6 October 1917. As a footballer, he was a brave and determined defender and won four Scottish championships north of the border with Celtic as well as four Scottish caps. McLeod hardly missed a game in his first three seasons at Ayresome, forming an excellent understanding with fellow former Celtic defender Jackie Weir and 'keeper Tim Williamson. By the time Boro were mounting a serious Championship bid in 1913–14, however, McLeod had turned 30 and his right full-back berth went to either John Walker or Joe Hisbent. On his retirement in 1914 he took over a Middlesbrough hotel before going off to the war and laying down his life for his country.

McMAHON Anthony

Defender
Born: Bishop Auckland, 24 March 1986.
Career: MIDDLESBROUGH 2005.

■ Tony McMahon was captain of Boro's FA Youth Cup-winning team in 2004 and a big future is predicted for the Evenwood-born right-back. Injuries have restricted him in the last couple of seasons, however. He made a hugely impressive first-team debut in a 1–1 draw against Manchester United at Old Trafford in October 2004 in a game featuring five Academy products. McMahon went on to make 19 appearances that season, including games against Egaleo, Lazio, Villarreal and Sporting Lisbon in the UEFA Cup. But he dislocated his right shoulder an hour into a reserve game against Aston Villa at Billingham at the start of the next season and didn't play his first senior match until February, featuring in a 2–0 FA Cup fifth round win at Preston. A further injury following a bad challenge truncated his next game, at Charlton, and he was out for another six weeks, returning to play just two more games that campaign. The 2006–07 season brought just one appearance after he broke a leg in a reserve game against Liverpool at Wrexham. McMahon was set to figure in the final game of the campaign until chipping a bone in his ankle in a reserve game a few days earlier. A strong, determined character, his ambition remains to captain Boro and play for his country. By summer 2007 he had made 24 appearances.

McMANUS Charles Eric

Goalkeeper
Born: Limavady, 14 November 1950.
Career: Coleraine. Coventry City 1968. Notts County 1972. Stoke City 1979. Lincoln City (loan) 1979. Bradford City 1982. MIDDLESBROUGH (loan) 1986. Peterborough United (loan) 1986. Tranmere Rovers 1986.

■ Times could hardly have been harder when experienced 'keeper Eric McManus was brought in to cover for the injured Stephen Pears. Boro were staring at relegation to Division Three and boss Willie Maddren had already stated he would go unless results improved. That made it imperative for the players to respond on McManus' debut at Brighton, on 18 January, and they came away with a 3–3 draw. He was required only once more, in the following 1–0 defeat at high-flying Portsmouth before Pears returned.

McMORDIE Alexander (Eric)

Midfield
Born: Belfast, 12 August 1946.
Career: Dundela. MIDDLESBROUGH 1964. Sheffield Wednesday (loan) 1974. York City 1975. Hartlepool United 1976.

■ When Eric McMordie decided Manchester wasn't for him, he could have altered football history by taking George Best back to Northern Ireland with him. The pair had been on trial at Old Trafford but became homesick. And while Best eventually answered Matt Busby's pleas to return, McMordie refused and stayed back in Northern Ireland, working as a plasterer and playing as an amateur for Dundella. Fortunately, United's loss was Boro's gain as Irish scout Matt Willis recommended him to the club.

He broke into a struggling Boro side in 1965, scoring in his second game and was part of the side that crashed out of the Second Division by losing the last match at Cardiff. He played only occasionally in the promotion season that followed but was called up for the run in and appeared on that famous night against Oxford at a packed Ayresome as promotion was clinched. In the following six seasons the clever and hard-working inside-forward became a mainstay of a team that included Maddren and Hickton. Time and again Boro went close to promotion but always fell near the finishing post. McMordie was a star of the side, a fact recognised by his international call-up for Northern Ireland against Israel in 1968 and he went on to become Boro's third most capped player with 21. In 1969, he was named the *Evening Gazette's* Player of the Year. Aggressive and with a fierce will to win, McMordie often found himself in trouble with referees.

He was looking to move on by 1972

and had a bitter dispute with the club after they put a £60,000 valuation on him which the player felt was too high. Boro had already rejected a swop deal proposed by Blackburn which would have seen Eamon Dunphy coming the other way. His Boro career was clearly drawing to a close after Jack Charlton's arrival in 1973. Charlton was unimpressed by a flair player of McMordie's type and wanted players with a longer passing range. His place went to Bobby Murdoch early in the Second Division championship winning season, though he did stay around to see out the remainder of his contract. During this time he spent his spare hours building houses and had a successful loan at Sheffield Wednesday before joining York and Hartlepool. He was only 32 when he retired from football to pursue business interests on Teesside.

McMURRAY John Daniel

Wing-half
Born: Billingham, 5 October 1931.
Career: Billingham Synthonia. MIDDLESBROUGH 1949. Poole Town.

■ Nothing for four years, then two come along at the same time... Former Billingham Synthonia player McMurray had to wait for his debut. That came at the start of the 1953–54 season in a goalless draw at home to Cardiff. He was retained for the next game against Preston three days later but was dropped after a 4–0 reverse and his number-four shirt went to Harry Bell. Boro went down to the Second Division in that disastrous season and McMurray was called upon only once more, for a home defeat against Stoke early in the following campaign. On being released, the half-back went into non-League football with Poole.

McNALLY John

Centre-half
Born: Details unknown.
Career: MIDDLESBROUGH 1895. Thornaby 1896. MIDDLESBROUGH 1898.

■ His professional Boro career certainly didn't amount to much but there is one moment of history that can never be taken away from John McNally. He was in the first ever Boro side to play in the Football League at Lincoln in 1899, which the side lost 3–0. He lost his defensive place after another defeat against Burslem Port Vale two days later as boss John Robson looked for a winning formula. A veteran of Middlesbrough sides in the amateur era, McNally was called upon just once more, the following season, and was released in 1901.

McNEIL Michael

Left-back
Born: Middlesbrough, 7 February 1940.
Career: MIDDLESBROUGH 1957. Ipswich Town 1964. Cambridge City.

■ For a player who ended up with nine England caps, it is surprising that Mick McNeil's talents could have been missed altogether were it not for the eagle eye of Boro coach Jimmy Gordon. After leaving school, the former Middlesbrough Boys player was studying to be an analytical chemist and turning out for Cargo Fleet when Gordon signed him on.

He made his debut as an 18-year-old in 1958 as a left-half in an extraordinary game at Brighton, which Boro won 6–4, but soon lost that place to Ray Yeoman. It was at the start of the following season that he was moved to left-back for the opening draw against Portsmouth and he made the place his own for the next two seasons. Despite being in the Second Division, he was called up by England, having already represented the Under-23 side. He was still only 21 when he was awarded the last of his nine full caps and the emergence of Ray Wilson, not to mention competition for his left-back slot at Boro had much to do with this. However, McNeil displayed his versatility by again switching to the central defence and then found his left-back berth taken by the emerging talents of another excellent player, Gordon Jones. He was moved to right-back for a while until Cyril Knowles broke into the first team, after which another run came on the left. Despite the nine caps he won, he was still only 21 when he was awarded the last and it remains a mystery why he was overlooked afterwards.

A quick, forceful defensive player who could carry the ball up field, his sale to Ipswich was greeted with derision by the fans, coming hard on the heels of the departures of Alan Peacock to Leeds and Knowles to Spurs. He had suffered injuries, however, and did not see eye to eye with boss Raich Carter either and handed in a transfer request. He won promotion while with Ipswich and was in his early 30s when he quit the game in 1971, opening a highly successful sports outfitters business in Suffolk.

McNEILL Alexander (Alan)

Midfield
Born: Belfast, 16 August 1945.
Career: Crusaders. MIDDLESBROUGH 1967. Huddersfield Town 1968. Oldham Athletic 1969. Stockport County 1975.

■ McNeill's brief Boro career started and ended in victory. He was drafted in to replace Derrick Downing for a match at Aston Villa in 1968, midway through Boro's first season back in the Second Division after promotion, and was on the winning side as Arthur Horsfield gave Boro a 1–0 win. A steady, hard working midfielder, he kept his place for the home draw with Charlton that followed but didn't appear again until the opening day of the following season when he took the number-four shirt for a 2–1 home win against Preston. After that Downing returned and McNeill was soon on his way to Huddersfield.

McPARTLAND Desmond

Goalkeeper
Born: Middlesbrough, 5 October 1947.
Career: MIDDLESBROUGH 1964. Carlisle United 1967. Northampton Town 1969. Hartlepool United 1970.

■ Brilliant form early in McPartland's career led some to tip the England youth player for full international success. The Middlesbrough-born 'keeper was only 15 when he broke into Boro's reserve side and he was called into the first team three years later after an injury to established keeper Connachan. It was a baptism of fire for McPartland as Boro were battling relegation to the Third Division for the first time in their history. But although he was still only 18, McPartland played a blinder on his debut at Bristol City on 11 December 1965. The game ended 2–2 but the quality of his performance led even the City fans to give him a standing ovation. Agile and slender, the teenager held his place until April when struggling Boro conceded six at Bolton. He was called back into action early in the promotion winning season that followed before being replaced by Willie Whigham as the new season got off to a bad start. He was never able to establish himself in the side and had a tendency to make fairly simple saves look spectacular. He was back to cover for Whigham in mid-season wins over Oldham and Scunthorpe and a 4–1 FA Cup win at York. McPartland started the 1967–68 season and played a further nine games before again losing the place to Whigham after a 6–1 defeat at Birmingham. Midway through that season he moved to Carlisle and finished his career at Hartlepool.

McPHAIL Donald Douglas

Winger
Born: Dumbarton, 17 February 1911.
Died: 1992.
Career: Dumbarton Academy. Dumbarton. South Bank (loan). MIDDLESBROUGH 1930. Bournemouth 1932. Barnsley 1933. Carlisle United 1933. Burton Town. Nuneaton Town. Swindon Town 1935. Dunfermline Athletic. Dartford. Burton Town.

■ Signed as a teenager from Dumbarton, McPhail had to wait more than two years for a debut in Boro's fine First Division season of 1930–31. That came in a 5–1 win over Blackpool when he replaced winger Billy Pease. There were only three more appearances in Boro colours for the Scot, the last of which, against Leicester, saw him score the opening goal in a 2–2 draw.

McPHERSON Kenneth

Centre-forward/Centre-half
Born: Hartlepool, 25 March 1927.
Career: Horden Colliery. Notts County 1950. MIDDLESBROUGH 1953. Coventry City 1955. Newport County 1958. Swindon Town 1961.

■ Big bustling striker McPherson managed to average almost a goal every other game for Boro, a statistic rendered largely irrelevant by the fact he played so few games over three seasons with the club. A courageous and free-scoring player, who was particularly strong in the air, he sadly suffered ill health in his time at Ayresome which restricted his appearances. In his first season he shared the number nine shirt with Johnny Spuhler, scoring eight goals as the side was relegated to Division Two. His next

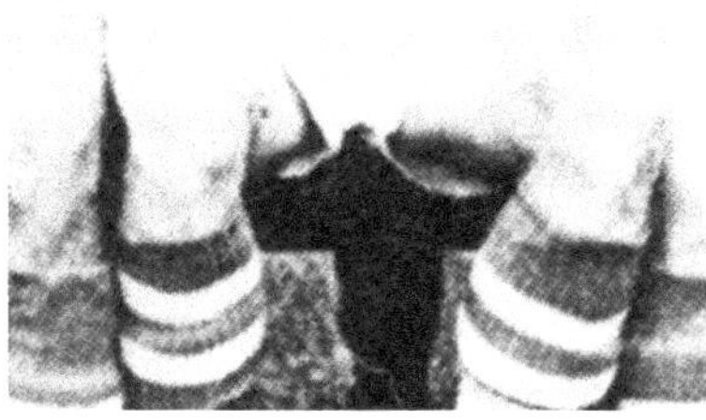

season started and ended with goals but there was nothing in between as he missed seven months. His final game, against Forest on Bonfire Night in 1955 at least saw some fireworks as he scored a late winner as Boro won 3–2. He moved on for a successful spell with Coventry and later in his career, which went on until he was 37, he was converted to centre-back.

McROBBIE Alan

Full-back
Born: Elgin.
Career: Elgin City. MIDDLESBROUGH 1911. Swindon Town 1913.

■ Short and very sweet is the only possible summary of McRobbie's one-game Boro career. He replaced James Weir at left full-back for a 4–0 home win over Notts County in the First Division in February 1912. He went to Swindon a year later.

MENDIETA Gaizka

Midfield
Born: Bilbao, Spain, 27 March 1974.
Career: Castellon 1991. Valencia (Spain) 1992. Lazio (Italy) 2001. Barcelona (Spain) (loan) 2002. MIDDLESBROUGH 2003.

■ Two years before joining Boro, initially

on loan, Gaizka Mendieta was the costliest player in Europe when he moved from Valencia to Lazio for £28.9 million. Born in Bilbao in the Basque region of Spain, Mendieta began his career with Castellon in 1991 before joining Valencia and initially playing for the club's B team. He made his debut for Valencia's first team in June 1993 and gradually established himself as the key member of the side. In the 1995–96 season he played 34 League games as Valencia finished runners-up to Atletico Madrid. He also starred in the Spainish team that finished runners-up in European Under-21 Championship. The following season he came close to leaving the club, but his fortunes were revived with the arrival of Claudio Ranieri. The Italian was switched to a more attacking role, playing 30 League games and scoring 10 goals. Mendieta's form came to the attention of his national coach and he made his debut for Spain in March 1999 in a 9–0 win over Austria. Hector Cuper took over as Valencia coach after Ranieri left for Atletico Madrid, but the club continued to go from strength to strength, winning the Spanish Super Cup with a 4–3 aggregate win over Barcelona. Inspired by Mendieta, Valencia reached the 2000 Champions League Final only to lose 3–0 to Real Madrid. That summer he helped Spain reach the quarter-finals of Euro 2000 before receiving a UEFA award as the best midfielder of the season. Valencia again reached the Champions League Final the following season, this time losing on penalties to Bayern Munich in Milan. The move to Lazio didn't work out and Mendieta played just 19 games in Serie A, mostly as substitute, after Lazio sacked coach Dino Zoff. Mendieta played three games in the 2002 World Cup, scoring one goal, before joining Barcelona on loan for the 2002–03 season. He joined Boro in August 2003 on an initial one-year loan deal before signing a four-year contract. He instantly became a hit with the Teesside public and was one of the club's outstanding players in the 2–1 Carling Cup Final success over Bolton in 2004. Mendieta missed most of Boro's 2004–05 campaign after damaging his cruciate ligaments against Portsmouth in October. In October 2005 he produced one of his best games in a Boro shirt, scoring the first and fourth goals and pulling the strings throughout as Boro crushed Manchester United 4–1. But injury again ended his campaign prematurely as he suffered a broken foot. The 2005–06 season brought 29 games but just three goals and he played only eight games in the 2006–07 campaign as he fell out of favour under new boss Gareth Southgate. By the end of the season he had made 83 appearances, scoring six goals.

MERSON Paul Charles

Forward
Born: Harlesden, 20 March 1968.
Career: Arsenal 1985. Brentford (loan) 1987. MIDDLESBROUGH 1997. Aston Villa 1998. Portsmouth 2002. Walsall 2003. Tamworth.

■ Rarely can a player have plummeted so quickly in the estimation of Boro fans. Merson was probably the club's most popular player at the start of the 1998–99 season after playing such a major role in helping Bryan Robson's team clinch promotion at the first attempt. But the manner of his departure, in which he appeared to criticise the culture of the club, left a bitter taste with many. It was a bizarre turnaround for a player who frequently professed his love for the club to suddenly announce his eagerness to leave.

His signing from Arsenal for less than £5 million in 1997 was something of a

coup and helped convince fans of the club's continued ambition after the departure of Juninho and the imminent sale of Fabrizio Ravanelli. He had been a legend at Highbury and instrumental in their championships of 1989 and 1991. He won the lot under George Graham, with League Cups, FA Cups and a European Cup-winners' Cup all heading to north London. In later years he had well-publicised problems with gambling, alcohol and drugs but fought back and regained his Arsenal place.

He quickly settled in at the Riverside and seemed to get better and better as the season went on. He was a class apart in the First Division and ended as second top scorer with 12 League goals, missing only one game, and helped Boro to the Coca-Cola Cup Final by scoring in either leg of the semi-final against Liverpool. It was no surprise that he was Boro's Player of the Year. Merson was full of skill, powerful running and inventiveness. His ability to pass the ball over long distances was best demonstrated with a superb ball to set up Marco Branca in Coca-Cola Cup semi-final win over liverpool. That summer he was named in the England World Cup squad and played as a substitute against Argentina, scoring one of England's penalties. As Boro geared up for the Premiership, Merson claimed he would one day like to manage the club, but everything changed dramatically while he was away with the England squad three games into the new season. Newspapers stated Merson was unhappy and set to sign for Aston Villa, though Bryan Robson appeared not to have been told of Merson's wish to leave. Within days the 'Magic Man' was gone, though Boro managed to make a hefty £2 million-plus profit on the deal. After joining Villa he missed numerous games with a back injury and returned to his problems of old. He rounded off his playing career with Walsall, whom he also briefly managed.

MILLAR James

Wing-half
Born: 1877.
Career: Elgin City. Glasgow Rangers. MIDDLESBROUGH 1900. Bradford City 1903. Aberdeen.

■ Somewhere along the line, Millar fell out of grace at Boro. Having started the 1900–01 season, the right-half lost his place after 10 games but came back to have another run near the end. Then he disappeared from the first-team picture and played no more games for the Second Division club. The former Port Glasgow Athletic and Rangers player moved to Bradford in 1903.

MILLAR William Mills

Outside-left
Born: Glasgow, 1902.
Career: Bo'ness. Heart of Midlothian. Ayr United. Rhyl Athletic. MIDDLESBROUGH 1927. York City 1929. Crewe Alexandra 1931.

■ Boro's dressing room was obviously short on wit in 1927. When Willie Millar signed from Rhyl the players came up with an uninspiring nickname by dubbing him 'Rhyl'. Millar was always a peripheral figure at Boro, replacing Owen Williams for a run in the side as the team fought in vain against relegation to Division Two. He did start the next campaign but was Williams' understudy throughout, playing only eight games, despite a healthy return of goals. The outside-left moved to York after Boro's immediate return to the First Division, the club getting £500 of any subsequent transfer fee and 25 percent of anything over that figure.

MILLER Alan John

Goalkeeper
Born: Epping, 29 March 1970.

Career: Arsenal 1988. Plymouth Argyle (loan) 1988. West Bromwich Albion (loan) 1991. Birmingham City (loan) 1991. MIDDLESBROUGH 1994. Grimsby Town (loan) 1997. West Bromwich Albion 1997. Blackburn Rovers 2000. Bristol City (loan) 2000. Coventry City (loan) 2000.

■ With Stephen Pears in the later stages of his career, new boss Bryan Robson swooped for Arsenal reserve Alan Miller just days before the 1994–95 season began. Miller arrived with an impressive CV and was tipped by Robson to play for England. He was among the first batch of youngsters to go through the FA School of Excellence and became its first graduate to play for the England Under-21 side. As understudy to England's David Seaman at Highbury, Miller's first-team chances with the Gunners were inevitably few, so a move to ambitious Boro looked a good one for the big 'keeper. Pears was injured for the opening game of the Robson reign, at home to Burnley on 13 August, so Miller stepped straight into the team. A chirpy character and a fine shot-stopper, he made an impressive start by keeping a clean sheet in his first four games. He went on to play a key role in Boro's Championship success that season, missing only a handful of games along the way. His list of appearances included the emotional last ever game at Ayresome Park against Luton.

Miller started the next season as first choice, despite the arrival from Manchester United of Gary Walsh, and played in the opening game at the new Cellnet Riverside Stadium as Chelsea were beaten 2–0. Miller's career took a sharp nosedive within weeks, however, as he was injured and then found Walsh in terrific form on his return to fitness. He didn't get another game until April. After three matches back in the side, including a superb performance against Liverpool at Anfield, Miller was furious to be dropped for the last game of the season against Manchester United when Walsh was recalled. He kept a diary of events that season, one of the most exciting in the club's history with the opening of the new stadium and the signing of Juninho, and the club published a book of his memoirs. Miller won the race to start as first choice in the 1996–97 season but, after a decent start, he lost form and never played for the club again. Miller got the blame for a dismal 3–0 home defeat against Spurs in October and Walsh and Ben Roberts played out the rest of the campaign. In March, Robson decided to cash in on Miller and sold him to West Brom for £500,000. He became a popular figure at The Hawthorns and was named their Player of the Year in 1998, as well as making it into the PFA's Division One team.

MILLER Joseph

Right-half
Born: Belfast, 27 April 1900.
Career: Morton. Johnstone. Nuneaton Town. Aberdare Athletic 1925. MIDDLESBROUGH 1926. Hibernian. Bournemouth 1931. Ballymena.

■ Boro's yo-yo existence of the late 1920s saw them swop divisions three times in three years, with two Second Division championships and a relegation sandwiched in between. Despite the club's rapidly changing fortunes, Joe Miller became a bedrock of the side. The wing-half had struggled at first after signing from Aberdare and found it hard to adjust to the pace of the game. But once he found his feet he became a fine acquisition, noted for his ability to intercept a pass and feed Boro's strikers. He missed only two games as Boro raced away with the Second Division championship in 1927 and was again a regular the next year, despite Boro's disappointing season, as they finished

bottom of Division One. He survived that setback and, now at right-half, was a lynchpin of the side the following year as promotion was secured once again. It was a successful season on the international front too as he made his debut for Ireland against Wales and later faced an England side that contained his Boro teammate George Camsell. Next time out in the top flight was not the same for Miller, however, as he found his place under threat from new skipper Joe Peacock. After being a regular in the previous three years he played only half the games as Boro finally achieved stability and finished mid-table. That summer boss Peter McWilliam had signed John MacFarlane from Celtic and though he started at wing-half he was converted to take Miller's right-half position the following year. Frozen out of the first-team picture, he moved on to Hibernian in November 1930.

MILLION Esmond

Goalkeeper
Born: Morpeth, 15 March 1938.
Career: Amble Juniors. MIDDLESBROUGH 1956. Bristol Rovers 1962.

■ The Geordie goalkeeper was always a peripheral figure at Ayresome Park but he will be remembered for his part in one of football's most shameful episodes. Million was jailed and banned from the game after taking part in an infamous bribery scandal in the early 1960s. He left Boro in 1962 for Bristol Rovers and admitted throwing the ball into his own net on two occasions for Rovers. He started out as an understudy to Peter Taylor, making his debut against Port Vale in October 1956 in a 3–1 win, with Brian Clough among Boro's goal scorers. He remained second choice to Taylor until 1960 but, as Taylor's Boro career came to an end, it wasn't Million who manager Bob Dennison turned to as a replacement. Young Bob Appleby, a 20-year-old, was brought in instead at the end of the 1959–60 season and Million was forced to shadow him for much of the rest of his Ayresome career. Million's last game for the club came in a 3–2 defeat at Derby in December, 1961. The following summer he was gone, transferred to Bristol Rovers. The rest, as they say, is history.

MILLS Daniel John

Right-back
Born: Norwich, 18 May 1977.
Career: Norwich City 1994. Charlton Athletic 1998. Leeds United 1999. MIDDLESBROUGH (loan) 2003. Manchester City 2004. Hull City (loan) 2006.

■ The combative right-back enjoyed a successful year-long loan from Leeds United, a period that saw him pick up a Carling Cup-winners' medal. He made 37 appearances for Boro during that campaign, picking up 10 yellow cards along the way. He made his debut against

his parent club, whom he had helped to a Champions League semi-final place two years earlier. Mills won 19 international caps and a reputation for a no-nonsense approach. After failing to agree personal terms, he returned to Leeds at the end of the season. The relegated West Yorkshire side couldn't afford to keep him and he was sold to Manchester City, with part of his wages being paid by his old club. He went on loan to Hull City for two months in September 2006.

MILLS David John

Forward
Born: Whitby, 6 December 1951.
Career: MIDDLESBROUGH 1968. West Bromwich Albion 1979. Newcastle United (loan) 1982. Sheffield Wednesday 1983. Newcastle United 1983. MIDDLESBROUGH 1984. Whitby Town. Darlington 1986.

■ David Mills overcame adversity to go on and become one of Boro's best ever strikers. He emerged through the youth ranks at the same time as his good friend Willie Maddren, making his debut as a sub at Birmingham on the last day of the 1968–69 season. He would have been relieved to get that far, as a serious back injury threatened at one time to rob him of a career at all.

The Thornaby lad had a chance to sign for a host of clubs on leaving school, having played for both Durham County and England Schoolboys. Those interested included Manchester United but Mills decided to join his local club. A hard-working and pacey front man, he could play as an out-and-out striker or behind the front two. Despite scoring against Swindon on his full debut, Mills remained on the fringes of the first team until midway through the 1971–72 season when he won the troublesome position at number nine. It was a boost for Maddren as well as Mills, as Maddren had been forced to play up front and was now able to return to defensive duties. Having waited patiently for a big breakthrough, Mills wasted no time in taking his chance, scoring in the first minute of a 4–3 defeat at Hull in December 1971. From that day on Mills became a key part of the Boro scene. It was rarely plain sailing, however, as he became a target for the Boro boo-boys

who criticised him for wasting opportunities. The frustration of his treatment from the terraces boiled over when he gave a V-sign to the crowd after scoring twice in a 2–0 home win over Blackpool in 1973, an act which cost him a club fine.

Mills was on the up by now though and was a star of Jack Charlton's promotion-winning team of 1974. He scored 11 goals in 40 games that year and had the honour of striking the goal that secured promotion in a 1–0 win at Luton in March. As Boro made an impressive start to life in the top flight, so Mills started to attract the attentions of the top clubs, with Liverpool reported to be interested in 1974. Mills stayed on and continued to produce the goods for Charlton. By the middle of the 1976–77 season, however, he was becoming restless and the board accepted his transfer request, slapping a £200,000 price tag on their star player. The transfer never actually came and Mills went on to finish as Boro's top scorer in both 1977 and 1978. That run included a memorable hat-trick as Boro crushed Arsenal 4–1 in an FA Cup fifth round tie in February 1977. Despite his form, Mills never managed to break through into the England side. He won a host of Under-23 caps and made it into England squads but, like Maddren and Boam, he was always overlooked.

With Boro consistently out of the running for major honours, it was only a matter of time before the transfer finally came and when it did it made headlines for more reasons than one. Ron Atkinson was reported to have paid £500,000 to take Mills to West Brom and, although the actual figure may have been less, he was widely credited as the first half million pound footballer. Things didn't work out at The Hawthorns, however. Atkinson tried to convert him to midfield but he suffered an Achilles injury early on at his new club and never seemed to settle. He had spells with both Sheffield Wednesday and Newcastle before his career went full circle as Maddren re-signed him for Boro in 1984. His 14 goals that season were crucial in keeping the club in the Second Division but he suffered another Achilles injury to miss out on the run-in. Mills must have wondered if the Boro he rejoined was the same club as Maddren's team slid towards relegation and finally bankruptcy. The Achilles problem and then a broken arm, suffered in a freak training accident, meant he didn't play at all in the relegation season of 1985–86 but helped Maddren with coaching and worked hard behind the scenes. In fact, the club was so desperate that Mills once had to drive the team coach on a pre-season trip to Scotland. He didn't get on with Maddren's successor Bruce Rioch and was released at the end of that season, just weeks after a poorly attended testimonial against Newcastle when only 3,500 turned up. It was a sad end to a distinguished Boro career. Mills had a brief spell in the Third Division with Darlington before giving up the professional game. Tragedy struck Mills' life in 1988 when he was seriously injured in a road accident in which his father was killed. Fortunately, Mills recovered despite horrific injuries and went on to work as a print sales representative. He has also done considerable media work. He returned to Newcastle under Bobby Robson to work within the scouting network, eventually becoming the club's chief scout. The Mills family's ties with Boro continued through to David's son Andrew, who was a youth player at the club in the mid-1990s.

MILNE John Vance (Jackie)

Winger
Born: Stirling, 25 March 1911.
Career: Glasgow Ashfield. Blackburn

Rovers 1933. Arsenal 1935. MIDDLESBROUGH 1937. Dumbarton.

■ Two Boro careers got underway on 18 December 1937. One of the debutants that day against Bolton, George Hardwick, went on to become a legend but the other, Jacky Milne, is less well known. Were it not for the outbreak of war in 1939, however, Milne's name might have lived much longer in the memory.

Winger Milne's goal for Blackburn had knocked Boro out of the FA Cup in 1935. After signing from Arsenal, he didn't make the most explosive of starts. But once he teamed up with Wilf Mannion he became a star of the side. He shone in the 1938–39 season as Boro finished fourth in the First Division as his ball control and ability to mask his intentions set him apart. Equally at home at outside-left or outside-right, he was capable of popping up on either wing and could swing in some majestic crosses. Boro turned in some stunning displays and Milne was in the side as Blackpool were crushed 9–2, though he was actually criticised for missing an easy chance to make it 10! He was never a prolific goalscorer but his flair helped set up chances for Micky Fenton. He made his debut for Scotland while with Boro, in a match against England in April 1938, when Fenton was on the other side and Boro 'keeper Dave Cumming also played for the Scots.

The outbreak of war sadly terminated his career in its prime and he worked in the shipyards during the war years. He played part-time for Dumbarton in 1941 but Boro held on to his registration and the Scottish club was fined £50 for an illegal approach to Milne over their manager's job. They were ordered to pay £1,000 for his transfer or £350 if they paid a fee within three years. He also earned himself a four-week ban in Scotland for misconduct in a game against Third Lanark. Boro wanted him back after the war, even though he was in his mid-30s by then, but Milne declined.

MITCHELL Albert James

Outside-left
Born: Burslem, 22 January 1922.
Died: 1997.
Career: Stoke City 1941. Blackburn Rovers 1948. Kettering Town. Northampton Town 1949. Luton Town 1951. MIDDLESBROUGH 1954. Southport 1956. Wellington. Kidderminster.

■ Although he was in his 30s when he arrived at Boro, boss Bob Dennison had been determined to sign Mitchell from Luton. The England B international had an impressive spell with the Hatters and Dennison was so keen to have him he allowed him to live in his hometown of Stoke while playing for Middlesbrough. It was actually the second time Dennison had signed Mitchell, having rescued him from non-League football by taking him to Northampton in 1949. His career had started at Stoke and then Blackburn before he drifted out of the professional game to join Kettering until Northampton stepped in. The tricky outside-left came into a Boro side that had just been relegated and lost its biggest star, Wilf Mannion. Boro's attempts to adjust to life out of the top flight had been disastrous and he came into a side that had just lost 6–1 and 3–0 in its last two games. Mitchell's arrival made absolutely no difference, as they lost his debut 4–1 against Forest at Ayresome Park. He didn't really make the expected impact at his new club and the goals didn't flow. Boro were again a very ordinary Second Division side the following year and Mitchell lost his place to Billy Day after a 2–0 defeat at Bristol City. He played only sporadically from then on and asked for a transfer, moving on to Southport in 1956. He also had spells with Wellington and Kidderminster. Bert Mitchell died in 1997.

MOCHAN Neil

Forward
Born: Larbert, 6 April 1927.
Died: 28 August 1994.
Career: Dunipace Thistle. Morton 1944. MIDDLESBROUGH 1951. Glasgow Celtic 1953. Dundee United 1960. Raith Rovers 1963.

■ A distinguished career north of the border was punctuated by a brief spell at Ayresome Park for Neil Mochan. When he arrived from Morton at the end of the 1950–51 season, Boro were one of the leading lights in the First Division but they were about to hit the slide. Mochan's first action for his new club was unusual, against Partisan Belgrade in the Festival of Britain series, and his League debut came against League champions Spurs before 44,000 at Ayresome Park on 18 August 1951. It was a fine start, as Boro ran out 2–1 winners. He scored twice in his second game as Boro went down 4–2 at Manchester United and, though the goals came regularly in his opening months at the club, all was not well for the side. They conceded too many goals and finished 19th, with Mochan losing his place towards the end to the man he had initially replaced, Johnny Spuhler.

A small but strong forward player, Mochan played mainly on the left and possessed a ferocious shot, but he struggled to get a game in his second season, losing out to Spuhler as Boro again flirted with relegation before finishing mid-table. His last game came in a 5–1 defeat at Manchester City midway through that campaign. The man they called 'Smiler' was presumably less than happy and moved on to Celtic in 1953, where he was a stalwart. He won a Scottish League and Cup double at Parkhead and earned himself three Scottish caps. He was used as a utility player at Celtic and had some moments of outstanding individual success, on one occasion scoring five in a Cup game against St Mirren. After spells at Dundee United and Raith, he became assistant trainer-coach at Celtic and then head trainer, a position he held when Jock Stein's men lifted the 1967 European Cup. He served Celtic right up to the 1990s. Neil Mochan died on 28 August 1994.

MOHAN Nicholas

Central defender
Born: Middlesbrough, 6 October 1970.
Career: MIDDLESBROUGH 1987. Hull City (loan) 1992. Leicester City 1994. Bradford City 1995. Wycombe Wanderers 1997. Stoke City 1999. Hull City 2001. Gateshead. Thornaby.

■ After producing a team full of local youngsters in the early and mid–80s, the Boro production line then seemed to dry up. One exception was former Coulby Newham School pupil Nicky Mohan. After starting in goal for Whinney Banks as a 12-year-old, he played for local sides Kader and Acklam Steelworks before starring for the Boro boys team that won the English Shield in 1986. His career actually started at Charlton but the

youngster could not settle in London and Lennie Lawrence agreed to release him. Instead he returned home and joined Boro on a YTS.

A tall and fast defender – he could run 100 metres in 10.8 seconds – Mohan could play in either full-back position but was primarily a centre-back. He was called up for first-team action at the end of 1988 as Bruce Rioch's side came to terms with the First Division. After being a non-playing sub for a goalless draw at Norwich, his full debut came a fortnight later in January 1989 as he replaced the injured Gary Parkinson for a Simod Cup win over Coventry at Ayresome Park. His League bow came in the following 3–1 win at Southampton. Mohan switched sides to play at left-back in place of the injured Colin Cooper for Boro's desperate run-in at the end of that season. He played the last three games, including the fateful final day defeat at Hillsborough which saw Boro relegated. Still only 18, he was in the starting line-up at left-back in the Second Division the following year as Boro struggled. He lost out on Cooper's return but did play in the ZDS Cup semi-final against Aston Villa that clinched Boro's place at Wembley. He lost out on the Final, named as a sub, and his career took a marked downturn when he suffered a serious knee injury in a reserve game against Preston. A frustrating series of failed comebacks followed and Mohan was out of the first-team picture for the best part of two years. When he came back, his old Charlton boss Lennie Lawrence was in the Boro hot seat and Mohan looked set for a £175,000 move to Plymouth. But Boro sold Tony Mowbray to Celtic in the same week and Mohan was handed the job of filling Mogga's boots.

Mohan became a regular as Boro won promotion and fought through to the League Cup semi-finals in an impressive partnership with Alan Kernaghan. He was actually sent off in the game that clinched promotion after trying to break up a fracas at Wolves. The arrival of Derek Whyte from Celtic that summer forced him out of the first team in the Premier League but he was recalled in place of Kernaghan for a 3–2 home win against Blackburn in December and went on to play 18 games in the top flight. Mohan replaced Kernaghan the following season but again lost out when Lawrence signed Steve Vickers from Tranmere. He was out of contract when Bryan Robson arrived and was allowed to move to Premier League Leicester. His boss there was Brian Little, and Little later signed him again, this time for Stoke, after Mohan's spells with Bradford and Wycombe Wanderers.

MOISES COSTA Emerson

Midfield
Born: Rio de Janeiro, Brazil, 12 April 1972.
Career: Flamengo (Brazil). Curitiba (Brazil). Belenenses (Portugal) 1992. FC Porto (Portugal) 1994. MIDDLESBROUGH 1996. Tenerife (Spain) 1998. Deportivo la Coruna (Spain) 2000. Atletico Madrid (Spain) 2002. Rangers 2003. Vasco da Gama (Brazil) 2004. Xanthi (Greece) 2005. AEK Athens (Greece) 2006. Apoel (Cyprus) 2007.

■ Samba star Emerson was an enigmatic performer who had the ability to turn on the style with flair and powerful running. He could also pop up with spectacular long-range goals. He was unfortunately prone to inconsistency and left under a cloud after going AWOL on a trip home to Brazil.

Signed shortly after the end of the 1995–96 season, Emerson was Brazilian by birth but played most his football in Portugal and has joint nationality. After beginning his career in his home country with Coritiba, he moved to Portuguese side Belenenses for a three-year stint. He had starred with Bobby Robson's Porto side, twice winning the League title and being named Portuguese Player of the Year in his last season. Emerson was an unknown quantity in the UK but Boro beat off competition from the likes of Sampdoria, Fiorentina, Roma and Inter Milan to secure his services.

Emerson joined fellow Brazilians

Branco and Juninho at Boro and looked to be a massive talent in his early matches. Indeed, it would not be an exaggeration to say he had the ability to become one of the best players in the world. With his astonishing array of tricks, dummies and body swerves, he delighted fans and bewildered opponents. Although rather casual in his passing and defensive duties, his immense strength meant he was a strong tackler and impossible to knock off the ball. With his long, curly black hair and effervescent smile, 'Emmo' was a truly unmistakeable sight. Reports of interest from Barcelona and Parma were unsettling and, when it emerged that his wife was struggling to settle on Teesside, Emerson returned to Brazil for a spell, insisting he would not be back. It was suggested that the player and his advisors were trying to force Boro's hand to sell him but the club refused to buckle. He was soon back in the side, though his form was rarely the same, despite scoring a long-range special against Chesterfield in the FA Cup semi-final. He was part of the team that reached the FA and Coca-Cola Cup Finals but suffered relegation, after which it was felt that he would leave along with Juninho and Ravanelli.

Instead, he stayed to play his part in the first half of Boro's First Division campaign, following the arrival of his cousin and look-alike Fabio. Emerson was given permission to return to Brazil over the 1997 Christmas period but failed to return on schedule amid speculation of interest from Tenerife. Bryan Robson lost patience with the errant star and agreed to sell Emerson to the Spanish club for £4.25 million. After a season and a half of struggle, he suffered relegation with Tenerife in 1999. It was reported that a return to Boro fell through when Tenerife demanded £8 million for the player. He instead moved on to Deportivo and Atletico Madrid before a brief and unsuccessful spell in Scotland with Rangers. In September 2005 he was given a hero's welcome when he returned to the Riverside with Greek side Xanthi for a UEFA Cup tie.

MOODY Alan

Defender
Born: Middlesbrough, 18 January 1951.

Career: MIDDLESBROUGH 1968. Southend United 1972.

■ When local lad Moody emerged during Stan Anderson's reign, he was thought the best of the crop of youngsters coming through. Indeed, Moody was part of Anderson's 'M-Squad' of talented youngsters – Willie Maddren, David Mills and Brian Myton being the others – which he said would save him thousands in the transfer market. He had been an outstanding player from the start, having won representative honours for his school, town, county and country. His debut, after recovering from a fractured skull suffered in a Northern Intermediate League game against Leeds, came on his 18th birthday. Moody replaced Bill Gates at right-back for a 1–1 draw at home to Millwall and despite playing 10 games in that season, the consistency of Alex Smith limited his opportunities. He had to be versatile and played games in midfield and at centre-back. The departure of George Smith to Birmingham in the 1970–71 season opened a door for him but he was never able to keep a place for long. Moody's last Boro game came in a 2–0 defeat at Orient early in the 1972–73 season. He was signed by Southend and gave sterling service on the south coast, playing well over 400 games and earning a testimonial against West Ham in 1973.

MOORE Alan

Left-winger
Born: Dublin, 25 November 1974.
Career: MIDDLESBROUGH 1991. Barnsley (loan) 1998. Burnley 2001. Shelbourne 2004. Derry City 2007.

■ Alan Moore's Boro career started brilliantly but went into steep decline following a succession of injuries. Perhaps the worst thing that could have happened to Irish winger Alan Moore was to be dubbed the 'new Ryan Giggs'. He found himself the centre of attention after a dramatic start to his Boro career under Lennie Lawrence in 1993. He had joined Boro from Irish Sunday League side Rivermount and had been on trial at Manchester United before opting for Boro. The Republic of Ireland's Young Player of the Year in 1993, his full Boro debut came the same year, on the opening day of the season with Boro newly relegated to the First Division. He scored twice that day – both from long range – as Boro beat Notts County and followed up with two more stunning goals at Barnsley a few weeks later. The side won their opening four matches and fans began to wonder just how far Moore could go. Inevitably, it was hard for a young player to keep up such a scorching pace and his form fluctuated. With close control and great skill, he could terrify opposing full-backs when running at them with the ball at his feet and played nearly every game in that season. He was again a regular under new boss Bryan Robson and a key part of the side that won promotion back to the Premier League in 1995. Moore's career dipped from then on, however. Robson employed a wing-back system in the top flight and, with star players like Juninho and Barmby drafted in, Moore's first-team chances were limited.

When he did play, he was asked to take on more defensive duties from a midfield role and his confidence was rarely the same as in his early years. He suffered injuries and required a double calf operation in November 1997 that kept him out for almost a year. Moore had been a peripheral figure in the side that went down in 1997, though he did appear as an extra-time sub in the Coca-Cola Cup Final replay against Leicester, and was again on the sidelines as promotion was won in 1998. He asked for a move at the end of 1998 and had a loan spell with John Hendrie's Barnsley. Moore made his last appearance for Boro in February 1999, spending two seasons in the wilderness before moving to Burnley in 2001. He was a limited success with the Clarets before turning his back on English football to return to Ireland with Shelbourne in 2004. The 2006–07 season found him making a few appearances from the bench for Derry City.

MORAN Martin

Outside-right
Born: Bannockburn, April 1878.
Died: 1950.
Career: Glasgow Celtic 1898. Hamilton Academical 1898. Clyde 1899. Sheffield United 1899. MIDDLESBROUGH 1900. Millwall 1902. Heart of Midlothian 1904. Chelsea 1905. Glasgow Rangers 1908. Glasgow Celtic 1908.

■ Nicknamed the muscular midget, Moran holds the honour of being one of Boro's smallest ever players. Standing only 5ft 5in, he was a regular in midfield in the second season in the Football League as Boro finished sixth in the Second Division. The Glaswegian, once a player with Glasgow Benburb, was forced out of his number-seven slot the following season by Willie Wardrope and played only three games as the side was promoted to the First Division for the first time. He is thought to have returned north to Celtic, his last Boro game coming in a 2–0 win at Blackpool on the closing day of that victorious 1901–02 season.

MORDUE John (Jackie)

Winger/Inside-left
Born: Edmondsley, 13 December 1886.
Died: 1957.

Career: Sacriston. Spennymoor United. Barnsley 1906. Woolwich Arsenal 1906. Sunderland 1908. MIDDLESBROUGH 1920. Hartlepool United 1922. Durham City 1922. Ryhope.

■ A veteran at Sunderland, Mordue had enjoyed great success at Roker Park as a fast outside-right, forming a partnership with Charlie Buchan. He won a League Championship medal at Roker and played in a Cup Final they lost in 1913 as well as earning England caps. Soon after World War One he was signed by new Boro boss Jimmy Howie but rarely reached the same heights at Ayresome Park. He lost his first-team place a few months after arrival when Howie signed Billy Birrell. Boro were a decent First Division side at the time, finishing eighth in both Mordue's seasons with the club. In the 1921–22 season he found it hard to get a regular game and was this time squeezed out by Jacky Carr, his last game coming in a 1–1 draw at home to Sheffield United on 14 January 1922. He refused a new contract and was transfer listed in May 1922, moving to Hartlepool. He later moved into management but had a fraught time as player-boss of Division Three North side Durham. The club forgot to apply for its exemption from the 1923–24 FA Cup qualifying round and was forced to play. He was sacked shortly afterwards as the directors considered him 'unsuitable for the post'. He died in Sunderland in March 1938.

MOREIRA DA SILVA Fabio

Midfield/Full-back
Born: Brazil, 14 March 1972.
Career: Flamengo (Brazil). Chaves (Portugal). MIDDLESBROUGH 1997.

■ The cousin and brother-in-law of Boro's wayward Brazilian Emerson, Fabio originally came to Teesside to visit him but after impressing in training he was given an 18-month contract. Like Emerson, he started out with Flamengo in his native Brazil but on being unable to hold down a regular spot, moved to Portugal to play for Chaves. At Middlesbrough, he was a regular in the club's reserve side before being given his chance during an injury crisis in the club's promotion-winning campaign of 1997–98. In what turned out to be Moreira's only appearance for the club, he impressed at left wing-back, especially going forward in a 3–0 defeat of Huddersfield Town. Not used again, he left the club before the season's end.

MORENO Jaime Morales

Forward
Born: Bolivia, 19 January 1974.
Career: Blooming (Bolivia) 1991. Medellin (loan) 1993. MIDDLESBROUGH 1994. DC United (US) 1996. MIDDLESBROUGH (loan) 1997. Metrostars (US) 2003. DC United 2004.

■ Boro's penchant for overseas signings under Bryan Robson started with a young Bolivian star of the 1994 World Cup. Jaime Moreno became an instant hit with the Teesside public after the club fought off competition from Brazil and Spain to complete his signing. Nicknamed 'Il Pichon' in Bolivia, which translates as roadrunner, he became the first Bolivian to play in England. He had come through the renowned Tahuici Football Academy and played for FC Blooming in the country's second city of Santa Cruz de la Sierra. His appearance at the World Cup was to be expected, as he had been in the national side's full squad at just 16.

After Bryan Robson saw a video of Moreno in action, the striker played in a Boro pre-season friendly at Darlington and instantly looked the part with his box of tricks and the reserve crowd. An

his second string debut in September, 1994 was 10 times the normal gate. He got few first-team chances, however, making his debut as a sub for Craig Hignett as Boro beat Millwall 3–0 and scoring his first goal in an Anglo-Italian Cup home draw with Cesena. He broke through for a couple of home games in March, replacing first Jamie Pollock and then Robson himself and looked good as the side beat Bristol City and Watford. His first League goal soon followed when he struck the opening goal of a draw against Barnsley. He made useful subs appearances as Boro clinched the First Division Championship but never looked comfortable after the step up to the Premier League and his chances were few. Although boasting a great touch, he was not a natural goaslcorer and was too easily bundled off the ball in the rough and tumble of English football.

He moved on to the USA and had a good spell with Washington DC before Robson brought him back on loan during the American off-season as Boro again fought for promotion in 1997–98. He was mainly restricted to substitute appearances but did strike the winner in a vital game at Stoke in February 1998. He is one of the all-time top scorers in the US Major League.

MORRIS Christopher Barry

Full-back
Born: Newquay, 24 December 1963.
Career: Sheffield Wednesday 1982. Glasgow Celtic 1987. MIDDLESBROUGH 1992.

■ It didn't take Lennie Lawrence long to realise Boro's desperate need for defenders as they prepared for life in the Premier League in 1992. The answer was to buy two Celtic defenders, centre-half Derek Whyte and full-back Chris Morris, with Andy Payton going the other way. Morris had enjoyed an impressive career to that point and, valued at £600,000, looked a useful signing.

He had missed out on the usual football apprenticeship and was rejected by West Country sides, Exeter and Plymouth. He made the grade, however, and was signed by Jack Charlton for Sheffield Wednesday after a trial. He won promotion with Wednesday before a successful move to Celtic. He won the lot at Parkhead, including a League and Cup double, and Charlton made him an established member of the Republic of Ireland squad. An attack-minded full-back, he played in both the European Championships of 1988 and the 1990 World Cup as Ireland became a force in the world game. His move to Boro was less impressive, however, and he often struggled for consistency. It was a poor year for the club as they went down and Morris shared the full-back role with Curtis Fleming. He covered as an emergency centre-back on a number of occasions but reverted to full-back as a young side took to the field back in the First Division.

It was while playing as a sub against Bolton in November 1993 that he suffered a serious knee injury that threatened his career. Morris was out for almost a year and when he came back,

under Bryan Robson, he found Neil Cox and Curtis Fleming were holding the full-back roles. When Fleming was injured it was usually Derek Whyte who played at left-back. He got a new lease of life with Boro back in the top flight and was the left wing-back for the first half of the 1995–96 season as Boro started very well, earning himself an international recall along the way. After that he once again became a peripheral figure as Cox and Fleming took the wing-back roles again. A diligent and hard-working professional, he was forced to quit the game in 1997 because of a persistent knee problem. The club awarded him a well-attended benefit match against Forest in 1998. He then set up a family business in Cornish pasties.

MORRISON James Clark

Midfield
Born: Darlington, 25 May 1986.
Career: MIDDLESBROUGH 2003. WBA 2007.

■ Morrison played an integral part as Boro won the FA Youth Cup in 2004, scoring two crucial goals in the 3–0 final first leg win at Aston Villa and terrorising the Midlands side's defence in the return leg. The Hummersknott School-educated player has represented England at every level except full. He is a skilful and quick central midfielder who can also play on the right. He made his first-team debut as a substitute for Michael Ricketts in the 2–0 FA Cup win over Notts County at the Riverside in January 2004, aged just 17. Morrison stepped up to the first team again in September 2004 and scored in Boro's 1–1 draw at Banik Ostrava in the UEFA Cup. He kept his place for a visit to Manchester United three days later and laid on Stewart Downing's early goal as an injury-hit side again drew 1–1. Morrison added to his honours collection in May 2006 with a UEFA Cup runners'-up medal after being named in the starting line-up for the final in Eindhoven. He agreed a new improved contract in August 2006, pledging his future to the club until summer 2009. He made 36 appearances in 2006–07, scoring twice, but was also sent off for the first time in his professional career after lunging at Cristiano Ronaldo in an FA Cup quarter-

final replay defeat at Old Trafford. In early summer 2007 Scotland manager Alex McLeish was exploring his Caledonian grandparentage with a view to calling him up. At the end of 2006–07 Morrison had made 97 appearances, scoring eight goals. He joined West Bromwich Albion in the summer of 2007 for £1.5 million, a fee that could rise to £2.2 million.

MOWBRAY Anthony Mark

Central defender
Born: Saltburn, 22 November 1963.
Career: MIDDLESBROUGH 1981. Glasgow Celtic 1991. Ipswich Town 1995.

■ An inspirational figure who will forever be a legend on Teesside. Tony Mowbray was the local lad with the heart of a lion who led the club from the hell of liquidation and back to the promised land of Division One.

He came through the youth ranks after playing for local clubs, including Nunthorpe and Grangetown, to make his debut at St James' Park as Kevin Keegan's marker in 1982. Boro drew that game and Mowbray ended the season as a regular under Malcolm Allison. Big Mal played the young Mowbray out of position for much of his time as a left-back and, never the fastest of players, he found it hard to adapt. There were plenty more hard times to come. When Willie Maddren took over he reverted to a more familiar role at centre-back but things were getting worse for the club. He helped stave off relegation in 1985 as a central defensive partner for Irving Nattrass but it was merely postponing the inevitable. He looked likely to leave the club the following season after a contractual dispute with Maddren saw him dropped from the team after a game against Bradford. On a week-to-week contract, Oldham boss Joe Royle twice tried to sign him but the club rejected offers of around £50,000. It was just as well he stayed, because there was light emerging at the end of the tunnel for Boro.

Mowbray signed a new contract when Bruce Rioch arrived and continued his increasingly promising pairing with the young Gary Pallister. Relegation still came, however, in a dismal closing day defeat at Shrewsbury...and worse was to follow. Mowbray, the Player of the Year in both 1985 and 1986, and the other local youngsters stayed loyal to a club that was bankrupt and could not pay their wages. They knew they could be facing the soccer scrapheap and were even barred from Ayresome Park by the official receiver. Mowbray later recalled training at Billingham Synthonia and on local parks while the consortium fighting to save the club tried to stave off disaster. When the club was saved, the day before the 1986–87 season, there was no time to prepare Ayresome Park and the players started out against Port Vale on Hartlepool's Victoria Ground. Mowbray led his men out for a battling 2–2 draw and a remarkable rise from the ashes was underway.

Mowbray didn't miss a game as promotion was won from the Third Division as Boro's young defence, which included Pallister, Cooper, Pears and Parkinson, got to grips with Third Division attacks. It just got better for Mowbray from then on. The following year he was once again an ever present and it was during this season that Rioch made his immortal remark about his skipper. Rioch said: 'If you were on a rocket ship going to the moon, the man you would want sitting next to you would be Tony Mowbray'. Boro's fanzine Fly Me To The Moon was named in honour of those words and Mowbray set about reinforcing the legend. His impact was at its height in February 1988, when he scored a last gasp equaliser in a Cup tie against Everton and then scored the winner in a live TV game against Aston Villa. By the last game of that season Boro were second and needed to beat Leicester at Ayresome Park to clinch promotion. Boro seemed to have blown their chance, losing 2–1, but it was only a setback. They beat Bradford in the Play-offs and then knocked out Chelsea to get back into the top flight against all odds. Captain Fantastic was the first scorer in the First Division, with a thunderous drive into the top corner against Norwich, but Boro were gradually brought back down to earth. Mowbray missed just one game but the naïve young side, despite some fine performances, fell through the relegation trap door at the end of that season. He did win England B honours in the summer of 1989 but the toll of his exertions seemed to catch up with Mowbray and he suffered a serious pelvic injury the following year as Boro struggled, missing out on the ZDS Final at Wembley in 1990. Rioch got the sack and an era was at an end.

Mowbray stayed around to help Boro to the 1991 Play-offs but he needed another challenge and, in November 1991, he joined Celtic, playing his last game in a 2–1 defeat at Barnsley. He was still only 27 but was ranked ninth in Boro's all-time appearance record. He suffered injuries at Parkhead but played in Europe and became a popular figure, starting the famous Celtic huddle on the pitch before games. He came back to Ayresome for an emotional testimonial with his new side and more than 20,000 turned out. Lennie Lawrence tried to re-sign him in 1993 but the clubs could not agree terms and [illegible]

signed Steve Vickers instead. He suffered tragedy in his personal life when he lost his wife Bernadette to cancer. He wrote a book about his life with Bernadette and her fight against the disease. His playing career later took him to Ipswich, where he narrowly missed out on promotion and was appointed their first-team coach in summer 1999. He went on to enjoy success as manager of Hibernian and is now in charge at West Bromwich Albion. Mowbray has said he would one day like to manage Boro.

MUIR John

Outside-left
Born: Details unknown.
Career: Leith Athletic. MIDDLESBROUGH 1902.

■ Muir was drafted in to strengthen Boro's squad for the first season in the First Division and played in the club's first ever match at the higher level, taking the number-11 shirt for a 1–0 win at Blackburn in 1902. Games were few and far between though and he was understudy to Chris Carrick for most of the season. He came back for the end of that season, playing in the last match at the Linthorpe Road ground against Stoke. He played just four more games in 1903–04, with Boro finishing mid-table in both his seasons.

MUIR William

Right-half
Born: Details unknown.
Career: Hamilton Academical. MIDDLESBROUGH 1902. Bradford City 1903.

■ Like his namesake John Muir, William was a member of the Boro side that played in the last game at the Linthorpe Road ground when he got a rare outing as a stand-in for half-back Abe Jones at number five in a First Division match against Stoke. He moved on that summer to Bradford along with Jimmy Millar.

MULHOLLAND Francis Gerard

Wing-half
Born: Belfast, 28 October 1927.
Career: Glentoran. MIDDLESBROUGH 1951. Poole Town 1958.

■ Irish left-half Mulholland was always on the fringes of the Boro side. He stayed on through Boro's decline from First Division front-runners to Second Division also-rans, making his debut in place of Jimmy Gordon against Charlton at Ayresome for a 2–1 win in January 1952, the side containing Mannion and Spuhler. A 5–0 defeat at Chelsea cost him his place soon after and he wasn't seen for almost a year, when he got another run in place of Russell. He was first choice at the start of the 1953–54 season but lost his place by mid-September as Gordon came back and got few further chances as Boro went down. He did play in the club's last First Division match, a 3–1 defeat at Arsenal which also ended Mannion's Boro career. He remained an occasional player for the rest of his spell at Ayresome but was awarded a benefit in 1957 and that earned him £750. He was put on the transfer list by Bob Dennison and released. He joined Poole in September 1958.

MURDOCH Robert White

Midfield
Born: Bothwell, 17 August 1944.
Died: 15 May 2001.
Career: Motherwell. Cambuslang Rangers. Glasgow Celtic 1959. MIDDLESBROUGH 1973.

■ Despite being one of the greatest players of his generation, it is hard to imagine a figure like Bobby Murdoch in the modern game. He was an inspired signing by Jack Charlton and completed the jigsaw that would take Boro to an easy Second Division Championship in 1973. Clearly overweight and famously fond of a cigar and a drink, he was said to enjoy gin as a pre-match tipple but his world class ball-playing skills still set him apart.

At Celtic he was a legend, winning eight consecutive titles and was one of the 'Lisbon Lions' who became the first British team to win the European Cup by beating Inter Milan 2–1 in 1967. A rampaging yet sophisticated player in his prime, he could lay on endless pinpoint passes and was the perfect link between defence and attack. He was admired by his own side and opponents alike. After that European night of 1967, the Inter coach Hellenio Herrara described him as 'my complete footballer' and Celtic boss Jock Stein rated him 'just about the best player I had as manager'.

Stein decided to accept Boro's audacious move for him because he felt Murdoch 'needed new challenges' and he stepped straight into the team against Blackpool in September 1973, replacing Eric McMordie. He scored a blistering goal against Bristol City on his home debut and pulled the strings for Boro from then on. He was on a different level to his Second Division opponents and helped along talented youngsters like Souness and Armstrong, dropping passes on a sixpence and controlling the pace of the game. His defence splitting passes opened the game up for Boro time after time and Alan Foggon was able to cash in by bursting clear to latch on to Murdoch's clever through balls. After that promotion year of 1974 he remained a regular for two more seasons in the First Division before becoming the club's youth coach in 1977.

He actually wanted to replace Charlton as boss that year but the directors appointed John Neal instead. He did a fine job in the backroom helping develop talent like Hodgson, Proctor and Johnston. He eventually got the top job in 1981 after Neal's departure but it coincided with the start of the club's fall from grace. The best players were sold and the replacements were not of the same standards and Boro went down in 1982. A disastrous start the following season, when the side lost their opening three home games 4–1, inevitably cost him his job, the last straw a dismal 4–1 defeat against Grimsby on a wet Ayresome night. He returned to live in Glasgow and died in 2001.

MURPHY David

Full-back
Born: Hartlepool 1 June 1984.
Career: MIDDLESBROUGH 2001. Barnsley (loan) 2003. Hibernian 2004.

■ Murphy, a strong-running left-back, looked an exciting prospect when he emerged from the Boro Academy in 2001. The powerfully-built youngster made his debut as a 17-year-old in a League Cup second-round win over Northampton, scoring the opening goal with a header to become the youngest Riverside goalscorer. He enjoyed a few outings from the bench the following spring during Steve McClaren's first season in charge. His Boro career never really took off, however. He suffered a metatarsal injury that took some time to heal. McClaren brought in Franck Queudrue as first-choice left-back and Murphy was given just four starts in 2003–04. Following a loan spell with Barnsley, he was surprisingly released to try his luck north of the border with Hibernian. It is in Scotland that he has enjoyed his best form, becoming a regular under former Boro great Tony Mowbray and his successor, John Collins. He has played in both the UEFA Cup and the Intertoto Cup during his spell at Easter Road and was also a member of the side that won the Scottish League Cup in March 2007.

MURPHY David Anthony

Left-half
Born: South Bank, 19 July 1917.
Died: September 1944.
Career: South Bank St Peters.
MIDDLESBROUGH 1937.

■ A promising career was brought to an end by the war and sadly Murphy did not come home, killed in the Middle East in September 1944. A South Bank lad, he was brought up with Wilf Mannion and the pair would travel in to Ayresome together. He was 20 when he made his debut in a 3–1 defeat against Bolton at the end of the 1937–38 season at half-back in place of Bill Forrest. His chances were always limited, though he did step in for Forrest a few more times the following season in a fine Boro side that finished fourth in Division One. He was in the side early in the 1939–40 season and played in the last match before the outbreak of war at home to Stoke on 2 September 1939. He continued to play for the club during the war years and was so dedicated he once borrowed a stranger's bike to get to Ayresome after missing the bus from Redcar. Forced to travel by train, he arrived late at Middlesbrough train station and needed to cycle on to Ayresome to make it for kick-off.

MURPHY Thomas Edwin

Inside-forward
Born: Middlesbrough, 25 March 1921.
Career: South Bank St Peters.
MIDDLESBROUGH 1939. Blackburn Rovers 1947. Halifax Town 1949.

■ To find a good footballer in the 1930s you could simply get the bus to South Bank and sign up the first teenager you came across. That's the way it must have seemed given the apparently endless list of players Boro signed up in that era. Murphy was a part of this tradition, signing from South Bank St Peter's in 1939 only for the war to put his professional career on a very lengthy hold. Standing only 5ft 5in, the little inside-forward served with the navy but did play war games for the club, blasting a hat-trick just before the Football League re-started against Blackburn. He was quickly introduced to the starting line-up, at Manchester United in 1946–47, as Boro lost 1–0 in a game switched to Maine Road because of bomb damage at Old Trafford. He took George Dews' place in that game and replaced Johnny Spuhler for the next at home to Preston, a 2–0 win. He was always on the fringes and scored only once, in a 5–0 win over Blackpool. His solitary appearance of the next season was as a stand-in for Wilf Mannion for a home defeat against Portsmouth. He moved on to Blackburn shortly after that. Rovers boss Jack Bruton remembered that wartime hat-trick against his side and beat off Grimsby to snap him up, with Boro pulling him out of a squad to face Manchester United so the move could go through. Relegated in his first season with Rovers, he enjoyed the satisfaction of scoring in a 1–1 draw at Ayresome Park five months after leaving Boro. He later had a long spell at Halifax before returning to live on Teesside.

MURPHY Joseph

Inside-left
Born: Ireland.
Career: MIDDLESBROUGH 1894.

■ Here's a good pub quiz question. What have Joe Murphy, occasional Boro forward of 1899, and Fabrizio Ravanelli got in common? The answer is they are the only two Middlesbrough players to score a debut hat-trick. Murphy has cheated here somewhat, as he did play for the club in the amateur days, but his first game as a professional against Burton Swifts in November 1899 saw him score three as Boro won 8–1 at Linthorpe Road. It took another 97 years for Rav to repeat the feat, against Liverpool. As for Murphy, the Irishman was soon left out of the side again and played only six games in all, scoring five goals. He was freed in 1900. During Boro's pre-League days, Murphy had played in the 1895 Amatuer Cup Final victory over Old Carthusians.

MURPHY Michael

Inside-left
Born: Details unknown.
Career: South Bank.
MIDDLESBROUGH 1899.

■ Like his namesake Joe, this Murphy is noted for a Boro goalscoring feat and absolutely nothing else. The former South Bank player replaced Bob Page to score Boro's first home League goal against Small Heath on 9 September 1899. The game was still lost, 3–1, and Murphy was dropped. He won a recall a few months later and scored again in a 3–0 win over Loughborough.

MURRAY Alan

Midfield
Born: Newcastle, 5 December 1949.
Career: MIDDLESBROUGH 1967. York City (loan) 1972. Brentford 1972. Doncaster Rovers 1973.

■ Murray played only a bit part as a Middlesbrough player but went on to have a long career in the lower divisions and moved into management and coaching. The midfielder could not have had a better start as a youngster when he replaced Joe Laidlaw for a Second Division game at home to Blackburn in January 1970. Primarily a fast and skilful winger, Murray marked his full debut with a goal in a 4–1 win. He played only

a handful of games that season and had to wait until the end of the following season for another chance, replacing Alan Moody for a draw at Portsmouth. Stan Anderson allowed him to go to Brentford and he later had a long spell at Doncaster. After his playing career, he spent three years back at Boro as the club's commercial manager before moving back into the football side. He was in a similar role at Hartlepool when he stepped in to replace Cyril Knowles, who was suffering from a brain tumour. He helped Pools to promotion from Division Four and they had a good season after going up, with a mid-table finish. A run of six defeats cost him his job in 1993 but he was soon to take over at Darlington. Graeme Souness appointed him to the backroom staff at Southampton and he followed Souness to Benfica, acting as a caretaker manager after Souness was fired. He was also a member of the Souness backroom team at Blackburn and Newcastle.

MURRAY Thomas

Inside-forward/Outside-left
Born: Middlesbrough, 7 April 1889.
Died: 1976.
Career: MIDDLESBROUGH 1905. Glasgow Rangers. Heart of Midlothian. Bradford City 1913. Hull City 1913.

■ A goal against Forest in his second game for the club wasn't enough to keep Thomas Murray in the side for long. Boro had lost 3–0 at Sheffield Wednesday and 4–0 at Manchester City either side of that result and boss Alex Mackie left him out for the rest of that season, Tom Green taking over. He managed another flurry of games in the number-11 shirt midway through the next season, mainly at Jim Thackeray's expense, but he scored only once more, in a 3–1 defeat at Manchester City. New boss Andy Aitken let him go to Aberdeen in 1907.

MURRAY William

Inside-left/Outside-left
Born: South Church, 1898.
Career: Eildon Lane. Bishop Auckland. Derby County 1920. MIDDLESBROUGH 1921. Heart Of Midlothian. Dunfermline Athletic.

■ Boro signed the England amateur international from Derby. He earned his cap while with Bishop Auckland, playing against Belgium, but the diminutive inside-left was rarely in the first-team picture at Ayresome. He replaced Tom Urwin for three games at the end of the 1921–22 season and had another run in 1922–23, again mainly for Urwin, scoring his only Boro goal in a 2–0 win over Spurs on 30 December 1922. At Derby, he had suffered relegation to the Second Division so the chance to join Boro was a step up. Murray later played in Scotland.

MUSTOE Robin (Robbie)

Midfield
Born: Witney, 28 August 1968.
Career: Oxford United 1986. MIDDLESBROUGH 1990. Charlton Athletic 2002. Sheffield Wednesday 2003.

■ Robbie Mustoe played under five managers and was fantastic value for his £375,000 transfer fee. He lies 18th in Boro's all-time list of appearance makers, his 367 games putting him one behind the immortal Wilf Mannion. Mustoe also holds the club record for the most League Cup appearances. He arrived at Ayresome Park in 1990 when gates were down to 6,000 and the club was struggling for its very existence. He left in 2002 having distinguished himself in top-class international company in front of 30,000-plus crowds at the Riverside. Colin Todd signed him on the same day as John Hendrie in 1990. Noted for his 'good engine', his debut was alongside John Wark in a goalless home draw against West Ham, when he did enough running for the two of them. His energy quickly endeared him to the fans and he made a seamless transition to a side challenging strongly for promotion. He was just as impressive under Todd's successor, Lennie Lawrence, and was a regular until he got injured in the Rumbelows Cup semi-final epic at Old Trafford in 1992, missing out as his teammates won promotion. Like the rest of the side, his first taste of the Premier League was hard going and Mustoe missed almost half the games as Boro went back down. That grim season of 1992–93 was illuminated by the pairing of Mustoe and Jamie Pollock in midfield and, when Bryan Robson took over, he

quickly realised the potential, keeping the dynamic duo together. Robson knew little about the unsung Mustoe on arrival and actually left him out so he could play himself at first. It didn't take him long to become an admirer of the player and he was once again given the job of holding Boro's midfield together. Mustoe was magnificent in the new formation that followed promotion. He was in the side that played the first game at the Riverside, forming a two-man midfield with Pollock in a new wing-back system. In the dramatic year of 1996–97, he played in the great Cup runs and both Wembley Finals, though he was injured early in the FA Cup Final against Chelsea. Mustoe was just as influential in the 1997–98 promotion season and was there as his old club Oxford were beaten 4–1 to clinch a rapid return to the Premier League in May. He appeared in his third Wembley Final, another Coca-Cola defeat, against Chelsea.

He was a mainstay of the side that achieved a ninth-placed finish the following year and went on to forge strong links with a succession of midfield partners, including Paul Ince. The arrival of Christian Karembeu, Noel Whelan and Paul Okon – and Terry Venables to select the team – in 2000 saw him having to take a seat on the bench for much of that season, but he was quickly back to first choice in Steve McClaren's first year in charge when he proved himself to be one of the fittest members of the squad.

With George Boateng, Geremi and Juninho added to the squad in summer 2002, Mustoe was on his way, despite being offered the chance to stay on Teesside. He chose to try his luck with Derby, but financial problems at Pride Park meant the Rams were unable to offer him a contract and he signed a short-term agreement with Charlton. He then spent a season with Sheffield Wednesday in 2003–04 before leaving for a new life in the USA, where he is involved in coaching and media work.

MUTTITT Ernest

Inside-left/Left-half
Born: Middlesbrough, 24 July 1908.
Died: August 1996.
Career: South Bank.
MIDDLESBROUGH 1929. Brentford 1932. Dartford. Dover.

■ Having made his name in the local Leagues with South Bank, local lad Ernie Muttitt could not have asked for a better debut when he took Owen Williams' place for a match at Arsenal in November 1929. He scored the winner to clinch a 2–1 win but was able to play only a handful more games before Fred Warren took his berth. He struggled to get a game in a good Boro side the following season and it was the same story in 1931–32, though he did replace George Camsell on the closing day of the campaign for a 1–1 draw with Leicester. That summer he was one of three Boro players snapped up by Brentford and he enjoyed a successful time in London, helping The Bees from Third to First Division and actually playing against Boro for Brentford. He also guested for Charlton during the war. A fan of horse racing, golf and swimming, Ernie Muttitt died of cancer near Brentford, aged 88, in August 1996.

MYTON Brian

Left-back
Born: York, 26 September 1950.
Career: MIDDLESBROUGH 1967. Southend United (loan) 1971.

■ Imagine waiting for your debut, getting called up, and then being sent off. That's what happened to Brian Myton. Stan Anderson gave him a place at centre-back in place of the injured Frank

Spraggon at Cardiff in September 1968 but he was given his marching orders in a 2–0 defeat and didn't get another chance for seven months. This time the tough-tackling, workmanlike Myton replaced Gordon Jones at left-back for a 2–0 defeat at Charlton. He didn't appear in a winning Boro side until April 1970, when Cardiff were beaten 2–1 at Ayresome. His last Boro games came at the start of the 1970–71 season when he took Jones' place after a disappointing start to the season, making his final appearance in a draw at home to Blackburn. He moved on for a brief spell at Southend.

NASH Carlo James

Goalkeeper
Born: Bolton, 13 September 1973.
Career: Clitheroe. Crystal Palace 1996. Stockport County 1998. Manchester City 2001. MIDDLESBROUGH 2003. Preston North End 2005. Wigan Athletic (loan) 2007. Wigan Athletic 2007.

■ Carlo Nash was spotted keeping goal for Clitheroe against Brigg Town in the 1996 FA Vase Final and signed by Crystal Palace. A part-time model, he helped the Eagles win promotion to the Premiership via the Play-offs in his first season at Selhurst Park. However, following the signing of Kevin Miller, Nash did not appear at all for Palace in 1997–98 and in the close season he moved to Stockport County. Arriving at Edgeley Park under the Bosman rule, he had a great first couple of seasons. Due to be out of contract in the summer of 2001, the club cashed in by selling him to Manchester City for £100,000. Nash had to bide his time at Maine Road, eventually making his debut against

Arsenal but finding himself picking the ball out of the net four times before he had the chance to make a save. Following City's relegation, he lost his place to Peter Schmeichel and joined Middlesbrough as cover for Mark Schwarzer. Nash patiently waited for his debut chance and this came in a 2–0 win at Villa Park in November 2003, but this was to be his only appearance of the season. He was out for over six months with a ruptured tendon in a finger and only returned to reserve-team football towards the end of the campaign. He fared a little better in 2004–05, playing some four games spread over as many months, but with Brad Jones gaining rave reviews he opted for a move to Preston North End. Nash made some telling contributions to the club's Play-off effort with some terrific saves in the Final against West Ham. Ever present in 2005–06, he set a new individual record for clean sheets in League games. He returned to the Premier League with Wigan in 2007.

NASH Frank Cooper (Paddy)

Goalkeeper
Born: Middlesbrough, 30 June 1918.
Died: 1989.
Career: South Bank.
MIDDLESBROUGH 1937. Southend United 194[illegible]

■ The ups and downs of life as a footballer were placed into sharp perspective for Paddy Nash. The South Bank lad's career was interrupted by the war in 1939. Nash was captured in enemy occupied France soon after and spent four-and-a-half years trapped in a prisoner of war camp. Goalkeeper Nash belonged to the same generation of talented South Bank youngsters as Wilf Mannion. He played as a centre-half for Prince's Street School and progressed to the South Bank East End club. When he signed on for Boro in 1937, he and Mannion would travel into Ayresome together. Nash was understudy to Dave Cumming and made his debut against Preston in a team containing Camsell and Fenton but got to play in only 16 games before the war began. After coming out of the POW camp he did play some war games but let in 11 as Boro were thrashed by Newcastle in 1945. Doubtless that was far from being the worst of his war experiences and he was still around when the League restarted in 1946. He replaced Cumming in games at Everton and Brentford before joining Southend. He returned to Teesside to work at ICI Billingham for 35 years and coached Billingham Synthonia. Paddy Nash was a well-known Teesside figure as chairman of both South Bank and Hemlington Social Club. He died in 1989.

NATTRASS Irving

Right-back
Born: Fishburn, 20 December 1952.
Career: Newcastle United 1970. MIDDLESBROUGH 1979.

■ A cool and refined defender, Irving Nattrass became Boro's record signing when John Neal paid £475,000 for him in the summer of 1979. That record lasted more than nine years until Peter Davenport signed in 1988. Nattrass started out with Newcastle United where he seemed destined for great things. He became captain at United and played in their League Cup Final defeat of 1976. His confidence at full-back and central defence led many to tip him for an England place. Injuries plagued his career, however, and he missed England's tour of South America in 1977 when a first cap loomed. A few years earlier a knee ligament injury had robbed him of

an FA Cup Final berth. When the Magpies were relegated in 1978 it was time for him to move on and within a year he had opted for Boro – ahead of Spurs and Manchester City.

The old injury jinx followed him to Teesside as his debut was delayed until September by an Achilles injury and the next six months brought no less than three hairline fractures of the leg. He had a better run the following year as Neal's team looked set for honours but from then on it was downhill for the club. Nattrass was made captain by Malcolm Allison in 1983 but he was often criticised for supposedly playing within himself. His career ended on a sad note when Boro were relegated to Division Three in 1986 and Nattrass was freed by Bruce Rioch. He later set up a retail clothing business in Chester-le-Street and Gateshead.

NEAL Richard Marshall

Wing-half
Born: Dinnington, 1 October 1933.
Career: Wolverhampton Wanderers 1951. Lincoln City 1954. Birmingham City 1957. MIDDLESBROUGH 1961. Lincoln City 1963. Rugby Town.

■ Tall wing-half Neal followed in the footsteps of his uncle Fred Gibson when he joined Boro in 1961. Gibson had been Boro's keeper in the 1930s. His nephew, an England Under-23 international, came in from Birmingham where he had established himself after an equally successful time at Lincoln. Things didn't work out so well at Ayresome where games came less frequently. He did play in one particularly memorable game for Boro in his first season, a 5–4 defeat at Norwich in which he scored. Capable of spraying passes out to wide positions, he was often vying for the number six shirt with Billy Horner. When Raich Carter replaced Bob Dennison as boss in 1963, Neal found himself out of favour and played only once under the new boss before being allowed to go back to Lincoln. After his playing days he worked in a brewery.

NEMETH Szilard

Forward
Born: Karmarna, Slovakia, 8 August 1977.
Career: Slovan Bratislava (Slovakia) 1994. Kosice (Slovakia) 1997. Sparta Prague (Czech Republic) (loan) 1998. Inter Bratislava 1999. MIDDLESBROUGH 2001. Strasbourg (France) (loan) 2006. Alemannia Aachen (Germany) 2006.

■ Following Vladimir Kinder, Szilard Nemeth became the second Slovakian to play for Boro when joining from Inter Bratislava. Nemeth was the last signing made by Bryan Robson, who allegedly beat off interest from Inter Milan for the player, but by the time he arrived Steve McClaren had taken over as manager. Having scored 24 goals in 29 starts for Inter Bratislava in 2000–01, Nemeth had been watched in action for his country by backroom staff Gordon McQueen and Ray Train before Robson travelled out with coach Terry Venables and chief executive Keith Lamb to get a second opinion. The free transfer deal was clinched when Nemeth scored twice in the opening minutes of the game. Much of his time at the Riverside was frustrating for Nemeth, who scored 29 goals in 146 appearances. His record at international level was much better, scoring 21 times in 55 games to become his young country's all-time top scorer. Despite arriving with an injury and consequently missing much of the pre-season, he made his Boro debut in August 2001 in a 2–0 defeat at Everton, but scored

on his home debut in a Carling Cup win over Northampton Town on 11 September 2001, a date forever synonymous with atrocities in New York when the twin towers were attacked. But the goals were slow to come at domestic level and the next season only brought three from 21 League games, while scoring six in seven for Slovakia. His third season with Boro brought a top-scoring nine goals but included a run of 16 games in which he scored just once. But there was always the feeling that there were goals in Nemeth, who often gave the impression that when used as a substitute he would take the field with a point to prove. Six goals came the following season, including a crucial strike at Anfield as Boro pushed for a UEFA Cup spot. With Mark Viduka, Jimmy Floyd Hasselbaink, Yakubu and Massimo Maccarone all ahead of him in the pecking order, the season that followed, 2005–06, proved to be his last in England as he was released in January 2006 and joined Strasbourg. He wasn't kept on by the French side at the end of that season and joined German side Alemmania Aachen. Having played just 15 minutes for his new club, he was taken seriously ill in November 2006 when he suffered a pulmonary embolism after thrombosis developed following a calf injury. Fortunately the life-threatening condition was discovered early enough and his life was saved. He made a goalscoring return in May 2007, though Aachen were relegated from the Bundesliga after finishing second bottom.

NIBLO Thomas Bruce

Centre-forward/Winger
Born: Dunfermline, 24 September 1877.
Died: Newcastle, July 1993.
Career: Hamilton Academical. Linthouse. Newcastle United 1897. MIDDLESBROUGH (loan) 1899. Aston Villa 1901. Nottingham Forest 1904. Watford. Hebburn Argyle. Aberdeen. Raith Rovers. Cardiff City. Blyth Spartans.

■ Things weren't going at all well as Boro's initial League season drew to a close in 1900. They had conceded 14 goals in four matches without reply and lost each of the last two away games 5–0. John Robson clearly knew it was time to act and brought in a forward from Newcastle by the name of Niblo. The story of Niblo's Boro career is as brief as it was successful. He made an immediate impact by scoring in both of his first two games and helped arrest the slide as we held Loughborough and beat Newton Heath – but then they were never very good. What happened next remains something of a mystery as Niblo played only once more for Boro, in the final game of that season when they lost 3–0 at Sheffield Wednesday. It is thought he came on loan but for whatever reason he didn't stay. Niblo, who could play in all five forward positions and was noted for his educated left foot, moved back to Newcastle instead. Niblo enoyed a varied career as a hard-working front runner with stylish dribbling skills, though he was criticised for trying to take on too many opponents and for his inconsistency. He later won a Scotland cap with Aston Villa and stayed in the game until well into his 30s, finishing at Cardiff in 1911. Niblo was wounded in World War One and later settled in Newcastle, working as a publican. His son Alan also made it on to Newcastle's books. Tom Niblo died in July 1933.

NICHOLL James

Outside-left/Inside-left
Born: Port Glasgow.
Career: MIDDLESBROUGH 1910. Liverpool 1913.

■ James Nicholl was the hero of one of Boro's big games of the pre-war era. Such was the interest in the clash with Sunderland on December 3 1910, the entire local League programme was cancelled and a crowd of 27,980 packed Ayresome. Boro ran out 1–0 winners thanks to wide man Nicholl's 25th minute goal. At the time both sides were riding high, though Boro faltered and ended up 16th. Nicholl's career by the Tees peaked in his first season with Eyre holding the number-11 shirt for most of his later seasons here. A bright and incisive inside or outside-left, he moved to Liverpool and played in the 1914 FA Cup Final when the Reds lost 1–0 to Burnley.

NOBBS Alan Keith

Right-back
Born: Bishop Auckland, 18 September 1961.

Career: MIDDLESBROUGH 1979. Halifax Town 1982. Bishop Auckland. Hartlepool United 1985.

■ Nobbs was part of the production line of juniors to make it to the first team under John Neal. He had been signed by Neal from school and could play at full-back or centre-back. His lack of height was a disadvantage at centre-back but he was good in the air for his height and a hard tackler. Nobbs played in only one senior game for Boro, a 1–0 home defeat against Coventry in April 1981 in the dying embers of Neal's reign. He was released the following year and played for Halifax before dropping out of the League to join his home town club, Bishop Auckland. Nobbs soon returned to the professional ranks with Hartlepool and gave sterling service at the Victoria Ground over many years.

NORRIS Oliver

Centre-forward
Born: Derry, 1 April 1929.
Career: MIDDLESBROUGH 1948. Worcester City. Bournemouth 1955. Northampton Town 1958. Ashford Town. Rochdale 1961. Gloucester City.

■ Norris is one of many players, from Shackleton to Gascoigne, to have been dubbed the 'clown prince of soccer'. Nicknamed 'Narker', the Irishman joined Boro from Londonderry juniors and worked his way through the ranks before finally making his debut in 1952 at Newcastle as an outside-right while Lindy Delapenha was out of the side. Boro won 2–0 but it was a false dawn for Norris. New boss Walter Rowley tried to sell him to West Brom soon after but the player refused. He made sporadic appearances from then on as a centre-forward or wing-forward, enjoying his best run early in the 1952–53 season. He took over the famous Johnny Spuhler's shirt and scored at Blackpool and Tottenham – the latter a 7–1 thrashing. He was finally placed on the transfer list at the end of the 1953–54 season. He tried to join Worcester but Boro held his registration and he moved to Bournemouth in 1955 where he had his best spell before a brief time at Northampton. Norris moved into player-management with Gloucester City in 1959 but was sacked after six months. He ended up emigrating to Australia and played for Hakouk while Down Under and worked as coach for the Australian Soccer Federation. He was also a director of coaching in Victoria.

NORTON Paul

Midfield
Born: Middlesbrough, 15 October 1975.
Career: MIDDLESBROUGH 1993.

■ Local lad Paul Norton progressed through the Boro ranks and, though his career was short-lived, he achieved the distinction of appearing for his home town club when replacing Robbie Mustoe in an Anglo-Italian Cup game in Udinese in 1994. A defensive, left-sided midfielder, he had been a sub in a League game at Portsmouth under Lennie Lawrence the previous season, though he didn't get on. A competitive player who was rated as a good passer, he was released by Bryan Robson in 1995.

NURSE Melvyn Tudor George

Centre-half
Born: Swansea, 11 October 1937.
Career: Swansea City 1955. MIDDLESBROUGH 1962. Swindon Town 1965. Swansea City 1968. Bury Town. Merthyr Tydfil.

■ Brian Clough's patience with Boro's notoriously porous defence had run out by the time Welsh centre-half Mel Nurse arrived. Clough was frustrated at Boro's inability to keep goals out at the other end while he banged them in by the sackful. A year after Clough went, boss Bob Dennison shored things up by bringing Nurse from Swansea for a club record fee of £25,000. A Welsh international, he had joined the Swans, his hometown club, from school having already won Schoolboy caps for Wales. At well over 6ft, he was the kingpin of a defence and quickly made it to

Swansea's first team and the national Under-23 side. He had marked Boro's Alan Peacock in an international shortly before coming to Ayresome, though Peacock did find the net.

Boro did well to get him for £25,000 as Manchester United made a £35,000 offer two years before, just after the Munich Air Disaster, but Swansea turned it down. He was actually keen to stay in Wales but was told by the Swansea directors that he would never play again if he did not join Boro. After signing for £25 a week, Nurse's debut came in a typically end-to-end Boro performance as they beat Grimsby 4–3. He must have wondered what he had come into as they conceded 21 goals in his first seven games. But Nurse impressed the boss and was made skipper within a week of joining. Boro finished fourth in that first season but from then on it was a struggle for the club and, in his final year, 1964–65, Boro ended up 17th. Nurse was unsettled under the reign of new boss Raich Carter and, with his wife homesick, Boro put him on the transfer list. A move back to the West Country followed with Swindon but he ended his professional days back home with Swansea, who he had the unfortunate experience of relegating by scoring a crucial goal against them for Boro in 1965. Boro certainly suffered after he went as the next season they were relegated to Division Three. Nurse played a dozen games for Wales but was unlucky that his time coincided with that of John Charles and Mike England. No profile of Nurse would be complete without mentioning a bizarre incident in 1963 when he and his wife were stopped by police outside a cinema – wrongly believing he was one of the great train robbers! Nurse's playing days ended when he broke a leg playing for Merthyr Tydfil. Nurse later joined the board at Swansea for a time and ran a country club hotel in the city as part of a property empire.

O'CONNELL Seamus

Inside-forward
Born: Carlisle, 1 January 1930.
Career: Queen's Park Rangers. MIDDLESBROUGH 1953. Bishop Auckland. Chelsea 1954. Crook Town. Carlisle United 1958. Crook Town.

■ What have the following got in common: Chelsea, Crook Town, Boro and Bishop Auckland? The answer is that Seamus O'Connell played for them all. He enjoyed a fine amateur career, representing England and winning an Amateur Cup at that level. Although his Boro record was limited to three games he had the distinction of replacing the injured Wilf Mannion at inside-forward for a game at Newcastle on Boxing Day 1953, when he scored in a 3–2 win. He hit the target again a few days later as Boro beat Spurs 3–0 but played only once more before Mannion returned. He could have extended his appearance record but withdrew from a game at Blackpool to play for Bishop Auckland in an Amateur Cup tie. After leaving Boro, he was part of a Chelsea Championship-winning side and, though he wasn't a regular, he did score a hat-trick in a game which Chelsea lost 6–5.

O'HAGAN Charles

Inside-left
Born: Buncrana, 1882.
Career: St Columb's College. Derry Celtic. Old Xaverians. Everton 1903. Tottenham Hotspur 1904. MIDDLESBROUGH 1906. Aberdeen 1906. Greenock Morton.

■ Inside-forward O'Hagan, described as a 'born entertainer', didn't hang around too long at Boro. He started out at Derry Celtic before moving to Liverpool to play for top local amateur side Old Xavierians. He later signed on for Everton but was restricted to their reserve side. O'Hagan played in the

Southern League for Spurs, scoring eight goals in 37 games, before joining Boro. He took the place of Alf Common and played three successive games, scoring once. O'Hagan played only twice more after that, the last a draw at Sheffield United, before heading north of the border to Aberdeen. His time in Scotland was his best and he became Aberdeen's first capped player. He made 11 appearances for Northern Ireland but his career was brought to an end by World War One, where he served with the Highland Light Infantry. He tried his hand at management with Norwich City but it took him until November to get his first victory and quit after winning only four out of 22 games.

O'HALLORAN Keith James

Midfield
Born: Dublin, 10 November 1975.
Career: Cherry Orchard BC (Ireland). MIDDLESBROUGH 1994. Scunthorpe United (loan) 1996. Cardiff City (loan) 1996. St Johnstone 1997. Swindon Town 2000. Shamrock Rovers (Ireland) 2004.

■ An injury crisis as Boro went for promotion in Bryan Robson's first season meant midfielder O'Halloran was pitched in to a game against Derby at Ayresome as a right full-back. But it turned out to be a baptism of fire as he came up against experienced winger Paul Simpson and Boro were three down at half-time. He was taken off at the interval with Boro eventually going down 4–2. A product of Ireland's Cherry Orchard Boys Club, he showed fine form for the reserves and got another chance the next year at Chelsea. Unfortunately for him, it was another bad day for Boro as they went down 5–0, this time with O'Halloran in midfield. His third and final start came a few weeks later at the Riverside against struggling Bolton. If Keith wasn't already beginning to feel jinxed he would have done after another thrashing, this time by 4–1. O'Halloran moved to Cardiff on loan and settled at Scottish Premier Division side St Johnstone, where he played alongside Alan Kernaghan, before spells with Swindon and Shamrock Rovers.

O'HANLON Kelham Gerard

Goalkeeper
Born: Saltburn, 16 May 1962.
Career: MIDDLESBROUGH 1980. Rotherham United 1985. Carlisle United 1991. Preston North End 1993. Dundee United. Preston North End 1996.

■ Local lad O'Hanlon worked his way through the Boro ranks and served his time as understudy to established keeper Jim Platt. When Malcolm Allison took over as boss in 1982 it was suddenly Platt who found himself in the shadows. O'Hanlon's debut came a few months after Allison signed, for a 1–1 draw at home to Sheffield Wednesday in January 1983, and he held his place until Steve Pears came in on loan the following season. A chirpy character in the dressing room, his form had dipped in that 1983–84 season, though Allison came up with a novel excuse, claiming O'Hanlon was put off by a terrorist death threat! Boro couldn't afford Pears on a permanent basis and in 1984–85 O'Hanlon became the only keeper on the books with any first-team experience so he was excused rigorous training on a Friday in case he got injured. His final game was a happy one as Boro beat Shrewsbury 2–0 to stay in the Second Division. When Pears did sign, in the summer of 1985, O'Hanlon was allowed to leave and became a much travelled 'keeper with clubs including Rotherham, Preston and Dundee United. In 1988, he was capped by the Republic of Ireland in a game against Israel.

OKON Paul Michael

Central defender/Midfield
Born: Sydney, Australia, 5 April 1972.
Career: Marconi Fairfield (Australia) 1989. Brugge (Belgium) 1991. Lazio (Italy) 1996. Fiorentina 1999. MIDDLESBROUGH 2000. Watford 2002. Leeds United 2002. Vicenza (Italy) 2003. Oostende (Belgium) 2004. Apoel (Cyprus) 2005. Newcastle Jets (Australia) 2006.

■ An Australia legend, Okon was a classy midfielder who suffered a serious knee injury when playing in Italy. It was an injury that robbed the player of his pace, but certainly didn't inhibit his ability to pass a ball. Former captain of the Australian national team, Okon arrived at the Riverside in the summer of 2000 on a Bosman free transfer from Fiorentina. Bryan Robson fought off stiff competition from Ajax, Lazio and Anderlecht to sign the cultured player, who could operate in the centre of defence or midfield. Okon made his debut in a 3–1 win away to Coventry City on the opening day of the 2000–01 season, with his final game coming in a 3–0 Boxing Day defeat by Newcastle at St James' Park in 2001. Okon started his

career at Sydney Marconi but after just two seasons he signed for Belgian side Brugges. Here he started on his outstanding record of success, winning the Belgian Player of the Year award before the lure of the Lira lead him to Lazio. Serie A caused him no worries as he was rated Lazio's best player in his debut season in Italy. Three years later he joined Fiorentina where he played in a world class line up including Gabriel Batistuta and Rui Costa. In total he won six trophies in Europe. A broken foot caused him to miss the Olympic Games in his hometown, Sydney, but he had represented his country at the Barcelona Olympics in 1992. Used as sweeper by Boro coach Terry Venables during the successful battle against relegation in 2000–01, Okon went on loan to Watford towards the end of his stay with Boro, having fallen out of favour under Steve McClaren's management. He eventually moved permanently to Leeds on a free transfer. From there he moved on to play for Vicenza in Italy, Ostende of Belgium, APOEL in Cyprus and latterly Newcastle Jets back in Australia. He announced his retirement at the end of the 2006–07 season.

OLIVER Michael

Midfield
Born: Middlesbrough, 2 August 1975.
Career: MIDDLESBROUGH 1992. Stockport County 1994. Darlington 1996. Rochdale 2000.

■ Middlesbrough born and bred, Michael Oliver was restricted to the fringes of the first team with Boro. Having played for Cleveland Juniors at Under-10 level alongside Phil Stamp and Paul Norton, he progressed to Middlesbrough juniors and Cleveland County schools. He was sounded out by Everton and Sunderland but chose to sign for Boro after attending the school of excellence. He supported the club as a boy from the Holgate End with Tony Mowbray his hero. He skippered the youth team as a hard-running midfielder and appeared alongside Phil Stamp and Mark Summerbell, signing professional on his 17th birthday. Despite being the club's Young Player of the Year in 1994, Oliver's first-team chances were restricted to a substitute's appearance at Ayresome against Ancona in November 1993 in the Anglo-Italian Cup, when he replaced John Gannon. He was a non-playing substitute in a League Cup defeat against Sheffield Wednesday a week earlier. Determined to leave, Oliver was allowed to join Stockport as Bryan Robson's reign got underway in 1994 and a Football League tribunal set his fee at £15,000. He became a frequent first teamer at Darlington before three years with Rochdale.

O'NEILL Keith Padre Gerard

Midfield
Born: Dublin, 16 February 1976
Career: Home Farm. Norwich City 1994. MIDDLESBROUGH 1999. Coventry City 2001.

■ Hard-working Irishman Keith O'Neill was an instant hit with Boro fans when Bryan Robson bought him from Norwich City in 1999 for £700,000. The Boro manager had watched him for three years and at one time it was rumoured that Newcastle were prepared to offer £4 million for him. But injuries affected his availability. He played almost 100 games for Norwich, whom he joined as a trainee, before Bruce Rioch allowed him to move to Teesside. Fast, strong and direct, he could play as winger, striker, midfielder or full-back and the fans loved his no-holds-barred tackling and willingess to run at defenders. He played for Ireland at all levels and won a dozen full caps. O'Neill was one of the first victims of Steve McClaren's squad overhaul and he left the club for Coventry in a £1 million deal shortly after the new manager's arrival in 2001. He played just 42 games for the Sky Blues. After impressing in his early games, O'Neill was struck down by a pelvic injury and he was sidelined until the end of the season when he suffered a double fracture of his left leg in a freak training ground incident. Despite making a brief substitute appearance in 2003–04, he was forced to announce his retirement from the game and took up a new role in the Christmas crackers business.

O'RIORDAN Donal Joseph

Centre-half/Midfield
Born: Dublin, 14 May 1957.
Career: Derby County 1975. Doncaster Rovers (loan) 1978. Tulsa Roughnecks (United States) 1978. Preston North End 1978. Carlisle United 1983. MIDDLESBROUGH 1985. Grimsby Town 1986. Notts County 1988. Mansfield Town (loan) 1989. Torquay United 1993. Scarborough 1995. Gloucester City. Dorchester Town.

■ Don O'Riordan was expected to be part of a Boro revival when Willie Maddren signed him from Carlisle in 1985. But it turned out to be a disappointing year for the player and Boro as they went down in his one and only season at the club. Maddren made him skipper and he played in all but one game but, although he was a good passer and calm on the ball, his goals return wasn't what was expected from the midfield driving force. When Boro went bust he exercised his right to leave and joined Grimsby. He had a varied career, joining Derby around the time they won the League in 1975, but became a journeyman in the lower divisions apart from a spell with Tulsa Roughnecks in the US where he played against the likes of Beckenbauer and Cruyff. The best times of his career came at Carlisle and Grimsby and his playing days had a late flourish as

he helped Notts County back into the old Division One – at Boro's expense in the Play-offs. Sadly, he was injured in the opening top flight game at Manchester United and missed the rest of the season. O'Riordan also had spells as assistant manager at Grimsby and as boss at Torquay.

ORMEROD Anthony

Winger
Born: Middlesbrough, 31 March 1979.
Career: MIDDLESBROUGH 1996. Carlisle United (loan) 1999. York City (loan) 1999. Hartlepool United (loan) 2001. Scarborough 2002. Whitby Town 2003.

■ Anthony Ormerod was one of a crop of young players who burst on to the scene under Bryan Robson but failed to live up to their early potential. Injuries also cost him the chance of a more extended career at the Riverside. The Brotton-born player came through the youth ranks with Andy Campbell and Steve Baker. Having trained with Boro's school of excellence from nine years old, he had trials with Manchester United, Leeds and at the FA National School at Lilleshall before signing on a two-year Boro training scheme. He edged towards the first-team scene in the relegation year of 1996–97 with appearances as a non-playing substitute. Skilful and hard working, he then had a dream debut the following season with a fine goal at Bradford in a 2–2 draw when he had expected to be turning out for the club's juniors against Crystal Palace. For the next few months he was a regular feature in the first team, playing mainly wide on the right. A former England Under-16 and Under-18 player, the pacy Ormerod fell out of favour when Bryan Robson turned to the club's more experienced stars and he struggled to get a look-in with Boro back in the Premier League. He had a loan spell at Carlisle and another with York early in the 1999–2000 season. Still unable to win a regular place at the Riverside, he had a further loan period with Hartlepool before a short spell with Scarborough. He later joined Unibond League side Whitby, where he had spent four years by 2007.

O'ROURKE John

Centre-forward
Born: Northampton, 11 February 1945.
Career: Arsenal. Chelsea 1962. Luton Town 1963. MIDDLESBROUGH 1966. Ipswich Town 1968. Coventry City 1969. Queen's Park Rangers 1971. Bournemouth 1974.

■ O'Rourke became a Holgate hero during his 18-month spell at Ayresome. The crowd would sing 'Give us a goal, John O'Rourke' as his goals blasted Boro to promotion from Division Three. Stan Anderson gambled on the young O'Rourke, a free scoring player with Luton Town. He arrived at Kenilworth Road after non-playing spells at Arsenal and Chelsea and was determined to make Blues' boss Tommy Docherty regret letting him go. When he signed he revealed he actually thought Boro were higher than Division Three but he soon set about getting them back up by bagging a brace on his debut at Colchester and scored 27 in 39 games as they clinched promotion. This included a hat-trick in the crucial last match against Oxford as Boro won 4–1 before 39,683 fans. Although naturally confident and fairly quick, O'Rourke's main strength was in the air where he could power in headers. Playing alongside John Hickton, he netted two Second Division hat-tricks in December 1967, at Derby and at home to Carlisle, but those were his final goals for the club. His career at Boro was over after he fell out with Anderson and left for Ipswich. He gained England Under-23 recognition when replacing Rodney Marsh. He later became a newsagent on the south coast.

ORRITT Bryan

Inside-forward
Born: Caernarfon, 22 February 1937.
Career: Bangor City. Birmingham City 1956. MIDDLESBROUGH 1962.

■ Bryan 'Taffy' Orritt was Boro's original super-sub. When the rules allowed for a substitute to be named it was Orritt who had the 'honour' of being the first ever first teamer to spend most of the game on the bench. As a versatile player who appeared in all 11 positions in his career, including goalkeeper, he was an ideal choice as sub. That milestone, when he replaced Nev Chapman in a 1–1 draw at Preston, was three years into Orritt's Boro career, having signed from Birmingham in March 1962 while suspended for an 'incident' during a reserve game. He had already played at Welsh Youth and Under-23 level and represented the army during his National Service days. At Brum he played in the 1960 and 1961 Inter-Cities Fairs Cup Finals. Orritt had signed as an

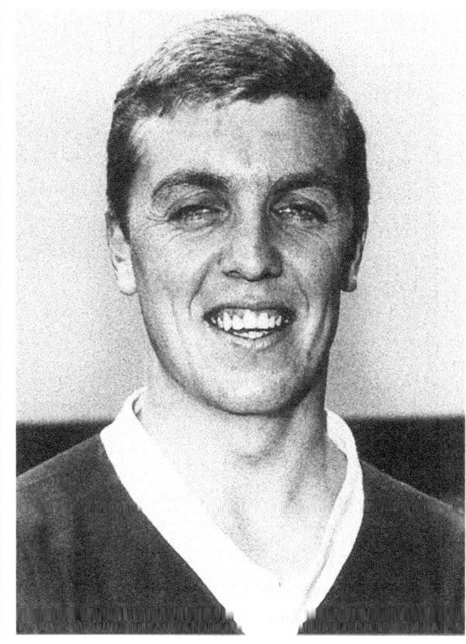

inside-forward but was quickly moved to wing-half, making his debut in a 3–2 win at Charlton and scoring twice in his second game as they beat Newcastle 3–0 a few days later. An enthusiastic and workman-like player, he emigrated to South Africa shortly before Boro were relegated to Division Three. Perhaps the rest of the squad should have done the same. The Orritt legacy could have returned to Boro in 1991, when Taffy's son Gareth had a trial at Ayresome.

OSBORNE Fergus

Inside-right
Born: Details unknown.
Career: Dykehead. MIDDLESBROUGH 1899.

■ Osborne was at the head of a long queue of Scottish strikers to make their way to the Boro. He first played in a 3–1 defeat at Port Vale but had few first-team chances as Boro chopped and changed in their first Football League season. He scored against Luton and little Manchester outfit Newton Heath but lasted less than a year.

OSTLER Jack

Centre-half/Inside-left
Born: Newarthill, 1873.
Died: Prestonpans, 1958
Career Motherwell. Newcastle United 1896. MIDDLESBROUGH (loan) 1899.

■ A dominating central midfield player, Ostler was one of the many to pass through Middlesbrough in the early League days. Thought to have been loaned from Newcastle near the end of the season, he made his debut in a draw at Loughborough but played only twice more. Ostler had been part of Newcastle's first promotion side in 1898. After his playing days he returned to Scotland and worked in the mines.

OTTO Hendrikus (Heine) Matheus

Midfield
Born: Amsterdam, 24 August 1954.
Career: Twente Enschede (Holland). MIDDLESBROUGH 1981. Den Haag (Holland) 1985.

■ Dutchman Otto provided a rare beacon of light in Boro's dark days of the

early 1980s. Bobby Murdoch signed him from Twente Enschede in 1981 as Boro tried desperately to plug the gaps left by the player exodus of 1981. He came highly recommended, having replaced Arnold Muhren at Twente when he joined Ipswich. Otto was a rare nugget for fans at that time, which was very appropriate since he worked in the gold industry before becoming a professional. With one Holland cap already behind him, he scored on his debut against Spurs at Ayresome, but it wasn't enough to prevent a 3–1 defeat and that pretty much set the pattern. Otto finished joint top scorer in 1981–82, though he only had four, as Boro went down...and down. A gifted technical player, his skills made him a terrace hero and, to his credit, he stuck at it despite the endless relegation battles, playing 139 consecutive games between 1982 and his departure in 1985. The feeling was that in a good side he would have been a great player. The fans were angry when Willie Maddren let him go but Boro could no longer afford his signing on fee and he joined Dutch Second Division side Den Haag, playing 221 games on the bounce for them. He later became an administrator, youth coach and assistant manager at the club before joining Dutch giants Ajax as part of their coaching team.

PAGE Robert

Left-half/Centre-half
Born: 1878.
Died: December 1949.
Career: Grove Hill. MIDDLESBROUGH 1899.

■ The name Bob Page will forever form a part of Boro history as he scored their opening Football League goal at Port Vale on 4 September 1899, a game Boro lost 3–1. He played sporadically in that first season, in a variety of attacking and defensive positions, and then disappeared from the League scene, but was still awarded a benefit game for Middlesbrough A against Newcastle A in 1903 but the game was poorly attended. Page returned to the League side from 1903–05. A member of the Old Middlesbrough Rifle Volunteers, he quit the game in 1906 and worked as a bookbinder for Jordisons. Page was also a publican at the Princess Alexandra, Dock Hotel, Marquis of Granby and the Albion. Bob Page died in December, 1949.

PALLISTER Gary Andrew

Central defender
Born: Ramsgate, 30 June 1965.
Career: Billingham Town. MIDDLESBROUGH 1984. Darlington (loan) 1985. Manchester United 1989. MIDDLESBROUGH 1998.

■ Gary Pallister started and finished his career at Boro in very different circumstances. As an up-and-coming centre-half, he experienced the desperate times of financial meltdown at Ayresome Park. When he returned to Teesside following a glittering career with Manchester United, Middlesbrough were a Premier League side with an opulent new ground and a squad packed with multi-million-pound players. Undoubtedly one of Boro's greatest ever players, Pallister was originally on trial in Malcolm Allison's day but he struggled with the physical side of the game. Coach Willie Maddren saw potential and decided to keep tabs on him as he toughened up in the Northern League with Billingham Town. When Maddren offered a second trial, Pallister was fitter and stronger and this time he was taken on. Pallister was on the dole at the time but Boro struggled to pay his wages – just £60 a week. Local businessman Dick Cordon agreed to pay the wage and Billingham were bought a set of strips by Steve Gibson as a transfer fee. At first he struggled and was dropped early in his first season, 1985–86, after a poor game

in a League Cup tie at Mansfield so Maddren loaned him to Darlington to get some experience. At the end of the loan Quakers boss Cyril Knowles offered £5,000 to keep him. Maddren's reponse was probably unprintable! Once he found his feet his potential became clear and Boro offered him a longer term contract as other clubs began showing an interest. In that first season he began his central defensive partnership with Tony Mowbray and continued to impress. But it all ended in tears as Boro went down by losing the last game at Shrewsbury and a disconsolate Pallister was sent off. In that long summer of 1986 he had the chance to join Crystal Palace but stuck by his beloved Boro despite the club facing extinction. It was a wise move as Bruce Rioch's young side won successive promotions and Pallister became one of the country's most sought after players. Classy and composed, he was the silk alongside Mowbray's steel at the heart of Boro's defence. He won an England cap in March 1988 against Hungary despite still being in the Second Division and rumours surfaced about his future at Ayresome. Rioch was said to have told Manchester United they could have him for £600,000 at one point. He played in the top flight for Boro but once they were relegated his departure was inevitable. Liverpool and United wanted him but Alex Ferguson was determined to get his man. The fee seemed to get higher by the day as Rioch and chairman Colin Henderson drove a hard bargain and eventually he went for a British record of £2.3 million. United struggled in his first year but Pallister became Player of the Year and the rest, as they say, is history. He won a League Cup, FA Cup and European Cup-winners' Cup before United landed the big one in 1993 by winning the League for the first time since 1967. He won three more titles and two more FA Cups plus appearances in the Champions League. In 1992 he was named the PFA Player of the Year. The main disappointment of his career was that he never played for England in a major Championship due to untimely injuries. He came back to where it all began when Bryan Robson brought him home in 1998 for £2.5 million and continued where he left off with many solid performances as a creditable ninth spot was achieved in the Premier League. Pallister increasingly struggled with a back injury, however, and retired in 2000 when Steve McClaren decided against offering him a contract extension. He then pursued a career in the media, often working for Sky Sports, while continuing to live on Teesside.

PARKIN Raymond

Inside-right/Right-half
Born: Crook, 28 January 1911.
Died: 1971.
Career: Newcastle United 1927. Esh Winning. Arsenal 1928. MIDDLESBROUGH 1935. Southampton 1937.

■ This North Easterner had a seven-year spell with Arsenal after doing the rounds in the local Leagues at Esh Winning Juniors and Bishop Auckland before being taken to Highbury by legendary boss Herbert Chapman. His appearances were few, however, and Boro boss Wilf Gillow tried to talk him into joining Boro over the phone. Gillow then travelled to London to complete the deal. Parkin made his debut at right-half in a 1–0 defeat at Brentford but vanished from the first team a few weeks later after a 5–2 defeat at Everton. That was his season over and his next game was on the day Wilf Mannion made his debut the following January against Portsmouth at Ayresome. He played just two more games before returning south to Southampton.

PARKINSON Gary Anthony

Right-back
Born: Thornaby, 10 January 1968.
Career: MIDDLESBROUGH 1986. Southend United (loan) 1992. Bolton Wanderers 1993. Burnley 1994. Preston North End 1997. Blackpool 2001.

■ Thornaby lad Parkinson found himself pitched into the first team earlier than he might have expected as an 18-year-old in the first game after liquidation. An attacking right-back, Parkinson made the place his own for the next four seasons as Bruce Rioch's young team stormed through the divisions. After playing for Cleveland and Stockton boys, he had gone to Everton but was homesick and returned to Boro as a YTS trainee three weeks later. After helping the reserves win promotion he was soon doing the same with the first team. Although not the greatest of defenders, he was a fine crosser of the ball and was capable of scoring long-range pile drivers, most notably against Sunderland and Everton. As the Rioch era drew to a close the famous side of 1986 began to

break up and new boss Colin Todd gave Parkinson's right-back place to Colin Cooper. At times he became a boo-boy target and his confidence suffered. Under Lennie Lawrence he competed for a place with Curtis Fleming but his appearances were becoming less frequent. He was made available for transfer and, after a loan spell at Southend, he rejoined Rioch at Bolton in 1993 on a free transfer. He didn't get many games and moved on to Burnley for £80,000 where he became a regular once again and scored the goal that secured promotion for the Lancastrians in the Second Division Play-off Final at Wembley. Preston then signed him in 1997.

PARLOUR Raymond

Midfield
Born: Romford, 7 March 1973.
Career: Arsenal 1991. MIDDLESBROUGH 2004. Hull City 2007.

■ Nicknamed 'the Romford Pele' – albeit with a hint of irony – after a distinguished career at Arsenal, Parlour initially impressed at the Riverside before injuries took their toll and he faded from the first-team picture. Instantly recognisable by a shock of red hair which had terrace wags likening him to TV gardener Charlie Dimmock, he joined Boro on a free transfer in summer 2004 after a long and distinguished Gunners' career, having established himself on the right wing or in central midfield under Arsene Wenger. Never afraid to get stuck in, Parlour had been a hugely popular figure at Highbury and although often considered something of an unsung hero, he won 10 England caps while with the club. After making his League debut for Arsenal against Liverpool at Anfield in January 1992, conceding a penalty in a 2–0 defeat, Parlour became an integral part of the club's engine room. He enjoyed an outstanding campaign when helping Arsenal win the FA and League Cups in 1992–93 before winning Premier League and FA Cup-winners' medals in 1997–98 as the Gunners stormed to the double. He was also an influential member of Arsenal's double-winning side in 2001–02, scoring a cracking effort to help the Gunners on their way to an FA Cup Final victory over Chelsea. But the following season a series of niggling injuries and a loss of form kept Parlour out of the side for long periods and, after appearing in 455 games for the North London club, he made the move north to Boro. He made his debut in a 2–2 home draw with Newcastle United and, despite missing games with a hip injury, managed to appear in 41 of the club's 52 games in that 2004–05 season. His first season was characterised by some typically no-nonsense tackling and he became a popular figure among the fans. Sadly, his second campaign was decimated by injury. He had been struggling with a knee problem – damaged in a 2–0 Riverside defeat against Sunderland – together with a hip complaint. He was an unused sub in the 2006 UEFA Cup Final but did not play a first-team game under new manager Gareth Southgate the following season. After failing to score for Boro in almost half a century of games, he was released in January 2007, signing a short-term deal with Hull City. Although he helped the Tigers avoid relegation, he was not offered a contract and was freed in summer 2007.

PARNABY Stuart

Defender/Midfield
Born: Bishop Auckland, 19 July 1982.
Career: MIDDLESBROUGH 1999. Halifax Town (loan) 2000. Birmingham City 2007.

■ An elegant defender who could also operate in midfield, Parnaby played at every England level expect the full side while with Boro. He emerged as one of the brightest starlets of Boro's successful Academy, which is managed by his father, Dave. However, his Boro career was hampered by a series of injuries, which often seemed to strike whenever he began to establish himself as the side's regular right-back. A key member of the Boro team to reach the FA Youth Cup semi-finals, in 1999–2000, Parnaby made his first-team debut in a Worthington Cup tie against Macclesfield. Shortly afterwards he joined Halifax Town on loan, where he showed a maturity beyond his years in half-a-dozen outings for the Shaymen. His 2001–02 season was virtually wiped out through injury but he came back with a bang the following campaign. Winning England Under-21 honours, he became a permanent choice in the right-back berth after Robbie Stockdale was sidelined with a foot injury. It was his turn to suffer more injuries in 2003–04 when he tore his anterior cruciate ligament in his right knee. Fortunately an operation was not needed but Parnaby was still out of action for over four months. On regaining full fitness, he found on-loan England right-back Danny Mills in his position and spent the rest of the season as cover, helping out in both defence and midfield. Another freak injury – a hairline fracture of his left fibula – was sustained while warming up, costing him another three months out of the side. In 2005–06 he played some of the best football of his Boro career and scored his first goal for

the club against Nuneaton in the FA Cup, then another against Sunderland at the Stadium of Light in the Premiership and again against VfB Stuttgart in the UEFA Cup. Probably Parnaby's most satisfying strike came in the Premiership against Bolton Wanderers at the Riverside. Boro had squandered a 3–1 lead and the final whistle was only moments away when he slid in from close range to earn all three points in a 4–3 win. His final season on Teesside was a frustrating one as he often played second fiddle to Abel Xavier and Andrew Davies. He was released in summer 2007, joining Premiership newcomers Birmingham City on a three-year contract.

PATERSON Thomas

Forward
Born: Ashington, 30 March 1954.
Career: Leicester City. MIDDLESBROUGH 1974. Bournemouth 1976. Darlington 1978.

■ Centre-forward Paterson had been a reserve at Leicester but was signed by Jack Charlton after a good goals return for the Foxes second team. Although he wasn't big for a target man, he was good on the ball and hard working but played only one game for Boro as a replacement for Alan Willey as they beat Birmingham 3–0 in December, 1974. He failed to score as a partner for John Hickton and was taken off 15 minutes from time. That was it for his Boro career and he moved on to Bournemouth. He later had a spell at Darlington.

PATTERSON Ronald Lindsay

Full-back
Born: Seaham, 30 October 1929.
Career: Whitehall Juniors. MIDDLESBROUGH 1949. Northampton Town 1952. Rothwell Town.

■ At 6ft 5in Ron Patterson was one of Boro's tallest ever players. He signed after a spell as an apprentice at Crystal Palace but played only once, at left-back, against Charlton in September 1951 as Boro lost 4–3. Later he became a stalwart at Northampton and was their skipper. He was also player-manager at Rothwell Town and managed Hendon.

PAYTON Andrew Paul

Forward
Born: Clitheroe, 23 October 1967.
Career: Hull City 1985. MIDDLESBROUGH 1991. Glasgow Celtic 1992. Barnsley 1993. Huddersfield Town 1996. Burnley 1998. Blackpool (loan) 2001.

■ Andy Payton scored goals for every club he played for – except Middlesbrough. Not for the first time, Boro signed a player who looked set to end Bernie Slaven's run as Boro's supreme goalscorer. Payton came in amid reported differences between Slaven and boss Lennie Lawrence and he seemed likely to partner Paul Wilkinson up front. In his first game against Bristol City in November 1991, Lawrence dodged the question by playing all three and the new boy got off to a dream start by scoring after only four minutes. But anything he could do Bernie could do better and the Scot responded by scoring two himself as Boro won 3–1. Payton picked up an injury in the game and was carried off just before half-time. Things never quite worked out for him after that and there were rumours he hadn't settled into the dressing room. Pacy and a natural goalscorer, Lawrence had made him the club's record signing and at Hull the nippy striker scored regularly and was Player of the Year. But at Ayresome he never managed more then two consecutive games and in the summer after Boro's promotion he was sold to Celtic as part of the deal that brought Chris Morris and Derek Whyte to Teesside. His family didn't settle in Scotland and he was soon sold on to Barnsley. A spell at Huddersfield was followed by a successful move to Burnley, the local club who had rejected him as a youngster.

PEACOCK Alan

Centre-forward
Born: Middlesbrough, 29 October 1937.
Career: MIDDLESBROUGH 1954. Leeds United 1964. Plymouth Argyle 1967.

■ Had Boro's defence been half as good as the attack in the late 50s and early 60s the club would have been a major force. Boro produced two England strikers in the same era and both were local lads. Alan Peacock and Brian Clough formed a formidable strike partnership but the leaky defence meant their efforts were often in vain.

Lawson Street School pupil Peacock had represented England's youth team in 1956, having made his Boro debut in the same year as Clough 1955, but had to endure a 7–2 defeat at Bristol Rovers. After his National Service he got the chance to make a forward's spot his own when he dislodged Arthur Fitzsimons to take the number-10 shirt. He was out-scored by Clough but was the perfect foil for him, leading the line and providing the knock-downs for his partner. When Clough moved on in 1961 he was left to carry the attack and gained further recognition for himself. He was selected for the England 1962 World Cup squad in Chile and actually made his debut in that tournament, playing against Argentina and Bulgaria. In total he gained six England caps, scoring twice.

Peacock headed Boro's goalscoring charts in 1962 and 1963 but, frustrated at the club's failure to win promotion, he left for Leeds, though Spurs and Everton were also interested. He helped Leeds to promotion under Don Revie and was an FA Cup Final loser in 1965. Sadly, a serious knee injury curtailed his career and, after a brief spell at Plymouth, he retired in 1968. Peacock, who will go down as one of Boro's finest players, later became a Middlesbrough newsagent and businessman and is now closely involved with the Middlesbrough Former Players' Association.

PEACOCK Joseph

Wing-half
Born: Wigan, 15 March 1897.
Died: 1979.
Career: Atherton Collieries. Everton 1919. MIDDLESBROUGH 1927. Sheffield Wednesday 1930. Clapton Orient 1931. Sliepner (Sweden).

■ Joe Peacock overcome adversity to win England caps as a Boro star. He was one of boss Peter McWilliam's first signings when he came in from Everton in 1927, where he been a stalwart at wing-half. He became a regular in a struggling Boro side that season which slid to relegation after failing to win any of the last five matches. Boro's last match in the top flight could hardly have been worse as they lost 3–0 at home to Sunderland before almost 42,000 at Ayresome. The club didn't stay down long, however, and

Peacock played in all but two Second Division games as a side containing 30-goal George Camsell and 27-goal Billy Pease swept to the Championship. That summer he toured with England, alongside Camsell, playing France, Belgium and Spain. Peacock was rewarded at Boro the following year when he took over the captaincy. Sadly, his season was heavily disrupted as he turned out just eight times. His career stuttered after that and he ended up coaching in Sweden before becoming trainer at Wrexham just before the war.

PEAKE Andrew Michael

Midfield
Born: Market Harborough, 1 November 1961.
Career: Leicester City 1979. Grimsby Town 1985. Charlton Athletic 1986. MIDDLESBROUGH 1991.

■ Andy Peake was a Mr Dependable figure for the clubs he played for. As a youngster he was considered good enough to play in the World Youth Cup in Australia and for England Under-21s. After serving his time with Leicester he established himself in the Foxes first team, playing in the First Division and then earning himself a Second Division Championship medal. Peake was part of a Leicester side that came close to FA Cup glory in 1982, only to lose a semi-final to Spurs. A close friend of the legendary Gary Lineker, who was his best man, he was soon to discover the harsh side of football life as a serious ankle injury kept him on the sidelines for a year. After that Leicester allowed him to leave and he was snapped up by Grimsby. Lennie Lawrence then took him to Charlton and he helped the Valiants' remarkable survival feats in the top flight.

When Lawrence took over at Boro in 1991, his former skipper became one of his targets and Peake needed only a 10 minute chat with Lawrence to agree to the move north. Peake made his Boro debut in a 2–1 defeat at Blackburn in November 1991 and became a useful member of a side which won promotion and enjoyed a run to the fifth round of the FA Cup. Peake could not play in the League Cup when Boro reached a semi-final against Manchester United. Despite his effort that year, he didn't set the world alight and became a boo-boy target. The problems were banished, however, as Boro got off to a flyer in the newly-formed Premier League with Peake a star in the side which crushed champions Leeds 4–1. Things got tougher for Boro though and at the end of that season they were relegated, despite Peake's assured promptings from the centre of midfield. His teammates certainly knew his worth as they voted him the 1992–93 Player of the Year. He was a reliable performer again the following season as cash-strapped Boro got used to life in a lower League once again. When Bryan Robson took over as boss in 1994, the club was

well stocked with midfielders and Peake, now nearly 33, was allowed to leave. He turned down a chance to rejoin Lawrence at Bradford and became a police officer back in Leicestshire.

PEARS Stephen

Goalkeeper
Born: Brandon, 22 January 1962.
Career: Manchester United 1979. MIDDLESBROUGH (loan) 1983. MIDDLESBROUGH 1985. Liverpool 1995. Hartlepool United 1996.

■ It is probably fair to say that all the regulars in Bruce Rioch's team of 1986 are heroes to Boro fans. But even among that group, the name of Pears stands out. Agile and a brilliant shot stopper, Pears is arguably the club's greatest ever 'keeper. Initially brought in on loan by Malcolm Allison during the 1983–84 season, the fans were desperate to have him permanently but the club couldn't afford the £80,000 deal.

He had learned his trade at Manchester United and managed four games as understudy to Gary Bailey. Dave Sexton had actually released him in 1981 but new boss Ron Atkinson wanted to give him another chance and he eventually spent seven years with United. It was always going to be hard for the athletic County Durham lad to get a regular place at Old Trafford though and Willie Maddren got his man in the summer of 1985. Even Pears' efforts – one mistake against Stoke apart – couldn't keep Boro up in the season of doom that followed but it was all celebrations for two years after that as Pears reached new heights to help Boro's double promotion effort. He set a new club record in 1987–88 with seven consecutive clean sheets and produced a wonder display in an FA Cup tie at Everton to earn Boro a replay the same year, one of many superlative performances. Pears earned a reputation for winning points with his stunning saves and was probably at his best in one-on-one situations with opposing forwards when his reflexes were a match for even the finest goalscorers.

Pears suffered a downturn as Boro battled for survival in the First Division and was replaced for the run-in by Kevin Poole after a 3–3 draw with Everton. He missed the first half of the following year through injury as Boro had a nightmare start in Division Two but made a sensational return against Leicester in December. Boro ran-out 4–1 winners but Pears produced some incredible saves from City's Kevin Campbell and was only beaten by a Gary McAllister penalty, a performance he dedicated to his late father. Pears suffered many injuries in his career, from a broken cheekbone to groin problems, but bizarrely one of the most serious came in a game of beach football in 1991 that could have ended his career. Fortunately, Pears battled back and even new boss Lennie Lawrence was surprised at just how good he was as Pears helped Boro to promotion in 1992 and was named the North East Player of the Year. The long overdue England recognition finally came that season, as he was called into a squad to play Czechoslovakia, but sadly he suffered a broken cheekbone in a collision with Cambridge striker Dion Dublin and missed out. Injuries interrupted his season in the Premier League as Boro once again went down, though he was ever present on Boro's drop to the new First Division. Bryan Robson's arrival in the summer of 1994 signalled the beginning of the end for Pears. Injury problems, particularly with his calf, persisted and he managed only five games as Boro again won promotion. He was released in 1995 but not before a testimonial match before 20,000 fans in which Boro paraded the championship trophy and Pears netted the last ever goal at Ayresome from the penalty spot in a modern Boro versus old Boro game. It was undoubtedly a fitting end for one of Boro's real greats. Pears moved on to Liverpool, where he was understudy to David James, and finished his career at Hartlepool. He is now a goalkeeping coach in Boro's academy. A talented builder, he also helped teammates Mark Proctor and Jamie Pollock build their houses.

PEARSON Nigel Graham

Central defender
Born: Nottingham, 21 August 1963.
Career: Heanor Town. Shrewsbury Town 1981. Sheffield Wednesday 1987. MIDDLESBROUGH 1994.

■ If Nigel Pearson had already had an eventful career on joining the Robson revolution in 1994, it was small beer compared to the drama of his time at Boro. When Bryan Robson arrived he knew his first job was to add defensive steel and he wasted no time in turning to Pearson. A fee of £750,000 was questioned at the time as warhorse Pearson had suffered knee problems and two broken legs. He had spent seven years at Sheffield Wednesday, winning promotion and a League Cup-winners' medal, but he had lengthy absences through injury and was unlucky enough to miss out on two Cup Finals at Hillsborough. The fans didn't need long to be convinced, however, as the new skipper, who had ironically played in a Shrewsbury side that relegated Boro in 1986, became a rock on which

promotion was built and the First Division Championship secured.

It was Pearson who led Boro into a bright new era as the Cellnet Riverside Stadium opened in 1995 and Boro got off to a flyer in the top flight. By the end of October Boro were sixth – and that was before Juninho arrived. Pearson barely missed a game that season and commanded great respect from teammates and fans alike. It was no coincidence that when Boro struggled amid the traumas of the following season, Pearson was often absent with injury. He suffered a serious neck injury in a collision with Marcus Gayle of Wimbledon and Boro were vulnerable at the back without him. Captain Courageous still played his part though and led the desperate fight to stave off relegation. He also twice led his team out at Wembley as Boro suffered the heartbreak of defeat at both the FA and Coca-Cola Cup Finals. Worse was to follow as the side crashed out of the Premiership at Leeds on the final day, ultimately sent down by the loss of three points for failing to play a match at Blackburn.

But with Pearson fighting on bravely despite his knee problems Boro were able to rally and win promotion at the first attempt in 1998. Once again he led Boro at Wembley when again they lost out, this time to Chelsea in the Coca-Cola Cup Final. He missed much of the run-in but returned for one last effort in a crucial match against Oxford. He had announced his decision to retire before the game, fearing the damage being done to his knees, so it was an emotional occasion as he helped the side to a 4–1 win to seal promotion. He had a brief spell as manager at Carlisle, avoiding relegation from the Football League in the last game, but his contract was not renewed. Pearson then became assistant boss at Stoke City and took on a coaching role with young England. He was later Bryan Robson's assistant at West Brom and was caretaker manager of the club before the appointment of another former Boro captain, Tony Mowbray. He spent much of 2006–07 as assistant manager to Glenn Roeder at Newcastle United but left the club following the appointment of Sam Allardyce in summer 2007.

PEASE William Harold

Outside-right
Born: Leeds, 30 September 1898.
Died: Redcar, 2 October 1955.
Career: Leeds City 1919. Northampton Town 1920. MIDDLESBROUGH 1926. Luton Town 1933.

■ Pacey Billy Pease became one of the Boro greats but, like so many who plied their trade at Ayresome, the England recognition he surely deserved rarely came. Pease was an entertainer, possessing great speed and may even be one of the fastest to play for the club. He could cross a ball well, didn't need a second touch and could cut inside and bear down on goal. He served with the Royal Northumberland Fusiliers during the Great War before beginning his football career. Boro boss Herbert Bamlett must have felt duty bound to snap him up from Northampton in 1926 after the trouble he had getting to see him play. A delegation headed south by car from Middlesbrough on a spying mission only to break down near Peterborough. The repairs were due to take some time so they found a hire car and got to Northampton at half-time – to find Pease wasn't playing! Northampton had signed him after his first club, Leeds City, were booted out of the League for irregularities. He played in Northampton's first season in the League and became a star in Division Three South. The price Boro paid was something of a snip, as Sunderland had been prepared to pay a five figure sum for Pease three years earlier. The new boy, a veteran of World War One with the Northumberland Fusiliers, took time to settle as Second Division Boro struggled early in the 1926–27 season. Pease's debut was an opening day 3–0 defeat at Chelsea but he scored in the first win of the campaign against Hull and from then on the only way was up. He teamed up with George Camsell and Boro stormed to the championship rattling in 122 goals in the process, Camsell hitting an astonishing 59 and Pease 23. He could have had more but for breaking his collarbone in a home game with South Shields in March. The injury probably served Pease right, however, as he had told teammate Jacky Carr he was going to feign injury so he could get off early and keep a date with a girl. He was ruled out for the rest of a glorious season but his contribution was recognised with a call-up to the England squad and he earned his one and only cap in a 3–3 draw with Wales in February 1927. He missed only one match on the return to the top flight and, though he and Camsell scored 52 times between them, it wasn't enough and Boro were down at the first attempt. As so often through Boro's history, the club was switching divisions with regularity and Pease and Camsell were able to help win promotion once again the next season as the goals continued to fly in. In one game Pease scored four and Camsell three as Wolves were beaten 8–3. The goals started to come less regularly as Pease got older but he was still a regular in a side that established itself in the top flight and finished seventh in 1931. Two years later his appearances were tailing off, however, and the Pease era was nearing an end. Boro decided it was time for the speed king to move on and he was transferred to Luton after more than 100 Boro goals. He did return to the North East after his career, working as a publican and at ICI Wilton in the late 1940s. He also had a spell coaching Redcar Albion. His career had been a great one, but it will remain a mystery why such a gifted player was so often overlooked by his country. Billy Pease died in Redcar in October 1955. He is buried in Redcar Cemetery.

PEGGIE James

Centre-forward
Born: Details unknown.
Career: Lochgelly United. East Fife. Hibernian. MIDDLESBROUGH 1910.

■ Brought down from Scotland in 1910, forward Peggie's Boro career was short and not so sweet. He played only six games over six months and was freed after less than a year. His second game, when he deputised for George Elliott, ended in a 5–0 defeat at Villa and he was rarely called upon again, finishing his time at the club by again replacing Elliott for a 3–1 defeat at Sunderland.

PENDER Robert

Left-half/Inside-left
Born: Dumbarton.
Career: Raith Rovers. Dunfermline Athletic. MIDDLESBROUGH 1919. St Johnstone.

■ Left-half Pender was drafted in to boost Boro as the club regrouped after World War One. He had to wait until November for a debut, in a 0–0 draw before 40,000 at Newcastle, and established himself for the rest of that First Division season. He remained a stop-gap performer for two more seasons until finally holding down a regular place in the 1922–23 season as Boro struggled to stay up. He made the number six berth his own, playing every game until a 3–0 defeat at Arsenal in March. Boro did stay up, though the following year the club fell through the relegation trap door and Pender's opportunities were few. He was recalled for the run-in but it was to no avail as Boro went down. His last game was a 1–0 defeat at Cardiff. He moved back to Scotland with St Johnstone in the summer of 1924.

PENTLAND Frederick Beaconsfield

Outside-right/Centre-forward
Born: Wolverhampton, 18 September 1883.
Died: Poole, March 1962.
Career: Avondale Juniors. Willenhall Swifts. Small Heath 1901. Blackpool 1903. Blackburn Rovers 1903. Brentford 1906. Queen's Park Rangers 1907. MIDDLESBROUGH 1908. Halifax Town 1912. Stoke 1913.

■ Fred Pentland was more than just a footballer, he was an ambassador who broke down the barriers of Europe. Perhaps his greatest achievements came

after his playing days as he followed a coaching career that led him into extraordinary trouble. He was a man with a distinguished background as the son of the Lord Mayor of Birmingham and as a player he was blessed with pace and excellent ball skills.

Strangely, he struggled to make the grade with local side Small Heath and became something of a journeyman with spells at Blackpool, Blackburn and Brentford before helping Queens Park Rangers to the Southern League title in 1908. From there he joined Boro for a fee that was a Rangers record. He found his feet at Ayresome and spent the longest spell of his career in Middlesbrough. A good crosser of a ball, he was a regular in a side that finished sixth in the top flight and remained a fixture for three seasons. He had also earned England international recognition with the club, his first cap coming against Wales in 1909. He then played in two eight-goal victories against Austria and Hungary. His Boro career fizzled out by 1912 and he finished his days in the lower Leagues.

Unlike many players, though, that was very much where Pentland's story began. He got a coaching job in Germany but when World War One broke out in 1914 he was interned by the Germans along with former Boro colleague, Steve Bloomer. He was free to move about within Germany but was not allowed out of the country. When the conflict ended he spent a short time in France before playing a major role in developing the game in Spain, taking Athletic Bilbao to five Spanish titles in seven seasons. To his great pride, it was his Spanish team that became the first foreign country to beat England in a full international. Conflict entered the picture again, however, and he left Spain in 1936 at the outbreak of the civil war. He returned home to be assistant boss at Brentford and took charge of Barrow for a year – but once again war intervened in 1939. Fred Pentland died at Poole in March, 1962.

PETERS Jeffrey

Left-back
Born: Gosforth, 7 March 1961.
Career: MIDDLESBROUGH 1979. Blyth Spartans.

■ Peters was converted from his original position as a left winger to make his Boro debut at left-back in a home draw against Spurs when he replaced Ian Bailey in November 1979. Peters, a graduate of Boro's youth programme, played six games in a row but lost his place after a 1–0 defeat at home to Southampton on 8 December and never played again. He had worked hard on and off the pitch, gaining a distinction in exams at Longlands College in 1979. Peters was with the club for a further three years but was released in March 1982. He joined Blyth Spartans.

PHILLIPS James Neil

Left-back
Born: Bolton, 8 February 1966.
Career: Bolton Wanderers 1983. Glasgow Rangers 1987. Oxford United 1988. MIDDLESBROUGH 1990. Bolton Wanderers 1993.

■ Quiet man Jimmy Phillips gave steady service to Boro over four seasons. The cultured left-back was perhaps not the best of players defensively but very good going forward and a fine crosser of a ball. His career began at his hometown club Bolton before he moved into the big time when Graeme Souness made him his first signing at Rangers for £100,000. Playing mainly in midfield, he won a Premier Division title medal and played in Europe while at Ibrox but was dropped by Souness and, with first-team chances restricted, returned to England with Mark Lawrenson's Oxford. Bruce Rioch and Colin Todd had tracked Philllips for some time but Boro didn't get him until March 1990, just before the Zenith Data Systems Cup Final. Todd had just taken over as boss and saw Phillips as a man to help the fight against relegation to the Third Division. It was a bad start, however, as Boro crashed 3–0 at home to Blackburn on his debut. Phillips became a fixture in the side until 1993, scoring in a Play-off semi-final against Notts County in 1991 and helping Lennie Lawrence's team to promotion a year later, when he captained the side for the crucial last game at Wolves. He found it tough going in the Premier League, as did the rest of the team, and despite taking over the captaincy for a time in Alan Kernaghan's absence, his confidence and form dipped. Boro were duly relegated and, as Lawrence tried to trim the wage bill, out-of-contract Phillips was allowed to leave, though the player was reluctant to go. He teamed up with Colin Todd again at Bolton, where Todd was deputy to Bruce Rioch, and enjoyed success in his second spell with his hometown club, savouring notable Cup victories and winning two promotions from Second Division to Premier League. Like Boro, they failed to hold their status and were relegated on both occasions.

PHILLIPS John Brian

Centre-half
Born: Cadishead, 9 November 1931.
Career: Altrincham. MIDDLESBROUGH 1954. Mansfield Town 1960.

■ Brian Phillips' football career led him to disgrace and imprisonment. Phillips joined Boro from non-League Altrincham just before being released from the forces in 1954. It took him a long time to establish himself in the side and he didn't become a regular until 1957. A craggy central defender noted for his mule-like kick, Phillips was embroiled in regular controversy with the club's goal machine hero Brian Clough. The pair were often in heated dressing room rows

and even fist fights, with Clough known to be extremely critical of the side's leaky defence. Phillips was instrumental in the notorious round-robin petition that sought to get Clough removed from the captaincy. But it was Phillips who was the loser as he was put on reduced contract terms and then sold on to Mansfield. In April 1962, two years after his departure from Boro, he was suspended from football and later banned for life and jailed for his part in a bribery racket. Phillips admitted offering a bribe to Boro 'keeper Esmond Million while at Mansfield. He did later move into management, where he took Nottinghamshire League club Railworth Miners' Welfare to the FA Vase Final. Sadly for Phillips, he will be remembered for other things.

PHILLIPSON Thomas F.

Inside-left
Born: Stanhope, 1886.
Career: Bishop Auckland. MIDDLESBROUGH 1904.

■ Inside-left Phillipson must have thought he'd made it as a professional after scoring just five minutes into his Boro debut. That was at Manchester City in February 1905, but there was little else to say about his Boro career. The game ended in a 3–2 defeat and he played just twice more. He was released by the club that summer. During his time with Boro he had been allowed to keep up his job as a teacher in Spennymoor despite being a professional at Middlesbrough.

PIERCY Frank R.

Left-back/Left-half
Born: Haverton Hill, 1880.
Died: 1931.
Career: South Bank. MIDDLESBROUGH 1897. West Ham United.

■ Piercy was very much a stop-gap for Boro in the early days of League football. A survivor from the amateur days, the left-half gave good service to the club and captained the reserve team, while his brother Bob captained the first team. He played just once in the first League season, a 4–1 defeat at Leicester, and then had to wait nearly four years for another chance. He became a coach and trainer at West Ham in 1912.

PIERCY Henry Robert

Full-back
Born: Details unknown.
Career: Port Clarence.
MIDDLESBROUGH 1894.

■ When Bob Piercy skippered Boro to an Amateur Cup win over Uxbridge in 1898 he couldn't have imagined it would be 77 years before another Boro captain lifted some Cup silverware. Sadly, it was 1975 by the time Stuart Boam's team won the Anglo-Scottish Cup. Former Port Clarence player Piercy won plenty of silver in the amateur days and was a regular in the Northern League side from the 1894–95 season, helping Boro win the title in 1895 and 1897. Among the left-back's other honours were an Amateur Cup win at Headingley in Leeds in 1895, when Boro beat Old Carthusians 2–1, and that 2–1 defeat of Uxbridge at Crystal Palace. Indeed he was one of only three players to appear in both of the club's Cup Final successes of the era. He struggled to make the transition to the Football League, however, and was released in 1900.

PLATT James Archibald

Goalkeeper
Born: Ballymoney, 26 January 1952.
Career: Ballymena. MIDDLESBROUGH 1970. Hartlepool United (loan) 1978. Cardiff City (loan) 1978. Ballymena. Coleraine.

■ Jim Platt was an outstanding goalkeeper whose Boro career spanned five managers and left him fifth in Boro's all-time appearance list. The young Platt had spent his school days as an outfield player but Irish League club Ballymena put his talents to better use between the posts. His performances as an amateur, when he was a member of a side which lost in the Irish Cup Final, alerted clubs on the mainland to his potential. Platt spent three weeks on trial at Liverpool but they had just signed Ray Clemence and it was Boro who stepped in, paying £7,000, rising to £10,000 after 10 games. He was spotted by Boro scout Bobby McAuley and recommended to the club by Ballymena's manager Alex McCrae, a former Boro player. At first he found himself third choice behind Willie Whigham and Pat Cuff – in fact he even managed to score a reserve hat-trick against Lincoln as an outfield player before breaking into the side. But Platt moved up the pecking order so he was the man to replace Whigham in 1971. Boro had lost a derby at Sunderland 4–1 and that spelled the end for long-serving Whigham, leaving Platt to seize his chance. So firm was the grip he established on the 'keeper's jersey, he did not miss another game until April 1974, by which time he had played 112 consecutive games and helped Jack Charlton's team to a runaway Second Division Championship. Over the course of his Ayresome career he kept more clean sheets than any other Middlesbrough 'keeper, much of the time behind that infamously miserly Charlton defence. A fall-out with Big Jack cost him his place in the 1976–77 season after the pair disagreed over whether Platt should stand at the near post for corners. Cuff took his place for 23 games before he was eventually restored to the side. The following season he again found himself frozen out, this time by youngster David Brown, and it became a more serious interruption to Platt's career. New boss John Neal brought in Scot Jim Stewart for the 1978–79 season and it was a year before he regained his place. During this period he was farmed out to Hartlepool and Cardiff on loan and almost joined John Pickering's Blackburn only for Neal to call him back as Stewart struggled. Once he got his place back Platt re-established himself to again become the commanding and consistent 'keeper of old. He was the 'keeper in the promising season of 1980–81 and stayed on as the club's young talent was sold off. An agile shot-stopper, his excellent performances weren't enough to keep Boro in the top flight in 1982, however, he had earned himself a testimonial against Sunderland, playing half the game outfield and scoring. The arrival of Malcolm Allison in 1982 spelled the end for Platt as youngster Kelham O'Hanlon was preferred to the old professional, even though Platt was skipper. Platt surprisingly chose to leave the English game for the comparitive back waters of

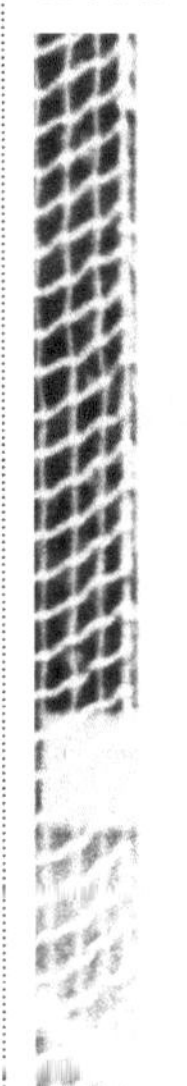

Irish football. Only a few months earlier he had been in Northern Ireland's 1982 World Cup squad, playing against Austria, and in all he won 23 caps, the first against Israel back in 1976. His international appearances would surely have been greater had it not been for the presence of the brilliant Pat Jennings, though Jack Charlton had once claimed Platt was the better 'keeper. His longest run in the Irish side was 13 games in a row, which took in the victorious side that won the 1980 Home International Championships. It had been a distinguished playing career, which twice saw him named Boro's Player of the Year, in 1972 and 1981, and he was also North East Player of the Year in 1981. After leaving Boro, he had spells as player-manager of Ballymena and Coleraine, taking the latter into Europe, before taking charge at Ballyclare Comrades. He even had a game in charge of the Northern Ireland team against Israel as stand-in for Billy Bingham. A season in charge of Assyryska in the Swedish First Division was followed by a returned to Northern Ireland, where he went into business with a Prontaprint franchise and working for the Irish FA. He teamed up with David Hodgson at Darlington. Platt later took over as sole boss and led the Quakers to a Wembley Play-off defeat in 1997. He spent some time with Gateshead before coming back to Boro as chief coach at Middlesbrough Football Community Centre.

POGATETZ Emanuel (Manny)

Defender
Born: Steinbock, Austria, 16 January 1983.
Career: Sturm Graz (Austria) 1999. Karnten (Austria) 2000. Bayer Leverkusen (Germany) 2001. Aarau (Switzerland) (loan) 2002. Grazer AK (Austria) (loan) 2003. Spartak Moscow (Russia) (loan) 2005. MIDDLESBROUGH 2005.

■ Fearless Austrian defender Pogatetz made one of the most remarkable turnarounds in Boro history as he became a huge fans' favourite after a shaky start to his career on Teesside. Having first caught Steve McClaren's eye starring against Boro for Grazer AK

during a UEFA Cup tie, it was some time before the then Riverside boss made his move for the player, in summer 2005. By then he was a Bayer Leverkusen player but was on loan at Spartak Moscow. The deal was almost complete when a Pogatetz tackle in his final game left opponent Yaroslav Kharitonskiy with a double leg fracture. He was banned for a massive 24 weeks by the Russian Football Association, putting the move in jeopardy. However, Boro stuck by the player and the ban was drastically reduced on appeal. He started his Premiership career challenging the popular Franck Queudrue for the left-back's shirt and scored his first goal for the club in a 2–0 win against Sunderland at the Stadium of Light. Though he broke his nose against Fulham, worse was to follow. In the UEFA Cup away leg at Basel, Pogatetz suffered a horrific facial injury after an accidental clash of heads. He flew back to England to face corrective surgery, knowing his 2005–06 season was over. The campaign also saw Pogatetz banned from playing for his country after falling out with Austria coach Josef Hickersberger. But the following year saw a dramatic change in fortunes as Pogatetz was transformed from an unconvincing left-back to a centre-half of genuine quality. Gareth Southgate's retirement and an injury to newcomer Robert Huth handed him his chance alongside Jonathan Woodgate and the partnership immediately gelled. His uncompromising displays inspired a memorable thread of fans' web forum correspondence on Fly Me To The Moon extolling his superhuman qualities. He also won the Middlesbrough Official Supporters Club's Player of the Year award as well as topping the players' own poll.

POLLOCK Jamie

Midfield
Born: Stockton, 16 February 1974.
Career: MIDDLESBROUGH 1991. Osasuna (Spain) 1996. Bolton Wanderers 1996. Manchester City 1998. Crystal Palace 2000. Birmingham City (loan) 2001.

■ When young Jamie Pollock burst on to the scene in 1991, Boro were still very much a shoestring club and local talent like Pollock was a godsend. From the moment he stepped out against Wolves in Colin Todd's only full season in charge he became a Holgate End hero. Despite his age, just 17, Pollock was never overawed by the senior players he came up against. Fearless in the tackle, he would drive Boro on from midfield, covering every blade of grass. He had been with the club since the age of 10, during which time he also represented Stockton West End, and chose his local club despite the offer of a contract from Nottingham Forest. He earned himself international recognition in the World Youth Cup in Australia and gained England Under-21 caps. The pride he showed in Boro's march to the Premier League inspired the fans and within a few months it was hard to imagine Boro without him. He impressed in the run to the semi-final of the Rumbelows Cup when he showed scant regard for Bryan Robson in Manchester United's midfield, the man who would later be his manager.

At the end of that season Pollock was named Boro's Young Player of the Year. He found games harder to come by in the top flight but never let Boro down. In one game against Blackburn he went on as sub and set about Rovers with some crunching tackles. Inspired by Pollock, Boro came back from 1–0 down and won 3–2. He showed his usual endeavour during the bleak 1993–94 season as Boro came to terms with life back in the First Division. Pollock gave the fans a rare beacon of hope for the future, though at times his passion boiled over and he was sent off that season in a Cup tie against Cardiff.

Life at the club changed after Bryan Robson's arrival in 1994 and Pollock hardly missed a game as Boro's midfield general in 1994–95 when the First Division Championship was clinched and he played a number of games as a hard-running stop-gap forward. The move to the Riverside saw a surprising downturn in Pollock's fortunes. At first he formed an impressive engine room with Robbie Mustoe as Boro got off to a fantastic start in the Premier League but, though he played most of the games, he looked out of sorts by the end and was substituted in his last Boro game against Manchester United in May 1996. That summer he moved to Spanish side Osasuna under the Bosman ruling but it was a nightmare time for Pollock and he was quickly back in England, joining Colin Todd's Bolton who were heading for promotion. He moved on to Manchester City the following year but endured relegation at Maine Road, though he was a hit with the fans. He lost the City captaincy as the club fought for promotion in 1998–99 and was injured as City went back up. He later moved into coaching and is now in charge of Northern League side Spennymoor, while running a glass-making business.

POOLE Kevin

Goalkeeper
Born: Bromsgrove, 21 July 1963.
Career: Aston Villa 1981. Northampton Town (loan) 1984. MIDDLESBROUGH 1987. Hartlepool United (loan) 1991. Leicester City 1991. Birmingham City 1997. Bolton Wanderers 2001. Derby County 2005. Burton Albion 2006.

■ Being an understudy to a goalkeeper like Stephen Pears was hardly the most promising position for Poole. Signed from Villa in 1987, in a deal that took Lee Turnbull to Villa Park, he played only one League game in his first 19 months with the club – a 2–1 defeat at Millwall. Boro won promotion that year but Poole took his chance in the top flight. When Pears was injured, Poole was handed the task of helping Boro's fight against relegation. He turned in some fine performances, notably against Villa in April 1989. He produced some great saves, only to be beaten in the last minute as Villa secured a draw that would ultimately keep them up and send Boro down. He started the 1989–90 season as the custodian but struggled for form. In the second game at Leeds, Boro were one minute away from a valuable draw when Poole allowed a Gary Parkinson back pass to elude him and roll into the net. It was a setback he seemed to struggle to overcome and, with the team in dire straits, Pears was recalled by December. Poole didn't get another game and was farmed out on loan to Hartlepool, who he helped to promotion. He eventually went to Leicester in 1991 where he had a successful time as the Foxes frequently made the Play-offs. A good shot-stopper but lacking in height, he was the Leicester fans' Player of the Year in 1995 and was a sub when they played Boro in the 1997 Coca-Cola Cup Final. He moved to Birmingham in the same year.

POSKETT Malcolm

Forward
Born: Middlesbrough, 19 July 1953.
Career: South Bank.

MIDDLESBROUGH 1973. Hartlepool United 1974. Whitby Town. Hartlepool United 1976. Brighton & Hove Albion 1978. Watford 1980. Carlisle United 1982. Darlington 1985. Stockport County 1986. Hartlepool United (loan) 1986. Carlisle United 1986. Morecambe.

■ From the moment he stepped on to the scene with South Bank, local lad Malcolm Poskett scored goals. One of football's journeymen, he travelled the land hitting the net wherever his services were required. His prolific Northern League record alerted Boro to his talents but he managed only 12 minutes of action for his local club, when Jack Charlton used him as a sub against Hull in 1973. He continued to score goals regulary for the reserves but got no further first-team oppportunities. He moved on the Hartlepool after Boro's 1974 promotion but soon drifted out of the League to Whitby Town. That was the making of him, however, and he was back at Pools in 1976 at the start of a career as a prolific goalscorer in the lower League. He was involved in some big money moves for his time as clubs sought his services. Brighton paid £60,000 for him and Graham Taylor's Watford paid £110,000 in 1980. He finished at Stockport in 1986.

POULTON Alonzo (Jerry)

Inside-forward/Centre-forward
Born: Wolverhampton, 28 March 1890.
Died: 1966.
Career: Priestfield Albion. West Bromwich

Albion 1912. Worcester City (loan). Merthyr Town (loan). MIDDLESBROUGH 1919. Bristol City 1921. Reading 1922.

■ A glamorous debut at Arsenal ended in a 2–1 defeat for Poulton in March 1920. He managed only one more game in that first season after signing from West Brom, though the Baggies had actually been loaning him out to Merthyr Tydfil when Boro stepped in. The inside-forward had to wait seven months for another game, but it was a memorable one. A crowd of 40,000 at Sunderland, then Roker's record attendance, saw the game which Boro lost 2–1. He then had a run in the side in place of Walter Tinsley and scored in four successive games. Poulton's final game came in an unhappy 4–1 home defeat against Villa in which he broke his collarbone. He moved on the Welsh side Llanelli in August 1923

POVEY William

Winger
Born: Billingham, 11 January 1943.
Career: MIDDLESBROUGH 1960. York City 1964.

■ Former Grangefield Grammar School boy Bill Povey came through the Boro ranks. He waited patiently for a debut and was 19 when he finally got a game – and what a game it was. The young outside-left, in for Bobby Hume, helped Second Division Boro win 4–3 at Norwich on 29 December 1962, with conditions so bad the lines had to be painted in blue. Bad weather meant the next game wasn't until 9 February but Boro were again in goalscoring mood as they won 5–4 at Plymouth, with Povey once again in the side. Although he played only six games, a total of 16 goals were scored when Povey made the side. His last Boro game was later that season in a 3–3 draw at Derby. He became frustrated at limited opportunities in the first team and, the following year, accepted a move to York.

PRATT Richard

Inside-left
Born: 1876.
Career: South Bank. MIDDLESBROUGH 1899.

■ Forward Pratt broke into Boro's team of Football League new boys a few weeks into the 1899–1900 season as one of three debutants for a 1–1 draw at New Brighton. Initially a centre-forward, he was also played at inside-forward but drifted in and out that season, scoring only once in a 5–1 defeat at Small Heath in January and was freed that summer.

PRIEST Alfred Ernest (Fred)

Outside-left/Left-back
Born: Darlington, 1875.
Died: Hartlepool, May 1922.
Career: South Bank. Sheffield United 1896. South Bank (loan). MIDDLESBROUGH 1906. Hartlepool United.

■ Priest earned an England cap in his Sheffield United days, against Ireland in 1900, but his time with Division One Boro was brief. He played in the full-back positions in his dozen games, the first of which was a draw at Bury in September and the last a best forgotten 4–0 defeat at Newcastle before a St James' crowd of 47,000. He had a significant spell at Hartlepool, where he became their first captain and manager in the North Eastern League days and was with the club as they turned professional. He won the Durham Senior Cup while with Pools. Priest also gave Boro service as an assistant trainer. He was also licensee of the Market Hotel in Hartlepool. Fred Priest died in Hartlepool in May 1922.

PROCTOR Mark Gerard

Midfield
Born: Middlesbrough, 30 January 1961.
Career: MIDDLESBROUGH 1978. Nottingham Forest 1981. Sunderland 1983. Sheffield Wednesday 1987. MIDDLESBROUGH 1989. Tranmere Rovers 1993. Blyth Spartans. St Johnstone. Hartlepool United 1997.

■ Accomplished midfielder Mark Proctor gave sterling service to his hometown club in two spells. He was a part of the generation of bright young talent that briefly threatened to deliver Boro to the promised land and win the club some trophies. Proctor, a former pupil of St Gabriel's and St Anthony's schools, joined the club as a schoolboy and then served his time as a junior. During that period he was given the task of cleaning the boots of his hero, Graeme Souness. and it wasn't long after his departure to Liverpool that Proctor was himself in Boro's midfield. He had to wait until only the second game of the 1978–79 season for a debut, as he replaced Tony McAndrew in a 3–1 win at Birmingham. He flitted in and out at first but established himself by December, a month when he scored his first goal in a 7–2 rout of Chelsea. David Hodgson and Craig Johnston broke in at a similar time but Proctor made quicker progress than any of them, playing 31 games in his first season and weighing in with nine goals. His neat passing skills became a permanent feature for the following two seasons and the future looked bright for the club with such promising youngsters. It all seemed to be falling into place as Boro reached the FA Cup quarter-final in 1981 but that ill-fated tie was lost and Boro's young side was broken up.

Having played so well, it was inevitable other clubs would be circling around the likes of Proctor and, with his local club showing little ambition, he moved on in the summer of 1981. Brian Clough returned to Boro to sign Proctor, having been impressed by a player who skippered his England youth side. Several clubs had been interested in Under-21 international Proctor but Clough got his man for £400,000. It didn't quite work out in Nottingham and, by 1983, he was back in the North East. A loan move to Roker Park was followed by a permanent deal, though his efforts weren't enough to keep Sunderland in the top flight as

they went down in 1985. Proctor suffered a serious injury at Roker and missed out on the 1985 League Cup Final. Worse was to follow for Sunderland as Lawrie McMenemy failed to arrest the slide and they found themselves in Division Three in 1987. A man of Proctor's talents was unlikely to stay at that level for long and Sheffield Wednesday took him back to the top, paying £275,000.

Then it was time to come full circle as Bruce Rioch, trying to stave off relegation from Division One in 1989, bought Proctor in a deadline day swoop. Sadly, relegation did come, ironically at Proc's old club Wednesday on the last day of the season. The following year he had the honour of leading out his hometown club at Wembley in the ZDS Cup as a replacement for injured skipper Tony Mowbray, though Boro lost 1–0 to Chelsea. He suffered injury troubles in 1990–91, fell out with boss Colin Todd and was linked with interest from Hartlepool but came back to help Lennie Lawrence's team to promotion in 1992. His relationship with Lawrence was strained as he was frequently dropped and even the manager admitted he didn't get a fair crack of the whip. He moved on to Tranmere after a loan in 1993 and had a spell with St Johnstone before going into local League football. He was working as a youth coach at Boro when he made a surprise comeback for Hartlepool in 1996–97 after an SOS call from Mick Tait.

Proctor later returned to Boro as an Academy coach, leading the club to their first FA Youth Cup triumph. After a brief spell as reserve team manager, he became David Hodgson's number two at Darlington. He then moved north of the border to assist another former Boro star, Tony Mowbray, at Hibernian before accepting his first sole managerial post at Livingston.

PROUDLOCK Paul

Winger
Born: Hartlepool, 25 October 1965.
Career: Hartlepool United 1984. MIDDLESBROUGH 1986. Luela (loan) (Sweden). Carlisle United 1989. Hartlepool United (loan) 1992. Gateshead.

■ A fee of £25,000 doesn't look much, but for Bruce Rioch in 1986 that was a risk. Having impressed in a reserve game at Old Trafford Rioch drafted Proudlock in from Hartlepool to boost a wafer-thin squad. A skilful forward, his debut brought two goals against Doncaster in the Freight Rover Trophy and he scored in one of his two League starts, against Mansfield at Christmas 1986. Sadly, he was injured in the game and didn't play again for nearly two years, appearing only as a non-playing substitute in 1987–88. Boro allowed Proudlock to play in Sweden with Luela in summer 1988, though he did get a run out as a substitute against Liverpool's star-studded team in the First Division as Boro lost 4–0 at home. He enjoyed a long spell with Carlisle before returning to the North East with Gateshead.

PUGH Charles Edwin

Outside-left
Born: Details unknown.
Career: St Augustine's. MIDDLESBROUGH 1899.

■ Red haired Pugh was part of Boro's big bang, playing at number 11 in the first ever League game at Lincoln in 1899 and went on to finish as top scorer with seven, most notably contributing two in an 8–1 home thrashing of Burton Swifts. The outside-left was not retained for the following season but was still playing in the Teesside League as late as 1913.

PUTNEY Trevor Anthony

Midfield
Born: Harold Hill, 9 April 1960.
Career: Brentwood Town. Ipswich Town 1980. Norwich City 1986. MIDDLESBROUGH 1989. Watford 1991. Leyton Orient 1993. Colchester United 1994.

■ A broken leg in the semi-final of the ZDS Cup against Aston Villa in 1990 severely disrupted Putney's Boro career. A clash with Villa's Gordon Cowans in the opening minutes of the second leg tie at Ayresome robbed him not only of a Wembley place but six months of football. He joined newly-relegated Boro in 1989, signing for Bruce Rioch after a proposed move to Leeds fell through. Putney came into the game late and worked as a postman and warehouse worker before Ipswich spotted him, aged 20, playing for Brentwood. His five years at Portman Road ended after a bust-up with boss Bobby Ferguson and he moved up the road to Norwich where he played almost 100 games. He was credited with ending the most irritating statistic in football by scoring against Liverpool and ensuring they finally lost in a game in which Ian Rush had scored. He was unlucky to lose in three Cup semi-finals with the two East Anglian clubs. A player known as something of a dressing room comedian, Putney's party trick was apparently to drop a full pint glass on to his foot without spilling it. Whether he could do this with a ball is not recorded. Sadly, he never reached his best form at Boro as the side struggled, though he was often played on the right flank and had the broken leg. A hard working and aggressive midfielder, he did come back early in the 1990–91 season and scored his only Boro goal with a piledriver against Leicester. Putney's final Boro game was a Play-off semi-final defeat against Notts County at the end of that season. When Lennie Lawrence took over, Putney, who could not sell his house in the south, was allowed to move to Watford with Paul Wilkinson and Willie Falconer coming the other way. He retired from the game in 1995.

QUEUDRUE Franck

Left-back
Born: Paris, 27 August 1978.
Career: Meaux. RC Lens (France) 1999. MIDDLESBROUGH 2001. Fulham 2006. Birmingham 2007.

■ One of the most popular and exciting players to have represented Boro in recent seasons, 'French Franck' could also be hot headed and occasionally error prone. A talented left-sided defender, he played the game with a cavalier, devil-may-care attitude that endeared him to the fans but sometimes left manager Steve McClaren tearing his hair out with frustration. Ever willing to represent the club off the field, he was rewarded by being named Community Player of the Year by Boro's Official Supporters Club. Queudrue joined Boro on an eight-month loan from French side RC Lens in October 2001 before the deal was made permanent, with Boro paying £2.5 million for his services. He endeared himself to the Boro faithful by scoring on his home debut against Sunderland and retained his place for the remainder of the campaign. The following season saw Queudrue show his excitable nature as he was sent off three times and booked on five occasions. On the plus side, he scored a stunning free-kick from way out to earn Boro a 1–0 win against Birmingham City. His poor disciplinary record saw him miss the start of the 2003–04 season through suspension, but after going through the campaign without a red card he received a crate of what was supposedly champagne from coach Steve Harrison – it was in fact cider! That season ended with Queudrue receiving a Carling Cup-winners' medal after the 2–1 defeat of Bolton Wanderers at the

Millennium Stadium. Though not a prolific goalscorer, he netted twice the following season in a remarkable 4–4 draw with Norwich City and was rewarded for some outstanding displays with an extension to his contract. His final game in a Boro shirt was the 2006 UEFA Cup Final defeat to Sevilla in Eindhoven before he moved to Fulham in summer 2006. However, by the following close season he was being linked with a move back to the North East with Newcastle. He was later signed by Birmingham for £2.5 million.

RAISBECK Luke

Centre-half
Born: Details unknown.
Career: Sheffield United 1898. Third Lanark. MIDDLESBROUGH 1899. West Ham United.

■ A participant in Boro's first ever League campaign, half-back Raisebeck was due to make his debut away at Leicester Fosse but the registration documents weren't processed in time so Bob Gray was Boro's only debutant. With Sheffield United for part of the 1898–99 season, his only goal for the Teessiders came in a 3–0 home triumph against Loughborough Trinity.

RAMAGE Alan

Central defender
Born: Guisborough, 29 November 1957.
Career: MIDDLESBROUGH 1975.
Derby County 1980.

■ A tall central defender, Ramage was also a fast bowler for Yorkshire between 1979–83 and some of his fierce Boro critics felt that's where his sporting efforts should have been concentrated. He had the unenviable task of taking over from Willie Maddren but never rose to the same heights and his better performances were often conveniently ignored by terrace snipers who chose to concentrate on the occasional clanger. A trialist at Ayresome, he'd been offered an apprenticeship after just three games and turned fully professional on his 19th birthday, eventually making his debut as sub for Ted Coleman in the final game of the 1975–76 season at Villa Park. He was a hard, physical defender and powerful in the air. He was not, however, a cultured player and, as replacement for the classy Willie Maddren, he did not compare favourably. After a largely unfulfilled Boro career, he joined Derby County but failed to settle and was forced into premature retirement with a knee injury, the same injury which put paid to his cricketing ambitions. He's currently living in Worcester.

RAMSAY Andrew

Left-back
Born: East Benhar, 1877.
Died: Leyton, 1908.
Career: East Benhar.
MIDDLESBROUGH 1899. Leyton.

■ Boro's left full-back in their first-ever League game against Lincoln City, Ramsay also played in their first Division One games three years later...and the first game at Ayresome 12 months after that! The only player to have appeared in all three big games, the Ayresome fixture proved a temporary swansong as, after it, Ramsay didn't taste first-team action again for more than four months, losing his place to Joe Blackett. His solitary goal came in a 1–1 draw at Port Vale in 1902. Awarded a benefit match against Newcastle in September 1904, he died tragically young, aged just 31, during his spell with Leyton.

RATCLIFFE Donald

Winger
Born: Newcastle-under-Lyme, 13 November 1934.
Career: Stoke City 1953.
MIDDLESBROUGH 1963. Darlington 1966. Crewe Alexandra 1968. Winsford Athletic.

■ Wing-forward Ratcliffe was unfortunately best remembered for being only the second Boro player to be sent off twice. He also struggled to break his goalscoring duck, hitting the post, bar, opponents' knees and heads, even his own teammates with the 'keeper beaten before notching his first goal in a 3–0 home win over Derby County. He signed for Boro the day after Raich Carter saw him playing for Stoke against Scunthorpe in September 1963. Bought following an injury to another new signing, Bobby Braithwaite, he played on the left wing initially but switched to the right when Braithwaite returned. The following season he was even played as an emergency right-back as Boro struggled in the lower reaches of the Second Division table. After just 71 appearances, he was one of four players transfer listed in September 1965 and was playing for the North Regional League reserve side when Darlington offered him first-team football. He moved to Crewe from Feethams and then into non-League soccer with Winsford Athletic.

RATCLIFFE Emor (Jack)

Full-back/Left-half
Born: Hyde, 1880.
Career: Loughborough Corinthians.
Derby County 1902.
MIDDLESBROUGH 1905.

■ Versatile defender Ratcliffe was used as a makeweight in the transfer game. Under transfer regulations at the time, clubs could pull in bigger transfer fees if two players were involved, so when Steve Bloomer came to Boro from Derby County, Ratcliffe – also known as Jack – came too. Usually a left full-back, he actually made his debut on the other flank in a 1–1 draw at Notts County. He did, however, operate in several defensive positions without ever commanding a regular place.

RAVANELLI Fabrizio

Forward
Born: Italy, 11 December 1968.
Career: Perugia (Italy) 1986. Avellino 1989. Casertana (loan) 1989. Reggiana 1990. Juventus 1992.
MIDDLESBROUGH 1996. Marseille (France) 1997. Lazio 1999. Derby County 2001. Dundee 2003. Perugia 2004.

■ Love him or loathe him, you couldn't argue with Ravanelli's goalscoring skills. Boro's record purchase at the time, his signing shocked the football world and was another indication that Middlesbrough Football Club meant business. His arrival on Teesside came after months of negotiation, a first approach at Christmas having been

turned down before a £12 million fee was slapped on his grey head. That was eventually whittled down to £7 million – a bargain for a player who had scored for Juventus against Ajax in the European Cup Final. In Italy, he didn't play in Serie A until the age of 24, having plied his trade in the lower divisions before Juve paid £3 million for La Penna Bianca – the White Feather.

Certainly, his Premier League debut on Teesside was typically flamboyant, bagging all three in a 3–3 home draw with Liverpool which had home supporters jubilant and, courtesy of TV coverage, football fans across the country gasping. Comfortably top scorer in 1996–97, goal machine Ravanelli's left foot was going down in Boro folklore. He also scored Boro's first ever goal at Wembley, the joyous scenes following his extra-time strike against Leicester being forever etched in the memory. Although totally left-footed, Rav was a clinical finisher from all distances and angles. With Juninho and Emerson supplying the chances, Boro fans drooled and Rav netted many great goals, perhaps most notably a spectacular strike against Derby to secure a first ever FA Cup semi-final appearance. Whatever the quality of the goal, it was always celebrated with a trademark shirt-over-the-head routine, launching a thousand copy cat celebrations in Sunday League games across the country.

But for all his skills, he was always a controversial figure and before too long, rumours of dressing room unrest swept Teesside. He didn't keep it behind closed doors either, with his frequent bickering at players on the pitch – notably poor Mikkel Beck – setting alarm bells ringing. He made further headlines with quotes attributed to him in the Italian press, criticizing the club and its training facilities. Apparently selfish and egotistical, his presence was becoming increasingly unwelcome and, after just two games in Division One – including a typically dramatic last-minute winner – he was on his way to France, ending a short but never-to-be-forgotten Boro career.

RAYMENT Joseph Watson

Outside-right
Born: Hartlepool, 25 September 1934.
Career: MIDDLESBROUGH 1951. Hartlepool United 1955. Darlington 1958.

■ Though starting out at Boro, it was Hartlepool and Darlington who got the most benefit from outside-right Rayment. He played his first football for TDS Old Boys in Hartlepool before joining Boro as a junior and turning professional in October 1951. He made his first-team debut just before his 18th birthday in a 4–1 defeat v Liverpool and continued to play for Boro on a part-time basis during 1953–54.

REAGAN Charles Martin

Winger
Born: York, 12 May 1924.
Career: York City 1946. Hull City 1947. MIDDLESBROUGH 1948. Shrewsbury Town 1951. Portsmouth 1953. Norwich City 1954.

■ A blistering performance against Boro helped seal Reagan's move to Ayresome, with then manager David Jack remembering his contribution during an

FA Cup with Hull. A quicksilver outside-right, he nevertheless failed to cement a first-team place during his four seasons at Boro, usually being in the shadow of Johnny Spuhler and Bill Linacre. He eventually headed for Gay Meadow, although he was later to make a surprise – and brief – return to Division One football with Portsmouth.

REDFERN J.

Left-half
Born: Details unknown.
Career: MIDDLESBROUGH 1899.

■ Redfern made his debut three games into Boro's first League season, wearing the number-six jersey in a 3–1 home defeat by Small Heath. His only other games came soon afterwards in a 3–0 reverse at Woolwich Arsenal and, a week later, a 3–0 home win over Barnsley. Like so many players of that era, he was released as the directors tried to bring in players of the right quality and experience.

REID George

Centre-forward
Born: Kilmarnock.
Career: MIDDLESBROUGH 1899. Millwall Athletic.

■ A keen golfer, Reid played for West Bromwich Albion in 1898–99 before his signing for Boro was reported on 2 November 1899. And he got off to a great start, bagging two goals in his debut match – an 8–1 thrashing of Burton Swifts. Clark and Murphy also played their first games for the club. Sadly, his final game wasn't quite so successful as Boro got turned over 5–0 at Gainsborough Trinity. All but one of his outings were in the coveted number-nine shirt at centre-forward.

REID George T. (Geordie)

Inside-left/Centre-forward
Born: Blackland Mill.
Career: Warmley. Thames Ironworks. St Mirren. MIDDLESBROUGH 1905. Bradford Park Avenue 1908. Brentford. Clyde.

■ Many have done it since, but 5ft 9in Scotsman Reid was Middlesbrough FC's first ever Division One hat-trick hero. Playing alongside the famous Alf Common, his triple strike came in a 5–1 home hammering of Bury on 7 October 1905, although he'd warmed up the previous month by scoring three in a friendly win over Sunderland. He scored just two other goals in 25 more League and Cup appearances before his release in 1906, converting from the forward line to half-back as the season progressed.

REIZIGER Michael John

Defender
Born: Amsterdam, 3 May 1973.
Career: Ajax 1990. Volendam 1993. Groningen 1993. Ajax (Holland). AC Milan (Italy) 1996. Barcelona (Spain) 1997. MIDDLESBROUGH 2004. PSV Eindhoven 2005.

■ Reiziger arrived on Teesside late in his career with a hatful of medals and a massive reputation but failed to make a major impact with Boro. A vastly-experienced player, having represented three of the game's giants in Ajax, AC Milan and Barcelona, Reiziger joined the club on a free transfer from Barca, where he had won two Spanish Championship medals, in the summer of 2004. Reiziger, who earned more than 70 caps for his country and won the Champions League with Ajax in 1995, turned down an offer to stay in Spain with Valencia to try his luck in the Premiership. He made his Boro debut in the 2–2 home draw against Newcastle United on the opening day of the 2004–05 season but a serious shoulder injury suffered in the 5–3 defeat by Arsenal at Highbury ruled him out of action for three months. Shortly after his return to action Reiziger celebrated his first goal for the club, a superb solo effort in a 3–0 defeat of Aston Villa. Although he figured in the first four Premiership games of the 2005–06 season, he struggled to match his previous reputation and in August 2005 returned to his native Holland, joining PSV Eindhoven.

RICARD Hamilton Cuesta

Forward
Born: Choco, Colombia, 12 January 1974.
Career: Deportivo Cali (Colombia) 1993. MIDDLESBROUGH 1998. CSKA Sofia (Bulgaria) 2002. Indepentiente Santa Fe (Colombia) 2002. Shonan Bellmore (Japan) 2003. Emelec (Ecuador) 2004. Apoel (Cyprus) 2004. Deportivo Cali (Colombia) 2005. Numancia (Spain) 2005. Danubio (Uruguay) 2006. Shanghai Shenhua (Japan).

■ One glorious season stands out in the Boro career of the enigmatic Ricard. The powerful Columbian looked like a fish out of water when he was thrust into the thick of the 1997–98 promotion campaign, with questions over his touch and tactical awareness. But once he had settled into his new surroundings, he began to win over his doubters. Ricard finished the first season back in the Premiership as 18-goal leading scorer and he became the leading marksman in the first decade at the Riverside, while also winning the club's Player of the Year title. A Colombian international with

more than 20 full caps, Ricard certainly had the pedigree to become the latest South American to make his mark in England. Signed for £2 million from Deportivo Cali in February 1998, after a scouting mission by coach Gordon McQueen and chief scout Ray Train, his speed and strength were obvious. Premiership defenders found him difficult to handle as his confidence soared and he scored some outstanding goals. At other times, he could appear frustratingly clumsy, but that was all part of the fascination. Ricard's long trips back to Colombia to represent his country began to take its toll in 1999–2000 when he looked jaded and out of form. Bryan Robson gave him a well-deserved rest to recharge his batteries and he survived a barren patch to finish leading scorer again in a season where goals were more difficult to find. It was a similar story the following year when he recovered from a slow start to finish second in the goals chart behind Alen Boksic. His form, and Boro career, were on the wane and he did not fit into the plans of new manager Steve McClaren and in 2002, following 43 goals in 134 League and Cup games, he moved to CSKA Sofia in search of regular action and helped his new club reach the Bulgarian Cup Final, where they were defeated by rivals Levski Sofia. Ricard played only a handful of games, however, and quickly headed back to Colombia to play for Santa Fe and Tulua. He became a journeyman player, heading backwards and forwards across the Atlantic for short spells with Cypriot side APOEL, former club Cali and Spanish second division outfit Numancia. Next came Danubio, of Uruguay, whom he helped to a League title. Summer 2007 found him appealing against a three-month prison sentence for dangerous driving and trying his luck in Chinese football.

RICHARDSON Paul

Forward
Born: Durham, 22 July 1977.
Career: MIDDLESBROUGH 1994.

■ A powerful young forward, Richardson signed a one-year professional contract in 1995 after impressing as a target man for the youth team. Sadly, a bad injury disrupted his progress and he never recaptured his early promise, playing only once for the Boro first team as sub in a 3–1 Anglo-Italian Cup defeat in Ancona, watched by only 1,500 fans in November 1994. He was released after failing to make the grade.

RICKABY Stanley

Full-back
Born: Stockton-on-Tees, 12 March 1924.
Career: South Bank. MIDDLESBROUGH 1946. West Bromwich Albion 1950. Poole Town. Weymouth.

■ Although he played 10 games for Boro, it's as manager of non-League Poole Town that Rickaby will probably be best remembered on Teesside. That's because in September 1955, he pulled off the extraordinary coup of signing former Boro teammate Wilf Mannion following the Golden Boy's ban from League football. Poole's crowd rocketed from 1,000 to 5,000 in a stroke! A decent left-back and captain of Boro reserves in the immediate post-war period, Rickaby yearned for regular first-team football but David Jack had an abundance of defensive talent. He finally got his chance v Derby County in March 1948, just four days before his 24th birthday, but he soon moved to The Hawthorns after being promised regular football by WBA boss Jack Smith. Once in the Midlands, he graduated to Football League representative honours and was capped by England against Northern Ireland in Belfast in 1954. He also managed Weymouth but later moved to Australia. Rickaby later wrote a book about his football career.

RICKETTS Michael Barrington

Forward
Born: Birmingham, 4 December 1978.
Career: Walsall 1996. Bolton Wanderers 2000. MIDDLESBROUGH 2003. Leeds United 2004. Stoke City (loan) 2005. Cardiff City (loan) 2005. Burnley (loan) 2006. Preston North End 2006. Oldham Athletic 2007.

■ Boro fans licked their lips on the day Ricketts was unveiled at Rockliffe Park, along with fellow striker Malcolm Christie and defender Chris Riggott. Sadly, the one-cap England international was to become one of the club's most disappointing signings of all time, looking overweight and out of touch during games and failing to find the goalscoring form which had built his considerable reputation. However, he did score a vital goal against Spurs as well as two penalty shootout goals on the way to Boro's 2004 Carling Cup success, and he picked up a winners' medal for his substitute appearance in the Final. Ricketts began his career with Walsall, leaving to join Bolton Wanderers for £500,000 in July 2000. He scored on his Trotters' debut and continued to find the net for the remainder of the campaign, finishing with 24 goals in all competitions as they won promotion to the top flight via the Play-offs. His spectacular rise continued as he made an immediate impression on the Premiership stage, scoring some eye-catching goals and earning that England cap as a substitute against Holland. But after that the goals dried up and he went almost a year before scoring again from open play. Hoping to refind his goalscoring touch, he joined Boro in a £2.5 million deal in January 2003. His only goal in nine games that season came on the final day as Boro lost 2–1 against his former club, a result that kept Wanderers in the Premiership. Though he scored just three more goals in 2003–04, he retained the support of manager Steve McClaren in the face of considerable criticism from the Boro faithful. He did score a crucial late equaliser at Tottenham on the way to Boro's Carling Cup success, but that was a rare highlight. However, McClaren's patience eventually waned and Ricketts joined Leeds United on a free transfer in June 2004. But his career continued in freefall and after loan spells with Stoke, Cardiff and Burnley, he signed a two-year deal with Southend. But he was released just two months later, the club accusing him of being overweight and out of condition. After a handful of games for Preston and still aged just 28, he was released by boss Paul Simpson in May 2007 before taking up an offer from Oldham.

RIGBY Arthur

Outside-left/Inside-left
Born: Chorlton, 7 June 1900.
Died: March 1960.

Career: Stockport County 1919. Crewe Alexandra. Bradford City 1920. Blackburn Rovers 1924. Everton 1929. MIDDLESBROUGH 1932. Clapton Orient 1933. Crewe Alexandra 1935.

■ England international Rigby was past his best by the time he joined Boro. An electrician by trade, he started out as a goalkeeper in the Manchester Amateur League but, after switching to outside-left, had a trial with Stockport before joining Crewe. He then moved to Bradford for £1,200 and Blackburn for £2,500, winning England caps along the way and the FA Cup in 1928. On losing his place at Blackburn, he joined Everton and helped the Toffees regain their Division One status before Boro boss Peter McWilliam signed him and left-winger George Martin for a combined £900 fee. During his time at Boro, his skill, cunning and class were obvious, but the cutting edge had gone and he returned to Crewe to end his career. He retired from the game in 1937 and lived in Crewe until his death in March 1960.

RIGGOTT Christopher Mark

Defender
Born: Derby, 1 September 1980.
Career: Derby County 1998. MIDDLESBROUGH 2003.

■ A talented central defender with an eye for goal, Chris Riggott joined Boro from Derby County together with striker Malcolm Christie on transfer deadline day 2003 in a deal worth a combined £3 million with bonuses rising to £5 million. At the Riverside he quickly developed into one of the brightest young central defenders in the country. Former manager Steve McClaren had seen Riggott emerge from close quarters while he was a coach at Pride Park. An England Under-21 international, Riggott was said to have been a £7 million target for Liverpool towards the end of the 2001–02 season but the deal never materialised. Initially he joined Boro on a three-month loan, with a guaranteed permanent transfer to follow on at the end. His task of breaking into the Boro first team meant breaking up the England international partnership of

Gareth Southgate and Ugo Ehiogu but he soon showed he was up to the task. A month after joining the club he scored twice in seven minutes during a 3–1 win at Sunderland. Gradually Chris has shaken off the deputy tag to become one of Boro's most reliable defenders. His 2003–04 season was interrupted by injury which restricted his Premiership appearances, but he was in the side for the two Carling Cup semi-final games with Arsenal and was unlucky not to start in the Final against Bolton. He did, however, have the consolation of a seat on the bench at the Millennium Stadium. The following season saw Riggott cement a place in the Boro side, but in the latter part of the campaign he struggled with a knee injury and was forced to undergo surgery. Having finally emerged from the shadows of Ehiogu and Southgate, Riggott became one of Boro's most consistent performers and in 2005–06 was voted the Players' Player of the Season. He also scored one of the goals in the dramatic UEFA Cup semi-final comeback against Steaua Bucharest at the Riverside and appeared in the final defeat to Sevilla. However, injuries and the form of Jonathan Woodgate and Emanuel Pogatetz meant he was a spectator for much of the following campaign.

RIPLEY Stuart Edward

Right-winger
Born: Middlesbrough, 20 November 1967.
Career: MIDDLESBROUGH 1985. Bolton Wanderers (loan) 1986. Blackburn

Rovers 1992. Southampton 1998. Barnsley (loan) 2000. Sheffield Wednesday (loan) 2001.

■ Pace frightens defenders and in blond winger Stuart Ripley, Boro had found a wide man to terrorise any full-back. Part of the Boro Boys team that shared the English Shield in 1983, he had trials with Chelsea and Man City before joining Boro and quickly made it into a youth team that also boasted Colin Cooper, Gary Hamilton, Alan Kernagan and Peter Beagrie. His first-team baptism was as substitute in a 2–1 home defeat by Oldham in February 1985, but it was during a loan spell with Third Division Bolton Wanderers that it became obvious Boro had unearthed a real talent. Immensely popular at Burnden Park, where he made his full scoring debut as a 17-year-old, Ripley returned to Ayresome and the fringes of a side battling unsuccessfully against relegation. With Boro on the brink, Ripley travelled to China on a goodwill trip with the England Youth team, which is where he heard news of the dreaded drop.

But it was in Bruce Rioch's famous Division Three side that Ripley first started regularly powering down opposition flanks with some exciting displays. A direct player, he mainly used power and pace to beat defenders and while his delivery was sometimes wayward, he became a firm favourite with the fans. 'Rippers' made his England Under-21 debut in the Toulon tournament v Soviet Union but, on a lower note, he was sent off in 1987–88 for fighting with Leeds' Glynn Snodin. He also missed out on an England B tour with Pallister and Mowbray through injury. The 1989–90 season wasn't plain sailing either, with hamstring injuries and a back injury sustained in a car crash contributing to below-par performances. Ripley, who was fluent in French, was back to his best in 1990–91 and although usually a winger, a run-out at centre forward bagged him a hat-trick in a 6–0 demolition of Sheffield United. Six goals in as many games then helped push Boro towards promotion, but he was injured again as Boro lost in the Play-offs. In 1991–92, he lost 10lb with flu over Christmas but at least he finally sorted out his long-running back injury, allowing him to star in that season's promotion side.

But even promotion to the top flight couldn't persuade him to stay, Ripley feeling the time was right for a new challenge. He also upset some Boro fans by saying he was sick of the club always living in the shadow of Newcastle and Sunderland, a situation he feared promotion wouldn't change. His move to Blackburn provided, initially at least, the success he feared he wouldn't taste with Boro and he was a key part of the side that lifted the Premiership title in 1995. He also made his full England debut against San Marino in Graham Taylor's last game as boss. Frequently linked with a move back to Boro, Ripley moved instead to Southampton and continues to make regular first-team appearances. And if his reception at the 1999–2000 season's Boro v Saints clash is anything to go by, Teesside fans are still immensely fond of a player who encapsulated the excitement and optimism of re-born Boro in the 1980s.

ROBERTS Alan

Right-winger
Born: Newcastle, 8 December 1964.
Career: MIDDLESBROUGH 1982. Darlington 1985. Sheffield United 1988. Lincoln City 1989.

■ Perhaps Roberts' finest Boro moment came after just 15 seconds of one game, as that's how long it took him to score from the kick-off at Manchester City in 1983. A right-sided wide midfielder, he was slightly built but tenacious, skilful and a good crosser. He certainly caught the eye of Malcom Allison, who gave him a new contract when it seemed he was on the way out at Boro after being released at the end of the 1982–83 season. His full League debut came in the opening game of the 1983–84 season – a 1–0 win at Portsmouth – but he struggled to hold down a regular first-team place and was dropped after a Milk Cup defeat against

Third Division Mansfield. A player-exchange deal saw him and Paul Ward join Darlington, with Boro getting £5,000 and Mitch Cook in return. And, as often happens, the Boro reject returned to shock his former club, scoring for the Quakers at Boro in 1986–87 to become the first opposition player to score at Ayresome for more than four months. A £15,000 move to Sheffield United was followed by a switch to Lincoln City, but a knee injury forced his retirement aged just 25.

ROBERTS Benjamin James

Goalkeeper
Born: Bishop Auckland, 22 June 1975.
Career: MIDDLESBROUGH 1993. Hartlepool United (loan) 1995. Wycombe Wanderers (loan) 1995. Bradford City (loan) 1996. Millwall (loan) 1999. Luton Town (loan) 2000. Charlton Athletic 2000. Reading (loan) 2002. Luton Town (loan) 2002. Brighton & Hove Albion 2003.

■ For such a good goalie, it's a shame his main claim to fame so far is an unwanted one – the 'keeper conceding the fastest ever goal in an FA Cup Final. That 42-second strike by Roberto Di Matteo would have dented anyone's confidence. He was first named as Boro's goalkeeping substitute in August 1992 at the tender age of 17 and played in a 3–1 Anglo-Italian Cup defeat in Ancona in 1994, but his League debut didn't come until January 1997. Until then, a succession of 'keepers – Ironside, Collett, Pears, Miller and Walsh – had kept him at bay. An England Under-21 international, he enjoyed loan spells with Hartlepool, Wycombe and Bradford before making the breakthrough at Boro, battling his way into the first team late in the 1996–97 Premiership campaign. Mark Schwarzer's form and a persistent back injury then kept him largely at bay, but he returned to competitive action in December 1998 and enjoyed a successful loan spell at Millwall, where he suffered another Wembley heartache in the Second Division Play-off Final. Millwall wanted to sign him but Boro preferred to hang on to Roberts. A good shot-stopper, he was also a talented cricketer who opened the batting for Crook Cricket Club.

ROBERTS J.

Outside-left
Born: Details unknown.
Career: MIDDLESBROUGH 1906.

■ Outside-left Roberts made just one Boro appearance and it wasn't a happy one, the side going down 3–0 at Newcastle United in October 1906. His namesake, William Roberts, replaced him for the next match and he was released soon after.

ROBERTS Richard James

Winger
Born: Redditch, 1887.
Died: 1931.
Career: Redditch Excelsior. West Bromwich Albion 1899. Newcastle United 1901. MIDDLESBROUGH 1903. Crystal Palace.

■ Roberts' Boro career began with a bang, scoring on his debut in gale force winds in a 1–0 triumph v Liverpool on 2 April 1904 and netting again in the next match v Bury. Indeed, 'Old Bird' in the *Sports Gazette* was moved to write: 'Roberts is proving to be a fine acquisition...the only question that needs to be asked of the directors is why he was brought to the club so late in the season?' A teetotaller and non-smoker, he was signed on the recommendation of director George Pickard after putting in some fast and direct performances at Newcastle United, although he'd made his name as a pacy winger at West Bromwich Albion. A big favourite at St James' Park and the leading scorer in 1901–02, he lost his place to Scottish international Bobby Templeton and Boro moved in. After his brief spell on Teesside, he followed manager John Robson to newly-formed Southern League club Crystal Palace. He died in 1931.

ROBERTS William S.

Outside-left
Born: Details unknown.
Career: MIDDLESBROUGH 1906.

■ Outside-left Roberts struggled to establish himself in the 1906–07 season, but boss Andy Aitken put him in from the start of the following campaign. However, his appearances remained spasmodic and he pulled on a Boro shirt for the final time in a 0–0 draw at Sheffield United on Christmas Day 1907, having lost his place to Jim Thackeray.

ROBERTSON Alexander (Sandy)

Centre-forward/Outside-left
Born: Dundee, 1878.
Career: Dundee Violet. Dundee. MIDDLESBROUGH 1900. Manchester United 1903.

■ A centre-forward, Scotsman Robertson scored Boro's first two goals in the top flight – each winning efforts in consecutive 1–0 triumphs against Blackburn Rovers and Everton. He was one of nine players who had made their Middlesbrough debuts against Lincoln on the opening day of the 1900–01 season – Boro's second in the League – and found the net in a 2–0 win at Linthorpe Road. There was a steady flow of goals, including a hat-trick against Kettering in the FA Cup. The club's top scorer in 1900–01, it is believed injury ruled him out for most of the following season but he returned with a hat-trick as Chesterfield were hammered 7–1 in March 1902 and he scored more vital goals as promotion to Division One was secured for the first time. Injury again disrupted his season in the top flight, though he was again top scorer. Robertson left Teesside to join Newton Heath – better known nowadays as Manchester United.

ROBERTSON James

Outside-right
Born: Details unknown.
Career: MIDDLESBROUGH 1901. New Brompton.

■ Outside-right Robertson played in the last game at Linthorpe Road but never trod the hallowed turf at Ayresome Park. Having made his debut along with Joe Blackett against Woolwich Arsenal in October 1901, he was the regular winger through the following First Division campaign but his final goal for Boro was the consolation in a 2–1 defeat by Sunderland, played at Newcastle's St James' Park on 18 April 1903.

ROBERTSON William George

Winger
Born: Glasgow, 4 November 1936.
Career: MIDDLESBROUGH 1953.

■ A Glaswegian, he cut short his first-team chances by opting to join the forces in 1955. An outside-right or left, his debut came in place of Bert Mitchell against Swansea in February 1955. His two goals came in a 3–1 defeat at Doncaster Rovers and on the final day of the 1954–55 season in a 2–2 draw at Bristol Rovers. He was released from his contract four years later after several seasons in the reserves.

ROBINSON John

Inside-forward
Born: Middlesbrough, 10 February 1934.
Career: MIDDLESBROUGH 1951. Hartlepool United 1959.

■ Robinson's debut came in the final game of the 1953–54 relegation season in a 3–1 home defeat by Arsenal. He then began the first two games in Boro's Division Two campaign but after Arthur Fitzsimons claimed the inside-forward position, Robinson never appeared for Boro again. His reserve team football was punctuated by National Service and he was allowed to join Hartlepool in 1959.

ROBINSON John William

Left-half/Inside-left
Born: Grangetown.
Career: MIDDLESBROUGH 1919. Portsmouth 1921. Guildford United. Queen's Park Rangers 1923.

■ Robinson's solitary outing in a Boro shirt came in a big local derby, but it wasn't a particularly happy occasion. With 30,000 people inside Ayresome, Newcastle clinched a 1–0 First Division win – and so ended Robinson's Boro career. The left-half position had been troublesome since the League restarted after the war, but Robinson was not the answer and Bill Fox returned for the next match against Chelsea.

ROBINSON Joseph Norman

Centre-half
Born: Middlesbrough, 5 January 1921.
Died: 1990.
Career: South Bank St Peters. MIDDLESBROUGH 1946. Grimsby Town 1948.

■ A tough, towering defender, Robinson was the brother-in-law of Wilf Mannion but his Boro career never scaled such heights. Yet another product of South Bank St Peter's, he made his debut at half-back at Sheffield United soon after League football returned following the Great War. He lost his place to Jimmy McCabe and, after just 17 games, was allowed to leave. He joined Grimsby Town in a part-exchange deal for Tom Blenkinsopp but after five games for the Blundell Park outfit, he revealed an injury that pre-empted his early retirement from the game. Town approached Boro for compensation and as a compromise, the Teesside club agreed to sell Paddy Johnston to the Mariners for a much-reduced fee. Robinson died in 1990.

ROBINSON Richard (Dicky)

Full-back
Born: South Shields, 19 January 1927.
Career: MIDDLESBROUGH 1945. Barrow 1959.

■ Few footballers can have had their boss as a golf caddy, but it was Boro manager David Jack who carried Robinson's clubs during the 1951 PFA Golf Championships! Indeed, it was Jack who'd brought Robinson to Boro after seeing him play for Mandale Juniors. Signed as a promising forward, he was tried as a left-winger but eventually settled in at full-back, although the player himself preferred the centre-half

slot. Reliable and stylish, Robinson went straight into the side after the war and clocked up over 400 games to stand 10th in the club's all-time appearance list. Golf was his other sporting love and as a boy, he earned extra money caddying for Sunderland players Johnny Mapson and Eddie Burbanks. But it was as a footballer that he really made people take notice and even during the war he was in demand, guesting for Dunfermline Athletic while he worked down the mines as a Bevin Boy. At Boro, he made his League debut in the club's first post-war League game with George Hardwick as his fellow full-back at Villa Park. Robinson soon made his name as a hard but classy, quick and intelligent defender. Rarely beaten by a winger, he was also extremely good in the air and a clutch of outstanding displays earned him Football League honours. His only goal for Boro was against Sunderland, more than 10 years after his debut, and he actually travelled back to his Whitburn home on the Sunderland team bus. He was given a two week suspension for an undisclosed incident after an away game at Wolves in November 1952 and asked for a transfer, but he withdrew the request a month later. A series of niggling injuries forced his retirement and he spent a year out of the game before joining Barrow as trainer. Robinson later worked in the Furness shipyards.

ROBSON Bryan

Midfield
Born: Witton Gilbert, 11 January 1957.
Career: West Bromwich Albion 1974. Manchester United 1981. MIDDLESBROUGH 1994.

■ History will judge Bryan Robson as the man who transformed Middlesbrough from an under-achieving second-tier club to a high-profile Premier League outfit packed with big-name stars. Boro achieved unparalleled growth and development on and off the pitch during his seven-year stewardship, with the signing of big-name players such as Juninho, Fabrizio Ravanelli and Alen Boksic and the opening of the Riverside Stadium and Rockliffe Park training ground. No wonder the former England great still inspires respect and affection from the club's fanbase. It was a considerable coup by chairman Steve Gibson to secure Robson for his first managerial post at the end of a distinguished career at Manchester United. Few could have guessed the scale of the transformation to come when he arrived as player-manager in May 1994, having turned down Wolves for Teesside. He wasted no time in getting started, guiding the club to promotion in his first management season and even becoming Boro's oldest-ever goalscorer with his strike against Port Vale on March 26 1995. Robson went on to guide the club to its first major Cup Finals and achieved a second promotion in 1997–98. One of the game's greatest players throughout the 1980s, he won 90 England caps and skippered the side an amazing 65 times. His playing career began at West Bromwich Albion before he moved to Old Trafford for a then British record fee of £1.5 million. And so began a quite extraordinary spell, winning League, FA Cup, League Cup and European glories during an unforgettable career, much of it alongside Gary Pallister. At Boro, niggling injuries, especially sciatica, restricted his first-team outings but he still had a great on-field presence and, when he played, he controlled midfield with his trademark tough tackling and slide-rule passing. Typically, he was still breaking records to the very end, becoming the oldest ever player to appear for the club in a New Year's Day 1997 clash at Arsenal. Even so, it wasn't until the following January that he finally announced his playing retirement to concentrate on a management career that bagged him three Manager of the Month awards and, during Terry Venables's reign, saw him as assistant England boss. Robson stabilised the club in the Premiership during the late 1990s with the signing of experienced players such as Paul Ince, Andy Townsend, Brian Deane and Gary Pallister. He was also not afraid to ask for help, in the shape of his former England mentor Venables, when Boro sunk to the bottom of the League in early 2000–01. Together they steered the club away from trouble, though Robson was hurt to be booed by a small section of fans when he went on to the pitch following the final match. Gibson decided it was time for a change and next season Steve McClaren was in charge for a very different style of Riverside revolution.

Surprisingly, it took Robson two years to win another shot at management, but he was unable to prevent trouble-torn Bradford City from being relegated to the third tier. He enjoyed better fortunes in a two-year stint at West Bromwich Albion, keeping them in the Premiership in a dramatic final day of the 2004–05 season. The Baggies succumbed to the drop the following year, however, and after an indifferent start to their Championship campaign he again found himself out of work before teaming up with another ex-Manchester United colleague, Brian Kidd, at Sheffield United in May 2007.

ROCHEMBACK Fabio

Midfield
Born: Soledade, Brazil, 10 December 1981.
Career: Internacional (Brazil) 2000. Barcelona (Spain) 2001. Sporting Lisbon (Portugal) (loan) 2003. MIDDLESBROUGH 2005.

■ Boro's penchant for Brazilian international midfielders continued when Rochemback was signed from Barcelona shortly before the closure of the August 2005 transfer window. Skilful and hard working, Rochemback mainly operates just in front of the defence, where he loves to spray the ball around, with a deceptive look-the-other-way pass among the weapons in his armoury. Rochemback arrived at the Riverside after ending a very successful loan spell with Sporting Lisbon. Having missed the club's pre-season friendlies and the opening Premiership game of the 2005–06 season, he made his top-flight debut in a 2–1 home win over Arsenal. However, he was unavailable for the initial stages of the UEFA Cup because he had played for Sporting Lisbon against Udinese in the Champions League before his transfer. Rochemback scored his first goal for the club in a 3–0 defeat of eventual champions Chelsea but in February 2006 damaged his ankle ligaments in the FA Cup win over Preston North End at Deepdale. The injury kept him sidelined until the latter stages of the campaign, but he was back for Boro's UEFA Cup Final against Sevilla in Eindhoven, finishing with a runners'-up medal for the second successive season. Rochemback experienced mixed fortunes during the 2006–07 campaign and was reported to be unsettled during the January transfer window. But he returned to the side at the end of the season and again showed glimpses of the form that helped him break into the Brazil side as a teenager.

RODGERSON Alan Ralph

Inside-forward
Born: Potters Bar, 19 March 1939.
Career: MIDDLESBROUGH 1956. Cambridge United. Hereford United.

■ A skilful inside-forward, former England Schoolboy Rodgerson came to Boro via non-League Potters Bar and scored twice on his debut in a 4–1 win at Rotherham United in 1958 while standing in for Derek McLean. He played in 10 more games during the 1958–59 season but only one game each season in the following two while he served his National Service in the Army and was deemed surplus to requirements in 1964. His career finished at non-League level with Cambridge United and Hereford United.

ROOKS Richard (Dickie)

Centre-half
Born: Sunderland, 29 May 1940.
Career: Sunderland 1957. MIDDLESBROUGH 1965. Bristol City 1969. Willington.

■ A popular blond centre-half, Rooks joined Boro after getting frustrated

playing understudy to Charlie Hurley at Sunderland. Ironically, Hurley got injured the day after Rooks left but Boro boss Raich Carter already had his man, signing Rooks as a replacement for Swindon-bound Mel Nurse. Although a powerful defender with an unquenchable spirit and aerial dominance, it was as a makeshift centre-forward that he grabbed the headlines on the final day of the 1965–66 season. Sadly his hat-trick in a 5–3 defeat at Cardiff City wasn't enough to prevent Boro being relegated to Division Three for the first time in their history. A dispirited Rooks asked for a transfer but was turned down and he stayed to help win promotion at the first attempt. And it was during those next two seasons that Rooks really cemented his place as a fans' favourite, winning the club's Player of the Year award in 1967–68 and 1968–69. He also returned to his goalscoring exploits, netting in Boro's first ever *Match of the Day* televised match – a 1–1 draw with Blackpool in December 1968. Unhappy at being dropped by boss Stan Anderson near the end of the 1968–69 campaign, so spoiling his ever-present record, Rooks left soon afterwards to join Bristol City. Anderson, however, felt he had a ready-made replacement in utility man Bill Gates. At Ashton Gate, Rooks was fined and censured after press comments that he was about to ask for a transfer because he didn't want to stay at a club fighting relegation. Soon afterwards, he returned to the North East to run a DIY shop in Sunderland but was tempted into Football League management by Scunthorpe United in 1974. Things didn't go smoothly and the club was forced to seek re-election in 1974–75, so he switched to East Africa where a three-year coaching spell was rudely ended by war in Tanzania. He now runs a building firm in Sunderland.

ROSS Albert Cyril

Full-back
Born: York, 7 October 1916.
Career: Arsenal 1933. Gainsborough Trinity. MIDDLESBROUGH 1935. Bradford Park Avenue 1936. Chester 1938.

■ Signed from Gainsborough Trinity, Ross made his debut at left-back in a 1–0 defeat at Brentford on 18 January 1936, covering for regular full-back Bobby Stuart. Further games came at right-back in 1937–38 in place of George Laking as Boro challenged for the title. Boro bought him for £50 and agreed to donate a further £150 if he played 12 games. And that's exactly how many he played, although Boro weren't complaining – they sold him for £750.

ROSS Colin

Midfield
Born: Dailly, 29 August 1962.
Career: MIDDLESBROUGH 1980. Chesterfield (loan) 1983. Darlington 1983. South Bank. Whitby Town.

■ Recruited from Ayr United Boys Club, midfielder Ross had always wanted to come to England and he duly arrived for trials aged just 15. He soon caught the eye with his tough-tackling central displays, although his first-team debut was delayed when tonsilitis forced his withdrawal from a squad to play Manchester City. John Neal eventually gave him his debut in a 1–0 defeat at Southampton, but Ross only became a regular under Bobby Murdoch as Boro were relegated. He was dropped after playing right-back in a 4–1 home defeat to Grimsby in the Second Division, though he won a recall under Malcolm Allison. However he was taken off at half-time against Blackburn with Boro 1–0 down. Blackburn eventually ran out 5–1 winners! His final game came after a loan spell with Chesterfield. Ross left for Darlington on a free transfer before the 1983–84 season. Sadly, a bad knee injury forced him to quit League football at the tender age of 22, although he later played for South Bank. He's also one of many Boro players who, having tasted Teesside life, decided to stay. He still played occasional games alongside Terry Cochrane for the Navigation pub team.

ROWELL Gary

Winger
Born: Sunderland, 6 June 1957.
Career: Sunderland 1974. Norwich City 1984. MIDDLESBROUGH 1985. Brighton & Hove Albion 1986. Dundee. Carlisle United 1988. Burnley 1988.

■ Having originally made his name as a prolific scorer at Sunderland, Rowell welcomed a North East return when Willie Maddren rescued him from a relatively barren spell at Norwich, where he had struggled with injuries. Capped once by England at Under-21 level, Rowell still had the finishing touch and ended the 1985–86 relegation season as Boro's top scorer with 10 goals to his name, often partnering the newly-signed Bernie Slaven. Although confident and composed in front of goal, he was something of a loner and didn't mix with his teammates off the pitch. But being top scorer wasn't good enough to impress new boss Bruce Rioch. Out in the cold under Rioch, Rowell moved on to Brighton but failed to hold down a first-team place. His career ended with spells at Dundee, Carlisle and Burnley.

RUSSELL Edward Thomas

Wing-half
Born: Cranwell, 15 July 1928.
Career: St Chads College. Wolverhampton Wanderers 1946. MIDDLESBROUGH 1951. Leicester City 1953. Notts County 1958.

■ Despite making his debut at right-back, Russell was actually a tall and talented wing-half. His Boro debut couldn't have gone much worse – they got thumped 7–1 at Burnley – but while always a fringe player, he often showed signs of ability and flair. His only Boro goal was a dramatic last-gasp equaliser against his former club Wolves at Molineux in 1952. He moved on to help Leicester City win promotion to Division One as Boro were going the other way, although Leicester's stay in the top League was for one season only. Russell was unable to help Notts County avoid relegation in his only season at Meadow Lane.

RUSSELL Martin Christopher

Midfield
Born: Dublin, 27 April 1967.
Career: Manchester United 1984. Birmingham City (loan) 1986. Leicester City 1987. Scarborough 1989. MIDDLESBROUGH 1990. Portadown.

■ They say home is where the heart is and that certainly seemed the case with Irish winger Russell. An apprentice at Manchester United for two and a half years without playing, he made his Football League debut in a loan spell at Birmingham before becoming Scarborough's record signing at £100,000. A nine goal blast for the Seasiders prompted Colin Todd to bring him to Teesside, but the exciting wing play which earned him an Eire B cap failed to fully materialise and a school of thought persisted that he wanted to return to Ireland. Although skilful and a fine crosser of the ball, Russell – signed at the same time as Jimmy Phillips – never impressed Todd enough for a long run in the first team. Allowed to leave in August 1991, with Boro waiving a fee, he joined Portadown and was voted Northern Ireland Player of the Year for the 1992–93 season.

SAXBY Michael William

Central defender
Born: Clipstone, 12 August 1957.
Career: Mansfield Town 1975. Luton Town 1979. Grimsby Town (loan) 1983. Lincoln City (loan) 1983. Newport County 1984. MIDDLESBROUGH 1984.

■ Having once been a £200,000-rated defender when bought by Luton, big things were hoped of from the 6ft 2in central back. Snapped up by Willie Maddren on a free transfer from Newport County in 1984, he made his debut in place of Darren Wood, who had been sold to Chelsea. Boro fans certainly liked what they saw as, on an impressive first home outing, he marshalled the defence superbly in a 1–0 victory over Charlton. Sadly, a training injury saw him spend a full year on the sidelines with knee cartilage trouble, the injury which eventually forced his retirement after just 17 starts for Boro.

SCHWARZER Mark

Goalkeeper
Born: Sydney, Australia, 6 October 1972.
Career: Blacktown. Marconi (Australia) 1990. Dynamo Dresden (Germany) 1994. Kaiserslautern (Germany) 1995. Bradford City 1996. MIDDLESBROUGH 1997.

■ Boro's longest-serving player is also the club's most capped player of all time, overtaking the immortal Wilf Mannion with his appearances for Australia. Schwarzer is one of only 13 players to make 400 League and Cup appearances for Middlesbrough and was on course to break into the top 10 list of the club's all-time appearance-makers at the end of 2006–07. A model of consistency, he has been No 1 between the posts for 10 seasons since his bargain £1.25 million move from Bradford City in February 1997. Boro were his fourth club in three years following spells with Dynamo Dresden, Kaiserslautern and Bradford City and he welcomed the stability the move to Teesside brought. He had started out as a 15-year-old in Australia with Marconi Stallions when his teammates included Christian Vieri, progressing to the first team by 19 and helping them win the Australian National League during a four-year stay. He won his first Australia cap as a sub in a qualifying match for the 1994 World Cup against Canada shortly after a training spell with Bayer Leverkusen in Germany. He failed to break into Dynamo Dresden's first team but played four times at Kaiserslautern, though they were eventually relegated from the Bundesliga. After deciding to move to England, he joined Bradford for £150,000 in November 1996 after City's Middlesbrough-born manager Chris Kamara had spotted him on trial with Manchester City. The tall and commanding player quickly came to the attention of Middlesbrough and made the move to Teesside after just four months at Valley Parade, turning down Everton for Boro. After making his debut at Stockport in the semi-final of the Coca-Cola Cup, he soon established himself at the Riverside as a commanding figure at the back and a terrific shot-stopper, so it came as no surprise when he was offered – and signed – a massive six-and-a-half year contract in November 1998. He was in goal for both the 1997 and 1998 Coca-Cola Cup Finals, although he missed the 1997 replay through a leg injury. He was also absent from the 1997 FA Cup Final against Chelsea, having appeared for Bradford earlier in the competition. Internationally, for a while, he opted to concentrate on his Boro career rather than keep playing second fiddle to Mark Bosnich. He had become frustrated under Terry Venables when Zejlko Kalac was preferred, despite the fact he was still playing his football back in Australia. But Schwarzer's form for Boro soon earned him No 1 status and he achieved a lifetime ambition by helping his country qualify for the World Cup Finals in Germany in 2006. One of his highlights was an unforgettable second-round match with eventual winners Italy, and he has set his sights on keeping the jersey for the 2010 tournament. Schwarzer was consistently impressive at club level and made one of his most crucial saves against Robbie Fowler of Manchester City from the penalty spot in May 2005 to assure Boro of a second successive season in Europe, a moment that resulted in commentator Alastair Brownlee memorably describing him as 'the greatest Australian since Ned Kelly'. He was a key figure in the run to the UEFA Cup Final, appearing in the defeat to Sevilla in Eindhoven wearing a protective face mask after fracturing his cheekbone in the FA Cup semi-final against West Ham. In January 2006, he asked to be placed on the transfer list following differences with the club but later withdrew the request 'for the good of the club and the team'. However, there was more talk of him leaving during the summer of 2007 when he was playing for his country in the Asia Cup.

SCOTT Geoffrey Samuel

Defender
Born: Birmingham, 31 October 1956.
Career: Solihull Boro. Highgate United. Stoke City 1977. Leicester City 1980. Birmingham City 1982. Charlton Athletic 1982. MIDDLESBROUGH 1984. Northampton Town 1984. Cambridge United 1985.

■ A well-travelled left-back, Scott's Boro career couldn't have got off to a much poorer start, making his first team bow in a 2–0 League Cup defeat at Bradford and then suffering with the rest in a 5–1 home pummelling by Grimsby Town on his League debut. His form never really recovered from such a bad start, a surprising fate for a player with more than 130 appearances under his belt by the time he joined Boro. He began his career with Stoke City but was relegated in his first season before winning promotion in his second. He was subsequently snapped up by Leicester City for £80,000 and Charlton Athletic for £40,000 before, on release from The Valley, Boro boss Willie Maddren moved in to bring him to Ayresome, initially on a one-month contract. The optimism at recruiting such an experienced performer soon waned and within three months, his contract was cancelled and he was on his way to Northampton Town.

SCOTT Joseph Cumpson

Inside-forward
Born: Fatfield, 9 January 1930.
Career: Newcastle United. Spennymoor United. Luton Town 1952. MIDDLESBROUGH 1954. Hartlepool United 1959. York City 1960.

■ Geordie Joe began his Boro career with a bang, firing an impressive 16 goals in 29 games during his debut season to make him runner-up in the scoring stakes to leading scorer and fellow new kid on the block, Charlie Wayman. He'd originally hoped to make it with Newcastle United but, after failing to make the breakthrough, he dropped into non-League soccer with Spennymoor before moving back into the League with Luton Town. Boro boss Bob Dennison snapped up the inside-forward for £5,000 and it proved money well spent as he became an established name in the first-team line-up between 1954–57. Boro were in desperate trouble at the bottom of the Second Division table when he joined but two goals on his home debut against Lincoln set the ball rolling and brought the first win of the season at the 10th time of asking. His appearances then began to dwindle following the emergence of Derek McLean and he eventually moved on to Hartlepool in 1959.

SCOTT William Reed

Inside-forward/Right-half
Born: Willington Quay, 6 December 1907.
Died: London, October 1969.
Career: Howden British Legion. MIDDLESBROUGH 1930. Brentford 1932. Aldershot 1947. Dover.

■ Signed as an amateur from Howden, County Durham-born Scott spent five years with Boro before moving to Brentford and really making his name. One of several ex-Boro players recruited at Griffin Park, his was probably the most regretted of sales as not only did he establish himself as a Brentford regular, he was capped by England and became a target for Arsenal, who had a huge offer for him turned down. An inside-forward, he made his Middlesbrough debut under Peter McWilliam on the opening day of the 1930–31 season. He lost his place in the side to Johnny McKay and appeared only once more all season, as a stand-in for winger Billy Pease, though he was on target in a 3–2 home defeat to Huddersfield. The following season he was given a long run in the side alongside George Camsell but was dropped after several heavy defeats. Having helped Brentford from Division Three to Division One, he was among five former Boro men who played against their old side at Ayresome Park in 1935–36. In January 1936, he scored the winner as the Teessiders went down 1–0. He died in London in October 1969.

SCRIMSHAW Charles Thomas

Left-back
Born: Heanor, 3 April 1909.
Died: Smallthorne, 4 June 1973.
Career: Hebden Bridge. Stoke City 1929. MIDDLESBROUGH 1938.

■ Middlesbrough proved to be a brief interlude for Scrimshaw, who was close to an England call-up while with Stoke City in 1935–36. Indeed, Stoke had a reputation for producing fine full-backs, so Boro boss Wilf Gillow was happy to bring one of them north. He made his League debut for Middlesbrough at left-back in a 3–2 home victory over Grimsby Town in October 1938 but went on to make just nine appearances. When war was declared, he returned to the Potteries where he played war games for both Stoke City and Port Vale. He never re-appeared for Boro, who released him in 1945. It is believed he went on to become a publican.

SENIOR Trevor John

Forward
Born: Dorchester, 28 November 1961.
Career: Dorchester Town. Portsmouth 1981. Aldershot (loan) 1983. Reading 1983. Watford 1987. MIDDLESBROUGH 1988. Reading 1988. Woking. Weymouth. Basingstoke Town. Dorchester Town. Farnborough Town.

■ Senior may have scored just four goals in his brief Boro career, but one proved to be among the most precious in the club's history – a 30-minute strike in the Chelsea Play-off home leg which helped set up that famous promotion party at Stamford Bridge. Boss Bruce Rioch had used most of the money from a good FA Cup run to sign Senior from Watford for £200,000, one day ahead of the transfer deadline. Club scouts had seen him play and were unimpressed but Rioch looked

up Senior's prolific goalscoring record in Rothman's Football Yearbook and decided to go for him. He repaid a chunk of the fee with that Play-off goal, but never really looked the part and became a boo-boy target in the top flight. By his own admission, Senior's finesse and touch was found wanting in Division One and, after being substituted and booed off following a nightmare showing in a League Cup tie with Tranmere, he was transfer-listed and soon joined Reading for just half the fee Boro had paid for him.

The Reading move – where he was Player of the Season – was a return to the club where he made his name, bagging a sackful of goals in both spells there. He even went in goal five times and kept a clean sheet on each occasion! His career began with hometown club Dorchester Town before he joined Portsmouth for £35,000. After few chances to shine at Fratton Park, he found good form in a loan spell at Aldershot before embarking on the first of those two sparkling Reading stints. He moved up the divisions to join top flight side Watford for £320,000 but scored only one goal before joining Boro. After his second Reading spell ended, he turned down Swansea to join non-League Woking before ending up at Beazer Homes outfit Weymouth as player-manager and community officer.

SHAND Hector

Right-half
Born: Inverness.
Career: Inverness Thistle. Southampton. Inverness Thistle. MIDDLESBROUGH 1906. Millwall Athletic.

■ Lured to Teesside from Inverness, Scotsman Shand made his debut in a 2–2 home draw with Everton on the opening day of the 1906–07 season but didn't reappear until April 1907 in a 1–0 reverse at Bolton Wanderers, his second and final Middlesbrough outing. In that time, Boro had changed managers from Alex Mackie to Andy Aitken – both Scots – and it was Aitken who let half-back Shand head south for Southern League Millwall, where he played for three seasons.

SHANNON Robert

Left-back
Born: Bellshill, 20 April 1966.
Career: Dundee 1982. MIDDLESBROUGH (loan) 1991. Dunfermline Athletic 1991. Motherwell 1993. Dundee United 1995. Hibernian 1997. East Fife 1999.

■ Faced with an injury crisis, Boro boss Lennie Lawrence moved to fill one of the gaps with a player he knew about – Rab Shannon, a beefy full-back or midfielder he had once bid £200,000 for while Charlton boss. Sterling service with Dundee earned Shannon seven Scotland Under-21 caps in the same national side as other Boro favourites Gary Hamilton and Willie Falconer, but by 1991 he was out of contract and Lawrence moved in to bring him to Teesside on loan. He moved from training with Dundee United to a Boro reserves outing against Hull City and hopes of a contract, but he had just two first-team run-outs – an appearance as substitute at Bristol Rovers and 120 minutes in an extra-time Rumbelows Cup triumph at Bournemouth. With his loan period ending, he joined Dunfermline and later, in a £100,000 move, Motherwell.

SHAW Thomas William

Right-back
Born: Details unknown.
Career: Stockton. MIDDLESBROUGH 1899.

■ An Amateur Cup-winning full-back with Stockton in 1899, Shaw was one of the pioneers – a member of Middlesbrough's first-ever Football League side in the 3–0 Division Two defeat at Lincoln City on 2 September 1899. A right full-back, his brother kept football in the family by representing Woolwich Arsenal.

SHEARER David John

Forward
Born: Inverness, 16 October 1958.
Career: Inverness Clachnacuddin. MIDDLESBROUGH 1978. Wigan Athletic (loan) 1980. Grimsby Town 1983. Gillingham 1984. Bournemouth 1987. Scunthorpe United 1988. Darlington 1988. Billingham Synthonia.

■ Arriving from Scottish non-League outfit Inverness Clachnacuddin, Shearer really set Boro fans talking when, on a sensational debut, he bagged both goals in the 2–0 home win over Chelsea. John Neal had beaten off competition from Hearts to sign him, playing him in a trial game before parting with a nominal fee. A powerfully-built young striker with a good hard shot, Shearer originally worked as a labourer on a building site after leaving school, so the move to English Division One was a dream come true. Sadly, he missed a big chunk of the 1979–80 season with ankle ligament trouble and on his recovery, was loaned to League newcomers Wigan, where he rediscovered his goal touch. Back at Boro, he became a regular in the 1980–81

season and was top scorer in 1982–83 following relegation from Division One. That haul included seven goals in the first nine games, although none in the last 14, and a curious appearance at full-back against Wolves, where Malcolm Allison's ploy backfired and Shearer was all at sea as Boro were thumped 4–0. Nicknamed 'Sheik', Shearer was never a prolific scorer but was courageous, dedicated and a brave, unselfish front-runner. He also had an uncanny knack of scoring against the great Liverpool side of the time, finding the net on four occasions between May 1980 and November 1981. In 1983, he was allowed to join Grimsby on a 'free' but made only one League start before moving on to a more fruitful spell at Gillingham, where he played alongside Terry Cochrane. He moved back to the North East when Darlington paid £10,000 for him and later switched to the Northern League with Billingham Synthonia. His Scottish international brother Duncan also played League football for Chelsea, Huddersfield, Blackburn and Swindon. David still lives on Teesside.

SHEPHERDSON Harold

Centre-half
Born: Middlesbrough, 28 October 1918.
Died: September 1995.
Career: MIDDLESBROUGH 1936.
Southend United 1947.

■ Simply one of Boro's biggest names, Shepherdson's greatest contributions to the game came off the pitch – for club and country. That's not to say he couldn't play. As a big, commanding centre-half he earned respect with some good shows on the rare occasions he stepped in for Bob Baxter. On one of those first-team outings, he did an excellent job marking Everton's star striker Dixie Dean. As an Army staff sergeant PT instructor in World War Two, he learned about physiology and anatomy, while still managing the occasional game for Boro in regional matches.

After just 17 games for Boro, he joined Southend but made no appearances and a knee injury suffered on an FA coaching course at Birmingham University forced his premature retirement aged just 28. A call to Boro's trainer Charlie Cole landed him the job of assistant trainer, where he put into practice the health and fitness expertise he'd learned during the war. Cole soon retired in 1948 and Shep replaced his successor, Tom Mayson, in 1949 to make training more interesting and varied and shift the emphasis away from purely running work. His work certainly impressed England officials and, in 1957, he became the national team's trainer – the start of a remarkable period covering four World Cups and 169 international matches. England's longest-serving trainer by a mile, he was awarded the MBE in 1969.

Yet despite all the international action, he never turned his back on his beloved Boro and was made assistant manager under Stan Anderson, a job he held into the 1980s as various managers came and went. He was also caretaker manager at Boro on four occasions and had several offers to manage other clubs, but he wanted to stay in Middlesbrough. He was also happy to keep out of the manager's chair, preferring to get on with the job without the added pressures of management. He retired in 1983 after nearly half a decade at the club, although the club's willingness to let him go as part of a cost-cutting exercise was disappointing. Not that Shep was one to make a fuss – his affable nature, light touch and easy humour made him one of football's true gentlemen. When Bobby Moore died in 1993, for example, Shep was happy to point out that reports he had also passed away were 'greatly exaggerated'. A true Boro legend, he died of a heart attack in September 1995. Four years later, his widow Peggy auctioned off some of his memorabilia, including Bobby Moore's World Cup Final shirt.

SHORT Maurice

Goalkeeper
Born: Middlesbrough, 29 December 1949.
Career: MIDDLESBROUGH 1967.
Oldham Athletic 1970. Grimsby Town (loan) 1971. Whitby Town.

■ A qualified grocer, Short was also a decent goalkeeper who was unlucky enough to find Willie Whigham and then Jim Platt in his way. He got a rare chance in December 1968 in bizarre circumstances when Whigham was suspended for assaulting coach Jimmy Greenhalgh in a dressing room fracas. Short made the most of his chance, keeping a clean sheet in a 1–0 home win over Blackpool, but Whigham was back between the sticks for the next match – and for the rest of the season. Although naturally laid back he was frustrated by Jim Platt's arrival, he moved on to Oldham in 1970 but again failed to establish himself. He eventually returned home to play for Whitby Town and other local sides.

SLADE Howard Charles

Wing-half/Inside-right
Born: Bath, 29 January 1891.
Died: Doncaster, April 1971.
Career: Bath City. Stourbridge. Aston Villa 1913. Huddersfield Town 1913. MIDDLESBROUGH 1922. Darlington 1925. Folkestone.

■ Slade's Teesside days were probably most memorable for being part of Boro's first ever relegated team in 1923–24, but his career before and after proved he had much to offer the game. A 5ft 7in left-half back, he started out playing inside-forward for Bath City and Stourbridge before joining Aston Villa and quickly moving on to Huddersfield, who he helped to promotion in 1919–20, an FA Cup Final defeat in 1920 and an FA Cup Final victory in 1922. Earlier in his Huddersfield career, he broke his leg against Derby in 1916 when a reservist with the Cavalry Regiment. He left Boro for Darlington in 1925, when his fee was reduced from £500 to £100 by the Football League, but retired in 1927 and moved into coaching – a career switch that took him around the world, including Venezuela, Mexico, Scandinavia and Turkey. Back in Britain, he had spells as trainer at Rotherham, coach at Aldershot and chief scout at Crystal Palace, where he had a spell as joint manager with Fred Dawes from 1950–51. He died in Doncaster in April 1971.

SLAVEN Bernard Joseph

Forward
Born: Paisley, 13 November 1960.
Career: Morton 1981. Airdrieonians 1983. Queen of the South 1983. Albion Rovers 1984. MIDDLESBROUGH 1985. Port Vale 1993. Darlington 1994. Billingham Synthonia.

■ One of Boro's leading post-war scorers, Bernie Slaven's story is pure Boy's Own stuff. His goals record speaks for itself – top scorer in six consecutive seasons between 1986–91 – while his appearance statistics are impressive indeed. Fourteenth in the all-time list, he played 136 consecutive League games between October 1985 and November 1988 and 116 between December 1988 and May 1991, the only Boro player to have had two runs of at least 100 straight games.

Yet such a phenomenal record had humble beginnings when, as top scorer in Scotland, Slaven fell out with his club, Albion Rovers. He even considered hanging up his boots to concentrate on his part-time gardening job with Glasgow Corporation. In desperation, he wrote to every English Division One and Two club asking for a trial. Luckily, Willie Maddren was short of strikers, replied ahead of Leeds and Bradford and Slaven was soon heading to Teesside. He played in two reserve games, although he needed some persuading to show for the second as fears of losing his council gardening job surfaced. Thankfully, he stuck around and Maddren made his move after seeing Slaven score twice in a one-man show. A midnight call to Albion Rovers followed and the deal was tied up. In truth, he took some time to adjust, suffering early homesickness and indifferent form to finish second to Gary Rowell in the 1985–86 goalscoring chart. But after finding his feet, he came into his own during the Division Two promotion season and never looked back. With his good close control, ability to get into the right place at the right time and unerring accuracy of shooting, the 'Wolfman' was already forging legendary status.

A great goalscorer rather than a scorer of great goals, some critics rounded on his tackling (or lack of it), workrate and heading ability, plus his seeming inability to conquer the offside rule. But as Slaven himself pointed out, he wouldn't have scored half his goals without playing on the edge. He also thought it a crime to pass to a teammate when he had a good chance himself. His 15 goals in Division One in 1988–89 were bettered only by Alan Smith and John Aldridge and included a memorable hat-trick at Highfield Road in the 4–3 triumph over Coventry City, while the 1989 Hennessy North East Player of Year award was richly deserved. International recognition followed too as, qualifying through his grandparents, he was chosen for Eire when Scotland continually overlooked him. Back at Boro, Bruce Rioch rated the Slaven sidestep and shimmy to score against Aston Villa in the Zenith Data Systems Cup northern final one of the best goals he'd even seen. He also netted two crucial last day goals against Newcastle to help Boro avoid a second successive relegation in 1990.

Things started to turn sour in the early 1990s when Colin Todd and particularly Lennie Lawrence failed to always see eye-to-eye with the teetotal Scot. In fact, Slaven was so furious at being substituted in a home game with Charlton in 1990–91, he stormed off and was walking his dogs while the second half was being played. With his Boro career winding up, Slaven was linked with Blackburn and Nottingham Forest before opting to join John Rudge's Port Vale, but the sight of him playing in anything other than a Boro shirt just didn't seem right. He did, however, score for Vale in the Auto Windshields Trophy final against Stockport at Wembley before an unhappy spell with Darlington. Later a pundit with Century Radio and Boro TV, the 'Living Legend' is still a regular visitor at the Riverside Stadium and remains a popular honorary Teessider. His autobiography *Legend?* was a big seller on Teesside, raising over £30,000 for charity, though his long-running commentary partnership with Alastair Brownlee came to an end after 400 games when Century lost Boro's radio rights in 2007.

SMITH David

Winger
Born: Thornaby, 8 December 1947.
Career: MIDDLESBROUGH 1964. Lincoln City 1968. Rotherham United 1978.

■ Boro's loss was Lincoln City's gain, with Thornaby-born Smith heading for Sincil Bank – and an impressive 371-game appearance record – after just a handful of games for his local club. The left winger still had something to boast about during his short Boro career, however, grabbing the winner in a 2–1 League Cup tie against Chelsea in front of 30,417 at Ayresome Park. Although skilful and happy go lucky, he lacked consistency. His only League start was in a 1–0 home reverse against Millwall.

SMITH David A.

Right-half
Born: Nottingham.
Career: Lochgelly United. Third Lanark. Chatham. Millwall Athletic. Notts County 1900. MIDDLESBROUGH 1900.

■ A right-half, Smith scored a memorable hat-trick by playing in Boro's first ever Division One fixture, the first game at Ayresome Park and the last at Linthorpe Road. Club captain between 1901–03, he was part of a promotion-winning half-back line in 1901–02 alongside 'Bullet' Jones and Andy Davidson – a trio supporters talked about for years to come. His career began

with Chatham and Southern League Millwall before he joined Nottingham Forest and then Middlesbrough where he lost his place on the arrival of Sam Aitken. After hanging up his boots, he became a club director and vice-chairman. Controversially, he was suspended for two years for paying two Eston amateurs. He was interred in Germany during World War One.

SMITH Edward George

Goalkeeper
Born: Details unknown.
Career: MIDDLESBROUGH 1899.

■ A prominent player in the Northern League side which finished third behind Bishop Auckland in 1898–99, Smith was Middlesbrough's goalkeeper in their first ever League game – a 3–0 defeat at Lincoln City. In the pre-League days, he'd been at the centre of a pre-match drama, pulling out of a home game against St Augustine's in February 1899 at the last minute through illness. Without a replacement, team manager Jack Robson went in goal and Boro won 2–1! In his 10 League starts for Boro, Smith kept four clean sheets and conceded 15 goals.

SMITH Ernest Edwin (Bert)

Centre-half
Born: Donegal, 4 January 1896.
Career: Cardiff City 1919. MIDDLESBROUGH 1923. Watford 1925. Emsworth.

■ An effective defender, Smith made his debut under boss Herbert Bamlett in a 2–1 home defeat by Preston North End midway through the 1923–24 season. He largely kept his place for the rest of the campaign at the end of which the team suffered a first ever relegation. He began 1924–25 well, but his fortunes dipped and he was soon on his way to Watford.

SMITH George

Midfield
Born: Newcastle, 7 October 1945.
Career: Newcastle United 1963. Barrow 1965. Portsmouth 1967. MIDDLESBROUGH 1969. Birmingham City 1971. Cardiff City 1973. Swansea City 1975. Hartlepool United 1977.

■ Boro fans like grafters, so it was no surprise that Smith – a midfield dynamo in the Billy Bremner mould – was voted Player of the Year in his first full season at Ayresome. He made his name at Portsmouth and was rated one of the best midfielders outside the top flight when Stan Anderson snapped him up in 1969 for a then club record fee of £50,000. A Geordie, he'd initially come through the youth ranks at Newcastle and was a professional for nearly two years before joining Division Four outfit Barrow, not having made an appearance at St James' Park. His terrific stamina and top class passing ability soon established him as an engine room of any team. Best man at Willie Maddren's wedding, Smith was a reliable ball-winner. He left Boro in an exchange deal with Johnny Vincent – who he later played with at Cardiff – and won promotion to the top flight with Birmingham. In the 1980s, he was

player-coach at Hartlepool, assisting Billy Horner, and worked for the FA as staff coach for the Teesside area. He later linked up with former Birmingham teammate Trevor Francis as youth team coach at Queen's Park Rangers before joining the scouting network, first for Sheffield Wednesday and then as Birmingham's North East talent spotter.

SMITH John

Right-back
Born: Hurlford.
Career: MIDDLESBROUGH 1933. Queen of the South.

■ John Smith's only game for Middlesbrough was at least a memorable one, playing right full-back in a 4–1 home drubbing of Leicester City in the final game of the 1933–34 season. He stood in for Jack Jennings that day but was not considered throughout the following season. Manager Wilf Gillow allowed him to leave for Queen of the South in 1935.

SMITH John (Jock)

Full-back
Born: Dalbeattie, 7 December 1898.
Career: Neilston Victoria. Ayr United. MIDDLESBROUGH 1926. Cardiff City 1930. Distillery.

■ A no-nonsense Scot, Smith forged a reputation as a pretty solid customer, shoring up the back to great effect. While he used his big physique with relish, he was also a good reader of the game and had many of the attributes a classy defender requires. Sadly, his occasional forays up front drew a blank, failing to score in 123 first-team outings. Smith joined Boro three games into the 1926–27 season after three straight defeats. He helped the club pick up a first point in a goalless draw at South Shields and made his home debut on the day George Camsell was called up to begin his phenomenal scoring feats that would lead to a record-breaking promotion success. A right full-back in that glorious first season, he was switched to the left in Division One and the following season when he picked up a second Division Two title medal. After losing his place to Don Ashman he moved on to Cardiff City.

SMITH Malcolm

Forward
Born: Stockton, 21 September 1953.
Career: MIDDLESBROUGH 1970. Bury (loan) 1975. Blackpool (loan) 1976. Burnley 1976. York City 1980.

■ Boro's 1973–74 promotion-winning side tended to pick itself and so did the substitutes, with either Peter Brine or Malcolm Smith usually sharing the honours. A centre-forward, Smith grew up in Ferryhill, played in the same County Durham side as David Armstrong and had trials with Newcastle, Leeds and Coventry before plumping for Boro. He certainly had a Roy of the Rovers start, scoring twice on his full debut against Sunderland on the opening day of the 1972–73 season. But with fans' expectations already sky high, the 18-year-old failed to score in his next nine starts. Alan Foggon's arrival then put paid to his hopes of a lengthy first-team run, although he did score a memorable winner against Manchester United in the League Cup. Rapidly becoming a forgotten man, despite a super sub tag, Smith had a spell in the North American Soccer League with Portland Timbers and eventually left for Burnley in 1976 in a £25,000 deal after a loan spell. After quitting playing, he became a sales rep for Hi-Tec.

SMITH Robert Alexander (Alex)

Defender
Born: Billingham, 6 February 1944.
Career: MIDDLESBROUGH 1961. Bangor City. Darlington 1974. Guisborough Town.

■ All good things come to those who wait, so it must have been with some relief that Smith made his Boro debut after nearly four seasons on the books. An honest full-back, he'd been an apprentice fitter at Haverton Hill before joining Boro where he eventually forged a reputation as a hard tackler and good organiser. After making his Second Division debut as sub for Billy Horner in a 4–2 win against Bristol City in March 1966, he suffered relegation two months later. He spent two years in the reserves as the club were promoted again before becoming regular right-back. Transfer-listed in May 1967, he stuck around and subsequently turned down a move to Blackburn Rovers in September 1971. He did leave Teesside in June 1972, however, becoming player-manager of Northern Premier League side Bangor City. He returned to League football in 1974 with Darlington before fixing his gaze at non-

League level where his posts included player-coach of the Guisborough side which reached the FA Vase Final and assistant to ex-Boro defender Peter Creamer at Evenwood Town in 1991. He also ran a sports shop and in 1996–97 returned to Boro as kit manager.

SOUNESS Graeme James

Midfield
Born: Edinburgh, 6 May 1953.
Career: Tottenham Hotspur 1970. MIDDLESBROUGH 1973. Liverpool 1978. Sampdoria (Italy) 1984. Glasgow Rangers 1986.

■ To be voted Player of the Year in Boro's 1973–74 team, you had to be pretty special and Graeme Souness was just that. A Scottish Schools and Youth international, he joined Spurs on leaving school and helped the White Hart Lane youngsters win the FA Youth Cup but even then, controversy wasn't far away and he was reported to have gone AWOL back to Edinburgh. Impatient at waiting for a first-team chance, he turned down Oxford in favour of Boro and became one of Stan Anderson's final signings, but had an unimpressive first season and was out of favour under Jack Charlton, who questioned his attitude. He won a first-team recall after injury to Brian Taylor, coming on as sub against Cardiff – and he never looked back.

Starting to show the aggression he would later be synonymous with, he benefited from playing alongside Bobby Murdoch and became a crucial part of the 1973–74 promotion side, rounding the home campaign off with a hat-trick in the 8–0 thrashing of Sheffield Wednesday. Three full Scotland caps followed the next season and he became known as a stylish but tough-tackling midfielder with a lethal shot and fearsome will to win. A natural leader, he could control the pace of a game by picking the ball up from the back four and spreading it to the wings with pinpoint passes.

Frustrated the club wasn't challenging for honours, he asked for a transfer at the start of the 1976–77 season, but it was another 18 months before he left to join Liverpool for a club record fee in bitter circumstances. In what proved to be his last game, a home clash with Norwich on New Year's Eve 1977, he was roundly barracked by fans who accused him of having no heart for the game. Indeed, he'd been unsettled since Jack Charlton's departure and didn't help his cause by flashing a V-sign as he left the pitch. Earlier that year, he famously went missing with a female friend on a Boro world tour in summer 1977, missing the flight from Hong Kong to Australia to earn a 'Hong Kong Souey' nickname! It was typical of the playboy nature which earned Souness a 'Champagne Charlie' reputation.

In seven seasons at Anfield, he captained club and country, winning five League titles, three European Cups and joining the Scotland party in World Cup 1978. He teamed up with Trevor Francis in Sampdoria in 1984 where he helped the club win the Italian Cup – its first major honour – before returning to Britain as player-manager at Rangers, where he resurrected flagging fortunes and led the 'Gers to three League titles. Subsequent managerial posts included Liverpool, where he won the 1992 FA Cup but failed to bring the title back to Anfield, and Galatasaray, where he clinched the Turkish Cup but still lost his job. More recent managerial appointments have included Southampton, Torino, Benfica, Blackburn and Newcastle, but on Teesside he'll always be known as one of the best players ever to pull on the famous red shirt.

SOUTHGATE Gareth

Defender
Born: Watford, 3 September 1970.
Career: Crystal Palace 1989. Aston Villa 1995. MIDDLESBROUGH 2001.

■ Voted Boro's greatest ever skipper by the club's fans, Southgate will forever be

remembered as the man who captained the club to their first ever major trophy after a 128-year wait. Capped 57 times by England, Southgate was a stylish and reliable central defender with two good feet who was able to bring the ball out of defence and distribute it effectively. He was Steve McClaren's first and, the manager maintained, best signing when he joined Boro from Aston Villa for £6.5 million in the summer of 2001. Southgate settled in well at the Riverside and went on to be a virtual ever present in defence for Boro, replacing Paul Ince as captain when the former England midfielder left the club. He deservedly won the club's Player of the Year award and as a valued member of the England set-up was in the squad for the 2002 World Cup Finals. His proudest moment with Boro came on 29 February 2004 with the 2–1 Carling Cup Final win over Bolton at the Millennium Stadium. He also led the team into UEFA Cup action and seventh place in the Premiership to ensure the club would be playing European football again in 2005–06. He struggled with back and ankle injuries during that season but still managed to lead the side in two-thirds of the 60 matches played, including the UEFA Cup Final in Eindhoven. Southgate began his career with Crystal Palace and was the only ever present when the Eagles dropped out of the Premiership in 1994–95. That summer he joined Aston Villa in a £2.5 million deal. Though he arrived at Villa Park as a midfielder, he joined Ugo Ehiogu and Paul McGrath in a three-man defensive system. After making his international debut as a substitute against Portugal, he forced his way into England's Euro '96 squad. Despite his infamous penalty shootout miss, he was one of the stars of the England team that reached the semi-finals. A member of England's World Cup party for France '98, he was injured in the opening match but returned for the last 50 minutes of the Argentina match after David Beckham's dismissal, only to have another nightmare experience of the penalty shootout system. Following the departure of Andy Townsend, he took over the Villa captaincy and led the club to the 2000 FA Cup Final, the last to be held at Wembley before the old stadium's reconstruction. The respect with which Southgate is held throughout the game was recognised when chairman Steve Gibson appointed him as the club's manager in succession to the England-bound McClaren in summer 2006.

SPRAGGON Frank

Defender

Born: Whickham, 27 October 1945.

Career: MIDDLESBROUGH 1962. Minnesota Kicks (US). Hartlepool United 1976.

■ With loyalty becoming a forgotten word in today's megabucks game, Frank Spraggon's Boro career was a model of dedication and dependability. A Newcastle fan as a boy, he was spotted playing for a district side by Harold Shepherdson – later to become his father-in-law – and chose Boro ahead of Preston, Newcastle and West Bromwich Albion. He went straight from the juniors into the reserves and made his first-team debut aged just 17 in a League Cup clash with Bradford. He had relatively few chances early on, although he did play in the 5–3 defeat by Cardiff that relegated Boro to Division Three for the first time. Once back in Division Two, he established himself as a regular, initially as a wing-half but later centre-half and finally left-back.

Hard working, consistent and a fine reader of the game, he was out for seven months in 1971–72 after an ill-fated cartilage operation, surgery which left him with blurred vision in one eye after too much anaesthetic. He remained virtually blind in one eye, but it didn't restrict a career which soared to new heights when, with the emergence of Willie Maddren at centre-half, Jack Charlton switched him to left-back and he became an integral part of Charlton's Champions. Never flamboyant but always reliable, he gave 13 years of loyal service to Boro and was rewarded with a testimonial against Dinamo Zagreb in 1975. On losing his Boro place to Terry Cooper, Spraggon moved on to US outfit Minnesota Kicks before returning for a short spell at Hartlepool. An arthritic knee forced his retirement, although he was offered the chance to manage Icelandic side Reykjavik in 1977. Spraggon returned to Boro in the 1990s to work as a coach in their Football Community Centre at Eston.

SPRIGGS Stephen

Midfield
Born: Armthorpe, 16 February 1956.
Career: Huddersfield Town 1973. Cambridge United 1975. MIDDLESBROUGH (loan) 1986.

■ He may only have started three games, but it's thought that pocket-sized midfielder Spriggs holds a distinction unlikely to be beaten – Boro's smallest-ever player. Standing just 5ft 3in, he was signed on a month-to-month contract from Cambridge after being released following an ankle injury. He made his Boro debut in a home derby with Darlington and his stature – or lack of it – was soon a talking point. He spent a spell in Cyprus after leaving Boro, only to return to Teesside in December 1987 to sign another month's contract. However, he left soon afterwards without playing a game.

SPUHLER John Oswald

Centre-forward
Born: Sunderland, 18 September 1917.
Died: 2007.
Career: Sunderland 1934. MIDDLESBROUGH 1945. Darlington 1954. Spennymoor United.

■ A committed centre-forward or winger, Johnny 'Sulphur' Spuhler wasn't renowned for his ball skills but used his natural ability to sprint from a stationary position to great advantage. He could also head the ball with strength and direction but would often drift into offside positions – much to the annoyance of the crowd! A brave player, he once played several games with a broken nose.

Spuhler was originally taken on as an office junior at Roker Park and, unsure of a football career, was set to become a joiner before Sunderland offered him a contract in September 1934. He guested for Boro during the war and, after several good displays, David Jack persuaded him to sign on in 1945–46, making his debut for the regional side in a 5–2 home defeat

by Barnsley. When League football returned, Spuhler became a mainstay of Boro's post-war line-up, keeping £18,000 forward Andy Donaldson out of the team. He even took over in goal for one game when Dave Cumming was sent off for thumping Arsenal's Les Compton in December 1947. After more than 200 appearances, Spuhler was placed on the transfer list and sold to Darlington following relegation to Divison Two in 1954. Following a brief stint with the Quakers, he was player-manager for Spennymoor United and later managed Shrewsbury for a short but unsuccessful spell. He was also full-time coach at Stockton FC, but lost his job through financial cutbacks. Many Teessiders also remember him for running Yarm Post Office for eight years. In later years, he lived near Barnard Castle. Spuhler died in 2007.

STAGE William

Outside-left/Inside-right
Born: Edinburgh, 22 March 1893.
Died: 1957.
Career: MIDDLESBROUGH 1913. Hibernian. St Bernard's. Bury 1921. Burnley 1928. Southampton 1930.

■ A regular for Boro reserves before World War One, playing inside or outside forward, Stage's three first-team appearances were made at outside-left. After the war, he moved north across the Border to play for Hibernian and Edinburgh St Bernard's in 1920. Later in the 1920s, he returned to England and played against Boro for Bury in 1928. Staying in the North West, he then moved to Burnley and turned out in the claret and blue at Ayresome Park in 1930. The Teessiders won 3–1.

STAMP Philip Lawrence

Midfield
Born: Middlesbrough, 12 December 1975.
Career: MIDDLESBROUGH 1993. Millwall (loan) 2001. Heart of Midlothian 2002. Darlington 2005.

■ Phil Stamp was another fringe player who did not survive Steve McClaren's regime change. Injuries were the bane of the midfielder's life and held up his progress at club and England junior level. Stamp spanned the Ayresome Park-Riverside divide, having made his debut under Lennie Lawrence, aged just 17, in an Anglo –Italian Cup match with Barnsley. Middlesbrough-born, and the product of the town's boys team, he impressed with his battling, attack-minded displays. He went on to make sporadic first-team appearances until finding more favour under Bryan Robson. He netted a brilliant individual goal against Manchester City in December 1995 – the day Juninho got his first goal – and scored another gem against Arsenal. Then, in 1997, he played

in the FA Cup Final against Chelsea. He also made his mark off the pitch, with his memorable one-liner 'You're joking, aren't ya?' a highlight of Boro's Cup Final record, Let's Dance. Several call-ups for England Under-21s followed, but unluckily he was injured each time and had to pull out. An England Youth international, Stamp missed the majority of 1998–99 through a series of injuries but returned to first-team action in the 1999–2000 campaign when he signed a bumper, four-and-a-half year contract. But his injuries increased and he found himself out in the cold when McClaren arrived. After a short loan spell with Millwall, Stamp tried his luck with Heart of Midlothian, where he played 80 matches in three successful seasons. He returned to the North East for a short spell with Darlington before retiring in 2006.

STEPHENS Arthur (Archie)

Forward
Born: Liverpool, 19 May 1954.
Career: Melksham Town. Bristol Rovers 1981. MIDDLESBROUGH 1985. Carlisle United 1987. Darlington 1989.

■ There have been some fine headers of the ball in Boro's history, but popular Scouser Archie Stephens ranks alongside the best – despite his relative lack of height. He was discovered by Bristol Rovers playing for Melksham Town in the Western League and was recommended to Willie Maddren by Bristol City boss and former Boro teammate, Terry Cooper. Maddren didn't even see him play but club scouts were impressed, so the Boro boss snapped him up – only to raise an eyebrow when he saw how small he was! He signed for Boro on the pitch at half-time in a match v Sheffield United, but a disappointing 1985–86 season saw Stephens struggle for goals and acceptance by the crowd. But true to his competitive nature, he won them over with his displays in Division Three, forging a fine partnership with Bernie Slaven (33 goals between them) in the memorable 1986–87 promotion season. He also holds the honour of scoring the first goals for 're-born' Boro, bagging both in the first game after liquidation – a 2–2 draw with Port Vale at Hartlepool's Victoria Ground.

While always determined and willing to get stuck in, he struggled in Division Two and lost his place to Alan Kernaghan. He went on the transfer list in October 1987 and by the end of the year, former Bristol Rovers manager Clive Middlemass had moved in to take him to Carlisle. Two years later, he returned to the North East with Darlington, where he was in the side which lost its League status but made an immediate return, before ending his playing career in 1990. To mark his retirement, his teammates decided to put a notice in the newspaper, only for it to be published in the 'deaths' column! He stayed in the North East for spells as manager of several Northern League teams.

STEVENSON Arthur Brown

Outside-left
Born: Padiham, 24 August 1896.
Died: 1976.
Career: Accrington Stanley. Darwen. Wigan Boro 1922. MIDDLESBROUGH 1923. Mid-Rhondda United. Sheffield United 1924. Bristol City 1930. Wigan Boro 1931.

■ Signed from Wigan, outside-left Stevenson made just eight appearances for Boro after replacing Tom Urwin for a defeat at Arsenal in November 1923. His final run-out came in a 1–0 defeat at Cardiff City on New Year's Day. That Welsh appearance proved something of an omen as, at the end of the season, he moved on to Rhondda, the League Committee setting the transfer fee at £750 on 24 May.

STEWART James Garvin

Goalkeeper
Born: Kilwinning, 9 March 1954.
Career: Troon Juniors. Kilmarnock 1971. MIDDLESBROUGH 1978. Glasgow Rangers 1981. Dumbarton. (loan). St Mirren. Partick Thistle.

■ When searching for goalkeeping cover for Jim Platt, Boro boss John Neal inquired about Scottish international Alan Rough – and signed his deputy Jim Stewart instead. Capped at Youth, Under-21 and Under-23 levels, Stewart was first called up for the Scotland squad in the 1974 World Cup while a 20-year-old part-timer with Kilmarnock, but had to wait until 1977 for his first cap, coming on as a substitute for Rough against Chile. He made just two full appearances, despite being in 50 squads. While with Kilmarnock, Stewart held down a job as an ICI engineer, but eventually made the switch to full-time soccer. At Boro, he started as first choice 'keeper, but Jim Platt regained the spot in March 1979 and condemned Stewart to a lengthy spell of reserve team soccer. Salvation came in March 1981 when Scottish giants Rangers snapped him up on the eve of the transfer deadline. It proved to be a fantastic move for Stewart, who clinched a Scottish Cup-winners' medal in 1981 and a League Cup triumph in 1982 with the 'Gers. After playing, he became a Ministry of Defence policeman and goalkeeping coach at Kilmarnock.

STILES Norbert Peter

Wing-half
Born: Manchester, 18 May 1942.
Career: Manchester United 1959. MIDDLESBROUGH 1971. Preston North End 1973.

■ Surely one of the most colourful characters to ever play for Boro, 'toothless terrier' Nobby Stiles was the short-sighted son of a football-mad undertaker who, having being knocked down by a bus as a child, recovered sufficiently to play for Manchester United and, memorably, do a jig of joy around Wembley in 1966 while holding aloft the World Cup! Little wonder, then, that when Stan Anderson signed him in 1971, Boro fans felt the club was at last showing the ambition needed to get into the top flight after years of near misses. Stiles captained Manchester Boys and England Schoolboys before the Munich disaster thrust him into the Old Trafford reserves at the tender age of 16. He became a first-team regular in 1964–65, winning the title and his first England cap in the process. While his 1966 World Cup exploits are now the stuff of legend, he also went to Mexico in 1970 and helped Manchester United win the European Cup in 1968. He joined Boro for a nominal fee and was immediately given the captaincy by Anderson, making his debut in the same game as Stuart Boam. But while he was obviously a born leader, his appearances were restricted by injuries and loss of form. His mobility wasn't all it used to be either, although his impudence, tenacity and grit still made him a formidable midfield opponent. He didn't fit into Jack Charlton's plans, though, and with his wife failing to settle on Teesside, Stiles took the chance to join former teammate Bobby Charlton's Preston as player-coach. As manager at Deepdale, he won promotion to Divison Two in 1977 but lost the job on relegation in 1981. Later jobs included assistant to Johnny Giles at Vancouver Whitecaps, boss at West Bromwich Albion and working with youngsters at the place it all began for him – Manchester United.

STIRLING John

Outside-right
Born: Clydebank.
Died: 1924.
Career: Clydebank. Clyde. MIDDLESBROUGH 1911. Bradford Park Avenue 1914. Stoke 1919. Coventry City 1919. Alloa Athletic.

■ A consistent wing-forward, Scotsman Stirling was an integral part of a Tom McIntosh side which, in 1913–14, finished third in Division One – Boro's highest-ever League placing. After making his debut on the opening day of 1911–12, he rarely missed a match in three seasons and supplied the ammunition for George Elliott to fire the goals. Although never a regular scorer himself, Stirling's creativity made him an automatic choice alongside Elliott and other talented players like Jacky Carr and goalkeeper Tim Williamson. One of his best moments came when he was on target in a 3–0 win over Newcastle in December 1913.

STOBBART George

Born: Morpeth, 9 January 1921
Career: Netherfield, May 1939. Newcastle United 1946.

■ A strong, stocky and quick forward, Stobbart's official Boro statistics – just two FA Cup games played – mask the real story. In fact, he made more appearances for Boro during World War Two than any other player, scoring a remarkable 125 goals in 168 games, while also finding time to guest for Darlington and South Shields. He'd signed for Boro from Netherfield Juniors just before the war, but a hefty fee persuaded David Jack to let him leave for Newcastle United in 1946 where he scored twice on his debut. Having helped the Magpies to promotion in 1947–48, he became Luton Town's record signing and later went on to play for Millwall and Brentford. On retirement, he returned north and lived in the Forest Hall area of Newcastle. He died in Newcastle in 1995.

STOCKDALE Robert Keith

Right-back
Born: Redcar, 30 November 1979.
Career: MIDDLESBROUGH 1998. Sheffield Wednesday (loan) 2000. West Ham United (loan) 2003. Rotherham United 2004. Hull City 2005. Darlington (loan) 2006. Tranmere Rovers 2006.

■ Robbie Stockdale showed immense promise as a youngster and made an impressive transition from the Academy to the Premier League. Despite being capped at England Under-21 level, he also became a full Scotland international after qualifying through grandparentage. The right-back showed early promise with Marske United and Cleveland Schools, leading to a call-up for trials at the FA National School of Excellence. He signed schoolboy forms with Boro aged 14, impressing in the youth and reserve teams and, while still a trainee, made his first-team debut at 18 in an FA Cup third-round replay with Queen's Park Rangers in January 1998. Although Stockdale made 20 starts in the 1998–99 season, he found himself behind Curtis Fleming in the pecking order the following season and it was not until the arrival of Steve McClaren in 2001 that he re-established himself. Stockdale became

the preferred number two and appeared in 28 Premiership games. His form also attracted the attention of Scotland manager Berti Vogts, who gave him his full debut against Nigeria in 2002. He has gone on to win three further caps. He also made an impact off the pitch, winning the club's Community Player of the Season award for his work in support of the club's charitable and education projects. That was as good as it got at the Riverside because the next season McClaren gave Stuart Parnaby his chance. Stockdale's prospects diminished even further in 2003 with the arrival of Danny Mills, and he went out on loan to first West Ham and then Rotherham, who offered him a permanent deal. Stockdale experienced relegation with the Millers before moving to Yorkshire rivals Hull City in 2003–04. His stay on Humberside was not a happy one, however, and in 2006 his former Rotherham manager, Ronnie Moore, gave him the chance to resurrect his career at Tranmere, where he has become a regular.

STONE John George

Full-back
Born: Redcar, 3 March 1953.
Career: South Bank. MIDDLESBROUGH 1970. York City 1972. Darlington 1976. Grimsby Town 1979. Rotherham United 1983.

■ Originally a forward, Stone soon proved to be a rock in defence and made his Boro debut at left-back against Cardiff on New Year's Day 1972 in place of Gordon Jones. He retained his place for his only other appearance against Bristol City a week later. Naturally a right-back, he was big, strong and a no-nonsense tackler. On leaving Boro, he joined York City on a free transfer and established himself as a sound and constructive full-back who wasn't averse to the occasional run-out as centre-forward. Having helped City to promotion, another 'free' took him to Darlington, where he put in some good displays. A £22,500 switch to Grimsby then saw him play alongside a young Paul Wilkinson.

STONEHOUSE Derek

Full-back
Born: Skelton, 18 November 1932.
Career: Lingdale. MIDDLESBROUGH 1951. Hartlepool United 1963.

■ Only one outfield player, Ray Bilcliff, played more first-team games for Boro without finding the back of the net. But despite his goal-shyness, Stonehouse was a more than useful full-back who gave years of sterling service. An England Youth international, he made his debut at left-back during the 1953–54 relegation season in a 3–0 home victory against Spurs. He remained in the side which tried unsuccessfully to avoid the dreaded drop, but made only four appearances in the subsequent Division Two season. Following a spell of National Service, he ran up decent first-team spells in the mid–1950s, but they waned as the decade progressed and once the 1960s dawned, Stonehouse was living on borrowed time at Boro. After failing to manage a single appearance in 1962–63, he moved on to Hartlepool where he played 34 games and failed to break that scoring duck.

STOREY Thomas

Inside-right/Outside-right
Born: Crook.
Career: Crook Town. MIDDLESBROUGH 1913. Crystal Palace 1921. Coventry City 1922.

■ Storey's story is a short one. His one and only Boro goal came in a bizarre 7–5 goal fest against Spurs, although he was on the scene before, during and after World War One. Replacing Jacky Carr for his debut in a 3–2 win over Bradford in January 1914, he only established in the second half of the following season as a wing forward. Released after the war, he was a first-team regular for Crystal Palace during the Eagles' first two seasons in the Football League.

STOTT James

Left-half/Inside-left
Born: Middlesbrough, 1871.
Died: Gosforth, 8 October 1908.
Career: South Bank. MIDDLESBROUGH 1891. Liverpool 1893. Grimsby Town 1894. Newcastle United 1895. MIDDLESBROUGH 1899.

■ A tough-tackling but swift and inspiring half-back, Stott had two spells at the Boro. He initially joined from South Bank in 1891 for a two-year spell and returned in 1900 after making his name at Liverpool, where he scored almost a goal a game in a promotion-winning side, and at Newcastle, where he skippered the Geordies to promotion. A snappy dresser, he was also snappy in the tackle and in 1896 was censured by the Newcastle board for the 'continual fouling of his opponent.' On arriving at Boro, he told boss John Robson he'd only be available for home games. More accurately, it turned out to be a single home game – a 1–0 victory over Grimsby Town. After football, he became a publican at the Star Hotel in Newcastle and died of a brain tumour in Gosforth in October 1908.

STRONG Andrew Forster

Left-back
Born: Hartlepool, 17 September 1966.
Career: MIDDLESBROUGH 1984. Billingham Synthonia. Whitley Bay. Spennymoor United.

■ A friend and contemporary of Colin Cooper, full-back Strong was actually the first of the pair to make a breakthrough, making his debut for Willie Maddren's struggling Division Two side in a home 0–0 draw with Leeds United in March 1985. More games came at left-back as Paul Ward's stand-in but after a long spell back in the reserves he was released. He went on to play for Billingham Synthonia, Whitley Bay and Spennymoor United.

STUART Robert William

Full-back
Born: Middlesbrough, 9 October 1913.
Died: 25 August 1987.
Career: South Bank.
MIDDLESBROUGH 1931. Plymouth Argyle 1947.

■ An accomplished left-back, Stuart was never one to lie down – except once. In one of the more eccentric moments in the club's history, he refused to captain the reserves in September 1946 and lay down near one of the goals when the teams ran out. He was unsurprisingly transfer listed at £3,500, although he countered with a transfer request of his own. It was all a bit strange from a tremendous servant for Boro, particularly during the war years when he made more than 100 appearances sandwiched between RAF service in Iceland. Originally signed as an amateur by Boro after playing for England Schools, he opted for football instead of a job as a motor mechanic. Certainly, he had a colourful Boro career, dislocating his shoulder in his reserves debut, getting hammered 5–0 at Arsenal on his first-team bow and compiling an unenviable record of five own goals, primarily because his job was to assist the 'keeper by standing on the line. Sadly, his attempts to kick the ball clear backfired more than he would have liked. He had two England trial games in 1936, but his career was curtailed by the war. In March 1947 – just a year after being club captain – he asked for a transfer after George Hardwick recovered from injury with England to step straight into Stuart's place. Annoyed at Hardwick's immediate return and with youngster Dicky Robinson waiting in the wings, Stuart moved to Plymouth with striker George Dews for a combined fee of £4,000. He later coached in Whitby but an accident in 1953 ended his active role in football. He died in August 1987.

SUDDICK James

Outside-right/Centre-forward
Born: Middlesbrough, 17 August 1875.
Died: 1932.
Career: MIDDLESBROUGH 1896. Aston Villa 1897. Nottingham Forest 1898. Thornaby. MIDDLESBROUGH 1902. Thornaby 1904.

■ Not many players can say they averaged a goal a game for Boro. But Suddick scored in his one and only Football League match for the club, a second half strike in a 3–1 defeat at Sunderland in January 1904. Playing at inside-forward, he was standing in for Ted Gettins with regular number eight Bobby Atherton switched to the wing. However, Dave Smith was preferred the following week against WBA and Suddick returned to Thornaby. He had originally played for Boro in the Northern League, helping them clinch the title in 1897 before moving into the Football League with Aston Villa.

SUGRUE Paul Anthony

Forward/Midfield
Born: Coventry, 6 November 1960.
Career: Nuneaton Boro. Manchester City 1980. Cardiff City 1981. Kansas City (US). MIDDLESBROUGH 1982. Portsmouth 1984. Northampton Town 1986. Newport County 1986.

■ Malcolm Allison's appointment as Boro boss was good news for Sugrue, who saw his chance to renew acquaintances with the man who gave him his League chance. Big Mal spotted the tricky midfielder at Nuneaton Boro and took him to Maine Road for £30,000, but he played only six games before joining Cardiff City on a free transfer. A spell with Kansas followed but Sugrue had noticed Allison's Boro appointment, phoned him and was invited for a three week trial. He passed with flying colours, impressing with his

determined effort and even shedding 9lb to help his cause. On his day, he was certainly capable of breathtaking dribbling skills – witness his brilliant goal against Grimsby in April 1983 when he beat three defenders before placing the ball in the corner. Other Boro highlights included being made captain for the day against Manchester City in October 1983 and scoring in a famous 3–2 FA Cup win over Arsenal in January 1984. However, he requested a transfer when Big Mal was sacked and didn't endear himself to new boss Willie Maddren, who told him he could leave if he wasn't prepared to knuckle down and fight for his place. Sugrue countered by demanding a move, believing the club would want a fee – but was shocked when Maddren told him he could leave for nothing. Placed on the transfer list, he joined Portsmouth on a 'free' and a month later, Portsmouth offered him back. Maddren declined, so Sugrue headed for Sweden before returning to Britain for spells with lower League clubs, including the death throes of Newport County as a Football League club. In January 1991, he was appointed manager of Nuneaton Town.

SUMMERBELL Mark

Midfield
Born: Durham, 30 October 1976.
Career: MIDDLESBROUGH 1995. Cork City (loan). Bristol City (loan) 2001. Portsmouth (loan) 2002. Carlisle United 2002. Spennymoor United.

■ A tigerish ball-winner, Mark Summerbell looked full of promise when he broke into the first-team under Bryan Robson in the late 1990s. But ultimately

he failed to fulfil the potential he had shown as a teenager in the club's School of Excellence. Very small as a youngster, Summerbell was given a two-year contract in 1995 after putting on a stone and gaining five inches in height in two years. The combative midfielder was a season ticket holder at Newcastle as a youngster but turned down his boyhood heroes after being spotted by Boro's youth development officer Ron Bone playing for Hilda Park in Chester-le-Street. After serving a two-year training scheme, he signed professional forms at 18 and made his debut as an early substitute at Tottenham in April 1996. After some impressive displays for the reserves, he was made second-string captain and looked set to follow in the manager's own image. His first goal came in a 2–1 Coca-Cola Cup home victory over Bolton in November 1997. Summerbell signed a three-and-a-half year extension to his contract in 1998, enjoying his best season in 1999–2000 when he made 16 starts. He drifted out of the picture in the latter days of Robson's reign and was never fancied as a contender by his successor, Steve McClaren. After loan spells with Bristol City and Portsmouth, he signed for Carlisle in 2002 and was a virtual ever present in his first season at Brunton Park. Injuries then restricted his first-team opportunities and Summerbell decided to leave Carlisle to play non-League for Spennymoor United and he later ran a pub.

SURTEES John

Inside-forward
Born: Percy Main, 2 July 1911.
Died: 1992.
Career: Percy Main. MIDDLESBROUGH 1931. Portsmouth 1932. Bournemouth 1933. Northampton Town 1933. Sheffield Wednesday 1934. Nottingham Forest 1936.

■ After just one Boro appearance – a 4–0 hammering at Chelsea – Geordie Surtees, an inside-left, headed for the south coast with Portsmouth and was about to emigrate when Sheffield Wednesday offered him a chance. After helping the Owls win the FA Cup, he moved on to Nottingham Forest and played against Boro in 1937–38.

SWALES Norman

Wing-half
Born: New Marske, 2 October 1908.
Career: Scarborough. MIDDLESBROUGH 1925. Aston Villa 1928. Scarborough. Whitley Bay.

■ Local lad Swales made his debut against Clapton Orient, but was surplus to requirements in Herbert Bamlett's team and bowed out from Boro on New Year's Day 1926 in a 2–1 home defeat by South Shields. A right-half, he stood in for Bob Ferguson for both defeats but was released the following close season.

TAYLOR Andrew Derek

Central defender
Born: Hartlepool, 1 August 1986.
Career: MIDDLESBROUGH 2003. Bradford City (loan) 2005.

■ Taylor recovered from the toughest of Premiership baptisms to establish himself as Boro's regular left-back during Gareth Southgate's first season in charge. He was part of the young Boro side handed their heaviest ever Premiership defeat as they were mauled 7–0 by a

rampant Arsenal at Highbury in the 2005–06 campaign. But he kept his nerve and played in a total of 20 League and Cup games before the season's end. Skilful and cool in possession, Taylor loves to get forward and support the attack and is capable of beating defenders and whipping in excellent crosses. Indeed, it was on the left side of midfield that Taylor helped Boro beat Aston Villa to lift the 2004 FA Youth Cup. A successful loan spell at Bradford City in the 2005–06 season underlined his potential and earned him an England Under-21 call-up. On his recall to the Riverside he was drafted straight back into the first-team squad and he was one of Boro's best performers in the 1–0 FA Cup semi-final defeat to West Ham at Villa Park. He deputised at left-back after Julio Arca broke his foot in the first game of the 2006/7 season at Reading, instantly becoming a fans' favourite and making the position his own.

TAYLOR Brian

Central defender
Born: Whitwell, 12 February 1954.
Career: MIDDLESBROUGH 1971. Doncaster Rovers 1975. Rochdale 1978.

■ For every winner there's a loser and Brian Taylor has every reason to curse the cruel finger of fate – or rather Joe Laidlaw's elbow. A tall, blond centre-half, Taylor was handed his debut by Stan Anderson as replacement for Stuart

Boam at Portsmouth just before Christmas 1972. He had impressed new boss Jack Charlton in the summer of 1973 with his hard work and commitment and was rewarded by being in the starting line-up as the 1973–74 season kicked off. But in only the fourth game, a home fixture against Carlisle, he was elbowed in a clash with ex-Boro striker Laidlaw. A depressed cheekbone meant Taylor was sidelined, Willie Maddren moved back from midfield to defence, Graeme Souness was brought into midfield...and the rest is history. He made only a handful more appearances before moving on to greater success in the lower divisions, with a Doncaster Rovers side managed by Stan Anderson his first port of call.

TAYLOR Carl Wilson

Outside-right
Born: Kirkby Stephen, 20 January 1937.
Career: Penrith. MIDDLESBROUGH 1956. Aldershot 1960. Darlington 1962. Burton Albion. Matlock Town.

■ Winger Taylor's debut came in place of Lindy Delapenha for a 2–0 Second Division defeat at Notts County in November 1957. His only goal for Boro came in his first season during a 3–2 home defeat by Sheffield United. After very sporadic appearances, Bob Dennison allowed him to leave for Aldershot, where he became a first-team regular.

MARK TAYLOR

Born: Saltburn, 8 November 1974
Career: Juniors, March 1993. Released, March 1995.

■ A product of Langbaurgh and Cleveland Schools, 6ft 3in Taylor's versatility saw him shuffled between the forward line, midfield, central defence and left-back. Indeed, it was at left-back that he made his debut in an Anglo-Italian clash at Piacenza but, despite good displays in the reserves, three Italian jobs provided his only first-team action. Cool under pressure and a good tackler, youth team coach George Shipley rated him one of the best footballers at the club, but he suffered from inconsistency and, after a loan spell at Darlington, was released.

TAYLOR Peter Thomas

Goalkeeper
Born: Nottingham, 2 July 1928.
Died: Majorca, August 1990.
Career: Nottingham Forest. Coventry City 1946. MIDDLESBROUGH 1955. Port Vale 1961.

■ A solid but unspectacular goalkeeper, Taylor's real talent would come in management – especially as Brian Clough's sidekick. After starting his career in the Midlands, Taylor was signed by Bob Dennison as a replacement for Rolando Ugolini and never let anyone down, but even as a player he would travel the country to watch games and spot talented performers. One such was Clough, who Taylor noticed playing in a Probables versus Possibles pre-season game. Having seen a star in the making, Taylor battered down Dennison's door to make him take notice. Within months, Taylor was keeping goal and Clough was banging them in at the other end. He was the club's regular 'keeper for several seasons until his spot to Bob Appleby. On leaving Boro, Taylor had one game for Port Vale before starting his famous managerial partnership with Clough. Hartlepool was first stop, but it was at Derby where the dynamic duo succeeded in spectacular fashion, helping the Rams to promotion and ultimately the Division One title. Then it was on to Brighton, where Taylor became manager in his own right on Clough's departure for Leeds, but soon they were back together again at Nottingham Forest, twice guiding the club to European Cup triumph. Sadly, an acrimonious split in 1981 soured the atmosphere with Clough, a split which some say never fully healed. Taylor briefly came out of retirement to manage Derby in the early 1980s and enjoyed initial success, but things took a turn for the worse and he left just before relegation to Division Three in 1984. He died in Majorca in 1990.

TENNANT James

Outside-left
Born: Glasgow, 1878.
Career: Linton Villa. Parkhead. St Bernard's. Woolwich Arsenal 1899. MIDDLESBROUGH 1901. Watford 1902. Royal Albert. Stenhousemuir.

■ Standing just 5ft 5in, Tennant began his Boro career with a bang by netting on his debut in a 3–1 triumph at Stockport County on the opening day of the 1901–02 campaign. The season was to result in promotion to Division One for the first time but Tennant didn't last that long. An ever present until December, he made just three more appearances before the end of the season – and the end of his Boro career.

THACKERAY James

Outside-left
Born: Hebburn.
Career: Hebburn Argyle. MIDDLESBROUGH 1904. Bradford Park Avenue 1910. West Stanley.

■ Part of an impressive forward line in the early 1900s, Thackeray was an outside-right who was more a maker of goals than a taker. Signed by John Robson, he retained his place under the managerial reigns of Alex Mackie and Andy Aitken, helping the latter's 1907–08 team finish in Boro's highest position – sixth – since joining the League. He remained a consistent performer in the top flight until a move to Bradford at the end of the 1909–10 season. He was also a decent cricketer and represented Northumberland.

THOMAS David

Winger
Born: Kirkby-in-Ashfield, 5 October 1950.
Career: Burnley 1967. Queen's Park Rangers 1972. Everton 1977. Wolverhampton Wanderers 1979. Vancouver Whitecaps. MIDDLESBROUGH 1982. Portsmouth 1982.

■ A winger with North-Eastern roots, Thomas' impressive career was on the wane by the time Bobby Murdoch brought him to Ayresome Park. A former Barnard Castle School pupil, he played for Durham and England Schoolboys and made his debut for Burnley aged 16. While at Turf Moor, he made his name and won England Under-23 honours before turning down Manchester United, Leeds and Everton to join Second Division Queen's Park Rangers for a club record £165,000. His speed, deadly crossing ability and socks rolled down made him an instantly recognisable figure and he became a full international while at Loftus Road. Big money moves to Everton and Wolves followed, although he headed Stateside to play for Johnny Giles' Vancouver Whitecaps after his Molineux move fell flat. Having signed a three-year contract, he expected to end his career in the US, but was released from his contract amid financial cutbacks and returned to England after only 10 matches. That's when Murdoch stepped in, bringing him to Boro on a no-fee, short-term basis after long negotiations. Not having played for months, Thomas was ring-rusty and his pace wasn't all it used to be. However, his class still stood out in a very poor team and while he was offered new terms after relegation to Division Two, he opted to sign instead for Portsmouth, where he became youth team coach. Latterly, he played for Bognor Regis Town.

THOMAS Martin Richard

Goalkeeper
Born: Senghenydd, 28 November 1959.
Career: Bristol Rovers 1977. Cardiff City (loan) 1982. Southend United (loan) 1983. Newcastle United 1983. MIDDLESBROUGH (loan) 1984. Birmingham City 1988. Cheltenham Town.

■ A goalkeeper who made his name with Bristol Rovers, Thomas was signed on loan by Willie Maddren for a month from Jack Charlton's Newcastle as cover for Kelham O'Hanlon. Despite some decent performances, he never finished on a winning side for Boro, although he did an excellent damage limitation job in a 2–0 defeat at Leeds United. Capped by Wales just once, his international career was hampered by Dai Davies's continuing excellence.

THOMAS Michael Lauriston

Midfield
Born: Lambeth, 24 August 1967.
Career: Arsenal 1984. Portsmouth (loan) 1986. Liverpool 1991. MIDDLESBROUGH (loan) 1998. Benfica 1998. Wimbledon 2000.

■ Cultured midfielder Thomas will always be remembered for something that happened nine years before his time at Boro – an extraordinary injury time winner for Arsenal at Anfield in the final game of the 1988–89 season to snatch the title for the Gunners. An England Schoolboy, Youth, Under-21 and full international, his 10-game loan spell at the Riverside was unspectacular but important, as he brought vital experience at a crucial time in the successful Division One promotion campaign. He had lost his place in the Anfield first team and there was talk of the move being made permanent. Thomas was a rather embarrassed spectator when Boro knocked his club out of the Coca-Cola Cup semi-final during his loan spell but he was delighted to link up again with his former Highbury teammate Paul Merson. He later joined Graeme Souness at Benfica.

THOMPSON Alexander

Centre-forward/Inside-right
Born: Details unknown.
Career: MIDDLESBROUGH 1900. West Ham United. Chesterfield 1905.

■ Forward McFarlane made his debut for Boro in only their second season of League football, in March 1901 at Burslem Port Vale. Christmas 1901 was a time to remember for Thompson as he bagged both goals from centre-forward in a 2–1 home victory over Blackpool on 28 December. However, he played only once more, on New Year's Day, that season and left the club after another season of reserve team football.

THOMPSON Norman

Inside-left
Born: Forest Hall, 5 September 1900.
Career: Newcastle United 1919. Seaton Delaval. Backworth. South Shields 1922. MIDDLESBROUGH 1925. Barnsley 1926. Chilton Colliery Welfare. York City. West Stanley. Nottingham Forest 1927. West Stanley. Carlisle United. West Stanley.

■ Hot-shot Thompson started the 1925–26 with a bang, scoring twice on his debut in a 5–1 away win versus Portsmouth on the opening day and netting again four days later in a 3–2 home win over Blackpool. Playing alongside fine forward players like Jacky Carr and Billy Birrell, he could not hold his place and spent most of the season in the reserves. Barnsley secured his services at the end of the season after just six more first-team outings for Boro.

THOMPSON William Thomas

Outside-right/Inside-left
Born: Morpeth, August 1886.
Died: 1933.
Career: Grangetown. MIDDLESBROUGH 1905. Morpeth Harriers. West Bromwich Albion 1907. Sunderland 1911. Plymouth Argyle. Queen's Park Rangers. South Shields.

Queen's Park Rangers. Newport County 1920. Hartlepool United 1921. Jarrow.

■ Local lad Thompson failed to build on an astonishing start to his Boro career. He was plucked from local League football with Grangetown to make his Division One debut in place of George Reid and scored twice on his debut, a 4–4 home draw with Bolton in December 1905. Partnering Alf Common, the world's first £1,000 footballer, it was a huge elevation for Thompson and he failed to live up to his billing as a young star. He did not find the net again in his five subsequent appearances before being released at the end of the season.

THOMSON Kenneth Gordon

Centre-half
Born: Aberdeen, 25 February 1930.
Died: Castle Eden, 1969.
Career: Caledonian Thistle. Banks O'Dee. Aberdeen. Stoke City 1952. MIDDLESBROUGH 1959. Hartlepool United 1962.

■ Centre-half Thomson made his Stoke debut against Boro – and nearly made his Boro debut versus Stoke. However, he arrived at Ayresome Park on the day before the two sides met and wasn't allowed to play in a match Boro won comfortably 5–2. Aberdeen's record sale at £22,000, he carved out a great career at the Victoria Ground, managing 278 appearances before switching to Teesside. A natural leader, he displaced Brian Phillips as Boro's regular centre-half and was named captain when Brian Clough relinquished the role in the summer of 1960. In September 1962, boss Bob Dennison signed Welsh international centre-half Mel Nurse and within a month, Thomson was on his way on to Hartlepool, where his career was to end in dramatic fashion. After just 28 games with Pools, he was suspended sine die by the Football League for 'illegal activities', having become ensnared by police in an alleged bribery probe. He died of a heart attack on Castle Eden golf course in 1969.

THOMSON Robert

Midfield
Born: Glasgow, 21 March 1955.
Career: St Johnstone. Morton. MIDDLESBROUGH 1981. Hibernian 1982. Blackpool 1985. Hartlepool United 1987. Colne Dynamos.

■ Ever said something you later regretted? No-nonsense midfielder Bobby Thomson once publicly vowed he would never miss a penalty for Boro, so it was with depressing predictability that in a home clash with Southampton in January 1982, he'd take – and miss – probably the worst spot-kick ever seen at Ayresome. Having screwed the ball wide in extraordinary fashion, his after-match comment that he was suffering from double vision and should have let someone else take it was the understatement of the season. He'd arrived at Boro from Morton with a big reputation, having interested Celtic at one stage, and it was Jock Stein who recommended him to Bobby Murdoch. As captain of Morton, he was sent off twice against Rangers in one season. Rugged and mean – quite a contrast to the man he'd been signed to replace, David Armstrong – he revelled in the nickname 'Desperate Dan' after one opponent remarked: 'It wouldn't surprise me if he shaved with a blow torch.' Referring to his famous North East comic namesake, he arrived on Teesside with the line 'I'm no comedian,' although anyone who saw THAT penalty might have begged to differ. His debut came as sub in a 3–2 win over Stoke and before long, his hardman style was embraced by the Boro faithful and he became the first Boro player to be sent off in a League Cup tie. He finished the 1981–82 season as joint top scorer with just five goals, having never hit any sort of form. With Boro relegated, he moved back to Scotland before returning to the North East in 1987 on a week-to-week contract at Hartlepool. In 1989 he could be found playing for Colne Dynamos, helping them to the HFS Loans League title.

TINSLEY Walter Edward

Inside-left
Born: Ironville, 10 August 1891.
Died: 1966.
Career: Alfreton Town. Sutton Town. Sunderland 1911. Exeter City. MIDDLESBROUGH 1913. Nottingham Forest 1921. Reading 1924.

■ Nicknamed 'One a Week', inside-forward Tinsley was a real goal machine. His record of a goal every two games was admirable and, with George Elliott also banging them in alongside him, he notched 19 in just 23 games in the 1913–14 season as Boro finished third in Division One – their highest ever League placing. Indeed, it was Tinsley's double strike on the final day at Aston Villa that took Boro to such lofty heights. Top scorer in 1914–15 with 26 goals, the tally included a hat-trick in an amazing 7–5 victory over Spurs in February – and he still had time for two more hat-tricks before the end of the season, against Liverpool and in an infamous match against Oldham which was abandoned when a Latics player refused to leave the pitch. The outbreak of war could not have come at a worse time for Tinsley who might well have pushed for international honours had he had the opportunity to carry on his scoring exploits. He scored in Boro's first match after World War One, a 1–0 victory at Sheffield Wednesday but his days as a goal machine were over and he joined Nottingham Forest in 1921.

TODD Andrew John James

Defender
Born: Derby, 21 September 1974.
Career: MIDDLESBROUGH 1992. Swindon Town (loan) 1995. Bolton Wanderers 1995. Charlton Athletic 1999. Grimsby Town (loan) 2002. Blackburn Rovers 2002. Burnley (loan) 2003. Derby County 2007.

■ The son of Colin Todd, Andy had the unenviable task of following in his England international dad's footsteps. A

Durham County Schools defender, he joined Boro as a YTS player but left to go to Forest. Failing to settle at the City Ground, he returned to Boro to complete his YTS apprenticeship and his first-team chance came in 1993–94 amid an injury crisis in Lennie Lawrence's small squad. Initially as centre-back and then as a midfielder, his comfort on the ball marked him out as a decent prospect. However, Bryan Robson's arrival saw Todd's chances restricted, although in one of his few outings, he was sent off in an Anglo-Italian Cup clash with Udinese in October 1994. He had a spell on loan at Swindon as part of the deal that brought Jan Aage Fjortoft to Boro and was eventually sold to Bolton, where he played under his dad and was named Player of the Year in 1997–98. He joined his dad's old club, Derby County, from Blackburn in 2007.

TOMLIN John

Centre-half
Born: Details unknown.
Career: Seaham White Star. Sunderland 1905. MIDDLESBROUGH 1906. Murton Red Star.

■ Half-back Tomlin's brief Boro career was sandwiched into four consecutive games, wearing the number-five shirt against Bury, Manchester City, Derby County and Preston North End early in the 1906–07 season. A bad start to the season resulted in the club's directors insisting that Alex Mackie made wholesale changes to the side and Tomlin was given his chance. But the risk didn't pay off and not one of the four games was won. Tomlin was dropped and Mackie quit the game to run a pub.

TOWNSEND Andrew David

Midfield
Born: Maidstone, 23 July 1963.
Career: Welling United. Weymouth. Southampton 1985. Norwich City 1988. Chelsea 1990. Aston Villa 1993. MIDDLESBROUGH 1997. West Bromwich Albion 1999.

■ A vastly-experienced left-sided midfielder, Townsend signed for Boro in August 1997 from Aston Villa and proved to be a snip at £500,000 with his excellent passing, powerful shot, defensive know-how and tackling ability. After playing non-League football for Welling and Weymouth while working as a computer operator in London, Townsend's career took off with a £35,000 move to Southampton where he played alongside David Armstrong. By his own admission, snooker and pubs had distracted him from his football but big money moves took him to Norwich, Chelsea and then Aston Villa for £2.1 million. He picked up two League Cup-winners' medals along the way – while internationally, he won 70 caps for the Republic of Ireland. A true leader on the pitch, Bryan Robson installed him as Boro club captain for the 1998–99 season following Nigel Pearson's retirement. He was part of the losing Coca-Cola Cup Final side at Wembley in March 1998 and helped Boro secure promotion back to the Premier League, where he continued to perform with great consistency. Despite being linked with a return to Aston Villa, he signed a one-year extension to his contract up to summer 2000, but the lure of the Midlands proved too strong when West Bromwich Albion boss Brian Little (the man who had sold him to Boro) moved in with a £100,000 offer. Knowledgeable about the game and a good motivator, he later became a successful TV pundit.

TOWNSEND James Clabby

Wing-half
Born: Greenock, 2 February 1945.
Career: St Johnstone. MIDDLESBROUGH 1964. St Johnstone. Heart of Midlothian. Morton.

■ Wing-half Jimmy Townsend was sent off in only his fourth game for Boro, a goalless draw at Sunderland in 1964. He'd joined from St Johnstone, where he made his debut aged just 17 and Partick Thistle had a £15,000 offer turned down before Boro moved in. A forceful player and confident going forward, he was a near ever-present in the 1964–65 season but was troubled by a thigh injury in the 1965–66 relegation season. Stan Anderson obviously didn't feel he fitted the bill in the battle to return to Division Two and allowed him to leave for Scotland during the 1966 close season. After 65 starts for Boro, he re-joined St Johnstone and went on to play for Hearts and Morton.

TRECHMAN Otto L.

Centre-forward
Born: Details unknown.
Career: West Hartlepool. MIDDLESBROUGH 1905. West Hartlepool.

■ An amateur, Trechman made just one appearance for Boro – a goalless draw at Wolves – although that's maybe not surprising as Alf Common was the usual occupant of the number-nine shirt. On leaving Boro, he returned to West Hartlepool as captain.

TUCKER William Henry

Centre-forward
Born: Details unknown.
Career: MIDDLESBROUGH 1906.

■ Tucker was another of those players lucky enough to score on their Boro debuts. His moment of glory came in a 4–2 defeat at Preston in October 1906 after being spotted playing local League football. But, like others before him, he couldn't oust £1,000 man Alf Common and was released after just three more appearances in the top flight.

TURNBULL Lee Mark

Midfield/Forward
Born: Stockton, 27 September 1967.
Career: MIDDLESBROUGH 1985. Aston Villa 1987. Doncaster Rovers 1987. Chesterfield 1991. Doncaster Rovers 1993. Wycombe Wanderers 1994. Scunthorpe United 1995. Darlington 1997. Gainsborough Trinity.

■ A midfielder or striker, Boro fan Turnbull made his full debut in one of the saddest matches in the club's history – the 2–1 defeat at Shrewsbury Town in May 1986 which meant relegation to Division Three and near oblivion. He was in tears in the dressing room after the game but happier times were round the corner. On the run-in to promotion the following season, he scored three vital goals in four games. In a surprise exchange deal with 'keeper Kevin Poole, Turnbull joined Aston Villa but the switch didn't pay off and, after falling out with Villa boss Graham Taylor, three months later he moved to Doncaster Rovers for £17,500, the start of an impressive career in the lower Leagues. Turnbull had progressed through the Boro ranks with several players who made it big, including Stuart Ripley, Alan Kernaghan and Colin Cooper.

TURNBULL ROSS

Goalkeeper
Born: Bishop Auckland, 4 January 1985.
Career: MIDDLESBROUGH 2002. Darlington (loan) 2003. Barnsley (loan) 2004. Bradford City (loan) 2004. Barnsley (loan) 2004. Crewe Alexandra (loan) 2005. Cardiff City (loan) 2007.

■ Strapping England Under-21 goalkeeper Turnbull has all the attributes for a top class career in the game. Unfortunately for him, the form of Boro number one Mark Schwarzer and his deputy Brad Jones has meant his first-team chances have been severely limited. Tall and strong, Turnbull joined the club as a schoolboy and kept goal for Boro when they reached the 2002–03 FA Youth Cup Final before being beaten by Manchester United over two legs. Early the following season he made his League debut for Darlington, impressing and keeping a clean sheet before his one-month loan spell was prematurely ended by an international call-up. Later in the season he went on loan to Barnsley and got further League experience as he covered for injured former Boro goalkeeper Marlon Beresford. He returned to Barnsley for a season-long loan at Oakwell but was recalled to the Riverside to cover for the injured Schwarzer at the end of the 2005–06 campaign. He responded with several outstanding displays, including a Man of the Match performance as a team of locally-born players went down to a late penalty at Fulham in May 2006. In summer 2007 he joined Cardiff City on long-term loan.

TURNER Peter

Inside-left
Born: Glasgow, 18 December 1876.
Died: East Kilbride, 8 February 1970.
Career: Parkhead. St Bernard's. Woolwich Arsenal 1900. MIDDLESBROUGH 1901. Luton Town 1903. Watford. Leyton.

■ Signed from Woolwich Arsenal for £90 at the end of the previous season, inside-forward Turner was an ever-present for the first half of the 1901–02 campaign. Though promotion – which was eventually achieved – always looked on the cards, manager John Robson shuffled his pack in February and Turner permanently lost his place, save for a swansong appearance at Burton United in April. He was allowed to leave that summer.

TWINE Frank William

Full-back
Born: Holborn, 1903.
Career: Army. MIDDLESBROUGH 1926. Aldershot. Rochdale 1931. Caernarvon United.

■ A sergeant in the army while playing for Boro's reserves in 1926–27, burly soldier Twine put in a solid display when given his chance at right full-back in a 4–1 win at Darlington in October 1926. It was a good week for Twine as just a few days earlier, he played for England Amateurs in a victory over Ireland in Belfast. Coolness personified under pressure and a determined tackler, he was called up for England Amateurs against Belgium in January 1927 and signed professional terms for Boro on the termination of his military service two months later, by which time he had become the club's first choice right-back. He helped secure the record breaking

promotion and was a regular throughout the First Division campaign which followed before joining Aldershot when relegation came.

TYLDESLEY James

Right-back
Born: Halesowen, 7 October 1882.
Died: Newcastle, January 1963.
Career: Halesowen St John. Newcastle United 1903. MIDDLESBROUGH 1906. Luton Town 1908. Leeds City 1909.

■ Right full-back Tyldesley started his career at Halesowen St John before joining Newcastle United as a reserve. A more-than-able defender, broad-shouldered and a tough competitor, he tackled with outstanding power to leave opponents in no doubt they'd been in a game. He had only one season in the Boro first team, playing regularly in the First Division in 1906–07. However, he then spent two years out of the spotlight before leaving for Leeds City. After his playing days, he scouted for Newcastle and discovered, among others, Bob Roxburgh and Micky Burns. Leeds United's trainer in the 1950s, he died in Newcastle in January 1963.

UGOLINI Rolando

Goalkeeper
Born: Lucca, Italy, 4 June 1924.
Career: Armadale Thistle. Heart of Midlothian 1943. Glasgow Celtic 1944. MIDDLESBROUGH 1948. Dundee United 1960.

■ Few Boro players are remembered with more fondness than colourful 'keeper Ugolini. A great crowd favourite, 'Ugo' came to Ayresome Park from Celtic, where he was on the fringes of first-team action but was kept at bay by Scottish international Willie Miller. And having opted to join Boro instead of Chelsea, he soon made sure he'd never be forgotten – not least by new signing Andy Donaldson, whose leg he broke in a practice match!

An Italian by birth, Ugolini's family moved to Scotland in 1925 and set up a fish and chip business. Young Ugolini built a big reputation in junior Scottish football and spent some time on Hearts' books before joining Celtic. He took up British citizenship shortly after joining Boro and made his debut against the team he turned down, Chelsea. His theatrical style of play soon had the terraces talking while, off the pitch, he was just as eccentric. A dressing room prankster, the directors at one time had unfounded doubts about his eyesight after one player commented that 'Ugo' was eating a lot of carrots! Joking apart, he was fit, agile and a very good goalkeeper, making the number one jersey his own in eight seasons at Ayresome Park to stand 20th in the club's all-time appearance list. Indeed, many thought him unlucky not be called up by his country.

Unluckily, he lost his place to Peter

Taylor for the last game of 1955–56 after dislocating his shoulder and, after a year out of the side, he moved on to Wrexham before ending his career with a brief spell at Dundee. Now living in Edinburgh, he ran a bookies' shop until retirement.

URQUHART Arthur

Outside-right
Born: Details unknown.
Career: Greenock Morton. MIDDLESBROUGH 1907.

■ Urquhart's Boro first-team career couldn't have been much more compact, his four games fitting snugly into a 12-day period over Christmas 1907. It started badly with a 6–0 drubbing at Aston Villa and reached its high point seven days later with a 3–1 home win over Liverpool. A wing-forward, Urquhart had been signed from Greenock Morton and went straight into Andy Aitken's side. However, Boro boasted a strong squad, eventually finishing sixth in the top flight, and Urquhart was released at the end of the season.

URWIN Thomas

Winger/Inside-right
Born: Haswell, 5 February 1896.
Died: Tynemouth, 7 May 1968.
Career: Fulwell. Lambton Star. Shildon. MIDDLESBROUGH 1914. Newcastle United 1924. Sunderland 1929.

■ Few players can have served North East football better than nippy winger Tommy Urwin, remarkably the recipient of benefits from all the region's big three clubs. An England Schoolboy, he served Boro first and made his debut against Sunderland in a New Year's Day derby at Ayresome Park, although his Teesside career was soon interrupted by World War One and he guested for Fulham while serving with the Royal Artillery.

Standing just 5ft 5in tall, he was full of craft, speed and cunning, combining those attributes with a deadly crossing ability from either flank. A fans' favourite, he was awarded a Middlesbrough benefit in 1921–22 and toured with England in 1923, winning two caps against Sweden. Sadly, he left Boro under a cloud, a row over payments following the club's first-ever relegation

in 1924 putting paid to his Ayresome career. Opportunist Newcastle boss Bill McCracken stepped in to sign him for £3,200 at Newcastle railway station as Urwin was on his way to meet Manchester United officials.

He helped Newcastle win the League in 1927 – the same year Boro won Division Two – although he was suspended for a month after getting sent off in a FA Cup tie at Liverpool. Then it was on to Sunderland in February 1930 for £525 where he saw out his playing days before stepping into youth coaching in 1936. He was also employed as an accounts clerk in Sunderland Royal Infirmary and later scouted for Sunderland, becoming assistant to Bill Murray in the 1940s. One story involving Urwin was that a telegram asking him to play for England never arrived and the place instead went to Derby's Alf Quantrill. Amazingly, the FA later confirmed the tale was true. He died at Tynemouth in May 1968.

VERRILL Edward

Left-half
Born: Staithes.
Career: South Bank. MIDDLESBROUGH 1907.

■ Also known as 'Fishy', half-back Verrill was a consistent performer under Andy Aitken, Andy Walker and Tom McIntosh, making the number-six shirt his own. However, after joining from South Bank, he was initially given his chance as a wing-forward before finding his niche at the back. He partnered player-manager Aitken and his namesake Sam in the Boro half-back line as they finished in the First Divison top 10 in his first two seasons at the club.

Two of his four goals for the club were particularly sweet – the second in a 3–2 home win over North East rivals, Sunderland in 1909, and the solitary strike in a 1–0 home triumph over Preston later in the same season. He retired following the outbreak of war as his first-team appearances had diminished over the previous two years.

VICKERS Stephen

Central defender
Born: Bishop Auckland, 13 October 1967.
Career: Spennymoor United. Tranmere Rovers 1985. MIDDLESBROUGH 1993. Crystal Palace (loan) 2001. Birmingham City 2001.

■ Few Boro players of the modern era have enjoyed such a long and eventful career on Teesside as Vickers, who played under four managers and became a key member of an ever-changing defence. The former Spennymoor United player joined Tranmere Rovers in September 1985 after turning down the chance to join Boro on YTS terms. He made rapid progress at Prenton Park and soon established himself as a first-choice centre-half, never missing a game in 1987–88 and 1988–89. Vickers chalked up 148 successive appearances for Rovers and celebrated two promotions and five Wembley appearances with the Wirral club. He was just short of 400 appearances for them when he was brought back to the North East by Lennie Lawrence in December 1993, and he quickly made himself at home at Ayresome Park. Boro were struggling in the lower half of the First Division when he made his debut and he boosted his popularity with a goal against Sunderland in one of his first appearances. Replacing Nicky Mohan as Derek Whyte's regular defensive partner, he hardly missed a match under Lawrence. The consistent centre-half won the Player of the Year title in 1995–96, Boro's first at the Riverside, while he was a vital member of Bryan Robson's promotion-winning team

alongside the powerful Nigel Pearson a year earlier. Calm and composed, with good distribution, Robson tipped him for England honours but the international call-up never came. His partners also included Viv Anderson, Craig Liddle, Phil Whelan, Gianluca Festa, Neil Maddison, Gary Pallister, Colin Cooper, Jason Gavin, Paul Okon, Ugo Ehiogu and Gareth Southgate in his eight years on Teesside. In 1998–99, Vickers completed 200 games for Boro and then reached the landmark of 500 career games. A non-playing substitute in the 1997 Coca-Cola Cup Final and an early sub for the injured Robbie Mustoe in the same season's FA Cup Final, he made up for the disappointment of not being in those starting line-ups by playing from the kick-off in the 1998 Coca-Cola Cup Final. Vickers enjoyed another excellent spell with Terry Venables in charge of team affairs as Boro fought for Premiership survival in 2000–01, but was not a first-choice under Robson's successor, Steve McClaren. After a loan spell with Crystal Palace, he rejoined Steve Bruce at

Birmingham City in November 2001. He had a big influence on the Blues defence but, following a spate of injuries, he retired to pursue a new career in property development.

VIDMAR Anthony

Defender
Born: Adelaide, Australia, 15 April 1969.
Career: Adelaide City (Australia) 1988. Ekeren (Belgium) 1992. NAC Breda (Holland) 1995. Glasgow Rangers 1997. MIDDLESBROUGH 2002. Cardiff City 2003. NAC Breda (Holland) 2005. Central Coast (Australia) 2006.

■ A committed, versatile and honest defender, Australian international defender Tony Vidmar struggled at times to come to terms with the rigours of the Premiership during his short spell at the Riverside. He was signed by Steve McClaren in the summer of 2002 after being released by Rangers, having won every domestic honour with the Glasgow club. At Ibrox he helped Rangers to the treble of Premier Division Championship, Scottish Cup and League Cup in 1998–99 and 1999–2000 and to a Scottish Cup and League Cup double in 2001–02. He had scored 11 goals, mainly from set pieces, in 159 games for Rangers, when he signed for Middlesbrough on a one-year contract in September 2002. The transfer went ahead after the deadline had passed because the player was out of contract. Happy to play anywhere across the defence, he made his debut as he replaced Gareth Southgate at centre-back against Birmingham, impressing in a 1–0 win. He found first-team chances limited due to the partnership of Southgate and Ugo Ehiogu, but he did make 12 starts that season. His last appearance in a Boro shirt came in a disastrous 5–2 defeat at home to Aston Villa in late January 2003. Vidmar later enjoyed a short but successful spell at Cardiff City before returning to Dutch side NAC Breda, where he had initially made his name after leaving Australia. In May 2006 Vidmar withdrew from World Cup selection because of an irregular heartbeat caused by a blood clot in his coronary artery. But after an operation in London he was given the all-clear to resume his professional career. He is now playing for Australian side Central Coast Mariners.

VIDUKA Mark Anthony

Forward
Born: Australia, 9 October 1975.
Career: Melbourne Knights (Australia). NK Croatia Zagreb (Croatia). Glasgow Celtic 1998. Leeds United 2000. MIDDLESBROUGH 2004. Newcastle United 2007.

■ One of the most gifted players to have pulled on a Boro shirt in recent years, Viduka's contribution to the club will sadly be overshadowed by his controversial move to neighbours Newcastle. But before that Boro fans were treated to some wonderful displays from the bulky but deceptively skilful striker, who joined the club from Leeds United for £4.5 million in summer 2004. Although born in Australia, it was in Croatia, birthplace of his parents, that Mark's talents as a goalscorer really began to flourish with Croatia Zagreb. The goals brought the attention of Celtic's scouts and he joined the Glasgow giants for £3.5 million in 1998. After being named Scottish Player of the Year in 1999–2000 and Oceania Player of the Year in 2000, he moved to Elland Road in a £6.5 million deal. He made his Leeds debut in a 2–1 win over Boro at the Riverside but will always be remembered for his superb four-goal display in the classic 4–3 win over Liverpool in November 2000. A regular marksman for the Elland Road club, Viduka scored 13 goals in a struggling Leeds team in his final season with the club. Viduka was something of a slow starter on Teesside. His first season was blighted by a string of injuries that brought to mind comparisons with the recently departed Alen Boksic, with some observers even questioning his commitment to the cause. But all that changed the following year when Viduka played a huge part in

Boro's progress to a historic UEFA Cup Final appearance, beating Massimo Maccarone to the club website's Man of the Match awards in the dramatic quarter-final and semi-final victories over Basel and Steaua Bucharest at the Riverside. He could have been the hero again in the 4–0 final defeat to Sevilla, being denied what looked like a clear penalty at 1–0 and then missing what turned out to be Boro's best chance of the game. Viduka had almost a talismanic presence for Boro that season as he hit 16 goals in all competitions and in the summer was chosen to captain Australia for the World Cup Finals in Germany, helping them reach the last 16. After a slow start he again hit top form the following season after returning to action from a broken toe early in the campaign. In all he hit 19 goals, including an incredible late streak as he overtook Yakubu to top the club's scoring charts. The campaign ended with Viduka out of contract and Boro and their fans still unsure where the player's future lay. Despite the club's best efforts, including personal calls from Steve Gibson during Viduka's family holiday, he signed for Newcastle in June 2007.

VINCENT John Victor

Midfield
Born: West Bromwich, 8 February 1947.
Career: Birmingham City 1964. MIDDLESBROUGH 1971. Cardiff City 1972. Atherstone Town.

■ For a player Stan Anderson predicted would 'set the River Tees on fire,' someone must have forgotten the matches as Johnny Vincent failed to light up Ayresome Park. An England Youth international, he made his name with Birmingham City before heading for Teesside in a deal which saw George Smith head the other way.

After a solid but unremarkable spell, he handed in a transfer request in November 1971 and was promptly dropped by Anderson. Vincent returned but was again put up for sale in August 1972 and met Cardiff's Jimmy Scoular on the same day Anderson was speaking to Alan Foggon about coming to Boro. With his prospects on Teesside obviously grim, Vincent agreed to head for Wales and he had the last laugh, scoring on his debut for Cardiff in a 2–0 win over Boro.

WAINSCOAT William Russell

Inside-left/Centre-forward
Born: Maltby, 28 July 1898.
Died: Worthing, July 1967.
Career: Maltby Main Colliery Welfare. Barnsley 1919. MIDDLESBROUGH 1923. Leeds United 1924. Hull City 1931.

■ Once dubbed the perfect inside-forward, Russell Wainscoat's time at Boro was merely a forerunner to a scintillating spell with Leeds. Signed from Barnsley, he scored on his Boro debut, playing inside-left in a 2–1 Division One defeat at Preston, but relegation more or less put paid to his Ayresome career and Leeds offered him another top flight chance. Ironically, they were also relegated but he helped them back to Division One at the first attempt. He played a deeper role with Leeds, where his attacking skills were allied to tactical mastery, a deceptive turn of speed and wonderful ball control. An extremely clever player with a powerful shot, he was selected for an FA tour of Canada in 1926 and was capped by England in 1929. Relegation in 1931 saw him leave Leeds for Hull City, where he helped his new side win Division Three North. After retiring in 1934, he held various jobs including railway clerk, licensee, shoe shop owner, confectioner and drapery store manager. He died in Worthing in July 1967.

WALDOCK Ronald

Inside-forward
Born: Heanor, 6 December 1932.
Career: Loscoe YC. Coventry City 1950. Sheffield United 1954. Scunthorpe United 1957. Plymouth Argyle 1959. MIDDLESBROUGH 1960. Gillingham 1961.

■ A contractual dispute enlivened the Boro career of journeyman Waldock, who came to Teesside after spells with Coventry, Sheffield United – where he'd been signed by ex-Boro player Reg Freeman – and Plymouth. His dispute in mid–1961 came about after some decent performances which he felt merited £2 a week more than the £18 a week he'd been offered. He left soon after for Gillingham and then became player-coach at Halifax Town. His first goal for Boro came in the heat of a Wear-Tees derby against Sunderland soon after his arrival but the form of Alan Peacock meant he was often switched from inside-forward to a wing role as Boro narrowly missed out on promotion in 1961. He signed off the season in style with a double strike against Portsmouth, Brian Clough grabbing the other goal, and hit two more in a 4–3 home defeat against Derby on the opening day of 1961–62. However, financial matters soon rose to the surface and his Boro spell came to an end.

WALKER Donald Hunter

Wing-half
Born: Edinburgh, 10 September 1935.
Career: Tranent Juniors. Leicester City 1955. MIDDLESBROUGH 1959. Grimsby Town 1963.

■ Walker was certainly kept waiting for his debut by Boro boss Bob Dennison after signing from Leicester – six months in fact. It eventually came in a 2–0 win v Swansea in March 1960 and heralded a nine-game run at the end of the season, but he wasn't in the side which kicked off the following campaign. A tidy left-half, Walker was made available in March 1962 and was officially placed on the transfer list in summer 1963. Only offered a monthly contract in 1963–64, he left after the second month when the Football League ordered Boro to give him a free transfer.

WALKER John

Left-back
Born: Beith, 1882.
Died: 1968.
Career: Eastern Burnside. Cambuslang Rangers. Burnbank Athletic. Raith Rovers. Beith. Glasgow Rangers. Swindon Town. MIDDLESBROUGH 1913. Reading 1921.

■ A Boro servant either side of World War One, steady left-back Walker started out as an outside-left in Scottish junior football but switched position during a makeshift dinner break game at a factory. Playing for Burnbank Athletic, he was spotted and signed by Scottish Division Two side Raith Rovers, but problems with a persistent leg injury saw him ask Celtic's trainer for a second opinion. That didn't impress Raith and in the ensuing fall-out, Walker vowed never to play for the Kirckaldy club again and he returned home to Beith. Rangers and Cowdenbeath provided his next first-team action until, in summer 1907, he switched to Southern League Swindon Town and made a great impression. In 1911 he won the first of his 11 Scotland caps and was rated the best full-back in the Southern League when signed by Boro manager Tom McIntosh. He was initially played at right-back on his arrival from Swindon but switched to the right as a highest-ever League placing of third was achieved in his first season at Ayresome Park. He was unfortunate to have the war interrupt his career and lost his place to the emerging Walter Holmes when peace returned. A year after joining Reading, Walker retired and later ran a fish shop in Swindon.

WALKER Joshua

Midfield
Born: Newcastle, 21 February 1989.
Career: MIDDLESBROUGH 2006. Bournemouth (loan) 2007.

■ When central midfielder Josh Walker replaced Malcolm Christie for the final 28 minutes at Fulham on the final day of the 2005–06 season, Boro fielded a team made up entirely of Academy graduates. That was Steve McClaren's last game in charge but the outgoing Boro boss had already recognised Walker's considerable potential when he plucked him out of obscurity and brought him on as a substitute for the first team in a pre-season friendly against Carlisle in July 2005. The youngster duly completed the scoring in a 4–2 victory after playing a one-two with Szilard Nemeth. Senior opportunities were difficult to come by the following season but he starred for the reserves and spent a successful loan spell at Bournemouth. A bright future is predicted for the England Under-16, Under-17 and Under-18 international, who has captained his country at each level.

WALKER Robert Geoff

Outside-left
Born: Bradford, 29 September 1926
Died: 1997.
Career: Bradford Park Avenue 1946. Doncaster Rovers 1954.

■ He may have played 259 games for Boro, but speedy outside-left Walker was a Bradford lad at heart. He didn't make any League appearances for Bradford Park Avenue but played for them during World War Two in a Football League North fixture at Ayresome, scoring a hat-trick in an 8–1 win. Not surprisingly, he caught the eye of Boro boss David Jack and soon signed for £8,000, but he refused to give up his Bradford roots. Indeed, during most of his time at Boro, he stayed in Bradford and trained with his old club, only travelling to join his teammates on the eve of matchdays. Incredibly, for one game at Ayresome against Huddersfield, he arranged a lift to Middlesbrough on the visiting team bus and was lucky to get a ride home after scoring two in a 4–1 win. He'd now be called an old-fashioned winger, with a game built on speedy runs, hard shots and dangerous centres. Possessor of an excellent left foot, he scored some great goals as well as creating them and soon became one of the most feared flank players in the game. In February 1949, he asked to be placed on the open transfer list but asked to come off when no other League clubs showed interest. Resigned to being with Boro, he fought his way back into the side and was a regular for the following five seasons, but he again requested a transfer in September 1951 after buying a house in the Bradford area to be closer to his family. After leaving Doncaster, he played on into his late 30s with Southern League Clacton Town before working as a sports master at a local public school. He retired to Chelmsford and died in 1997.

WALKER Robert Henry

Inside-left
Born: Northallerton, 1884.
Career: Heart of Midlothian. MIDDLESBROUGH 1906. Tottenham Hotspur 1906. New Brompton 1908. Northampton Town 1909. Millwall Athletic 1910. Luton Town 1911. Bristol Rovers 1912.

■ Walker's 14 first-team appearances were sandwiched into the first three months of 1906 before fellow Scot Alex Mackie allowed him to leave for Spurs. An inside-forward, he played alongside Alf Common before being ousted following the arrival of Fred Wilcox. However, Boro fans were doubtless extremely grateful for his goal in a 1–0 home victory against arch rivals Newcastle United.

WALLEY Ernest

Wing-half
Born: Caernarfon, 19 April 1933.
Career: Tottenham Hotspur 1951. MIDDLESBROUGH 1958. Crystal Palace 1960. Gravesend. Stevenage Athletic.

■ He only played eight games for Boro, but at least Walley's debut came in a 9–0 victory. A wing-half, Welshman Walley's great start came in a famous thrashing of Brighton when a certain Brian Clough netted five of the goals. Signed from Spurs, he played only seven more games before badly injuring his knee in a match with Rotherham United. He failed to regain his first-team place and moved to Crystal Palace, where he forgot his playing aspirations to join the coaching staff. And he was still there in 1980 when Terry Venables relinquished the manager's post, allowing Walley to take over for two months before Malcom Allison stepped in.

WALSH Alan

Midfield/Forward
Born: Hartlepool, 9 December 1956.
Career: Horden Colliery. MIDDLESBROUGH 1976. Darlington 1978. Bristol City 1984. Besitkas (Turkey). Walsall 1991. Huddersfield Town 1991. Shrewsbury Town 1992. Cardiff City 1992. Southampton 1993. Backwell United. Hartlepool United 1994.

■ An apprentice bricklayer, Walsh was spotted playing part-time for Horden Colliery but only ever played for Boro as a substitute. Greater success came at Darlington, where he became the club's all-time top goalscorer, and Bristol City, where boss Terry Cooper signed him after being tipped off by ex-Boro teammate Maddren. Some years later, Cooper returned the favour by alerting Maddren to Archie Stephens. Walsh was converted to full-back in later years and even helped Besiktas win the Turkish championship, but his return to England saw him on non-contract terms at all his clubs from Walsall onwards. He also had a spell at Southampton without playing before being brought back into the League by Hartlepool from Taunton Town, where he'd been player-coach. His Pool spell lasted just four games before he again headed south to join Bath City.

WALSH Colin David

Left-winger
Born: Hamilton, 22 July 1962.
Career: Nottingham Forest 1979. Charlton Athletic 1986. Peterborough United (loan) 1989. MIDDLESBROUGH (loan) 1991.

■ For several years as boss of Charlton, Lennie Lawrence had watched the creative Walsh weave his left-wing magic at The Valley. So when Boro's 1990–91 promotion campaign needed bolstering, Lawrence stepped in to bring Walsh north on loan and the skills which saw him win five England Under-21 caps were still in evidence in flashes. An attacking midfielder with a fine passing range and strong shot, Walsh endeared himself to Boro fans by scoring a splendid goal in a 3–1 hammering of Newcastle at Ayresome Park. There was talk of the move being made permanent as Walsh was not keen to return to Charlton but nothing materialised. He returned south to play his part in history, scoring Charlton's first goal on their emotional return to The Valley in December 1992. His career had been hampered by two broken legs, but he remained a classy performer until a knee injury in 1995–96 forced his retirement.

WALSH Gary

Goalkeeper
Born: Wigan, 21 March 1968.
Career: Manchester United 1985. Airdrieonians (loan) 1988. Oldham Athletic (loan) 1993. MIDDLESBROUGH 1995. Bradford City 1997. MIDDLESBROUGH (loan) 2000. Wigan Athletic 2003.

■ Gary Walsh was Boro's first-choice 'keeper in the club's first season at the Riverside and his form was so good that he was talked about as an England possibility. After 10 years of sporadic appearances at Old Trafford, he relished the chance of regular football and gave Alan Miller stiff competition for the number-one jersey. The formidable figure of Peter Schmeichel blocked his path at Manchester United and England Under-21 international Walsh had to be content with occasional European action. He did not have to wait long for his chance at Boro, an injury to Miller seeing him step into the team in September 1995. He held on to his place for seven months, surviving a dip in form that featured some embarrassing howlers. Miller returned towards the end of the season amid reports of a bust-up between Walsh and goalkeeping coach Mike Kelly, although Walsh played in the final game of the season as his old club, Manchester United, won the title at the Riverside. Gastro-enteritis and a bowel infection early in 1996–97 saw him lose a stone in weight and his place in the team, with Ben Roberts stepping in. Bradford, who had sold Mark Schwarzer to Boro, rescued him from reserve team football and Walsh said thank-you with some fine displays to earn him the Player of the Year title at Valley Parade. In 1999–2000,

Walsh was back in the Premiership following Bradford's dream promotion, keeping a clean sheet as they started with a shock win over Boro in the opening match. He had been an ever present in their promotion campaign but injuries and the arrival of Matt Clarke saw him slip from the limelight a little. Walsh made a brief return to Boro in September 2000 when he was brought in on loan to answer a goalkeeping crisis and was still at Valley Parade when they slipped out of the top flight the following May. He spent the next couple of seasons recovering from knee surgery before, having played in 144 games for the club, he was released in May 2003 to join his home-town club, Wigan Athletic, to act as cover for John Filan. He retired at the end of the 2005–06 season to pursue a coaching career with the Latics.

WANLESS Robert

Outside-right
Born: Middlesbrough, 19 July 1876.
Died: Middlesbrough, July 1963.
Career: MIDDLESBROUGH 1898.

■ Marine fitter Wanless was nicknamed 'Blue' because his waistcoat split and he repaired it with a blue patch. Sartorial matters apart, he was a prominent player in Boro's Northern League team and helped clinch the 1898 FA Amateur Cup Final with a 2–0 win over Uxbridge at Crystal Palace. He'd also scored one of the goals in the 2–0 semi-final win over London Casuals. With Boro in the Football League, Wanless played outside-right in the first game at Lincoln City but managed just nine more appearances. He died in Middlesbrough in July 1963.

WARD Paul Terence

Midfield
Born: Fishburn, 15 September 1963.
Career: Chelsea 1981. Colombus Waterside (New Zealand). MIDDLESBROUGH 1982. Darlington 1985. Leyton Orient 1988. Scunthorpe United 1989. Lincoln City 1991.

■ Boro tried to sign midfielder Ward as a schoolboy but he opted to try his luck at Chelsea, where he failed to make the grade. Instead, he emigrated to New Zealand and had some success with Kiwi outfit Colombus Waterside before returning to Britain six months later. Offered a trial by Boro by Bobby Murdoch, this time he impressed enough to be taken on, although he had to receive clearance from the New Zealand FA before he could play in a match. His debut, on the same day Tony Mowbray began his Boro career, couldn't have been much bigger – a 1–1 draw with Newcastle at St James' Park – and he was offered a contract by new manager Malcolm Allison in November. An honest, utility player, he switched from midfield to full-back and put in some good displays, but Willie Maddren opted to let him and Alan Roberts leave for Darlington, with Mitch Cook and £5,000 coming in return. While at Feethams and aged just 23, he was made caretaker manager when Cyril Knowles was sacked in 1987 before moving to Orient.

WARDLE George

Outside-right
Born: Kimblesworth, 24 September 1919.
Died: 1991.
Career: MIDDLESBROUGH 1937. Exeter City 1939. Cardiff City 1947. Queen's Park Rangers 1949. Darlington 1951.

■ Wardle's solitary Boro run-out came in a goalless draw with Portsmouth in January 1938, but he forged a decent career in the game on both sides of the touchline. While playing, he helped Chelsea win a wartime Cup Final, but it was as a coach that he truly found his niche, guiding Crook Town to Amateur Cup Final wins at Wembley in 1959 and 1962. During a spell as a Durham PE lecturer, he was asked by Stan Anderson to take charge of Boro's youth policy and he unearthed some real gems who went on to make the grade in the 1970s. He died in 1991.

WARDROPE Alexander (Sandy)

Centre-half
Born: Stewarton, 1886.
Career: Airdrieonians. MIDDLESBROUGH 1910. Portsmouth.

■ Boro fans hoping Alex be as good as his elder brother Willie, who'd starred for the team at the turn of the century, were sorely disappointed. Brought from Scotland, where he had made his name with Airdrie, Alex stepped in for the dominating half-back Andy Jackson for his debut at Aston Villa in November 1910 with Boro riding high in Division One. Both team and player were brought to earth with a bump as Villa hammered in five goals. His home debut was more memorable, being a win over North East rivals Sunderland but Wardrope was used only in emergencies from then on before his release at the end of the season.

WARDROPE William

Winger
Born: Wishaw, 1876.
Career: Dalziel Rovers. Motherwell. Linthouse. Newcastle United 1895. MIDDLESBROUGH 1899. Third Lanark 1902. Fulham 1904. Swindon Town 1906. Hamilton Academical 1907. Third Lanark. Raith Rovers 1908.

■ Wardrope's signing from Newcastle underlined Boro's ambition to become a serious force in professional football. An inside or outside-left, he was small but well-built, astute and skilful and the possessor of a terrific shot. Little wonder, then, that Newcastle fans took him to their hearts after he joined them from Scottish non-League football. A first-team regular for five years, he was an international trialist shortly before the end of the century but was later suspended by the Scottish FA for alleged irregularities. He initially joined Boro on loan in their first season of League football, but the signing became permanent a month later and he ended his first full season as the club's top League goalscorer. He helped the team to promotion in 1902, supplying many of the assists for Jack Brearley's 22 goals. Other footballing honours included winning the Scottish League with Third Lanark and the Southern League Championship at Fulham before he emigrated to the USA in 1910, where he lived in Pittsburgh. Willie's brother, Alex, also played for Middlesbrough.

WARK John

Midfield
Born: Glasgow, 4 August 1957.
Career: Ipswich Town 1974. Liverpool 1984. Ipswich Town 1988.

MIDDLESBROUGH 1990. Ipswich Town 1991.

■ Former PFA Player of the Year Wark seemed past his best during his one season at Ayresome Park, but a return to first club Ipswich Town would prove there was life in the old dog yet. His love affair with Ipswich began in the 1970s, becoming a first-team regular, helping win the FA Cup in 1978 and scoring 14 goals in 10 games as Ipswich won the UEFA Cup in 1980–81, a feat which made him the European Young Player of the Year. Bizarrely, he also appeared in the film *Escape to Victory* alongside Pele and Bobby Moore. He won the League title with Liverpool and scored in all three of Scotland's 1982 World Cup games, but he struggled to recreate former glories when he came to Boro in 1990. Signed by Colin Todd at the same time as Robbie Mustoe and John Hendrie, he looked quite calm and unruffled in front of the defence, particularly in away games, but his surging runs and tigerish tackling had largely disappeared. Dropped by Todd towards the end of the season, he was told he wasn't talking enough to players in the dressing room. Chairman Colin Henderson was also unimpressed by his refusal to move to Teesside, so it was little surprise when Lennie Lawrence let him return to Ipswich for an amazing fourth spell. He went on to have several more good years in Suffolk, playing in defence as Ipswich won Division Two in 1991–92. Not surprisingly, he then joined the coaching staff.

WARREN Frederick Windsor

Outside-left
Born: Cardiff, 23 December 1907.
Died: 1986.
Career: Cardiff City 1927. MIDDLESBROUGH 1929. Heart of Midlothian 1936. Barry Town.

■ Boro's management team travelled to Cardiff to sign one player and ended up with three – including nippy winger Warren. Already a Welsh international, he still may not have come to the attention of Boro but for Jack Jennings. It was Jennings that Peter McWilliam and chairman Phil Bach travelled to Ninian Park to sign, only to be told that reserve winger Warren and goalkeeper Joe Hillier were also available for a combined fee of £8,500. All three switched to Teesside and made their debuts in a 4–1 away defeat at Leicester City in February 1930. Injuries then often cost Warren his place in the Boro side, particularly in 1931–32, but he played well while fit and was recalled by Wales for clashes with Ireland in 1931 and England in 1932. Sadly, injuries flared up again in 1932–33 and he needed an operation, but then went on to be part of the first Welsh side to play an international on foreign soil against France in Paris.

WATKIN Thomas William Steel

Inside-forward
Born: Grimsby, 21 September 1932.
Career: Grimsby Town 1949. Gateshead 1952. MIDDLESBROUGH 1954. Mansfield Town 1955.

■ Schoolboy international Watkin started his career with Grimsby, but he failed to register a first-team appearance for his hometown club. He moved on to Gateshead – then a Football League side – before switching to Ayresome Park, where boss Walter Rowley pushed him straight into the side. His debut came as outside-left in an exciting 3–3 home draw with Chelsea but despite staying in the team for the rest of the season, he couldn't help Boro avoid the drop to Division Two. After just two starts in 1954–55, he was sold by boss Bob Dennison to Mansfield Town for less than half the fee Boro had paid.

WATSON Arnold

Right-half
Born: Ferryhill, 26 December 1903.
Died: 1978.
Career: Chilton Colliery Welfare. MIDDLESBROUGH 1925. Darlington 1926.

■ County Durham-born Watson found favour with Boro boss Herbert Bamlett as the 1925–26 season drew to a close. His six appearances came consecutively, starting with a 3–0 home win against Southampton on 20 March and ending on 17 April with a 2–1 home defeat by Derby County. The regular holder of the wing-forward role, George Jones, returned for the final two games and Watson was not called upon again.

WATSON Herbert Leonard

Left-half
Born: Springwell, 20 November 1908.
Died: 1939.
Career: Pelton Fell. MIDDLESBROUGH 1929. Brentford 1932. Bristol Rovers 1936.

■ Signed from Durham club Pelton Fell by Herbert Bamlett, Watson struggled to make an impact at Boro and made just 15 appearances in six years at Ayresome. A half-back, he played all his League games for Boro in Division One but played far more football for the club's reserves. He fared better with Brentford, where he helped the side to the Division Three South title.

WATSON Robert

Inside-right/Outside-right
Born: Middlesbrough, 1883.
Career: South Bank. MIDDLESBROUGH 1901. Woolwich Arsenal 1903. Leeds City 1905. Rochdale. Exeter City. Stalybridge Celtic.

■ Inside-forward Watson scored on his Boro debut, a 7–1 win over Chesterfield in March 1902, but it was at his next club Arsenal that he really came into his own. In one match, he scored seven goals in a friendly against a Paris XI which Arsenal went on to win 26–1! He joined the production line that led from South Bank to Ayresome Park in 1902, shortly before the club were promoted to Division One for the first time and was a regular during the early part of the following campaign. However, he ended the season out of the side and moved on. In the South West, he was Exeter's first professional captain.

WATSON James

Left-back
Born: Motherwell, 4 October 1877.
Died: 1915.
Career: Burnbank. Sheffield United 1898.Clyde. Sunderland 1899. MIDDLESBROUGH 1906. Shildon.

■ With a nickname like 'Daddy Long Legs', you may guess Watson's style wasn't exactly elegant. A left full-back, his career began with Clyde before a move to Roker Park paid real dividends, earning him his first Scottish cap and helping Sunderland to the League Championship in 1902. An important signing for Boro, he helped turn things round under player-manager Andy Aitken after the club had flirted with relegation for several seasons and was an ever present in 1907–08. His insect-related nickname came because he tended to throw his legs and arms around when pursuing opponents, while his appearance was distinctive to say the least – dark hair parted down the middle and an impressive moustache. The first Boro player to be sent off in an FA Cup tie, he briefly became assistant trainer and 'A' team coach before joining non-League Shildon. He later became manager of the Leviathan Hotel in Sussex Street.

WAYMAN Charles

Centre-forward
Born: Bishop Auckland, 16 May 1922.
Died: 27 March 2006.
Career: Spennymoor United. Newcastle United 1941. Southampton 1947. Preston North End 1950. MIDDLESBROUGH 1954. Darlington 1956.

■ Goal machine Charlie Wayman was past his very best by the time he joined Boro, but his strike rate of 31 goals in 55 League appearances was still pretty phenomenal. A miner, his League football career began with Newcastle United in September 1941, where he was overshadowed at first by Jackie Milburn and Len Shackleton but he came into his own after the war. Small but hard working and skilful, he once revealed that a secret of his success was lightweight Brazilian football boots bought by Southampton manager Bill Dodgin on a tour of South America. He'd joined Southampton after a dispute with officials at Newcastle, but the journey south didn't diminish his appetite for goals and he finished top scorer in Division Two, including a five-goal haul against Leicester City. He then moved to Preston for family reasons and again found the net regularly, winning promotion to Division One in his first season and scoring in every round of the 1954 FA Cup, including the Final. Top scorer in the Football League for three seasons, it's believed only his lack of height cost him England honours.

On arrival at Boro, he found a club rooted to the bottom of Division Two and his debut saw the club's eighth successive defeat, but his signing to bolster a non-existent attack was a calculated risk which paid off...eventually. He didn't score in his first five games and the fans were getting restless, but a four-goal haul against

West Ham was quickly followed by a brace against Fulham – although the little matter of a 9–0 thumping by Blackburn was sandwiched in between. Having found his scoring touch again, Wayman helped Boro's slow push up the table to comparative safety and he finished top scorer in 1954–55. An injury early in 1955–56 gave young Brian Clough his first chance, but Wayman returned and continued to score goals. With youngsters coming through and time marching on, however, he was allowed to join Darlington at the age of 35, where a knee injury forced his retirement in 1958. He then coached Evenwood Town and worked for the Scottish and Newcastle brewery.

WEBB Stanley John

Forward
Born: Middlesbrough, 6 December 1947.
Career: MIDDLESBROUGH 1967. Carlisle United 1971. Brentford 1972. Darlington 1974. Whitby Town. Guisborough.

■ Lanky striker Webb made a sensational debut, scoring both goals in a 2–1 win over Bristol City at Ayresome in the final game of the 1967–68 season. He had signed as a professional under Stan Anderson and put in some good displays for the reserves alongside Willie Maddren and David Mills, but had to wait in line for first-team selection behind Arthur Horsfield and John Hickton. He scored again on his recall against Bury in a 3–2 win but, after a handful of games, he was back in the second string again. His yo-yo career continued with a recall against Sheffield United and again he was in scoring action, netting twice in a 3–1 triumph. For a while, his partnership with Hickton looked likely to bear fruit, only for Joe Laidlaw to step into the breach and send Webb into the reserves again. Early in 1969–70, he got another chance to partner Hickton but, without a goal in three starts, he made way for new signing Hugh McIlmoyle. Opportunities were then largely restricted to a few midfield run-outs before he left for Carlisle. He later played non-League football for Whitby and Guisborough.

WEBSTER Maurice

Centre-half/Right-half
Born: Blackpool, 13 November 1899.
Died: 1978.
Career: Fleetwood. Lytham. Blackburn Rovers 1920. Stalybridge Celtic 1921. MIDDLESBROUGH 1921. Carlisle United 1935.

■ Not many people kept George Camsell quiet on the pitch, but accomplished defender Maurice Webster did just that – even though he was a Boro teammate at the time. Webster's magnificent marking job came in an England trial match at Liverpool and he did it with distinction in a 6–1 win. Suitably impressed, the England management team kept him in mind and he went on to get three caps in 1930 – against Scotland and on a summer tour to Germany and Austria, where he broke his nose. Originally from Lancashire, Webster enlisted aged just 17 and saw active service in World War One in the 4th Duke of Wellington's Regiment. After the war, he joined Lytham in the West Lancashire League and Fleetwood in the Football Combination before signing professional terms with Stalybridge Celtic during their brief stay in the Football League. After just one year, Boro boss Jimmy Howie beat Liverpool to his signature and he made his debut in a 2–1 defeat at Huddersfield at the end of the 1921–22 season. For the next three seasons he was Boro's defensive lynchpin only for a bad injury in 1926–27 to leave him largely on the sidelines for the best part of two years. The end of the 1920s saw him back on top form until injury struck again at Leeds in October 1930, limping off with an injured knee after just 15 minutes of a game Boro lost 7–0. Club captain in 1932–33, his distinguished Boro career lasted until 1934 when, aged 36, he left for Carlisle, only to break his leg in his unlucky 13th game. He stayed on as trainer until the war before returning to Teesside, where he was trainer, coach and groundsman at Stockton FC from 1948 to 1954. He worked at Dorman Long's Port Clarence Works and, until his death in 1978, was a regular at Ayresome Park with his old teammate Walter Holmes.

WEDDLE Derek Keith

Winger/Forward
Born: Newcastle, 27 December 1935.
Career: Sunderland 1953. Portsmouth 1956. Cambridge City. MIDDLESBROUGH 1961. Darlington 1962. York City 1964.

■ A Geordie, Weddle had already tasted Football League action with Sunderland and Portsmouth before Boro snapped him up from non-League Cambridge City. His debut came at centre-forward alongside Alan Peacock in a 2–1 home defeat to Scunthorpe, which was followed by almost four months in the reserves. His only goal was the third in a 3–1 home win over Southampton in February 1962 when he played at inside-forward but, having failed to establish himself, he was made available the following month for £2,500. Firm offers came in from Workington and Brighton but he had a house in Newcastle and wanted to remain in the North East, so he headed for Feethams.

WEIGHTMAN Eric

Left-half
Born: York, 4 May 1910.
Career: Scarborough. MIDDLESBROUGH 1933. Chesterfield 1936. Notts County 1939.

■ Boro failed to find the net in central defender Weightman's three League games. Having joined from non-League Scarborough the previous season, he was elevated to the first team to cover for Jack Martin in a Division One match with deadly rivals Sunderland in December 1933. It could not have been a worse start, Boro losing 4–0 in front of their own embarrassed supporters. It was not until another two-and-a-half years later that the half-back was given another opportunity, appearing in the final two line-ups of the 1935–36 campaign, again as stand-in for Martin. A goalless draw with Stoke was followed by another 4–0 mauling at Wolves. He fared a little better in his single Cup appearance, helping Boro to a 1–0 home win against Southampton in FA Cup round three in January 1936.

WEIR James

Left-back
Born: Muirkirk, 23 August 1887.
Career: Benfoot Hill Thistle. Ayr United. Glasgow Celtic. MIDDLESBROUGH 1910.

■ Described as 'strong, truculent and fearless,' proud Scot Weir was noted for his ability to recite Rabbie Burns' Tam O' Shanter. His footballing ability wasn't bad either for, as a consistent left full-back, he kept many a flank man quiet. He certainly impressed for Boro in a massive Division One derby game with Sunderland in December 1910, a match so huge all local League fixtures were cancelled that day! And, in front of nearly 28,000 fans, Boro won 1–0 to end Sunderland's record of being the country's only unbeaten team. A native of Ayrshire, Weir started at Ayr United before going to Celtic, only to leave Parkhead in a dispute over terms after figuring in four consecutive Championship seasons and helping win the Scottish Cup in 1908. At Boro, he joined former Celtic teammate Don McLeod and, although he played his final League game in 1915, he turned out three times for Boro's 1918–19 Northern Victory League side before retiring in 1920.

WHEATER David James

Central defender
Born: Redcar, 14 February 1987.
Career: MIDDLESBROUGH 2005. Doncaster Rovers (loan) 2006. Wolverhampton Wanderers (loan) 2006. Darlington (loan) 2007.

■ Towering central defender Wheater has a knack of coming up for set pieces and grabbing important goals. At 6ft 4in, perhaps it's no surprise that the former pupil of the Sacred Heart School in Redcar is often the target of corners and free-kicks. A star of Boro's 2004 FA Youth Cup-winning side, he played all eight games in the competition, scoring three goals. He had also appeared in the previous year's Final, against Manchester United, while still a schoolboy. Has also scored a number of goals while representing England at Under-16, Under-17, Under-18 and Under-19 levels, helping the Under-17s to fourth place in the European Championships in France in 2004. Like many of Boro's young players, he benefited from the club's UEFA Cup adventures and was on the bench for their historic first game away in Europe, against Banik Ostrava in September 2004. His first-team debut came as replacement for Stuart Parnaby a couple of minutes from the end of the UEFA Cup Round of 16 game away to Sporting Lisbon in March 2005. He then made a number of impressive appearances for the first team in the latter stages of the 2005–06 season, as Steve McClaren rested his senior stars and experimented with some of his younger players. He gained valuable experience on loan at Doncaster that season and, when Rovers boss Dave Penney moved to Darlington, he clearly remembered Wheater's contribution and came calling at the Riverside once again. A lengthy loan spell with the Quakers followed and he scored twice in 15 games. On his return to the Riverside he was named in the starting line up for the final game of the 2006–07 season, against Fulham. Once again he was on the scoresheet, restoring Boro's lead with a header just before half-time.

WHELAN Noel David

Forward
Born: Leeds, 30 December 1974.
Career: Leeds United 1993. Coventry City 1995. MIDDLESBROUGH 2000. Crystal Palace (loan) 2003. Millwall 2003. Derby County 2004. Aberdeen 2004. Boston United 2005. Livingston 2006.

■ A combination of poor form and injuries meant Whelan rarely threatened to recapture at the Riverside the form that had made him one of England's brightest prospects in his youth. Off the field problems blighted his early career but on joining Boro he vowed he would put his bad boy image behind him. Mainly used in an attacking midfield role, the Yorkshireman is perhaps best remembered on Teesside for his coolly struck winner in the North East derby at Sunderland during Steve McClaren's first season in charge, as well as a spectacular long-range effort against Southampton at the Riverside in January 2003. He also struck one of the goals in a 2–0 FA Cup win over Manchester United. But sadly for Whelan and Boro, the goals were too few and far between. An England Youth and Under-21 international, he came up through the ranks at the club and looked set to be a permanent fixture at Elland Road until his surprise move to Coventry City for £2 million. He was signed by Bryan Robson for £2.25 million and ended the 2001–02 season as second top scorer behind Alen Boksic with seven goals. Struggling to hold down a first-team place, Whelan went on loan to Crystal Palace but picked up an injury and returned to the Riverside. He joined Millwall on a free transfer in August 2003 but midway through the campaign switched to Derby County. He was released after a couple of months and then went north of the border to play for Aberdeen, later returning to join Boston United. But in January 2006 he was admitted to the Sporting Chance clinic to have treatment for alcoholism, revealing in interviews he had been drinking heavily throughout much of his career. Afterwards he returned to Scotland with Livingston and later Dunfermline, but at the age of just 32 he found himself without a club.

WHELAN Philip James

Centre-half
Born: Reddish, 7 March 1972.
Career: Ipswich Town 1990. MIDDLESBROUGH 1995. Oxford United 1997. Rotherham United (loan) 1999. Southend United 2000.

■ Phil Whelan began his career with Ipswich Town, showing great composure at the heart of the Suffolk club's defence as they swept to the 1991–92 Second Division Championship and promotion to the Premiership. Even though he was occasionally played out of position the following season, he impressed enough to be called up by the England Under-21 side before being released to concentrate on preparing for his final accountancy exams. He suffered a horrendous ankle injury in the club's final game of the 1993–94 season and was expected to be out of action for a long time. However, Whelan made good progress and was back in the first team in November 1994, although four months later he was transferred to Middlesbrough for £300,000. Following a registration mix-up, he did not make his debut until the following season – as a substitute at Arsenal on the opening day of the 1995–96 season. However, a broken jaw suffered in an off-the-field incident and suspensions limited Whelan's first-team opportunities – although he did score his first goal for the club in a 1–1 draw with Spurs. Transferred to Oxford United, his first season at the Manor Ground was a nightmare as, after a back injury in the opening game following a clash with a teammate, he had the misfortune to suffer a bad leg break. On recovery he fell out with the manager and went on loan to Rotherham. Eventually transferred to Southend United, Whelan was appointed the Shrimpers captain – going on to play in 119 games – before a serious knee-ligament injury forced his retirement.

WHIGHAM William Murdoch Morrison

Goalkeeper
Born: Airdrie, 9 October 1939.
Career: Falkirk. MIDDLESBROUGH 1966. Dumbarton 1974. Darlington 1974.

■ Football's a game of highs and lows and Scotsman Willie Whigham had more than his fair share of both in a lengthy Boro career. A qualified motor mechanic, he made his name at Falkirk to such an extent that five coachloads of Falkirk fans travelled to see him make his Boro debut. Known as 'The Whig', he proved popular among players and fans alike by encouraging defenders on the pitch and putting in some brave and commanding performances himself. But 'keepers tread a fine line between success and failure and he was also capable of letting in some very soft goals.

Signed by Stan Anderson, he made his debut in a 2–0 defeat at Watford in October 1966 and, by and large, kept his place for the rest of the successful promotion campaign. In Division Two, he was a virtual ever present as Boro tried and always just failed to get out of Division Two. But that erratic style refused to go away, so one week he'd play a blinder and the next he'd concede a howler. Always considered a rebel at the club, he was suspended indefinitely without pay in December 1968 for assaulting coach Jimmy Greenhalgh in the dressing room after being sent off in

a practice game. Dropped for the game at Blackpool, apologies to Greenhalgh and the board did the trick and his ban was quickly lifted. He missed 14 games in 1969–70 after he slapped in a transfer request, but it was smartly withdrawn when he was offered better terms and he went on a run of 80 consecutive games. However, two early season blunders in 1971–72 were to prove very costly indeed. Tamely letting in a long-range free-kick at Bristol City was bad enough, but another soft error in an embarrassing 4–1 defeat by Sunderland proved the final straw. Jim Platt was handed his debut in the next game and Whigham had played his final game for Boro.

WHITAKER William

Centre-half
Born: Chesterfield, 7 October 1923.
Died: 1995.
Career: Chesterfield 1942. MIDDLESBROUGH 1947.

■ A casual remark that Boro was the sort of team he'd love to play for proved fateful indeed for ice-cool centre-half Whitaker. A wartime Bevin Boy, Bill Whitaker was still working as a miner when he joined hometown club Chesterfield, but he was out of the side through injury when the Spireites visited Ayresome Park for an FA Cup tie in 1947. The watching Whitaker remarked to a club steward how impressed he was with the set-up, the remark got back to Boro boss David Jack and Whitaker was soon a Boro player. Pale-faced and the possessor of a lolloping run, he had few peers at centre-half and was a regular first-teamer in the late 1940s and early 1950s alongside talented stars like Wilf Mannion, George Hardwick and Jimmy Gordon. Despite boasting a number of excellent individuals, Boro were never able to win a first major trophy, though they did threaten to take the title in 1950–51 when Whitaker – who had represented the Football League in April 1950 – partnered Harry Bell and Gordon in the centre of defence. In October 1949, he had asked for a transfer after losing his place to Tom Blenkinsopp but he won his place back soon afterwards, only to lose it again when he tore knee ligaments. Club captain in 1952–53, he was increasingly dogged by injury and never really recovered after having his cartilage removed in 1953, an injury which ultimately prompted his retirement and a return to the coal mines. He died in 1995.

WHITE Alan

Centre-half
Born: Darlington, 22 March 1976.
Career: MIDDLESBROUGH 1994. Luton Town 1997. Colchester 2001. Leyton Orient 2004. Boston United 2005. Notts County 2006. Peterborough (loan) 2006. Darlington 2007.

■ The much-maligned Anglo-Italian Cup gave White his sole Boro first-team appearance, turning out at centre-half in a 3–1 defeat in Ancona. Yet at one time, he was poised to turn his back on soccer altogether when, after a spell as a schoolboy at Derby, he opted to go to college and study. But when Boro moved in after seing him playing for Shildon, he gave football another go and he was soon putting in good displays for the club's junior sides. He got his chance in the reserves when Andy Todd went on loan to Swindon and he was a non-playing first-team sub at Coventry in December 1996. But the major breakthrough never came and just weeks after signing a new contract in summer 1997, Luton boss Lennie Lawrence – who remembered him from Boro's youth team – took him to Kenilworth Road. He signed for £60,000 after a successful trial and went on to be a regular with the Hatters.

WHITE William

Inside-right
Born: Broxburn.
Career: Dundee. MIDDLESBROUGH 1903.

■ His League figures don't show it, but Willie White scored one of the most important goals in Middlesbrough Football Club's history – the first ever goal at Ayresome Park. White's golden strike wasn't the best the ground would ever see – it was a penalty – but the goal, in a friendly against Celtic which Boro won 1–0, marked the start of a wonderful new era. He also played in the first League game at the new ground, a 3–2 defeat by Sunderland on 12 September 1903. However, the inside-forward lost his place to Bobby Atherton and returned to Scotland with Aberdeen at the end of the season, just a year after leaving Dundee.

WHYTE Derek

Central defender
Born: Glasgow, 31 August 1968.
Career: Glasgow Celtic 1985. MIDDLESBROUGH 1992. Aberdeen 1997. Partick Thistle 2001.

■ Popular defender Derek Whyte had played for Scotland at every level – Schools, Youth, Under-21, B and full – so it's not surprising his arrival at Ayresome Park was eagerly anticipated. Boro's record signing at the time, he came as part of a deal which also brought Chris Morris to Boro and saw Andy Payton head the other way. Whyte was valued at £900,000 and with his composure on the ball, he soon made himself at home in

Boro's 1992–93 Premier League side. His career had begun at Celtic, where he made his full debut aged just 17 and went on to win the title in 1986–87, two Scottish Cups and, while still a teenager, his first international call-up. Strong, quick and a good tackler, he took over the Boro captaincy in 1993–94 when Alan Kernaghan left but, on the downside, he scored an own goal and was sent off in a match against Millwall. Bryan Robson's arrival saw Whyte initially partner club captain Nigel Pearson at the heart of the defence but when Curtis Fleming was injured Whyte switched to left-back and settled in so well that he earned the supporters' club Player of the Year award for 1994–95. He also set up the final goal at Ayresome Park, feeding John Hendrie in a 2–1 victory over Luton Town that all but guaranteed promotion. Returning to centre-back in the Premier League, he lost his place when Robbo changed the team formation on Juninho's arrival. He returned the following year as part of the new five-man defence but was dropped again and missed out on both Cup Finals that season. But with his first-team chances becoming increasingly limited, Whyte returned to Scotland when Aberdeen moved in and quickly became a first-team fixture at Pittodrie, earning a recall to the full Scotland squad.

WILCOX Frederick Jeremiah

Inside-left/Centre-half
Born: Bristol, 7 July 1880.
Died: 1954.
Career: Glendale. Bristol Rovers. Small Heath 1902. MIDDLESBROUGH 1905. Plymouth Argyle.

■ Signed in the same month as England internationals Steve Bloomer and Billy Brawn, Wilcox formed part of a formidable forward line along with Alf Common and Jim Thackeray as manager Alex Mackie moved to safeguard Boro's Division One status. It worked, too, with Boro staying in the top flight and Wilcox becoming a near permanent fixture in the first team before heading for Plymouth in 1909. An inside-forward, Wilcox netted 12 goals in his first full season at Ayresome – the same number as £1,000 Common – and was again a regular scorer as the club finished sixth in 1907–08.

WILKIE Derrick

Centre-half
Born: Lanchester, 27 July 1939.
Career: MIDDLESBROUGH 1957. Hartlepool United 1961.

■ Standing 5ft 9in tall, Wilkie wasn't the biggest centre-half you'll ever see but he was an effective performer nevertheless. His debut came in a 1–0 win at Huddersfield in November 1959, when he stepped in for Brian Phillips. However, the arrival of Ken Thomson limited his chances and he played twice at right-back before switching to Hartlepool.

WILKIE John

Inside-left/Outside-left
Born: Govan.
Career: Partick Thistle. Blackburn Rovers 1895. Glasgow Rangers. MIDDLESBROUGH 1900. Glasgow Rangers. Partick Thistle. Hibernian.

■ By scoring five goals in one game, hotshot Scot Wilkie achieved a feat managed by just three other players in the club's history – legends Andy Wilson, Brian Clough and George Camsell. However, those five goals in a 9–2 Second Division drubbing of Gainsborough Trinity in March 1901 were somewhat deceptive as he bagged just three more goals in his 27 other League outings for Boro. The inside-forward had joined John Robson's side from Rangers for Boro's second season of League football. In 1901, he returned to Glasgow Rangers.

WILKINSON Paul

Forward
Born: Louth, 30 October 1964.
Career: Grimsby Town 1982. Everton 1985. Nottingham Forest 1987. Watford 1988. MIDDLESBROUGH 1991. Oldham Athletic (loan) 1995. Watford (loan) 1995. Luton Town (loan) 1996. Barnsley 1996. Millwall 1997. Northampton Town 1998.

■ Rarely can such a bad goal have been so important. But when Paul Wilkinson managed to comically mis-head the ball

into the net at Wolves on the final day of the 1991–92 season, Boro were promoted to Division One and 'Wilko' had further heightened his popularity rating with the Boro faithful. An old-fashioned target man, he had already forged an impressive career in League football before he arrived at Ayresome Park. Originally a promising cricketer, he was offered terms by Nottinghamshire CC but opted instead to join Grimsby Town where he started out as a midfielder before moving into the forward line when a teammate was injured. He scored just five minutes into his debut against Charlton and never looked back, earning four Under-21 caps while at Blundell Park and scoring a memorable winner in an FA Cup tie at Everton. Soon he was on his way to Goodison Park to become an Everton player and made himself an instant hero by scoring in a 1–0 win over Liverpool. He won a League Championship medal with Everton before moving to Nottingham Forest and then Watford, where he was top scorer for three seasons before becoming one of Boro boss Lennie Lawrence's first major signings. Watford wanted £800,000 but, after a tribunal, £500,000 was agreed at the eleventh hour, with Willie Falconer joining Wilko on the trip north and Trevor Putney heading the other way.

A big hit from the start, Wilkinson thrived on the crosses of John Hendrie and Stuart Ripley, while still managing to set up numerous chances for others. However, relentless mickey-taking from his teammates meant his long hair had to go! The only ever present in 1991–92, he also ended Bernie Slaven's long run as top scorer by bagging 24 goals in League and Cup – including 'that' Wolves effort described by an unimpressed goalscorer as 'the worst header of my career'. In August 1992, he notched Boro's first ever Premier League goal in a 2–1 defeat at Coventry and his impressive early form saw Lennie Lawrence tip him for England. But the goals began to dry up as, with midfield support badly lacking, he was often asked to plough a lone furrow up front.

With Boro relegated, Everton tried to re-sign Wilko for £1.1 million but he was offered, and accepted, an improved contract to stay at Boro. However, Bryan Robson's arrival coincided with a slump in Wilko's form, with a hat-trick in the League Cup against Scarborough one of the season's few highlights. And when German marksman Uwe Fuchs and Norwegian Jan-Aage Fjortoft arrived to push Boro towards the Premiership, the writing was on the wall for Wilko. Told he could leave at the end of the season, he had loan spells at three clubs in 1995–96 before getting a surprise recall in mid-season during an injury crisis. When he eventually left to join Barnsley, the sun went down on a Boro career in which he'd averaged nearly a goal every three games and established himself as a distinctive and popular figure. He later worked with his old boss Lennie Lawrence as assistant manager at Grimsby.

WILKSHIRE Luke

Midfield
Born: Wollongong, Australia, 2 October 1981.
Career: AIS Australia. MIDDLESBROUGH 1999. Bristol City 2003. Twente (Holland) 2006.

■ Wilkshire's Boro career could have been so different if he had converted one of several excellent chances that came his way during the 2001 FA Cup semi-final against Arsenal at Villa Park. Instead they got away and so did the biggest opportunity of the midfielder's career on Teesside. Wilkshire, then aged just 19, was handed his chance as injuries bit into

Steve McClaren's squad. The game finished in a 1–0 defeat for Boro, who dominated much of the game but were undone by Gianluca Festa's own goal. He originally came to Teesside on the same 'Big Brother' scheme that brought Harry Kewell to Leeds United.

He made his first-team debut against Southampton on 6 March 2002. But it was his home debut against Liverpool 10 days later that really caught the eye.

A week after that Luke was back on the bench as Boro visited Old Trafford to take on then Premiership favourites Manchester United. Just 21 minutes had gone when he was called into action to replace the injured Jonathan Greening and he went on to play his part as Boro pulled off a heroic 1–0 win.

While on the club's books he appeared for his country at Under–23 level but was allowed to join Bristol City for £250,000. He finally found his shooting boots at Ashton Gate, scoring 10 goals in 2004–05, many of them from long distance. He went on to make senior appearances for Australia, notably as a surprise starter in the 2006 World Cup games against Japan and Brazil after receiving warm praise from boss Guus Hiddink. His performances earned him a three-year contract with Dutch top flight side Twente Enschede, where he became a first-team regular.

WILLEY Alan Steven

Forward
Born: Houghton-le-Spring, 18 October 1956.
Career: MIDDLESBROUGH 1974. Minnesota Kicks (United States).

■ Trying to oust John Hickton as centre-forward was an unenviable task, but somebody had to do it – and Alan Willey was that somebody in the mid-1970s. He broke into the team as a youngster after prolific displays in the youth team and made his debut in a 3–0 win over Manchester City in September 1974. He then made the starting line-up at the dawn of the 1975–76 season, playing alongside Hickton for several games, but he drifted out of favour as the season progressed. In September 1976, he headed stateside with Frank Spraggon and Peter Brine to play for Minnesota Kicks and, of the three, it was Willey who settled in best to become a popular figure in the North American Soccer League. His Boro contract was cancelled in February 1978 when he joined Minnesota permanently.

WILLIAMS Jesse Thomas

Winger
Born: Cefn-y-Bedd, 24 June 1903.
Died: 1972.
Career: Oak Alyn Rovers. Wrexham 1923.

MIDDLESBROUGH 1924. Clapton Orient 1927. Rhyl Athletic. Ashton National. Shrewsbury Town. Wellington Town.

■ Outside-left Williams won his one Welsh cap while with Boro, taking his place in a match against Northern Ireland. But while the 1924–25 season saw him regularly in the first XI, ironically his best form was probably for the reserves in 1926–27, when he fired in 20 goals but managed only four first-team starts as promotion was secured. He spent another season out of the limelight before leaving for Clapton Orient. After a spell refereeing in the Welsh League, he emigrated to Canada and lived in Toronto, although he did return for a nostalgic visit to Ayresome Park in 1965.

WILLIAMS Joseph Joshua

Winger
Born: Rotherham, 4 June 1902.
Career: Rotherham Town. Rotherham County 1921. Huddersfield Town 1924. Stoke City 1925. Arsenal 1929. MIDDLESBROUGH 1931. Carlisle United 1935.

■ Nicknamed 'Yo-Yo', Williams was a bit part player at Arsenal but did at least set up a goal for future Boro boss David Jack which took the Gunners to the 1930 FA Cup Final. However, regular winger Joe Hulme recovered from injury to take Williams' place at Wembley. His Boro debut came in a 1–0 home defeat by Sunderland in March 1932, although things did pick up and he was a regular winger for four fruitful seasons as the club fought relegation. He was placed on the transfer list at the end of the 1934–35 campaign. Priced at £750, the fee was reduced by the Football League to £300 and Carlisle paid in £75 instalments.

WILLIAMS Owen

Outside-left
Born: Ryehope, 23 September 1896.
Died: 1960.
Career: Ryehope Colliery. Sunderland 1913. Manchester United 1914. Easington Colliery. Clapton Orient 1919. MIDDLESBROUGH 1923. Southend United 1930. Shildon.

■ A fast, direct winger who caused havoc among opposition defences, speedy and persistent Williams supplied the ammunition for George Camsell among others. Born in County Durham, the England Schools international played for Ryhope Colliery, was once on Sunderland's books and had trials at Manchester United but ended up signing for Easington Colliery Welfare. Spotted by a scout at the end of World War One, he was taken to London where his speed and excellent ball control brought him to the attention of England's selectors and he played against Ireland in October 1922 to become Orient's first international.

He joined Boro late in the 1923–24 season and experienced immediate relegation but bounced back to be top scorer the following season, albeit with just seven goals. Knocked out of the FA Cup in 1926 by his old club Orient, things picked up for the short and stocky outside-left and he won two Division Two championship medals in 1927 and 1929 as part of a famous forward line boasting such names as Birrell, Pease, Camsell and Jacky Carr. The 1926–27 side in particular won the title by a mile and Williams' ability to get behind defences and supply the killer cross proved crucial. Placed on the transfer list in summer 1930 at £400, he joined Southend for a cut-price £250 but played only one more season before retiring to live back in Easington.

WILLIAMSON Reginald Garnet (Tim)

Goalkeeper
Born: North Ormesby, 6 June 1884.
Died: Redcar, August 1943.
Career: Redcar Crusaders. MIDDLESBROUGH 1901.

■ Goalkeeper Tim Williamson holds a record that will surely never be beaten. Middlesbrough FC's all-time record appearance maker, he played over 600 League and Cup games for the club, of which a staggering 130 were consecutive.

Ironically, he played centre-forward for Coatham Grammar School as a boy but had taken over between the sticks when he played for Boro, aged 17, in a friendly against Cliftonville. Boro wanted him to sign professional terms, but Williamson was reluctant and only put pen to paper on the understanding he could follow his business interests as a qualified draughtsman in Middlesbrough. Known as Tiny – he was barely 5ft 10in tall – he rarely talked of football, but soon football supporters were talking of him. Goalkeeper in the first League game at Ayresome Park and last at Linthorpe Road, he was initially understudy to Scottish international Rab MacFarlane but made the goalie's jersey his own in 1903–04.

Clever at anticipating shots and decisive at clearing, he would often stand for long periods during the game with both hands on his hips. He also never dropped on one knee to pick up the ball, preferring instead to gather it with both feet together and scoop it up in a clutching embrace. And, in moments to give his managers heart failure, he would

often deftly sidestep his opponent, lob the ball over him and run round the player to catch the ball! He even scored two goals from the penalty spot but, after missing one against West Ham, he never took another, feeling the race back to guard his goal was too risky...and tiring. Work commitments with the Teesside Bridge and Engineering Company meant he missed Boro's first ever European 'tour' to Denmark in May 1907 but by 1910 he was becoming a legend on Teesside, with his name chalked between imaginary goalposts across the area.

He was exempted from service in World War One because he had a reserved occupation but the Football League then refused to grant him a benefit in 1921, ruling those years did not contribute to League service. Despite the League's benefit snub, he did have a benefit game in 1913 against Chelsea which raised £300. He was also paid £1,000 at the end of his career and received a silver tea and coffee service from Boro chairman Phil Bach at a board meeting on 23 May 1923.

Internationally, Williamson had become England's youngest and Boro's first capped 'keeper when he played against Ireland in February 1905 but, during a quiet game, he dropped the ball into own net, was credited with an own goal and ended up waiting six years for his next cap. The sparkling form of Liverpool's Sam Hardy didn't help either. Back at Boro, the Williamson era ended with a 1–0 home defeat by Cardiff City on 24 March 1923 – an unremarkable game but memorable because Williamson, at 38 years nine months, was the oldest to represent the club until Bryan Robson finally broke the record 74 years later.

On retirement in 1923, Williamson continued in goal for his works football team and rarely went to Ayresome, preferring golf and shooting to watching football. 'Tiny' died in Redcar in August 1943 following an operation at North Ormesby Hospital and is buried in Coatham churchyard.

WILSON Andrew Nesbit

Inside-forward/Centre-forward
Born: Newmains, 14 February 1896.
Died: 15 October 1973.
Career: Cambuslang Rangers. MIDDLESBROUGH 1914. Heart of Midlothian. Dunfermline Athletic. MIDDLESBROUGH 1921. Chelsea 1923. Queen's Park Rangers 1931. Nimes.

■ Not many players attract a crowd to greet them off the train, but such was the case with star striker Andy Wilson – the man with the black glove. He was originally signed by Boro chairman Phil Bach in the waiting room at Sunderland station after playing in a friendly for Cambuslang Rangers v Sunderland Reserves, one season before war broke out.

During wartime service with the 6th Highland Infantry – commonly known as the Footballers' Regiment – he lost his Lance-Corporal's stripe in what was described as a disagreement with another soldier. He also lost the use of his left hand when a German shell exploded at Arras in 1918 and, invalided out of the war, he spent eight months in hospital. Yet when he went back to football, he never let his disability affect him and he played with a black glove covering his injured hand. The outbreak of war meant all footballers reverted to amateur status, which allowed Wilson to turn out for Hearts in Scottish League and score 42 goals in 28 games. He also played in two Victory internationals against England and Ireland but, all the while, Boro retained his registration. He was keen to stay north of the border and several Scottish clubs made approaches but Boro turned them down, insisting he return to Ayresome Park for the 1919–20 season. However, Wilson started playing for breakaway club Dunfermline Athletic in the rebel Scottish Central League, scoring 104 goals in two seasons. When Dunfermline joined the Scottish League, so making Andy ineligible to play, he joined a Scottish party on a goodwill tour of Canada and the USA and scored 62 goals, the Americans dubbing him the 'Babe Ruth of Soccer'.

He finally returned to Teesside in August 1921 and a big crowd turned out at the railway station to greet him. A huge cheer went up when Wilson alighted from the train with his golf clubs slung over his arm. He then went back to business as Boro's top scorer in 1921–22 and 1923–24, including a five-goal blast against Nottingham Forest in October 1923. He had the centre-forward's mean streak, too, and was twice sent off including, rarely and uniquely for Boro, a Division One dismissal.

Sold for a large fee to Chelsea, he switched to inside-forward but his new club was relegated along with Middlesbrough. Remarkably, he was leading scorer for both clubs in the same season. In the early 1930s, he had a spell in France with Racing Club de Paris and Nimes before becoming a manager at Clacton Town and Walsall. A fine all-round sportsman, he played golf, bowls and billiards and represented England at bowls in 1948. He died on 15 October 1973.

WILSON Archibald

Outside-right
Born: Cambuslang, 1890.
Died: 1916.
Career: Tottenham Hotspur 1909. Southend United. MIDDLESBROUGH 1914.

■ Known as Baldy, Wilson's Boro career was tragically cut short when he was killed in action during World War One. An Ayrshire Scot, he achieved junior representative honours in Scotland before spending two years at Nottingham Forest. Spells at Spurs and Southend followed before a move to Middlesbrough, which started promisingly but was to end prematurely. A wing-forward, the highlight of his short time on Teesside was probably a two-goal haul in a 5–1 mauling of Everton at Ayresome Park in January 1915, when his namesake Andy Wilson also scored two.

WILSON Frederick Peter

Full-back
Born: Newcastle, 15 September 1947.
Career: MIDDLESBROUGH 1966.

■ A career 'Down Under' meant Wilson would again cross swords with Boro, nine years after his only appearance for the club. That came in February 1968 when, as right-back, Wilson played in a 1–1 home draw with Charlton Athletic. Released at the end of the season, he emigrated to Australia and became an Australian international, playing in a qualifying tournament for the 1970 World Cup. Transformed to a shaggy-haired centre-half, Wilson's form with South Coast United saw him voted the Australian *Sunday Telegraph's* Soccer Player of the Year in 1969–70. Then, while doing the business for Safeway United, he captained Australia in the 1974 World Cup Finals, losing to East and West Germany and drawing with Chile. And then there was that reunion with Boro when, as part of the Teessiders' World tour, Wilson played in midfield and captained an Australian XI against his old side. The match, a World Cup warm-up game for the hosts, ended in a 5–0 win for Boro.

WILSON John

Right-back
Born: Chilton, 29 October 1904.
Career: Chilton Colliery Welfare. MIDDLESBROUGH 1924. Southend United 1927.

■ Right-back Wilson was one of those players who found it hard to please the fans. When on form, he was capable of some sterling displays, but all too often he was criticised. He eventually lost his place and, probably to the benefit of all concerned, he left for Southend after playing four games in the record-breaking promotion year of 1927.

WILSON Mark Antony

Midfield
Born: Scunthorpe, 9 February 1979.
Career: Manchester United 1996. Wrexham (loan) 1998. MIDDLESBROUGH 2001. Stoke City (loan) 2003. Swansea City (loan) 2003. Sheffield Wednesday (loan) 2004. Doncaster Rovers (loan) 2004. Livingston (loan) 2005. Dallas Burn (US) 2005. Doncaster Rovers 2006.

■ Wilson moved to Boro in a £1.5 million deal at the same time as his Manchester United and England Under-21 teammate Jonathan Greening in August 2001. The transfer was trailed in the press almost from the minute Steve McClaren moved from his coaching job at Old Trafford to the Riverside hotseat. When it was eventually completed, Boro fans hoped McClaren was bringing with him two stars of the future, having seen them develop from close quarters. In fact, while Greening became a first-team regular, a combination of injuries and poor form meant Wilson never really proved himself as a Premiership player and he played just a handful of first-team games in four years at the club. Wilson had made sporadic appearances for United but found his route to the first

team blocked by established stars like Roy Keane and David Beckham. Injuries restricted him to just two starts in his first season with Boro and though he appeared more frequently in 2002–03, he was allowed to go on loan to Stoke City. The following season he had loan spells with Swansea and Sheffield Wednesday, but during his spell at Hillsborough he suffered cruciate-ligament damage and returned to the Riverside. The 2004–05 campaign saw a fully-recovered Wilson on loan at Doncaster Rovers and then Scottish League Livingston, before returning to Boro. There were some highs for Wilson – he played his part in defeating his old Manchester United teammates in Boro's 3–1 win at the Riverside in the 2002–03 season as he deputised for the injured George Boateng. But it was no surprise when he was allowed to join US outfit Dallas Burn on a free transfer in September 2005. He was released less than a year later and, after an unsuccessful trial at Bradford, Wilson signed an 18-month contract with Coca-Cola League One Doncaster in January 2007.

WILSON Thomas T.

Centre-half/Left-half
Born: Newcastle.
Career: Morpeth Harriers. MIDDLESBROUGH 1907. Heart of Midlothian.

■ An effective defender, Wilson made his debut at the back end of the 1907–08 season and started well in a 4–1 home victory over Bury. But in the next two seasons, first-team opportunities were hard to come by for the half-back and he moved on to Hearts.

WINDASS Dean

Forward
Born: Hull, 1 April 1969.
Career: North Ferriby. Hull City 1991. Aberdeen 1995. Oxford United 1998. Bradford City 1999. MIDDLESBROUGH 2001. Sheffield Wednesday (loan) 2001. Sheffield United (loan) 2002. Sheffield United 2003. Bradford City 2003. Hull City (loan) 2007. Hull City 2007.

■ One of the more colourful stars to have played for Boro in recent years, Windass was Terry Venables's sole

signing during his short tenure as head coach alongside Bryan Robson. Popular with the supporters for his all-action style and willingness to chase lost causes, he was, however, unable to make the impact in the Premiership that he did before and afterwards as a prolific goalscorer outside the top flight. Distinctive due to a stocky build that made him look more like a rugby League player, Windass made his name as a striker with his hometown club, Hull City, before temporarily switching to a midfield role later in his career.

His goals for the Tigers brought the attention of scouts and he moved to Scottish Premier League side Aberdeen for £700,000 in December 1995. There he had the distinction of being shown three cards in one game, the final one for taking his frustration out on a corner flag after being sent off. He moved to Oxford United for a club record £400,000 in 1998, joining Bradford City for £1 million less than a year later. It came as something of a surprise when Venables swooped to sign the then 32-year-old, whose best years appeared to be behind him. But he scored on his debut in a 2–1 defeat at Chelsea and was a useful squad player, without ever being a permanent fixture in the side. The goals were few and far between, although he did come off the bench to head home Benito Carbone's corner to earn Boro a 2–2 draw at home to Leeds United in February 2002. Windass went on loan to first Sheffield Wednesday and then their city rivals United, before signing permanently for the Blades. But his spell at Bramall Lane was short and he moved back to Bradford City in July 2003, aged 34. His career looked to be on the wane, but then came a remarkable renaissance as he spectacularly rediscovered his goalscoring touch.

Putting off a double-hernia operation, he scored a number of vital goals for the club from his central-midfield position but then in 2004–05, after being moved back up front, he had his most prolific season, scoring 27 League goals, including a hat-trick against Bournemouth on the final day of the season. Finishing the campaign as League One's joint leading scorer with Hull's Stuart Elliott, Windass netted over 20 goals again the following season. At the age of 37, Premiership side Wigan Athletic tried several times to sign him. In January 2007 his career completed a full circle as he rejoined Championship strugglers Hull on loan, scoring eight vital goals in 18 games to help save the Tigers from relegation, while Bradford dropped from Coca-Cola League One to League Two. The deal became permanent in summer 2007.

WINDRIDGE James Edwin

Inside-left
Born: Sparkbrook, 21 October 1882.
Died: 1939.
Career: Small Heath Alma. Small Heath 1902. Chelsea 1905. MIDDLESBROUGH 1911. Birmingham 1913.

■ A true all-rounder, inside-left Windridge was also a Warwickshire county cricketer. Known as 'Windridge the Wizard' at Chelsea, he played in the London club's first ever League game and scored a hat-trick in their first home game against Hull. At Boro, he scored the winner in his second game, a 1–0 home triumph against Bradford City, but goals subsequently proved hard to come by and boss Tom McIntosh let him leave for Birmingham City.

WINDROSS Dennis

Wing-half
Born: Guisborough, 12 May 1938.
Died: 1989.
Career: MIDDLESBROUGH 1956. Brighton & Hove Albion 1960. Darlington 1961. Doncaster Rovers 1962.

■ A Bob Dennison signing, Windross was unfortunate to be reserve to the great Brian Clough. He was 21 by the time he got his first-team chance, standing in for Cloughie at centre-forward in a 1–0 Second Division defeat at Villa Park in October 1959. He managed three consecutive games at inside-right in 1960–61, scoring his only goal in a 5–0 win over Southampton at Ayresome Park, but he accepted an offer from Brighton and set off for the south coast. Before long, though, he was heading back north to join Darlington. He was working at Saltburn Leisure Centre at the time of his death in 1989. He also worked at ICI.

WINNIE David

Left-back
Born: Glasgow, 26 October 1966.
Career: St Mirren. Aberdeen. MIDDLESBROUGH (loan) 1994.

■ Full-back Winnie was no stranger to Ayresome Park, having scored for Scotland in a Schoolboy international played on Teesside. He made his St Mirren debut aged 16 and tasted

European football straight away before moving to Aberdeen in a £265,000 move. With Boro's 1993–94 promotion effort running out of steam, Lennie Lawrence brought Winnie to Teesside with a view to a permanent signing. But after a disastrous single game – a 4–0 defeat at Tranmere – Winnie was allowed to return to Pittodrie and Boro's season petered out.

WOOD Alfred Edward Howson

Central defender/Forward
Born: Macclesfield, 25 October 1945.
Career: Manchester City 1963. Shrewsbury Town 1966. Millwall 1972. Hull City 1974. MIDDLESBROUGH 1976. Walsall 1977. Stafford Rangers.

■ With John Hickton approaching the end of his career, Jack Charlton knew that finding a replacement goalscorer was a priority. Malcolm Smith, Billy Woof, Phil Boersma, Alan Willey and Peter Brine were all tried without lasting success. Charlton then turned to much-travelled Alf Wood, a footballing journeyman who started off as a centre-half at first club Shrewsbury but went on to become a feared striker in the lower Leagues.

A Manchester City apprentice and England youth international, he became Millwall's record signing at £45,000 when he joined from Shrewsbury, where he'd been the country's joint top scorer with 32. His career floundered at Hull amid contractual problems and Jack Charlton stepped in, offering him terms until the end of the 1976–77 season with a review to follow.

But it soon became apparent that while Wood was a tryer, the step-up to Division One might prove beyond him. The goals didn't come and, in an FA Cup quarter-final at Liverpool, he had a header scooped away by Clemence when it looked to be over line. A goal then would have put Boro 1–0 up and left them eyeing the semi-final but instead, Liverpool capitalised on their good fortune and won 2–0. After scoring just two goals in 22 apearances, the two-year contract he'd been offered by Charlton was withdrawn when John Neal arrived and Wood was soon on his way to Walsall. He later played at Wembley for Stafford Rangers in an FA Trophy Final and ran his own promotions business in the West Midlands.

WOOD Darren Terence

Right-back/Midfield
Born: Scarborough, 9 June 1964.
Career: MIDDLESBROUGH 1981. Chelsea 1984. Sheffield Wednesday 1989.

■ In the dark days of the early 1980s, Darren Wood was one of Boro's few shining stars. Centre-half and captain of England Schoolboys – as his father Terry had been – Wood was wanted by Ipswich, WBA and Brighton among others before he opted for Boro, making his reserves debut at the tender age of 15. Handed a tough first-team debut as a 17-year-old in a relegation-threatened team, his display against Southampton – who included Kevin Keegan – impressed Boro boss Bobby Murdoch greatly and Wood was tipped for a very bright future.

Quick to tackle and with decent pace, he performed well in a poor team and was even tipped as a future England captain, with his composure on the ball and all-round defending skills attracting attention across the country. He was linked with Sheffield Wednesday and Liverpool, with the Anfield club having a £250,000 bid turned down in 1982. Yet two years later, the board accepted a much smaller bid from John Neal's Chelsea as financial crisis loomed and Wood – National Young Player of the Month in January 1984 – was on his way to Stamford Bridge for £40,000 plus Tony McAndrew. His career was cut short by injury while at Sheffield Wednesday and he retired from the game aged just 25.

WOODGATE Jonathan

Central defender
Born: Middlesbrough, 22 January 1980.
Career: Leeds United 1998. Newcastle United 2003. Real Madrid (Spain) 2004. MIDDLESBROUGH (loan) 2006. MIDDLESBROUGH 2007.

■ One of the finest central defenders of his generation, Woodgate was the one that got away who eventually found his way home – via Real Madrid! Born in Middlesbrough, he signed for Leeds United as a junior, having been spotted at the age of 13 by a scout while playing for local side Marton Juniors. After progressing through the Academy he helped Leeds win the FA Youth Cup in 1997 and in November the following year made his full senior debut. Woodgate was capped five times for England during his time at Elland Road, making his debut for the national side in the 1–1 Euro 2000 qualifier with Bulgaria under Kevin Keegan. His 123 appearances for Leeds included memorable UEFA Cup and Champions League runs, as well as Premiership title challenges in the club's brief heyday before financial troubles ended the Yorkshire club's big time dream. A £9 million move north to Newcastle United followed in January 2003. He impressed quickly and became an instant fans' favourite, although he was troubled by injuries while at St James' Park. But in

August 2004 he swapped the black and white of Newcastle for the all white of Real Madrid in a £13.4 million deal. He didn't play for Real during his first year in Spain, eventually making his debut 13 months later in a League match against Athletic Bilbao. But his relief at starting a La Liga match quickly turned into a nightmare as he scored an own goal and was then sent off for a second bookable defence. From February 2006 Woodgate established himself as a regular first teamer but further injury setbacks prevented him from being named in England's 2006 World Cup squad after he was tipped to be a surprise choice. Woodgate joined Boro on a year's loan on transfer deadline day before the start of the 2006–07 season. The deal included an option for a permanent deal, which was activated in April 2007 after a hugely-successful loan spell. Putting his injury troubles behind him, Woodgate became a regular starter for Boro, his classy displays earning him the 888.com Player of the Year award as well as an England recall. He signed a four-year contract making him a Boro player from 1 July 2007 in a deal worth £7 million.

WOODWARD Thomas

Outside-right
Born: Horwich, 8 December 1917.
Died: 1994.
Career: White Horse Temperance. Bolton Wanderers 1935. MIDDLESBROUGH 1949. Wigan Athletic.

■ Tom Woodward's time at Boro is perhaps best remembered for him winning the PGA Golf Championship at Liverpool in October 1950. He arrived on Teesside after years of sterling service at Bolton Wanderers, as well as guesting for Manchester United during World War Two. Aged 31 when signed by David Jack, doubts were expressed about the size of the fee, with many feeling his best days were probably behind him. He made his debut at outside-left in a 1–1 draw with Arsenal at Ayresome and went on to start the next eight games, more than playing his part in a revival of the team's fortunes by bagging seven goals. Injury disrupted his progress the following season and he was placed on the transfer list for £3,000 in March 1951, training back at Bolton before joining non-League Wigan in September. He died in 1994.

WOOF William

Forward
Born: Gateshead, 16 August 1956.
Career: MIDDLESBROUGH 1974. Peterborough United (loan) 1977. Blyth Spartans. Cardiff City 1982. Gateshead. Hull City 1983.

■ Patience is a virtue Billy Woof had to show bags of during his eight years at Ayresome Park, for he rarely got more than the occasional taste of first-team action. Signed from Redheugh Boys Club, he made his debut aged 18 as substitute for the injured Bobby Murdoch, playing for almost an hour of a 3–1 home defeat by Queen's Park Rangers in November 1974. He didn't figure again until 15 months later when he was rewarded for his patience with a string of outings as substitute. His first start came as Boro's number nine in a 2–0 home win over Ipswich and his first goal came nine days later in a 3–1 reverse at Everton.

But while he made only one more substitute appearance under Jack Charlton, new boss John Neal made him first choice at the start of the 1977–78 campaign. After failing to score in the first three games, Neal signed Billy Ashcroft and Woof's only call-ups came in the League Cup when Ashcroft was Cup-tied. Woof got yet another chance at the start of 1978–79 and scored after just four minutes of the new season at Coventry, but he was soon out in the cold again and made only fleeting appearances until Bobby Murdoch suprisingly made him first choice in 1981–82. He managed only three goals as Boro were relegated and was released at the end of the season.

Following a spell at Blyth Spartans, he went on a non-contract basis to Cardiff City but walked out after being dropped for a League Cup game. He wound up his playing days at Gateshead and Hull.

WORRALL William Edward

Goalkeeper
Born: Shildon, 1886.
Career: South Bank.
MIDDLESBROUGH 1905. Shildon.
Sunderland 1910. Wingate Albion.

■ Goalkeeper Worrall probably thought things could only get better after making his debut in a 6–1 hammering at Liverpool in March 1906. Sadly Worrall, who was signed as an amateur from South Bank while Tim Williamson was out injured, didn't make another appearance for Boro and left for Sunderland.

WORTHINGTON Peter Robert

Left-back
Born: Halifax, 22 April 1947.
Career: Halifax Town 1965.
MIDDLESBROUGH 1966. Notts County 1968. Southend United 1974. Hartlepool United (loan) 1975.

■ Left-back Worthington's biggest claim to fame was probably his brother, footballing playboy Frank. Signed from Halifax, Peter made his Boro debut in the same game as Mike Kear as stand-in for Gordon Jones but it was a nightmare start as Birmingham achieved a 6–1 rout. First team chances were like gold-dust and he moved with Don Masson to Notts County, where he became a popular figure.

WRIGHT Alan Geoffrey

Left-back
Born: Ashton-under-Lyne, 28 September 1971.
Career: Blackpool 1989. Blackburn Rovers 1991. Aston Villa 1995.
MIDDLESBROUGH 2003. Sheffield United 2003. Derby County (loan) 2006. Leeds United (loan) 2006. Cardiff City (loan) 2006. Doncaster Rovers 2007. Nottingham Forest 2007.

■ An England Schoolboy and Youth international, Alan Wright started out with Blackpool, becoming the youngest player to turn out for the Seasiders when he made his Football League debut as a substitute against Chesterfield in May 1988 at the age of 16 years 217 days. Wright made his first-team breakthrough the following season, appearing in a variety of positions. After playing in 121 games he became Kenny Dalglish's first signing for Blackburn Rovers. He assisted the club through the Play-offs to the Premiership and the England Under–21 international enhanced his chances of picking up a full cap when injury struck. In March 1995 Wright joined Aston Villa in a £1 million deal and at the end of his first season won his first medal as Villa beat Leeds United to lift the League Cup. He was also selected by his fellow professionals to the PFA award-winning Premiership side. One of the smallest defenders in the Premiership, he was ever present in three of his first four seasons at Villa Park, going on to play in 330 games. In the summer of 2003, Steve McClaren brought Wright to the Riverside as full-back cover. Sadly, his chances of first-team football were restricted to just two games. He made his debut against Fulham on the opening day of the 2003–04 season, while his final game was the 4–0 home defeat by Arsenal later in the campaign. After a loan spell with Sheffield United the move was made permanent, but he suffered a cruciate-ligament injury and was sidelined for months prior to making a comeback on loan with Derby County.

WRIGHT Thomas Elliot

Left-winger
Born: Dunfermline, 10 January 1966.
Career: Leeds United 1983. Oldham Athletic 1986. Leicester City 1989.
MIDDLESBROUGH 1992. Bradford City 1995. Oldham Athletic 1997. St Johnstone.

■ 'It's now or never' proclaimed Lennie Lawrence for flying winger Wright, a talented player who tended to promise more than he achieved. A Scotland Youth international, he scored on his Leeds debut aged 17 but lost his place through injury and moved to Oldham for £80,000. Initially a striker, he was converted to a winger at Oldham and his form earned him an Under-21 cap. From Boundary Park, he moved to Leicester City for £350,000 and did a decent job before leaping at the chance of Division One football with Boro.

Signed as a replacement for Stuart Ripley, injuries and loss of form meant he didn't do himself justice, although he got off to a good start. His performance in the 4–1 home thumping of old club Leeds United – the reigning champions

was particlarly sweet for Wright, but his obvious talent remained frustratingly unfulfilled and he became increasingly anonymous as Boro sank towards relegation. He missed the first half of the following season through injury and, on finding himself out in the cold when Bryan Robson arrived, he opted to rejoin Lennie Lawrence at Bradford City. Small, slightly built but fast and tricky, Wright provided good service for frontmen on his day but, sadly, those days were few and far between at Boro.

WYNN Richard

Outside-left
Born: Details unknown.
Career: Chester. MIDDLESBROUGH 1913.

■ Winger Wynn made a scoring debut, netting the sixth in a 6–0 home trouncing of Spurs in April 1914. But the form of John Cook in the number-11 shirt kept Wynn's opportunities to a minimum and he was released on the outbreak of war in 1915.

XAVIER Abel Luis da Silva Costa

Central defender
Born: Nampula, Mozambique, 20 November 1972.
Career: Estrela Amadora (Portugal) 1990. Benfica (Portugal) 1993. Bari (Italy) 1995. Oviedo (Spain) 1996. PSV Eindhoven (Holland) 1998. Everton 1999. Liverpool 2002. Galatasaray (Turkey)

(loan) 2003. Hannover (Germany) 2004. Roma (Italy) 2004. MIDDLESBROUGH 2005. LA Galaxy (US) 2007.

■ The phrase 'larger than life' is sometimes overused but in Abel Xavier's case it is an apt description in every sense. An impressive physique and striking looks are enhanced by his ever-changing but always outrageous hairstyle and facial hair, while off the field his dress sense is equally eye-catching. Xavier's Boro career was interrupted by a ban for alleged drug use, although the player always denied any wrongdoing. A hugely experienced and much-travelled Portugal international defender, Mozambique-born Xavier played more than 20 times for Portugal and was involved in controversy in the Euro 2000 semi-final against France when he was adjudged to have handled a shot in the dying seconds of Golden Goal overtime. Despite fierce protests from Xavier and his teammates, Zinedine Zidane converted the resultant spot-kick to put his side in the final. Xavier started his career with Estrel Amadora in Portugal before he moved on to Benfica, Bari, Real Oviedo and PSV. He signed for Everton in 1999, spending two seasons at Goodison before becoming one of the select band of players who have crossed Stanley Park as he joined Liverpool. After a brief loan spell in Turkey with Galatasaray he joined Hanover and then took in a spell with Roma. He joined Boro on a one-year deal on transfer deadline day, 31 August 2005. Better known as a central defender, he also operated for Boro as a right-back, slotting in to replace Dutch defender Michael Reiziger, who left the club on the day Xavier arrived. He made a very impressive debut for Boro in a 2–1 win over Arsenal at the Riverside and then started each of the club's next five games before the premature end to his first spell with the club. His drugs ban, which was shortened on appeal from 18 months to 12, followed a positive test after Boro's UEFA Cup tie against Skoda Xanthi in Greece. As it drew to an end he returned to train with Boro and was offered a contract to the end of the 2006–07 season. He played an important part in the remainder of the campaign, celebrating wildly after his goal in the 5–1 win over Bolton in January. However, he left the club at the end of the season, finding a new challenge alongside David Beckham at US Major League side LA Galaxy.

YAKUBU Ayegbeni

Forward

Born: Benin City, Nigeria, 22 November 1982.

Career: Okomo Oil. Julius Berger (Nigeria) 1998. Hapoel Kfar-Saba (Israel) 2000. Maccabi Haifa (Israel) 2001. Portsmouth 2003. MIDDLESBROUGH 2005.

■ One of the most prolific Premiership goalscorers of recent years, powerfully-built Yakubu was linked with Boro several times before finally making the move from Portsmouth for £7.5 million in summer 2005. The Nigerian international experienced Champions League action for Maccabi Haifa of Israel during the early part of the 2002–03 season, netting a hat-trick against Olympiakos. In January 2003 he joined Pompey on loan and was a great success, netting seven goals from just 12 starts as he helped the club to promotion. In his two-and-a-half years at Pompey, Yakubu blasted 29 Premiership goals in 68 games – only Arsenal's Thierry Henry hit the back of the net more over the same period. On his arrival at the Riverside he told reporters he wanted to improve and become as good a player as the France legend. Yakubu first came to Boro's attention with a stunning four-goal show in the Teessiders' 5–1 defeat at Fratton Park on the final day of the 2003–04 season. At £7.5 million he became the third biggest signing in the club's history, after £8.15 million Massimo Maccarone and £8 million Ugo Ehiogu. Nicknamed 'The Yak', he was granted a work permit on appeal after the original application was turned down because he had not played the required 75 percent of competitive internationals over the previous two years. It took Yakubu until his fourth game before he scored his first goal for the club, but when it came it ended Arsenal's run of six games without defeat at the Riverside. He finished the campaign as the club's top scorer with 19 League and Cup goals, also scooping the 888.com Player of the Year award as well as the official supporters' club award. One of the highlights came as he gave the complete centre-forward's performance as a lone striker in the 3–0 win over champions Chelsea at the Riverside, terrorising England defender John Terry all afternoon before scoring a brilliant individual goal to complete the scoring. In his second season he again challenged the leaders in the Premiership's top scorers charts, although for the second successive term the goals dried up towards the end of the season and he endured another long barren streak. He was linked with a £12 million move to Portsmouth or Manchester City over the summer of 2007.

errea
5

YEOMAN Ramon Irvine

Wing-half
Born: Perth, 13 May 1934.
Career: St Johnstone. Northampton Town 1953. MIDDLESBROUGH 1958. Darlington 1964.

■ Craggy Scot Yeoman's dependability was summed up when he played 207 consecutive games for Boro in a four-and-a-half season spell. A tough-tackling and fearless wing-half, his honest style, integrity, dedication and determination made him a fans' favourite at Ayresome Park, with supporters recognising that what he lacked in natural silky skills, he made up for in effort.

Originally signed by Bob Dennison for Northampton, he was the only player Dennison took with him to Boro. That remarkable 207-game run ended when he was dropped by Raich Carter for the start of the 1963–64 season but, in typically determined fashion, he fought his way back into the team after just a few games.

As manager at Darlington, Yeoman nearly took the Quakers to promotion in 1968–69, only to be pipped by Bradford who went up after winning an end-of-season showdown 3–1. The following season, Darlington finished third bottom of Division Four. He lost his job soon after and became youth team manager at Sunderland. He also scouted for Northampton and Everton.

YORSTON Benjamin Collard

Inside-forward/Centre-forward
Born: Nigg, 14 October 1905.
Died: London, November 1977.
Career: Aberdeen Mugiemoss. Montrose. Aberdeen. Sunderland 1931. MIDDLESBROUGH 1933.

■ Hard as nails Scotsman Benny Yorston was surely one of the most colourful characters ever to play for Middlesbrough Football Club. A pocket-sized dynamo, the bald inside-right was well-known for his hair-raising tackles. He was also renowned for enjoying a good Friday night out before running off any ill effects on Saturday. Decades before Jack Charlton started his little black book with the names of opponents who had crossed him, Yorston had a list in his changing room locker headed 'To Be Got', with offending opponents' names regularly added to the list in preparation for retribution in the return fixture! And he didn't just look after himself – crimes perpetrated against his teammates were also logged. Such benevolence extended to his partnership with inside-forward Wilf Mannion, who Yorston protected by shielding him from any defenders giving him a hard time. He was also crucial in honing Mannion's heading ability by teaching him how to time his jump.

When Yorston was in the side, Boro had backbone as his fierce self-confidence inspired his teammates. The son of an Aberdeen trawler captain, Yorston began his career with Montrose and Aberdeen, where in 1929–30 he scored 38 goals to set a club record that still stands to this day. A £2,000 move to Sunderland followed. In his early days, he enjoyed the thrill of racing around the Brookland motor racing circuit, but was advised to give it up if he wanted to be successful at football. Sunderland thought he had seen better days and offered him for sale in 1934, with Boro the takers when their approach for Raich Carter was turned down.

He soon became a crucial part of the pre-war side that looked set to challenge for the Division One title, but he broke his leg at Blackpool in December 1937 and, aged 34 when war broke out, he decided to hang up his boots. After the war, he briefly served Bury and Barnsley as chief scout before going into business letting flats in South Kensington. He died in November 1977.

YOUNG Ernest William

Centre-forward
Born: Middlesbrough, 1893.
Career: MIDDLESBROUGH 1920. Darlington 1922. Leadgate Park.

■ Young's one and only Boro appearance came in the number-nine shirt usually worn by George Elliott. For the record, centre-forward Young's debut and farewell came in a home goalless draw with Chelsea in April 1921. He left for Darlington soon after.

YOUNG Michael

Born: Chester-le-Street, 15 April 1973
Career: Newcastle United 1991. Released 1993.

■ Given a chance in Lennie Lawrence's injury-ravaged squad, Young's only League appearance came as a 63rd minute substitute for Gary Parkinson in a 1–1 home draw with Southend United in November 1991. The previous month, the former Newcastle youth trainee made his debut in a Zenith Data Systems Cup tie against Tranmere, but following the Southend game, his only involvement with the first team came as a non-playing substitute against Bristol City and Newcastle United. On release, he went for a trial at Darlington but did not make the grade.

YOUNG Robert Thomas

Centre-half/Right-half
Born: Swinhill, 1886.
Died: 1955.
Career: St Mirren. West Ham United 1907. MIDDLESBROUGH 1908. Everton 1910. Wolverhampton Wanderers 1911.

■ Young had the difficult task of replacing player-manager Andy Aitken, the supporters' favourite who left to join Leicester Fosse in the summer of 1908. He did well enough but wasn't in the same class. He did, however, score some vital goals to help stave off relegation in his second season, scoring five times in just eight games – four of the goals from the spot as Young displayed an ice cool head. He left for Everton once safety was secured and, in 1911, rejoined the club Boro had bought him from, West Ham United.

ZENDEN Boudewijn (Bolo)

Midfield
Born: Maastricht, Holland, 15 August 1976.
Career: PSV Eindhoven (Holland) 1994. Barcelona (Spain) 1998. Chelsea 2001. MIDDLESBROUGH (loan) 2003. MIDDLESBROUGH 2004. Liverpool 2005. Marseille (France) 2007.

■ Bolo Zenden will always be remembered on Teesside as the man who scored the goal that earned Boro the first major trophy in their 128-year history. In doing so he upset Bolton boss Sam Allardyce, who felt the penalty kick should have been disallowed. Zenden slipped and made double contact with the ball, which travelled almost straight forward to deceive the diving Jussi Jaaskelainen and send the Boro contingent in the Millennium Stadium wild with delight. But by the time Big Sam let rip, the Carling Cup was safely in Boro's possession. Nicknamed Bolo as English fans had such trouble pronouncing his full name, Zenden was considered the natural successor to Marc Overmars when he burst on to the scene with PSV Eindhoven in the 1994–95 season. After giving a glimpse of what was to come, he then played an instrumental part the next season as PSV lifted the Dutch championship. He continued to build his reputation as a pacey and hard-working goalscoring left-winger and was a regular on the scoresheet in his next two seasons. He was named Dutch Player of the Year in 1998 before earning a big money move to Barcelona, where he helped the Catalan giants win the Spanish title. Chelsea signed him for £7.5 million in August 2001 but he was not a major success at Stamford Bridge and he joined Boro on a year's loan on 30 August 2003. Initially he competed with Stewart Downing for the left-wing berth but he struggled to make an impact, lacking the pace to get behind opposition defenders. But a decision by manager Steve McClaren to convert the Dutch

international to a left-sided central midfield position alongside his close friend George Boateng proved inspirational. Boateng was able to spot Downing's runs and, knowing the kind of passes the young winger needed, he gave him a regular supply, as well as scoring more than his fair share of goals. The move prompted a humorous chant from supporters which included the line 'He used to be s***e, but now he's all right, walking in a Zenden wonderland', although the player made it known he was not amused by the song. At the end of his loan he signed a permanent one-year deal with Boro on a free transfer after taking part in the Euro 2004 Finals in Portugal. He suffered an early setback by breaking his hand in the game against Everton but was allowed to wear a soft-cast tape and went on to miss only two of Boro's 51 games. He made more Boro history by scoring both goals in a brilliant 2–0 win over Lazio at the Riverside in one of the highlights of the club's first ever European campaign. But he was out of contract in the summer and Boro were unable to persuade him to stay and he instead joined newly-crowned European champions Liverpool. His first season at Anfield was cut short by a serious knee injury, which required surgery in the United States. While he was never a regular starter, his second campaign was capped by a place in the team as the Merseysiders were beaten by AC Milan in the Champions League Final. Shortly afterwards Liverpool announced that Zenden's contract would not be renewed. He signed for Marseille.

ZIEGE Christian

Left-back
Born: Berlin, Germany, 1 February 1972.
Career: Hertha Zehlendorf. Bayern Munich (Germany) 1990. AC Milan (Italy) 1997. MIDDLESBROUGH 1999. Liverpool 2000. Tottenham Hotspur 2001. Borussia Mönchengladbach (Germany) 2004.

■ Ziege's sole season at the Riverside was highly successful. The talented German reclaimed his place in his national team on the back of his outstanding displays for Boro and won the club's Player of the Year title. But his controversial departure

left a bitter taste. When the versatile left wing-back triggered a release clause in his contract to join Liverpool, it sparked a huge controversy with chairman Steve Gibson pursuing the Reds in the courts. The row overshadowed Ziege's huge contribution on the field following an astute piece of transfer business by Bryan Robson, who rescued him from AC Milan reserves. The Boro boss turned to Ziege after being priced out of the market for Ipswich's Kieron Dyer, who switched to Newcastle for £6.5 million, and following an audacious attempt to prise Roberto Carlos from Real Madrid. Robson had been impressed by Ziege's performances in Euro 96, where he came face to face with Paul Ince and England in the semi-finals, and rated him alongside Carlos and Paulo Maldini as one of the best wing-backs in the world. The player was keen to move on following two unhappy years in Milan, where injuries marred his first season and he then suffered loss of form. His early career had been with Hertha Zehlendorf and his big break came with a £200,000 move to Bayern Munich, with whom he won two Bundesliga titles and one UEFA Cup. Robson fought off interest from top European clubs for Ziege's signature and he made an instant impact at the Riverside. He scored from a sensational free-kick in a 3–1 win at Derby in only his third game for the club and looked equally adept in midfield alongside Ince and Juninho. Recalled to the Germany squad after a two-year absence, he responded with a hat-trick in a 4–0 Euro 2000 qualifying victory over Northern Ireland to become the first Boro player to net an international hat-trick since Wilf Mannion half a century earlier.

Ziege angered Boro fans by pledging his loyalty to the club before exercising his get-out clause to join Liverpool in summer 2000 for £5.5 million. Steve Gibson claimed the Reds had made an illegal approach for the player and accused both parties of 'lies and deceit'. Boro won a lengthy legal case, with Liverpool forced to stump up more cash for the player. Ziege must have wondered whether it was all worth it as he flopped at Anfield, where he never looked at home in a flat back four and raised questions about his attitude and workrate. Tottenham snapped him up in 2001 and he played 27 games in his first season with them. The next two seasons were marred by injuries and he returned to Germany with Borussia Mönchangladbach in 2004. He announced his retirement in October 2005 due to a persistent ankle injury. Ziege was appointed as director of football at Borussia Mönchengladbach in 2007.

Three of Middlesbrough's close-season signings for 2007–08

ALIADIERE Jeremie

Forward
Born Rambouillet 30 March 1983
Career: Arsenal 2001. Celtic (loan) 2005. West Ham United (loan) 2005. Wolverhampton Wanderers (loan) 2005. MIDDLESBROUGH 2007.

■ A product of France's famous Clairefontaine Academy, Aliadiere found it difficult to break into the Arsenal side due to the consistency of Thierry Henry and Robin van Persie. The speedy forward was signed by Boro in summer 2007 for £2 million and is looking forward to the chance of regular first-team football. He enjoyed a successful run in the Gunners' Carling Cup line-ups in 2006–07 when they went all the way to the Final before being beaten by Chelsea.

TUNCAY Sanli

Forward/Midfielder
Born Sakarya, Turkey 16 January 1982
Career: Sakaryaspor 2001. Fenerbahce 2002. MIDDLESBROUGH 2007.

■ Tuncay is ambitious to prove himself in English football after achieving superstar status in Turkey. He is major news in his home country and his progress will be keenly monitored back home. Turkey's first-choice striker, he has scored 13 goals in 43 internationals, while hitting 59 goals in 154 League games for Fenerbahce over the past five seasons. In December 2004, the 25-year-old made worldwide headlines when he scored a Champions League hat-trick in Fenerbahce's 3-0 win over Manchester United. Tuncay is known as 'Braveheart' in Turkey and is determined to live up to the nickname.

YOUNG Luke

Right-back
Born Harlow 19 July 1979
Career: Tottenham Hotspur 1997. Charlton Athletic 2001. MIDDLESBROUGH 2007.

■ The vastly-experienced defender was signed from Charlton for £2.5 million in summer 2007. Young captained the Addicks in their relegation season and is a former colleague of Jason Euell at The Valley. He has won seven England caps but missed the 2006 World Cup Finals with injury. Young, who is also adept at centre-back, brings specialist experience to the problem right-back position at the Riverside.

Managers

John Robson

May 1899 to May 1905

Division Two runners-up 1901–02

John Robson was connected with Middlesbrough for many years and became their first manager, having previously played in goal in the club's reserve side, Middlesbrough Swifts. Initially, he was assistant secretary when Boro reverted to amateur status and took over as manager following their admission to the Football League. Robson moulded a Northern League club into a side ready for Second Division football in the space of just three months, with Middlesbrough gaining promotion to the First Division at the end of the 1901–02 season. Untarnished by the irregular payments to players' scandal which shook the football world in 1905, he in fact had the foresight to have a document signed by the club chairman completely absolving him of any dubious involvement in the unsavoury episode. After parting company with the club he ran a tobacconists for a while, but the urge to return to football proved too strong and he moved south to become manager of Crystal Palace. Robson was in charge of the London club for a couple of seasons before taking over the reins at Brighton & Hove Albion. There he drove the players hard but looked after their welfare and recreational activities. Brighton finished third in the Southern League in 1906–07 and 1910–11 and won the title in 1909–10, with 59 points and conceding only 29 goals. They then surprisingly beat Aston Villa 1–0 in the FA Charity Shield match. Initially team manager at Manchester United, Robson also took over secretarial duties when J.J. Bentley resigned in 1916. Ill health led to him stepping down to assistant in 1921 and, shortly afterwards, he died of pneumonia.

Alex Mackie

June 1905 to October 1906

An administrator who never played professional football, Alex Mackie was associated with several Scottish clubs before becoming Sunderland's manager in the summer of 1899. In 1901–02 Sunderland won the League Championship and the following season were third, just a point behind Sheffield Wednesday. The FA investigated Sunderland's books after a player called Andy McCrombie claimed that the Wearsiders had made him a gift of £100 to start a business. The club said it had been a loan but when the books were examined, irregularities were found and Mackie was banned for three months. When he returned he sold Alf Common to Middlesbrough for £1,000, the first four-figure transfer fee in football history. Shortly afterwards, Mackie followed Common to Ayresome Park when he obtained the post of Boro's manager from 70 applicants. It was his swoop into the transfer market that saved the club from relegation. He signed the legendary Steve Bloomer and fellow England international Billy Brawn in March 1906, but yet again accusations began to fly and the FA looked into the matter. Illegal payments had been paid and the books had not been kept properly. Suspended for a second time, Mackie was so disillusioned with the game that he left to run the Star and Garter Hotel in the town.

Andy Aitken

November 1906 to February 1909

Andy Aitken was one of Newcastle United's all-time great wing-halves, who made 345 appearances and scored 41 goals for the club. He also gained full international honours for Scotland and won many League and Cup medals while at St James' Park. Costing Boro £500 when he joined them as player-manager, in his first season with the club he lifted Middlesbrough from bottom of the League at Christmas to a safe mid-table position at the close. The following season, Boro finished sixth, their best-ever position. Sadly, a clash of personalities forced Aitkin to leave the Teesside club and he joined Leicester Fosse as player-manager. They were relegated at the end of his first season in charge. Things were even worse the following season and he returned north of the border to become just a player again, turning out for both Dundee and Kilmarnock before a groin injury forced his retirement from playing. Aitkin had a spell as manager of Gateshead Town and later scouted for Arsenal.

Andy Walker

June 1910 to January 1911

Andy Walker did not get off to the best of starts at Middlesbrough, being suspended for four weeks for an illegal approach to one of his former Airdrie players. There was even more trouble when Boro chairman Thomas Gibson-Poole, a local Conservative parliamentary candidate, wanted the club to beat local rivals Sunderland in an attempt to enhance his chances of being elected at the forthcoming elections. Walker offered Sunderland's captain Charlie Thomson £30 to draw the game, yet Thomson reported the incident to his own club chairman and an FA Commission was set up to investigate. In January 1911 Gibson-Poole and Walker were permanently suspended from football. Despite a big petition, the FA refused to review Walker's case, although there were many who felt he had been used by his chairman and the ban was eventually lifted. Walker returned to management 18 years later but at the end of his only season in charge of Barrow, the club had to seek re-election.

Tom McIntosh

August 1911 to December 1919

Tom McIntosh was a right-half with Darlington when the club offered him the secretary's job at Feethams in the summer of 1902. The Quakers turned professional in 1908 and had an excellent FA Cup run in 1910–11, when they reached the third round proper before losing 9–3 at home to Swindon Town. They had beaten League clubs Sheffield United and Bradford Park Avenue in the previous rounds. Following the suspension of Andy Walker, McIntosh was installed as the new Middlesbrough manager in August 1911. He was at Ayresome Park in 1913–14 as the club achieved their highest-ever placing of third in Division One, but the outbreak of World War One brought an end to a successful period when the club closed down. McIntosh joined the Teesside Pioneers in August 1914 and saw active service as a sergeant in France. He guided Middlesbrough to the Northern Victory League title in 1918–19, then accepted an offer to join Everton as secretary without team responsibilities and remained there until his death. While on Merseyside, McIntosh signed an 18-year-old Dixie Dean, who, of course, went on to become one of the great names in the Toffees' history.

Jimmy Howie

April 1920 to July 1923

Known as 'Gentleman Jim', Howie's playing career only really took off when he joined Newcastle United, where he gained three League Championship medals and played in three FA Cup Finals before gaining a winners' medal in 1910. He had scored 83 goals in 235 League and Cup games for the Magpies and appeared in three full internationals for Scotland when he was appointed manager of Southern League Queen's Park Rangers. He left the club before they joined the Football League to take over the reins at Middlesbrough. At Ayresome Park, he had a fine attack but a poor defence and his side struggled in the First Division. Howie, who once scored both Scotland's goals in a 2–1 defeat of England, stayed on Teesside until the summer of 2003, after which he ran a tobacconists in London.

Herbert Bamlett

August 1923 to January 1927

Herbert Bamlett made his name as a referee rather than as a player, taking charge of the 1914 FA Cup Final between Burnley and Liverpool – the last Final to be played at Crystal Palace. His first managerial post was at Oldham Athletic, who he joined just after the outbreak of World War One. Despite falling crowds, the Latics had the best season in their history in 1914–15 when they finished runners-up in the First Division. When football resumed after the hostilities, the Boundary Park club had lost some great players and they proved difficult to replace. Bamlett resigned in May 1921 to take charge of Wigan Boro, who had just been elected to the Football League's Third Division North. After a disappointing first season, he led them to fifth place in 1922–23 before being appointed manager of Middlesbrough in the close season. Bamlett didn't endear himself to Boro supporters when he allowed star forward Andy Wilson to join Chelsea and George Carr to join Leicester City. The club had lost their only regular goalscorer in Wilson and ended the season relegated to the Second Division. A disastrous start to the 1926–27 season saw Boro lose their opening three games before a point was secured in a bruising encounter with South Shields. Middlesbrough then went on to break all records over the remaining part of the season, their star being George Camsell who was signed by Bamlett from Durham City. He scored 59 goals in 37 League appearances and the side netted 122 in all. Bamlett left the club in January 1927 before he could see his side win its place back in the top flight. Three months after his surprise dismissal, he joined Manchester United as manager. He was at Old Trafford for four years until the club suffered relegation in 1930–31, conceding 115 goals along the way.

Peter McWilliam

January 1927 to March 1934

Second Division Champions 1926–27, 1928–29

Peter McWilliam excelled as both a player and a manager. He played for a number of local clubs before joining Newcastle United. With the Magpies he gained three League Championship medals and also won an FA Cup-winners' medal against Barnsley in 1910, after picking up three runners'-up medals. After making his Scotland debut against England in April 1905 he received a knee injury against Wales in March 1911, which ended his playing career. In May 1913 McWilliam was named as the new manager of Tottenham Hotspur, but after the north London club were relegated in 1914–15 they had to wait four years before they could seek to restore their place in the First Division. They ran away with the Second Division title in 1919–20 and then won the FA Cup in 1921. Spurs also finished runners-up in Division One in 1921–22 but went into decline after this. McWilliam was in the process of rebuilding the Spurs team when he was approached by top of the Second Division Middlesbrough, who offered him £1,500 per annum to become their manager – £200 more than Spurs were paying. After asking for a pay rise and being refused, he resigned and joined Boro as manager in January 1927. At Ayresome Park, McWilliam was given complete control of team selection without any interference from the board. It was an up-and-down period for the Teesside club and McWilliam never won the hearts of the supporters. Boro went on to clinch the title that season but were relegated the following term, yet with McWilliam still at the helm they again took the Division Two title in 1928–29 and stayed in the top division while he was manager. He was sacked in March 1934 and then scouted in the North East for Arsenal until returning to White Hart Lane to manage Spurs in May 1938. Although remaining with the club for little more than a year, in that time he also began to promote the famous Northfleet Nursery. Deciding he was too old to remain in football, he ended his involvement with the game during World War Two. McWilliam died in Redcar in October 1951 and was buried at nearby Kirkleatham Cemetery.

Wilf Gillow

March 1934 to March 1944

Wilf Gillow was a capable, skilled footballer who played League football for Blackpool, Preston and Grimsby as well as for Middlesbrough in the North Yorkshire League. Having made just under 200 Football League appearances, he built the foundations for his future success as player-manager at Blundell Park. When he took over the reins, the Mariners were a moderately-placed Third Division North side. Five years later, they were in the First Division. A quietly-spoken pipe-smoker, Wilf Gillow had to sell players to make the books balance. He found life in the top flight difficult and resigned in April 1932, yet he remained in office until the end of the campaign when Grimsby were relegated. Two years later he joined Middlesbrough as manager, the club just avoiding relegation in his first season at Ayresome Park. Much respected by players and fans alike, Boro under Gillow improved season by season, finishing fourth in 1938–39. He was too old for active service, so during the hostilities he worked in Middlesbrough Council's treasury department during the day and for Boro part-time in the evenings and at the weekend. Gillow was also a good cricketer, and he once fielded as a substitute for England in an Ashes Test at Old Trafford while a member of the Lancashire groundstaff. Sadly, he died while in office after complications set in following an operation.

David Jack

November 1944 to April 1952

A tall, elegant player with brilliant dribbling ability and deadly finishing, David Jack scored the first goal in a Wembley Final as Bolton Wanderers beat West Ham United 2–0 in 1923. He also scored the winner three years later when the Wanderers beat Manchester City 1–0. Arsenal's Herbert Chapman broke the British transfer record when he paid £10,890 for his signature in 1928. Jack had five successful seasons at Highbury, playing in two FA Cup Finals and winning three League Championship medals. A full England international, winning nine caps, he didn't have the same success when a manager. With his first club Southend United, he found it difficult just to keep them in business. On the untimely death of Wilf Gillow, Jack gave up his job as manager of Sunderland Greyhound Stadium to become manager at Ayresome Park in November 1944, and at the time Boro were playing Wartime League North football. His best season on Teesside was 1950–51, a campaign in which Boro were challenging for the League Championship but injuries and a loss of form saw the club slip away and eventually finish sixth. It was felt that Jack lacked the personality needed to motivate players. After resigning his post in April 1952, he was so disillusioned with the game that he became a publican in Islington before returning to management with League of Ireland side, Shelbourne. Later he took a job with the Air Ministry.

Walter Rowley

June 1952 to February 1954

Walter Rowley gave Bolton Wanderers 38 years' service as a player, coach and manager before resigning through ill health. Having made his Bolton debut against West Bromwich Albion in 1913, he was the 12th man for the club's 1923 FA Cup success, having just finished a suspension following his sending-off in the fifth round. After 19 years as the Wanderers' coach, Rowley succeeded Charlie Foweraker as Bolton's manager. The club soon had some success when they beat Manchester United 3–2 on aggregate to win the League North Cup in May 1945. Wanderers also reached the FA Cup semi-finals in 1946, although there had been a disaster at the Burnden Park ground earlier in the year when many spectators died during the game with Stoke. The Trotters continued to make progress under Rowley but never won anything and in October 1950, he resigned through ill health. Once fully recovered, Rowley succeeded another former Bolton player David Jack as Middlesbrough manager. After finishing 13th in his first season, the club were struggling in the relegation zone in 1953–54 and the doctors advised him to undergo an operation for a stomach ulcer. Before entering hospital he tendered his resignation, saying that a football club fighting for survival in the First Division should have a fully-fit man at the helm. A month later, the board announced it had parted company with their manager but, by then, Rowley was fully fit and wanted to withdraw his resignation. Unfortunately, the board had begun to canvas for a new manager leaving no place for Rowley any more on Teesside and he left to take charge at Shrewsbury Town.

Bob Dennison

July 1954 to January 1963

One of a family of 10, Bob Dennison started his career with Newcastle United before playing for Nottingham Forest, Fulham and Northampton Town. His first managerial post was with Northampton – he had began working in a timber business in the town – but he wanted to work on his own terms and this was too much for some directors. Released from his contract at the County Ground, he joined Middlesbrough for the start of the club's first season back in Division Two after relegation and assumed the secretarial duties at the club from 1955 to 1961. Dennison spent nine very eventful years at Ayresome Park and though he might have been unable to get the club back into the top flight, he produced many fine players including Brian Clough, Edwin Holliday, Mick McNeil and Alan Peacock. Dennison also brought goalkeeper Peter Taylor to the club, thus bringing together the men who would one day form one of the most successful managerial partnerships in football. On 10 January 1963 Bob Dennison was told that his contract, which still had 19 months to run, would be terminated, although a press conference was told that this was by 'mutual consent'. Dennison later sued Middlesbrough for unfair dismissal and was eventually awarded £3,200 damages. He then went into non-League management with Southern League Hereford United. After a successful spell at Edgar Street, he returned to League football with Coventry City as their chief scout. Dennison was later the caretaker and assistant manager between the reigns of Noel Cantwell and Gordon Milne.

Raich Carter

January 1963 to February 1966

Raich Carter was one of the greatest inside-forwards ever produced by England. He was capped by England for the first time in 1934 against Scotland at Wembley, but thereafter he was only spasmodically recalled to the side and of course the war robbed him of many caps. He started out with Sunderland, helping them win the League Championship in

1935–36 and a year later he skippered the Wearsiders to an FA Cup Final success. So by the time he was 25, he had won every major honour open to an English footballer. During the war he served with the RAF and appeared for Derby County. Unsettled at Sunderland, Carter then joined Derby on a permanent basis and helped the Rams to FA Cup success over Charlton Athletic in 1946. In March 1948 he joined Hull City as player-assistant manager, later succeeding Major Frank Buckley as manager, and in 1948–49 the Tigers set a new record by winning the first nine games of the Third Division North season and reached the FA Cup quarter-finals. While at Hull he was persuaded to play again, ending his career in 1952 with a total of 216 goals in 451 League appearances for his three clubs. In May 1953 Carter took over the reins of Leeds United, steering the club into the First Division in 1955–56. It was a great surprise when, in the summer of 1958, the Elland Road club decided not to renew his contract. He was out of the game for a while before being appointed manager of Mansfield Town in January 1960. After two seasons of struggle, he led the Stags to promotion from Division Four and this success at Field Mill brought an offer from Middlesbrough to manage them. It was a constant struggle for Carter at Ayresome Park as the Boro fought against relegation to the Third Division. His dealings in the transfer market were disappointing as he allowed promising players like Cyril Knowles and Alan Peacock to leave the club. With Boro on the brink of relegation, Carter was dismissed and Harold Shepherdson appointed caretaker manager until a replacement could be found. He finished with the game after this and returned to Hull to run a sports department of a local store.

Stan Anderson

April 1966 to January 1973

Division Three runners-up 1966–67

Stan Anderson had the distinction of skippering all three major North East clubs, Sunderland, Newcastle United and Middlesbrough. With Sunderland, he scored 31 goals in 402 League games and helped the club reach two FA Cup semi-finals in 1955 and 1956, losing to

Manchester City and Birmingham City respectively. A tough-tackling wing-half, he moved to Newcastle in November 1963 and played an important role in the Magpies Second Division Championship side of 1964–65. After joining Middlesbrough as player-coach in November 1965, Anderson found things difficult at first and had trouble maintaining his form due to his responsibilities off the field. He retired from playing when he was appointed manager in April 1966 and brought about a revival at Ayresome Park, greatly improving the Teesside club's team spirit. Unfortunately, his appointment had come too late to save the club from relegation to the Third Division but he soon devised new training schedules, bringing much greater interest to these day-to-day tasks. Promotion back to the Second Division was achieved the following season after a great run from November 1966 and, after twice going close to further promotion, he decided to accept an offer to manage AEK Athens. Anderson later had spells with Queen's Park Rangers, Manchester City and Doncaster Rovers before joining Bolton as coach. When Ian Greaves was dismissed Anderson took over as manager, but he didn't have a happy time at Burnden Park and was sacked in May 1981 with two years of his contract still to run.

Jack Charlton

May 1973 to April 1977

Division Two Champions 1973–74, Anglo-Scottish Cup winners 1976

An earthy, uncomplicated man who believes in speaking his mind, Jack Charlton became as famous for his forthright comments as a manager as he ever was for his build and style as a player. He made 629 appearances for Leeds United from 1953 to 1973 and scored 70 goals, mainly at free-kicks and corners. His early career was overshadowed by his brother Bobby at Manchester United, but after the departure of John Charles to Juventus, his career came into its own. Leeds boss Don Revie developed Charlton into a much better centre-half and in April 1965 he made his England debut against Scotland at Wembley. He and Bobby became the first brothers to play for England in the 20th century and Jack went on to gain 35 caps, winning a World Cup-winners' medal in 1966. After Leeds gained promotion, the honours came thick and fast and in 1967 he was voted Footballer of the Year. When he decided to retire from playing, he was offered the Middlesbrough job. This was in May 1973 and at the end of his first season in charge, Boro, aided by new signing Bobby Murdoch, ran away with the Second Division Championship. As early as 23 March 1974, with eight games still to play, Boro ensured promotion back to the top flight for the first time since 1954. They then established themselves as a

First Division club, mostly finishing in mid-table. In 1975 they reached the quarter-finals of the FA Cup and the following year lost to Manchester City in a League Cup semi-final. Middlesbrough did win the Anglo-Scottish Cup, beating Fulham in a two-legged Final. After four years at Ayresome Park Charlton resigned, feeling he needed a six-month break from football but later returning to the game in October 1977 as manager of Sheffield Wednesday. The Owls were languishing near the foot of the Third Division, but within two years he had created a team that won promotion to the Second Division. Two years later they missed a further promotion by just one point. Charlton resigned in 1983, just after the Owls had reached the FA Cup semi-finals. After a brief spell as caretaker manager at Middlesbrough, he took control at Newcastle United, where he had an unhappy time and resigned at the start of the 1985–86 season. In February 1986 he was approached by the FA of Ireland to take over the running of the Republic of Ireland national team on a part-time basis. In 1988 Ireland reached the European Championship Finals for the first time and in the 1990 World Cup Finals the club reached the quarter-finals, where they lost to Italy. He led Ireland to a second consecutive World Cup Finals in 1994, but resigned in December 1995. Charlton's reign had exceeded all expectations and had taken Ireland to the Finals of three major tournaments, not to mention the dizzy heights of sixth place in the FIFA world rankings.

John Neal

May 1977 to July 1981

John Neal gained a reputation as a keen-tackling full-back. After 60 games for Hull City, he moved into non-League football with King's Lynn before Swindon Town gave him the chance to resurrect his League career. Joe Mercer then signed him for Aston Villa, where he made over 100 appearances and won a Second Division Championship medal in 1959–60 and a League Cup-winners' tankard in 1961, when they won the inaugural competition. On leaving Villa Park he made over 100 appearances for Southend United before entering the

world of management at Wrexham. Neal enjoyed great success at the Racecourse Ground, taking the Welsh club to promotion to Division Three in 1969–70 and to the quarter-finals of the European Cup-winners' Cup in 1976. He left a strong side when he moved to Middlesbrough and Wrexham were soon in the Second Division. Neal instilled attacking flair in Boro's side but sold some excellent players, including Graeme Souness to Liverpool and David Mills to West Bromwich Albion. He left the Teesside club after a disagreement over the sale of Craig Johnston to Liverpool and was soon snapped up by Chelsea chairman Ken Bates. Neal took Chelsea to the Second Division Championship in 1983–84, but after undergoing heart surgery in 1985 he was replaced by John Hollins.

Bobby Murdoch

June 1981 to October 1982

Bobby Murdoch was one of Scotland's most influential post-war players, helping Celtic to eight consecutive League Championships. He also appeared in eight Scottish Cup Finals and another eight Scottish League Cup Finals. Celtic's greatest achievement, though, was as the first British team to win the European Cup in 1967 when Inter Milan were beaten 2–1 in Lisbon. Three years later they lost in the Final to Feyenoord 2–1 in Milan, with Murdoch

again in the side. After 61 goals in 291 League appearances, Murdoch moved south to join Middlesbrough. On hanging up his boots, he became Middlesbrough's youth-team coach before replacing John Neal as manager in the summer of 1981. The loss of stars like David Armstrong and Craig Johnston greatly weakened the side and relegation to Division Two was the result. He was sacked soon afterwards.

Malcolm Allison

October 1982 to March 1984

Malcolm Allison's coaching and management days overshadowed a playing career with Charlton and West Ham United. He started his career at The Valley but was soon on his way to West Ham United to replace the ageing Dick Walker as centre-half. He played in 255 League and Cup games for the Hammers before being struck down with tuberculosis at the beginning of the club's 1957–58 promotion-winning season. Allison lost a lung as a result of this illness but carried on playing Southern League football for Romford, ignoring the medical advice. He took up his first management post at Bath City in October 1962 before being appointed boss of Plymouth Argyle in May 1984. He stayed at Home Park until the following April, accepting the assistant manager's post at Manchester City three months later. At Maine Road, Allison combined with Joe Mercer to make one of the most successful partnerships in English football. They revived the City club, combining an attractive style of play with sustained success. The Second Division Championship was won in 1965–66 and two years later the League title was gained, with other trophies soon following. City won the FA Cup in 1969 and the European Cup-winners' Cup and Football League Cup the following year. After Mercer left Maine Road, Allison was sole manager but was not as successful and, with the team in disarray, he left to join Crystal Palace. After losing his job at Selhurst Park in 1976, he moved abroad to coach Galatasaray of Turkey. He later managed Plymouth again and returned to Maine Road as coach. There followed another spell in charge at Crystal Palace and one at Yeovil before he went to manage Sporting Lisbon, taking them to the Portuguese League and Cup double in 1981–82 but the following October arriving back in England as boss of Middlesbrough. At Ayresome Park, Allison had the job of reviving morale and creating a Boro team that believed in itself. They eventually pulled themselves off the bottom of the table to finish 16th, but his period in charge on Teesside ended in controversy in March 1984 after he blocked the £100,000 transfer of Darren Wood to Chelsea – Boro were on the brink of bankruptcy at the time. After parting company with the club, Allison became a wanderer and moved from one club to another, including spells in Kuwait and Portugal and a brief period as caretaker manager of Bristol Rovers, though Allison was then dogged by ill health.

Willie Maddren

June 1984 to February 1986

Willie Maddren was, of course, a defender of the highest quality. During his time at Ayresome Park, he developed a superb partnership at the heart of the Boro defence with Stuart Boam and they had a marvellous understanding on the field. Maddren made 341 appearances for Boro before a serious knee injury ended his career. After a spell as coach at Hartlepool United, he returned to Ayresome Park as coach and physiotherapist. He had rejoined the Teesside club on the advice of Jack Charlton, who was at Ayresome Park for a short spell following the dismissal of Malcolm Allison. Though the fans wanted Charlton to stay, he was adamant that the arrangement should only be short-term. Maddren was offered the manager's job and appointed as successor to Allison in the summer of 1984. He had a tough time as Boro boss. The club were already £1.2 million in debt, which meant that he could buy very few players. Even so, he resisted pressure to blood youngsters during this traumatic time in the club's history. In October 1985 Maddren threatened to resign but stayed on. During the early part of 1986, he appointed Bruce Rioch as the club's coach but in February, Maddren was sacked and Rioch took over. Sadly, for the last five years of his all-too short life, Willie suffered from motor neurone disease.

Bruce Rioch

February 1986 to March 1990

Division Three runners-up 1986–87, Division Two promotion 1987–88

As a player, Bruce Rioch possessed power, pace and a lethal shot, and he played in three divisional Championship sides. He gained a Fourth Division medal with Luton Town in 1967–68, a Third Division medal with Aston Villa in 1971–72 and a League Championship medal with Derby County in 1974–75. Rioch also played in Villa's losing League Cup Final side in 1971. He captained Scotland to their ill-fated 1978 World Cup in Argentina and, from midfield, once scored four goals in a match for Derby against Spurs in October 1976. Rioch made a name for himself in management at Torquay United where he got his first break. After being appointed Middlesbrough's first-team coach in January 1986, the following month, after the departure of Willie Maddren, he became Middlesbrough's boss. Too late to prevent the club's relegation to the Third Division, Rioch found success in 1986–

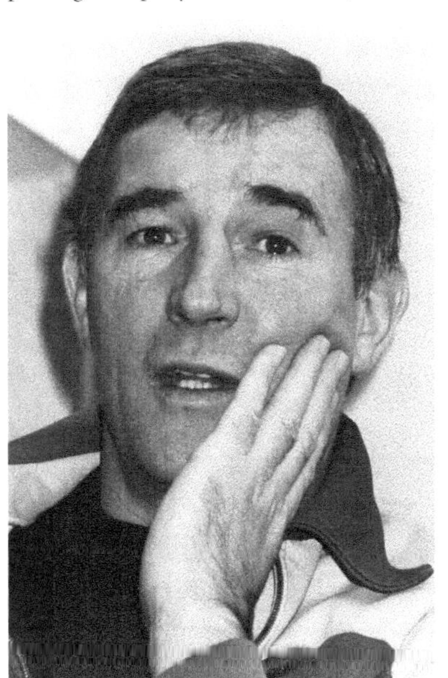

87 when taking the club from the brink of liquidation to promotion to Division Two as runners-up to Bournemouth. The following season the club were promoted to the First Division via the Play-offs against Bradford City and Chelsea. Though Rioch was the first Boro manager to take the club to two successive promotion successes, sadly, Boro were relegated immediately. In March 1990, with the club languishing near the foot of Division Two, Rioch left Ayresome Park. In less than a month he was in charge at Millwall and in 1990–91 took the club to the Second Division Play-offs, but after their form slumped he resigned to take charge at Bolton Wanderers. He achieved promotion in his first season at Burnden Park, while in 1993–94 he led Bolton to the FA Cup quarter-finals. The following season he took Bolton to the League Cup Final and promotion to the Premiership via the Play-offs. In June 1995 Rioch left Bolton to manage Arsenal, but lost his job after 15 months and joined Queen's Park Rangers as Stewart Houston's assistant. He later managed Norwich City before taking over the reins of Wigan Athletic. His stay at the JJB Stadium was brief and he resigned after just eight months.

Colin Todd

March 1990 to June 1991

Zenith Data Systems Cup runners-up 1990

Colin Todd was that rarity – a defender

who excited crowds. He developed a great partnership with Roy McFarland at Derby County, which was later transferred into the England team. Todd, who had cost the Rams a record £180,000 when he joined them from Sunderland, won two League Championship medals at the Baseball Ground. At the end of the second of those seasons, 1974–75, Todd was named the PFA's Footballer of the Year. Later in his playing career, he helped Birmingham City win promotion to the First Division and Oxford United to the Third Division title. After managing Whitley Bay, he was assistant manager to former Derby teammate Bruce Rioch at Middlesbrough, eventually succeeding him as manager. Boro made the Second Division Play-offs in 1990–91 after finishing seventh, but lost to Notts County in the semi-final. Todd had been employed too late to save the club from relegation the previous season. In June 1991 he surprisingly resigned and a year later became assistant manager to Bruce Rioch again, this time at Bolton Wanderers. He was later joined by McFarland after Rioch moved to Highbury, but Todd's former Derby teammate was dismissed with Bolton at the wrong end of the Premiership. Todd became manager but was unable to prevent the Trotters' relegation. In 1996–97 he was at the helm as the club won the First Division Championship with 100 goals and 98 points, and although the club then lost their top flight status, Todd remained with the club until a poor start to the 1999–2000 season saw him replaced by Sam Allardyce. He made his comeback with Swindon Town but resigned after a few months to become Derby's assistant manager for a second time. When Jim Smith stepped down, Todd was promoted to the hot seat but lost his job after just three months in charge. He then became Bryan Robson's assistant at Bradford City and after Robbo's short-term contract was not renewed, Todd became manager. Despite being the longest-serving boss at Valley Parade in the last 20 years, he was unpopular with City fans and sacked in February 2007.

Lennie Lawrence

July 1991 to May 1994

Division Two runners-up 1991–92

In his eight years as manager of Charlton Athletic, Lennie Lawrence experienced just about everything. As well as promotion and relegation, the London club nearly went bankrupt, lost their Valley ground, shared with Crystal Palace and won an exciting Play-off match to avoid relegation. In June 1991 with Charlton on the point of returning to The Valley, Lawrence resigned to take the manager's job at Middlesbrough. He took the then Ayresome Park club to promotion to the newly-formed Premiership at the end of his first season in charge as they finished runners-up to Ipswich Town. Boro also reached the semi-finals of the League Cup. Relegated in 1992–93, Lawrence resigned his post in May 1994 after the club had ended the campaign in ninth place in the First Division. Three weeks later he was appointed manager of Bradford City. Feeling that he had to recruit new players, he spent £1.5 million but City finished 14th after a disastrous end to the season saw them win just one of their last 12 games. Lawrence lost his job in November 1995 but a month later took charge of Luton Town, leading the Hatters to the Second Division Play-offs in 1996–97. After three seasons of mid-table placings, he took charge of Grimsby Town but his time at Blundell

Park was not a happy one. In February 2002 he was appointed manager of Cardiff City and led the Bluebirds to the Play-offs. Though they were unsuccessful, Lawrence took the Welsh club to the Play-offs for a second successive season in 2002–03, this time beating Queen's Park Rangers in the Final. The club have remained in this division ever since but at the end of the 2004–05 season, Lawrence announced he was stepping down as the Cardiff boss. He acted as the club's consultant for a while but was then appointed director of football at Bristol Rovers, working alongside coach Paul Trollope.

Bryan Robson

May 1994 to December 2000 (with Terry Venables December 2000 to May 2001)

Division One Champions 1994–95, FA Cup runners-up 1997, Football League Cup runners-up 1997 and 1998, Division One runners-up 1997–98

After an outstanding career with West Bromwich Albion and Manchester United, England midfielder Bryan Robson accepted the player-manager's job at Middlesbrough in the summer of 1994. He made a dream start to his managerial career on Teesside as Boro won the Division One Championship and promotion to the Premiership in their final season at Ayresome Park. Following relocation to the new 30,000 seater Riverside Stadium on the banks of the River Tees, Middlesbrough made an ambitious return to the top flight by signing big-name players like Nick Barmby and Juninho. They went up to fourth in the Premiership in October 1995 but an injury crisis demoralised the side and they ended the campaign in 12th place. In the summer of 1996, Robson splashed out millions of pounds to sign Italian striker Fabrizio Ravanelli. Though the club were deducted points for postponing a fixture at Blackburn at short notice, they reached the Finals of both domestic Cup competitions. In the League Cup Final, Boro drew 1–1 with Leicester City after extra-time but lost 1–0 in the replay. The club's eventful season ended in relegation on the final day of the season, whereas they would have avoided relegation and finished in 14th place had it not been for the points deduction which was not overturned despite appeals. The club then endured further disappointment with a 2–0 FA Cup Final defeat at the hands of Chelsea. The board kept faith in Robson and he rewarded them with automatic promotion back to the top flight in 1997–98, the only downside of the season being a League Cup Final defeat by Chelsea. Robson then spent three more seasons at the club, but from December 2000 he turned to his former boss at England level, Terry Venables, for help. The combination had the desired effect and after a campaign that ended in mid-table respectability, Venables was given a rapturous ovation while Robson was barracked by a small section of the Riverside crowd. He handed in his resignation and was out of the game for two years before managing Bradford City. His spell at Valley Parade was short-lived and unsuccessful, as the club were relegated to Division Two. Robson's third management job began in November 2004, when he took charge of West Bromwich Albion 23 years after leaving them as a player. Under Robson, the Baggies defied all the odds and stayed up after being bottom of the Premiership at Christmas. He strengthened the squad in the close season but from a position of safety the club had a disappointing end to the 2005–06 campaign and lost their top flight status. Robson was later replaced by Tony Mowbray. In the summer of 2007 he took charge of Sheffield United.

Steve McClaren

June 2001 to May 2006

Football League Cup winners 2004, UEFA Cup runners-up 2006

Steve McClaren's unspectacular playing career was spent mostly in the lower Leagues of English football. He started out with Hull City and played for Derby County, Lincoln City (on loan), Bristol City and Oxford United before an injury forced his retirement in 1992. Moving into coaching, he became Oxford United's reserve-team coach before his talent was spotted by Jim Smith at Derby County. McClaren joined the 'Bald Eagle' in 1995 and as the assistant manager he helped to engineer Derby's promotion to the Premiership in 1995–96. The duo then led County to two consecutive mid-table finishes in their new Pride Park surroundings, but McClaren's influence hadn't gone unnoticed and he was invited to become Alex Ferguson's assistant at Manchester United. Success came early at Old Trafford as United claimed an unprecedented treble of League Championship, FA Cup and European Cup titles during the 1998–99 season. In recognition of his coaching abilities, McClaren was asked in 2000 along with Peter Taylor to become caretaker manager to the England team prior to Sven-Göran Erikkson's appointment as coach. He was interviewed for the West Ham vacancy before being offered the Middlesbrough manager's job in the summer of 2001 by club chairman Steve Gibson. In his first season in charge, he took the club to the FA Cup semi-finals, where they were beaten by Arsenal. He was then in charge as Middlesbrough won their first-ever major honour, winning the League Cup in 2004 against Bolton Wanderers at the Millennium Stadium. McClaren took the club into European football for the first time and helped recruit many big-name international players, including Chelsea's Jimmy Floyd Hasselbaink. McClaren had also taken Boro to their highest Premiership finish of seventh in 2004–05, which gave them another run in Europe. In the 2005–06 season, Middlesbrough achieved a semi-final place in the FA Cup and reached the UEFA Cup Final, where they went down 4–0 to Sevilla of Spain. In August 2006, following England's disappointing showing in the World Cup, McClaren was named as the new England manager, with Terry Venables as his assistant. He caused an early storm by dropping captain David Beckham from the squad and, though early results were good, his England team was criticised for poor performances. If England fail to qualify for Euro 2008, pressure will doubtless increase for him to lose his job.

Gareth Southgate

June 2006 onwards

England defender Gareth Southgate had played for both Crystal Palace and Aston Villa before joining Middlesbrough for £6.5 million in 2001. He won the club's Player of the Year award in his first season at the Riverside and was then awarded the captaincy for 2002–03. He became the first Middlesbrough captain to lift a major trophy when the club won the Carling Cup in 2004, although his season ended shortly after. Southgate later committed his final playing years to Middlesbrough, his last appearance as a professional footballer coming in the 2006 UEFA Cup Final as captain in a 4–0 defeat to Sevilla. McClaren's departure from Middlesbrough, coupled with Terry Venables taking the decision not to return to Teesside, saw Southgate emerge as chairman Steve Gibson's choice as the next Boro manager. Southgate does not currently hold a UEFA Pro Licence but has been granted special dispensation by the Premier League to acquire his qualifications. He was unveiled as Boro's new manager in June 2006. Effectively retired from playing to concentrate on management, Southgate's biggest win of the 2006–07 season came at home against Bolton Wanderers when Boro ran out winners 5–1, ending the season in 12th place. The club also reached the FA Cup quarter-finals before losing to Manchester United in a replay.

Statistics Section

Progressive Scoring Records

Charlie Pugh set the first target for Middlesbrough's opening League season, scoring seven goals. This table shows how individual scoring records have been equalled and beaten since then.

	League		All Matches	
1899–1900	Charlie Pugh	7	Charlie Pugh	7
1900–01	Bill Wardrope	11	Alex Robertson	16
1901–02	Jack Brearley	22	Jack Brearley	23
1912–13	George Elliott	22	George Elliott	25
1913–14	George Elliott	31	George Elliott	31
1919–20	George Elliott	31	George Elliott	34
1921–22	Andy Wilson	32		
1925–26	Jimmy McClelland	32	Jimmy McClelland	38
1926–27	George Camsell	59	George Camsell	63

100+ Consecutive Appearances

League

305	David Armstrong	March 1972 to August 1980
190	Ray Yeoman	December 1958 to May 1963
136	Bernie Slaven	October 1985 to November 1988
130	Tim Williamson	October 1907 to January 1911
129	Bill Harris	September 1954 to September 1957
125	Willie Maddren	April 1972 to March 1976
121	Tony Mowbray	November 1985 to September 1988
105	Stuart Boam	December 1972 to August 1975

All Matches

358	David Armstrong	March 1972 to August 1980
207	Ray Yeoman	December 1958 to May 1963
159	Bernie Slaven	October 1985 to November 1988
149	Willie Maddren	April 1972 to March 1976
142	Tony Mowbray	November 1985 to September 1988
138	Tim Williamson	October 1907 to January 1911
135	Bill Harris	September 1954 to September 1957
122	Stuart Boam	December 1972 to August 1975
117	Stuart Boam	September 1975 to December 1977
113	Gordon Jones	December 1964 to March 1967
105	Jimmy Mathieson	August 1926 to November 1929
101	Roland Ugolini	February 1950 to April 1952

Individual Scoring Feats

Five Goals in a Game

J. Wilkie v Gainsborough Trinity (h) 9–2	Football League	2 March 1901
A.N. Wilson v Nottingham Forest (h) 5–2	Football League	6 October 1923
J. McClelland v Leeds United (h) 5–1	FA Cup	9 January 1926
G.H. Camsell v Manchester City (a) 5–3	Football League	25 December 1926
G.H. Camsell v Aston Villa (a) 7–2	Football League	9 September 1935
B.H. Clough v Brighton HA (h) 9–0	Football League	23 August 1958

Four goals in a game

J. Brown v Bishop Auckland (h) 4–0	FA Cup	8 December 1900
J. Brearley v Barnsley (a) 7–2	Football League	22 February 1902
S. Bloomer v Woolwich Arsenal (h) 5–3	Football League	5 January 1907
G.W. Elliott v Bradford City (h) 4–0	Football League	17 April 1920
G.H. Camsell v Portsmouth (h) 7–3	Football League	6 November 1926
G.H. Camsell v Fulham (h) 6–1	Football League	20 November 1926
G.H. Camsell v Swansea Town (h) 7–1	Football League	18 December 1926
G.H. Camsell v Everton (h) 4–2	Football League	3 September 1927
G.H. Camsell v Bury (h) 6–1	Football League	10 March 1928
J. Pease v Wolverhampton W (h) 8–3	Football League	9 February 1929
G.H. Camsell v Leeds United (h) 5–0	Football League	28 February 1931
G.H. Camsell v Manchester United (a) 4–4	Football League	2 May 1931
G.H. Camsell v Sheffield United (h) 10–3	Football League	18 November 1933
G.H. Camsell v Sheffield Wednesday (h) 5–0	Football League	13 April 1936
T. Cochrane v Manchester City (a) 6–1	Football League	9 March 1938
M. Fenton v West Brom Alb (h) 4–1	Football League	7 May 1938
W.J. Mannion v Blackpool (h) 9–2	Football League	10 December 1938
M. Fenton v Stoke City (h) 5–4	Football League	7 September 1946
C. Wayman v West Ham United (h) 6–0	Football League	30 October 1954
B.H. Clough v Huddersfield Town (h) 7–2	Football League	22 April 1957
B.H. Clough v Doncaster Rovers (h) 5–0	Football League	11 September 1957
B.H. Clough v Ipswich Town (h) 5–2	Football League	23 November 1957
B.H. Clough v Swansea Town (h) 6–2	Football League	21 March 1959
A. Peacock v Derby County (a) 7–1	Football League	29 August 1959
B.H. Clough v Plymouth Argyle (h) 6–2	Football League	5 September 1959
A. Peacock v Rotherham United (h) 5–1	Football League	30 August 1961
J. Hickton v Hull City (h) 5–3	Football League	22 March 1969
M. Burns v Chelsea (h) 7–2	Football League	16 December 1978
C. Hignett v Brighton HA (h) 5–0	League Cup	21 September 1993

Three goals in a game

24 times	G.H. Camsell
17	B.H. Clough
13	G.W. Elliott
10	M. Fenton
7	A. Peacock, B. Slaven
6	J. Hickton, W. Tinsley
5	W.J. Mannion
4	J. McClelland, J. O'Rourke
3	A. Common, J. Hendrie, A. McCrae, D. Mills, J. Pease, F. Ravanelli, A.N. Wilson
2	G. Carr, J. Carr, J. McCormack, A. Robertson, C. Wayman
1	I. Baird, R. Birkett, H. Blackmore, S. Bloomer, Branca, J. Brearley, J. Brown, R. Bruce, M. Burns, J. Cassidy, T. Cochrane, I.W. Dickson, G. Emmerson, U. Fuchs, S.C. Gail, T. Green, J.H. Hall, W.C. Harris, J. Hartnett, J.F. Hasselbaink, C.J. Hignett, D. Hodgson, A. Horsfield, J.D. Irvine, A. Kernaghan, T. McAndrew, J. Murphy, G.T. Reid, H. Ricard, D. Rooks, J.C. Scott, G. Souness, J. Wilkie, P. Wilkinson, B.C. Yorston

Ever Presents in a Football League Season

1901–02	34	A. Davidson, A. Jones
1903–04	34	J. Cassidy, R.G. Williamson
1906–07	38	R.G. Williamson
1907–08	38	S. Atkins, J. Watson

1908–09	38	R.G. Williamson
1909–10	38	R.G. Williamson
1919–20	42	S. Davidson
1920–21	42	R.G. Williamson
1924–25	42	J. Clough
1925–26	42	W. Birrell
1926–27	42	J.A. Mathieson
1927–28	42	J.A. Mathieson
1930–31	42	J. Jennings
1935–36	42	F. Gibson; B.C. Yorston
1936–37	42	R.W. Stuart
1937–38	42	G.E. Laking
1950–51	42	H.D. Bell, R. Ugolini
1953–54	42	R. Ugolini
1955–56	42	W.C. Harris
1956–57	42	W.C. Harris
1958–59	42	B.H. Clough
1959–60	42	M. McNeil, R.I. Yeoman
1960–61	42	R.I. Yeoman
1961–62	42	R.I. Yeoman
1962–63	42	R.I. Yeoman
1963–64	42	I.S. Gibson
1964–65	42	J.D. Irvine
1965–66	42	G.E. Jones
1967–68	42	J. Hickton
1969–70	42	J. Hickton, G.E. Jones
1970–71	42	W. Whigham
1972–73	42	J. Platt
1973–74	42	D. Armstrong, S. Boam, W. Maddren
1974–75	42	D. Armstrong, S. Boam, W. Maddren, J. Platt
1975–76	42	D. Armstrong
1976–77	42	D. Armstrong, S. Boam, J. Craggs
1977–78	42	D. Armstrong
1978–79	42	D. Armstrong
1979–80	42	D. Armstrong, J. Craggs
1981–82	42	J. Platt
1982–83	42	S. Bell, D. Wood
1983–84	42	I. Nattrass, H. Otto, D. Wood
1985–86	42	B. Laws
1986–87	46	C. Cooper, T. Mowbray, G. Pallister, S. Pears, B. Slaven
1987–88	44	T. Mowbray, G. Pallister, B. Slaven
1989–90	46	B. Slaven
1991–92	46	P. Wilkinson
1993–94	46	S. Pears
1998–99	38	D. Gordon
2002–03	38	J. Greening, M. Schwarzer

Leading Scorers 1899–1900 to 2005–07

	League Matches		All Matches	
1899–1900	C.E. Pugh	7	C.E. Pugh	7
1900–01	W. Wardrope	11	A. Robertson	16
1901–02	J. Brearley	22	J. Brearley	23
1902–03	A. Robertson	7	A. Robertson	8
	J. Cassidy	7		
1903–04	A. Brown	12	A. Brown	17
	J. Cassidy	12		
1904–05	H. Astley	4	H. Astley	5
	R.H. Atherton	4		
1905–06	A. Common	19	A. Common	24
1906–07	S. Bloomer	18	S. Bloomer	20
1907–08	S. Bloomer	12	S. Bloomer	12
	S.G. Cail	12	S.G. Cail	12
1908–09	J.H. Hall	18	J.H. Hall	18
1909–10	J.H. Hall	12	J.H. Hall	12
1910–11	G.W. Elliott	10	G.W. Elliott	10
1911–12	G.W. Elliott	17	G.W. Elliott	19
1912–13	G.W. Elliott	22	G.W. Elliott	25
1913–14	G.W. Elliott	31	G.W. Elliott	31
1914–15	W. Tinsley	23	W. Tinsley	26
1919–20	G.W. Elliott	31	G.W. Elliott	34
1920–21	G.W. Elliott	26	G.W. Elliott	26
1921–22	A.N. Wilson	32	A.N. Wilson	32
1922–23	G.W. Elliott	23	G.W. Elliott	23
1923–24	A.N. Wilson	8	A.N. Wilson	8
1924–25	I.W. Dickson	7	I.W. Dickson	7
	O. Williams	7	O. Williams	7
1925–26	J. McClelland	32	J. McClelland	38
1926–27	G.H. Camsell	59	G.H. Camsell	63
1927–28	G.H. Camsell	33	G.H. Camsell	37
1928–29	G.H. Camsell	30	G.H. Camsell	33
1929–30	G.H. Camsell	29	G.H. Camsell	31
1930–31	G.H. Camsell	32	G.H. Camsell	32
1931–32	G.H. Camsell	20	G.H. Camsell	20
1932–33	G.H. Camsell	17	G.H. Camsell	18
1933–34	G.H. Camsell	23	G.H. Camsell	24
1934–35	G.H. Camsell	14	G.H. Camsell	14
1935–36	G.H. Camsell	28	G.H. Camsell	32
1936–37	M. Fenton	22	M. Fenton	22
1937–38	M. Fenton	24	M. Fenton	26
1938–39	M. Fenton	34	M. Fenton	35
1946–47	W.J. Mannion	18	W.J. Mannion	23
	M. Fenton	18	M. Fenton	23
1947–48	M. Fenton	28	M. Fenton	28
1948–49	M. Fenton	12	M. Fenton	12
1949–50	P.S. McKennan	15	P.S. McKennan	16
			A. McCrae	16
1950–51	A. McCrae	21	A. McCrae	21
1951–52	L. Delapenha	15	L. Delapenha	17
1952–53	W.J. Mannion	18	W.J. Mannion	18
1953–54	L. Delapenha	18	L. Delapenha	18
1954–55	C. Wayman	16	C. Wayman	17
	J.C. Scott	16		
1955–56	L. Delapenha	17	L. Delapenha	18
1956–57	B.H. Clough	38	B.H. Clough	40
1957–58	B.H. Clough	40	B.H. Clough	42
1958–59	B.H. Clough	43	B.H. Clough	43
1959–60	B.H. Clough	39	B.H. Clough	40
1960–61	B.H. Clough	34	B.H. Clough	36
1961–62	A. Peacock	24	A. Peacock	32
1962–63	A. Peacock	31	A. Peacock	32
1963–64	I.S. Gibson	14	I.S. Gibson	14
1964–65	J.D. Irvine	20	J.D. Irvine	24
1965–66	J.D. Irvine	15	J.D Irvine	17
1966–67	J. O'Rourke	27	J. O'Rourke	30
1967–68	J. Hickton	24	J. Hickton	29
1968–69	J. Hickton	18	J. Hickton	18
1969–70	J. Hickton	24	J. Hickton	30
1970–71	J. Hickton	25	J. Hickton	27
1971–72	J. Hickton	12	J. Hickton	16
1972–73	J. Hickton	13	J. Hickton	15
1973–74	A. Foggon	19	A. Foggon	20
1974–75	A. Foggon	16	A. Foggon	18

1975–76	D. Mills	10	J Hickton	18
1976–77	D. Mills	15	D. Mills	18
1977–78	D. Mills	10	D. Mills	16
1978–79	M. Burns	14	M. Burns	14
1979–80	D. Armstrong	11	D. Armstrong	14
1980–81	B. Jankovic	12	B. Jankovic	13
1981–82	W. Ashcroft	6	W. Ashcroft	7
1982–83	D. Shearer	9	D. Shearer	13
	H. Otto	9		
1983–84	D. Currie	15	D. Currie	15
1984–85	D. Mills	14	D. Mills	14
1985–86	G. Rowell	10	G. Rowell	12
1986–87	B. Slaven	17	B. Slaven	21
1987–88	B. Slaven	21	B. Slaven	22
1988–89	B. Slaven	15	B. Slaven	18
1989–90	B. Slaven	21	B. Slaven	32
1990–91	B. Slaven	16	B. Slaven	19
1991–92	B. Slaven	16	P. Wilkinson	24
1992–93	P. Wilkinson	14	P. Wilkinson	15
1993–94	P. Wilkinson	15	P. Wilkinson	17
1994–95	J. Hendrie	15	J. Hendrie	17
1995–96	N. Barmby	7	N. Barmby	9
1996–97	F. Ravanelli	16	F. Ravanelli	31
1997–98	M. Beck	14	M. Beck	15
1998–99	H. Ricard	15	H. Ricard	18
1999–2000	H. Ricard	12	H. Ricard	14
2000–01	A. Boksic	12	A. Boksic	12
2001–02	A. Boksic	8	A. Boksic	8
2002–03	M. Maccarone	9	M. Maccarone	9
2003–04	S. Nemeth	9	S. Nemeth	9
			Juninho	9
2004–05	J.F. Hasselbaink	13	J.F. Hasselbaink	16
2005–06	A. Yakubu	13	A. Yakubu	19
2006–07	M. Viduka	14	M. Viduka	19

Top 20 Scorers

All Matches			League Matches		
1	George Camsell	345	1	George Camsell	325
2	George Elliott	214	2	George Elliott	203
3	Brian Clough	204	3	Brian Clough	197
4	John Hickton	192	4	John Hickton	159
5	Mickey Fenton	162	5	Mickey Fenton	147
6	Bernie Slaven	146	6	Alan Peacock	125
7	Alan Peacock	141	7	Bernie Slaven	118
8	David Mills	111	8=	Wilf Mannion	99
9	Wilf Mannion	110		Billy Pease	99
10	Billy Pease	102	10=	Lindy Delapenha	90
11	Lindy Delapenha	93		David Mills	90
12=	Jackie Carr	81	12	Jackie Carr	75
	Johnny Spuhler	81	13=	Bill Harris	69
14	David Armstrong	77		Johnny Spuhler	69
15	Bill Harris	72	15=	David Armstrong	59
16	Paul Wilkinson	66		Billy Birrell	59
17	Alf Common	65		Steve Bloomer	59
18	Billy Birrell	63	18	Alf Common	58
19	Steve Bloomer	62	19	Andy Wilson	56
20	Andy Wilson	57	20	Benny Yorston	54

Top 20 Appearances

All Matches			League Matches		
1	Tim Williamson	603	1	Tim Williamson	564
2	Gordon Jones	527/5	2	Gordon Jones	457/5
3	John Craggs	487/1	3	Jackie Carr	421
4	Jim Platt	481	4	George Camsell	418
5	John Hickton	473/26	5	John Craggs	408/1
6	George Camsell	453	6	Jim Platt	401
7	Jackie Carr	449	7	John Hickton	395/20
8	David Armstrong	428/3	8	Dickie Robinson	390
9	Stephen Pears	424	9	Bill Harris	360
10	Tony Mowbray	419/6	10	David Armstrong	357/2
11	Dickie Robinson	416	11	Tony Mowbray	345/3
12	Mark Schwarzer*	407	12	George Elliott	344
13	Colin Cooper	396/27	13	Wilf Mannion	341
14	Stuart Boam	393	14	Stephen Pears	339
15=	David Mills	378/20	15	Mark Schwarzer*	333
	Bill Harris	378	16=	Colin Cooper	322/24
17	Wilf Mannion	368		Stuart Boam	322
18	George Elliott	365	18	Ronnie Dicks	316
19	Bernie Slaven	355/26	19	Tony McAndrew	311/2
20	Tony McAndrew	353/5	20	David Mills	309/19

* still playing in 2006–07

Middlesbrough Career Records

Below are the career records of every Middlesbrough player to have played League football for the club since 1899–1900. The years given are the first years of the season. For example, 1927 means 1927–28. The Others column includes all the competitions not accounted for in the rest of the table – Anglo-Italian Cup, Anglo-Scottish Cup, Freight Rover Trophy, Full Members' Cup, Simod Cup, Texaco Cup, UEFA Cup and Zenith Data Systems Cup. Substitute appearances are given to the right of full appearances. eg 13/4

		LEAGUE		FA CUP		FL CUP		OTHERS		TOTAL	
Player	Played	A	G	A	G	A	G	A	G	A	G
Agnew W.B.	1904–06	66	2	7	0	0	0	0	0	73	2
Aitken A.	1906–09	76	1	3	0	0	0	0	0	79	1
Aitken G..B.	1951–53	17	0	1	0	0	0	0	0	18	0
Aitken S..	1903–10	227	6	15	0	0	0	0	0	242	6
Allen M.	1967–72	32/2	0	2	1	10	0	0	0	35/2	1
Allport H.G.	1899–1900	31	0	1	0	0	0	0	0	32	0
Anderson J.R.	1947–48	1	0	0	0	0	0	0	0	1	0
Anderson S.	1965–66	21	2	1	0	0	0	0	0	22	2
Anderson V.A.	1994	2	0	0	0	0	0	0	0	2	0
Angus M.A.	1979–82	35/2	1	1/1	0	4	0	0	0	40/3	2
Appleby R.	1959–67	99	0	6	0	5	0	0	0	110	0
Arca J.	2006–07	18/3	2	7	1	0	0	0	0	25/3	3
Armes S.	1938–39	3	0	0	0	0	0	0	0	3	0
Armstrong A.	1997–2000	10/19	4	0	0	4	0	0	0	14/19	4
Armstrong D.	1970–81	357/2	59	29	8	27/1	6	15	4	428/3	77
Arnold I.	1990–91	0/3	0	0	0	0	0	0	0	0/3	0
Ashcroft W.	1977–82	139/20	21	12/2	3	6	1	0	0	157/22	25
Ashman D.	1924–32	160	2	14	0	0	0	0	0	174	2
Askew W.	1980–82	10/2	0	0	0	0	0	0	0	10/2	0
Astley H.	1904–05	14	4	2	1	0	0	0	0	16	5
Atherton R.W.	1903–05	60	13	6	1	0	0	0	0	66	14
Auld W.B.	1950–51	2	1	0	0	0	0	0	0	2	1
Bailey I.C.	1975–82	140/4	1	13/1	1	10/1	0	6	1	169/6	3
Baird I.J.	1989–90	60/3	19	3	1	5/1	0	4	1	72/4	21
Baker S.R.	1997–2000	6/2	0	0/1	0	2/2	0	0	0	8/5	0
Barham M.F.	1988–89	3/1	0	0	0	0	0	0	0	3/1	0
Barker F.M.	1906–07	1	0	0	0	0	0	0	0	1	0
Barker W.C.	1905–13	105	2	8	0	0	0	0	0	113	2
Barmby N.J.	1995–96	42	8	3	1	4	1	0	0	49	10
Barnard R.S.	1951–60	113	0	5	0	0	0	0	0	118	0
Barron M.J.	1993–96	1/1	0	0	0	1/1	0	2/1	0	4/3	0
Bates M.D.	2005–07	14/6	0	2/2	0	1/2	0	5	0	22/10	0
Baxter M.J.	1981–84	122	7	9	1	7	0	0	0	138	8
Baxter R.D.	1932–39	247	19	19	1	0	0	0	0	266	20
Beagrie P.S.	1983–85	24/9	2	0	0	1	0	1/1	0	26/10	2
Beaton S.	1909–10	2	0	0	0	0	0	0	0	2	0
Beattie T.K.	1982–83	3/1	0	1	1	0	0	0	0	4/1	1
Beck M.V.	1996–98	66/25	24	5/3	2	14/2	5	0	0	85/30	31
Bell H.D.	1946–55	290	9	25	1	0	0	0	0	315	10
Bell I.C.	1977–81	10	1	0	0	0	0	0	0	10	1
Bell J.	1904–05	10	3	10	0	0	0	0	0	11	3
Bell J.N.	1934–35	2	0	0	0	0	0	0	0	2	0
Bell S.	1981–85	79/6	12	6	2	2/1	0	0	0	87/7	14
Bell W.	1899–1900	1	0	0	0	0	0	0	0	1	0
Beresford M.	1997–2001	8/2	0	0	0	3	0	0	0	11/2	0
Best C.	1910–11	5	1	0	0	0	0	0	0	5	1
Bilcliff R.	1951–61	182	0	8	0	0	0	0	0	190	0
Birbeck J.	1953–59	38	0	4	0	0	0	0	0	42	0
Birkett R.J.E.	1934–38	93	35	8	1	0	0	0	0	101	36
Birrell W.	1920–28	225	59	10	4	0	0	0	0	235	63
Bissett J.T.	1924–26	33	0	0	0	0	0	0	0	33	0
Blackburn C.	1980–81	1	0	0	0	0	0	0	0	1	0
Blackett J.	1901–05	78	4	6	0	0	0	0	0	84	4
Blackmore C.G.	1994–98	45/8	4	4/1	0	4/2	0	1	0	54/11	4
Blackmore H.A.	1932–33	19	9	4	3	0	0	0	0	23	12
Blenkinsopp T.W.	1948–52	98	0	2	0	0	0	0	0	100	0
Bloomer S.	1905–10	125	59	5	3	0	0	0	0	130	62
Boam S.W.	1971–79	322	14	29	0	27	2	15	0	393	16
Boardman H.	1909–10	4	0	0	0	0	0	0	0	4	0
Boateng G.	2002–07	148/1	6	12	1	8	0	16	1	184/1	8
Boddington H.	1903–04	1	0	0	0	0	0	0	0	1	0
Boersma P.	1975–77	41/6	3	3/1	0	1	0	3	1	48/7	4

Player	Played	LEAGUE A	LEAGUE G	FA CUP A	FA CUP G	FL CUP A	FL CUP G	OTHERS A	OTHERS G	TOTAL A	TOTAL G
Boksic A.	2000–03	59/9	22	4/3	0	1/1	0	0	0	64/13	22
Bolton J.	1981–83	59	1	5	0	5	0	0	0	69	1
Bottrill W.G.	1922–24	17	0	1	0	0	0	0	0	18	0
Braithwaite R.M.	1963–67	67/1	12	1	0	3	0	0	0	71/1	12
Branca M.	1998–99	11/1	9	0	0	2	1	0	0	13/1	10
Branco C.IVL.	1996–97	6/3	0	0	0	2	2	0	0	8/3	2
Brawn W.F.	1905–08	56	5	2	1	0	0	0	0	58	6
Brearley J.	1900–02	32	22	2	1	0	0	0	0	34	23
Brennan M.R.	1988–90	61/4	6	4	0	6	0	8	1	79/4	7
Briggs W.	1946–48	2	0	0	0	0	0	0	0	2	0
Brine P.K.	1972–77	59/20	6	7/2	1	4/1	1	6/2	0	76/25	8
Brown A.	1903–05	44	15	5	5	0	0	0	0	49	20
Brown A.S.	1912–13	4	0	0	0	0	0	0	0	4	0
Brown D.J.	1977–78	10	0	0	0	0	0	0	0	10	0
Brown James	1900–01	4	0	0	0	0	0	0	0	4	0
Brown John	1900–01	19	5	9	5	0	0	0	0	28	10
Brown J.R.	1906–08	25	0	1	0	0	0	0	0	26	0
Brown Joseph	1949–51	11	0	0	0	0	0	0	0	11	0
Brown T.	1920–23	5	0	0	0	0	0	0	0	5	0
Brown T.E.	1954–58	44	0	3	0	0	0	0	0	47	0
Brown W.H.	1931–46	256	2	18	0	0	0	0	0	274	2
Brownlie J.J.	1982–83	12	0	1	0	2	0	0	0	15	0
Bruce R.F.	1927–35	237	64	16	7	0	0	0	0	253	71
Bryan P.A.	1962–65	4	0	0	0	1	0	0	0	5	0
Bryan R.	1936–37	1	0	0	0	0	0	0	0	1	0
Buckley M.J.	1984–85	27	0	2	0	2	1	0	0	31	1
Buckley S.	1899–1900	1	0	0	0	0	0	0	0	1	0
Burbeck R.T.	1956–63	139	24	9	1	4	4	0	0	152	29
Burke M.S.	1987–90	32/25	6	2/1	0	3	0	2/1	0	39/27	6
Burluraux D.	1970–72	4/1	0	0	0	0	0	0	0	4/1	0
Burns M.E.	1978–81	58/3	24	2/1	0	3	0	0	0	63/4	24
Burton G.	1909–10	2	0	0	0	0	0	0	0	2	0
Butler G.	1965–67	54/1	1	5	0	2	0	0	0	61/1	1
Butler R.	1919–20	27	11	1	0	0	0	0	0	28	11
Butler T.	1938–39	2	0	0	0	0	0	0	0	2	0
Butler W.	1922–23	2	0	0	0	0	0	0	0	2	0
Caig H.	1914–15	1	0	0	0	0	0	0	0	1	0
Cail S.G.	1906–13	136	52	7	3	0	0	0	0	143	55
Callaghan J.	1899–1900	2	0	0	0	0	0	0	0	2	0
Cameron K.	1929–34	99	30	6	0	0	0	0	0	105	30
Campbell A.	1906–09	34	0	2	0	0	0	0	0	36	0
Campbell A.P.	1996–2001	28/28	4	2/3	2	5/5	1	0	0	35/36	7
Camsell G.H.	1925–39	418	325	35	20	0	0	0	0	453	345
Carbone B.	2002	13	1	0	0	0	0	0	0	13	1
Carr A.	1930–33	5	0	0	0	0	0	0	0	5	0
Carr G.	1919–24	67	23	3	0	0	0	0	0	70	23
Carr H.	1910–11	3	3	0	0	0	0	0	0	3	3
Carr J.	1910–30	421	75	28	6	0	0	0	0	449	81
Carr W.	1910–24	116	3	2	1	0	0	0	0	118	4
Carrick C.	1900–04	26	6	6	4	0	0	0	0	32	10
Cartwright H.P.	1925–26	6	0	0	0	0	0	0	0	6	0
Cassidy J.	1901–06	126	34	9	0	0	0	0	0	135	34
Cattermole L.B.	2005–07	32/13	2	11/1	1	1	0	3/2	0	47/16	3
Chadwick C.	1933–39	93	27	4	0	0	0	0	0	97	27
Chadwick D.E.	1966–70	100/2	3	7/1	0	6	1	0	0	113/3	4
Chapman N.	1961–67	51/2	0	2	0	5	0	0	0	58/2	0
Charlton H.	1970–75	8/2	0	1	0	1	0	1/2	0	11/4	0
Chipperfield F.	1919–20	1	0	0	0	0	0	0	0	1	0
Christie M.N.	2003–07	27/16	7	2/2	1	0/1	1	0/1	0	29/20	9
Clark E.	1899–1900	1	0	0	0	0	0	0	0	1	0
Clark J.	1899–1900	1	0	0	0	0	0	0	0	1	0
Clark W.	1919–21	8	0	1	0	0	0	0	0	9	0
Clough B.H.	1955–61	213	197	8	5	1	2	0	0	222	204
Clough J.	1922–26	124	0	4	0	0	0	0	0	128	0
Cochrane A.F.	1922–26	67	8	1	0	0	0	0	0	68	8
Cochrane G.T.	1978–83	96/15	7	12	4	5	1	0	0	113/15	12
Cochrane J.K	1973–74	3	0	0	0	0	0	1	0	4	0
Cochrane M.	1900–01	6	0	0	0	0	0	0	0	6	0
Cochrane T.	1936–39	80	16	1	0	0	0	0	0	81	16
Coleman Edward	1975–76	1	0	0	0	0	0	0	0	1	0
Coleman Ernest	1934–37	85	21	5	0	0	0	0	0	90	21
Coleman S.	1989–90	51/4	2	5	0	0	0	10	1	[illegible]	[illegible]

Player	Played	LEAGUE A	LEAGUE G	FA CUP A	FA CUP G	FL CUP A	FL CUP G	OTHERS A	OTHERS G	TOTAL A	TOTAL G
Collett A.A.	1992–94	2	0	0	0	0	0	3	0	5	0
Comfort A.	1989	15	2	0	0	3	1	0	0	18	3
Common A.	1905–10	168	58	10	7	0	0	0	0	178	65
Connachan E.D.	1963–66	95	0	4	0	6	0	0	0	105	0
Cook H.	1912–15	23	0	2	0	0	0	0	0	25	0
Cook J.	1911–15	52	3	2	0	0	0	0	0	54	3
Cook M.C.	1985–86	3/3	0	0	0	0	0	1/1	0	4/4	0
Cooper C.T.	1984–91 and 1998–06	322/24	11	18/1	0	32/1	0	24/1	3	396/27	14
Cooper D.	1955–57	5	0	0	0	0	0	0	0	5	0
Cooper T.	1974–78	105	1	7	0	11	0	10	0	133	1
Corbett R.	1951–57	92	0	5	0	0	0	0	0	97	0
Corden S.	1985–86	1	0	0	0	0	0	0	0	1	0
Cowan J.	1899–1900	17	0	0	0	0	0	0	0	17	0
Cox N.J.	1994–96	103/3	3	5	1	5/2	0	1/1	0	114/6	4
Coxon T.	1905–06	11	1	0	0	0	0	0	0	11	1
Coyle R.P.	1986–87	1/2	0	0/1	0	0	0	0	0	1/3	0
Craddock T.	2005–	0/1	0	0	0	0	0	0	0	0/1	0
Craggs J.E.	1971–82	408/1	12	33	0	31	1	15	1	487/1	14
Craig T.	1904–05	2	0	0	0	0	0	0	0	2	0
Crawford A.	1983–84	8/1	1	0	0	0	0	0	0	8/1	1
Crawford J.	1901–03	24	1	2	0	0	0	0	0	26	1
Creamer P.A.	1972–75	9	0	0	0	1/1	0	0	0	10/1	0
Crosier J.	1910–14	27	0	4	0	0	0	0	0	31	0
Crossan J.A.	1967–70	54/2	7	5	1	2	0	0	0	61/2	8
Crossley M.G.	2000–02	21/2	0	3	0	5	0	0	0	29/2	0
Cuff P.J.	1973–78	31	0	5	0	0	0	2/1	0	38/1	0
Cumming D.S.	1936–47	135	0	22	0	0	0	0	0	157	0
Cummins M.T.	1995–99	1/1	0	0	0	0	0	0	0	1/1	0
Cummins S.	1976–80	39/4	9	7	1	0/1	0	0	0	46/5	10
Cunliffe A.	1935–37	27	5	4	2	0	0	0	0	31	7
Currie D.N.	1982–86	94/19	30	5/1	0	6	1	2	0	107/20	31
Currie R.	1902–03	3	1	0	0	0	0	0	0	3	1
Curtis J.J.	1919–20	5	0	0	0	0	0	0	0	5	0
Davenport P.	1988–89	23/1	4	1	0	0	0	3	1	27/1	5
Davidson A.C.	1900–06	181	8	20	0	0	0	0	0	201	8
Davidson I.	1964–67	46	0	1	0	5	0	0	0	52	0
Davidson S.	1913–23	208	4	8	0	0	0	0	0	216	4
Davidson W.	1910–11	16	0	3	0	0	0	0	0	19	0
Davies A.S.	1914–15	1	0	1	0	0	0	0	0	2	0
Davies A.J	2002–07	36/13	0	2/1	0	3	0	4	0	41/14	0
Davies B.E.	1910–15	31	0	0	0	0	0	0	0	31	0
Davies W.A.	1904–05	10	0	2	0	0	0	0	0	12	0
Davison J.W.	1919–20	1	0	0	0	0	0	0	0	1	0
Day W.	1955–62	120	18	9	2	2	1	0	0	131	21
Deane B.C.	1998–2001	72/15	18	3	1	4/1	0	0	0	79/16	19
Debeve M.	2002	1/3	0	1/1	0	0	0	0	0	2/4	0
Delapenha L.L.	1949–58	260	90	10	3	0	0	0	0	270	93
Desmond P.	1949–50	2	0	0	0	0	0	0	0	2	0
Dews G.	1946–48	33	8	6	0	0	0	0	0	39	8
Dibble A.G.	1991 and 1998–99	21	0	0	0	0	0	2	0	23	0
Dickinson P.E.	1924–25	6	1	0	0	0	0	0	0	6	1
Dicks R.W.	1947–58	316	10	18	0	0	0	0	0	334	10
Dickson I.W.	1923–25	37	12	1	0	0	0	0	0	38	12
Dixon C.	1919–21	12	0	0	0	0	0	0	0	12	0
Dixon T.	1907–11	27	8	2	1	0	0	0	0	29	9
Dobbie H.	1946–50	23	6	1	2	0	0	0	0	24	8
Doig T.	1900–01	3	0	1	0	0	0	0	0	4	0
Donaghy P.	1919–23	30	2	0	0	0	0	0	0	30	2
Donaldson A.	1948–51	21	7	0	0	0	0	0	0	21	7
Doriva G.D.	2003–	56/23	0	4/1	1	9/1	0	15/1	0	84/26	1
Douglas H.	1902–03	4	0	0	0	0	0	0	0	4	0
Douglas J.S.	1946–47	2	0	0	0	0	0	0	0	2	0
Dow J.M.	1900–02	34	0	7	0	0	0	0	0	41	0
Downing D.G.	1965–72	173/10	39	22/1	7	5	2	3	1	203/1	49
Downing S.	2001–07	82/24	8	17	0	3/2	1	17/1	1	119/27	10
Dowson F.	1920–21	7	2	0	0	0	0	0	0	7	2
Duffy C.F.	1905–06	4	0	0	0	0	0	0	0	4	0
Duguid W.	1910–13	23	0	1	0	0	0	0	0	24	0
Eckford J.	1900–01	4	0	3	0	0	0	0	0	7	0
Edwards W.I.	1952–55	16	4	0	0	0	0	0	0	16	4

Player	Played	LEAGUE A	LEAGUE G	FA CUP A	FA CUP G	FL CUP A	FL CUP G	OTHERS A	OTHERS G	TOTAL A	TOTAL G
Eglington R.	1899–1900	5	2	1	1	0	0	0	0	6	3
Ehiogu U.	2000–	122/4	7	9/1	1	7	0	4/3	0	142/8	8
Elkes A.J.	1929–33	105	4	8	0	0	0	0	0	113	4
Ellerington W.	1919–24	127	0	4	0	0	0	0	0	131	0
Elliott G.W.	1909–25	344	203	21	10	0	0	0	0	365	213
Emerson M.C.	1996–97	32	4	5	1	8	2	0	0	45	7
Emmerson G.A.H.	1928–30	7	3	0	0	0	0	0	0	7	3
Emmerson M.	1962–63	10	0	3	0	0	0	0	0	13	0
Euell J.	2006–07	9/8	0	0/2	0	0/1	0	0	0	9/11	0
Eustace J.M.	2003	0/1	0	0	0	0	0	0	0	0/1	0
Evans R.W.	1899–1900	2	0	0	0	0	0	0	0	2	0
Eyre E.	1911–14	63	13	6	2	0	0	0	0	69	15
Falconer W.H.	1991–92	47/6	10	3	2	2/1	0	0	0	52/7	12
Featherstone T.F.	1903–04	1	0	0	0	0	0	0	0	1	0
Fenton M.	1932–50	240	147	29	15	0	0	0	0	269	162
Ferguson C.	1933–36	19	7	1	1	0	0	0	0	20	8
Ferguson R.	1936–38	10	0	0	0	0	0	0	0	10	0
Ferguson R.G.	1924–31	149	2	10	0	0	0	0	0	159	2
Fernie W.	1958–61	65	3	2	0	1	0	0	0	68	3
Festa G.	1997–2001	132/6	10	14/1	1	18	1	0	0	164/7	12
Fitzsimons A.G.	1949–59	223	49	8	2	0	0	0	0	231	51
Fjortoft J.A.	1994–96	37/4	10	0/2	1	7	2	0	0	44/6	13
Fleming C.	1991–2000	248/18	3	16/1	0	24/2	1	7/1	0	295/22	4
Flint W.	1909–10	1	0	0	0	0	0	0	0	1	0
Foggon A.	1972–76	105/10	45	10/1	2	9/1	2	4/1	1	128/13	50
Forrest W.	1929–39	307	7	26	1	0	0	0	0	333	8
Forrester P.	1993	0/1	0	0	0	0	0	0	0	0/1	0
Fowler H.N.	1937–39	7	0	0	0	0	0	0	0	7	0
Fox W.V.	1919–24	107	1	5	0	0	0	0	0	112	1
Frail J.M.	1900–05	63	0	11	0	0	0	0	0	74	0
Fraser A.	1911–13	5	0	0	0	0	0	0	0	5	0
Freeman R.V.	1923–30	179	0	8	0	0	0	0	0	187	0
Freeman T.	1930–33	74	0	4	0	0	0	0	0	78	0
Freestone C.M.	1994–98	2/7	1	0/2	0	1/1	1	0	0	3/10	2
French J.P.	1924–25	1	0	0	0	0	0	0	0	1	0
Fuchs U.	1995	13/2	9	0	0	0	0	0	0	13/2	9
Gallacher C.	1946–47	1	0	0	0	0	0	0	0	1	0
Gallagher J.	1920–21	1	0	0	0	0	0	0	0	1	0
Gannon J.S.	1993	6/1	0	0	0	0	0	2	0	8/1	0
Garbett T.G.	1965–66	7	1	0	0	0	0	0	0	7	1
Gascoigne P.J.	1997–99	39/2	4	2	0	3/2	0	0	0	44/4	4
Gates W.L.	1961–74	277/6	12	26/2	0	18	0	4	1	325/8	13
Gavin J.J.	1996–2002	19/12	0	1/2	0	5/1	0	0	0	25/18	0
Geremi N.F.S.	2002	33	7	1	0	0	0	0	0	34	7
Gettins E.	1903–05	43	5	4	0	0	0	0	0	47	5
Gettins J.H.	1899–1903	10	1	0	0	0	0	0	0	10	1
Gibson F.W.	1932–36	110	0	10	0	0	0	0	0	120	0
Gibson I.S.	1961–66	168	44	9	1	7	2	0	0	184	47
Gibson R.J.	1910–11	28	3	3	0	0	0	0	0	31	3
Gill G.	1983–89	69/8	2	4/1	0	4/2	0	6/1	0	83/12	2
Gittens J.A.	1991–92	22/3	1	1	0	0/1	0	0	0	23/4	1
Glover D.V.	1987–89	44/6	5	5	0	4	0	3	2	56/6	7
Godley W.	1902–04	2	0	0	0	0	0	0	0	2	0
Good H.J.	1924–26	10	0	0	0	0	0	0	0	10	0
Goodfellow D.O.	1947–48	36	0	3	0	0	0	0	0	39	0
Goodson L.	1902–05	35	6	1	0	0	0	0	0	36	6
Gordon D.	1908–09	1	0	0	0	0	0	0	0	1	0
Gordon D.D.	1998–2001	53/10	4	3	0	5	0	0	0	61/10	4
Gordon J.	1946–54	231	3	22	1	0	0	0	0	253	4
Gowland N.	1925–29	5	0	0	0	0	0	0	0	5	0
Graham D.A.W.	2004–07	1/14	1	0/2	0	0/2	1	1/1	0	2/19	2
Gray R.S.M.	1899–1900	3	0	0	0	0	0	0	0	3	0
Green T.	1904–06	37	9	5	0	0	0	0	0	42	9
Greening J.	2000–03	91/8	4	4/1	0	5	0	0	0	100/9	4
Griffiths T.P.	1932–35	88	1	4	0	0	0	0	0	92	1
Groves J.A.	1907–10	27	2	0	0	0	0	0	0	27	2
Hall B.A.C.	1927–30	7	2	0	0	0	0	0	0	7	2
Hall J.H.	1908–10	59	30	3	0	0	0	0	0	62	30
Hamilton G.J.	1982–88	217/12	25	14	1	13	1	11/1	1	255/13	28
Hamilton W.M.	1960–62	10	1	0	0	2	0	0	0	12	1
Hankin R.	1982–83	19/2	1	3	1	2	1	0	0	24/2	3
Hanlon E.	1906–07	1	0	0	0	0	0	0	0	1	0

Player	Played	LEAGUE		FA CUP		FL CUP		OTHERS		TOTAL	
		A	G	A	G	A	G	A	G	A	G
Hardwick G.F.M.	1937–50	143	5	23	2	0	0	0	0	166	7
Harkins J.	1906–07	39	0	2	0	0	0	0	0	41	0
Harris J.	1922–25	56	0	2	0	0	0	0	0	58	0
Harris W.C.	1953–65	360	69	14	2	4	1	0	0	378	72
Harrison C.	1996–99	19/5	0	2	0	4/2	0	0	0	25/7	0
Harrison H.	1919–22	20	0	0	0	0	0	0	0	20	0
Hartnett J.B.	1948–55	48	8	1	0	0	0	0	0	49	8
Hassell A.A.	1907–08	1	0	0	0	0	0	0	0	1	0
Hasselbaink J.F.	2004–05	48/10	22	7/1	3	3	1	17/3	7	75/14	33
Hastie J.	1920–21	1	0	0	0	0	0	0	0	1	0
Hawkins G.H.	1935–36	1	0	0	0	0	0	0	0	1	0
Haworth J.H.	1911–15	61	0	3	0	0	0	0	0	64	0
Healey R.	1913–15	4	2	0	0	0	0	0	0	4	2
Heard T.P.	1985–86	25	2	1	0	0	0	2	0	28	2
Hedley G.T.	1905–06	3	0	0	0	0	0	0	0	3	0
Hedley G.	1976–81	36/14	6	3	0	4	0	3	0	46/14	6
Henderson G.H.	1905–06	10	0	3	0	0	0	0	0	13	0
Henderson R.	1957–61	9	5	0	0	0	0	0	0	9	5
Hendrie J.G.	1990–96	181/11	44	10/2	2	22/2	6	6	3	219/15	55
Hepple G.	1946–54	41	0	0	0	0	0	0	0	41	0
Hewitt C.W.	1904–06	33	12	5	2	0	0	0	0	38	14
Hewitt J.	1991	0/2	0	0	0	0	0	0	0	0/2	0
Hick W.M.	1923–25	16	7	1	0	0	0	0	0	17	7
Hickling W.	1906–07	5	0	0	0	0	0	0	0	5	0
Hickton J.	1966–77	395/20	159	37	13	26/4	13	15/2	7	473/26	187
Higgins W.	1900–01	24	1	5	3	0	0	0	0	29	4
Higham N.	1935–39	49	10	1	0	0	0	0	0	50	10
Hignett C.J.	1992–97	126/30	33	9/2	3	19/3	12	5/1	0	159/36	48
Hillier E.J.G.	1929–35	63	0	2	0	0	0	0	0	65	0
Hisbent J.S.	1911–15	44	0	3	0	0	0	0	0	47	0
Hodgson D.J.	1978–86	118/9	16	9	4	6	0	1	0	134/9	20
Hodgson G.	1900–01	4	0	0	0	0	0	0	0	4	0
Hodgson J.P.	1947–55	13	0	0	0	0	0	0	0	13	0
Hogg J.	1902–06	90	0	10	0	0	0	0	0	100	0
Holliday E.	1957–66	157	21	6	3	6	1	0	0	169	25
Holliday J.W.	1930–32	6	4	0	0	0	0	0	0	6	4
Holmes W.	1914–27	167	1	7	0	0	0	0	0	174	1
Honeyman J.W.	1919–20	1	0	0	0	0	0	0	0	1	0
Horne B.S.	1992	3/1	0	0	0	0	0	0	0	3/1	0
Horner W.	1960–69	184/3	11	17	0	12/1	1	0	0	213/4	12
Horsfield A.	1963–69	107/4	51	12/2	5	2	0	0	0	121/6	56
Howling E.	1910–11	1	0	0	0	0	0	0	0	1	0
Hudson M.	1999–2003	0/5	0	0/1	0	0	0	0	0	0/6	0
Hughes M.	1899–1900	24	0	1	0	0	0	0	0	25	0
Hume R.	1962–63	19	5	0	0	2	0	0	0	21	5
Hunter H.	1905–06	3	0	0	0	0	0	0	0	3	0
Huth R.	2006–07	8/4	1	0/1	0	1	0	0	0	9/5	1
Illman N.D.	1993	0/1	0	0	0	0/1	0	3/1	0	3/3	0
Ince P.E.C.	1999–2001	93	7	7	1	6	1	0	0	106	9
Ironside I.	1991–92	12/1	0	0	0	2	0	0	0	14/1	0
Irvine J.	1964–67	90/1	37	4	3	5	3	0	0	99/1	43
Jackson A.	1910–15	123	3	14	0	0	0	0	0	137	3
James W.E.	1910–13	24	8	3	1	0	0	0	0	27	9
Jankovic B.	1978–81	42/8	16	7	1	3/2	1	0	0	52/10	18
Jarvis S.	1927–35	86	1	4	0	0	0	0	0	90	1
Jennings J.	1929–37	195	10	10	0	0	0	0	0	205	10
Jennings S.	1919–20	10	2	0	0	0	0	0	0	10	2
Job J.D.	2000–06	62/30	16	4/1	2	4/4	1	4/2	2	74/37	21
Johnson A.	2005–07	12/7	1	1	0	1	0	2/2	0	16/9	1
Johnson I.	1994–95	1/1	0	0	0	0	0	0/1	0	1/2	0
Johnson P.E.	1977–80	42/1	0	3	1	0	0	0	0	45/1	1
Johnston A.	2001–03	13/4	1	2/1	0	3	0	0	0	18/5	1
Johnston C.P.	1947–48	2	0	0	0	0	0	0	0	2	0
Johnston Craig	1977–81	61/3	16	5/2	0	4/2	0	0	0	70/7	16
Jones A.	1901–06	140	9	9	0	0	0	0	0	149	9
Jones B.	1999–2007	17	0	5/1	0	0	0	4	0	26/1	0
Jones G.W.	1925–26	24	1	2	0	0	0	0	0	26	1
Jones G.E.	1960–73	457/5	4	40	0	26	1	4	0	527/5	5
Jones J.	1899–1905	7	0	2	0	0	0	0	0	9	0
Jones J.L.	1908–10	14	0	0	0	0	0	0	0	14	0
Jordan B.A.	1958–59	5	0	0	0	0	0	0	0	5	0
Juninho J.G.O.	1995–96, 1999										

Player	Played	LEAGUE A	LEAGUE G	FA CUP A	FA CUP G	FL CUP A	FL CUP G	OTHERS A	OTHERS G	TOTAL A	TOTAL G
	and 2002–04	113/12	29	10/1	2	18/1	3	0	0	141/14	34
Kamara C.	1993	3/2	0	0	0	0	0	0	0	3/2	0
Karembeu C.L.	2000–01	31/2	4	1/1	0	0	0	0	0	32/3	4
Kavanagh G.A.	1991–95	22/13	3	2/2	1	1	0	7	0	32/15	4
Kay J.	1984–85	8	0	0	0	0	0	0	0	8	0
Kaye A.	1960–65	164	38	13	4	8	2	0	0	185	44
Kear M.P.	1967–70	56/2	7	5	0	3	0	0	0	64/2	7
Kelly B.	1910–11	4	0	0	0	0	0	0	0	4	0
Kennedy F.	1927–29	23	5	1	0	0	0	0	0	24	5
Kennedy J.B.	2005–	1/3	0	0	0	0	0	1/2	0	2/5	0
Kennedy M.F.M.	1982–84	68	5	7	0	4	0	0	0	79	5
Kent H.	1908–09	6	0	0	0	0	0	0	0	6	0
Kernaghan A.N.	1985–93	172/40	16	7/4	3	22/7	1	14/2	2	213/53	22
Kerr P.A.	1986–90	114/11	13	9/2	3	10	1	13/3	1	146/16	18
Kilgannon S.	1999–2001	0/1	0	0	0	0	0	0	0	0/1	0
Kinder V.	1996–97	29/8	5	3/1	0	7/1	0	0	0	39/10	5
Kinnell G.	1968–69	12/1	1	1	0	0	0	0	0	13/1	1
Kirby F.	1913–14	2	0	0	0	0	0	0	0	2	0
Kirk H.J.	1963–64	1	0	0	0	1	0	0	0	2	0
Kite P.D.	1985–86	2	0	0	0	0	0	0	0	2	0
Knowles C.B.	1962–64	37	0	1	0	1	0	0	0	39	0
Laidlaw J.D.	1967–72	103/5	20	9/2	1	5	1	4	1	121/7	23
Laking G.E.	1936–47	94	1	3	0	0	0	0	0	97	1
Lamb T.J.	1899–1900	23	6	1	0	0	0	0	0	24	6
Lawrie S.	1951–57	36	5	1	0	0	0	0	0	37	5
Laws B.	1984–87	103/5	12	8/1	0	6/1	2	5	0	122/7	14
Lawson J.J.	1965–68	25/6	3	4	1	2	0	0	0	31/6	4
Layton A.E.	1911–12	7	0	1	0	0	0	0	0	8	0
Lee D.G.	2006–07	3/6	0	0/20	0	0	0	0	0	3/8	0
Le Flem R.P.	1964–66	9	1	1	0	0	0	0	0	10	1
Leonard H.D.	1910–12	13	3	0	0	0	0	0	0	13	3
Leslie J.	1901–02	7	3	0	0	0	0	0	0	7	3
Liburd R.J.	1992–93	41	1	2	0	4	0	5	0	52	1
Liddle C.G.	1994–97	20/5	0	2	0	3/2	0	2	0	27/7	0
Lightening A.D.	1962–63	15	0	0	0	3	0	0	0	18	0
Linacre W.	1949–50	31	2	4	1	0	0	0	0	35	3
Linton T.	1899–1900	4	0	0	0	0	0	0	0	4	0
Linwood A.B.	1946–47	14	3	1	0	0	0	0	0	15	3
Livingstone J.	1960–63	20	7	0	0	2	0	0	0	22	7
Lloyd E.	1919–20	2	0	0	0	0	0	0	0	2	0
Longstaffe G.	1899–1900	19	3	1	0	0	0	0	0	20	3
Lugg R.	1966–70	34/3	3	2	1	1/2	0	0	0	37/5	4
Lynch P.	1971–72	0/1	0	0	0	0	0	0	0	0/1	0
MacAulay W.	1902–03	21	2	0	0	0	0	0	0	21	2
MacDonald G.	1980–85	40/13	5	4/1	1	2/1	0	0	0	46/15	6
MacFarlane J.	1929–33	95	0	6	0	0	0	0	0	101	0
MacFarlane R.	1902–03	18	0	1	0	0	0	0	0	19	0
MacFarlane T.	1901–02	2	0	1	0	0	0	0	0	3	0
Maccarone M.	2002–06	45/29	17	0/5	0	5/2	1	3/5	5	53/41	23
Madden G.	1899–1900	3	0	0	0	0	0	0	0	3	0
Maddison J.	1946–47	1	0	0	0	0	0	0	0	1	0
Maddison N.S.	1997–2000	32/24	4	4	0	7/1	0	0	0	43/25	4
Maddren W.D.	1968–77	293/3	19	23	0	24	2	11	0	351/3	21
Mahoney J.F.	1977–79	77	1	7	1	6	0	0	0	90	2
Maitland A.E.	1923–24	25	0	1	0	0	0	0	0	26	0
Malan N.F.	1946–47	2	0	0	0	0	0	0	0	2	0
Malcolm G.	1912–15	94	1	7	0	0	0	0	0	101	1
Mannion W.J.	1936–54	341	99	27	11	0	0	0	0	368	110
Marcroft E.H.	1931–32	1	1	0	0	0	0	0	0	1	1
Marinelli C.A.	1999–2001	18/25	3	3/2	0	3/2	1	0	0	24/29	4
Marshall D.W.	1993	0/3	0	0	0	0	0	0	0	0/3	0
Marshall J.	1919–23	116	0	5	0	0	0	0	0	121	0
Marshall S.K.	1965–66	2	0	0	0	0	0	0	0	2	0
Martin G.S.	1932–33	6	0	0	0	0	0	0	0	6	0
Martin J.	1932–39	129	3	8	0	0	0	0	0	137	3
Marwood B.	1991	3	0	0	0	2	0	0	0	5	0
Masson D.S.	1964–68	50/3	6	7	1	4	0	0	0	61/3	7
Mathieson J.A.	1926–33	245	0	19	0	0	0	0	0	264	0
Mattinson H.	1946–47	3	0	0	0	0	0	0	0	3	0
McAllister W.	1924–26	19	0	2	0	0	0	0	0	21	0
McAndrew A.	1973–86	311/2	15	23/1	2	15/2	1	4	0	353/5	18
McCabe J.J.	1946–48	34	0	8	0	0	0	0	0	42	0

Player	Played	LEAGUE		FA CUP		FL CUP		OTHERS		TOTAL	
		A	G	A	G	A	G	A	G	A	G
McCallum D.	1904–06	25	0	2	0	0	0	0	0	27	0
McClelland J.	1924–28	81	42	4	6	0	0	0	0	85	48
McClure S.	1910–11	11	3	1	0	0	0	0	0	12	3
McCormack J.C.	1946–49	37	15	2	1	0	0	0	0	39	16
McCorquodale D.	1899–1900	2	0	0	0	0	0	0	0	2	0
McCowie A.	1900–01	16	5	4	2	0	0	0	0	20	7
McCracken P.J.	1899–1900	33	0	1	0	0	0	0	0	34	0
McCrae A.	1948–53	122	47	8	2	0	0	0	0	130	49
McCreesh A.	1981–82	2	0	0	0	0	0	0	0	2	0
McCulloch A.	1907–08	3	1	0	0	0	0	0	0	3	1
McGee O.E.	1989–90	18/3	1	1/1	0	2/4	0	2/2	0	23/10	1
McGuigan A.	1902–04	1	0	0	0	0	0	0	0	1	0
McIlmoyle H.	1969–71	69/1	19	8	2	2	1	2	0	81/1	22
McKay J.R.	1926–34	104	19	5	1	0	0	0	0	109	20
McKennan P.S.	1949–51	40	18	3	1	0	0	0	0	43	19
McKenzie D.	1938–39	28	1	0	0	0	0	0	0	28	1
McLean J.D.	1955–62	119	30	3	0	1	0	0	0	123	30
McLeod D.	1908–13	138	0	10	0	0	0	0	0	148	0
McMahon A.	2005–07	15/1	0	1/1	0	1/1	0	4	0	21/3	0
McManus C.E.	1985–86	2	0	0	0	0	0	0	0	2	0
McMordie A.	1965–74	231/10	22	20./1	1	11	2	4	1	266/11	26
McMurray J.D.	1953–55	3	0	0	0	0	0	0	0	3	0
McNally J.	1899–1901	3	0	1	0	0	0	0	0	4	0
McNeil M.	1958–64	178	3	9	0	6	0	0	0	193	3
McNeill A.	1967–69	3	0	0/1	0	0	0	0	0	3/1	0
McPartland D.	1965–68	35	0	2	0	3	0	0	0	40	0
McPhail D.D.	1930–31	4	1	1	0	0	0	0	0	5	1
McPherson K.	1953–56	33	15	0	0	0	0	0	0	33	15
McRobbie A.	1911–12	1	0	0	0	0	0	0	0	1	0
Mendieta G.	2003–07	56/6	4	7	1	7	1	6/1	0	76/7	6
Merson P.C.	1997–98	48	11	3	1	7	3	0	0	58	15
Millar J.	1900–03	19	0	3	0	0	0	0	0	22	0
Millar W.M.	1927–29	16	6	0	0	0	0	0	0	16	6
Miller A.J.	1994–96	57	0	2	0	3	0	2	0	64	0
Miller J.	1926–30	140	0	13	0	0	0	0	0	153	0
Million E.	1956–62	52	0	1	0	0	0	0	0	53	0
Mills Danny	2003	28	0	2	0	7	0	0	0	37	0
Mills David	1969–85	309/19	90	29	10	23/1	8	17	3	378/20	111
Milne J.V.	1937–39	59	7	7	0	0	0	0	0	66	7
Mitchell A.J.	1954–56	50	6	2	0	0	0	0	0	52	6
Mochan N.	1951–53	38	14	1	0	0	0	0	0	39	14
Mohan N.	1987–93	93/6	4	9/1	0	11	0	11	0	124/7	4
Moody A.	1968–73	44/2	0	3	0	0	0	0/2	0	47/4	0
Moore A.	1991–2000	98/20	14	3/2	2	9/6	1	3/1	0	113/29	17
Moran M.	1900–02	36	5	9	1	0	0	0	0	45	6
Mordue J.	1920–22	35	1	0	0	0	0	0	0	35	1
Moreira F.S.	1997	1	0	0	0	0	0	0	0	1	0
Moreno J.M.	1994–96 and 1997	9/17	2	2/1	0	3	0	3	1	17/18	3
Morris C.B.	1992–96	75/7	3	6	0	12	0	4	1	97/7	4
Morrison J.C.	2003–07	40/27	3	6/7	1	3/1	1	11/3	3	60/38	8
Mowbray A.M.	1982–91	345/3	25	23	1	28/2	2	23/1	1	419/6	29
Muir J.	1902–04	13	0	0	0	0	0	0	0	13	0
Muir W.	1902–04	4	0	0	0	0	0	0	0	4	0
Mulholland F.G.	1951–58	46	0	4	0	0	0	0	0	50	0
Murdoch R.W.	1973–76	93/2	6	7	1	13	0	9/1	2	122/3	9
Murphy D.A.	1937–38	120	3	0	0	0	0	0	0	15	0
Murphy T.E.	1946–48	9	1	0	0	0	0	0	0	9	1
Murphy J.	1899–1900	6	5	0	0	0	0	0	0	6	5
Murphy M.	1899–1900	2	2	0	0	0	0	0	0	2	2
Murray A.	1969–71	6/4	1	0	0	0	0	0	0	6/4	1
Murray T.	1905–07	12	2	0	0	0	0	0	0	12	2
Murray W.	1921–23	15	1	2	0	0	0	0	0	17	1
Mustoe R.	1990–01	327/38	25	29/1	2	44/3	7	12/1	0	412/43	34
Muttit E.	1929–32	20	3	5	1	0	0	0	0	25	4
Myton B.	1968–71	10	0	0	0	2	0	0	0	12	0
Nash C.J.	2003–04	3	0	0	0	2	0	0	0	5	0
Nash F.C.	1937–48	19	0	0	0	0	0	0	0	19	0
Nattrass I.	1979–86	186/5	2	18	0	10/1	0	1	0	215/6	2
Neal R.M.	1961–63	33	4	2	0	3	0	0	0	38	4
Nemeth S.	2001–06	62/55	23	4/3	1	7/3	4	8/4	1	81/65	29
Niblo T.B.	1899–1900	3	2	0	0	0	0	0	0	3	2

Player	Played	LEAGUE A	LEAGUE G	FA CUP A	FA CUP G	FL CUP A	FL CUP G	OTHERS A	OTHERS G	TOTAL A	TOTAL G
Nicholl J.	1910–14	52	13	4	0	0	0	0	0	56	13
Nobbs A.K.	1980–81	1	0	0	0	0	0	0	0	1	0
Norris O.	1951–54	12	3	1	0	0	0	0	0	13	3
Nurse M.TG.	1962–66	113	8	8	1	3	0	0	0	124	9
O'Connell S.	1953–54	3	2	2	0	0	0	0	0	5	2
O'Hagan C.	1906–07	5	1	0	0	0	0	0	0	5	1
O'Halloran K.J.	1994–96	3/1	0	2	0	0	0	1	0	6/1	0
O'Hanlon K.G.	1982–85	87	0	6	0	4	0	0	0	97	0
Okon P.M.	2000–01	24/4	0	2	0	0	0	0	0	26/4	0
O'Neill K.P.G.	1999–2000	32/5	0	1	0	3/1	0	0	0	36/6	0
O'Riordan D.J.	1985–86	41	2	1	1	2	0	2	1	46	4
Ormerod A.	1996–2001	8/11	3	2	0	2/2	0	0	0	12/13	3
O'Rourke J.	1966–68	63/1	38	3	3	5	1	0	0	77/1	42
Orritt B.	1961–66	115/3	22	4	1	6	0	0	0	125/3	23
Osborne F.	1899–1900	12	2	0	0	0	0	0	0	12	2
Ostler J.	1899–1900	3	0	0	0	0	0	0	0	3	0
Otto H.M.	1981–85	163/4	24	12	2	9	2	0	0	184/3	28
Page R.	1899–1904	22	4	10	0	0	0	0	0	23	4
Pallister G.A.	1984–88 and 1998–2000	211	6	12	1	14	0	13	0	250	7
Parkin R.	1935–37	6	0	0	0	0	0	0	0	6	0
Parkinson G.A.	1986–92	194/8	5	17	1	20	1	19	0	250/8	7
Parlour R.	2004–	43/3	0	2/2	0	0	0	8/2	0	53/7	0
Parnaby S.	1999–2007	73/18	2	11/1	1	5/3	0	13/3	1	102/26	4
Paterson T.	1974–75	1	0	0	0	0	0	0	0	1	0
Patterson R.L.	1951–52	1	0	0	0	0	0	0	0	1	0
Payton A.P.	1991–92	8/11	3	1/3	0	0	0	0	0	9/14	3
Peacock A.	1955–64	218	125	13	8	7	8	0	0	238	141
Peacock J.	1927–30	80	2	5	2	0	0	0	0	85	4
Peake A.M.	1991–93	83/3	1	8	0	6	0	0	0	97/3	1
Pears S.	1983 and 1985–94	339	0	25	0	32	0	28	0	424	0
Pearson N.G.	1994–97	115/1	5	9	0	14	0	0	0	138/1	5
Pease W.H.	1926–33	221	99	17	3	0	0	0	0	238	102
Peggie J.	1910–11	6	0	0	0	0	0	0	0	6	0
Pender R.	1919–24	104	10	6	0	0	0	0	0	110	10
Pentland F.B.	1908–11	92	11	4	0	0	0	0	0	96	11
Peters J.	1979–80	6	0	0	0	0	0	0	0	6	0
Phillips J.N.	1989–92	139	6	10	0	16	0	5/2	0	170/2	6
Phillips J.B.	1954–60	121	2	3	0	0	0	0	0	124	2
Phillipson T.F.	1904–05	3	2	0	0	0	0	0	0	3	2
Piercy F.R.	1899–1903	4	0	1	0	0	0	0	0	5	0
Piercy H.R.	1899–1900	8	1	0	0	0	0	0	0	8	1
Platt J.A.	1971–83	401	0	34	0	33	0	13	0	481	0
Pogatetz E.	2005–07	56/3	3	12	0	2/1	0	9	0	79/4	3
Pollock J.	1991–96	144/11	17	13/1	1	17/2	1	4/1	0	178/15	19
Poole K.	1987–90	34	0	2	0	4	0	2	0	42	0
Posket M.	1973–74	0/1	0	0	0	0	0	0	0	0/1	0
Poulton A.	1919–22	18	5	10	0	0	0	0	0	19	5
Povey W.	1962–63	6	0	0	0	0	0	0	0	6	0
Pratt R.	1899–1900	16	1	1	0	0	0	0	0	17	1
Priest A.E.	1906–07	12	0	0	0	0	0	0	0	12	0
Priest F.	1906–07	1	0	0	0	0	0	0	0	1	0
Proctor M.G.	1978–80 and 1988–92	208/21	18	14/3	1	13/2	1	11/1	0	246/27	20
Proudlock P.	1986–89	2/3	1	0	0	0	0	1	2	3/3	3
Pugh C.E.	1899–1900	31	7	1	0	0	0	0	0	32	7
Putney T.A.	1989–90	45/3	1	2	0	5	0	5	0	57/3	1
Queudrue F.	2001–05	145/5	11	14	0	11/1	1	18/5	0	188/11	12
Raisbeck L.	1899–1900	19	1	0	0	0	0	0	0	19	1
Ramage A.	1975–80	65/4	2	6	0	5	0	1	0	77/4	2
Ramsay A.	1899–1904	124	1	12	0	0	0	0	0	136	1
Ratcliffe D.	1963–66	65	3	6	0	0	0	0	0	71	3
Ratcliffe E.	1905–07	9	0	0	0	0	0	0	0	9	0
Ravaenelli F.	1996–97	35	17	7	6	8	9	0	0	50	32
Rayment J.W.	1952–55	24	4	0	0	0	0	0	0	24	4
Reagan C.M.	1947–51	24	4	1	0	0	0	0	0	25	4
Redfern J.	1899–1900	3	0	0	0	0	0	0	0	3	0
Reid G.	1899–1900	15	5	0	0	0	0	0	0	15	5
Reid G.T.	1905–06	24	5	20	0	0	0	0	0	26	5
Reiziger M.J.	2004–05	15/3	1	2	0	0	0	4/1	0	21/4	1
Ricard C.H.	1998–2002	92/23	33	6	2	11/2	8	0	0	109/25	43

Player	Played	LEAGUE A	LEAGUE G	FA CUP A	FA CUP G	FL CUP A	FL CUP G	OTHERS A	OTHERS G	TOTAL A	TOTAL G
Rickaby S.	1947–50	10	0	0	0	0	0	0	0	10	0
Ricketts M.B.	2002–03	12/20	3	2	0	3/2	1	0	0	17/22	4
Rigby A.	1932–33	10	3	0	0	0	0	0	0	10	3
Riggott C.M.	2002–07	65/6	4	8/1	1	8/1	0	21	2	102/8	7
Ripley S.E.	1985–91	210/39	26	17/1	1	21/2	3	20/1	1	268/43	31
Roberts A.	1983–84	28/10	2	0/1	0	2/1	0	0	0	30/12	2
Roberts B.J.	1993–99	15/1	0	6	0	2/1	0	1	0	24/2	0
Roberts J.	1906–07	1	0	0	0	0	0	0	0	1	0
Roberts R.J.	1903–05	23	5	0	0	0	0	0	0	23	5
Roberts W.S.	1906–08	12	0	0	0	0	0	0	0	12	0
Robertson A.	1900–03	48	24	8	8	0	0	0	0	56	32
Robertson J.	1901–03	32	3	0	0	0	0	0	0	32	3
Robertson W.G.	1954–55	5	2	0	0	0	0	0	0	5	2
Robinson J.	1953–55	3	0	0	0	0	0	0	0	3	0
Robinson J.W.	1919–20	1	0	0	0	0	0	0	0	1	0
Robinson J.N.	1946–48	16	0	1	0	0	0	0	0	17	0
Robinson R.	1946–59	390	1	26	0	0	0	0	0	416	1
Robson B.	1994–97	23/2	1	1	0	1	0	0	0	25/2	1
Rochemback F.	2005–07	39/3	4	6/1	1	3	0	5/1	0	53/5	5
Rodgerson A.R.	1958–64	13	3	0	0	1	0	0	0	14	3
Rooks R.	1965–69	136	14	7	0	7	0	0	0	150	14
Ross A.C.	1935–37	11	0	1	0	0	0	0	0	12	0
Ross C.	1980–83	37/1	0	2	0	0	0	0	0	39/1	0
Rowell G.	1985–87	27	10	1	0	2	2	1	0	31	12
Russell E.T.	1951–53	29	1	3	0	0	0	0	0	32	1
Russell M.C.	1990–91	10/1	2	0	0	2/1	0	0	0	12/2	2
Saxby M.W.	1984–85	15	0	2	0	0	0	0	0	17	0
Schwarzer M.	1996–2007	333	0	27	0	26	0	21	0	407	0
Scott W.R.	1930–32	26	5	2	0	0	0	0	0	28	5
Scott G.S.	1984–85	2	0	0	0	1	0	0	0	3	0
Scott J.C.	1954–58	93	26	6	4	0	0	0	0	99	30
Scrimshaw C.T.	1938–39	9	0	0	0	0	0	0	0	9	0
Senior T.J.	1987–89	9/1	2	0	0	1	0	4	2	14/1	4
Shand H.	1906–07	2	0	0	0	0	0	0	0	2	0
Shannon R.	1991	0/1	0	0	0	1	0	0	0	1/1	0
Shaw T.W.	1899–1900	12	0	1	0	0	0	0	0	13	0
Shearer D.J.	1977–83	88/9	23	10/2	4	4/2	3	0	0	102/13	30
Shepherdson H.	1936–47	17	0	0	0	0	0	0	0	17	0
Short M.	1967–70	16	0	2	0	1	0	0	0	19	0
Slade H.C.	1922–25	68	2	2	0	0	0	0	0	70	2
Slaven B.J.	1985–92	286/21	118	16/3	4	26/2	10	27	14	355/26	146
Smith D.	1967–68	1/1	0	1	0	2	2	0	0	4/1	2
Smith D.A.	1900–1905	108	12	6	0	0	0	0	0	114	12
Smith E.G.	1899–1900	10	0	0	0	0	0	0	0	10	0
Smith E.E.	1923–25	21	0	0	0	0	0	0	0	21	0
Smith G.	1968–71	74	0	5	1	3	0	4	0	86	1
Smith J.	1926–30	113	0	10	0	0	0	0	0	123	0
Smith J.	1933–34	1	0	0	0	0	0	0	0	1	0
Smith M.	1972–76	32/24	11	0/2	0	5/1	2	2/2	0	39/29	13
Smith R.A.	1965–72	119/2	1	9	0	3	0	4	0	135/2	1
Souness G.J.	1972–78	174/2	22	13	1	15	0	12	4	214/2	27
Southgate G.	2000–05	160	4	15/1	0	9	0	19	0	203/1	4
Spraggon F.	1963–76	277/3	3	23	0	18/1	0	8/1	0	326/5	3
Spriggs S.	1986–87	3	0	0	0	0	0	0	0	3	0
Spuhler J.O.	1946–54	216	69	25	12	0	0	0	0	241	81
Stage W.	1913–14	3	0	0	0	0	0	0	0	3	0
Stamp P.L.	1993–2001	75/41	6	9/6	1	13/4	1	5/1	0	102/52	8
Stephens A.	1984–88	87/5	24	3	0	8/1	1	3	2	101/6	27
Stevenson A.B.	1923–24	8	0	0	0	0	0	0	0	8	0
Stewart J.G.	1978–80	34	0	2	0	2	0	0	0	38	0
Stiles N.P.	1971–73	57	2	7	0	5	0	0	0	69	2
Stirling J.	1911–14	103	8	9	0	0	0	0	0	112	8
Stockdale R.K.	1998–2003	62/13	2	7	0	8/1	0	0	0	77/14	2
Stone J.G.	1971–72	2	0	0	0	0	0	0	0	2	0
Stonehouse D.	1953–61	174	0	11	0	2	0	0	0	187	0
Storey T.	1913–20	33	1	0	0	0	0	0	0	33	1
Stott J.	1899–1900	1	0	0	0	0	0	0	0	1	0
Strong A.F.	1984–85	6	0	0	0	0	0	0	0	6	0
Stuart R.W.	1931–48	247	2	21	0	0	0	0	0	268	2
Suddick J.	1903–04	1	1	0	0	0	0	0	0	1	1
Sugrue P.A.	1982–85	66/3	6	8	3	4	1	0	0	78/3	10
Summerbell M.	1995–2001	35/16	1	0	0	4/3	3	0	0	39/19	4

Player	Played	LEAGUE		FA CUP		FL CUP		OTHERS		TOTAL	
		A	G	A	G	A	G	A	G	A	G
Surtees J.	1931–32	1	0	0	0	0	0	0	0	1	0
Swales N.	1925–26	2	0	0	0	0	0	0	0	2	0
Taylor A.D.	2003–07	41/6	0	11	0	1	0	1/2	0	54/8	0
Taylor B.	1972–76	14/4	1	0	0	1/1	0	1	0	16/5	1
Taylor C.W.	1957–60	11	1	0	0	0	0	0	0	11	1
Taylor P.T.	1955–61	140	0	6	0	0	0	0	0	146	0
Tennant J.	1901–02	17	7	0	0	0	0	0	0	17	7
Thackeray J.	1904–10	157	16	13	2	0	0	0	0	170	18
Thomas D.	1981–82	13	1	0	0	0	0	0	0	13	1
Thomas M.R.	1984–85	4	0	0	0	0	0	0	0	4	0
Thomas M.L.	1997	10	0	0	0	0	0	0	0	10	0
Thompson A.	1900–03	7	3	1	0	0	0	0	0	8	3
Thompson N.	1925–26	8	3	0	0	0	0	0	0	8	3
Thompson W.T.	1905–06	6	2	0	0	0	0	0	0	6	2
Thomson K.G.	1959–63	84	1	4	0	2	0	0	0	90	1
Thomson R.	1981–82	18/2	2	2	2	2	1	0	0	22/2	5
Tinsley W.E.	1913–21	86	46	3	3	0	0	0	0	89	49
Todd A.J.J.	1991–94	7/1	0	0	0	1/1	0	5	0	13/2	0
Tomlin J.	1906–07	4	0	0	0	0	0	0	0	4	0
Townsend A.D.	1997–99	73/4	3	4	1	7	0	0	0	84/4	4
Townsend J.C.	1963–66	65/2	6	4	0	10	0	0	0	70/2	6
Trechman O.L.	1905–06	1	0	0	0	0	0	0	0	1	0
Tucker W.H.	1906–07	4	1	0	0	0	0	0	0	4	1
Turnbull L.M.	1985–87	8/8	4	0	0	0/1	0	1/1	1	9/10	5
Turnbull R.	2002–07	2	0	1	0	0	0	0	0	3	0
Turner P.	1901–02	23	6	2	0	0	0	0	0	25	6
Twine F.W.	1926–27	52	0	6	0	0	0	0	0	58	0
Tyldesley J.	1906–07	23	0	2	0	0	0	0	0	25	0
Ugolini R.	1948–56	320	0	15	0	0	0	0	0	335	0
Urquhart A.	1907–08	4	0	0	0	0	0	0	0	4	0
Urwin T.	1914–24	192	14	8	0	0	0	0	0	200	14
Verrill E.	1907–15	181	4	8	0	0	0	0	0	189	4
Vickers S.	1993–2001	248/11	8	17/1	0	27/2	3	2	0	294/14	11
Vidmar A.	2002	9/3	0	1	0	2	0	0	0	12/3	0
Viduka M.A.	2004–07	56/16	26	9/3	7	4	1	11/2	8	80/22	42
Vincent J.V.	1970–72	37/3	7	0	0	2/1	0	0	0	39/4	7
Wainscoat W.R.	1923–25	34	5	2	0	0	0	0	0	36	5
Waldock R.	1959–62	34	7	1	0	0	0	0	0	35	7
Walker D.H.	1959–62	23	1	1	0	0	0	0	0	24	1
Walker John	1913–21	106	0	3	0	0	0	0	0	109	0
Walker Joshua	2005–	0/1	0	0	0	0	0	0	0	0/1	0
Walker R.G.	1946–55	240	50	19	3	0	0	0	0	259	53
Walker R.H.	1905–06	9	2	5	1	0	0	0	0	14	3
Walley E.	1958–59	8	0	0	0	0	0	0	0	8	0
Walsh A.	1977–78	0/3	0	0	0	0	0	0	0	0/3	0
Walsh C.D.	1991	10/3	1	1	0	0	0	0	0	11/3	1
Walsh G.	1995–97 and 2000	47	0	4	0	9	0	0	0	60	0
Wanless R.	1899–1900	10	0	0	0	0	0	0	0	10	0
Ward P.T.	1982–86	69/7	1	3/1	0	5	0	0	0	77/8	1
Wardle G.	1937–38	1	0	0	0	0	0	0	0	1	0
Wardrope A.	1910–11	10	0	1	0	0	0	0	0	11	0
Wardrope W.	1899–02	62	21	11	3	0	0	0	0	73	24
Wark J.	1990	3/1	2	2	0	5	0	0	0	10/1	2
Warren F.W.	1929–36	160	49	4	1	0	0	0	0	164	50
Watkin T.W.S.	1953–55	11	2	0	0	0	0	0	0	11	2
Watson A.	1925–26	8	0	0	0	0	0	0	0	8	0
Watson H.L.	1929–32	13	1	2	0	0	0	0	0	15	1
Watson R.	1901–03	16	5	1	0	0	0	0	0	17	5
Watson J.	1906–10	103	0	4	0	0	0	0	0	107	0
Wayman C.	1954–56	55	31	3	2	0	0	0	0	58	33
Webb S.J.	1967–71	20/9	6	0	0	0	0	1/1	0	21/10	6
Webster M.	1920–34	262	3	19	0	0	0	0	0	281	3
Weddle D.K.	1961–62	3	1	0	0	0	0	0	0	3	1
Weightman E.	1935–36	2	0	1	0	0	0	0	0	3	0
Weir J.	1910–15	113	0	12	0	0	0	0	0	125	0
Wheater D.J.	2004–07	20/2	2	0	0	0	0	0/1	0	20/5	0
Whelan N.D.	2000–02	33/28	6	5/3	3	4	2	0	0	42/31	11
Whelan P.J.	1995–96	18/4	1	3	0	5	0	0	0	26/4	1
Whigham W.M.M.	1966–72	187	0	17	0	6	0	4	0	214	0
Whitaker W.	1947–55	177	1	7	0	0	0	0	0	184	1
White W.	1903–04	7	0	0	0	0	0	0	0	7	0

Player	Played	LEAGUE		FA CUP		FL CUP		OTHERS		TOTAL	
		A	G	A	G	A	G	A	G	A	G
Whyte D.	1992–97	160/7	2	4/2	0	15/1	1	6	0	185/10	3
Wilcox F.J.	1905–10	106	12	4	0	0	0	0	0	110	12
Wilkie D.	1959–61	4	0	0	0	0	0	0	0	4	0
Wilkie J.	1900–01	28	8	7	2	0	0	0	0	35	10
Wilkinson P.	1991–95	161/5	49	14	5	16	8	5/1	4	196/6	66
Wilkshire L.	1999–02	13/8	0	1	0	2	0	0	0	16/8	0
Willey A.S.	1974–78	27/22	7	1/3	1	3/1	0	3	3	34/26	11
Williams J.T.	1924–28	37	8	1	0	0	0	0	0	38	8
Williams J.J.	1931–35	78	11	7	2	0	0	0	0	85	13
Williams O.	1923–30	184	40	10	4	0	0	0	0	194	44
Williamson R.G.	1901–23	563	2	39	0	0	0	0	0	602	2
Wilson A.N.	1914–24	86	56	4	1	0	0	0	0	90	57
Wilson A.	1914–15	21	4	2	0	0	0	0	0	23	4
Wilson F.P.	1967–68	1	0	0	0	0	0	0	0	1	0
Wilson J.	1924–27	18	0	0	0	0	0	0	0	18	0
Wilson M.A.	2001–	6/10	0	2/1	0	5	2	0	0	13/11	2
Wilson T.T.	1907–10	10	0	0	0	0	0	0	0	10	0
Windass D.	2000–02	16/21	3	4/3	0	2	0	0	0	22/24	3
Windridge J.E.	1911–14	68	11	8	1	0	0	0	0	76	12
Windross D.	1959–61	4	1	0	0	0	0	0	0	4	1
Winnie D.	1994	1	0	0	0	0	0	0	0	1	0
Wood A.E.H.	1976–77	22/1	2	5	0	0	0	0	0	27/1	2
Wood D.T.	1981–84	101	6	8	0	6	0	0	0	115	6
Woodgate J.	2006–07	30	0	6	0	0	0	0	0	36	0
Woodward T.	1949–51	19	6	0	0	0	0	0	0	19	6
Woof W.	1974–82	30/16	5	0/1	0	7/1	1	0	0	37/18	6
Worrall W.E.	1905–06	1	0	0	0	0	0	0	0	1	0
Worthington P.R.	1967–68	2	0	1	0	0	0	0	0	3	0
Wright A.G.	2003	2	0	0	0	0	0	0	0	2	0
Wright T.E.	1992–94	44/9	5	3	1	3/1	0	5/1	0	55/11	6
Wynn R.	1913–15	7	1	0	0	0	0	0	0	7	1
Xavier A.	2005–07	18	1	6	0	0	0	2	0	26	1
Yakubu A.	2005–07	65/6	25	15	8	1/1	0	5/9	2	86/16	35
Yeoman R.I.	1958–63	210	3	10	0	7	0	0	0	227	3
Yorston B.C.	1933–39	152	54	7	0	0	0	0	0	159	54
Young E.W.	1920–21	1	0	0	0	0	0	0	0	1	0
Young M.S.	1991	0/1	0	0	0	0	0	0/1	0	0/2	0
Young R.T.	1908–10	34	5	3	0	0	0	0	0	37	5
Zenden B.	2003–04	67	9	3/1	1	6/1	2	10	3	86/2	15
Ziege C.	1999–2000	29	6	1	0	3/1	1	0	0	33/1	7

ND - #0344 - 270225 - C0 - 260/195/19 PB 9781780911229 - Gloss Lamination